The
LEGAL HANDBOOK
of
BUSINESS TRANSACTIONS

The
LEGAL HANDBOOK
of
BUSINESS TRANSACTIONS

A GUIDE FOR MANAGERS AND ENTREPRENEURS

E. C. Lashbrooke, Jr.,

and

Michael I. Swygert

FOREWORD by ROBERT E. GINSBERG

QUORUM BOOKS

New York • Westport, Connecticut • London

Library of Congress Cataloging-in-Publication Data

Lashbrooke, E. C.
   The legal handbook of business transactions.

   Bibliography: p.
   Includes index.
   1. Commercial law—United States. 2. Business
enterprises—United States. I. Swygert, Michael I.
II. Title.
KF889.L35   1987   346.73'07   86-30595
                    347.3067

ISBN 0-89930-179-7 (lib. bdg. : alk. paper)

British Library Cataloguing in Publication Data is available.

Library of Congress Catalog Card Number: 86-30595
ISBN: 0-89930-179-7

First published in 1987 by Quorum Books

Greenwood Press, Inc.
88 Post Road West, Westport, Connecticut 06881

Printed in the United States of America

The paper used in this book complies with the
Permanent Paper Standard issued by the National
Information Standards Organization (Z39.48-1984).

10 9 8 7 6 5 4 3 2 1

To my parents, Elvin C. and Lois L. Lashbrooke

E. C. L.

To my father, Luther M. Swygert, and the memory of
my mother, Mildred Kercher Swygert

M. I. S.

Contents

Figures

Foreword

"The first thing we do, let's kill all the lawyers." (W. Shakespeare, *2 Henry VI*, act 4, sc. 2.) Shakespeare's seventeenth-century phrase probably best summarizes the collective frustration felt by managers and entrepreneurs in the United States as the twentieth century comes to an end. Managers and entrepreneurs feel that they are trying to survive in the most overlawyered and litigious society the world has ever known. They regard the law as permeating every area of their business endeavor—and they are right. The law does affect every action of managers and entrepreneurs, and it often affects those actions in unforeseen and unfortunate ways. Shakespeare's solution will not work to eliminate the pervasive intrusion of the law and lawyers into business for a couple of reasons. First, there are too many lawyers in the United States to make such an approach practical. At most recent count, there were more than 650,000 lawyers in this country, with law schools churning out thousands of new lawyers every year. Second, despite arguments to the contrary, lawyers are human beings, and lawyers have made sure that the killing of human beings is illegal and that the penalties are severe.

Instead, the easier way for managers and entrepreneurs to deal with the fact that the law pervades all business transactions is the same way that lawyers deal with it—with knowledge of the law. Those who know the law can anticipate its consequences in most instances and thus avoid unforeseen and unfortunate results. People can understand much of the law and deal with it to their advantage. Despite its archaic and sometimes arcane language, the law, particularly commercial law, is not that hard to grasp.

Much of commercial law simply represents a statement of common sense or business sense. Thus, the concept of offer and acceptance in contract law simply means that both parties must agree before there can be a contract, a concept which is not foreign to most business people. By the same token, the Latin phrase *respondeat superior*, i.e., let the master answer, simply means that if an employee hurts somebody while working for the boss, the boss should be liable to the victim. This simply puts in writing what most people would regard as a basic rule of common sense and fairness. Rules prohibiting trading securities based on undisclosed insider information simply implement the idea of the notion that nobody should have an unfair advantage in securities markets by virtue of their position as opposed to their ability to analyze the information available in the marketplace.

Of course, some areas of law are governed by apparently arbitrary statutes or rules. Tax rates and tax laws do not lend themselves to easy rational analysis. OSHA laws and consumer protection laws represent governmental interpretations of social policy. Sometimes these rules make sense. However, most of the time, these rules appear arbitrary. Anyone who has ever dealt with the IRS (Internal Revenue Service) or OSHA (Occupational Safety and Health Administration) can appreciate how arbitrary rules can appear. However, these rules are neither difficult to learn nor hard to apply to particular situations.

The point is that much of the law, if not most of it, is not difficult to understand. More importantly, knowledge of the basics of commercial law enables managers and entrepreneurs to plan transactions in a way which minimizes exposure to litigation and threats of litigation. Thus, for example, it is not difficult for a manager or entrepreneur to understand that when a debtor files any kind of bankruptcy petition, all creditor collection efforts of any kind in any forum other than the bankruptcy court are automatically stayed or suspended by operation of law. A creditor who is armed with this information can avoid wasting time and money trying to collect after bankruptcy in any forum except the bankruptcy court and can also avoid having to defend damage and contempt actions by the debtor for violating the bankruptcy automatic stay. In addition, such a creditor can immediately maximize its rights by quickly taking whatever action is appropriate in the bankruptcy court. This is but another example of the advantages that managers and entrepreneurs gain in knowing the basis of commercial law.

None of this should suggest that even in an ideal world managers and entrepreneurs can or should operate without lawyers. The simple answer is that they cannot. Law, particularly commercial law, is often arbitrary and full of traps for the unwary. Many areas of commercial law, such as bankruptcy law and tax law, are replete with arbitrary deadlines and time periods. A single day of inaction can be fatal. Only a lawyer can be expected to know all these deadlines or how and where to find them. That is one of the things lawyers, hopefully, learn in three years of law school. However, a manager or entrepreneur who has an understanding of the issues can better utilize the services of an attorney. By understanding the basics of even the most complex areas of law, the manager or entrepreneur can know when a lawyer should be called in as a preventive element in transactional planning and when the lawyer must be called in remedial and litigation situations. Equally important, the manager or entrepreneur who has a basic understanding of the law is in a much better position to know what questions to ask of the lawyer, to know what information the lawyer needs, to be able to measure the competence of the attorney who may be employed, and to understand the answers given by the lawyer, even if couched in legalese rather than English. In the end, knowledge of the law will ensure the manager or entrepreneur receiving high-quality legal advice for a fair price, as well as the opportunity to prevent costly legal problems.

The purpose of this book, therefore, is to teach those interested in business and related areas the basics of American law governing the entire gamut of commercial relations. The authors bring the best of all worlds to their task. They are both experienced teachers at the university and law school levels. They have each taught commercial law to both lawyers and nonlawyers. Thus, they each know the law and its language, and they each know how to translate that language into something understandable to people. They have come up with a practical volume that teaches managers and entrepreneurs the basics of commercial law and how to use that knowledge in preventing problems in planning business transactions and in dealing with the law and lawyers. They have filled a void by providing a comprehensive legal analysis of the common business transactions managers and entrepreneurs face day-to-day. In today's American society, the solution offered by Professors Lashbrooke and Swygert for dealing with law and lawyers may not be as appealing but is far more useful than that offered by Shakespeare.

Robert E. Ginsberg

Preface

This book is the result of our conviction that every business needs a manual of preventive law for its legal health. Our experience as legal advisors, researchers, and academicians has made us aware of countless situations where businesses get into legal difficulties because their managers or owners lack knowledge of legal rules, regulations, and principles applicable to everyday business transactions.

In this "age of the lawsuit," knowledge of the law permits a firm to conduct its operations within permissive and safe legal parameters. Regardless of a business' size or form, a firm will benefit and save money by having a sound and comprehensive knowledge of business law. Knowledge of the law may even act as a form of self-insurance; or, at a minimum, may cause the number of claims (and costs) to be reduced over time.

Preventive law begins with knowledge that specific laws exist and of what these laws are designed to accomplish. Learning what these laws precisely require is the next step. Having this knowledge, a manager or entrepreneur may prevent situations from arising that could end in liability judgments and jeopardize the health of the business. But not only is knowledge of the law often necessary to prevent or minimize legal liability, it also is crucial for effective business planning. Certainly, every business needs accurate knowledge of the sweeping changes resulting from the new federal tax law.

We have attempted in this volume to cover the principal laws, rules, regulations, and legal principles that every manager or entrepreneur should be familiar with in conducting his or her business. Our desire has been in writing this volume to be accurate and comprehensive. Reader comments are welcome.

Several individuals have assisted the authors in researching, typing, reviewing, and preparing this volume for publication. In St. Petersburg, Dawn Carapella,

Denise Des Rosiers, and Will Smith, Stetson University College of Law students, aided in the research, while Veronica Richardson, Beth Curnow, and Dianne Swygert typed multiple drafts of the manuscript. In East Lansing, Debra North was responsible for typing manuscript drafts and collating and assembling the completed manuscript. The Honorable Robert E. Ginsberg, U.S. Bankruptcy Judge for the Northern District of Illinois; Calvin A. Kuenzel, the L. LeRoy Highbaugh, Sr. professor of contracts and commercial law, Stetson University; and W. Gary Vause, director, Center for Labor and Management and professor of labor law at Stetson University, reviewed portions of the manuscript. We thank each of these people for their contributions.

The
LEGAL HANDBOOK
of
BUSINESS TRANSACTIONS

1

Introduction to the Law of Business Transactions

LEGAL RIGHTS AND LIABILITIES

Businesses seek profits for their owners, be they entrepreneurs, partners, or stockholders. Profits may not be forthcoming, however, should the enterprise incur legal liability in conducting its affairs. This book concerns both the legal liability of businesses, the real and at times ruinous costs of failing to comply with legal obligations, and the legal rights afforded businesses under law. In the following pages, the authors discuss the ways a business can preserve and protect its legal rights while avoiding or at least minimizing the potential for legal liability.

For better or worse, the pervasive legal regulation of business is a reality of modern commercial life. Regulated business activities include raising capital; extending credit; collecting accounts; advertising and selling goods; maintaining a safe office, store, factory, or other work place; hiring, paying, promoting, and discharging employees; and making and preserving various tax and business records. From the very formation of a business through its eventual sale or forced liquidation, various laws prescribe the "legal way" of doing things. Any other way creates the potential for legal liability and loss of legal rights.

This volume sets out the important laws and regulations applicable to everyday business transactions. Federal securities, tax, trade regulation, commercial, consumer protection, and employment statutes and regulations are covered. In addition, various state statutes and common law principles affecting the sale of property, goods, and services are also treated. Awareness and knowledge of these rules are essential if a business is to avoid the potentially staggering cost of regulatory noncompliance and protect its legal rights. Consequently, the minimization of legal liability and the protection of legal rights are this volume's principal themes.

Forms of Legal Liability

Criminal

Legal liability takes several forms. On occasion liability may have minimal significance, but in some instances it may be devastating. This is especially true if criminal sanctions are imposed as a consequence of a violation. For example, entrepreneurs and executives have gone to jail for not fully reporting financial data required to be reported, for failing to obey an order mandating a business to cease and desist from a particular business practice, and for charging an illegal (usurious) rate of interest in the extension of credit.

Civil

Business liability, however, more typically involves civil rather than criminal sanctions. Foremost among civil sanctions are monetary damages designed to compensate the injured person or firm for harm caused by breach of contract or other legal wrong. Civil damages may also include punitive awards which, although not in essence criminal fines, are intended to have similar deterrent and punitive impacts on the defendant and on other potential violators. In a few situations, a business's liability for punitive damages may automatically arise upon adjudication of compensatory liability. This happens, for example, in private antitrust lawsuits where the plaintiff may be entitled to a punitive award in the amount of (and in addition to) three times the amount of the actual damages that the plaintiff sustained.

Civil sanctions may also include judicial and administrative orders calling for specific performance—orders which mandate that a business do or refrain from doing some act or course of conduct. Under the regulatory scheme of the FTC (Federal Trade Commission), for example, the FTC after appropriate hearings may issue a cease and desist order directing a business to refrain from engaging in what the FTC has found to be an illegal or deceptive trade practice. One such practice is bait and switch selling. This legally objectionable selling technique along with other deceptive selling practices are discussed in Chapter 10.

How Legal Liability Arises

The nature of legal liability involves not only various forms and sanctions noted above, it also arises in different ways. First, any knowing and intentional disregard of an applicable statute, regulation, or common law rule renders the business enterprise liable (in some cases criminally so) for the violation. But so too, generally speaking, may an inadvertent, unintentional, mistaken, and unknowing deviation from a mandated regulation or rule create potential liability. Thus, the cliché—ignorance of the law is no excuse—is emphatically true.

Legal liability of a business enterprise may result from non-compliance with a regulation promulgated by a federal, state, or local administrative agency. Liability may also arise from violating the provisions of an applicable state or federal statute, or of a local municipal or county ordinance. And, of course, a business may incur liability as a result of infringing upon a person's legally protected rights as guaranteed by the federal or state constitutions.

A business also faces potential liability for breaches of contract and for tortious conduct. The law of contracts and the law of torts both have their foundations in the English-based and still-evolving common law (discussed in Chapter 2). Breaches of contracts (defined as non-compliance with the terms of binding legal agreements) create liability usually in the form of monetary damages. Specific performance, recission, and other equitable remedies, however, may also lie. These matters are discussed in Chapter 8.

Torts result from acts which cause harm for which the law affords the victim relief, again, usually in the form of money awards. The redressable injury occurs as a result of either negligence (carelessness) or an intentional act (for example, an assault and battery). Businesses ordinarily are liable for the torts they, their employees, and their agents commit. A business also faces potential liability for many "business torts," for example, for intentionally interfering with existing contractual relations. Moreover, a business which deals in goods—a manufacturer, processor, jobber, or retailer—may incur strict liability in tort (without regard to carelessness or intention) for injuries sustained by users of products which turn out to be defectively manufactured, designed, packaged, or assembled. These important matters are discussed in Chapters 10, 16, and 17.

In summary, legal liability may arise from innocent as well as intentional noncompliance with legal rules; from employer, employee, and agent inattention and carelessness; from not living up fully to the terms of binding agreements; and from simply having been involved in the manufacture, processing, or distribution of an article which in time injures a user or even a bystander.

EFFECTIVE USE OF LEGAL COUNSEL

Ignorance of the law is not only inexcusable under the law, it is also both imprudent and unnecessary. It is imprudent because it may contribute both to the business's being held liable and to a forfeiture of its rights; it is unnecessary because lawyers and this book are both available to assist the enterprise.

Through the pages of this volume, together with the periodic assistance and advice of legal counsel, the business person today has the means of acquiring an extensive knowledge and understanding of the laws and regulations that impact on the business enterprise. From purchase orders through withholding state and federal taxes, the law of business transactions affects the rights, liabilities, and ultimately the profit or loss of any firm or corporation. This volume, *The Legal*

Handbook of Business Transactions, was conceived and written to make available
to the entrepreneur, small business owner, manager, executive, accountant, consultant, business lawyer, and business student the knowledge necessary "to do
it legal."

Although no book can take the place of legal counsel, this volume will assist
the business person in knowing when to consult an attorney, the relevant questions
to ask, and how to use effectively legal representatives. This volume, moreover,
provides a comprehensive resource for the business person to become specifically
informed about the regulatory and legal framework in which business must
operate today. It answers many questions while alerting the reader to the multitude
of legal rules, statutes, regulations, and doctrines applicable to business
transactions.

In the process of avoiding liability, a business should be willing whenever
the need arises to obtain the advice of a competent attorney experienced in
business law. To be sure, good lawyers do not come cheaply. Consequently,
this volume emphasizes throughout the efficient use of legal counsel.

Lawyers' services tend to be most cost effective when used to help avert future
disputes and legal difficulties. Such "preventive law" involves an attorney's
reviewing current practices and advising a business on how to conduct its future
activities in compliance with applicable laws and regulations. It is less expensive,
in many cases dramatically so, to pay legal fees for advice on protecting rights
or preventing legal liability than having to pay a much larger sum for a legal
defense which, despite competent legal representation, may culminate in a judgment holding the business liable for monetary damages. Indeed, the amount of
the judgment could be calamitous to the enterprise. Moreover, although liability
insurance may often cover such potentially catastrophic risks, the escalating cost
of such coverage is forcing many businesses to self-insure. Prevention of liability-
producing conduct, consequently, becomes all the more vital.

This book alerts the reader to those highly technical and complex regulatory
areas where legal counsel to aid in compliance is clearly advantageous and thus
advisable. In many areas of business activity, however, the discussions set forth
in this volume, if followed, will assist an enterprise, be it large or small, in
minimizing its exposure to potential liability. To this extent, a lawyer's fees
may be greatly reduced or avoided.

Preparation

On those occasions when an attorney is consulted, a few things should be
kept in mind. Remember that time costs money. The first principle, therefore,
for controlling legal fees is adequate preparation. Lawyers representing businesses usually compute their fees on the basis of the total time expended, including telephone calls, conferences, consultations, letter writing, legal research,
fact investigation, and travel time. Thus, before seeking legal advice, the business
person should carefully formulate the questions to ask the attorney; he or she

should prepare for the meeting by assembling all documents, correspondence, and notes which *might* bear on the matters intended to be raised. Copies of these papers and documents should be made available to the lawyer at the initial conference. In addition, it is usually expedient for the client to prepare a memorandum of the problem summarizing the relevant facts and events chronologically. For example, should a business organization have a dispute with the Internal Revenue Service over a claimed tax deficiency, a memorandum summarizing all the correspondence, phone conversations, and meetings, if any, in chronological order would be very useful. This summary enables the attorney to reach a quicker (and consequently less expensive) understanding of the history and current status of the dispute.

Record Keeping

A second principle for the effective use of legal counsel concerns keeping appropriate and extensive records of ongoing, developing, and potential disputes. Understand, however, that all relevant business records, not privileged, may later have to be produced in litigation. Nonetheless, the side with the best records more often than not wins lawsuits. Thus, if a possible disagreement with a governmental agency or other regulatory board, commission, or body exists or may develop, the business should keep a diary of all related events, conversations, and correspondence. The written notes or records should include the names and addresses of possible witnesses and other interested parties. For example, when dealing with representatives of regulatory agencies, be sure to record their full names and to summarize all conversations shortly after they occur. All of the above steps can save many hours of lawyering time and, thereby, many dollars in fees that otherwise would be payable.

Being Candid

A third principle for the efficient use of counsel is for the business person to be completely candid at all times with his or her attorney. Never hold back information, once the lawyer-client relationship is established. The information which the client supplies counsel is considered under the law to be privileged. This means that the attorney, with certain exceptions, may not divulge that information to any other person including competitors, prosecutors, regulators, judges, or police officials without the client's prior authorization. Important exceptions to this principle are if a client commits perjury in court or if the client were to disclose to the lawyer that the client was planning to commit a felonious crime. In such circumstances, attorneys, under both the American Bar Association Code of Professional Responsibility and under substantially similar state mandated professional responsibility rules, must divulge the knowledge to appropriate authorities or tribunals.

Attorney Fees

Being candid with a lawyer includes the willingness on the part of the business client to discuss and agree on fees *before* they are incurred. The client should understand exactly how the lawyer computes fees and what services are to be rendered.

Retainer Agreements

Retainer agreements, where money is advanced to the lawyer, generally should be avoided by smaller firms because the cost tends to be high in comparison with the services rendered. Although various retainer plans exist, a common form involves a client's agreeing to pay an annual or monthly fee in return for which the lawyer or firm promises to be available for advice and consultation. Under many retainer fee arrangements, however, the client must pay over and above the retainer amount, additional fees based on actual services rendered, especially for the attorney's preparing for and conducting litigation. These additional fees usually are computed on an hourly basis. In talking with business people, we have found that retainer agreements at times tend to promote mistrust between the lawyer and client as one or the other comes to believe he is not getting out of the arrangement an equivalent of what he or she has put into it.

Contingency Fees

Another type of payment arrangement involves plaintiff's "contingency fees," where the lawyer charges the litigatory client only for actual out of pocket expenses, but pursuant to the fee agreement, will receive a fixed percentage of the actual damages awarded the plaintiff should the litigation succeed. The agreed-upon percentage is often 33 percent to 50 percent and, on occasion, even higher. Plaintiffs' lawyers in bringing tort suits alleging negligence, product liability, and malpractice claims generally represent their clients pursuant to such contingency fee agreements. These contingency plans are highly controversial as many persons both within and without the legal profession believe they encourage lawsuits and contribute to large damage awards. Over time, contingency fees, so the argument proceeds, have contributed appreciably to the costs of doing business, both directly through uninsured judgments and indirectly through escalating liability insurance rates. This is especially true for sellers of products and for service renderers, notably physicians and other health care providers.

Time-Fee Arrangements

The attorney-client fee agreement that may be the most suitable for many small and medium size businesses is the straight hourly or time-fee arrangement. For one thing, lawyers customarily charge larger fees for courtroom (litigation) time than they do for non-litigative activities. This emphasizes another cost advantage of using lawyers in a planning fashion rather than in a defensive and remedial manner. Employing an attorney in a preventive law capacity on an hourly basis emphasizes the efficiency of the client's doing as much of the preparatory work as possible. The business person who goes to his or her attorney and says—"Here are the facts; here are all the possibly relevant correspondence, notes and documents; here is a chronological summary; this appears to be the problem; what can I do?"—is effectively using legal counsel.

Whether the lawyer responds to such a well-prepared and documented inquiry from a business client by engaging in edifying discussions and giving sound legal advice depends on whether the attorney is experienced and competent in business law matters. We turn now to answering this crucial question. How does a business go about selecting competent legal counsel?

ATTRIBUTES OF A GOOD COUNSELOR

Before choosing a legal representative, the business person should understand the attributes of a good lawyer. First, it should be understood that the lawyer chosen will work for the client, not the other way around. The client should always make the final decisions whether to sue, defend, negotiate, settle, comply, bear the risk of non-compliance, and so forth. The lawyer, in short, is there *to assist the client* in making rational, knowledgeable, and reasonable business-legal decisions in light of all the circumstances. The client, therefore, needs a person who can efficiently and competently counsel, who is an able and responsible representative, who has an expertise in business law, who has unimpeachable personal integrity, who is knowledgeable about business practices and needs, who is trustworthy, and who, preferably, has experience in representing other similarly situated businesses or corporations over time.

In addition to the above-listed attributes, the lawyer chosen should be one who cares about the total well-being of his or her client. The lawyer does not serve his or her client best by necessarily doing immediately what the client initially believes he or she wants. An able counselor cares about the best interests of the client even when that means lower fees. A lawyer who merely accedes to a client's wishes without exploring the total legal and nonlegal context should be avoided. Professor Thomas L. Shaffer, former dean of the Notre Dame Law School, has suggested that the law office conversation between client and attorney should be one of moral discourse. According to Shaffer, the lawyer should not preach, but should engage the client in a moral conversation in which all the issues—legal, ethical, practical, and moral, as well as the long-run and short-run ramifications of a course of action—are explored. In the course of this exploratory conversation, both the lawyer and the client will come to view the "problem" with additional insight and understanding.

A good counselor, in short, listens, explains, asks questions, discusses, and, together with the client, explores what is ultimately in the client's best interests. The final decision as to which available alternative should be taken in reference to a problem or situation is always one for the client to make. In this decisional process, the competent, caring business lawyer can be of enormous assistance, not just in explaining how the law applies, but also in illuminating the whole picture for the client.

SELECTING A COMPETENT LAWYER

How does a business locate such a responsible, caring, and able lawyer? The best method has always been and continues to be by word-of-mouth. Business and professional acquaintances, friends, and associates may be excellent potential sources for recommendations. Talk with as many business people as possible. Whom do they respect and like? If a business acquaintance is satisfied with the services of a particular attorney, then pursue a meeting with that lawyer to explore a possible attorney-client relationship.

Lawyer referral services provided by state or local bar associations may also be utilized. One possible drawback, however, is that relatively inexperienced lawyers may be included on the referral list. Still, lawyer referral services, in many instances, do provide a satisfactory method of obtaining legal counsel, recognizing that it is a hit or miss procedure.

Other than lawyer referral services and personal recommendations from trusted associates, friends, and acquaintances, another method of locating a lawyer is to study a list or lists of lawyers. The best list of lawyers is not found in the yellow pages, but rather is set out in a multi-volume library reference work known as the *Martindale-Hubbell Law Directory*. The directory is divided into an alphabetical listing by city and state on one hand, and into a "card" or advertisement section on the other. The card section contains descriptive narratives of firms and practitioners who list their areas of practice and also give names of representative clients. The representative clients often tell a great deal about the firm, its reputation, and the kind of law it practices. For many business firms, using *Martindale-Hubbell* often proves advantageous. Most public libraries have a set as do virtually all law school libraries. The lawyers advertising in *Martindale-Hubbell* tend not to be inexpensive, however.

Although the cost of legal services is an important consideration in selecting a lawyer, the cost factor must be carefully weighed. Attempting to obtain the least expensive counsel may be unwise. For example, a recent law school graduate may advertise fees of $55 per hour, with no charge for the initial consultation. But given the lack of experience, this neophyte attorney may have to spend numerous hours researching a relatively simple business law problem (at $55 for each hour of research). On the other hand, the $125 per hour or more expert may be able to give an accurate answer to the question in significantly less time. Consequently, it pays to be cautious when responding to advertisements of discount legal services.

Finally, in selecting a business or corporate lawyer, it is important that the entrepreneur, executive, or manager have confidence in the lawyer chosen. Indeed, to support and foster an effective working relationship, the client must have confidence in the integrity, ability, fairness, trustworthiness, and experience of counsel. Whenever a lack of confidence even appears or begins to develop, it should be openly and immediately discussed. If not resolved, the mistrust may grow, and a change in legal counsel may become necessary. Changing counsel has many drawbacks, not the least of which is the reeducation of the new attorney in the ways of the particular business—often a timely and costly undertaking.

ORGANIZATION OF MATERIALS

The majority of law books, including those pertaining specifically to business law, are written and organized according to traditional *legal* topics—for example, torts, contracts, administrative law, property, criminal law, and civil procedure. Although such curricular oriented law books serve the pedagogical needs of legal education, they have limited utility for either the business person or the general business lawyer. Even undergraduate business students are routinely exposed to the legal topic approach, often encompassed under the umbrella of "the legal environment," in their college business law courses. For the most part, traditional college business law books have little usefulness beyond final examinations.

To make this volume about business law more useful and, therefore, valuable to the executive, manager, entrepreneur, business lawyer, and student, a transactional or situational approach has been taken throughout. The materials are organized not by traditional legal topics, but rather under common business situations. These transactions serve as the bases for the chapters which follow, and include formation of a business, raising of capital, negotiating contracts, contracting with the federal government, selling goods, collecting accounts, making the workplace safe, and so forth. In each of these transactional settings, the principal regulatory laws, rules, and governing decisions applicable to the particular business situation are discussed contextually. For example, in the material dealing with collecting accounts (Chapter 13), the relevant laws and regulations dealing with civil procedure, the judicial process, the Uniform Commercial Code, the tort of wrongful collection, and bankruptcy considerations, are set forth and discussed. Similarly, the chapter dealing with required records to be kept (Chapter 19) includes various statutory and regulatory rules, including those under the Equal Employment Opportunity Commission, the Occupational Health and Safety Administration, the Internal Revenue Service, and the Federal Trade Commission.

HOW TO USE THIS BOOK

The contextual and transactional format of this volume should make it valuable as a guide and reference beyond its immediate instructional and informational functions. A perusal of the Table of Contents will disclose that the most common business transactions and areas of regulation are covered. The authors recommend that the book initially be read through completely. Subsequently, it can serve as a reference resource to be used when needed by locating topics in the detailed Table of Contents and the Index related to the reader's concern.

Source notes are also included to aid the reader. These follow the text of each chapter as endnotes. In addition to giving necessary attribution to source materials, these endnotes also set out the official citations and names of many of the public laws, court decisions, and regulations discussed in the text. Copies of the statutes and regulations ordinarily are available at any law school library as well as at many public libraries. Given the reality that laws and regulations often change through amendments and revisions, it is advisable to check the latest statutory supplements to verify the current status of any law or regulation.

A few caveats need to be mentioned. No book about law can declare with absolute authority what the law will be at any given point of time in the future because of the fluid and uncertain nature of legal rules and their interpretations. This is especially true in highly technical and fluid areas such as administrative law and tax law. Moreover, agency enforcement policies and interpretations of legislative mandates change as administrations change. All of this suggests, of course, that although this book can serve as a very useful legal handbook and resource, it should neither be used nor relied upon to take the place of legal counsel when up-to-the-minute authoritative information and specific advice are required.

Moreover, space limitations prevent a comprehensive exposition of the multitudinous and, at times, conflicting judicial interpretations of the rules and regulations discussed in this volume. It is these thousands of interpretations that fill up the shelves of law libraries. The authors in this volume set out and discuss the basic regulatory frameworks and legal principles applicable to common business transactions.

2

The Legal Environment

The three primary sources of law in the United States are legislatures, courts, and administrative agencies. Legislatures enact laws for the benefit of society as a whole. Most legislatures are prohibited from enacting special legislation applicable only to particular individuals rather than entire classes. Courts adjudicate disputes between the particular parties before them whether they be private citizens, corporations, or governments. In determining the outcome of the case before it, a court sets a precedent to be followed in other cases similar to the one before the bench. Such precedent is called the doctrine of *stare decisis*. The common law developed in precisely this manner. One court within the jurisdiction develops a rule which other inferior courts in the same jurisdiction are bound to follow. The rule of law must be tested through the appellate process and adopted by the court of highest competence to hear the case within the jurisdiction before it becomes binding on the other courts in that jurisdiction Alternative dispute resolution through arbitration is rapidly expanding and playing a large role in relieving the congestion of court dockets. Today, the largest body of law is created by administrative agencies which are created by either legislation or executive fiat.

LEGISLATURES

Legislatures are composed of elected officials generally arranged in two deliberative bodies having various names. Representation is based on population and residence in geographical districts. At the federal level the legislature consists of the United States Senate and the House of Representatives. All state legislatures also consist of two houses with the exception of Nebraska, which is a unicameral system consisting of a single elected body.

The legislative process begins with the introduction of a bill by a member of the legislature. Generally, a bill may be introduced in either house of the legislature, except for appropriation or tax bills which must generate on the house or lower body side. After a bill is introduced it is assigned to a committee which deals with the particular subject matter. The committee will hold hearings on the subject and decide whether to report the bill out of the committee favorably or unfavorably. If the bill is reported out of the committee favorably it then goes to the floor for debate. If the committee reacts unfavorably to the bill it may or may not be reported out. If it is not reported out favorably or unfavorably the bill dies in the committee; however, the bill could be reported out with an unfavorable recommendation. If the bill is passed after debate, it is sent to the other house of the legislature for consideration. The process is essentially the same; the bill is sent to a committee which holds hearings and then reports on the bill. Once the bill has passed both houses of the legislature in the same form, it is sent to the executive, the president in the case of federal legislation or the governor in the case of state legislation, for action. If the bill contains substantial differences, a conference committee consisting of members of both houses of the legislature will meet to work out a compromise provision. The compromise provision will then be reported back to both houses of the legislature for action; if it is passed, the bill is then sent to the executive for action. The executive may either sign it, in which event the act becomes law, or veto it. At the federal level, the president's veto must consist of a veto of the entire legislative act; however, at the state level, many governors have the power of line item veto; that is, they may veto a part of a legislative enactment while the rest of the act becomes law on signature. If the act is vetoed the legislature has an opportunity to override the veto. To override a veto requires a super-majority such as a two-thirds vote of each house to override the veto.

Once the legislative act has become law, it is the duty of the executive to give it effect and enforce it.

COURTS

In the United States we have two parallel court systems. The federal court system is created in Article III of the United States Constitution, which establishes the Supreme Court and gives Congress the power to create other federal courts as it sees fit. Because the states are individual sovereigns in our system of federalism each of the states retains the right under the Constitution to set up and maintain its own court system. The result is that there are more than 51 separate court systems in the United States. Moreover, there is a variety of different court systems in the different states.

State Courts Systems

Because there is such a variety of state court systems with different names for the courts and different jurisdictional divisions, it is advisable to consult the

Figure 1
State Court System

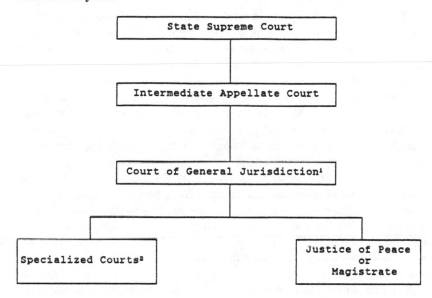

1. May be called District Court, Superior Court, Circuit Court, or Supreme Court (New York).

2. Probate, Orphans, or Surrogate Court; County Court; Municipal Court; Family Court; Juvenile Court; other nonrecord courts.

court jurisdiction in your own state. What follows is a general description of the state court systems (see Figure 1).

Each state has a court of general jurisdiction. That court of general jurisdiction may be called by different names such as district court, circuit court, superior court, court of common pleas, or even supreme court as in New York. Whatever its name, the court of general jurisdiction is the basic trial court of record in the state. All court proceedings in the court of general jurisdiction are recorded by a court reporter in order that a record or trial transcript may be prepared. In the court of general jurisdiction a jury trial is available, and in most cases the court is authorized to hear both civil and criminal cases.

Many states have lesser courts such as probate, surrogate, orphans, county, municipal, or justice of the peace courts. These lesser courts are not courts of record in that no trial transcript is prepared. Appeals from these lesser courts are generally to the court of general jurisdiction de novo. In a trial de novo, the evidence is re-presented to the trier of fact of the court of general jurisdiction since there are no records of the proceedings below. The court of general jurisdiction re-decides the case.

The decision as to which court a person should apply for redress of a grievance depends in part on subject matter jurisdiction. Subject matter jurisdiction refers to the type of case that the particular court may hear. Typically, courts have dollar limits which define their jurisdiction. For instance, a county court may hear cases where the amount in controversy does not exceed $300, and the district court would hear cases where the amount exceeds $300. Some of the lesser courts are specialized in subject matter jurisdiction such as the probate court which deals with estate administration and the probate of wills. A court is called a court of competent jurisdiction if it is authorized to hear the subject matter of the suit.

In general, if one of the parties to the lawsuit is not satisfied with the judgment rendered at the initial court trial, he or she may appeal to an appellate court. Only about half of the states have intermediate appellate courts in the absence of which the appeal goes to the highest court in the state. An appeal to the appropriate appellate court is an appeal on law and not fact. Appellate courts do not review findings of fact except in unusual circumstances such as lack of evidence in the record to support the finding of the lower court. At the appellate level the parties to the suit do not appear but are represented by their attorneys. There are no witnesses and no cross-examination before an appellate court. Each side presents a written brief and is allowed approximately one-half of an hour for oral argument. The appellate judges may ask questions of the attorney to clarify points. The appellate court subsequently issues a written opinion which may uphold the judgment of the lower court, may reverse the finding of the lower court, or may remand the case to the lower court for subsequent proceedings. Appeals beyond the first appeal to an appellate court are generally discretionary in the judgment of the next higher appellate court if one exists.

Federal Courts

The basic trial level court of general jurisdiction in the federal scheme is the federal district court. Each state has at least one federal district which may be divided into several divisions (see Figure 2).

Federal subject matter jurisdiction has two components. Federal courts have federal question jurisdiction and diversity of citizenship jurisdiction. Federal question jurisdiction refers to controversies where a federal constitutional claim or federal statutory right is at issue. Diversity of citizenship refers to situations involving lawsuits between citizens of different states in cases involving other than federal question jurisdiction. Note that there must be complete diversity of citizenship. For example, all plaintiffs must have different state citizenship from that of the defendants. No one plaintiff or defendant can be a citizen of the same state for diversity of citizenship to exist. Congress has further required that the

Figure 2
United States Court System

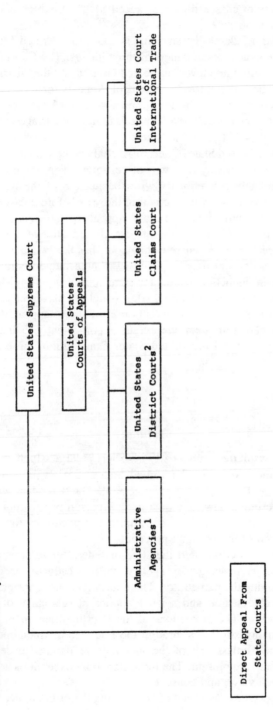

1. Tax Court, Federal Trade Commission, National Labor Relations Board, Securities and Exchange Commission, etc.

2. Includes United States Bankruptcy Courts

claim in a diversity of citizenship case exceed $10,000, which is referred to as the amount in controversy.

An appeal from a federal district court is taken to a United States Court of Appeals which generally sits in panels of three judges. The Court of Appeals is divided geographically into eleven numbered circuits and the District of Columbia. In addition, there is a thirteenth Court of Appeals for the Federal Circuit. Being appellate courts, U.S. Courts of Appeals do not hear witnesses or have cross-examination. The U.S. Court of Appeals reviews the trial court proceedings for errors or mistakes of law and not fact.

An appeal from a United States Court of Appeals to the United States Supreme Court is discretionary by way of a writ of certiorari. The granting of a writ of certiorari is completely discretionary with the justices of the Supreme Court. Four justices must vote in favor of granting the writ before a case can be heard before the Supreme Court. In certain cases, appeals may be made directly to the United States Supreme Court instead of to a United States Court of Appeals. For instance, in certain cases where a state court has held a federal statute to be unconstitutional, an appeal may be taken to a three judge district court panel which may issue an injunction against the state court proceeding. In such cases, an appeal from the three judge district court panel is sent directly to the United States Supreme Court. The other exception is of direct appeals to the United States Supreme Court from the highest court of competent jurisdiction in a state proceeding which involved the United States Constitution; these are primarily criminal cases.

Procedure

Criminal

In a criminal lawsuit the injured party is society at large which may be referred to as the state, the people, or the United States. Society is represented by a prosecutor, district attorney, or attorney general. The defendant who is charged with violating a criminal law may be a natural person or a corporation.

There are both state and federal constitutional protections for defendants at virtually every step of the criminal procedure.

If a crime has been committed the state or federal government, through its police force or other investigatory agency, will investigate the crime for the purpose of identifying the perpetrator. The Fourth Amendment right to be secure against unreasonable search and seizure applies at this stage of the criminal investigatory process. The protections of the Fourth Amendment also apply to the states in their investigations through the Fourteenth Amendment. A search warrant is required unless one of the judicially recognized exceptions to the warrant requirement are present. The more important exceptions are hot pursuit, plain view or open view, and consent.

The person or persons suspected of committing the criminal act are taken into custody which constitutes an arrest. At this stage police must have sufficient evidence to show probable cause that the person is the perpetrator of the crime. An arrest may be made by a police officer or a citizen if the crime is committed in their presence; otherwise, police may arrest only if they have a warrant. Subsequent to the arrest, the alleged perpetrator is taken to the police station and booked to record the arrest. At the arrest stage the arresting officers must read the Miranda warnings to the suspect so that the suspect is fully apprised of his or her constitutional rights.

Next, the suspect will be taken before a lower level court such as a justice of the peace or a magistrate where the case may be disposed of if it is a lesser offense such as a misdemeanor or a traffic violation, or the suspect may be bound over for trial if it is a more serious crime. If the suspect is bound over for trial, the lower court may set bail. For lesser offenses the suspect may be released on his or her own recognizance, which means that no bail is required. The more serious the crime, the higher the bail is set. Since most suspects do not have large amounts of cash available, bail is met by posting a bail bond, which in effect is an insurance policy by which the bail bondsman guarantees appearance of the suspect in court. Should the suspect be released on bail and flee to avoid prosecution, the bail bondsman must forfeit the entire amount of the bail.

The formal complaint is issued either by a grand jury or by information. A grand jury is a blue ribbon panel of citizens who hear evidence presented by the prosecutor against criminal suspects who are not present and have no right to be represented. If the grand jury believes that there is sufficient evidence presented that the person has in fact committed a crime, it will issue an indictment. If the grand jury is not convinced that there is sufficient evidence that the person has committed the crime, the charges are dismissed. For lesser crimes prosecutors generally do not make presentations to grand juries but instead issue an information, which is based on information supplied by citizens or the police. It is important to remember that grand juries do not determine the guilt or innocence of a suspect. The grand jury's function is merely to decide whether or not the prosecutor has sufficient evidence to justify the expense of a trial and to check possible prosecutorial abuse of the system.

At all times during the criminal process, the prosecutor may exercise discretion. The prosecutor has the discretion whether or not to present the case to the grand jury or whether or not to issue an information. In either event the result may be that the prosecutor declines to prosecute the suspect. Prosecutorial discretion also applies to plea bargaining, which is a negotiation between defense counsel and the prosecutor ostensibly to save the cost of trial by having the defendant plead guilty to a lesser charge. If an information is issued or a grand jury indicts the suspect, formal charges are made at the arraignment where the defendant will enter a plea of guilty, not guilty, or nolo contendere. A plea of nolo contendere, or no contest, is an admission by the defendant that he or she committed the criminal act but only for purposes of criminal prosecution and cannot subsequently be used as evidence in a civil suit arising out of the same transaction. As far as result is concerned, a plea of nolo contendere is equivalent to a plea of guilty. The defendant may also stand mute, in which event the judge will enter a plea of not guilty.

It is at this point that the defendant makes the decision as to whether or not he or she wants a jury trial. If no jury trial is requested, the case will be presented to and decided by the judge. If the defendant is indigent, counsel will be appointed for him or her.

The Sixth Amendment provides for a speedy trial in criminal cases. Criminal trials are generally held in the court of general jurisdiction. At the federal level this is a federal district court.

One of the more important steps in the trial process is the selection of the jury. Proper selection of the jury can be critical to the outcome of the case. If possible, defense counsel will select jurors who would be sympathetic to the defendant because of social status or other empathy. It may be that, in a case that shocks the public's morals, the defense would not want to risk a jury.

After the jury is selected or if no jury is requested, opening statements are made by the prosecutor and the defense attorney to the jury or the judge. The prosecutor proceeds to present his or her case against the defendant. The burden of proof is on the prosecution to prove every element of its case beyond a reasonable doubt. This heavy burden is placed on the prosecutor to overcome the presumption of innocence accorded all defendants in criminal actions. The Sixth Amendment also accords every defendant the right to face his or her accuser. This is manifested in the opportunity to cross-examine the prosecutor's witnesses. After the prosecution has completed its case, defense counsel may introduce evidence to rebut the evidence presented by the prosecutor and to introduce new evidence to support an affirmative defense such as insanity. After the defense has presented its case each side, in turn, has an opportunity to sum up the case before the judge or the jury.

After due deliberation the judge or jury will enter its verdict, and, if found guilty, the defendant will be sentenced, generally at a later date. If found not guilty, the defendant is discharged and may not be tried again for the same offense by the same sovereign. The double jeopardy clause of the Fifth Amendment does not, however, prohibit a person from being tried by both the state and the federal government on charges arising out of the same transaction.

If convicted, the defendant has a right of appeal. The appellate process is similar to that previously discussed. If acquitted, the defendant is discharged, and in most states the state may not appeal the acquittal.

Civil

In order to bring a civil suit, one must have standing. In order to have standing, a potential plaintiff must have suffered some actual harm or loss of some legally recognizable interest. Assuming that one does have standing as a result of a legal wrong and resulting damages, the lawsuit must be filed within a specified period of time known as the statute of limitations. Statutes of limitations are set by the states and vary in time depending upon the cause of action involved. Of course, in order to bring the suit one must know what cause of action he or she has. Except for certain small claims courts, an attorney is required to proceed further.

After determining whether or not the client has a recognizable cause of action for a legal wrong, the attorney must decide which court is the proper forum to resolve the issue. Jurisdiction depends on geography and subject matter. A state court only has jurisdiction within the territorial limits of the state.

The general rule is that a defendant is entitled to be sued in the state of his or her domicile. There are major exceptions to this rule such as the right to assert jurisdiction over a person who has an automobile accident in a state other than the state of his or her domicile (guest motorist statutes). For a state court to assert jurisdiction there must be some nexus between the state that seeks to assert jurisdiction and the person over whom jurisdiction is sought.

Subject matter jurisdiction on the other hand deals with those matters over which a court has power to hear a case. For instance, a probate court has the power to administer estates and probate wills but does not have any criminal jurisdiction or other civil jurisdiction.

The suit is started by filing a complaint in the proper court. After the complaint is filed, the clerk of the court will record the suit, and a copy of the complaint will be delivered to an official process server, such as a sheriff's office, to be delivered to the defendant. The summons directs the defendant to answer the complaint within a specified period of time. If the defendant fails to respond within the specified period of time, a default judgment will be entered against the defendant.

If the defendant does answer within the specified period of time, the suit is joined. Under the rules of civil procedure, each party has an opportunity to discover the evidence in the possession of the other side and whom the other party intends to call as a witness. This discovery is made at pre-trial conferences and by way of pre-trial motions. The original intent of the discovery rules was to simplify the trial by disposing of all of those issues which were not in controversy prior to the actual trial. Unfortunately, pre-trial discovery has become a game played by lawyers to subvert the original intent of the discovery rules which was to expedite the trial process. Discovery can become a burdensome and expensive process utilized primarily as a delaying tactic. After all the pre-trial motions have been filed and ruled upon, the case may actually get to trial.

At the trial the plaintiff must prove his or her case. The burden of proof on the plaintiff is a preponderance of the evidence. A preponderance of the evidence means that it is more likely than not that the plaintiff is telling the truth. In essence it is a balancing of the plaintiff's testimony against the defendant's testimony to establish the truth. A preponderance of the evidence is a much lesser standard than beyond a reasonable doubt in a criminal case.

In a civil suit, the plaintiff may or may not have a right to a trial by jury. If a jury trial is available, the plaintiff may elect to have the case tried by jury or by the judge. In either event the trier of fact will reach a resolution of the facts in the case. Once the facts are determined, the judge will apply the law to the facts. In some states the jury performs that function. Not only does the jury determine the facts, the jury also applies the law and reaches a verdict for one party or the other.

If a jury trial is held there are several post-verdict motions which may be made by the losing party. The losing party can ask the court for a "judgment notwithstanding the verdict." A judgment notwithstanding the verdict is a device by which a judge can curb abuse by a jury. If the evidence does not support the jury verdict, the judge may overrule it and enter judgment notwithstanding the verdict. Either party dissatisfied with the judgment or other disposition of the case may appeal to a higher court.

Assuming a judgment is entered and all appeals are resolved in favor of the defendant, the plaintiff takes nothing. Conversely, however, if the ultimate prevailing party is the plaintiff and the plaintiff has been awarded a money judgment, the plaintiff becomes a judgment creditor.

In all probability, the judgment creditor plaintiff will not be able to collect the judgment directly. The defendant may have been insured, in which case the insurance carrier will ultimately pay, or the defendant may be judgment proof, which means that he or she simply has no assets with which to pay the judgment. The judgment does not die though just because it is uncollectible at that point. A judgment will be entered for a number of years and can be renewed. A judgment creditor then will have several years in which to collect the judgment. Alternatively, the plaintiff creditor may be able to sell the judgment to a third party who, in turn, will try to collect from the defendant-judgment debtor.

If the judgment debtor has property that is not exempt under law, the judgment creditor may attempt to attach, seize, and sell the property to satisfy the judgment debt. The attachment and seizure are accomplished by obtaining an order directing the sheriff to seize the property. This is the execution of the judgment. Most states provide for a homestead exemption, which means that the house in which the debtor lives may not be seized. Certain household furnishings and tools of the trade are also generally exempt from seizure. Whether or not a judgment debtor's wages may be garnished depends on state and federal law as to whether or not wages may be garnished at all or whether or not a limitation is placed on garnishment.

In some cases, the plaintiff instead of or in addition to money damages may be seeking to make the defendant refrain from doing something or to make the defendant perform a particular act. Such an order is called an injunction. A negative injunction orders the defendant to refrain from some action such as dumping sewage into a stream. A positive injunction orders the defendant to do something such as convey good title to property. A defendant who disobeys an injunction may be punished for contempt of court by fine or imprisonment.

Except for certain small court claims, where a plaintiff may represent him-

or herself in relatively minor actions, civil litigation is an expensive and time-consuming process and should not be undertaken lightly.

ARBITRATION AND DISPUTE RESOLUTION

Arbitration is the submission of a dispute to an impartial arbitrator or tribunal for decision. The parties agree in advance to accept the arbitrator's award as a final and binding resolution of their controversy. Arbitration, like litigation, is an adjudicatory process. An arbitrator renders a judicial decision which can be overturned by a court only if it is established that the arbitrator in deciding or framing the award went beyond delegated powers (as stipulated in the parties' labor agreement). Unlike litigation, arbitration tends to be a rather informal procedure. Although witnesses are heard and usually sworn, the formal rules of evidence are not strictly adhered to. Thus, the arbitrator is permitted to receive evidence, for example, hearsay which is not admissible in formal litigation. The arbitrator must still weigh the probative value of the evidence adduced at the hearing.

Despite the differences between arbitration and litigation, the trend in recent years has been for arbitrations to take on more of the trappings of judicial trials. Increasingly, arbitrations involve stenographers, lawyers, and post-hearing briefs. This movement toward more formality (and expense) has fostered a counter-development—the proliferation of less formal and less costly "expedited" arbitration procedures. These typically do not involve briefs, transcripts, or lawyers. An expedited procedure usually requires the arbitrator to render a short written decision within a few days of the hearing. As a general rule, expedited awards rarely if ever set precedents governing the subsequent conduct of the parties.

The Arbitration Hearing

Following the introduction of the arbitrator or tribunal, an arbitration hearing usually begins with each side being afforded the opportunity of making an opening statement. The initiating party then presents its evidence and witnesses followed by the defending party's cross-examination. Next, the defending party presents its evidence and witnesses followed by the initiating party's cross-examination. Following presentations of all the evidence, the parties make their closing arguments and summations.

Throughout the hearing, the arbitrator keeps order, marks exhibits introduced into evidence, swears the witnesses, and rules on objections. When all the evidence has been presented and all the arguments have been made, assuming no post-hearing briefs are to be filed, the arbitrator declares the hearing closed. Normally, the arbitrator will issue an award within 30 days of the hearing (or less if the dispute has been submitted under expedited procedures rules).

Arbitration of Rights; Interest Arbitration

The most frequent use of arbitration arises out of collective bargaining agreements between employees and employers. The employer may be a governmental agency or body, for example, a local school board or county council, in which case the collective bargaining agreement is referred to as a public sector contract. More typically, however, the employer is a private business, in which case the contract is called a private sector labor agreement.

Whether public or private, labor agreements usually contain an agreed-upon grievance procedure. Although a grievance is defined variously under different agreements, a typical definition reads as follows: A grievance under this contract consists of any claimed violation, misinterpretation, or misapplication of the terms of this labor contract. Arbitrations involving grievances under labor contracts are sometimes referred to as arbitrations of rights. A rights arbitration commences with a "demand" for arbitration. This occurs when either party sends written notice to the other, as provided for in the contract's grievance procedure, that arbitration of a grievance is being demanded and initiated.

In contrast to arbitration of rights, arbitration of interests involves an arbitrator's or tribunal's binding determination of what terms are to be included in the final labor agreement of the parties. Interest arbitration (at times referred to as binding fact finding and final offer arbitration) usually grows out of an impasse in bargaining; in other words, a breakdown in the parties' negotiations for a new or renewal contract. Interest arbitrations occur much less frequently than do rights (or grievance) arbitrations. When they do occur, a panel of arbitrators (a tribunal) rather than one arbitrator is often selected.

The Arbitration Clause

An arbitration clause is that portion of the parties' labor agreement which allows or mandates that disputes under the contract be submitted to arbitration. Although in the public sector such arbitration clauses may call for either advisory or binding awards, in the private sector, virtually all arbitration clauses include the parties' stipulation agreeing to accept arbitration awards as final and binding. An advisory award, in contrast, need not be accepted by either of the parties. Consequently, many labor experts believe advisory awards tend to promote rather than resolve disputes.

Submission Agreements

Certain controversies are submitted to arbitration even when the disputants are not parties to a basic labor agreement, or if they are, there is no arbitration clause. In either case, the disputants may voluntarily agree to submit their controversy to arbitration pursuant to a "submission to arbitration agreement." Under a submission agreement, the parties agree ahead of time to be bound by and to perform the award of the arbitrator. The parties themselves may agree on the arbitrator in their submission agreement, or they may utilize the services of the American Arbitration Association (AAA) or Federal Mediation and Conciliation Service (FMCS) in the selection and appointment of the arbitrator.

Selection of the Arbitrator

The arbitration clause often stipulates a method or methods for selection of a single arbitrator or for the appointment of a tribunal (three arbitrators). The use of a single arbitrator, also called an umpire, naturally is less expensive than a full tribunal. The parties may agree on the use of a "permanent" umpire, a person both sides believe to be fair and competent. More often, however, parties agree to use the arbitrator selection and administrative services of either the FMCS or those of a private organization such as the AAA. Both the FMCS and the AAA maintain current national panels of labor as well as commercial arbitrators. Through regional offices, these services respond to requests for voluntary arbitration of disputes by submitting names of impartial arbitrators. The parties may then strike names until one remains, who, if available, will be appointed to arbitrate the dispute. FMCS or AAA, as the case may be, is the "administrator" of their respective arbitration systems. Each has a set of rules applicable to both their arbitrators and the parties.

In the case of the AAA, an arbitration under their procedures is begun by the initiatory party filing three copies of the "notice" or demand for arbitration with any AAA regional office, together with a copy of the collective bargaining agreement in effect. The notice must contain a statement setting forth the nature of the dispute and the remedy sought.

Commercial Arbitration

In addition to the interest and grievance arbitrations growing out of labor controversies, arbitration increasingly is being utilized as a less costly alternative dispute resolution mechanism for all sorts of commercial disputes. Thus, in addition to the well-publicized professional athlete compensation cases, controversies being submitted to arbitration in recent times have included questions concerning product quality under sales agreements, the issue of whether a contractor's performance is in accordance with an architect's specifications on a building project, various consumer small claims disputes with merchants, and property settlement controversies in marital dissolution cases. In a few instances, courts have undertaken to promote an alternative arbitration mechanism for specific kinds of disputes. In other settings, community groups, merchants, or trade associations have sponsored arbitration forums. Regardless of the nature and origin of the procedure, the parties to the dispute ordinarily (but not always) must agree to submit their disagreement to arbitration in consideration for their agreement not to (initially) litigate.

Costs of Arbitration

The direct costs of arbitration consist of the arbitrator's fee, the administrator's charges, the stenographic record (if any), and the cost of preparing for and presenting the evidence at the hearing. Arbitrators charge from $300 per hearing and writing day, up. During 1986–87, a $400 to $450 per day fee was not unusual. Most grievance hearings last one day or less. Arbitrators as a general rule bill one day for the hearing and two or three days for preparing, deciding, and writing the award depending on the complexity of the evidence and issues involved. If lawyers are not used and the parties rely on their own union and management representatives, the costs may be modest when compared with court contested adjudication involving lawyers, delays, briefs, etc. Nearly all labor agreements with arbitration clauses provide that the parties will split the arbitrator's fee and administration charges attributable to the arbitration.

Advantages

In addition to the cost factor, arbitration of disputes affords other advantages to a business. First, it tends to resolve issues more quickly than does litigation. Second, it brings disputes to a point of finality, a desirable objective in maintaining to the extent possible harmonious labor relations. Third, it provides a potential decisional scapegoat for the losing party. And fourth, arbitrators (the good and widely used ones, at least) develop an "industrial relations" expertise and wisdom which ultimately benefit both employees and employers in their employment relations. The suitability of arbitration for resolving disputes other than labor controversies is less clear. Still, less costly dispute resolution mechanisms arguably are needed and arbitration may in the years ahead help fill that need.

ADMINISTRATIVE LAW

Administrative Agencies

The vast majority of government regulations are promulgated by administrative agencies at the federal, state, and local levels. An administrative agency is a nonlegislative, nonjudicial governmental rulemaker.

Administrative agencies were created to perform functions that the traditional legislative, executive, and judicial branches of government were unable or unwilling to perform. Most legislators and judges do not have the technical expertise to deal with the more complex issues of today's society such as pollution, solid waste disposal, and nuclear regulation. Administrative agencies deal with many problems that have but a slight impact on an individual but an overwhelming impact on society as a whole. This is an important aspect of the need for administrative agencies because law develops primarily through the selfish efforts of an individual vindicating his or her claim through the court system. An individual who is not significantly affected by a particular social problem will not seek redress through the court system thereby leaving the social welfare without a champion. Another function of administrative agencies has been to regulate big business in those situations where individuals are in disadvantaged bargaining positions. The Interstate Commerce Commission is a prime example. Unfortunately, the regulated eventually become the regulators. Administrative agencies get results faster than legislatures or courts. The legislative process is time consuming and political by its very nature. The court dockets are crowded, and litigation can take years. Moreover, judges tend to lag behind public conceptions of desired social goals.

After a particular social problem is brought to the attention of the legislature, it may create an administrative agency to deal with the problem. The act creating the agency is called the *organic act*. The organic act usually creates the agency, delegates legislative authority to the agency to make rules and regulations to deal with the defined problem, grants judicial authority to hear and decide cases regarding the agency's subject matter jurisdiction, and provides executive authority to investigate and administer the subject of its jurisdiction. Hence, an administrative agency is all three branches of government rolled into one. It has legislative, executive, and judicial functions under a single authority which may be an individual or board or commission. You have already encountered and will encounter many administrative agencies in this book. The Federal Trade Commission, the Securities and Exchange Commission, the National Labor Relations Board, and the Occupational Safety and Health Administration are but a few.

Federal agencies are governed by the Administrative Procedures Act which was enacted in 1946 and subsequently substantially amended.[1] The more important amendments are the Freedom of Information Act,[2] the Privacy Act of 1974,[3] and the Government in the Sunshine Act.[4] Rulemaking procedures and internal agency enforcement and adjudication are governed by the Administrative Procedures Act. In addition to the federal act, each state has a similar administrative procedures act which governs its own administrative agencies.[5]

Rulemaking

Most federal rulemaking is informal. Congress authorizes an agency to informally make rules and regulations regarding a subject involving relatively little controversy over its regulation. Informal rulemaking requires notice in the Federal Register and inviting written comments from interested parties concerning the proposed regulation. The regulation is then issued as proposed, or it may be changed in response to the written comments received. Such a regulation is reviewed under the arbitrary, capricious, and unreasonable evidentiary standard. The arbitrary, capricious, and unreasonable rule standard is not a strict standard, and the administrative agency does not have to produce much evidence in order to justify its action. Virtually any evidence will suffice to show that the action was not whimsical.

Formal rulemaking, on the other hand, is generally required by Congress where there is controversy over the regulated subject matter such as hazardous work in coal mines, textile mills, and chemical and industrial plants, in which case a considerable amount of evidence is necessary to make an informed decision. This process involves notice, hearings with witnesses, and cross-examination of those witnesses. Such a regulation is reviewed under the substantial evidence test. The substantial evidence test requires the reviewing court to consider the evidence presented by both sides and then decide if there is substantial evidence in the record to support the agency's decision.

A problem may be brought to an agency's attention by its own staff, Congress, or the executive. If the problem is within the scope of the agency's authority, it will conduct the study either in-house by its own staff or private contractor such as a consulting firm or university. The study is important because it represents the fact-finding which is the basis of the regulation.

Once the study is concluded and the action is determined to be in order, a proposed regulation will be drafted. Generally the proposed regulation will be reviewed in-house before it is sent to the Federal Register office for publication. The Federal Register is published every business day Monday through Friday and contains important public notices such as Presidential Proclamations, notices of public meetings, proposed regulations, and publication of final regulations. The Federal Register is intended to give public notice of official acts of the federal government. Citizens are presumed to know what is published in the Federal Register. This presumption is completely unwarranted because most citizens do not have access to the Federal Register, and if they did would be unable in all probability to find anything because it is published chronologically as items are received in the office of the Federal Register. The notice published in the Federal Register must contain time, place, and nature of the public rulemaking; a statement identifying the law the agency uses as justification for its rulemaking; and either publication of the proposed rule or a description of the subject and issue involved in the rule.

In 1980 the Regulatory Flexibility Act[6] was passed for the benefit of the small business. Congress recognized that most small business people do not have access to nor do they read the Federal Register. The Regulatory Flexibility Act encourages but does not require federal agencies to send notices of proposed rules to journals likely to be subscribed to or read by small businesses such as small hospitals, municipal governments, and small business organizations.

After notice has been published in the Federal Register, public comment is invited for at least 30 days unless some other exception applies. The agency may, but is not required to, hold a public hearing. If a public hearing is not held, public comment is obtained by written data submitted by virtually anyone who desires to do so. No standard or particular form is required.

After public comment has been solicited and received, the agency in response to that public comment may modify or withdraw the proposed regulation. However, the agency is required only to consider relevant material presented; it need not react or incorporate the material in the proposed regulation. The agency may proceed to promulgate the regulation as proposed. The agency could modify and promulgate the modified regulation, or it may modify and re-propose the regulation by publication in the Federal Register and invite subsequent public comment. Finally, in response to adverse public comment, the agency may withdraw the proposed regulation.

The best and most efficient way to oppose a proposed regulation is to submit public comment or attend a public hearing and oppose the regulation or attempt to modify it. If the regulation is in fact finally promulgated, subsequent challenges must be made through the federal court system. Under the Administrative Procedure Act, challenges to regulations must fit into one of the following categories: violation of the United States Constitution; arbitrary, capricious, abuse of discretion, or otherwise not in accordance with the law; or the regulation is ultra vires (lacking authority). Most appeals from agency actions are made to the United States Courts of Appeals.

Enforcement

The administrative agency's executive function is primarily one of enforcement of its own statutes and rules and regulations. The executive function also includes the issuing of permits and licenses such as dumping permits or, in the case of a state agency, occupational licensing.

Congress in many enabling acts has provided civil penalties for violation of agency rules or regulations. Such civil penalties are hybrids between civil actions and criminal sanctions. The agency generally has the power to enforce its own rules and regulations with appeals taken to the federal courts, generally a United States Court of Appeals. The civil penalty has raised some concern regarding safeguards provided to defendants in criminal cases. In general, most of the safeguards apply, such as the presumption of innocence until proven guilty, prosecutorial discretion, and Fourth Amendment protection against unreasonable warrantless searches by government officials. However, an enabling act which provides for both civil penalty and criminal sanction does not violate the proscription against double jeopardy. An administrative agency can subject a person to a civil penalty and in turn request the Justice Department to proceed against the individual for violation of the criminal section.

Judicial Function

Administrative agencies also function as courts within the scope of their subject matter jurisdiction. The Administrative Procedures Act governs the administrative agency's procedure. The judicial officer presiding at an agency hearing may be either the governing body of the agency itself, such as the Federal Trade

Commission commissioners sitting as an adjudicatory body, or an administrative law judge who is employed by the agency but is required to be technically separate and apart from the agency's prosecutorial staff.

Administrative law judges are granted the following powers under the administrative procedures act: to administer oaths and affirmations, to issue subpoenas authorized by law, to take and receive relevant evidence and rule on motions affecting such evidence, to order depositions, to regulate the course of the hearing, to hold conferences to promote a settlement or simplify the issues, to rule on procedural matters, to make or recommend decisions, and to take any other action authorized by agency rule.

A party subpoenaed or forced to appear before an agency has the right to be accompanied by, represented by, and advised by an attorney. The party may introduce evidence, bring witnesses, and make arguments in support of his or her position.

Rules of evidence in an administrative hearing are not as strict as the Federal Rules of Civil Procedure used in federal courts. However, certain constitutional guarantees, particularly due process of the Fifth or Fourteenth Amendments, must be accorded. Due process requires that notice and a fair hearing be granted which, after *Goldberg v. Kelley*,[7] requires the following: the opportunity to be heard at a meaningful time and in a meaningful manner; prior notice of the hearing; a statement as to the subject matter of the hearing; the opportunity to confront and cross-examine adverse witnesses; the opportunity to present evidence in behalf of the party; the right to retain and be represented by a lawyer; the right to a decision based solely on the evidence presented at the hearing and based on legal rules, such decision to be accompanied by reasons therefore and supported by the evidence; and the right to have the matter impartially tried.

Before a party to an administrative hearing may appeal outside the agency to a federal court, he or she must exhaust all internal agency remedies. Often, a decision by an administrative law judge is appealable to the commission or agency head sitting as a judge. After all internal procedures have been exhausted, an appeal may be made to a federal court. Most often, the appeal is taken to a United States Court of Appeals. An appeal taken to a United States Court of Appeals does not involve a retrial of the evidence. The Court of Appeals accepts the evidence as developed within the agency. Some appeals may be made to a federal district court for trial de novo; in a trial de novo, the district court will retry the entire matter by hearing the evidence and ruling on such evidence. On appeal, the reviewing court may issue an injunction either ordering an agency to act or prohibiting it from acting. It may also declare the agency action unlawful or unconstitutional. Alternatively, it may send the case back to the administrative agency for further action.

Administrative agencies wield a great deal of power which is subject to abuse. The potential for abuse is curbed by the Constitution and the Administrative Procedures Act. If problems arise with an administrative agency, competent legal counsel should be retained to guarantee your rights, particularly that of due process.

NOTES

1. 5 U.S.C. §§ 551–59, 701–6, 1305, 3105, 3344, 6362, 7562.
2. 5 U.S.C. § 552.
3. 5 U.S.C. § 552a.
4. 5 U.S.C. §§ 551, 552, 552b, 556, 557; 2 U.S.C. § 10; 39 U.S.C. § 410.
5. *See*, Uniform Law Commisioner's Revised Model State Admin. Proc. Act, 1970 version.
6. 5 U.S.C. §§ 601, *et seq.*
7. 397 U.S. 254 (1970).

3

Formation of a Business

The sole proprietorship, partnership, limited partnership, and corporation are the four common forms of business enterprises utilized in the United States today. Of these, the corporate form is the most favored largely as a result of misconception and myth. There are, of course, other forms such as the business trust, joint stock company, joint venture, and syndicate, but when examined closely they are really special cases of the four common types. A business trust and joint stock company are treated as corporations for tax purposes. A joint venture is merely a partnership limited to a particular activity or project. A syndicate can be a partnership, a limited partnership, or a corporation.

This chapter is devoted, in part, to discussing the basic structure and characteristics of each form, factors to be considered when selecting the form to be used, and tax considerations of starting a new business in each form. The remainder of the chapter will be devoted to the methods of acquisition of an ongoing business and the consequences of doing so.

STRUCTURE OF COMMON FORMS

Sole Proprietorship

The simplest method of doing business is the sole proprietorship. It requires no formal organizational form. There are no legal requirements imposed as a condition to begin business as a sole proprietor. The owner of the business is the sole proprietor who is the business.

Although sole proprietorships are generally considered to be small businesses, there is no legal limit to the size or scope of activities in which a sole proprietor may engage.

Partnership

The Uniform Partnership Act defines a partnership as an association of two or more persons to carry on as co-owners of a business for profit. A partnership is created by agreement of the parties. The agreement may be oral or written; however, it is in the best interest of all parties that a formal written partnership agreement be executed. There is no formal requirement to create a partnership other than the agreement of the parties. The agreement controls the relationships among the parties. In the absence of a formal agreement or omission in a formal agreement, the state partnership act applies and fills the interstitial spaces. Relationships between the partnership and third parties established in the state partnership act cannot be altered by the partnership agreement without the consent of affected third parties.

As is the case with sole proprietorships, there are no limits to the size or scope of a partnership operation. Partnerships are widely used in business and play an important role in business activities.

Limited Partnership

The limited partnership is a creation of the state which combines the attributes of a partnership with limited liability for the limited partners. A limited partner, in essence, is merely an investor who contributed capital and exchanged powers of management for limited liability. The general partner is subject to all the rights, powers, and liabilities of a partner in an ordinary partnership. A limited partnership is a partnership created in accordance with state law by two or more persons at least one of whom is a general partner and at least one of whom is a limited partner. A limited partnership does not exist until a valid certificate of limited partnership has been filed with the proper state authority.

Corporation

Creation and organization of a corporation require strict adherence to the statutory scheme in the state of incorporation. The corporate form is the most widely used form of business organization in the United States. Size can range from an operation of one person to the giant multinationals. A corporation, unlike a partnership, is a juridical person separate and apart from its owners, the shareholders.

The primary attributes of the corporate form are limited liability of shareholders, centralized management (board of directors), perpetuity of life, and free transferability of interests (stock).

Shareholder participation in management is only indirect through the election of a board of directors which is legally responsible for the management of the corporation. The board of directors delegates its managerial powers to the officers and agents of the corporation who operate it on a daily basis.

Variant Forms

Joint Venture

A joint venture is a partnership organized to accomplish a particular purpose or to have a limited life. Some legal commentators argue that a joint venture is a separate legal form from a partnership. This is a minority view. Whatever limitations on the implied authority of one of the principals to bind the other exist, they do so as a result of the limited scope of the agreement rather than the existence of a new legal form. A joint venture requires a business purpose since it is a form of partnership. The confusion arises out of the nontechnical application of the term to nonbusiness situations such as a car pool. Sometimes lawyers and judges confuse themselves.

Joint Stock Company

A joint stock company is an unincorporated association of persons for business. Membership is evidenced by shares of transferable stock, and management is delegated to a small group. The joint stock company lacks limited liability; however, the members are not generally considered to be agents of each other. Thus, a joint stock company has attributes of both a partnership and a corporation. For tax purposes, a joint stock company is taxed as a corporation. This is one of the primary reasons that joint stock companies are rarely used today.

Syndicate

Syndication is a popular form of joint investment. Depending on the terms of the agreement, syndication may result in the joint ownership of property, which is not a recognized form of business, or in a partnership, limited partnership, or corporation. The syndication agreement should be carefully scrutinized to determine potential liability resulting from the business form of organization.

Business Trust

A business trust, sometimes referred to as a Massachusetts Trust, is a form of organization created by agreement whereby legal ownership of income-producing property is transferred to a trust while beneficial ownership is retained by the transferors. Management control rests with the trustee(s). Profits are divided among the beneficiaries according to the agreement. One of the primary advantages of a business trust is the limited liability of the beneficiaries.

Business trusts were popular in the first half of the twentieth century. In some states such as Illinois, early corporation acts forbid corporations from holding title to real property. Real property was acquired, and title was held by a business trust. The trust in turn leased the real property to the corporation for its use. The change in corporation statutes allowing corporations to hold title to real property and treatment of business trusts as corporations for tax purposes brought about the demise of the business trust as a popular form of business organization.

SELECTING THE APPROPRIATE FORM

The choice of organizational form is an important one and should be made only after careful analysis of the goals and needs of the business. One form should not be chosen over the other merely because it is in vogue. There is generally no one required form of doing business although some business organizations such as insurance companies and banks must conform to the requirements of special legislation.

There are seven primary factors to be considered in choosing an organizational form: management control, liability of owners, continuity, free transferability of interest, capitalization, startup costs, and tax consequences.

Management Control

Generally, the degree of control diminishes from a sole proprietorship to a partnership to a corporation. The extent to which a person wishes to exercise control over his or her business is an important factor in the decision-making process. A sole proprietor exercises complete control over the business. In fact, the sole proprietor is the business. Formation of a partnership results in sharing management control with the other partners. Similarly, creating a limited partnership means shared management control among the general partners while the limited partners are prohibited by law from exercising managerial control. Incorporation of a business results in surrender of direct control of management by the owners, the shareholders. Corporate shareholders elect a board of directors which has managerial control.

The structural constraints aside, managerial control is often determined by other, more practical factors. A sole proprietor may be limited by conditions imposed by creditors to secure their investments or loans. A partnership agreement may modify control by appointing a managing partner or allocating partnership interests other than on an equal basis. Control of a corporation generally depends on the amount of common stock held. A majority shareholder may be able to dominate the election of directors and may be a director him- or herself, thus depriving minority shareholders of any say in management.

Liability of Owners

Shareholders and limited partners have limited liability from business obligations under the law. Liability is limited to the amount of their investment. All others, sole proprietors and general partners in either a partnership or limited partners, are exposed to liability for business obligations in excess of their investments. Sole proprietors and general partners are personally liable. Partners are jointly and severally liable; that is, a creditor may collect from one or all of the partners. It is up to the partners to allocate the liability among themselves after the creditor is satisfied.

Other factors to be considered are the degree of commitment of personal finances to the business, availability of insurance, and credit terms. A sole proprietor or partner can protect him- or herself from personal liability from business torts by purchasing liability insurance. If a sole proprietor or partner has committed substantially all of his or her financial assets to the business, there is little or nothing left to lose. The business may have considerable assets and be able to afford substantial losses without impacting the owners' assets. Even though the law accords corporate shareholders limited liability, creditors may require shareholders to assume personal liability in the event that the corporation defaults. This is particularly true in the case of a small corporation with limited assets.

Continuity

The life of a sole proprietorship is coterminous with that of the owner. If the owner withdraws, is incapacitated, or dies the sole proprietorship ceases to exist. A partnership is created by association and agreement among the partners. Any event, such as death, withdrawal, expulsion, bankruptcy, or agreed dissolution, works a dissolution of the partnership. The partnership is then terminated. In a limited partnership, any event which works a dissolution of the general partners will bring about a termination of the limited partnership. However, the limited partners' interests are generally transferable so that withdrawal, death, or incapacity of a limited partner does not work a dissolution of the limited partnership. A corporation may exist in perpetuity unless the charter limits its life.

Frequently, a business continues to operate even though technically dissolved. The business of a sole proprietor may be carried on by family members, or it may be sold to a third party who continues to operate it. The same is true of a partnership. The remaining partners may continue to operate the business. Nonetheless, the organizational form ceases to exist in the eyes of the law. The sole proprietorship may become a sole proprietorship operated by another person, a partnership, or a corporation. The business continues, but the organizational form changes.

Free Transferability of Interest

Often a business person wants to be able to disinvest whether it be to reinvest in another business or to retire. A sole proprietor may sell his or her business but in doing so terminates the sole proprietorship. A general partner in a regular or limited partnership who wishes to disinvest or withdraw from the partnership cannot do so without dissolving the partnership; however, a limited partner can generally transfer his or her interest without dissolving the limited partnership. Corporate shares are freely transferable without dissolving the corporation. Both stock and limited partnership shares may be subject to certain restrictions on transferability but are nonetheless transferable.

Capitalization

Obtaining the needed capital to start or expand a business may be a compelling reason for changing organizational form. A sole proprietor must look to his or her own resources and ability to borrow. A general partnership allows the partners to pool their assets while a limited partnership allows third parties to invest with limited liability. The corporate form provides the most flexibility in raising capital. Capital stock can be sold to many investors without diluting managerial control as with a partnership. Moreover, acquisition of capital through sale of stock enhances the ability of the corporation to leverage by borrowing money either through the sale of corporate bonds or loans from third-party lending institutions. To expand a corporation, one need only issue more stock to acquire additional capital assuming a healthy, prosperous corporation.

Startup Costs

A sole proprietorship may begin operations with only small startup costs. No formal organization costs are incurred. Filing may be required under an assumed name statute if doing business under a name other than the proprietor's own. The cost of filing is usually modest. The assumed name statutes are for the protection of creditors so that they know who is actually the owner of the business. A partnership may be formed without incurring significant costs; however, for everyone's protection a formal agreement should be drafted by an attorney. Legal fees vary from locality to locality. A limited partnership certificate is required before doing business. In addition to legal fees, if an attorney drafts it, there are filing fees which are relatively small. Of the organization forms, the cost of incorporation is highest. There are legal fees, filing fees, and franchise taxes to be paid before operations begin. If a public stock issue is contemplated, the cost rises sharply due to registration requirements.

Startup costs should not be a determining factor in deciding which organizational form to use; however, it is wise to avoid unnecessary expenses.

Taxation

Of all the factors to be considered, taxation is generally regarded as the most important. A wrong decision could have adverse tax consequences not just at formation but also during the life of the organization.

For the sole proprietor or partner, there is only one level of taxation, that of the individual. In a sole proprietorship, the owner is the business so that all tax attributes of income, deductions, credits, and so on are those of the individual. A partnership, general or limited, is not considered to be a separate taxable entity from the partners. The partners are the taxpayers. All tax attributes of the partnership are passed through to the partners who incorporate them into their individual returns. The partnership is required to file a return, but it is an informational return only.

A corporation is a taxable entity. A corporation is taxed on its income in much the same manner as an individual except that personal deductions such as medical and moving expenses are disallowed. When the corporation distributes or is deemed to distribute a dividend, the dividend will constitute income to the shareholder who in turn includes that amount on his or her individual tax return. This form of double taxation can have serious consequences and should be given serious consideration when choosing an organizational form.

When choosing an organizational form, the lay person should be wary of some traps. The Internal Revenue Code defines corporation by merely stating what the term includes. For tax purposes, a corporation includes associations, joint stock companies, and insurance companies. However, this list is not exclusive and includes other organizational forms.

In general, corporation includes business enterprises organized under a state corporation act including professional corporation or association acts, after Treasury Regulations section 301.7701–2(h) was revoked, and also includes unincorporated associations which more closely resemble corporations than not.

The test for whether an unincorporated association more closely resembles a corporation than not was articulated by the U.S. Supreme Court in *Morrissey v. Commissioner.*[1] In *Morrissey* the Court listed six basic characteristics of a corporation: (1) associates, (2) an objective to conduct a business enterprise, (3) centralized management, (4) continuity of life, (5) free transferability of interests, and (6) limited liability of the participants to the property of the organization. If the association has more of these basic characteristics than not, it is treated as a corporation for tax purposes.

Morrissey is applied to partnerships and trusts by discarding those characteristics that the entities have in common. A corporation and partnership have the characteristics of associates and an objective to conduct a business enterprise in common, while a corporation and trust have the remaining four characteristics in common but not associates and an objective to conduct a business enterprise. After discarding the common characteristics, the remaining characteristics are examined. If more than half the remaining characteristics are in common with a corporation, the entity is treated as a corporation for tax purposes.

The Treasury Regulations are slanted against finding that a partnership or limited partnership is a corporation for tax purposes if the partnership agreement conforms substantially with the provisions of the Uniform Partnership Act or the Uniform Limited Partnership Act. State partnership acts which deviate from the uniform acts may create tax problems. In *Phillip G. Larson,*[2] the Internal Revenue Service contended that a California limited partnership be treated as a corporation for tax purposes because the California limited partnership act did not provide for dissolution of the partnership on bankruptcy of a general partner and, therefore, had continuity of life which shifted the balance and made the partnership more like a corporation than not.

Conversely, there are cases in which a corporation exists under the basic corporation law of a state, but the corporate entity is disregarded for tax purposes. The corporate form will be disregarded for tax purposes if the corporation is purely a passive dummy or is solely used for tax avoidance.

In order to mitigate the harshness of the corporate double tax scheme, Congress added Subchapter S to the Internal Revenue Code in 1958. Subchapter S is an elective tax provision, not a form of incorporation as is commonly believed. Shareholders of a qualified corporation may elect the Subchapter S provisions which in essence allow tax treatment similar to that of partnerships. The corporation itself is not treated as a taxable entity; instead the tax attributes are passed through to the shareholders. Professional tax advice is recommended for those contemplating Subchapter S. It is not for all.

FORMATION

Sole Proprietorship

There are no formal legal requirements to organize and do business as a sole proprietor. In the case of a professional, such as a doctor, lawyer, or beautician, an occupational license may be required by the state before engaging in business. If the business is to be operated under a fictitious name, it must be registered under the assumed name statute. The assumed name statute is for the benefit of creditors so that they may ascertain the true owner of a business.

Partnership

A partnership is formed by an agreement among the partners. The agreement may be formal or informal, oral or written. While there are no statutory requirements to create a partnership, it is usually in the best interests of all the parties to have a formal written agreement. A formal written agreement at the beginning can save time, expense, and misunderstanding later. The best time to consult your attorney is before trouble happens. The partnership agreement which manifests the intent of the parties is controlling in all situations addressed in the agreement. The state partnership act is designed to fill in the interstitial spaces of the partnership agreement. If the parties themselves do not address the issue, the state does in the state partnership act.

To make sure that it is the partners' intent that prevails and not the intent of the drafters of the state partnership act, the partners should be explicit in their intent and comprehensive in their coverage. There are certain basic provisions that should be included in the agreement. Although a partnership is not required to have a name, it generally does. Whether the name is the name of the partners, a name of one of the partners and associates, or a fictitious name, a good name can have beneficial advertising effects and contribute to the goodwill of the business. If a fictitious name is used, the name must be filed under the assumed name statute of the state. The assumed name statute is for the benefit of creditors, so that creditors are able to obtain the identity of the true owners of the business. The nature and scope of the partnership business should be discussed and agreed upon in the partnership agreement. The nature of the business must be legal; the law prohibits an association for an illegal purpose. It is important that each of the potential partners knows exactly what his or her contribution to the partnership is to be. All property to be contributed to the partnership should be specifically described, and all amounts of money to be contributed should be set out in sum certain. It is recommended that the potential partners be required to make their contribution to the partnership within a specific time. The partners should agree on the division of net profits or losses; otherwise, the state partnership act will impose an equal division of both profits and losses upon the partners. If the partners are to draw salary or have a drawing account, each should be specified. If a managing partner is to be appointed or the work or duties of the partners are to be divided in a particular manner, those provisions should be clearly set out. Likewise, if the power of any individual partner is to be restricted, then that should be clearly delineated. In case of dissolution, the partners should agree as to what procedure will be followed for giving notice to partners and creditors, which partner or partners will be in charge of the winding up process, and what the division of the assets on dissolution will be. The partners should anticipate future disputes and agree upon some procedure for settling them, such as arbitration. Finally, the method of bookkeeping or accounting should be determined along with where the books will be located and access to the books by the partners.

The partners must make a capital contribution to the partnership consisting of money, property, or services past rendered but avoid services to be rendered in the future. Any proposal to exchange a partnership interest for future services to be rendered should be submitted to competent tax counsel before proceeding. This is an uncertain area of the tax law and can cause adverse tax consequences to the partners.

The Internal Revenue Service will recognize a partnership created by a gift to family members.[3] It is treated as a transfer of money or property from one family member to another, which will be considered a gift and which in turn is transferred to the partnership in exchange for a partnership interest. The Internal Revenue Service imposes certain restrictions on a partnership created in this manner. The interest transferred must be a capital interest in a partnership in which capital is a material income-producing factor, which means that a partnership interest in a service partnership, such as a partnership of doctors or lawyers, cannot be acquired by gift. The donee's distributive share of the partnership income cannot exceed the proportionate share acquired by gift, that is a donee who receives a twenty-percent interest in a partnership by gift cannot have allocated more than twenty percent of the partnership income after a reasonable allowance for compensation for services rendered to the partnership by the donor.

Limited Partnership

The persons forming a limited partnership must sign and swear to a certificate of limited partnership which contains the following:

1. The name of the partnership
2. The character of the business
3. The location of the principal place of business
4. The name and place of residence of each member; general and limited partners being respectively designated
5. The term for which the partnership is to exist
6. The amount of cash and a description of and the agreed value of the other property contributed by each limited partner
7. The additional contributions, if any, agreed to be made by each limited partner and the times at which or events on the happening of which they shall be made
8. The time, if agreed upon, when the contribution of each limited partner is to be returned
9. The share of the profits or the other compensation by way of income which each limited partner shall receive by reason of his contribution
10. The right, if given, of a limited partner to substitute an assignee as contributor in his place, and the terms and conditions of the substitution
11. The right, if given, of the partners to admit additional limited partners
12. The right, if given, of one or more of the limited partners to priority over other limited partners, as to contributions or as to compensation by way of income, and the nature of such priority
13. The right, if given, of the remaining general partner or partners to continue the business on the death, retirement, or insanity of a general partner
14. The right, if given, of a limited partner to demand and receive property other than cash in return for his contribution.

After execution, the certificate must be filed with the appropriate state authority.

It is recommended that legal advice be obtained before forming a limited partnership not only because a written filing is required but also because of the securities aspect.

A limited partnership interest is a security and is subject to regulation under both the state and federal securities laws. An offer to sell or a sale of a nonexempt security is a violation of both state and federal securities law. The reader is referred to Chapter 5 for a more detailed discussion of securities regulation.

Incorporation

The organization of a corporation requires strict adherence to the statutory scheme in the state of incorporation.

Jurisdiction

The choice of jurisdiction for incorporation can be an extremely important consideration given the variety of corporation statutes available. While there is a tendency to utilize local jurisdictional statutes, it may be in the best interests of the corporation in the long run to incorporate in another state.

In making the choice of jurisdiction, consider the following factors:

1. Number of incorporators required
2. Qualifications of incorporators
3. Purposes for which a corporation made be incorporated
4. Restrictions on ownership of property
5. Organizational costs such as fees and taxes
6. State securities laws
7. Form of governance allowed
8. Reporting requirements
9. Liabilities of shareholders and directors
10. Requirements for meetings
11. Compensation restrictions for officers and directors
12. Merger or consolidation requirements
13. Dissolution procedures and requirements
14. Foreign corporation restrictions.

Corporate Name

After the decision is made as to where to incorporate, the corporate name should be selected and reserved or registered. Certain restrictions are placed on the choice of a corporate name. A corporate name may not be (1) misleading or deceptive, (2) so similar to another corporate name as to cause confusion, (3) merely descriptive indicating geographical location or type of association, (4) vulgar or offensive, or (5) a prohibited name expressly forbidden by the statute.

All state corporation statutes require that corporations be identified as such in the corporate name by the use of such words as "Corporation," "Incorporated," "Limited," or an abbreviation thereof.

Reserving or registering a corporate name is a relatively simple process. An application to reserve or register a corporate name and the required fee are submitted to the Secretary of State or other designated authority setting forth the name and address of the applicant, the name to be reserved or registered, and the basis of the application.

If the name is not otherwise in use or reserved, a certificate of reservation will be issued reserving the name for a short period of time, generally from 30 to 180 days depending on the state.

A corporate name which has been registered may be transferred by the registrant to another person or entity. Notice must be given to the Secretary of State or designated authority so that the change in registration is officially recorded.

A corporation which desires to change its corporate name must comply with the statutory requirements concerning amendment of its Articles of Incorporation since the corporate name is therein stated. Failure to comply with the statute may result in the abandonment of the corporation.

Articles of Incorporation

Each state specifies the contents of articles of incorporation in the business corporation act. Some states merely state the required content while other states also set forth the required form to be used. Strict adherence to the applicable statutory provision is required.

While no one form is applicable to every jurisdiction, certain essential items are required by almost all states:

1. Heading or title (*e.g.*, Articles of Incorporation)

2. Reference to the act or statutory provision under which incorporation is sought

3. Name of the corporation

4. Purpose(s) for which formed (any legal purpose allowed)

5. Location of corporate office or principal place of activity

6. Duration of the corporation's life (perpetual or for term of years)

7. Number of shares authorized for each class of stock

8. Par value or no par value

9. Names and addresses of first directors

10. Name and address of registered agent for service of process

11. Names and addresses of incorporators and their qualifications, if any

12. Signatures and acknowledgements as required.

The drafter must adhere to the statutory requirements of the jurisdiction. After the Articles of Incorporation have been drafted in final form, the Articles must be executed by the incorporators and notarized and acknowledged, if required by statute.

Filing and Approval

Once fully executed and approved as required by the statute, the completed forms together with the required fee (check or money order) are sent to the Secretary of State or designated authority for approval and filing. When the Secretary of State or designated authority approves the Articles of Incorporation or issues the certificate of incorporation, corporate existence begins. Issuance of the certificate of incorporation is prima facie evidence of incorporation.

Defective Incorporation

If the incorporation procedure has been adhered to and the incorporation statute has been substantially complied with, the corporation is a de jure corporation. But, if the incorporation procedure was not followed or if there is substantial noncompliance with the incorporation statute, the organization is not technically a corporation as far as the state is concerned. The state Attorney General may bring a *quo warranto* proceeding to revoke the charter or Articles of Incorporation on the grounds of defective incorporation.

Nonetheless, an organization that does not attain de jure status may be a de facto corporation. Traditionally, to be considered a de facto corporation, there must be a statute under which the organization could validly have been incorporated, there must be a colorable attempt in good faith to comply with the statute, and there must be some use or exercise of the corporate privileges. A determination of de facto status by a court prevents collateral attack by persons other than the state against the corporateness of the organization. The usefulness of the de facto corporation doctrine can be seriously debated. Many courts are hesitant to use it because it is a judicially created concept in opposition to specific statutory requirements. The Model Business Corporation Act, which has been adopted in a substantial number of states, has been interpreted as abolishing the de facto corporation doctrine. The Model Business Corporation Act makes the certificate of authority "conclusive evidence" of incorporation except as against the state.

The de facto corporation doctrine cannot be used to cure serious defects in the incorporation process. There is simply no corporation and, hence, no limited liability. The organizers are personally liable for torts and in contract unless the "corporation by estoppel" doctrine is applicable. A person who dealt with a defectively incorporated organization believing it to be a corporation may not later collaterally attack the corporateness of the organization to impose personal liability on the organizers unless it is the only way to prevent injustices.

Promoters and Incorporators

An organizer of a corporation is called a promoter and may or may not be an incorporator, director, officer, or shareholder of the corporation after incorporation. A promoter is the moving force behind the creation of a corporation. The promoter is the person with the idea who interests others in the idea and solicits their contribution to the effort. The promoter starts the wheels of incorporation in motion and sees the project through to incorporation at which time his function ceases to exist.

Promoters and promoters' activities generally are not the subject of legislation. Most of the law dealing with promoters is of case law origin. Promoters are subject to certain fiduciary duties and liabilities with respect to their activities, but no qualifications are imposed other than the implicit capacity to contract.

A promoter owes obligations to other promoters jointly engaged, the non-existent corporation, and future shareholders or members of the corporation.

Promoters are joint venturers. A joint venture is generally considered to be a partnership for limited purposes short of the conduct of an ongoing business. As joint venturers they are partners and hence agents of each other. Each has the power within the limits of the joint venture agreement to contractually bind the other joint venturers. Likewise, the joint venturers are liable for torts committed by one of them within the scope of the joint venture. The joint venturers are jointly and severally liable to third parties in both contract and tort.

Joint venturers are in a fiduciary relationship similar to that of partners. That relationship is characterized by Judge Cardozo's now-famous words: "Not honesty alone but the punctilio of an honor the most sensitive, is then the standard of behavior."[4] Breach of that fiduciary duty is actionable in equity by the other joint venturers.

A promoter cannot be an agent for a nonexistent corporate principal prior to incorporation. The liability of a promoter for any agreement entered into before incorporation depends on the type of agreement in question.

The first kind of agreement is an offer contingent upon formation of the corporation or acceptance by the newly formed corporation. This type of agreement is not a contract at all but a revocable offer. The promoter has neither enforceable rights nor liabilities under the agreement. If the proposed corporation is not formed or, if formed, it refuses to accept the offer, if not revoked, then no contract is created. This type of agreement must be carefully worded because courts are reluctant to find that the parties did not intend to create immediate, legally enforceable rights. While a promoter has no liability under the agreement, the promoter may be liable for misrepresentations or breach of warranty arising out of the agreement.

Another type of agreement is a contract between a promoter and third party whereby the promoter promises to form the corporation and use his best efforts to have the newly formed corporation accept the irrevocable offer given in exchange for the promoter's promise. The promoter is personally liable for failing to form the corporation or not using his best efforts to get an acceptance of the offer in addition to potential liability for misrepresentation or breach of warranty. If the proposed corporation is not formed or refuses the offer, if formed, no contract exists between the corporation and the third party, and the corporation has no liabilities or rights under the promoter's contract. If the offer is accepted by the newly formed corporation, the corporation is bound by the terms of the contract between it and the third party, and the promoter's obligations and liabilities under his contract are extinguished except for misrepresentation or breach of warranty.

A contract between a third party and a promoter on behalf of a proposed corporation is binding on the promoter as principal unless otherwise qualified. If the proposed corporation is not formed or does nothing with respect to the contract, the promoter remains liable. Moreover, even if the corporation is formed and ratifies or adopts the contract or becomes the assignee of the promoter, the promoter remains personally liable on the contract as well as liable for misrepresentation or breach of warranty. Only in case of a novation, in which the corporation is substituted for the promoter, is the promoter released from liability. In the event of breach of the contract by the corporation where the promoter remains personally liable, the promoter has a cause of action against the corporation based on either *quantum meruit* or reliance and estoppel against the corporation to deny liability.

However, before a contract or act of a promoter is adopted or ratified, the promoter must make full disclosure. Promoters owe a fiduciary duty to the newly formed corporation which consists of good faith, fair dealing, and full disclosure. If the board of directors of the newly formed corporation is an independent board, then full disclosure to the board is sufficient to satisfy the obligation of full disclosure. But if the board of directors is not independent, full disclosure must be made to the shareholders or membership. There is a split of authority as to whether full disclosure extends to the group of shareholders or membership existent at the time of ratification or adoption or whether it extends to contemplated shareholders or members.

The corporation either in its own stead or by shareholder derivative suit may bring a cause of action against the promoters for breach of fiduciary duty. The typical suit is for disgorgement of secret profits made by the promoters at the expense of the corporation.

Promoters owe fiduciary duties to potential shareholders. Separate from any corporate cause of action are claims of fraud against the promoters in connection with the sale of stock or membership subscription, the primary claim being one of misrepresentation or omission of a material fact in connection with the sale of stock or membership subscription.

Since the corporation is controlled by the board of directors, the organizers are in a position to appoint themselves to such positions and control the corporation. Preincorporation agreements to perpetuate control are not uncommon in business corporations. The agreement is not binding on the corporation, but as long as the organizers control the board of directors, it will be effective.

Generally, anyone who performs services in connection with the formation of a corporation expects to receive compensation for such services. The preincorporation contract for the services provided is with the promoter because the corporation is nonexistent. The promoter remains personally liable until the corporation is formed and assumes responsibility for the contracts by acceptance of the offer, ratification, adoption, assignment, or novation. A third party may recover against a corporation that accepts the benefits of the services without formal action assuming that responsibility is based on *quantum meruit*.

Compensation for promoters of business corporations is expected and generally received. Compensation must be fair and reasonable, and full disclosure must be made. Determining the value of such services is the most difficult step in the process.

Incorporators

Incorporators, technically, are persons who sign the original articles of incorporation. They derive their status strictly from the corporation statutes. Qualifications are expressly set out in the appropriate state statute.

The qualifications for an incorporator of a corporation are *de minimis* under the laws of the several states. The number of incorporators required to sign the original articles of incorporation varies from state to state. Capacity to contract is a requirement which may not be specifically stated but is implicit in the age requirements for natural persons and in the nature of other juridical persons. Capacity to contract in a natural person is a function of age unless the person is otherwise incapacitated by insanity or incompetence. Some states have a residency or citizenship qualification.

Taxation

When setting up a new corporation, stock may be subscribed for cash, property, or services past rendered. If money is used to purchase the stock, no gain or loss is involved, and the purchaser acquires the stock with a tax basis equal to the amount of money paid. If property is exchanged for stock, there may be a realized gain or loss. Under certain conditions, the gain or loss will not be recognized.

To qualify for nonrecognition: (1) the property transferred must be solely in exchange for stock or securities of the corporation and (2) immediately after the transfer the transferors must be in control of the corporation. Control can be held by a group who transferred property pursuant to a plan; however, all transfers need not be made at the same time under the plan. Control means owning at least 80 percent of the total combined voting power of all classes of stock entitled to vote plus at least 80 percent of all other classes of stock. Control does not have to be acquired by the transfer of property in question but includes all stock however acquired.

An exchange of stock for services past rendered is a taxable event resulting in income to the renderer of the services. The exchange will be treated as if the services were compensated in cash and then the stock were purchased with the cash.

ACQUISITION

An alternative to forming a new business and starting from scratch is to acquire an already existing business in the same line of business. Acquisition of an existing business saves the time and cost of developing an organization and starting up. The target business is already in operation; there are no startup costs. The existing business already has the necessary expertise or know-how, suppliers, markets, and good will. More importantly, acquisition of an existing business eliminates it as a competitor.

Sole Proprietorships

Acquisition of a sole proprietorship is merely a purchase of the assets of the sole proprietor. The assets may be purchased by another sole proprietor, partnership, limited partnership, or corporation. The seller may be offered a contract of employment, if desirable, or may merely wish to sell out. The purchaser as a part of the negotiation should insist on a noncompetition covenant to prevent the seller from moving across the street and starting his or her business again. Noncompetition clauses are enforceable if reasonable with respect to time and distance. Obviously, it would be unreasonable to prohibit a person from ever engaging in that particular business again anywhere in the country. Conversely, an agreement not to compete in the city or county for a period of one or two years is not unreasonable.

Assuming an arm's length transaction, the purchaser acquires the assets of the sole proprietorship with a tax basis equal to cost. The seller computes gain or loss on the transaction based on the difference between the amount of money and property received for the assets and his or her tax basis in the assets.

Partnership

Sale of a partnership interest works a dissolution of the partnership although the business may continue under a new partnership. If a new partnership is formed, the purchaser's basis in his or her partnership interest is the amount of money and other property paid. The seller recognizes gain or loss based on the difference between the amount received and his or her partnership basis. The basis of the remaining partners remains the same as before.

Rather than buy a partnership interest, the purchaser may purchase the partnership assets in which event the consequences are similar to purchasing the assets of a sole proprietorship except that the gain or loss recognized on the sale of the assets by the partnership is passed through to the individual partners according to the partnership agreement.

Limited Partnership

Sale of a general partnership interest or sale of a limited partnership's assets are the same as for a partnership. Sale of a limited partnership interest is the purchase and sale of a security and not the business since limited partners are prohibited by law from exercising any managerial power. Purchasing a limited partnership interest is merely an investment. The antifraud provisions of state and federal securities laws apply whether the limited partnership interest is registered or not.

Corporations

Corporate acquisitions are more complicated and require strict adherence to the state corporation act and Internal Revenue Code to avoid adverse consequences. Mergers and consolidations involve two or more corporations and their boards of directors. Stock acquisitions for cash or other stock involve only the shareholders of the target corporation. Acquisitions of corporate assets for cash or other stock generally involve the target corporation's board of directors. Most of these corporate acquisitions are tax reorganizations subject to special treatment under the Internal Revenue Code. Corporate acquisition also involves both state and federal securities laws.

Mergers and Consolidations

A merger takes place when one corporation absorbs another. After the merger, only one corporation survives, and it may be either the acquiring corporation or the target corporation. If the acquiring corporation is the survivor, it is called a forward merger. Conversely, if the target corporation is the survivor, it is called a reverse merger.

A consolidation is a procedure by which two or more corporations combine and form a new corporation, after which the old corporations terminate.

A person or persons who want to acquire a corporation but do not control an acquiring corporation can incorporate a new corporation, the sole purpose of which is to acquire and merge with the target corporation. The new corporation in essence is merely a corporate shell.

The procedure for a merger or consolidation is prescribed by statute. Procedures vary from state to state but generally are similar to one another. All states allow two or more domestic corporations to merge, and most allow a domestic and a foreign corporation to merge. Foreign corporation means a corporation incorporated in another state.

The board of directors of both the acquiring corporation and the target corporation must adopt a plan of merger. Depending on the state, the shareholders of one or both of the corporations may also have to approve the merger at a special shareholders meeting.

In general, the plan of merger must contain the following items:

1. The name of each corporation a party to the merger and the name of the surviving corporation into which each of the other corporations plans to merge;
2. The terms and conditions of the merger;
3. The manner and basis of converting the shares of each corporation into the shares, obligations, or other securities of the surviving or any other corporation or into cash or other property; and
4. Any amendments to the Articles of Incorporation of the surviving corporation resulting from the merger.

After the plan of merger has been adopted by both corporations at either an annual or special meeting, the plan must be submitted to the Secretary of State or other designated official in a document called Articles of Merger or Consolidation. After submission and review of the Articles of Merger or Consolidation by the Secretary of State or designated state official, a certificate of merger or consolidation is issued to the surviving or the new corporation. Immediately after the certificate of merger or consolidation is issued, the corporations party to the merger become a single corporation; all of the corporate parties to the merger other than the surviving corporation cease to exist; the surviving or new corporation possesses all of the rights, privileges, and powers of the combining corporations; the surviving or new corporation acquires all the property of the combining corporations directly; the surviving or the new corporation is liable for all the debts and obligations of the parties to the merger; and the amendments to the Articles of Incorporation of the surviving corporation become effective.

Most state corporation acts provide for a streamlined procedure for merging a parent corporation into a subsidiary corporation. A parent corporation that owns at least 90 percent of the outstanding shares of each class of a subsidiary corporation's stock may merge the subsidiary into the parent without the approval of the shareholders of either the parent or the subsidiary.

In any merger or consolidation there will probably be a small group of dissenters opposed to the merger or consolidation. It would be in the best interests of the surviving corporation and dissenters if they could be bought or cashed out.

Originally, under common law a merger or consolidation required unanimous consent of all shareholders of each corporation. The common law rule was a hindrance to corporate acquisitions. Modern corporation statutes have reduced the requirement for the number of shareholders voting in favor to effect a merger or consolidation to a majority in most states. In exchange for this reduction in voting rights, dissenting shareholders are given appraisal rights by statute. Dissenters who object to being shareholders in the merged or consolidated corporation have the right to be cashed out.

As with other procedures involving corporations, strict adherence to the statutory procedure for securing appraisal rights is required. Failure of the dissenters to follow the statutory procedure will result in the loss of dissenters' appraisal rights.

A dissenting shareholder is generally required to give notice of his or her intent to demand payment before the vote is taken and must not vote in favor of the merger or consolidation. If no shareholder vote is taken, then dissenters must make demand for payment within the time prescribed by statute.

Within ten days after the merger or consolidation is effective, the corporation commonly must deliver a written dissenter's notice along with copies of the dissenter's rights statutory provision and financial statements of the corporation whose stock the dissenter holds. The dissenter must demand payment and deposit his or her stock in accordance with instructions. The amount of the payment is the fair market value of the shares plus accrued interest. Fair market value of the shares is the value of the stock on the day before the merger or consolidation. A dissenting shareholder is not entitled to any synergistic value resulting from the merger or consolidation.

If the corporation fails to provide dissenter's rights or if the shareholder is not satisfied with the corporate offer, resort may be had to the courts. The court will determine the fair value for the stock probably through the appointment of an appraiser who will hear evidence and make a recommendation to the court on fair value.

A corporate merger or consolidation is an "A" reorganization for tax purposes. Reorganizations are classed alphabetically according to the order in which they appear in I.R.C. section 368(a)(1). The tax benefit of a valid "A" reorganization is that neither gain nor loss is recognized by a party to the corporate reorganization. For a merger or consolidation to be a valid "A" reorganization, the state merger or consolidation statute must be strictly complied with, and there must be continuity of interest in a proprietory right not merely that of a creditor. For ruling purposes, the IRS requires that one or more of the shareholders of the acquired corporation receive, in the aggregate, stock with a value greater than or equal to 50 percent of the value of the outstanding stock of the acquired corporation before reorganization.

If the stock or securities received are greater in principal amount than the securities given up, the fair market value of the excess is treated as boot. When boot is received in a reorganization, no loss is recognized; however, gain is recognized but not in excess of the fair market value of the boot received. The rules concerning corporate distributions apply, which may result in the boot's being treated as a dividend to the extent of the earnings and profits of the corporation.

The tax basis of the stock or securities received in exchange by the distributee-shareholder in a reorganization is equal to the basis of the stock or securities exchanged in the hands of the distributee-shareholder, decreased by: (1) the amount of money received, (2) the fair market value of other property received, and (3) any recognized loss on the exchange and increased by any gain recognized on the exchange.

Sale of All or Substantially All the Assets

An alternative to a merger or consolidation is to purchase the assets of the target corporation. Originally, the sale of assets provision was a means to avoid the higher shareholder vote required for merger or consolidation. Today, the vote requirements are generally the same. Purchase of the assets avoids the problem of having to absorb the shareholders of the target into the surviving corporation and thereby diluting ownership control. A purchase of the assets allows acquisition without the attendant personnel problems.

Generally, the purchasing corporation's board of directors may act without shareholder approval. Depending on the state, the selling corporation's board of directors may approve the sale with or without shareholder approval. If the selling corporation's shareholders are entitled to vote, they possess an appraisal right similar to that in a merger or consolidation.

After the selling corporation sells its assets, it may dissolve and distribute the proceeds to its shareholders in exchange for its stock, or it may continue as a holding company whose assets are the proceeds from the sale.

The consideration given by the purchasing corporation in exchange for the assets of the target corporation may be cash, property, or stock or securities. An acquisition for cash or property is not a tax reorganization, but a purchase. Any gain or loss realized on an exchange of property other than cash for assets would be recognized unless protected by another nonrecognition provision. An exchange of voting stock for all or substantially all the assets is a "C" reorganization. At least 80 percent of the fair market value of the target's assets must be acquired solely in exchange for the voting stock of the acquiring corporation. The other 20 percent of the fair market value of the assets may be acquired by nonstock properties. The transactions must be accomplished in a single step. The acquiring corporation may assume liabilities of the target provided there is no boot involved. If boot is involved, then assumed liabilities count as nonstock consideration. No gain or loss is recognized in a valid "C" reorganization except for boot received.

Tender Offers

Mergers and sales of all the assets require action by the board of directors of the target corporation. A hostile board of directors means instant doom to the merger or sale. A direct confrontation with a hostile board of directors may be avoided by dealing directly with the shareholders of the target corporation by offering to buy their stock for cash, property, or other stock. This procedure is known as a tender offer.

A hostile board of directors of the target corporation may engage in defensive manuevers and frustrate the takeover attempt by stopping it or making it too expensive. A wide array of defensive manuevers, such as a friendly merger with a more desirable corporation, a counteroffer to buy by a friendly party, or a repurchase of its own stock by the target corporation, are available to thwart the takeover.

Cash or property offered in exchange for stock is considered a straight sale for tax purposes. An offer to exchange voting stock solely in exchange for the voting stock of the target corporation is a "B" reorganization. Immediately afterward, the acquiring corporation must be in control of the target. Control means owning at least 80 percent of the voting stock of the target plus at least 80 percent of the target's nonvoting stock. Unlike a "C" reorganization, which must be accomplished in a single step, a "B" reorganization may be accomplished in steps over a twelve-month period. No boot whatsover is allowed in a "B" reorganization. Once control is acquired, each successive acquisition by means of an exchange of voting stock for voting stock is a "B" reorganization.

A word of caution: A valid "B" reorganization followed by a liquidation of the target corporation is a "C" reorganization and falls under those rules. In a valid "B" reorganization, no gain or loss is recognized on the exchange. The acquiring corporation receives a carryover basis in the target stock. The carryover basis is the basis that the target shareholder had in the stock immediately prior to transfer. A similar rule applies to the target shareholders' basis in the acquiring corporation's stock.

Tender Offers-Securities Regulation

A tender offer for the stock of a publicly held corporation is subject to sections 13(d) and 14(d) and (e) of the Securities Exchange Act of 1934. Under section 13(d), any person or group of persons who becomes the owner of more than 5 percent of any class of securities registered under section 12 of the Securities Exchange Act of 1934 must file with the issuer of the securities and with the Securities and Exchange Commission a statement setting forth (1) the background of the person or persons, (2) the source of the funds to be used in the acquisition, (3) the purpose of the acquisition, (4) the number of shares actually owned, and (5) any relevant contracts, arrangements, or understandings concerning the ownership of the stock or its acquisition. The statement must be filed within ten days of acquisition of the required percentage of the stock.

Under section 14(d) of the Securities Exchange Act of 1934, no person may make a tender offer that would result in his owning more than 5 percent of a class of securities required to be registered under section 12 of the Securities Exchange Act of 1934 unless the filing has been made with the commission and a copy of which is furnished to each offeree. The information to be contained in the statement is essentially the same information that is required to be filed under section 13(d) of the Securities Exchange Act of 1934.

Section 14(e) of the Securities Exchange Act of 1934 makes it unlawful for any person to misstate or omit a material fact, or to engage in any fraudulent, deceptive, or manipulative acts or practices, in connection with a tender offer. While there is no specific private cause of action granted to shareholders of the target corporation under section 14(e), the Supreme Court of the United States has implied one in *Piper v. Chris-Craft Industries*.[5]

More than 30 states have also enacted laws regulating takeovers of companies incorporated or doing business in their respective states. These statutes tend to be more extensive than the federal statute and tend to favor the incumbent management of the target corporation. The most debilitating part of these state statutes generally imposes a waiting period from 10 to 60 days from the announcement and the commencement of the tender offer. It is this waiting period that allows hostile incumbent management of the target corporation to marshall their forces to ward off the tender offer and frustrate the attempt of the acquiring corporation's management to take over the target company. There have been inconsistent decisions in the federal courts as to whether or not these more extensive state statutes infringe upon the federal perogative of regulating securities.

NOTES

1. 296 U.S. 344 (1935).
2. 66 T.C. 159 (1976).
3. I.R.C. § 704(e).
4. Meinhard V. Salmon, 249 N.Y. 458, 463–464, 164 N.E. 545, 546 (1928).
5. 430 U.S. 1 (1977).

4

Sale of a Business

A business may be sold for any number of reasons including disinvestment, retirement, bankruptcy, and profit-taking. Although the ramifications and consequences of the sale of a business depend in large part on the organizational form of the business, certain aspects are common to all organizational forms.

The sale of a business regardless of its organizational form involves certain common issues. Buyers and sellers have a common interest in having the sales transaction characterized as they thought they had structured it. In any sales transaction, creditors seek protection of their interests in the assets of the business. Determination of a fair market value is an important part of the negotiations. Buyers need to protect their newly acquired business from competition by the previous owners.

Other issues are peculiar to a particular enterprise form and are discussed by organizational form.

Finally, the tax consequences of the sale of a business are discussed in the framework of the recent tax reform measures.

CHARACTERIZATION OF THE TRANSACTION

The parties to the sales transaction should be aware that the transaction as structured may not be treated by the courts in the manner intended by the parties. Sales contracts should be carefully worded and structured to avoid unwanted results. An option to purchase or a lease followed by an option to purchase may be treated as a de facto sale. The sale of a corporate business by a sale of substantially all the stock will be treated as a securities transaction rather than a sale of business. The sale of a business may be treated as a sale of goods under the Uniform Commercial Code.

Option to Purchase; Lease with Option to Purchase

If a potential buyer does not have the available capital to purchase the assets outright, the seller has two options. First, the seller may consider accepting a down payment and carrying the balance on a promissory note. The seller may lend with or without recourse. A loan with recourse means that the seller would be able to take back the business plus any amount owed on the note above the value of the business at the time it is repossessed. Under a nonrecourse loan, the seller is limited to taking the business back. Repossession, however, is not cost free. It may require a lawyer and court costs and can be a time-consuming process—a process it would be wise to avoid. A nonrecourse loan should mean a higher sales price to compensate for the risk.

An alternative to a sale subject to indebtedness is an option to purchase. The seller sells the buyer an option to purchase the business at a later date at a price which represents the total sales price less the price of the option. The option price is applied to the sales price if and when the option is exercised. If the buyer does not or cannot exercise the option, the seller keeps the option price. The benefit derived from an option to purchase is that the seller retains title to the assets until the option is exercised. In the event of default, there are no costs to recover the assets as in the case of a sale subject to indebtedness.

If contemplating such an alternative, be forewarned that a court might construe the option to purchase as a de facto sale requiring formal court proceedings to repossess.

A variation on the option to purchase is a lease with an option to purchase at the end of the lease. The buyer signs a lease and operates the business under the lease. The option to purchase is at a price which represents the total sales price less the cost of the lease.

A lease with an option to purchase is not as likely to be considered a de facto sale as would the option to purchase plan standing alone.

Sale of a Business as a Sale of Goods

Depending on the state, the sale of a business may constitute the sale of goods within the scope of Article Two of the Uniform Commercial Code. The general rule is that the sale of a business is not a sale of goods under the Uniform Commercial Code. Nonetheless, in some states, if the sale consists of tangible property which falls within the statutory definition of goods in the Uniform Commercial Code, the entire purchase price may be allocated among the goods and become subject to the provisions of Article Two. To prevent Article Two from applying to the sale, the sale must involve some nongoods such as goodwill and real property, but, even then, if the sale is predominantly one of goods, some state courts will subject the sale to Article Two of the Uniform Commercial Code. Where there is a mixture of goods and nongoods, state courts look to see whether or not the sale is predominantly one of goods or nongoods. If the essential bulk of the assets sold qualifies as goods, Article Two will apply. Some state courts have gone so far as to divide the sale into a sale of goods and a sale of nongoods, in which case, that part of the sales contract dealing with goods is subject to Article Two of the Uniform Commercial Code while the nongoods part of the transaction is not.

If a sales transaction involves both goods and nongoods, the parties to the sale may wish to treat everything as coming within Article Two of the Uniform Commercial Code. If so, there is nothing to prevent them from doing so. See Chapter 10 for a detailed discussion of Article Two.

Sale of Business Doctrine

In 1985, the United States Supreme Court rejected the "sale of business" doctrine.[1] As a result, all stock transactions, at a minimum, are subject to the antifraud provisions of the federal securities law. Registration may be required if no appropriate exemption is available.

The "sale of business" doctrine was a judicially created exception from the registration and antifraud provisions of the federal securities law. It meant that the sale of all the common stock of a closely held corporation was exempt as well as the sale of a controlling interest in a closely held corporation. The rule applied to professional corporations as well as general corporations.

This change in treatment creates a problem since many states adopted the sale of business doctrine. While the sale of all the common stock or a controlling interest may still be exempt from the state registration and antifraud provisions, it is no longer exempt under federal law.

See Chapter 5 for a discussion of securities regulation.

Successor Corporation's Liability for Predecessor Corporation's Defective Product

There is a growing trend in product liability cases to hold successor corporations liable for injuries sustained as a result of using a defective product manufactured by the predecessor corporation. At the heart of this development is the desire of many judges to provide an equitable remedy for injured plaintiffs who have no defendant to sue.

Corporate acquisitions may be accomplished by (1) merger or consolidation, (2) acquisition of the stock of the target corporation, or (3) purchase of the assets of the target corporation.

Under a statutory merger or consolidation, the surviving corporation succeeds to the assets and liabilities of the participating corporations; therefore, the successor corporation is liable for injuries incurred from using a defective product of one of the merged or consolidated corporations.

In an acquisition of the stock of a target corporation, whether it be by cash, assets for stock, or stock for stock exchange, the target corporation continues in existence. Only the shareholders have changed. Hence, the liabilities of the target corporation continue. A subsequent merger or consolidation does not alter existing corporate liability.

To avoid assuming liabilities of a target corporation, an acquiring corporation may purchase the assets of the target corporation. A purchase of the assets is in effect a purchase of property. As a result, the legal theory shifts from corporation law to property law. Under property law, a bona fide purchaser for value without notice of any unknown claims cannot be held liable for those unknown claims after acquisition. Moreover, any cash or stock received by the target corporation for its assets is generally distributed to the shareholders, and the target corporation is dissolved leaving no defendant for subsequent product liability claims.

Under traditional corporate law, no successor liability is imposed in a sale of the assets transaction unless:

1. There is a fraudulent transfer of assets to defraud creditors;
2. The successor expressly or impliedly agrees to assume all of the debts and liabilities of the selling corporation;
3. The successor is merely a continuation of the selling corporation; or
4. The transaction is held to be a de facto consolidation or merger of the buying and selling corporations.

The first two exceptions listed above rarely occur in corporation law today. The last two exceptions can really be treated as one—the de facto merger doctrine. It is the de facto merger doctrine that judges use as the vehicle to provide relief for the defendantless product liability plaintiff.

The de facto merger doctrine is an equitable remedy used to provide relief in cases where the economic effect of a statutory merger or consolidation and a sale and purchase of the assets is the same in that the essential business or enterprise of the target corporation continues. The rationale is that, if the effect is the same, then the consequences should be the same. The de facto merger doctrine is traditionally used to protect creditors, assess taxes, and provide dissenting shareholders' rights.

A de facto merger will be found where:

1. There is a continuity of shareholders;
2. There is a cessation of ordinary business and dissolution of the target corporation immediately following the sale or as soon as practical;
3. There is an assumption of all liabilities of the target corporation that are necessary for uninterrupted continuance of the target's normal business operation; and
4. There is a continuity of management, personnel, physical location of facilities and assets, and general business operation.

The de facto merger doctrine is now being used to impose liability on the purchasing corporation for injuries sustained as a result of use of a defective product manufactured by the selling corporation regardless of whether the product was sold before the sale of the assets and the injury occurred after the sale of the assets.

The de facto merger doctrine has been recognized to impose successor corporation liability in California, Florida, Illinois, New Jersey, New York, and Pennsylvania.[2] The Texas Legislature has prohibited use of the de facto merger doctrine in product liability cases.

PROTECTION OF CREDITORS

Sale or Transfer of Secured Property

A debtor may sell or transfer property which is collateral for a loan whether or not any security agreement prohibits such transfer or the transfer constitutes a default. The Uniform Commercial Code (UCC) prohibits an enforcement of a prohibition of sale or transfer except to the extent that the transfer constitutes a default. In this situation, the debtor has the right to transfer his or her interest in the collateral, and his or her creditors may take appropriate action to reach that interest. The right of any transferee or buyer with respect to the collateral is subject to the rights of the secured party in accordance with the priority provisions of UCC section 9–312.

A security interest continues in collateral notwithstanding sale, exchange, or other disposition unless such disposition was authorized by the secured party in the security agreement or otherwise. The buyer or transferee takes the property unencumbered by any unperfected security interest.

For a more detailed explanation of Article Nine of the Uniform Commercial Code and its provisions, see Chapter 6.

Bulk Sales

Today in nearly every state, bulk transfers or sales are governed by Article Six of the Uniform Commercial Code. This article is the successor to bulk sales acts previously in force in most states. Those earlier statutes were designed to prevent the secret disposition of the substantial assets of a business to a transferee for valuable consideration to the detriment of the transferor's unsecured creditors. A dishonest merchant could cheat its unsecured creditors by selling its whole inventory of goods in one transaction, taking the proceeds, and disappearing. So the purpose of bulk sales law is to regulate a merchant's or manufacturer's extraordinary or secret transfer of stock in trade.

The law in this area employs an extraordinary notion—a transfer of title valid between the parties is invalid as to creditors of the transferor even if it is for good consideration to a bona fide transferee. More specifically, Article Six is designed to prevent the following two types of commercial fraud:

1. The merchant, owing debts, who sells out its stock in trade to a friend for less than it is worth, pays its creditors less than it owes them, and hopes to come back into the business through the back door some time in the future; and

2. The merchant, owing debts, who sells out its stock in trade to any one for any price, pockets the proceeds, and disappears leaving its creditors unpaid.

While the first type of transaction would fall into the category of a voidable fraudulent conveyance under the common law fraudulent conveyance doctrines, the second, in the absence of bulk sales law would be free from attack. Article Six, however, regulates both transactions.

Unless the specific Article Six requirements are complied with by *both* the seller-transferor and buyer-transferee, a bulk transfer is ineffective against all creditors of the seller-transferor-in-bulk. The creditors' claims can be secured or unsecured, contingent or absolute, liquidated or unliquidated, in tort or in contract. In the case of a sole proprietor, personal as well as business creditors would be protected by Article Six. The basic requirement of Article Six is that timely notice be given to all creditors of the seller-transferor that a bulk sale is about to occur. Then it is up to the creditors to take further affirmative action to protect their interests.

Bulk Transfer Defined

The practical and legal problems inherent in any "bulk transfer" can be understood only through an analysis of the statutory provisions. Section 6–102 defines a "bulk transfer" as any transfer in bulk and not in the ordinary course of the transferor's business of a major part of the materials, supplies, merchandise, or other inventory (section 9–109) of an enterprise subject to Article Six.

A transfer of a substantial part of the equipment of such an enterprise is a bulk transfer if it is made in connection with a bulk transfer of inventory. Enterprises subject to Article Six include all whose principal business is the sale of merchandise from stock including those which manufacture what they sell.

The article's scope, consequently, is limited to sales of inventory or equipment. Unless there is a disposition of inventory, however, there is no bulk transfer. The rationale of the inventory scope restriction is that, since inventory is more readily removable than equipment, the danger of fraud inherent in sales of inventory in bulk is not present when only equipment is sold. The fallacy of such reasoning is that, although equipment may not be easily removable, the proceeds of an equipment sale certainly are.

Not all sales of inventory by merchandisers are included. Article Six regulates only those, first, which are *not* in the ordinary course of the transferor's business and, second, which constitute a *major part* of the transferor's merchandise or inventory. Of these two qualifiers, the "major part" language presents the more serious interpretative problem. Court decisions are inconsistent in interpreting the "major part" requirement.

To determine the applicability of Article Six to a particular transfer, not only must the nature of the transfer be examined, so also must the nature of the transferor's business be scrutinized since section 6–102(3) limits a bulk transfer to enterprises whose principal business is the sale of merchandise from stock. This language includes manufacturers, distributors, and retailers whose principal business is the sale of *goods*. Services are clearly excluded. What about enterprises which sell both goods and services, for example, restaurants or taverns? The courts are divided as to whether they are covered.

In addition to the "major part" and "principal business" limitations on the scope of Article Six, there is a third limitation: The transfer, to be a covered transaction, must be one *not* in the ordinary course of business.

The scope of Article Six is also restricted by section 6–103 which specifically excludes the following transfers:

1. Those made to give security for the performance of an obligation;

2. General assignments for the benefit of all the creditors of the transferor and subsequent transfers by the assignee thereunder;

3. Transfers in settlement or realization of a lien or other security interest;

4. Sales by executors, administrators, receivers, trustees in bankruptcy, or any public officer under judicial process;

5. Sales made in the course of judicial or administrative proceedings for the dissolution or reorganization of a corporation and, of which, notice is sent to creditors of the corporation pursuant to order of the court or administrative agency;

6. Transfers to a person maintaining a known place of business in this state who becomes bound to pay the debts of the transferor in full and gives public notice of that fact and who is solvent after becoming so bound;

7. A transfer to a new business enterprise organized to take over and continue the business, if public notice of the transaction is given and the new enterprise assumes the debts of the transferor and it receives nothing from the transaction except an interest in the new enterprise junior to the claims of creditors; and

8. Transfers of property which are exempt from execution.

Duties of Buyer and Seller

Article Six imposes upon both buyer and seller strict requirements designed to insure adequate notice of the impending transfer to creditors. These requirements consist generally of first, preparation and preservation of a list of creditors; second, the scheduling of property; and third, the timely transmitting of adequate notice to creditors of the seller-transferor by the buyer-transferee.

Section 6–104 provides that in order for the transfer to be effective against creditors:

1. First, the *transferee* must require the transferor to furnish a list of existing creditors.

2. Second, the *parties together* must prepare a schedule of the property transferred, sufficient to identify it.

3. Finally, the *transferee* must preserve the list and schedule for six months following the transfer and permit inspection of either or both and copying therefrom at all reasonable hours, or must file the list and schedule with the recorder of deeds of each county where any part of the property is located.

The list of creditors must be signed and sworn to or affirmed by the seller or its agent. It must contain the names and business addresses of all creditors, including those whose claims are disputed. Section 6–104(3) provides that responsibility for the completeness and accuracy of the list of creditors rests with the seller. The transfer is not rendered ineffective by errors and omissions unless the buyer has actual knowledge thereof.

Note that, notwithstanding section 6–104(3), virtually the entire responsibility for compliance rests on the buyer-transferee. It is the buyer who must first demand the list, who must assist in the preparation of the schedule of property, and who is responsible for the preservation and filing of both documents. Finally, and most important, it is the buyer who will suffer the major consequences of non-compliance if the sale is ultimately held defective as the buyer will be subjected to the claims of the seller's creditors.

While section 6–104(3) relieves the buyer of responsibility for completeness and accuracy of the list of creditors, no similar provision exists with regard to the schedule of property. Errors or omissions in the designation or description of the property transferred will subject the buyer to creditors' claims; the buyer must, therefore, make sure that the schedule of property is complete and accurate in every respect.

Obviously, the only creditors who can be listed are those existing at the time the list is prepared. In most instances, practical considerations will require the list to be prepared at least several days in advance of the sending of notices pursuant to section 6–105. A question thus arises whether creditors whose claims come into existence during the intervening period should be listed and notified. The answer is probably "yes." Caution, at least, would require that an amended list be prepared adding such additional creditors, if any, as may arise in the interim. Note also that, other than express limitations to "existing" creditors, there is no other restriction as to the types of creditors required to be listed. Consequently, the required list of creditors must include those whose claims are contingent, unmatured or unliquidated, and all combinations thereof.

With regard to the schedule of property, the statute states only that it must be "sufficient to identify it." There is no requirement that the cost, price, or other valuation of the property be shown. The schedule must be detailed, however.

As to preservation of the list and schedules, the articles allows two options. The buyer may keep and preserve the list and schedules for a period of six months and permit copying and inspection during reasonable hours, or, in the alternative, he or she may file them with the recorder of deeds of each county in which any part of the goods is located.

The key requirements imposed by Article Six are those of sections 6–105 and 6–106 which state the form, manner, and extent of notice that must be given to creditors. Two types of notice are prescribed. A *short form* may be used where creditors of the seller are to be paid in full while the so-called *long form* is required where creditors are not to receive full payment or where the buyer is in doubt in this respect.

If creditors are to be paid in full, the notice need only state:

1. That a bulk transfer is about to be made;
2. The names and business addresses of the transferor and transferee, and all other business names and addresses used by the transferor within the three years last past so far as known to the transferee; and
3. Whether or not all the debts of the transferor are to be paid in full as they fall due as a result of the transaction and, if so, the address to which creditors can send their bills.

If the debts of the seller are not to be paid in full or if the buyer is in doubt, then the notice must also state:

4. The location and general description of the property to be transferred and the estimated total of the transferor's debts;
5. The address where the schedule of property and list of creditors may be inspected;
6. Whether the transfer is to pay existing debts and, if so, the amount of such debts and to whom owing; and
7. Whether the transfer is for new consideration and, if so, the amount of such consideration and the time and place of payment.

The notice must be in writing and is to be given by the buyer at least ten days before taking possession of the goods *or* paying for them, whichever happens first. It must be transmitted either by personal delivery or registered mail to all persons shown on the list of creditors furnished by the seller and to all other persons who are known to the buyer to hold or assert claims against the seller.

Section 6–106(3) provides that the notice shall be delivered personally or sent by registered or certified mail to *all* persons shown on the list of creditors and to *all other persons known to the transferee* to hold or assert claims against the transferor.

Effect of Noncompliance

Noncompliance does not affect the validity of the transfer as between the transferor and the transferee. Nor does noncompliance give rise to any tort action against any party. Instead, the parties may choose not to comply and to accept the risks and potential consequences that Article Six provides. The effect of noncompliance, except in case of auction sales, is to render the sale ineffective against any creditor of the transferor.

The possible harsh effect of these provisions is abated to a certain extent by the short limitation period prescribed by section 6–110 which provides that no action shall be brought, nor levy made more than six months after the date on which the seller-transferee took possession of the goods unless the transfer has been concealed. Where the transfer has been concealed, actions may be brought or levies made within six months after discovery.

It is probably safe to say that, in many instances, bulk sales have been defective, but the ultimate running of the six-month period without action saved the day for the buyers of the businesses involved. Creditors, had they acted more diligently, might have been able in many cases to upset the transaction on some ground or another and to enforce their claims against the sold property.

Creditors' Rights

The preceding discussion has examined the bulk transfers primarily from the point of view of the party who wishes to consummate a bulk sale without running the risk of liability to the seller's creditors. It is now appropriate to examine the problem from the other side—that of the creditors of a transferor who is about to effect a bulk transfer.

If Article Six has not been complied with, the creditor has the right to proceed against the goods in the hands of the transferee and to levy against them or take such other action as would have been available if the transfer had not taken place. This right of action may be asserted by a bankruptcy trustee of a bulk transferor. The trustee may recover the property from the transferee if Article Six is not complied with even if the transfer is neither a preference nor a fraudulent conveyance.

Where a creditor has reason to believe that the sale may be fraudulent or for an excessively inadequate consideration, he or she may be able to obtain relief by injunction. However, this would ordinarily require the posting of substantial bond, and, if it turned out that the proposed sale was proper, the creditor might find him- or herself substantially liable in damages as a result of interference with the sale. Consequently, this is a remedy to be exercised only in extreme cases.

Fortunately, in most instances it is feasible to obtain cooperation from the parties and their attorneys which will both satisfy creditors as to the adequacy of the price and assure them as to prompt and proper distribution of the proceeds. Often provision is made for payment to be made to a committee of creditors or other creditor body so that no dissipation can occur. In the absence of such voluntary safeguards, however, the creditors' remedy may be quite limited.

In summary, the "bulk transfer" article meets a need and, in general, services it fairly well. There are, however, many areas of uncertainty, extensive gaps in the protection provided, and in some instances traps for the unwary. Parties to a bulk transfer, particularly the buyer on the one hand and the seller's creditors on the other, must be unusually diligent if their rights are not to be jeopardized.

The commercial bar is not unaware of the weaknesses and ambiguities of Article Six as presently written. Accordingly, the American Bar Association's Section on Corporation, Banking, and Business Law has established a committee to propose a revision of Article Six. The proposals for revision of Article Six were first published in August 1983. As of this writing, however, no state has enacted the proposed revisions.

VALUATION

The sale of a business generally presumes a willing buyer and seller negotiating at arm's length. The key element in the negotiations is price. If the seller is buying the assets or stock of a business where market prices are readily available for the assets or stock, determination of the price is relatively easy. For example, if the buyer is purchasing the stock of a publicly held corporation, market quotations are widely available in newspapers and from brokers. Similarly, the value of an asset can be determined from recent sales of identical or similar assets in arm's-length transactions. Valuation by reference to market value is customary.

Some sales are at book value. Book value, which refers to the balance sheet of the business, is calculated by subtracting liabilities from assets. This is the owner's equity. Book value generally does not reflect the true value of the business. First, asset entries on the balance sheet are made at historical cost and do not reflect appreciation or depreciation of the assets. Second, book value does not take into account any synergistic or going concern value or goodwill.

Problems arise where there is no readily available market for assets or stock or when purchasing a going concern which has synergistic value above the value of the assets. Where there is no definable market, valuation may be made by capitalizing the income stream of the business. This method is applicable to the sale of a going concern that will be continued. Two values need to be determined—the annual average income for a three-to-five-year period preceding the sale and the capitalization rate. The annual average income can be calculated from the business records of the concern. The capitalization rate, however, is more difficult to determine. Theoretically, the capitalization rate should reflect an acceptable rate of return on the investment plus compensation for risk. The income stream is capitalized by dividing it by the capitalization rate. For example, a business may have an annual average income over the past five years of $30,000. Given the nature of the business and current interest rates, a 15-percent capitalization rate is appropriate. The value of the business is determined by dividing the annual average income of $30,000 by fifteen percent which yields a value of $200,000.

Capitalization rates for different kinds of businesses may be found in financial publications. Anyone unfamiliar with capitalization rates and calculations of present value should seek the professional advice of an accountant or business lawyer.

COVENANT NOT TO COMPETE

Part of the consideration in the sale of a business may be a covenant not to compete. The buyer would be wise to insist upon one if the success of the business is largely due to the personal efforts of the seller. It would be unwise to purchase a business only to have the seller start a new, competing business across the street.

A restrictive covenant not to compete is a direct restraint on competition and may violate federal antitrust and state laws. Such restrictive covenants are allowed only in employment contracts and in contracts for the sale of a business. They must be narrowly worded and must protect a legitimate business interest.

To be valid, a covenant not to compete must be reasonable with respect to both time and place. What constitutes a reasonable time and place depends on the type of business involved, the nature of the industry, and the length of time that the seller ran the business. An agreement not to deal with former customers or clients for a reasonable period of time will be enforceable against the seller of a commercial activity but not against a seller engaged in a profession because the restriction infringes on the rights of third parties to deal with a professional of their own choosing.

SOLE PROPRIETORSHIP

The sale of a business by a sole proprietor is merely the sale of the assets and goodwill of the business. The identifiable tangible assets of the business can readily be assigned a value as can identifiable intangibles such as securities. Valuation of the goodwill presents a problem.

Goodwill is neither identifiable nor tangible. Goodwill may include:

1. The abilities of the management team
2. The lack of ability of competitors
3. The ownership of trade secrets or lists
4. Good labor relations
5. Reputation in community
6. Location
7. Superior training programs
8. Favorable tax position
9. Favorable regulatory climate.

Goodwill can be realistically valued only at the time of a sale of the business. To the extent that the sales price exceeds the value of the net assets, the difference is attributable to goodwill. (A brief discussion of valuation methods appears in the preceding section.) Accountants use several different methods to calculate the value of goodwill depending on the circumstances. Should difficulties arise in evaluating goodwill, professional advice should be sought.

The cost of goodwill must be amortized like other intangible assets over a period of time not to exceed 40 years. The cost of goodwill is not tax deductible.

PARTNERSHIP

Sale of an entire partnership business is similar to the sale of a sole proprietorship. The sale consists of a sale of the assets and goodwill of the partnership. Partnership assets are owned by the partnership and not the individual partners.

Sale of the partnership assets usually means that the individuals are no longer carrying on a business for profit; therefore, the partnership is dissolved. The proceeds of the sale are first allocated to liabilities of the partnership including liabilities owed to individual partners. After the liabilities have been satisfied, each partner is entitled to be repaid his or her contributions (capital or advances to partnership property) to the partnership. Any profit or surplus remaining is then distributed to the partners according to the partnership agreement or in the absence of an agreement, equally. If the proceeds of the sale are insufficient to satisfy the liabilities, the partners must contribute toward the losses or deficit according to how they share profits. General partners are personally liable for losses or deficits beyond the value of the assets.

In a limited partnership, the limited partners are entitled to be paid before the general partners take anything in their capacity as general partners. Limited partners are not liable for any losses or deficit above their contribution unless they take part in the control of the business.

An individual partner may sell his or her partnership interest. In this event, the former partnership is dissolved, and a new partnership may be formed without interruption of the business by unanimous agreement among the continuing partners. The buyer and seller independently agree to a price to be paid for the partnership interest equal to the sales price. The buyer who is admitted as a new partner is liable for all obligations of the partnership, even those that arose before becoming a partner, but limited to his or her partnership interest.

SALE OF A CORPORATION

The sale of a corporate business may be accomplished by (1) a merger or consolidation with one or more other corporations, (2) a sale of all or substantially all of the assets of the corporation, or (3) sale or exchange of at least a controlling interest in the common stock.

A merger or consolidation and sale of the assets are transactions involving the boards of directors of the participating corporations. The shareholders may be entitled to vote if provided in the articles of incorporation or bylaws; however, the decision regarding merger, consolidation, or sale of assets is initially that of the board of directors. A sale or exchange of stock on the other hand bypasses the board of directors and directly concerns the shareholders who are willing to sell or exchange their stock.

Merger or Consolidation

Any two or more corporations may merge or consolidate pursuant to the state corporation statute by adopting a plan of merger or consolidation. The plan typically sets forth the following:

1. The names of the corporations proposing to merge or consolidate; the name of the surviving corporation, if a merger takes place; or the name of the new corporation, if a consolidation takes place;
2. The terms and conditions of the proposed merger or consolidation;
3. The changes or required statements to be included in the articles of incorporation of either the surviving corporation or the new corporation being organized;
4. The right to withdraw from the plan of merger or consolidation at any time prior to filing the certificate of merger or consolidation with the appropriate state authority; and
5. Other provisions desired or deemed necessary.

The plan is approved by the board of directors at a regular or special meeting which must comply with the statutory requirements for meetings. If no share-holders are entitled to vote, the plan is approved or disapproved. If shareholders are entitled to vote on the merger or consolidation, then the proposed plan is submitted to the shareholders for approval at a regular or special meeting which also must comply with the statutory requirements.

After approval, the articles of merger or consolidation are executed by the corporate officers and filed with the appropriate state authority, usually the secretary of state. The merger or consolidation generally is effective upon issuance of a certificate of merger or consolidation by the appropriate state authority.

A merger involves two or more corporations, one of which will be the surviving corporation. Any one of the corporations may be chosen as the survivor. In a consolidation, a new corporation is created which will be the surviving corporation. The previously existing corporations are merged into the new corporation which was created solely for that purpose.

The effect of the merger or consolidation is that the separate existence of the corporations, except for the surviving corporation or new corporation, ceases. The surviving or new corporation succeeds to all the rights, privileges, immunities, and franchises of each of the merging or consolidating corporations as well as all property and debts due on whatever account, all other choses in action (a personal right not reduced to possession but recoverable in a lawsuit), and all other interests belonging to each of the merged or consolidated corporations. All title to real estate, or any interest therein, vested in any of the corporations shall not revert or be in any way impaired because of the merger or consolidation.

If one of the corporations involved is a foreign (incorporated in another state) corporation, additional requirements may be imposed such as providing authenticated articles of merger or consolidation from the appropriate foreign state authority.

Any stock issued which is used in the merger or consolidation may be subject to the registration requirements of federal and state securities laws. For a discussion of federal and state securities laws, see Chapter 5.

Sale of the Assets

A sale, lease, exchange, mortgage, pledge, or other disposition of all, or substantially all, the property and assets of a corporation may be made on such terms and conditions and for such consideration as may be authorized by the board of directors in the ordinary course of business. Ordinary course of business refers to the actual business being conducted by the corporation. Sale of all, or substantially all, the assets not in the ordinary course of business generally requires the approval of the shareholders of the selling corporation. Some states leave it to the articles of incorporation to determine whether or not the shareholders are entitled to vote. All meetings must meet the statutory requirements for corporate meetings.

Sale of the assets is used to accomplish certain objectives such as avoidance of shareholder approval or a higher shareholder vote requirement for mergers or consolidations or nonassumption of liabilities of the selling corporation.

The bulk sales requirements of the Uniform Commercial Code may be applicable. For details, see the section concerning bulk sales above.

Dissenting Shareholder's Rights

State corporation statutes generally provide an appraisal remedy for certain dissenting shareholders in exchange for reducing the common law unanimous shareholder consent requirement to a lesser requirement. Appraisal rights may be granted to dissenting shareholders entitled to vote for a merger or consolidation or sale of the assets not in the ordinary course of business. No appraisal rights are granted for dissenters from voluntary dissolution decisions. Appraisal rights are generally limited to shareholders of record entitled to vote on the matter in question. If entitled to appraisal rights, the dissenting shareholders must strictly follow the statutory requirements which, at a minimum, consist of timely objection and demand for payment. Failure to do so results in a denial of appraisal rights.

Dissenting shareholders are entitled to the fair market value of their stock on the day preceding the accomplishment of the transaction objected to by the shareholders. This is readily provided by the market price if the stock is publicly traded. Controversy usually arises when there is no readily available market price to serve as a benchmark. In case of dispute, courts will make an evaluation of the corporation often by capitalizing the income stream at an agreed-on rate and allocating that value to the securities in the capital structure of the corporation.

Voluntary Dissolution

A corporation may be voluntarily dissolved by expiration of the period of duration as provided in the articles of incorporation or action taken by the board of directors and shareholders pursuant to the articles of incorporation or the bylaws.

Following a merger or consolidation the corporate identity of the absorbed corporation ceases, and that corporation is voluntarily dissolved pursuant to the plan of merger or consolidation. After a sale of the assets, the selling corporation may continue in existence as a holding company for the proceeds of the sale, or it may distribute the proceeds of the sale to its shareholders and voluntarily dissolve.

At common law, unanimous consent of the shareholders was necessary to dissolve a corporation. State statutes have reduced the required vote, which ranges from a simple majority to two-thirds of the shareholders. The articles of incorporation may require that a higher percentage of the shareholders vote to adopt a resolution of dissolution than that stated by the statute.

Procedurally, the board of directors by majority vote adopts a resolution recommending that the corporation be dissolved. If there are no shareholders entitled to vote, the dissolution is authorized by the vote of the board of directors. If shareholders are entitled to vote, the board of directors gives notice of a meeting of shareholders to decide whether the corporation should be dissolved. The resolution to dissolve is effective on passage by the requisite vote of the members.

After the resolution to dissolve is authorized, a plan of distribution of the assets must be adopted. The plan is adopted by majority vote of the board of directors if there are no shareholders entitled to vote. Otherwise, the board resolution is submitted to the shareholders at a regular or special meeting of the shareholders for their approval by the requisite vote. The meeting must conform to the statutory requirements for calling and holding a meeting of the shareholders.

After the resolution to dissolve is passed, a statement of intent to dissolve or articles of dissolution must be filed with the appropriate state authority, usually the secretary of state. The statement of intent or the articles of dissolution generally contains the name of the corporation; the manner in which the resolution to dissolve was approved; a statement providing that all debts, obligations, and liabilities of the corporation have been paid and discharged or adequate provision has been made to do so; a statement that there are no suits pending against the corporation in any court for which provisions have not been made for the satisfaction of any judgment, order, or decree which may be entered against the corporation; and a plan for distribution of the remaining assets.

On the adoption of the resolution to dissolve, the corporation must cease to conduct its affairs except for winding up its affairs, marshalling the assets, and distributing them.

Sale of Stock

A direct way to sell a corporate business is to sell the ownership interests— the common stock. One of the more desirable attributes of a corporation is the free transferability of the stock. Transferability, however, may be restricted in some cases such as closely held corporations and professional corporations. Such restrictions generally must appear on the stock certificate itself to be valid.

The decision to sell the stock belongs to the individual shareholders and not the corporation's board of directors. However, the board of directors may influence the shareholders' decisions by actively opposing a sale or buying back the stock and holding it as treasury stock or retiring it.

If the stock is publicly traded on a securities exchange or over-the-counter, a sale may be readily effected. Market price is established, and willing buyers are available. If the stock is in a closely held, nonpublic corporation, a sale is more difficult. Market price is difficult to establish, and willing buyers are hard to find. Many closely held corporations, therefore, have buy-out arrangements.

In the event that a shareholder wants to sell his or her stock in a closely held corporation, several options may be made available. First, the corporation itself may have an option or right of first refusal. A shareholder desiring to sell must first offer the stock to the corporation. The corporation would have a specified period of time such as 60 or 90 days in which to buy the stock. If the corporation refuses to buy the stock, the shareholder may offer it for sale elsewhere. In some cases, the other shareholders have the second chance to purchase after the corporation. Thereafter, the selling shareholder may offer the stock to third parties. An alternative plan is to reverse the roles of the corporation and nonselling shareholders. The first option or right of first refusal would belong to the other shareholders with the second option belonging to the corporation. Buy-sell agreements such as these are designed to provide dissatisfied shareholders with a market for otherwise nonmarketable stock and to provide the remaining shareholders in the closely held corporation with control over stock ownership.

For a discussion of issues related to buying stock see Chapter 3.

Sale of Control

A controlling shareholder owes his or her corporation the duty of due care and fiduciary duties.[3] The rationale for imposing these duties is that control is not the personal property of the controlling shareholder but rather belongs to all the shareholders. The controlling shareholder or shareholders hold control as fiduciaries for the benefit of all shareholders. As a result, controlling shareholders are liable for any damage to the corporation and profits derived from the control premium. The control premium is the increase in the sales price attributable to the fact that a control block is being sold over the market price for single shares. Minority shareholders are entitled to recover their proportionate share of the control premium from the controlling shareholders.

Use of corporate assets to finance the purchase of a controlling interest has been held to violate section 10b of the Securities Exchange Act and Rule 10b–5.

Transfer of Stock

Sale of stock generally does not transfer shareholder rights until the stock has been transferred on the corporation's books. Certificated shares are transferred by delivery of the certificate to the corporation's transfer clerk or secretary. The certificate may be endorsed in blank, or the assignment, usually printed on the reverse side of the certificate, may be endorsed on behalf of the buyer thereby giving the transfer clerk a power of attorney. A separate form of assignment may be used. On receipt, the transfer clerk or secretary will record the transfer on the corporate books, cancel the old certificates, and issue new certificates to the buyer. Uncertificated shares are transferred by registration. The bylaws should contain provisions for transferring ownership of stock in the corporation.

The corporation may be held liable if the transfer was not authorized by the registered owner or if the transfer was negligent and a fiduciary duty to the beneficial owners was breached. Approximately three-fourths of the states have adopted the Uniform Act for Simplification of Fiduciary Security Transfers. The act provides that a corporation may register stock in the name of a fiduciary without inquiring into the nature or extent of the relationship. The corporation is not charged with notice regarding any court record or document concerning the fiduciary relationship even if it is in the corporation's possession. These provisions apply to fiduciary relationships such as guardianships and estates.

The Uniform Commercial Code regulates the transfer, negotiability, and registration of the transfer of securities. UCC section 8–401 provides that the corporation is under a duty to register the transfer if:

1. The security is endorsed or the instruction was originated by the appropriate party;
2. Reasonable assurance is given that the endorsements or instructions are genuine and effective;
3. The corporation has no duty as to adverse claims or has discharged such duty;
4. Applicable law is complied with; and
5. The transfer, pledge, or release is in fact rightful or is to a bona fide purchaser.

The transfer clerk or secretary should rigorously examine the documents. If in doubt, transfer should be delayed pending the opinion of legal counsel. Unreasonable delay, however, may impose liability on the transfer clerk and corporation for damages resulting from nonrecognition.

TAXATION

Computation of Gain or Loss

The gain or loss on the sale is calculated by subtracting the adjusted basis of the assets from the sales price. This computation is to be made on an asset-by-asset basis. The sales price is allocated among the assets in the same proportion that the adjusted basis of the asset bears to the aggregate adjusted bases of the assets. Gain or loss is calculated per asset and is characterized as ordinary income unless the asset is a capital asset, then as long- or short-term capital gain or loss depending on the holding period. The holding period for a long-term capital gain or loss is more than six months and six months or less for a short-term capital gain or loss for assets acquired between June 22, 1984 and January 1, 1988. A capital asset is property other than:

1. Stock in trade of the taxpayer or other property included in inventory at the close of the taxable year
2. Property held primarily for sale to customers in the ordinary course of business
3. Real property used in a trade or business
4. Depreciable property used in a trade or business
5. Accounts or notes receivable acquired in the ordinary course of business for services rendered or from the sale of stock in trade or inventory
6. Certain copyrights, compositions, and letters
7. Certain government publications.

In the sale of a business, most gains or losses will be treated as ordinary income rather than capital gains or losses.

All gains or losses are recognized unless nonrecognition is specifically granted in the Internal Revenue Code. Recognized gains or losses must be included in income computations for the appropriate taxable year. If a gain or loss is not recognized, it may be excluded all together or merely deferred to a subsequent taxable year or the happening of a particular event.

Corporate Liquidations

A complete liquidation is not defined in the Internal Revenue Code, but Treasury Regulations section 1.332-2(c) states that a complete liquidation occurs when a corporation ceases to be a going concern and its activities are merely for the purpose of winding up its affairs, paying debts, and distributing any remaining balances to its shareholders. Dissolution of the corporation is not a requirement for a complete liquidation. The corporation may retain a minimal capital account to preserve the corporation's legal existence. Dissolution under state law is not the same as a complete liquidation for tax purposes.

There are two types of technical liquidations that are not treated as liquidations for tax purposes. First, an acquisition of a majority of the voting stock of a corporation followed by its liquidation is treated as a purchase of the assets and subsequent sale. The second is a liquidation followed by a reincorporation of the business of the liquidated corporation such that the business of the liquidated corporation is carried on by another corporation which is controlled by essentially the same persons.

General Rules

The board of directors of the corporation must adopt a plan of liquidation. The liquidating corporation must file IRS Form 966 and attach a certified copy of the plan to it. Failure to comply with this requirement does not disqualify the liquidation but may subject the corporation to criminal penalties for not supplying the required information. In addition to a certified copy of the plan, a copy of the minutes of the stockholders' meeting at which the plan was formally adopted is required, as well as a statement of assets sold after the plan was adopted and the dates of those sales, a statement of the assets retained to pay liabilities and the nature of these liabilities, and the date of the final liquidating distribution. IRS Forms 1099L and 1096 must be filed for each shareholder who receives a liquidating distribution of at least $600 during any calendar year.

Under the Tax Reform Act of 1986, Congress has reverted to its prior stance and generally requires complete liquidations to be taxed at both the corporate and shareholder levels. Section 337's nonrecognition by a liquidating corporation of gain or loss provision is repealed for transactions after July 31, 1986. The transition rules provide relief for certain transactions if the plan of liquidation was adopted before August 1, 1986 and under certain other circumstances. The transition rules for the Tax Reform Act of 1986 are extensive and should always be checked.

In a complete liquidation, a corporation is treated as if it had sold its assets at their fair market values and distributed the proceeds. Gain or loss is computed as the difference between an asset's fair market value and the corporation's adjusted basis in the asset. The gain or loss from this deemed sale is recognized by the corporation. However, a loss cannot be recognized by the liquidating corporation if property is distributed to a shareholder who, directly or indirectly owns more than 50 percent, in value, of the liquidating corporation's stock on a non-pro rata basis. Nor may losses be recognized on recently acquired property distributed to such a shareholder to prevent related shareholders from transferring property to a corporation to cause a loss on the liquidation at the corporate level.

A liquidating distribution to a distributee-shareholder is treated as a sale of the shareholder's stock to the corporation in exchange for cash or property or both. This treatment is contrary to what would have to be considered as the logical approach, which would be to treat that part of the liquidating distribution that represents the earnings and profits as a dividend and any excess over the earnings and profits as a sale of the stock. However, the Internal Revenue Code treats all amounts distributed to shareholders in a complete liquidation as if they were in full payment in exchange for the stock. IRC section 301 (dividends) does not apply to complete liquidations. A gain or loss is calculated by subtracting the shareholder's basis in his or her stock from the amount of cash plus the fair market value of any assets received. If the stock is a capital asset in the hands of the holder, it is a capital gain or loss.

The general rule is that a shareholder who receives property from a liquidating corporation in a complete liquidation takes the property with a basis equal to its fair market value. This rule does not apply to the liquidation of a subsidiary under section 332.

Complete Liquidations of Subsidiaries

No gain or loss is recognized by a corporation on receipt of property including money distributed in complete liquidation of another corporation. In exchange for nonrecognition of gain or loss, section 334(b) provides that the parent corporation acquires a basis in the property distributed by the subsidiary equal to the basis that the subsidiary had in the property immediately prior to the transfer.

Certain requirements must be met for nonrecognition of gain or loss by the parent corporation. The parent corporation must own at least 80 percent of the total combined voting stock of the subsidiary plus at least 80 percent of the nonvoting stock, except for nonvoting, nonparticipating preferred commencing with the date of adoption of the plan of liquidation through the distribution date. If the plan of liquidation is adopted before the parent corporation has acquired at least 80 percent of the total combined voting stock of the subsidiary, the distribution does not qualify under section 332. Likewise, if the parent corporation sells off an amount of stock such that its holding is less than 80 percent of the total combined voting stock of the subsidiary at any time during the requirement period, there is no nonrecognition under section 332. For certain corporations who want to recognize a loss on a distribution, it would be advantageous to sell off a sufficient amount of stock to disqualify itself under section 332. If a plan of liquidation is adopted without dates, the subsidiary must distribute its assets within one taxable year in complete cancellation or redemption of all of its outstanding stock. Some corporations routinely adopt liquidation plans at their annual meetings as contingency plans without specifying dates to execute the plan. If a plan of liquidation is adopted specifying the time frame for liquidation, the subsidiary must acquire all outstanding stock in complete cancellation or redemption in accordance with the plan within three years after the first distribution under the plan is made. It is important to note that section 332 provides nonrecognition of a gain or loss only to the parent corporation, not to any minority shareholder.

If a subsidiary is indebted to the parent corporation, then to the extent that the distributions represent satisfaction of the debt, those distributions are not treated as a redemption of the stock. If the subsidiary is solvent and is indebted to the parent corporation, the subsidiary does not recognize a gain or loss on the transfer in satisfaction of the indebtedness, but if the subsidiary is insolvent, it may recognize a gain or loss because section 332 does not apply unless the distribution is made by virtue of stock ownership.

Section 338

Prior to the 1954 Internal Revenue Code, the Kimbell-Diamond rule was articulated by federal courts. Under the Kimbell-Diamond rule, a corporation that acquired all or substantially all of the stock of a corporation for the purpose of immediately liquidating the corporation and acquiring the target corporation's assets was treated as if it had directly purchased the assets. The aggregate basis in the target corporation's assets was equal to the purchase price of the stock. The Kimbell-Diamond rule was partially codified in section 334(b) (2). Because of difficulties in applying section 334 (b) (2) and the uncertainty as to whether or not the Kimbell-Diamond rule was preempted by it, section 334 (b) (2) was repealed and replaced by section 338. Essentially, under section 338, an acquiring corporation that purchases control of another corporation within a twelve-month acquisition period must make an election. The parent corporation may elect to have the newly acquired subsidiary treated as if: (1) the subsidiary had sold all of its assets and had undergone a complete liquidation on the acquisition date and (2) on the day following the acquisition date, the same subsidiary as a fictional new corporation had purchased all of those assets at the purchase price that the parent corporation paid for the target corporation's stock. The result is that the parent corporation owns a controlling interest in a subsidiary whose asset basis is stepped up to equal the grossed up purchase price paid by the parent for the subsidiary's stock. The alternative treatment is to use the basis rule of section 334 (b) (1) which provides that the parent corporation acquires a basis in the acquired assets equal to the basis that the subsidiary had in the assets immediately prior to the acquisition.

One-Month Liquidations

Under certain circumstances, a shareholder's gain on the complete liquidation of a corporation may go unrecognized under old section 333. The primary purpose of section 333 was to allow a corporation holding appreciated property but having no earnings and profits or cash to be liquidated without the recognition of gain on the transaction by its shareholders until the shareholders subsequently sold the assets received in the liquidation. When the shareholder subsequently sells the asset, gain is computed by subtracting the shareholder's basis in the surrendered stock from the amount received from the sale.

Section 333 applied only to gains attributed to qualified electing shareholders on the complete liquidation of a domestic corporation before the effective dates set out in the Tax Reform Act of 1986. It does not apply to losses attributed to a qualified electing shareholder, gains or losses attributed to a nonelecting shareholder, or gains or losses of excluded corporations. An excluded corporation was a corporation that owned 50 percent or more of the total combined voting power of all classes of stock entitled to vote on the plan of liquidation. For section 333 to be effective, elections had to be timely filed by noncorporate shareholders who owned at least 80 percent of the total combined voting power of the noncorporate owned stock entitled to vote on the adoption of the plan when the plan was adopted. Likewise, elections had to be timely filed by corporate shareholders not including excluded corporations holding at least 80 percent of the total combined voting power of corporate owned stock entitled to vote on the plan on the date that the plan was adopted. Section 333 could apply to one group, or the other, or both. Once the election was made, it could not be revoked.

If a corporation had earnings and profits, the electing shareholders recognized gain to the extent of their ratable share of the earnings and profits. Consequently, there was a disadvantage to electing section 333 treatment if the corporation had more than an insignificant amount of earnings and profits.

Section 333 was repealed by the Tax Reform Act of 1986. Nevertheless, many former shareholders of these liquidated corporations are still affected by Section 333. The basis in the assets received pursuant to a one-month liquidation is determined under old section 333.

NOTES

1. Landreth Timber Co. v. Landreth, 471 U.S. 681 (1985); Gould v. Ruefenacht, 471 U.S. 701 (1985).

2. *See, e.g.*, Ray v. Alad Corp., 19 Cal.3d 22, 136 Cal. Rptr. 574, 560 P.2d 3 (1977); Bernard v. Kee Manufacturing Co., Inc., 409 So.2d 1047 (1982); and Turner v. Bituminous Casualty Co., 397 Mich. 406 (1976).

3. Perlman v. Feldmann, 154 F.Supp. 436, 219 F.2d 173 (2d Cir. 1955).

5

Capitalization

A new business must have an initial capital contribution to cover startup costs and initial operations until a reliable income stream is established. The amount and source of that initial capital depends on the kind of business and other attendant factors. The sole proprietor must look to his or her own resources to finance a business and obtain as much credit as is necessary to operate the business; the capital of a partnership is obtained by pooling the partners' assets and getting credit. Limited partnerships and corporations are capitalized by investors through offerings of securities.

CREDIT

To the extent that a business may need operating capital beyond its contributed capital, recourse may be had to lenders. Terms and conditions vary with general economic conditions and the relative bargaining power of the borrower. A new business entrepreneur generally has little leverage and must deal with the lender on the lender's terms. Consumer protection laws have been enacted at both the federal and state levels during recent years to afford some protection to borrowers from onerous terms and conditions. A complete discussion of these laws is in Chapter 11 and will not be repeated here. A careful review of Chapter 11 is urged because these laws do not apply to all organizational forms of business.

Loans

A loan is a transaction wherein one party (creditor) transfers to the other (debtor) a sum of money which that other (debtor) promises to repay absolutely, generally with interest. The loan may be secured or unsecured, recourse or nonrecourse.

A secured loan is one where the claim is secured by specific property, and in the event of default the secured creditor has first claim to the proceeds of the sale of that property or has the right to repossess it. A general creditor cannot look to any specific property for repayment, and his or her claims are subordinate to all secured creditors' claims. To avoid personal liability on a business debt, the debtor may obtain a nonrecourse loan. A nonrecourse loan is a secured loan whereby the creditor agrees that his or her sole recourse in the event of default is to sell the secured property and apply the proceeds to the outstanding loan balance. The creditor does not have recourse against the debtor for the unpaid amount. Obviously, creditors are reluctant to give nonrecourse loans to sole proprietors, partnerships, and small business corporations. Unless the loan is a nonrecourse loan, the debtor is personally liable for the amount of the loan plus interest in the event that the business defaults. Sole proprietors and general partners are personally liable because limited liability is not an attribute of these forms of business. Corporations do have limited liability, and, in the event of default, recourse may be had only against the assets of the corporation. To protect themselves, creditors usually require corporate directors, officers, or shareholders of small business corporations personally to guarantee the loan.

The document evidencing the loan is a promissory note. The note contains the elements of the loan: (1) the name of the borrower(s), (2) the amount of the loan, (3) due date, (4) interest rate, and (5) penalty for past due payments. If the note is secured, the security interest must be perfected in accordance with the state's commercial code (see Chapter 6). If the person is a corporate officer signing on behalf of the corporation and does not intend to be personally liable, the signature line should clearly state the capacity in which the officer signed to avoid unnecessary disputes at a later date.

Operational financing is discussed in Chapter 6.

CORPORATE FINANCE

Typically, a corporation's financial structure contains secured debt, general or trade debt, bonds, preferred stock, and common stock.

Common Stock

The common stock of a corporation is the residual equity interest. The equity interest is the interest of the shareholders as owners of the corporation. The equity interest is often thought of as the residual interest because it represents a claim to the assets of the corporation after all of the senior claims have been satisfied. The articles of incorporation specify the number of authorized shares of common stock of the corporation, but not all of the authorized shares of common stock have to be issued. Typically, a large number of shares is authorized but not issued and held in reserve to be issued at a later date. Should an additional number of authorized shares be needed, the articles of incorporation may be amended to increase the number of shares authorized.

Initially, prospective investors execute a stock subscription to buy the common stock of the corporation. The stock subscription is a contract which may be revoked prior to acceptance by the corporation unless the subscription itself contains a provision that the subscription is irrevocable for a certain time period; for example, the Model Business Corporation Act provides for a six-month period of irrevocability.

Each share of common stock represents an initial contribution of money, property, or services past rendered to the corporation. The value of the stock may be set in the articles of incorporation; that is, an amount called the par value may be specified below which the stock may not initially be sold. Setting the par value too high can result in some unnecessary legal problems. Sale of the stock for less than the par value results in watered stock. A shareholder who pays less than the par value for the stock is personally liable for the deficiency in the amount. This liability is generally owed to the corporation itself, but in certain cases the liability is directly owed to the corporation's creditors if their claims cannot otherwise be satisfied out of the corporate assets. To avoid the problem of watered stock, the par value should be set very low in relationship to the initial selling price or the stock should be declared to be no par value stock. No par value stock is merely stock for which no par value was specified in the articles of incorporation. After the shares have been authorized, but before they are actually issued, the board of directors determines a stated value of each share. Each share of no par stock must be sold in an amount at least equal to the stated value; otherwise, a watered stock problem arises.

Each share of common stock carries with it voting rights and the right to participate in the earnings and profits of the corporation through dividends. However, dividends can be paid to the common stockholders only after the more senior security obligations have been satisfied. For example, debt service on bonds has a prior claim on the earnings and profits of the corporation; similarly, preferred stock dividends are a prior claim on the earnings and profits of the corporation. Tax treatment of dividends is contained in Chapter 19.

Preferred Stock

Preferred stock is a cross between an equity security and a corporate bond. Preferred stock has some of the attributes of debt and some of the attributes of equity. This cross or hybrid results from the tradeoff of a more secure return, that is a specific dividend rate, and priority over common stock with respect to dividends for the loss of control over the management of the corporation. Preferred shareholders do not participate in the election of directors unless the preferred stock dividend is in arrears for some specified period of time.

Preferred stock may be cumulative or noncumulative. Preferred stock that is cumulative means that, even though a prior year's dividend may have been passed at the discretion of the board of directors, no common stock dividend can be paid unless the preferred stock's passed unpaid dividend or arrearage and the current year's dividend are paid. The board of directors declares the dividend at its own discretion and is not required to declare a dividend in any particular year; however, the preferred stock cumulative stock dividend in arrears must be made up before any dividend can be declared on a common stock. If cumulative preferred stock dividends are not declared over a specified period of time, the preferred stockholders succeed to the voting rights of the common stockholders until the arrearage is made up. Noncumulative preferred stock means that if any year's preferred stock dividend is passed by the board of directors, it is lost forever. A common stock dividend can be declared after the current year's preferred stock dividend is paid. There is no right to the preferred shareholders for passed dividends undeclared. Obviously, noncumulative preferred stock is not very desirable from an investor's standpoint. Moreover, even if the preferred stock is cumulative, preferred shareholders are generally not entitled to any interest on the arrearage.

In the event that the corporation is liquidated, preferred shareholders have priority over the common stockholders and are entitled to a fixed amount plus any cumulative dividends and liquidation premium.

The preferred stock may be participating or nonparticipating. Participating preferred stock is entitled to its fixed rate of return before any dividend is declared on the common stock and is subsequently entitled to share in the earnings and profits with the common shareholders after the common stock has been paid a specified minimum dividend. Nonparticipating stock entitles the preferred shareholder only to the fixed dividend called for in the preferred stock contract.

While some preferred stock is issued for an indefinite period, other preferred stock is callable or redeemable by the corporation under terms set out in the preferred stock contract. The redemption option may be exercised only by the corporation and not by the preferred shareholders. Preferred shareholders have no right to a return of their investment from the corporation at some date in the future. If the corporation calls in the preferred stock, it is generally at a modest premium over the face amount of the preferred stock plus any cumulative dividends in arrears.

The preferred stock may be convertible into common stock. The preferred stock may be exchanged for common stock under terms and conditions set out in the preferred stock contract. The conversion option price will generally be set above the value of the common stock at the time the conversion feature is offered. The conversion option then should be exercised only when the value of the common stock rises above the option price. As long as the market value of the common stock remains below the option price it is uneconomic to convert. As the price of the common stock rises in the market, the corporation may perceive an economic disadvantage to having convertible preferred outstanding. If the convertible preferred is callable, the corporation may call in or redeem the preferred stock before the common stock price exceeds the convertible option price thereby defeating the benefits of the conversion privilege.

Bonds and Debentures

A corporate bond or debenture is a debt obligation of the corporation. It does not represent an ownership or equity position in the corporation. Technically speaking, a bond is a debt obligation secured by a mortgage on some property of the corporation, while a debenture is an unsecured debt obligation. Corporate bonds and debentures are generally issued in a denomination, that is a face or par value, which is the amount that must be repaid at the end of the term of the bond on maturity.

A bond will carry a fixed rate of interest payable at regular intervals. It is quite common for corporate bonds to sell at a discount or premium depending on the interest rate to be paid. A below-market interest rate means that the bonds will sell at a discount sufficient to bring the total return up to the market rate. The opposite is true for above-market interest rates.

The bondholders in the corporation are bound by an agreement or covenant called an indenture. If the bonds are a public issue, the indenture must comply with the Trust Indenture Act of 1939. Under the act, once the bonds have been sold, the protection of the bondholder's interests and the enforcement of his rights are assigned to an indentured trustee, which ordinarily is a bank appointed at the time of issuance of the bonds. The indenture will contain provisions in case of default of the corporation. Bondholders have prior rights over preferred and common stockholders but may be subordinated to other secured creditors.

Like preferred stock, bonds may be callable and redeemed at face value plus a call premium. Callable bonds are more advantageous to a corporation in a fluctuating interest market. Bonds issued at a high interest rate may be called in, and a new bond issued at the lower market interest rate.

Bonds, like preferred stock, may also be convertible. The bonds may be convertible into a preferred or common stock. Again, the convertible option price of the underlying stock is set higher than the then current market price of the underlying stock. Convertible bonds justify the premium only when the market price of the underlying stock is rising. The bondholder should be cautious of buying any callable convertible bond in a rising market because the corporation in all likelihood will call the bonds before the conversion privilege can be exercised economically.

Warrants and Options

An option is just that; it is a right to purchase common stock at a set price. The option has a value of its own. The price at which the option holder may purchase the common stock is set at a value higher than the then current market value of the common stock. For the option to become valuable, the market price of the common stock has to increase above the value set as the option price plus the amount paid for the option. In other words, an option is a bet by the option holder that the price of the common stock will rise higher than the option price. If it does not, the option holder loses, and the option becomes worthless.

There are two kinds of options, only one of which involves the corporation directly. A common stock option may be issued by a corporation to its officers or employees as compensation or a work incentive. The more common type option is merely a contract between two or more persons to buy or sell a security, in which event the corporation is not directly involved. The buying, selling, and trading of options are subject to securities regulation.

A warrant, on the other hand, is a stock right or option issued by the corporation. The terms of a warrant are generally not exercisable for a substantial period of time. The warrant gives the holder the right or option to purchase a security of the corporation at a price above the then current market price of the security. Warrants, if they are issued, are most commonly issued in companion with a bond or debenture to make the offering of the bond or debenture more attractive.

An option issued by the corporation or a warrant may result in dilution of the existing equity interest in the corporation if they are exercised. There will be more owners having a claim against the corporation. This will have an effect on the control and the distribution of dividends and assets in the event of liquidation. Moreover, an option or warrant holder benefits from increases in value of the corporation without being exposed to the same risks as are the other equity shareholders. For these reasons, warrants and options issued by the corporation are disfavored in publicly held corporations. Options and warrants are more likely to be issued in privately negotiated transactions.

SECURITIES REGULATION

In response to perceived abuses in the securities market that contributed to the disastrous crash of 1929, Congress enacted a series of federal statutes dealing with the problems. Six major pieces of legislation were enacted between 1933 and 1940, with additional major enactments in 1970 and 1984. Federal securities law consists mainly of the Securities Act of 1933,[1] the Securities Exchange Act of 1934,[2] the Public Utility Holding Company Act of 1935,[3] the Trust Indenture Act of 1939,[4] the Investment Company Act of 1940,[5] the Investment Advisers Act of 1940,[6] the Securities Investor Protection Act of 1970,[7] and the Insider Trading Sanctions Act of 1984.[8]

In addition to federal securities regulation, each of the states regulates issues of securities and their distribution within the boundaries of each state.

The Federal Acts

Securities Act of 1933

The Securities Act of 1933 regulates the registration and initial sale of securities by an issuer. The primary purpose of the act is to provide full disclosure of all material facts so that the investor may make an informed decision concerning the investment.

Section 5 of the Securities Act makes it unlawful to offer for sale or to sell, in interstate commerce or through the mail, a security that is subject to the act unless a registration statement has been filed with the Securities and Exchange Commission and a prospectus has been provided to potential purchasers of the security.

Section 11 of the Securities Act provides for civil liability for misstatements or omissions of material facts in the registration statement. This liability extends to the issuer, underwriters, directors, every person who has signed the registration statement, and specialists or professionals who prepared or certified part of the registration statement.

Section 12 of the Securities Act provides a private cause of action for damages by a purchaser against a seller who offers or sells a security in violation of section 5 or who makes an untrue statement of or omits a material fact by means of the prospectus or any oral communication.

Section 17 of the Securities Act is a general antifraud provision which applies to the sale of any security whether it is required to be registered or not.

Securities Exchange Act of 1934

Unlike the Securities Act of 1933, which is devoted exclusively to registration and initial distribution of securities issues, the Securities Exchange Act is a hodgepodge. Among other things, the act establishes the Securities and Exchange Commission; requires registration of reporting companies; regulates and requires registration of national exchanges, brokers and dealers, and their associations; regulates secondary distributions; regulates certain intracorporate financial affairs; and contains antifraud provisions.

Section 10 of the Securities Exchange Act and its progeny, rule 10b–5, have been the workhorses for redressing fraud and misrepresentation in the sale or purchase of a security. Section 10 provides an implied private cause of action for damages to anyone who can prove the necessary elements of a violation of section 10 or rule 10b–5. It is broadly applied to all sales or purchases in interstate commerce or the mails whether the security is registered or not and is in addition to other remedies.

Trust Indenture Act of 1939

Certain debt securities, even though registered under the Securities Act of 1933, may not be issued unless they are issued under a trust indenture which qualifies under the Trust Indenture Act of 1939. The act provides for minimum qualifications for corporate trustees with respect to minimum combined capital and surplus. The trust indenture must also contain the powers and duties that the trustee must exercise in the event of default by the issuer.

Investment Company Act of 1940

Publicly owned companies that are primarily engaged in the business of investing, reinvesting, or trading in securities are investment companies regulated by the Investment Company Act of 1940. Excluded from the definition of an investment company are companies organized and operated exclusively for religious, educational, benevolent, fraternal, charitable, or reformatory purposes, in which no part of the net earnings inures to the benefit of any private shareholder or individual.

Investment Advisers Act of 1940

The Investment Advisers Act of 1940 regulates the capital structure of investment companies and the composition of their managements. The Securities and Exchange Commission must approve advisory contracts, changes in investment policy, and transactions between the investment company and its directors, officers, or affiliates. Management compensation and sales charges became subject to supervision following the 1970 amendment.

Insider Trading Sanctions Act of 1984

The Insider Trading Sanctions Act of 1984 increased the civil and criminal penalties that can be imposed on insiders. The statute of limitations is increased to five years.

Definition of a Security

The definition of a security is far broader than that of stock or shares and encompasses many instruments issued by organizations. The definition of a security is critical since none of the federal securities laws applies if the instrument is not in fact a security. If the instrument is a security, it must be registered unless it is otherwise exempt; however, the antifraud provisions apply whether registration is required or not.

The starting point is section 2 (1) of the Securities Act of 1933, which defines a security as any note; stock; treasury stock; bond; debenture; evidence of indebtedness; certificate of interest or participation in any profit-sharing agreement; collateral-trust certificate; preorganization certificate or subscription; transferable share; investment contract; voting-trust certificate; certificate of deposit for a security; fractional undivided interest in oil, gas, or other mineral rights; or, in general, any interest or instrument commonly known as a security or any certificate of interest or participation in, temporary or interim certificate for, receipt for, guarantee of, or warrant or right to subscribe to or purchase any of the foregoing.

A share of stock by definition is a security; however, the mere designation of a certificate as stock does not necessarily make it a security. In *United Housing Foundation v. Forman*,[9] United Housing required each prospective purchaser of low-cost housing to buy eighteen shares of stock for each room desired. The instruments were identified on their face as stock. The Supreme Court, however, refused to consider the instruments to be securities merely because they were called stock, reasserting disregard of form for substance and placing the emphasis on economic reality. Since the "stock" had none of the attributes of stock, such as the right to receive dividends, the right to vote, appreciation in value, free transferability, and right to pledge or hypothecate, it was not a security but rather a security deposit. The economic reality test has been used in one line of cases which holds that notes evidencing ordinary bank loans are not securities because they are commercial transactions rather than investments.

The touchstone for whether or not an instrument is a security is *SEC v. W. J. Howey*.[10] The issue in *Howey* was whether a land sales contract and service contract involving orange groves in Florida constituted an investment contract which is a security as defined in section 2 (1) of the Securities Act. The test promulgated by the Supreme Court in *Howey* is whether "the person invests his money in a common enterprise and is led to expect profits solely from the efforts of the promoter or a third party." The last part of the test dealing with the efforts of others has been modified in subsequent decisions to read "the efforts made by those other than the investor are the undeniably significant ones, those essential managerial efforts which affect the failure or success of the enterprise." While the *Howey* case involved an investment contract, the *Howey* test is generally applicable to any security.

Registration

The thrust of the Securities Act of 1933 is to provide the ordinary investor with all relevant and material facts necessary to make an informed investment decision. Hence, registration is a disclosure process designed to elicit that information for the benefit of the investor. Unlike many state securities commissions, the U.S. Securities and Exchange Commission does not pass on the worth or desirability of a particular issue.

The registration statement is really two documents: The prospectus is the selling document provided to all potential purchasers, and Part II contains other information and exhibits not furnished to potential purchasers but kept on file by the commission and made available for public inspection. Section 7 of the Securities Act of 1933 prescribes the information that must be included in the registration statement; section 10 prescribes the information that must be included in the prospectus.

Registration is accomplished by filing one of the prescribed forms. Form S–1 is the basic form required for registration when no other form is prescribed or authorized. Form S–1 requires the greatest degree of disclosure of all registration forms primarily because the users of form S–1 have little or no previous contact with the Securities and Exchange Commission.

In 1979, the commission adopted a new form, S–18, for use by small issuers. The disclosure requirements are essentially the same as for form S–1 except that the format is simpler and it is not keyed to regulation S–K which regulates disclosure requirements under both the Securities Act of 1933 and the Securities Exchange Act of 1934. Form S–18 may be used only by issuers who are not registered under the Securities Exchange Act of 1934 and only for cash offerings of $5 million or less. Form S–18 may be filed at the nearest commission regional office rather than with the commission in Washington, D.C.

In addition to the forms and instructions contained within it, regulation C, which consists of rules 400 to 485, provides registration procedures and general forms. Registration is a time-consuming, expensive, and complex task not to be undertaken lightly.

Section 8 (a) of the Securities Act of 1933 provides that a registration statement becomes effective twenty days after it is filed with the commission. Once the registration statement is effective, the issuer may begin to sell the securities. However, most registration statements do not automatically become effective. The commission expends an enormous amount of its resources on reviewing registration statements. In practice, the commission staff will issue a letter of comment or a deficiency letter concerning changes, deletions, or additions or will request other materials prior to making further comment. The twenty-day waiting period begins anew with each change or amendment.

The heart of the Securities Act of 1933 is section 5 which is difficult reading as a result of the amendment process altering the chronological order of the section. There are two dates to keep in mind: the registration filing date and the effective date of the registration.

Section 5 (c) prohibits any offer to sell or offer to buy from being made before the filing date except for negotiations between the issuer and underwriters or among the underwriters. No offer may be made to dealers or made by dealers.

Between the filing date and the effective date, offers may be made but not sales. While no restrictions are placed on oral offers, an offer in writing is a prospectus and must comply with the requirements of section 10. Rule 431 provides for a preliminary prospectus which may be used in the waiting period, and rule 134 allows "tombstone ads," so named because of the black borders generally placed around these notices.

After the effective date, offers and sales may be made to anyone, provided that a prospectus is delivered on any sale of securities that is part of an under-writer's unsold public offering and on resales by dealers within a specified time period following the beginning of the public offering.

Exemptions from Registration

Section 3 (a) (4) of the Securities Act of 1933 exempts from registration "any security issued by a person organized and operated exclusively for religious, educational, benevolent, fraternal, charitable, or reformatory purposes and not for pecuniary profit, and no part of the net earnings of which inures to the benefit of any person, private stockholder, or individual."

To be exempt from registration under the Securities Act of 1933, an organization must meet the same standards that it does for tax exempt status. They must meet both the exclusive organizational and operational test and the non-distribution prohibition.

The Securities and Exchange Commission brought an action against Children's Hospital of Phoenix, Arizona, to stop the distribution of 8-percent first mortgage bonds that the hospital did not register. The hospital did not claim that the bonds were exempt from registration under section 3 (a) (4). Since the burden of proof of the exemption is on the person asserting it, the hospital failed to carry its burden of proof. The court went on to discuss the section 3 (a) (4) exemption in terms of the requirement that the organization must be exclusively organized and operated for charitable purposes. Any substantial noncharitable purpose would disqualify the organization from taking advantage of the section 3 (a) (4) exemption. The court found a substantial purpose of the promoters to be self-enrichment. An organization must establish that it is not organized or operated for the benefit of private purposes. Failure to do so means loss of the benefits of the exemption.

Section 3 (a) (4) is intended to facilitate fund raising by eleemosynary issuers and not to allow promoters or managers to issue securities without registration for their own private benefit.

Section 3 (b) of the Securities Act of 1933 gives the commission the authority to exempt certain securities from registration by rules and regulations provided that registration is not in the public interest or for the protection of the investor and that the aggregate amount of the issue is $5 million or less. Small offerings are included in regulation D along with private offerings.

Section 4 of the Securities Act of 1933 provides for transactional exemptions as opposed to providing an exemption for a class of securities. Section 4 (2) exempts transactions by an issuer not involving any public offering.

The bulk of private placements are with institutional investors, which is consistent with the policy underlying the section 4 (2) exemption. Registration is required to provide the ordinary investor with information he or she could not otherwise obtain; therefore, investors who have access to the same kind of information that registration would disclose and who are sophisticated investors do not require the protection of the Securities Act of 1933.

To facilitate private offerings, the Securities and Exchange Commission issued rule 146 in 1974. Rule 146 was a safe harbor provision but was not the exclusive means by which a section 4 (2) exemption could be obtained. Rule 146 was not workable; therefore, to simplify matters, rule 146 was repealed in 1982 and regulation D was adopted.

Regulation D consists of rules 501 to 506. No general solicitation or general offering is permitted under regulation D. Since the purchase of a security under regulation D is not purchased in a public offering, it cannot be resold without registration unless another exemption is available under section 4 (1) or rule 144.

Rule 504 allows an issuer to sell an aggregate of $500,000 of securities in any twelve-month period to any number of purchasers without providing any information to the purchasers. The offer must be made in states that require registration of the securities and a disclosure document to be delivered to purchasers prior to sale. Any issuer except an investment company or company registered under the Securities Exchange Act of 1934 may use this exemption.

Rule 505 allows aggregate sales up to $5 million in any twelve-month period to any number of accredited investors and up to 35 other purchasers. An accredited investor is defined in rule 501 as follows.

1. Any bank, insurance company, investment company, or employee benefit plan

2. Any business development company

3. Any charitable or educational institution having assets of more than $5 million

4. Any director, executive officer, or general partner of the issuer

5. Any person who purchases at least $150,000 of the offered securities, provided such purchase does not exceed 20 percent of his net worth

6. Any person with a net worth of more than $1 million

7. Any person with an annual income of more than $200,000.

If there are any nonaccredited purchasers, then the following information required by rule 502 must be furnished to all purchasers: (1) if the issuer is not registered under the Securities Exchange Act of 1934, (a) the information contained on form S–18 or (b) if the offering exceeds $5 million, the information required on a registration statement on the form that the issuer is entitled to use; (2) if the issuer is registered under the Securities Exchange Act, (a) the most recent annual report to shareholders and proxy statement or (b) updated information contained in the last annual report to the commission. Rule 505 is not available to an investment company or an issuer disqualified from using regulation A by rule 252.

Rule 506 provides that any issuer may sell an unlimited amount of securities to any number of accredited investors and up to 35 other purchasers if, prior to the sale, the issuer reasonably believes that each nonaccredited purchaser or his purchaser representative has such knowledge or experience in financial and business matters that he is capable of evaluating the merits and risks of the prospective investment. The information required by rule 502 must be disclosed to nonaccredited purchasers.

Notices of sales pursuant to regulation D must be filed with the commission under rule 503. An issuer who restricts sales solely to accredited investors in an aggregate amount of $5 million or less may take advantage of the section 4 (6) exemption as an alternative to regulation D.

For business organizations that are local in nature and not proximate to a state line, the intrastate exemption is available. Section 3 (a) (11) provides for an exemption for securities offered or sold solely to residents of a single state or territory in which the issuer is a resident and is conducting business or, if the issuer is a corporation, in which the issuer is incorporated and is doing business. Intrastate offerings may make use of the mails or other interstate commerce facility. The exemption is not based on the jurisdictional requirements of the Securities Act of 1933.

The rationale for the intrastate exemption is local financing through local investment. The exemption is strictly construed according to its rationale, and an offer or sale to a single nonresident destroys the exemption for all. The offering will remain exempt under the intrastate exemption if no resales are made to nonresidents for at least nine months after the initial distribution is completed.

Regulation A, which consists of rules 251 to 263, was promulgated under the authority of section 3 (b) of the Securities Act. Regulation A, however, in practice is not an exemption but is rather a simplified registration process for small issues. Regulation A permits an issuer to offer a maximum of $1.5 million and any other person to offer a maximum of $100,000 of the securities during any twelve-month period.

The exemption may not be used by an issuer, underwriter, or other related person convicted of securities offenses, subjected to disciplinary action by the commission, or involved in certain other proceedings within specified periods of the issuance of the securities.

To use regulation A, an offering statement must be filed with the regional office of the commission where the issuer has its principal place of business at least ten days before the offering is to begin. The offering statement must contain an offering circular which includes information similar to a prospectus but much less detailed. The "letter of comment" procedure is used for regulation A offerings as well as registration statements.

A copy of the offering circular must be provided to each person to whom a written offer is made or to whom a sale is confirmed. Civil liabilities imposed under section 11 do not apply to regulation A offerings because of the exemption from registration under section 3 (b); however, section 12 liabilities may be imposed.

Antifraud Provisions

The antifraud provisions of the federal securities laws apply to securities whether they are exempt from registration or not or whether they are transactionally exempt or not. The primary antifraud provisions are section 17 of the Securities Act of 1933, section 10 (b) of the Securities Exchange Act of 1934, and section 206 of the Investment Advisers Act of 1940.

Section 10 is the catchall provision of the Securities Exchange Act of 1934. Its purpose is to provide relief from abuses not otherwise addressed in the act. However, section 10 itself is not a self-executing provision. It is only effective through rules and regulations promulgated by the commission pursuant to the authority of section 10 to make such rules as are necessary or appropriate in the public interest or for the protection of investors. In 1942, rule 10b–5 was issued by the commission. Interestingly, rule 10b–5 is merely modified language of section 17 (a) of the Securities Act of 1933; the principal modification is that section 17 (a) only applies to sales of securities whereas section 10 applies to purchase or sale.

Rule 10b–5 provides that

It shall be unlawful for any person, directly or indirectly, by the use of any means or instrumentality of interstate commerce, or of the mails, or of any facility of any national securities exchange,

(1) to employ any device, scheme, or artifice to defraud,

(2) to make any untrue statement of a material fact or to omit to state a material fact necessary in order to make the statements made, in the light of the circumstances under which they were made, not misleading, or

(3) to engage in any act, practice, or course of business which operates or would operate as a fraud or deceit upon any person, in connection with the purchase or sale of any security.

Section 10 and rule 10b–5 are stated as prohibitions and give rise to administrative proceedings, suits for injunction by the commission, and criminal actions referred to the Justice Department for prosecution upon conviction for which an individual could be fined up to $10,000 or be imprisoned for a period of not more than five years, or both. However, it was established as early as 1946 that there was an implied civil cause of action for damages in behalf of the defrauded victim.

The elements of a cause of action under rule 10b–5 are (1) use of the mails, an instrumentality of interstate commerce, or any facility of a national securities exchange; (2) a purchase or sale of a security; (3) fraud or deceit or a misstatement or omission of a material fact; (4) scienter; (5) causation; (6) reliance; and (7) damages in a civil action. A private cause of action must be brought by a purchaser or seller. This requirement is strictly applied.

Two of the three clauses of rule 10b–5 deal with fraud or deceit. Fraud does not include overreaching by a controlling shareholder unless it is accompanied by actual deception. A cause of action for fraud under rule 10b–5 is similar to common law fraud in that there must be a relationship between the parties which gives rise to a duty that is violated. In insider trading cases, the insider by virtue of his position gains access to information intended for corporate purposes and not personal benefit. The corresponding duty is to abstain from the marketplace until the information is made public. The insider must not take unfair advantage of information unknown to persons with whom the insider is dealing. In many instances the courts are not clear as to which clause of rule 10b–5 the court is applying, particularly in insider trading cases.

Clause 2 of rule 10b–5 deals with misstatements and omissions of material facts. A fact is material if it is the kind of information that a reasonable investor would consider important in making his investment decision. In the context of an untrue statement of a material fact, the intentional misstatement is akin to common law fraud. In the case of an omission of a material fact where there is a duty to disclose, an element of conjecture is introduced. The test of materiality then becomes whether the reasonable investor would have acted differently had he known of the undisclosed fact.

Since the Supreme Court's decision in *Ernst & Ernst v. Hockfelder*,[11] scienter is a requirement of a cause of action under section 10b and rule 10b–5. Scienter requires an intent to deceive, manipulate, or defraud. Negligence will not support a cause of action under section 10b and rule 10b–5. The Supreme Court reserved the issue of whether recklessness was equivalent to intentional conduct.

Causation is a necessary element of a cause of action under section 10b and rule 10b–5. The misrepresentation or fraud must be the proximate cause of plaintiff's loss. If the misrepresentation is of a material fact on which plaintiff relied but is not the reasonable direct cause of the pecuniary loss, no recovery is allowed.

In fraud cases and cases involving affirmative misstatements of material facts, plaintiff must show actual reliance. The Court of Appeals for the Ninth Circuit, however, has held that if the misleading statement constitutes a fraud on the market, plaintiff does not have to show reliance but only that he bought or sold a security at a price that was affected by the misleading statement. Nondisclosure or complete omission cases present another problem. Plaintiff would have to show that he would have relied on the facts if they had been made known to him, which, in effect, means that the omitted facts were material facts. In a nondisclosure case, if the plaintiff proves materiality, he has in fact proved reliance.

The measure of damages in most cases is the "out of pocket" rule. The damages award is based on the difference between what the plaintiff gave up and the value of what was received in the transaction. The potential for liability is great especially in insider trading cases since liability extends to all persons who traded in the market during the time that the inside information was undisclosed.

Whether there exists an implied private cause of action for damages under section 17 (a) is a matter of conflict in the different courts of appeals. The Supreme Court has left the issue unresolved.

Since rule 10b–5 is a modified version of section 17 (a), one would suspect that the same elements would apply to each, but there are some significant differences. Section 17 (a) applies only to the sale of a security and not to a purchase. Fraud by a purchaser is not addressed by section 17 (a). The Supreme Court has ruled that only the first clause of section 17 (a) requires scienter while negligence will suffice for a cause of action under clauses 2 and 3.

Section 206 of the Investment Advisers Act of 1940 is an antifraud provision similar to section 10b and rule 10b–5 of the Securities Exchange Act of 1934 and section 17 (a) of the Securities Act of 1933. Section 206 provides that

It shall be unlawful for any investment adviser, by use of the mails or any means or instrumentality of interstate commerce, directly or indirectly—(1) to employ any device, scheme, or artifice to defraud any client or prospective client; (2) to engage in any transaction, practice, or course of business which operates as a fraud or deceit upon any client or prospective client; (3) acting as a principal for his own account, knowingly to sell any security to or purchase any security from a client, or acting as broker for a person other than such client, knowingly to effect any sale or purchase of any security for the account of such client, without disclosing to such client in writing before the completion of such transaction the capacity in which he is acting and obtaining the consent of the client to such transaction. The prohibitions of this paragraph shall not apply to any transaction with a customer of a broker or dealer if such broker or dealer is not acting as an investment adviser in relation to such transaction; (4) to engage in any act, practice, or course of business which is fraudulent, deceptive, or manipulative. The Commission shall, for the purposes of this paragraph (4) by rules and regulations define, and prescribe means reasonably designed to prevent, such acts, practices, and courses of business as are fraudulent, deceptive, or manipulative.

Unlike section 10b and rule 10b–5 of the Securities Exchange Act of 1934 and possibly section 17 (a) of the Securities Act of 1933, section 206 of the Investment Advisers Act of 1940 will not support an implied private cause of action for damages. In a decision in which four justices dissented, the Supreme Court held that Congress provided an express action under section 215 of the Investment Advisers Act of 1940 for the recision of the contract and that there was no evidence to indicate Congress intended an implied private cause of action for damages. This case is representative of the recent trend of the Supreme Court to restrict implied causes of action for damages by private parties.

Actions under section 206 of the Investment Advisers Act are restricted to Securities and Exchange Commission administrative proceedings and civil or criminal suits brought by the commission.

State Securities Laws

Each of the four major pieces of federal securities regulation carefully preserves the rights of the states to regulate securities within their respective jurisdictions. As a result, any issuer contemplating a national issue must comply with the "blue sky" laws[12] of each state and the District of Columbia in addition to federal securities laws.

Uniform Securities Act

The commissioners on Uniform State Laws drafted a Uniform Securities Act for adoption by the states in 1956 and amended it in 1958. Since 1956 more than 30 states have adopted, in whole or in part, the Uniform Securities Act; however, national uniformity even among the adopting states is still lacking. Most states that adopted the act did so with substantial changes. Over time, different state courts have interpreted the language of the uniform act differently. The large commercial states such as New York, California, Texas, and Illinois have not adopted any part of the uniform act.

Definition of a Security

The definition of a security in section 401 (2) of the Uniform Securities Act is essentially the same as the definition of a security in section 2 (1) of the Securities Act of 1933. The drafters of the Uniform Securities Act intended to coordinate the Uniform Securities Act with the federal securities law. There is a slight variation in the wording of the provision regarding oil, gas, and mineral rights or interests, and the last sentence of section 401 (2) dealing with insurance, endowment, and annuity contracts does not appear in the federal statute.

In other states the definition of a security has taken an interesting turn. The risk capital test for investment contracts was developed by the California Supreme Court in 1961. Since that decision, other states, such as Alaska, Florida, Georgia, Hawaii, Michigan, Oklahoma, and Oregon, have turned to the risk capital test to avoid the restrictive nature of the *Howey* test.

In *Silver Hills Country Club*,[13] the promoters had purchased land on which to build and operate a country club. In order to finance the operation, they sold memberships in the club which entitled the members to use the facilities but did not entitle them to share in the profits of the enterprise. The membership was likened to a beneficial interest in title to property since it was irrevocable except for misconduct or failure to pay dues. The California Supreme Court held that the memberships were securities because the members had supplied the risk capital anticipating a return for their risk—the benefits of club membership.

Exemptions

Section 402 (a) (9) of the Uniform Securities Act exempts the following securities:

any security issued by any person organized and operated not for private profit but exclusively for religious, educational, benevolent, charitable, fraternal, social, athletic, or reformatory purposes, or as a chamber of commerce or trade or professional operation.

Some states require certain documents to be filed even though the security is exempt. It appears that in many states, the exemption is not mandatory but is merely at the discretion of the state authorities.

State reaction to the federal exemption for issues not involving a public offering under section 4 (2) of the Securities Act of 1933 is not uniform and is uncertain after the adoption of regulation D. Some states adopted the language of section 4 (2) of the Securities Act of 1933 while other states substantially adopted rule 146 in addition to the statutory language of section 4 (2). Other states merely coordinate their exemption with compliance with the federal requirements.

This area of state securities law is in a state of flux following the adoption of regulation D by the Securities and Exchange Commission. The reader should check the latest requirements for particular states.

Registration

Part III of the Uniform Securities Act provides for registration of a security prior to offer or sale of the security. There are three alternative registration procedures: notification, coordination, and qualification.

Section 302 of the Uniform Securities Act provides for registration by notification. This is the simplest of the three registration procedures. To qualify for registration by notification, the issuer must (1) have been in continuous operation for at least five years; (2) not have defaulted in the payment of principal, interest, or dividends of any security within the three fiscal years immediately preceding the registration; and (3) show an average earnings of at least 5 percent on its shares of common stock.

The registration form must contain the following information:

1. Name and address of the issuer
2. Issuer's form of organization
3. State in which organized
4. Date of organization
5. Character of the business
6. Description of the security
7. Offering price
8. Existence of any stock options
9. Certain financial data.

A copy of the prospectus or other sales materials must accompany the registration form.

Registration by notification takes place at 3:00 P.M. on the second full business day after filing or sooner if the state authority so determines, provided no stop order is in effect.

Coordination is available to an issuer who has filed a registration statement relating to the same offering with the Securities and Exchange Commission under the provisions of the Securities Act of 1933.

Registration by coordination is accomplished by filing the required number of copies of the federal prospectus with the state authorities.

Registration by coordination is automatically effective at the same time that the federal registration is effective, provided there is no stop order in effect, the registration statement has been on file with the state for at least ten days, and a statement regarding proposed offering prices and underwriter discounts and commissions has been on file with the state for at least two full business days unless otherwise waived by the state.

Section 304 of the Uniform Securities Act provides for registration by qualification, which is to be used by issuers who do not qualify for notification or coordination. The filing requirements for registration by qualification are roughly similar to those for registration under the Securities Act of 1933. Registration by qualification is not effective until it is approved by the state authority.

Under Uniform Securities Act sections 306 (a) (2) (E) and (F), registration may be denied if the offering tends to work a fraud upon purchasers or if underwriting compensation, promoter's profits, or options are unreasonable in amount. This represents a significant difference in philosophy between the federal securities law and the states'. The federal government is primarily concerned with disclosure and makes no value judgment.

Antifraud Provisions

As is the case with the antifraud provisions of the federal securities law, antifraud provisions of the state securities law represent a relaxation of the more stringent requirements of common law fraud. The manifestation of this proposition is contained in section 401 (d) of the Uniform Securities Act, which provides that " 'Fraud,' 'deceit,' and 'defraud,' are not limited to common law deceit."

The antifraud provision of the Uniform Securities Act bears a striking resemblance to sections 12 and 17 (a) of the Securities Act of 1933 and rule 10b–5 under the Securities Exchange Act of 1934. Section 101 of the Uniform Securities Act provides that:

It is unlawful for any person, in connection with the offer, sale or purchase of any security, directly or indirectly
(1) to employ any device, scheme, or artifice to defraud,
(2) to make any untrue statement of a material fact or to omit to state a material fact necessary in order to make the statements made, in the light of the circumstances under which they are made, not misleading or,
(3) to engage in any act, practice, or course of business which operates or would operate as a fraud or deceit upon any person.

All of the states except New Hampshire authorize the state authority to bring suit for an injunction against fraudulent conduct in the sale of a security, and most states extend that power to the purchase of a security.

The Uniform Securities Act provides only for a cause of action by a defrauded purchaser against his seller and makes no provision for a cause of action by a defrauded seller against his purchaser. This rule is adopted by a majority of the states. New York and Rhode Island make no provision for a private civil cause of action; however, in New York a private civil cause of action may be implied.

The elements of a cause of action for fraud under state securities law are essentially the same as under federal securities law; however, there are some important differences. The scienter requirement, which has played an important role in the development of federal rule 10b–5, is treated quite differently under state law. The scienter requirement exists as an element of a civil action, but the burden of proof is shifted from the defrauded purchaser to the seller to prove that the seller was unaware of any misrepresentation or omission of material facts and in the exercise of reasonable care could not have known of any. The reasonable care standard means that negligence is sufficient scienter.

Common law reliance is not required as an element of a civil fraud case under state law; however, the buyer must show that he did not know of the untruths or an omission to recover. Purchaser's reliance generally must be reasonable, but some states allow a purchaser to accept the statements made at face value and rely on them.

Generally, materiality is the same under both federal and state securities law, utilizing the reasonable man test that the representation be one to which the reasonable man would take into consideration or attach importance to in determining his course of action.

The express civil cause of action in most states is granted to the purchaser as against his seller. The remedies granted to a successful plaintiff are recision of the sale or suit for damages if he no longer owns the securities. The Uniform Securities Act and state securities laws require privity of contract between the purchaser and seller. The antifraud provisions of state securities law are more in the nature of the express civil liability provision of section 12 rather than section 17 (a) of the Securities Act of 1933 or section 10 (b) and rule 10b–5 of the Securities Exchange Act of 1934, which support a civil cause of action by any person whether in privity of contract or not. Since section 410 (h) of the Uniform Securities Act provides that no cause of action not specified therein may be created, a parallel development of implied civil causes of action for damages to rule 10b–5 is foreclosed.

Indemnification and Liability Insurance

Potential liabilities which may arise under sections 11, 12, and 17 (a) of the Securities Act of 1933 and section 10b and rule 10b–5 of the Securities Exchange Act of 1934 may be draconian. Officers, directors, controlling persons, and underwriters may be exposed to substantial financial liability. The right to indemnification for litigation expenses or for liabilities and fines incurred in direct or derivative actions brought on behalf of the corporation or in third-party actions arising out of actions taken in a representative capacity is first determined under state law. However, an indemnification agreement permissible under state law may not be enforceable with respect to violation of the federal securities law.

Indemnification of officers, directors, controlling persons, and underwriters for violation of federal securities law is contrary to public policy.[14] The goal of the civil liability provisions of federal securities law is deterrence and not compensation of victims. Indemnification would thwart that goal by passing on the cost of the liability ultimately to the corporation and its shareholders, many of whom might be victims of the fraud.

The Securities and Exchange Commission refuses to accelerate the effective date of a registration statement if an indemnification agreement is in existence unless the issuer agrees to submit the question of indemnification to a court before making any indemnification payment.[15]

Conversely, contribution among joint wrongdoers is allowed and is expressly provided for in section 11 of the Securities Act of 1933 and sections 9 and 18 of the Securities Exchange Act of 1934. Contribution is also allowed when liability is predicated on section 10b and rule 10b–5 of the Securities Exchange Act of 1934 so that one or more of the joint wrongdoers may not escape liability by leaving the prompt or diligent wrongdoer with the burden of payment.

Ironically, the Securities and Exchange Commission does not view liability insurance in the same way as indemnification regardless of who pays the premium. In either event, the deterrent power is thwarted. Nonetheless, liability insurance seems to be permissible.

NOTES

1. 15 U.S.C. §§ 77a, *et seq.*
2. 15 U.S.C. §§ 78a, *et seq.*
3. 15 U.S.C. §§ 79–79Z–6.
4. 15 U.S.C. §§ 77aaa–77bbb.
5. 15 U.S.C. §§ 80a–1–80a–52.
6. 15 U.S.C. §§ 80b–1–80b–21.
7. 15 U.S.C. §§ 78aaa, *et seq.*
8. Codified at 15 U.S.C. §§ 78a note, 78c, 78c note, 78o, 78t, 78u, and 78ff.
9. 421 U.S. 837 (1975).
10. 328 U.S. 293 (1946).
11. 425 U.S. 185 (1976).
12. So called because of the reference to "blue sky" in Hall v. Geiger-Jones Co., 242 U.S. 539 (1917).
13. 55 Cal.2d 811, 13 Cal. Rptr. 186, 361 P.2d 906 (1961).
14. Globus v. Law Research Service, Inc., 418 F.2d 1276 (2d cir. 1969), *cert. denied*, 397 U.S. 913 (1970); 17 C.F.R. § 230.460.
15. Item 512(i), Regulation S-K, 17 C.F.R. part 229.

6

Obtaining Operational Financing

The financing of American business operations is staggering in its dimensions. By one report, U.S. corporations near the beginning of 1986 were $1.56 trillion in debt.[1] Regardless of the ramifications of holding and servicing this indebtedness, demands for financing of business continue to be made not only in the equity and debt marketplaces (see Chapter 5) but also from financial institutions and suppliers of goods and services. This chapter focuses on the legal controls involved when a business obtains credit from financial institutions and suppliers.

THE NEED FOR BUSINESS FINANCING

Regardless of size, a business requires financing for both long- and short-term objectives. Obtaining affordable financing may be necessary not only for a business to expand, but also may be needed to service a firm's accounts payable requirements. Indeed, the cash flow of retailers, distributors, franchisees, processors, manufacturers, and other producers often dictates that a line of credit be available on a regular basis to finance normal business operations. Although it is true that becoming overextended creditwise may contribute to a firm's financial weakness and even lead to its insolvency or to a bankruptcy proceeding, credit which is both affordable and in reasonable proportion to a firm's assets is often the only way a business may successfully deal with its cash flow needs.

Sources of Credit

Credit sources range from governmental agencies such as the Small Business Administration to international banking houses. The problem is rarely one of credit availability. Rather, the more typical problem is obtaining credit at competitive rates pursuant to non-oppressive lending agreements. Preferred sources of credit are regulated financial institutions which lend within a state's usury limits. (See Chapter 11 for a discussion of usury.) Regulated and preferable sources of financing include national and state banks and savings institutions, insurance companies, mortgage houses, commercial credit lenders, purchasers of accounts receivable, and licensed small loan companies.

Factors Considered in Extending Business Credit

Three factors predominate in the evaluation of business loan requests: first, the credit history and current financial condition of the credit applicant; second, the availability and quality of the applicant's free and clear assets which may be used as security (the collateral); and third, the applicant's personal and business reputation for integrity and fair dealing. These three factors—creditworthiness, security, and business and personal reputation—are often important not only in the decision to extend business credit but also in influencing the terms and conditions of the credit when offered. This chapter focuses primarily on one of these criteria—security. Creditworthiness is discussed in Chapter 11.

SECURED VERSUS UNSECURED LOANS

An unsecured loan means that the borrower has neither conveyed an interest in property nor conditionally given collateral to the lender to secure the repayment of the credit. Should the debtor default by not paying an installment when due, the unsecured lender has only what the law calls a *chose in action*, that is, a right to enforce the claim in court. An unsecured lender as well as a seller of goods on credit where no security interest has been reserved may neither take possession nor sell any of the debtor's property. Other than trying to persuade or "dun" the debtor to cure the default by tendering the overdue payments, the unsecured creditor is left with the costly, uncertain, and often difficult remedy of collecting the indebtedness in court. (For a discussion of the law applicable to collections including the dunning process see Chapter 13.)

A secured creditor, on the other hand, is one to whom the debtor has conveyed a security interest in specified property called the collateral. Depending on certain factors (discussed in Chapter 13), a secured creditor may take possession of the collateral in which it had earlier been granted a security interest, then sell or dispose of the property and apply the proceeds against the amount owed plus the costs of repossession and disposition. When available, these self-help remedies mean that the secured creditor may not have to go to court to seek recourse from a debtor in default.

Self-Help Remedies

Although constituting an efficient means to collect and satisfy a delinquent indebtedness, self-help remedies are available only to certain secured creditors—

those who have lent or sold on credit pursuant to a conveyed or reserved security interest in specified personal property of the debtor. These remedies are expressly authorized by Article Nine of the Uniform Commercial Code,[2] a lengthy and comprehensive commercial statute enacted in all states, except Louisiana, and in the District of Columbia.

Personal property subject to self-help remedies include not only goods,[3] but also such intangibles as accounts receivable. The UCC defines an account broadly as the right to receive payment for goods sold or leased or for services rendered, whether or not yet earned by performance.[4]

When accounts are used as collateral and the principal debtor defaults, the creditor may notify the account obligors (called the "account debtors" under the UCC) to make all future payments directly to the creditor.[5] Because of this self-liquidating feature, accounts represent in many financing contexts the most desirable form of collateral.

Priority: The Key Legal and Practical Concept

Despite the ease and certainty the self-help remedies afford secured creditors (in contrast to the complexity and uncertainty typifying the judicial collection of unsecured obligations), a more important reason why many lenders and credit sellers extend credit only on a secured basis is because of the priority legal status a secured creditor may attain over the debtor's other creditors. Thus, the primary object of a secured loan or sale is to elevate a creditor's legal claim to one of priority which may allow the creditor to take and sell the collateral and to apply the proceeds of the disposition to satisfy its claim before any other creditors of the debtor may do so. Significantly, a secured creditor having priority does not have to share pro rata the proceeds with other creditors of the debtor. Priority status, in short, insures that the value of the collateral is available to the creditor having that status. Consequently, it is not the collateral per se that ultimately secures the lender. Rather, it is having priority rights in that collateral, ahead of all others, that is the true "acid test" of security.

THE LAW OF SECURED FINANCING

Article Nine—Secured Transactions

Although common law principles of law and equity apply to all credit extensions, secured financing is governed primarily by the provisions of Article Nine of the UCC, titled "Secured Transactions."[6] Article Nine has been described as a "code within a code" because its provisions seek to establish a unified set of legal principles which apply to the creation and priority of all security interests regardless of form in personal property or fixtures.

Depending on the type of collateral and who the claimant is, other laws may also apply. Security interests in aircraft, for example, are governed by the Federal

Aviation Act.[7] When the claimant is the Internal Revenue Service, priorities in part depend upon application of the Federal Tax Lien Act.[8] Security interests in motor vehicles usually are subject to state "title registration" laws in addition to Article Nine.

Scope of Article Nine

Article Nine applies to any transaction regardless of form which is intended to create a security interest in personal property or fixtures.[9] A security interest is an interest in personal property or fixtures which secures either the payment or performance of an obligation. A security interest includes the right reserved by a seller of goods to secure the balance of the purchase price when words such as "title reserved" or the like are used. A security interest also includes the interest of a lessor of goods when the lease is deemed to be one "intended for security."[10] Under this conceptual definition, secured loans, secured sales, and leases intended for security are all covered transactions.

The important thing to keep in mind regarding Article Nine's scope is that the form of the transaction does not matter provided evidence exists that the parties intended to create a security interest. Whether labelled a chattel mortgage, conditional sale, retail installment sales contract, long form promissory note, assignment of accounts, pledge, or lease, if the terms of the arrangement objectively considered reveal the parties' intention to use the device for security, Article Nine declares it to be a security agreement. As such, the arrangement is subject to the rules of Article Nine.

Virtually all business financing involving the extension of credit against inventory, equipment, accounts, chattel paper, documents of title, or other forms of personal property come within the scope of Article Nine, as do sales of accounts and chattel paper (a writing or writings evidencing both a payment obligation and a security interest, for example, a retail installment contract involving the secured sale of an automobile).[11]

Sales of Accounts and Chattel Paper

Sales of accounts and chattel paper are included within Article Nine because these assets may be either sold or assigned as security to raise funds for the seller or assignor. Thus, to assign or sell accounts or chattel paper in essence accomplishes an identical objective—obtaining needed funds by using existing assets having a high level of liquidity.

With the exception of sales of accounts and chattel paper, all other Article Nine secured transactions may be considered "layered"; that is, the secured transaction overlays an underlying obligation that either was preexistent to or created concurrently with the conveyance of the security interest. With this concept in mind, it is easy to understand why a conveyance of an interest in personal property to discharge a preexisting indebtedness is *not* a secured transaction. An example is where a debtor assigns a contract right to a creditor to discharge an obligation owed the creditor. The assignment is *not* one intended to secure any ongoing obligation but rather is made to extinguish and satisfy a preexisting obligation. Except for the sale of accounts and chattel paper, security interests are conveyed to secure newly created or preexisting obligations of a debtor which in either case continue to exist after the security interest has been created.

The Essential Components of a Secured Transaction

Every secured transaction involves five essential components: a debtor, a secured party, the collateral, a security interest, and a security agreement. These elements are present in both secured loans and in secured sales of goods on credit.

The Debtor, Secured Party, Collateral, and Security Interest

A *debtor* is the person to whom secured credit has been extended or to whom accounts or chattel paper have been sold. The *secured party* is the creditor, or the seller, or the assignor of accounts or chattel paper.[12] The *collateral* is personal property or fixtures in which the debtor has legal rights and in which the debtor has conveyed a security interest to the secured party. A *security interest* is one which secures an obligation of the debtor (normally, a payment obligation) but also includes the rights acquired by a purchaser of accounts or chattel paper.

The Security Agreement

The *security agreement* is the agreement between the debtor and the secured party which evidences the debtor's conveyance of an Article Nine security interest in his or her specified personal property.[13] A security agreement also includes an agreement to sell accounts or chattel paper. To qualify as an Article Nine security agreement, a document need not be called a security agreement but only must evidence the creation of a security interest in personal property.

Types of Security Interests

PMSIs and Non-PMSIs

Article Nine differentiates two types of security interests: purchase money security interests (PMSIs) and non-purchase money security interests (non-PMSIs). A PMSI is one either expressly retained by a credit seller of goods to secure the balance of the purchase price (a seller's PMSI),[14] or one which is conveyed to a lender who advances funds or credit for the purpose of enabling the debtor to acquire new property, which funds or credit in fact are so used (a non-seller's PMSI).[15]

Understand that sellers of goods who sell on credit do not automatically have a PMSI in the goods sold. The sales agreement must include language which evidences an Article Nine security agreement or the seller's reservation of a security interest in the goods sold. Language such as "title reserved" or "rights reserved" written on a sales slip describing the goods sold and signed by the debtor ordinarily will be sufficient to establish a non-seller's PMSI.

Evidence of the Security Agreement

A security agreement must be evidenced by a writing unless the secured party has possession of collateral subject to a possessory security interest. The writing must contain language which reasonably identifies or describes the collateral and must be signed by the debtor.[16] Several courts have added an additional requirement not explicitly required by the UCC. The additional requirement is that the language must contain "words of conveyance" or "reservation" such as "the debtor conveys to the secured party a security interest in the following described property, to wit: . . . "[17] Merely describing property and identifying it as "collateral" may be insufficient.

Floating Liens

The security agreement's description must reasonably identify what is included.[18] In the case of a blanket or floating security interest covering all of a business's equipment, inventory, or accounts, meeting the description requirement is a relatively easy task. An agreement covering all of a firm's accounts, for example, need only describe the collateral as "all accounts whenever acquired." The UCC permits a security interest to attach to after-acquired collateral, that is, collateral in which the debtor first acquires a property interest after the security agreement has been executed.[19]

Security interests which by agreement automatically attach to after-acquired collateral are commonly referred to as "floating liens," particularly if the collateral is inventory. In a floating inventory lien, the secured party's security interest is in a continually changing mass of inventory, where new inventory is constantly replacing items being sold (merchandise) or consumed (raw materials). Although not using the terminology of "floating lien," the UCC does use the language of "after-acquired collateral" clauses.

The Financing Statement

A *financing statement* is an important legal document filed with public authorities which puts a secured transaction on public notice. To be effective, a filed financing statement must contain the names and addresses of the debtor and the secured party, be signed by the debtor, and describe the collateral by types.[20] Once properly filed, a financing statement is effective for five years. Prior to its lapse, the secured party may file a "continuation statement," which continues the effectiveness for five years from its filing.

The Function of a Financing Statement

Whereas a security agreement is necessary both to evidence the secured relationship between the debtor and the secured party and to specify their respective rights and duties thereunder, a financing statement is intended to notify other potential creditors of the debtor that the debtor has entered into a secured transaction and that certain types of the debtor's personal property are subject to a prior security interest.

Not only must a financing statement (in most states known as "UCC-1's") be properly completed and signed to be effective, it must also be filed in the correct state and in the right location within that state. Creditors may need to consult an attorney for assistance in completing and in properly filing UCC-1 financing statements. The proper state to file is determined largely by Article Nine's choice of law rules set out in section 9–103.[21] The proper place within a state depends on that state's version of UCC section 9–401.[22]

Article Nine provides for both central and local filing. The proper place to file within a state depends on the kind of collateral and the kind of security interest involved. Most business forms of collateral—including accounts, chattel paper, equipment, and inventory—require central filing, usually with the secretary of state's UCC office located in the state's capital city.

The Effect of a Proper Filing

Filing of a financing statement by the secured party usually is necessary to gain priority status over other creditors or potential creditors of the debtor or over subsequent purchasers of the collateral. This is not to say that a proper filing, which results in a security interest's being perfected, automatically results in priority—far from it. It is to say, however, that perfection of a security interest (which in most instances may result only from a proper filing of a properly completed financing statement) is often a necessary requirement for priority. Perfection and priority are not synonymous but represent legally distinct phases of a secured transaction.[23]

Preemptive Filing

As part of a loan documentation or workup, a lender often requires that the prospective borrower sign a UCC-1 financing statement. This may occur before any required guarantees, subordinations, affidavits, or certified financial statements are completed. The signing of a UCC-1 may be requested even prior to the borrower and lender agreeing on terms of the credit arrangement. This practice is called "preemptive filing" and has a sound basis in law. By filing a debtor's signed financing statement before giving value (defined in the UCC as becoming committed to extend credit),[24] the lender enhances its priority rights. The UCC's residual, but far from only, rule of priority provides that if two or more secured parties have perfected security interests in the same collateral of a debtor, the first secured party to perfect or to file, whichever occurs first, has priority.[25]

Thus, if a lender has searched the public records under the prospective debtor's name and has found no financing statements of record and then files a financing statement before any other lender or purchaser does so, the lender can reasonably be assured that no subsequent lender or purchaser will have a better right to the debtor's covered property during the duration of the filing of the financing statement. It is this kind of assurance that Article Nine's rules make possible and that encourage lenders to extend loans against personal property (especially accounts) to assist a business in meeting its financing and liquidity needs.

TYPES OF COLLATERAL

Article Nine's classification of the types of personal property collateral may be grouped into three categories:

1. Tangible personal property including goods, accessions, and fixtures;
2. Intangible personal property including accounts, contract rights, and other general intangibles such as rights in intellectual property (patents, copyrights, trademarks, and tradenames);[26] and
3. Tangible-intangible personal property, in other words, intangible contract rights that are evidenced by tangible, specialized documents including chattel paper, documents of title, letters of credit, investment securities (stocks and bonds), and commercial paper (checks, drafts, and promissory notes).

Tangible Personal Property

Goods

Goods are "things" including chattels movable at the time a security interest attaches. Article Nine subdivides goods into four categories depending on their use in the hands of the debtor. *Consumer goods* are goods used or bought primarily for "personal, family, or household purposes."[27] *Equipment* consists of goods used or bought for use primarily in business which are not otherwise classified as inventory, farm products, or consumer goods.[28] *Farm products* are crops, livestock, or supplies which are used or produced in farming operations if in the possession of a debtor engaged in farming operations.[29] *Inventory* consists of goods held for sale or lease or to be furnished under service contracts, or goods in the form of raw materials, work in process, or materials used or consumed in a business.[30]

Accessions

Accessions are goods installed or affixed to other goods. Article Nine has a specific rule of priority which determines the rights of a secured party having a security interest in a good (for example, a truck engine) which is installed onto a whole (for example, a truck chassis) as against a secured party's having an interest in the whole.[31] Normally the accession claimant prevails over the "whole" claimant with certain exceptions.[32]

Fixtures

Goods are *fixtures* when they become so related to the real estate that an interest in them arises and is recognized under state real estate law.[33] Fixtures represent a hybrid of personal and real property. Article Nine seeks to reconcile and prioritize conflicting security interests asserted in fixtures by a secured party on the one hand and by the real estate's owner or encumbrancer, such as a mortgagee, on the other.[34]

Intangible Personal Property

Accounts and Contract Rights

Under the official UCC Permanent Editorial Board's revised version of Article Nine (enacted by over 40 states as of this writing), the definition of an account is a right to receive payment for goods sold or leased or for services rendered which is not evidenced by an instrument or chattel paper. This definition includes contract rights not yet earned by performance.[35] Thus, an assignment for security of executory contract rights (for example, the provisional right to receive future progress payments when earned under a Defense Department contract) is a secured transaction involving accounts as the collateral.

General Intangibles

Contract rights involving rights to receive performances other than the payment of money fall under the Article Nine category known as general intangibles. Also coming within this classification are choses in action which are rights to pursue claims in court (other than tort and judgment claims) and rights to receive payments under licenses, patents, and copyrights.[36]

Tangible-Intangibles

Chattel Paper

Chattel paper refers to a writing or group of writings which evidence both a monetary obligation and a security interest in, or a lease of, specific goods.[37] A written security agreement with or without a separate promissory note in either case constitutes chattel paper. This means that the assignment or transfer of a security agreement is itself a secured transaction, for example, where an automobile dealer assigns to a bank or finance company a customer's retail installment sales contract evidencing a reserved security interest in the vehicle sold.

Document of Title

A document of title is any document which, in the regular course of business or financing, is treated as evidencing that the person in possession of it is entitled to receive, hold, or dispose of the document and the goods it covers.[38] The most common form of document of title used in secured lending situations is a warehouse receipt, a receipt issued by a person or firm engaged in the business of storing goods for hire.[39] When warehouse receipts are pledged or assigned to raise capital, the arrangement involves a debtor or bailor who bails or stores the goods, the secured party who advances credit or distributes loan proceeds against the receipts (often the holder of the documents), and a warehouseman or bailee who issues the receipt upon taking receipt of the deposited goods.

Instruments

Another form of tangible-intangible under Article Nine is the category of instruments, defined as either a negotiable instrument under UCC Article Three or an investment security such as stocks and bonds recognized under the federal securities laws or under UCC Article Eight.[40] Stocks, bonds, and other investment paper are subject to a perfected Article Nine security interest but only if the secured party takes possession of the securities.[41] Thus, a non-possessory security interest in securities when they are not registered in the lender's name ordinarily has little security value to a creditor.

A security arrangement involving Article Three commercial paper typically consists of promissory notes where the maker promises to pay a sum of money to the holder on demand or at a definite time. (See Chapter 12 for a description of the forms of commercial paper.) Although promissory notes may serve as original collateral for a credit extension, they will more likely constitute "proceeds" collateral.

Proceeds

Proceeds include whatever is received when collateral (including proceeds) is sold or disposed of, and include cash, accounts, instruments, documents, chattel paper, or goods (when exchanged).[42] Because a security interest automatically extends to proceeds, the importance of proceeds to business lenders cannot be overstated, especially when equipment or inventory financing is involved. These matters are discussed subsequently in this chapter, but first, an overview of the legal phases of a secured transaction is presented.

LEGAL PHASES OF A SECURED TRANSACTION

Since Article Nine applies to any transaction intended to create a security interest in personal property or fixtures, an understanding of its provisions is necessary for structuring and analyzing secured financing arrangements. Although complex, the provisions are not particularly difficult provided one has mastered the article's internal construct, in other words, its organizing and conceptual principles. This section sets out an analytic procedure which affords the recognition of the legal issues that arise in secured financing arrangements. We begin with a hypothetical situation.

Hypothetical Situation

Assume that Oblet Supply Co. is a jobber engaged in wholesaling machine tools to industrial buyers. Oblet desires to acquire a new line of "widget" machine tools manufactured by Iblet Manufacturing Co. Iblet has informed Oblet, however, that it will sell widgets only on a cash basis because of Oblet's deteriorating credit rating.

To finance the purchase of new machine tools and to pay off a portion of existing accounts payable, Oblet goes to Secure Bank which agrees to advance the firm $15,000. Under the agreement, Secure Bank takes a security interest in Oblet's inventory whenever acquired and proceeds. Secure Bank files a financing statement covering the collateral. Oblet takes $5,000 of the $15,000 loan proceeds and pays its unsecured (accounts-payable) creditors. Oblet advances the remaining $10,000 to Iblet with a purchase order for 100 widget machine tools to be shipped upon completion. Subsequently, Oblet defaults on its obligation to Secure Bank. Only $500 of Secured Bank's $15,000 loan against Oblet's inventory and proceeds has been repaid. The 100 widgets which Oblet paid for in advance (using funds extended by Secure Bank) have not yet been shipped by Iblet. Their wholesale value approximates $10,000.

An officer of Secure Bank wonders whether the bank "owns" these 100 widgets which are awaiting shipment at Iblet's factory. The bank officer knows that another customer of the bank might purchase the widgets from the bank provided it has clear title.

The officer asks the bank's attorney the following questions:

1. May the bank take possession and sell the on-hand inventory of Oblets?

2. If the bank does have the right to take control over the 100 widgets, may the bank sell these items to the bank's customer?

Secure Bank's attorney will need to consult Article Nine. The issue to be analyzed is whether Secure Bank has a priority right to the 100 widgets.

Identification and Phase Analyses

To understand how Article Nine's provisions apply to the above hypothetical situation, an attorney or business person needs an analytic framework. Fortunately, Article Nine contains the structure necessary for legal analysis. A set of definitions facilitates an identification process whereby all the parties (and collateral) are defined in terms of their legal relationships to each other.

To answer the bank officer's questions requires first an analysis of the Oblet–Secure Bank loan transaction from its incipiency through its eventual breakdown (Oblet's default). The suggested methodology involves two processes—an identification analysis followed by a transactional phase analysis.

In the identification analysis, the secured transactions are identified. Next, the parties to each transaction are identified and labeled on the basis of their legal relationship with each other. The type of collateral is then designated within Article Nine's classification. Then, the particular kind of security interest (PMSI or non-PMSI) is identified. Finally, third parties (trustees, buyers in the ordinary course of business, unsecured creditors, purchasers of the collateral, lien creditors, and holders of instruments or documents of title) are identified and labeled according to the UCC's definitions.

After completing the initial identification analysis, the second step of the methodology—the transactional phase analysis—becomes applicable. Every commercial transaction may be viewed conceptually in a time-sequential fashion. The parties meet, negotiate, and enter into a legally binding relationship. Following the agreement and execution of the appropriate documents, the parties commence their performances, completing over time their respective obligations and ultimately receiving their mutual benefits. This assumes that the transaction ran smoothly, that it did not break down.

When difficulty arises, however, the legal relationships between or among the parties and in the collateral become altered. To analyze a financing arrangement, it is helpful to have a conceptual understanding of the various legal phases of the transaction. To view the transaction in a time-sequential manner does not go far enough, whereas to structure the transaction through its various legal stages is to study it sequentially as to when legal events occur, rather than when factual events take place. Phase analysis makes it easier to recognize potentially legally dispositive issues.

Consider a secured transaction. A sequential legal-phase analysis views an ordered sequence of legal events from the negotiation phase through the creation, enforcement, attachment, perfection, priority, default, and remedial phases. This phase-process model is helpful not only for analyses of transactional breakdowns (default, insolvency, improper care of collateral, or non-maintenance of a required collateral-to-loan ratio), but also for competent transactional planning since the model highlights drafting and planning pitfalls. An ordered sequential perception of legal events places potentially legally dispositive issues into the distinct legal phases which may be summarized as follows.

Negotiations

The negotiation phase includes all events, dealings, communications, and statements between or among the parties occurring before the creation of the security interest. These dealings and events may be relevant to issues relating to warranties, disclaimers, parol evidence, basis of the bargain, and good faith. (See Chapter 8 for an extended discussion on negotiations.)

Creation

The creation phase is that stage in a secured transaction when the security interest arises. This occurs when the secured party enters into a security agreement with the debtor. A lawyer will study the language of the security agreement and related documents to identify issues relating to conveyancing language, unconscionability, and description of the collateral.

Enforcement-Attachment

The enforcement-attachment phase consists of those legal events constituting conditions precedent to the secured party's having rights as against the debtor's collateral. Attachment of a security interest also means that it is enforceable. Before a security interest becomes enforceable, there must be an agreement, value must be given by the secured party, and the debtor must have rights in the collateral. At the moment all three events have taken place, under UCC section 9–203 (2), the security interest "attaches" in the collateral. Attachment is one of the essential requirements for a security interest to be properly "perfected," the next legal phase.

Perfection

The perfection phase is where a secured party takes steps to maximize his or her rights to a debtor's collateral versus third persons. Consequently, perfection often is determinative of a secured party's rights against other creditors of the debtor. Although perfection under certain circumstances occurs automatically at the moment of attachment, in most cases, the filing of an appropriate financing statement is required. Dispositive issues relate not only to the fact of filing, but also to the proper state, place, and time of filing as well as to the contents of the financing statement.

Priorities

The priority phase involves the application of the Article Nine rules of priority to determine the relative ranking of creditors and purchasers who claim rights in the debtor's collateral. In other words, a determination must be made as to which claimant among the various claimants has the best right to satisfy an indebtedness by taking and disposing of the collateral. Priority determinations may involve resolution of conflicting claims among both secured and unsecured creditors, lien creditors, bankruptcy trustees, purchasers of the collateral, and holders of instruments or documents of title. (As to the impact of bankruptcy on priority rights, see Chapters 13 and 14.)

Default

The default phase involves, first, a determination of exactly what factual events as defined in the security agreement constitute default; second, whether an agreed-upon default event has occurred; and, if it has, third, a determination of when the default occurred.

Remedies

The remedial phase concerns the remedies available to an aggrieved party following default. General principles of law and equity outside of Article Nine may also apply. Issues including the manner in which collateral is taken, the notice of sale, the commercial reasonableness of the sale, the availability of a deficiency judgment, and the remedies of subordinate creditors may be involved. (These issues are discussed in Chapter 13.)

It is helpful, moreover, to understand the relation of the legal phases. For example, for a secured party to have a right to take possession without judicial process of collateral, an earlier default event must have occurred. The non-payment of an installment due would constitute a default event which makes available to the secured party the Article Nine remedies but only if its interest in the collateral is deemed to have priority over other creditors who might claim an interest in collateral. Priority status usually depends upon the secured party's having timely perfected its security interest. Secure Bank, in the above hypothetical situation, did file a financing statement (often required for perfection under section 9–302). But perfection in part is predicated upon the security interest's having properly attached. Attachment requires that there be an agreement, that value be given, and that the debtor have rights in the collateral.

In the above hypothetical situation, there was an agreement and value was given by Secure Bank, but did the debtor, Oblet Co., have rights in the 100 widgets which had not yet been shipped by Iblet Co.? This rights-in-the-collateral requirement for attachment turns out to be analytically dispositive in answering the bank officer's inquiries. If Oblet did not have rights in the 100 widgets, then Secure Bank's security interest neither became enforceable under section 9–203 (1) nor attached under section 9–203 (2). Since perfection requires attachment, Secure Bank's security interest is unperfected. Consequently, Secure Bank's claim would be subordinate to the interest of any lien creditor under both the Bankruptcy Reform Act and the rule of UCC section 9–301 (1) (b). Thus, to properly analyze problems involving secured financing, one needs to be aware of the legal phases of a secured transaction and to be cognizant, moreover, of the relationship of the seven phases to each other.

THE LOAN WORKUP

Loan documentations or workups are necessary steps which a lender and a prospective borrower must take before the loan commitment is made. From a lender's perspective, good documentation is basic preventive law.

The Loan Agreement

The principal enabling document is the loan agreement. Although the UCC requires only that minimum terms be included,[43] most lenders will want many additional provisions including events of default and maintenance of collateral clauses. Provisions relating to a debtor's warranties of title to the collateral, covenants to do or to refrain from doing specified acts in reference to the collateral, and the duty to maintain casualty insurance on the collateral are also normally included. In addition, a lender's rights to monitor or police the collateral, such as the right to enter upon the debtor's premises to conduct an inventory, should be spelled out.

The Promissory Note

A lender may require, as a condition for extending a secured or unsecured loan, that the prospective borrower agree to execute a promissory note (discussed in Chapter 12). The note may or may not be negotiable. In either event, it personally obligates the maker to its repayment terms. "Long form notes" are not negotiable and typically contain all the terms and conditions of the loan. So-called short form notes, however, often will be negotiable and are executed together with a separate loan agreement. One purpose of the note is to establish clear evidence of the borrower's personal liability for repayment of the credit extended. Another purpose is to have the obligation in an easily marketable or transferable form.

The Guarantee Agreement

A separate, written guarantee agreement which renders the signer or signers personally liable to pay the indebtedness should the principal debtor default may be required as a condition for a business loan. A guarantee agreement should clearly specify the obligations that are guaranteed. In many cases, a guarantee provides for immediate recourse to the guarantor for the full amount of the principal debtor's obligations should the debtor default on any of its obligations. Thus, a guarantee agreement may be written with a default-acceleration provision (see Chapter 11).

The Subordination Agreement

When a loan is to be secured by a security interest in a business' personal property, such as equipment, inventory, farm products, or accounts, it is common for the lender to require that existing creditors of the debtor agree to subordinate their claims in the specified collateral to that of the lender. A creditor's subordination is one form of a subordination agreement recognized under the UCC.[44]

Subordination agreements are also used where the shareholders of a company agree to subordinate their claims to that of a "preferred" lender. Should the debtor default in repaying the lender, become insolvent, or go into bankruptcy, the preferred lender will be paid before the subordinated equity holders.

Understand, however, that no creditor who has a claim under the law either equal to or prior to the claim of another creditor may be subordinated to the other creditor's claim unless they both so agree. In bankruptcy reorganizations, however, a class of claims may be "adjusted" and "crammed down" as part of an approved plan, even against the wishes of the creditors in the class (see Chapter 14).

Compensating Balance

Certain lenders require that borrowers, as a condition for loans or other financial assistance, maintain a deposit account equal to a stated minimum percentage of the outstanding loan balance. This is called a compensating balance. Typically, these accounts are noninterest or low interest bearing. The reasons for requiring them include not only to increase a bank's deposits but also to enable the lender to monitor the cash flow of the business. Of course, a compensating balance of $10,000 on a $100,000 loan means that the borrower in effect has only $90,000 but is paying interest on a $100,000 loan.

Other Documents

Depending on the circumstances, a lender may require affidavits of ownership, certified financial statements, and proof of legal or corporate names. Finally, a financing statement (or UCC–1) must be completed and signed before it is filed with the proper public agency which, as mentioned previously, may occur at an early point in the loan's workup.

We turn now to a discussion of the law of personal property security as applied to particular business financing arrangements. We consider the legal problems involved in equipment financing.

FINANCING OF EQUIPMENT

Equipment purchases are financed through credit extended by sellers and lessors of the equipment or by third persons, including commercial banks or other financial institutions. The financing may take the form of a lease intended for security, a conditional sale contract, a chattel mortgage, or simply a secured sale. Regardless of form, each is an Article Nine secured transaction because each evidences that the seller or lessor has a security interest in the equipment, which is the subject matter of the transaction.

Equipment Leases

Leasing is widely used by businesses to finance the acquisition of personal property, especially equipment. By one report, nearly $150 billion in lease receivables was outstanding near the beginning of 1980, an amount reportedly representing at that time more than 20 percent of the total U.S. capital investment.[45]

Possible Tax Advantages

The explanation for the popularity and growth in leasing rather than purchasing equipment stems in part from firms not having the necessary funds to make cash purchases and in part from real and perceived advantages of leasing under the federal income tax laws.[46] These tax benefits have included at various times under the changing tax laws:

1. Accelerated depreciation
2. Deductibility of rental payments
3. The investment tax credit for personal property.

The investment tax credit especially has made the leasing of everything from compressors to company cars attractive to business.

Stretching Out Payments

In addition to the former and possible real tax benefits still remaining after the 1986 tax changes (see Chapter 20), an equipment lease enables a business to acquire and use equipment for its projected useful life while permitting the payments to be stretched out for the entire period. This cash flow advantage is especially attractive to firms not having large sums of cash to pay for the equipment outright.

Equipment leases in many respects are considered bailments for hire under the law. A bailment is where one party called the bailor relinquishes his or her right to possess and use personal property to another party, called a bailee, for consideration, usually in the form of a promise to pay periodic rental or lease payments. As such, an equipment lease is subject to the common law of personal property regarding bailments. This body of legal principles deals with issues such as whether a bailor or a bailee has the risk of loss should the equipment be destroyed in the bailee's possession, what a bailee's duty of care is in reference to the equipment, and what the rights are of a bona fide purchaser for value of the equipment who purchased it from the lessee vis-à-vis the original owner or lessor. (The purchaser normally prevails.)

Leases Intended for Security

When a lease of equipment is deemed to be one intended for security, UCC Article Nine applies to the transaction in several important respects.[47] First, the rights of the lessee's other creditors in the leased property are determined by Article Nine. Second, the rights of purchasers of the equipment are also delineated by Article Nine rather than by the common law's bona fide purchaser principle.

In acquiring equipment, the parties may choose to use a lease not only for possible tax and cash flow advantages but also to afford the seller security should the purchaser default. A lease where the lessor is not relinquishing title to the property may appear especially attractive to an owner of a chattel who wants to sell it yet be sure he or she can take it back should the buyer cease to make payments. In such a case, it is not unusual for the seller to become a "lessor," the buyer a "lessee," and the subject matter of the sale the "leased property." In these situations, the "lease" may contain a clause to the effect that, upon payment of all obligations, the lessee either will become the owner or will have the option of becoming the owner for a nominal consideration. Inclusion of an option to purchase clause in a lease does not automatically make it one intended for security.[48] On the other hand, inclusion of an option to purchase, which is exercisable upon the payment of no or of a nominal consideration at or near the scheduled expiration of the lease, does make the lease one intended for security,[49] meaning that the lessor is an Article Nine secured party having a security interest in the "leased" goods.

Any lease intended for security is an Article Nine covered secured transaction and is subject to its rules. It makes little difference what the parties call their agreement. Even declaring that "this lease is *not* intended for security" may not avoid Article Nine's reach because the courts tend to use an objective rather than a subjective test in making the determination. This means that a court analyzes the lease's terms to determine if the parties intended when beginning the lease that at its expiration the lessee would automatically become the owner or, for a nominal consideration, had the right of becoming the owner of the equipment. If the answer is yes, the parties' intention, as evidenced not by the title on their "lease" document but, as revealed by its substantive terms, would be one to sell the property using the lease as a security device.

Options to purchase with a stated price may or may not cause the lease to be one intended for security. It depends on the relationship of the stated option price to the anticipated fair market price of the chattel at the time the option is exercisable (not the *actual* fair market price, but rather the fair market price at the time of expiration of the lease as projected or anticipated by the parties at the commencement of the lease).

Consider this example: Lessee leases "Big Wheel" from lessor for a total lease price of $48,000 for four years with a monthly "rental" of $1,000. The lease grants the lessee the option to purchase the Big Wheel during the final month of the lease or within 30 days thereafter for the price of $5,000. To decide whether this lease is one intended for security or not requires additional information: first, the fair market retail value of the Big Wheel at the outset of the lease and, second, the anticipated fair market value it would have four years later. Assume the fair market value at the outset was $40,000 and that the anticipated fair market value that the Big Wheel would have four years later was $20,000 (assume that the Big Wheel had an expected thirteen-year life under normal use). Having this additional information, a court would likely conclude that the lease was intended for security because, first, the total lease payments plus option price ($53,000) approximates the original fair market price ($40,000) plus reasonable interest ($13,000) over a four-year period on the declining balance and, second, because the stated option price of $5,000 was nominal in comparison with the anticipated fair market price at the expiration of the loan ($20,000). Unless the Big Wheel had been destroyed or seriously damaged in the interim, the lessee would be foolhardy not to exercise the option. Even if the Big Wheel were no longer needed by the lessee, it still could be resold for a profit. The "lease" was thus intended for security.

The Need to Perfect Security Interest

The issue of whether Article Nine applies to a given lease may often be crucial to a lessor. In the above Big Wheel case, suppose a creditor of the "lessee" has a sheriff, pursuant to a writ of execution (see Chapter 13), "levy" on the Big Wheel. A levy is a required step in a judicial process designed to obtain proceeds to pay a judgment creditor. May the lessor upon learning of the levy enjoin the sale or, if sold, recover the proceeds of the Big Wheel's disposition? If the lease is under Article Nine, the answer is no, *unless* prior to the sheriff's levy the lessor or his or her counsel filed a signed UCC–1 properly describing the collateral with the appropriate public filing office.[50]

The lessor, having the interest of a secured party and having not timely filed a UCC–1, loses out to the levying creditor under one of Article Nine's basic rules of priority—an unperfected Article Nine security interest is subordinate to the rights of a lien creditor whose lien existed before the security interest is perfected.[51] A lien creditor is a creditor under Article Nine who has acquired a lien by attachment, levy, or the like and who sometimes is referred to outside of Article Nine as a "judicial lienor."[52]

The important lesson for a lessor of equipment is that it may find itself without any security and without the rights either to have the leased goods returned or to reclaim the proceeds of sale. This could happen if, at the time the lease was executed, the lessor failed to file a UCC–1. These dangers underscore the importance of filing in equipment leasing situations.

Precautionary Filings

Lessors and lessees of equipment do have a way to protect themselves should Article Nine be held to apply to their transactions. They may file a precautionary financing statement, a device specifically authorized by UCC section 9–408 (which has been enacted in at least 39 states). The section permits a lessor to file a UCC–1 using the terms "lessor" and "lessee." Moreover, the section also provides that the filing "shall not of itself be a factor in determining whether or not the . . . lease is intended as security."[53]

Net, Full-Payout Leases

Financial institutions as well as equipment leasing companies typically offer "net, full-payout" leases. Under a net lease arrangement, the lessee's payment obligations are "net" of costs and expenses for insurance, repairs, maintenance, and normal operations, all of which the lessee is obligated to pay. The "full-payout" aspect means that the lessee is obligated to pay a sum that approximates the original fair market value of the item plus an unstated "interest" amount. Net, full-payout leases may be either true leases not subject to UCC Article Nine or may constitute a secured sale (a lease intended for security) depending on the terms, market values, and prices involved.

Remedies of Lessor Upon Lessee's Default

Many equipment leases "financed" by lending institutions allow the lessor or lender, after the lessee or borrower has defaulted, to take possession of the leased property, dispose of it, and apply the proceeds to the entire indebtedness. The lender may also recover from the lessee under specific lease provisions all accelerated future rentals which may or may not be reduced to "present value" (the equivalent of a rebate of unearned interest).[54] This contractually based remedial scheme essentially reflects the rights permitted secured parties by law under the self-help remedies of the UCC.[55]

Secured Sales and Loans Involving Equipment

In addition to leases intended as security, equipment may be directly sold to a purchaser whereby the seller extends or a financer furnishes the necessary credit. When equipment purchases are either seller or bank financed, the seller or lender may demand a security interest in the equipment. If a security interest is involved, the seller or lender will obtain a purchase money security interest.[56] A lender may also loan money or extend credit against either existing or existing plus after-acquired equipment. In these instances, the lender has a non-purchase money security interest in equipment.

Secured lenders sometimes use older forms labeled conditional sales contracts or chattel mortgage agreements in lending against equipment. The form is not significant as each is considered an enforceable Article Nine security agreement.[57]

The lender may require that a detailed description of the equipment be included in the loan agreement and may also require that a financing statement be filed in another state. The "other state filing" may be mandated under Article Nine's choice of law rules, which apply when a transaction either in its execution or performance may involve parties or property located in two or more states. Filing in the proper state is necessary if a secured party is to perfect its security interest.

State of Filing

If the debtor's equipment is "mobile," that is, normally used in more than one jurisdiction (for example, shipping containers, trailers, motor vehicles, and rolling stock), the UCC requires that the lender must file in the state where the debtor is deemed to be legally located, that is, in the state where his or her place of business (if one place) is located or in the state where the chief executive officer is located (if the debtor has more than one place of business), otherwise in the state of his or her residence.[58]

In the case of equipment used or located principally within one state, that state is the state where the financing statement should be filed; in other words, in the state where the goods are located when the financing statement is filed or attempted to be filed.[59] When goods subject to a filed financing statement are removed to another state, the effectiveness of the originally filed financing statement continues for four months after the removal, beyond which the security interest ceases to be perfected in the state where the property has been removed unless a new financing statement is properly filed in the new state.

Fixtures

Equipment has the potential of becoming fixtures, that is, so related to real estate that an interest in them under real estate law may arise.[60] Should this occur, a lender may lose its priority interest in the equipment unless it has made a fixture filing, that is, the filing of a financing statement not only describing the fixtures but also including a legal description of the related real estate in the office where interests in real estate are recorded.[61] This means that an Article Nine equipment lender or seller should file both centrally with the state's secretary of state and locally with the local recorder of deeds in the county where the equipment is or may become attached to specific realty. Article Nine sets out an elaborate set of priority rules concerning creditors' claims in fixtures.[62] Fixture filings help maximize a secured party's position in these priority disputes.[63] In this area, however, many states including Florida have significantly altered the provisions of the standard fixture priority rules of Article Nine.

Priorities

Purchasers of equipment subject to an earlier security interest normally take the equipment subject to the security interest. They do not qualify as "buyers in the ordinary course of business" (BIOCOBs) under the UCC because the debtor does not as a normal part of its business sell equipment (in contrast to its inventory which it does normally sell). To be a BIOCOB, or one who buys free and clear of existing security interests under the UCC, the buyer must buy from one who normally sells goods of that kind.[64] Consequently, equipment purchasers buy at risk of being subordinate to earlier security interests under the UCC's residual rule that a security interest is good against all purchasers of the collateral and against all other creditors unless Article Nine specifically provides otherwise.[65]

As between two secured lenders each having a properly *perfected* security interest in the same equipment, the first to have properly filed or perfected, whichever occurs first, has priority.[66] An exception to this rule is a purchase money seller or lender who has financed the debtor's acquisition of new equipment. The purchase money secured party prevails even against an earlier perfected non-purchase money lender provided the PMSI was perfected at the time or within ten days of the debtor's taking possession of the new collateral.[67]

What this means to manufacturers and suppliers of equipment who sell on a secured basis is that they should not delay filing their UCC–1s but should attempt to file before the financed equipment arrives at the buyer's plant or other location.

INVENTORY FINANCING

Inventory is defined as goods held for sale or lease, raw materials, work in process, or materials used or consumed in business. Inventory represents a significant business asset for raising funds, assuming the inventory is paid for and is free of claims of prior creditors. Of course, acquisitions of new inventory often need to be financed. Although a supplier may be willing to sell on open credit, it may "demand security" by reserving a security interest in items sold.

Whether a creditor lends money against existing inventory or finances the acquisition of new inventory under reservation, the arrangement is an Article Nine secured transaction. Many variations in secured inventory financing exist including both purchase money and non-purchase money arrangements. We briefly discuss three of the more significant varieties here: general inventory financing, floor planning, and field warehousing.

General Inventory Financing

The Floating Lien

A lender who extends revolving credit in the form of a credit line to a business and takes back a security interest in its entire inventory including after-acquired inventory is said to have a "floating lien." Article Nine validates the floating lien (also called a continuing general lien) by several provisions when considered together.[68]

The Collateral-to-Loan Ratio

What concerns a general inventory financer is that there be on hand sufficient collateral to secure the loan balance. The inventory lender understands that when the debtor sells any of the covered inventory items to purchasers, they take the items free of the lender's security interest under the rule that a BIOCOB cuts off the inventory lender's security interest in the items sold.[69]

Consequently, the general inventory lender is (or should be) continually concerned about the amount of unsold inventory and its value in relation to the loan balance. Since both the loan balance and the value of the unsold inventory constantly change, a lender often desires a formula which places limits on how much the debtor may use of the credit line in reference to the value of the current unsold inventory. This may be accomplished by including a collateral-to-loan formula in the security agreement.

In a well-drafted collateral-to-loan clause, the parties first agree on how the inventory is to be valued, for example, by agreeing that value is to be based on the invoice price of the goods to the dealer. Next, they agree that the value of the on-hand collateral must at all times equal at least, for example, 150 percent of the outstanding loan balance. This is a 1.5 to 1 collateral-to-loan ratio.

The security agreement may also provide that the secured party has the right to make, without prior notice, spontaneous visits during normal working hours to conduct inventory checks or to perform other monitoring measures. Periodic reports of certified public accountants may also be required. In any event, legal counsel should be consulted in drafting general inventory or floating lien security arrangements where collateral-to-loan ratios and monitoring measures are used or contemplated.

Priorities

As between two general inventory lenders each having a security interest in the same inventory of their common debtor, the perfected lender prevails over an unperfected lender should the debtor default, while the first lender to file or to perfect, whichever occurs first, prevails when both are perfected. When a later in time seller of inventory reserves or a lender takes a PMSI, the PMSI lender will prevail over the earlier secured party but only if the PMSI lender, first, gives any earlier inventory secured party of record personal notice of the expected PMSI interest, then, second, perfects its own security interest, provided it perfects prior to the delivery of the new inventory to the buyer.[70] The sequence of these steps is as important as the taking of them to attain the priority.

The Danger of Losing One's Security

Because a security interest in inventory is cut off upon its sale to BIOCOBs, the inventory lender's security ultimately may depend on its priority right to *proceeds* which the sale of inventory generates. Proceeds of inventory often take the form of accounts or chattel paper or non-cash items. The UCC awards the priority in non-cash proceeds to the party that filed first. In other words, the purchase money exception to the usual first-in-time, first-in-right rule does not apply.[71] This may create a special problem for manufacturers, processors, jobbers, and other sellers of goods to buyers where the goods are inventory in the buyer's hands. The danger is that the debtor may over time sell its entire "purchase money" inventory and then default on paying the balance due its supplier who will *not* have priority to the accounts or other non-cash proceeds of the purchase money inventory. Suppliers of goods may attempt to protect themselves by either selling for cash or on a short thirty-to-ninety-day basis, reserving a security interest in the goods sold, notifying earlier secured parties of record of the pending sale or sales, and then perfecting by a proper UCC–1 filing.

Field Warehousing

A variation of the floating lien—one much more elaborate and expensive— is where a third party known as a warehouseman polices the collateral and oversees maintenance of the collateral-to-loan ratio. A knowledgeable commercial lawyer must be consulted to help put together this arrangement because of the risks to both lender and borrower that may result if done improperly. Although the UCC does not use the term "field warehousing," it permits this financing arrangement to be set up under the provisions of Articles Seven and Nine.

A field warehouse "comes to the goods" so to speak as it is set up on the debtor's property either inside its plant or within an outside stacking area. Unlike the more common "terminal" warehouse located off the debtor's premises and used by a business primarily to store goods, a field warehouse is used almost exclusively for financing purposes.

The Warehouse Agreement

The prospective debtor in a field warehouse arrangement must enter into a warehouse agreement with a commercial field warehousing company under which the company agrees to set up and manage the field warehouse. Pursuant to the agreement's terms, the warehouse company, upon the debtor's deposit of goods, is obligated to issue warehouse receipts covering the goods. Although non-negotiable receipts are issued in most field warehouse arrangements,[72] they may be issued in negotiable form, which makes them easier to sell or transfer. The warehouse agreement is between the debtor-bailor of the goods and the warehouse company-issuer of the warehouse receipts.

The Security Agreement

In a field warehouse arrangement, the debtor-bailor also executes a security agreement with a lender who agrees to lend money or advance credit against the issued warehouse receipts. What is important from the secured lender's perspective is that it have control over the release of goods from the warehouse. This may be accomplished by drafting the warehouse agreement and the security agreement contemporaneously so that the warehouseman is obligated to release deposited goods only upon the tender of signed delivery orders issued by the secured lender. By requiring that all the issued receipts be turned over to the lender, the warehouse agreement facilitates creditor monitoring of the agreed-upon collateral-to-loan ratio.

Advantages of Field Warehousing

In addition to its rights under Article Nine, the secured lender has legal protections under Article Seven should the warehouse company issue receipts for goods not deposited,[73] misdescribe what was deposited,[74] issue duplicate receipts without a conspicuous notification appearing on the face of the duplicates,[75] negligently cause the goods to be lost or damaged,[76] or misdeliver the goods by tendering them to a person not legally entitled to the goods under a negotiable receipt or according to the terms of the warehousing agreement when non-negotiable receipts are outstanding.[77]

Field warehouses are suitable either where inventory is largely seasonal or where it consists of raw materials or other work in process which may easily be moved in and out of the warehouse dependent upon the debtor's needs so long as a sufficient volume remains to satisfy the collateral-to-loan ratio. The principal disadvantage is its cost of implementation. Still, a field warehouse may be the only arrangement under which a creditor may be willing to extend credit to a business.

Floorplanning

A more common form of three-party financing is "floorplan financing." Floor-planning is used extensively to finance a dealer's acquisitions of inventory. As such, it involves the manufacturer or supplier of the inventory in addition to the dealer and the lender or "floorplanner."

Approval Numbers

Floorplans are set up in a variety of ways. Under one method, the manufacturer obtains from the floorplan lender an approval number which, pursuant to the floorplanning agreement, commits the lender to finance a shipment or partial shipment of inventory which a dealer desires to purchase and for which it needs financing. Upon obtaining the lender's authorization, the manufacturer then ships the goods with the assurance that it will be paid by the lender the agreed-upon portion of the dealer's invoice price. Meanwhile, the lender files a UCC–1 covering the shipped goods. Thus, when properly executed, the arrangement results in the lender's having a perfected, non-seller's PMSI in the goods shipped to the dealer.[78]

Should the dealer default in its obligations to the lender, the lender may not issue the approval number for the next scheduled shipment. The manufacturer may then stop shipment or, if the dealer is a franchisee, may even terminate the franchise. Franchise agreements typically require that an "in-place" line of credit be available for the purchase of inventory.

A dealer may have more than one floorplan financer. So long as each floor-planner perfects a security interest in only the inventory it finances, no priority problems between or among them results. Indeed, most floorplanners attempt to limit their security interests so as not to be classified as a general inventory financer since the purchase money priority status is necessary to protect a floor-planner's interest.[79]

The Repurchase Agreement

Another attraction of floorplanning to lenders is the repurchase agreement, which most manufacturers provide the lender. Under a repurchase agreement, the manufacturer agrees to repurchase from the lender any repossessed inventory either at cost or for the outstanding balance, whichever is less, plus costs of repossession. Repurchase agreements frequently include various provisions such as a flexible repurchase price clause. Repurchase agreements should be drafted with the assistance of counsel.

Priorities

To gain a purchase money priority over earlier general inventory financers, a floorplan lender must mail original notification of floorplanning letters to all earlier inventory financers of record,[80] along with periodic renotifications.[81] Again, advice of counsel is important in this area.

ACCOUNTS RECEIVABLE FINANCING

The most common form of asset based lending is extending credit on a revolving basis against inventory and accounts or against accounts only. As noted in the preceding section, general inventory financers to a large extent have security in the accounts which normally derive upon the sale of inventory. General inventory financers typically look to the proceeds rather than to the original collateral for recourse should the debtor default in repayment of the inventory loan.[82] The reason is the self-liquidating nature of accounts versus the impractical and burdensome task of repossessing and attempting to sell inventory items. If a secured party has an attached security interest in accounts, following a debtor's default it may notify the obligors of those accounts, the account debtors,[83] to make their future payments directly to the lender.[84]

Forms of Account Financing

Accounts may be sold or assigned to a purchaser or assignee for cash or assigned or pledged to a lender as security for credit. Regardless of the form, the transfer may be with or without recourse. To transfer accounts *with recourse* means that if the account debtor defaults for any reason in making a payment when due, the transferee may "throw back" the account or otherwise hold the transferor liable for the amount. If the transferee is a purchaser or assignee who had paid cash or given credit for the account, the amount will either be added back to the credit balance or deducted from a "bad debt" pool set up under provisions of the account transfer agreement. If the transfer is *without recourse*, the risk of non-collection falls on the transferee.

It is important to understand that Article Nine treats the sale, assignment, or discounting of accounts for cash; the assignment of accounts to discharge preexisting indebtedness; and the transfer or pledge of accounts as security for new or previously extended credit as being legally identical transactions.[85] In each case, the transferor is the debtor; the transferee is the secured party; the accounts are the collateral; and the transferee's interest is an Article Nine security interest.[86]

Notification (Direct Collection)

In a direct collection accounts financing arrangement, the transferee or assignee of the accounts notifies the account debtor (or obligor of the account) to make future payments to the assignee. On the other hand, the transfer or assignment of accounts, which is only for the purpose of collecting the accounts for the benefit of the assignor, is not an Article Nine secured transaction.[87]

Non-Notification (Indirect Collection)

Under a non-notification, indirect collections accounts arrangement, the principal debtor continues to collect the payments as they become due from the various account debtors. These payments are either periodically remitted to the secured party or otherwise credited to the secured party's account. Should the principal debtor default in any of its obligations to the secured party, the latter may notify the account obligors to make future payments to it.[88]

Factoring of Accounts

Although the factoring of accounts predated Article Nine, as a form of financing factoring, it is still used today, especially in the textile industry. Under a typical factoring plan, the assignee assumes the credit loss risk by purchasing accounts without recourse or charge-back rights should the account debtor default. In factoring arrangements, other creditors of the principal debtor have little concern about what the "factor" (more properly called the secured party) does with the accounts should they become delinquent. This is not the case, however, when the secured party has been assigned or has purchased accounts with reserve or charge-back rights. In these instances, other creditors of the transferor debtor have a legitimate commercial interest in the accounts. Thus, the secured party may not "dump" delinquent accounts but must proceed in a "commercially reasonable" manner to collect them.[89]

Creating and Perfecting Security Interests in Accounts

Because accounts are intangibles and cannot be possessed, they may not serve as the subject of an oral or possessory security agreement. Rather, to create a security interest in accounts by sale, pledge, discount, assignment, or factoring, there must be a written agreement evidencing the transfer of the legal interest in the accounts, signed by the transferor, and describing the principal debtor's receivables or portion thereof that constitute the subject matter of the transaction.[90] The typical accounts financer desires that its security interest attach automatically to after-acquired accounts, and the transfer (or security) agreement usually so provides.[91]

A security interest in accounts other than those arising out of the sale of farm products may be perfected only by filing a financing statement in the state where the debtor is legally located (usually the state of its chief executive office)[92] with the secretary of state's office.[93] This perfection rule applies to all transfers of interests in accounts. Thus, a purchaser of accounts who has given cash but who has not filed a financing statement has only an unperfected security interest in them and will lose out to a bankruptcy trustee or to perfected secured creditors should the debtor go into bankruptcy or become insolvent under the Article Nine rules of priority.[94]

Priorities

The first-in-time, first-in-right rule of priorities applies to security interests in accounts.[95] Consequently, in this area, preemptive filing by creditors is highly recommended. Note also that, even though a purchase money lender with a perfected security interest in equipment may gain a priority in the accounts generated upon the sale of the equipment as against an earlier, filed accounts financer,[96] that rule does not apply to purchase money inventory financers who have a subordinate interest in the inventory's non-cash proceeds including accounts as against an earlier filed accounts lender whose priority in after-acquired accounts includes those subject to later purchase money interests.[97]

Rights of Transferees of Accounts

Normally, a purchaser, assignee, or other transferee of an account takes the account subject to all of the terms of the underlying contract between the account debtor and assignor including any defense or claim that might arise.[98] Also, the assignee takes subject to any other defense or claim the account debtor might have against the assignor which accrues before the account debtor receives notification of the assignment.[99] An exception to these rules occurs, however, if the account debtor in the underlying contract with the assignor made an enforceable agreement not to assert defenses or claims arising out of the transaction.[100] These rules incorporate pre-Article Nine law for the most part, which made assignees of accounts subject to defenses or setoffs existing before an account debtor is notified of the assignment.

Where the accounts arise out of sales of goods defined as consumer goods in the hands of the purchasers, the waiver-of-defense exception noted above, which would avoid the liability for defenses or claim, does not apply because of a specific Federal Trade Commission rule, "Preservation of Consumers Claims and Defenses"[101] (discussed in Chapter 11).

CHATTEL PAPER FINANCING

Chattel paper is similar to accounts except that the account debtor's payment obligations are secured. Moreover, both the payment and secured obligations are evidenced by one or more written documents.[102] Article Nine applies to all transfers of chattel paper including sales, assignments, discounts, and pledges except for transfers intended only for collections.[103]

Creating and Perfecting a Security Interest in Chattel Paper

Unlike accounts, a secured party may create a security interest in chattel paper and perfect that interest by taking possession of the paper pursuant to a written security agreement.[104] A secured party may also perfect its interest in chattel paper by filing in the same manner and in the same location as it would to perfect a security interest in accounts.[105]

Rights of Purchasers of Chattel Paper

A purchaser of chattel paper, who gives new value (taking it neither as security for nor in discharge of a preexisting indebtedness owed by the assignor) and who takes possession of the paper in the ordinary course of his or her business, has a priority in the chattel paper over most earlier secured parties, including a secured party who filed to perfect its security interest in chattel paper whenever acquired.[106] This rule applies, however, only when the purchaser takes the paper without actual knowledge that it is subject to the earlier security interest or, even with knowledge, if the earlier security interest in the chattel paper was claimed merely as proceeds of inventory subject to an earlier security interest.[107]

As to whether a purchaser of chattel paper is subject to the claims and defenses of the account debtor, the issue depends first on whether the account debtor was using the goods purchased on credit for a consumer purpose. If so, the FTC rule on preservation of consumers' claims and defenses will likely apply.[108] If not, it depends on whether the chattel paper contract contained a waiver-of-defense clause or whether the buyer (account debtor), as part of the transaction, signed both a negotiable instrument (usually a promissory note) and a separate security agreement.[109] If a buyer did sign both documents, the purchaser of the chattel paper takes free of all claims and defenses (except defenses based on legal incapacity, duress, or fraud) that the account debtor could have asserted against paying the assignor of the chattel paper.[110]

ROLE OF COUNSEL

In asset based financing, lender's counsel is used to conduct UCC filing searches, to draft the enabling documents, to assist in the necessary documentation for the loan workup, and, most importantly, to render a legal opinion on the priority rights of the lender should the debtor default or go into bankruptcy.

The role of borrower's counsel, on the other hand, is to make sure that a lender does not overreach in tying up too much of the debtor's assets, in placing unworkable demands for collateral maintenance, or in too tightly defining the default events so as not to allow the debtor a little breathing room. In sophisticated lending arrangements, counsel is needed to draft and oversee the execution of guaranty and subordination agreements.

A lender's or credit seller's security is only as good as its legal basis. A missed or delayed perfection, for example, might negate entirely the value of one's security should a bankruptcy petition be filed by or against the debtor (see Chapter 14). Consequently, lenders, manufacturers, and suppliers of goods who intend to lend or sell on a secured basis should consult a knowledgeable, commercial lawyer to assist in setting up the transaction in order to maximize the value of the security by seeing that all the required legal steps are properly taken. Preventive law in this area may pay high dividends indeed.

NOTES

1. Wilson, "High Debt Could Strangle the Economy," *New York Times*, November 24, 1985, § 3 at 2, col. 4.
   2. U.C.C. §§ 9–503, 9–504, and 9–505.
   3. U.C.C. § 9–109.
   4. U.C.C. § 9–106.
   5. U.C.C. § 9–502.
   6. *See*, U.C.C. §§ 9–101, *et seq.*
   7. 49 U.S.C. §§ 191, *et seq.*
   8. 31 U.S.C. §§ 191, *et seq.*
   9. U.C.C. § 9–102 (1).
   10. U.C.C. § 1–201 (37).
   11. U.C.C. § 9–102 (2).
   12. U.C.C. § 9–105.
   13. *Id.*
   14. U.C.C. § 9–107 (a).
   15. U.C.C. § 9–107 (b).
   16. U.C.C. § 9–203.
   17. American Card Co. v. H.M.H. Co., 97 R.I. 59, 196 A.2d 150 (1963).
   18. U.C.C. § 9–110.
   19. U.C.C. § 9–204.
   20. U.C.C. § 9–402.
   21. U.C.C. §§ 9–103 (1)-(u).
   22. U.C.C. §§ 9–401 (1), (2), and (3).
   23. U.C.C. § 9–303.
   24. U.C.C. § 1–201 (44).
   25. U.C.C. § 9–312 (5) (a).
   26. U.C.C. § 9–105 (1) (h).
   27. U.C.C. § 9–109 (1).
   28. U.C.C. § 9–102 (2).
   29. U.C.C. § 9–102 (3).
   30. U.C.C. § 9–102 (4).
   31. U.C.C. § 9–314.
   32. U.C.C. §§ 9–314 (1), (2), and (3).
   33. U.C.C. § 9–313 (1) (a) (1972, rev. ed.).

34. U.C.C. §§ 9–313 (4), (5), (6), and (7) (1972, rev. ed.).

35. U.C.C. § 9–106.

36. *Id.*

37. U.C.C. § 9–105 (1) (b).

38. U.C.C. § 9–201 (15).

39. U.C.C. § 9–201 (45).

40. U.C.C. § 9–105 (1) (i).

41. *See*, U.C.C. §§ 9–304 (1) and 9–305.

42. U.C.C. § 9–306 (1).

43. U.C.C. § 9–203 (1).

44. U.C.C. § 9–316.

45. Mooney, *Personal Property Leasing: A Challenge*, 36 Bus. Law. 1605, 1605 n.3 (1981).

46. *Id.* at 1606.

47. *See, e.g.*, U.C.C. §§ 9–301 (1) (b), 9–102, 1–201 (37), 9–206 (1), and 9–408.

48. U.C.C. § 1–201 (37).

49. *Id.*

50. *See*, U.C.C. §§ 9–401 and 9–408.

51. U.C.C. § 9–301 (1) (b).

52. U.C.C. § 9–301 (3).

53. U.C.C. § 9–408.

54. Mooney, *Personal Property Leasing: A Challenge*, 36 Bus. Law. 1605, 1617 (1981).

55. U.C.C. § 9–503–9–507.

56. U.C.C. §§ 9–107 (a) and (b).

57. U.C.C. § 9–201.

58. U.C.C. §§ 9–103 (3) (a), (b), and (d).

59. U.C.C. § 9–103 (1) (b).

60. U.C.C. § 9–313 (1) (a).

61. U.C.C. §§ 9–402 (1), (3), (5), and (6). *See also*, U.C.C. § 9–403 (7).

62. U.C.C. § 9–313.

63. *See, e.g.*, U.C.C. §§ 9–313 (4) (a) and (b).

64. U.C.C. §§ 1–201 (9) and 9–307 (1).

65. U.C.C. § 9–201.

66. U.C.C. § 9–312 (5) (a).

67. U.C.C. § 9–312 (4).

68. *See, e.g.*, U.C.C. §§ 9–108, 9–203, 9–204, and especially, 9–205.

69. U.C.C. § 9–307 (1).

70. U.C.C. § 9–312 (3).

71. *See*, U.C.C. §§ 9–312 (3) and 9–312 (5).

72. U.C.C. § 7–104.

73. U.C.C. § 7–203.

74. *Id.*

75. U.C.C. § 7–402.

76. U.C.C. § 7–204.

77. U.C.C. §§ 7–403 (1) and (4).

78. U.C.C. § 9–107 (b).

79. *See*, U.C.C. §§ 9–312 (3) and 9–107 (b).

80. U.C.C. § 9–312 (3).
81. U.C.C. § 9–312 (3) (c).
82. *See*, U.C.C. §§ 9–312 (3) and 9–306 (1).
83. U.C.C. § 9–105 (1) (a).
84. U.C.C. § 9–502 (1).
85. *See*, U.C.C. §§ 9–102 (1) (a) and (b), and 9–102 (2).
86. *See*, U.C.C. § 1–201 (37).
87. U.C.C. § 9–104 (f).
88. U.C.C. § 9–502 (1).
89. U.C.C. § 9–502 (2).
90. U.C.C. § 9–203 (1) (a).
91. *See*, U.C.C. § 9–204 (1).
92. U.C.C. § 9–103 (3) (b) (d).
93. U.C.C. § 9–401 (1) (b) or 9–401 (1) (c) (depending on which alternative of § 9–401 a particular state has enacted).
94. *See*, U.C.C. §§ 9–301 (1) (b) and 9–201.
95. U.C.C. § 9–312 (5).
96. U.C.C. § 9–312 (4).
97. U.C.C. § 9–312 (3).
98. U.C.C. § 9–318 (1) (a).
99. *Id.*
100. *Id. See also*, U.C.C. § 9–206 (1).
101. 16 C.F.R. § 433.
102. U.C.C. § 9–105 (b).
103. *See*, U.C.C. §§ 9–102 (2) and 9–104 (f).
104. *See*, U.C.C. §§ 9–203 (1) (9) and 9–305.
105. U.C.C. § 9–304 (1). *See also*, U.C.C. §§ 9–103 (b) and 9–401.
106. U.C.C. § 9–308.
107. U.C.C. §§ 9–308 (a) and (b).
108. 16 C.F.R. § 433.
109. U.C.C. § 9–206 (1).
110. *Id. See also*, U.C.C. § 3–305 (2).

7

Real Estate and Real Estate Financing

It is safe to say without fear of contradiction that private ownership of property is one of the cornerstones of American jurisprudence. It permeates the Declaration of Independence and the Constitution and finds countless expressions in the statutes and court decisions issued from the beginning of the Republic. Private ownership of property is held in such high regard that a person may be deprived of it only by due process and just compensation.

PRIVATE PROPERTY

The concept of private property includes the exclusive right of a person or persons to possess, control, enjoy, and convey the property. To give effect to the concept of private property, there must be a private party who asserts a claim of ownership to a recognizable economic unit (the property) and a government policy to protect and enforce the ownership interests and rights of the private party.

Limitations on Private Property

Ownership or possessory rights are not unlimited or free from government interference, however. Governments have the power to tax and levy special assessments on the property.

A governmental unit may take or condemn the property under its power of eminent domain if in the public interest. Eminent domain is subject, however, to constitutional restrictions under the Fifth and Fourteenth Amendments to the U.S. Constitution and state constitutions. For property to be taken, the owner must be accorded due process and receive just compensation. Due process requires notice and an opportunity to be heard. Most controversies under eminent domain do not concern the right to take the property but rather just compensation. It is a question of valuation for a particular use that is subjective and hence debatable.

Private property cannot be used in such a manner as to affect adversely public health, welfare, safety, or morals. A government under its police power may regulate the use of property with regard to these items. The common law doctrine of public nuisance has been widely used to control the noxious use of private property.

Nuisance

A nuisance is defined to be anything that is injurious to health, is indecent or offensive to the senses, is an obstruction to the free use of property so as to interfere with the comfortable enjoyment of life or property, or unlawfully obstructs the free passage or use in the customary manner of any waterway, public park, square, street, or highway. A public nuisance is one that affects an indefinite number of persons within the range of its operation or locality. A private nuisance affects only a small number of persons different from any injury suffered by the general public. Not all persons affected by a public nuisance must suffer equally. For instance, a noxious odor emanating from a plant will affect individuals differently depending on distance from the plant and wind direction. The operation of a slaughterhouse inside the city limits and an overgrowth of vegetation (weeds) are public nuisances although, in the case of the slaughterhouse, there is the issue of which came first. A preexisting slaughterhouse that now finds itself within the city limits is not a public nuisance by right of being first in time. Examples of private nuisances are failure to provide lateral support (digging a hole near adjacent property and causing it to collapse) and blocking air and light by constructing tall buildings. Naturally occurring events are not public nuisances, for example, water flowing from a higher piece of property to a lower property.

Zoning

Land use is also restricted by zoning ordinances. Zoning is the regulation and restriction of real property by a local government under its police power. It involves a classification of territory based upon the character of land and structures and their fitness for particular uses. Consideration is given to the conservation of the value of property as well as encouragement of the most appropriate use of land throughout a particular locality.

Through zoning, a local government seeks control and direction of the development of property within its borders, according to present and potential uses of the property. Zoning laws are intended to promote the health, safety, welfare, convenience, morals, and prosperity of the community and are meant to further the welfare of the general public as opposed to furthering the economic interests of any particular property owner. They are designed to stabilize neighborhoods and preserve the character of the community by guiding its future growth.

The main purpose for the existence of most zoning ordinances is to segregate residential, commercial, and industrial areas from one another. Use of the property within a particular area is, for the most part, uniform. For example, if an area is zoned for industrial use, no residential buildings will be permitted there although existing structures might be allowed to remain.

For the purpose of protecting the public health, safety, morals, and general welfare, local governments exercise wide discretion in fixing the boundaries of commercial and industrial areas. A number of ordinances have been enacted to protect residential zones from encroachment by service stations, public parking, liquor stores, and smoke- or odor-producing factories.

Nonetheless, the power to zone is not unrestricted. Zoning amounts to the taking of property in the sense that it restricts private land use. Zoning ordinances must be reasonable and not arbitrary or capricious and must be nondiscriminatory. There must be a rational basis for the classification, and the property should be classified to insure its best use.

When enacting zoning ordinances, a zoning board takes into consideration factors such as density of population, site and physical attributes of the land, traffic and transportation, fitness of the land for the permitted use, location of the land, character of neighborhoods in the community, existing uses and zoning of neighboring property, the effect of permitted use on land in the surrounding area, effect of zoning on income from the property, potential decrease in property values, the gain to the public at large weighed against economic hardships imposed upon individual property owners, and the amount of time that the property has remained unimproved considered in the context of land development in the area as a whole.

Exclusionary zoning is the practice of utilizing zoning power to further the parochial interests of a particular local government entity at the expense of surrounding regions. Its purpose is to establish or advance economic and social segregation. Exclusionary zoning involves the use of zoning to take advantage of the benefits of regional development without being forced to bear the burdens of such development, as well as the use of zoning to maintain particular areas as enclaves of affluence or social homogeneity. Examples of exclusionary zoning are minimum house square feet requirements, minimum lot frontage requirements, prohibition of multifamily housing, and prohibition of mobile homes. These ordinances violate the fundamental principle that zoning ordinances should advance the general welfare.

Spot zoning, like exclusionary zoning, is generally invalid. Spot zoning consists of classifying a particular parcel of land differently from the classification of other land in the immediate area. Such classification is arbitrary, capricious, and unreasonable because it is a deviation from a comprehensive zoning plan for the area.

Some deviation from the comprehensive plan is permitted. A preexisting use of private property may be continued after the area is zoned for some other purpose. In general, the preexisting use may be continued but may not be expanded. Nonconforming use is terminated by abandonment of the use, changing the use, passage of a predetermined time during which the nonconforming use was permitted, or rezoning.

An owner of real property who suffers a hardship disproportionate to other owners in the immediate area from the zoning restrictions may be granted a variance. A variance may be granted if the property cannot yield a reasonable return if used as zoned, if the property is unique compared to others in the area, or if the variance will not disrupt the comprehensive plan of the area. Certain exceptions to zoned use may be included in the comprehensive plan itself.

Real Property

All property is divided into real and personal property. Classification is usually relatively easy. Land and things permanently fixed or attached to the land are real property. Problems arise when the permanence of the attachment is questioned. It is clear that the structures erected on the land are real property. It is not as clear in regard to things put in the structure such as a furnace, carpeting, or bay window. Such things are referred to as fixtures of real property. The question becomes one of intent. Did the person intend to attach the thing permanently so that it becomes real property? If the thing is attached so that the structure is damaged if it is removed or if it was custom made for that particular structure, then it is a fixture and is real property.

Real property includes not only the surface and structures but also the subsurface and airspace above the surface. Part of the real estate may be conveyed separately from the rest. For example, mineral rights may be conveyed separately or retained when the surface is conveyed. The same is true for the airspace above the land to a reasonable height.

Both natural vegetation and cultivated vegetation are real property until severed from the land. Trees, shrubs, flowers, wheat, corn, or other crops are real property and are conveyed with the land. Once severed from the land, they cease to be real property and become goods (personal property).

Personal Property

Personal property is all other property not classed as real property. Anything movable, not permanently attached to land that is capable of ownership is personal property.

REAL PROPERTY INTERESTS

Traditionally, all land belongs to the sovereign whether it be king, tyrant, or republic. The sovereign granted private ownership in exchange for services or money. The private party acquires the estate in land subject to restrictions placed on it by law or contract. Ultimately, the sovereign may reacquire the land by escheat when no private owner is known to exist.

The type of estate or interest conveyed is of the utmost importance because it determines what rights the parties have with respect to the property.

The legal terminology describing real property interests has roots in the common law of England and today seems obscure and unnecessary. Nevertheless, one needs to be familiar with some of the more important terms to understand the nature of the transactions. Real property interests are classed as either possessory or nonpossessory depending upon whether or not the interest entitles the holder to enjoy actual possession of the property.

Possessory Interests

Fee Simple

The most complete form of ownership is the "fee simple." A fee simple estate is of unlimited duration and allows the holder to use the land in any way provided the holder does not interfere with the property rights of adjoining owners and abides by the law. When the holder of a fee simple estate conveys the property, it is presumed that the entire fee simple estate is conveyed. To do otherwise requires a clear, express intent in the conveyance document.

A fee simple may be limited in such a way that it will terminate under certain conditions. Such a limited fee simple is called a "fee simple defeasible." One of the more common uses of the fee simple defeasible is to insure that the property will be used for the purpose conveyed. For example, property is conveyed to a city (grantee) in fee simple for use as a park, and, in the event that it is not used as a park, the property reverts back to the conveyor (grantor). Both the grantor and grantee have a property interest in the same piece of property. The grantee's interest continues as a fee simple until the designated event occurs. The grantor's interest is a future interest which, in the example, is called a "possibility of reverter." Instead of a reversion back to the grantor, the conveyance may give the interest to a third party if the designated event occurs. The interest held by the third party is called an "executory interest."

Life Estate

A more limited possessory interest is the life estate. The duration of the life estate is determined by the life of a designated party, not necessarily the holder of the life estate. For example, one spouse may convey property by will to the other spouse for as long as he or she lives, then to their children. The surviving spouse has the right to occupy and use the property during his or her lifetime in any manner except that he or she may not injure the interests of the remaindermen (children). For example, the life estate holder could not cut down and sell all the standing timber on the property without permission from the remaindermen. Outside of life estates created by wills for the benefit of a surviving spouse, life estates are rare.

Leasehold

A leasehold is a possessory interest that entitles the holder to possess the property temporarily in exchange for rent. The agreement that provides for the transfer of possession in exchange for the payment of rent is called the lease. The lessor transfers possession to the lessee who pays the rent.

Until fairly recently, the law governing leaseholds was a development of the common law. In 1972, the National Conference of Commissioners on Uniform State Laws promulgated a uniform residential landlord and tenant act which has been adopted in thirteen states. Hence, in those states, the law is a mixture of common law and statutory law. There are fundamental differences in the underlying philosophies of law regarding the common law and the statutory law. The common law developed in a rural society and economy and concerns itself with a transfer of an interest in real estate; therefore, the basic principles governing real estate law apply to leasehold arrangements. The statutory law tends to be based on a contract theory and has grown out of the consumer protection movement of the middle part of the twentieth century.

The lease itself contains the terms of the agreement and sets forth the rights and duties of the respective parties. Most controversies arise out of a neglected or omitted term from the lease. While a lease may be oral, it should be reduced to writing for the protection of both parties. In most states, the statute of frauds requires that a lease exceeding a specified period of time must be in writing. The rule varies from state to state but is generally effective for leases for a period greater than one year; however, some states use a three-year period. Whatever the form, oral or written, a valid lease agreement must manifest an intent to create a leasehold, identify the contracting parties who must have contractual capacity, specifically describe the leased property, and state the amount of the rent and how it is to be paid.

Other provisions in the lease are called covenants or conditions. A covenant is merely a promise by one or the other of the parties to the lease to do or not do a particular thing. If the promise is breached, the injured party's recourse is to file suit for money damages. Breach of a covenant does not terminate the lease nor relieve the injured party from any obligation arising under the lease, nor does the breaching party forfeit any rights under the lease. Conversely, the failure of a condition relieves the injured party of any further obligation under the lease. A condition is a future or uncertain event the happening of which determines the existence of an obligation. In most states, promises made in leases are construed to be covenants unless there is a clear indication it was intended to be a condition; however, lessee's default on payment of rent is a forfeiture whether there is an express term in the lease to that effect or not.

There are four basic types of tenancies under a leasehold. A tenancy for years exists if the lease states a specific duration for the lease regardless of the length of time. A tenancy for years does not have to be in increments of a year; the period could be 30 days, 6 months, or some other specified duration. The lease terminates automatically on the expiration of the time period. A periodic tenancy refers to a leasehold which has no set duration but specifies a rental payment to be made periodically or at a particular interval. The tenancy exists from period to period whether it be monthly, semiannually, or annually. A periodic tenancy terminates when one party gives notice to the other of termination. Such notice is generally required to be at least one period before actual termination. In some states, statutory law modifies the termination notice rule for those periods in excess of one month, in which event 30 days' notice is sufficient. A tenancy at will exists when neither lessor nor lessee has agreed to the duration or rent to be paid and is terminable without notice by either party. A tenancy at sufferance exists when a lessee stays beyond a termination date of a valid leasehold estate. The lessor has a choice of either agreeing to another lease or evicting the lessee from the property.

A leasehold estate is not terminated by a sale of the property. The purchaser takes the property subject to the lease. What the lessor actually sells is what he or she has, which is the right of reversion at the termination of the lease. Purchaser in effect merely buys the right of reversion. A purchaser does not have to honor an existing lease if its existence was unknown to the purchaser because the lease was not recorded and the lessee was not in possession of the property at the time of the sale.

Since a leasehold is a possessory interest in the property, the lessee is entitled to possession, but in some states the lessor is required only to transfer the legal right to possession and not give actual possession. In those states that require only a transfer of the legal right to possession, the lessee must take the necessary legal steps to remove any holdover from a prior lease from the property. If the lessor was required to convey actual possession, the lessor is responsible for evicting any holdover.

While the lease is in force and effect, the lessor may not interfere with the tenant's lawful possession and use of the property. This is known as the covenant of quiet enjoyment which, if not expressly stated in the lease, is implied in most states. The covenant of quiet enjoyment may be breached only by the lessor and not by a third party. The most common breaches of the covenant of quiet enjoyment are eviction and constructive eviction of the lessee.

Eviction is depriving the lessee of his or her right to possession by physically barring entry, changing a key, or padlocking the premises. In the event of an eviction, the lessee may either sue for damages or treat the eviction as a breach of a condition and be relieved of any obligations arising under the lease.

Constructive eviction consists of action taken by the lessor which makes the property unsuited to the use for which it was leased. Failure to provide heat in the winter in a cold climate is constructive eviction. The lessee may abandon the premises and treat the constructive eviction as a breach of condition and be relieved of any further obligation to pay rent, or the lessee may remain on the premises and sue for damages, but if the lessee remains on the premises he or she is still liable for the payment of rent.

While a leasehold is a possessory interest in the property, the lessee may not make any use of the property that would harm the lessor's interest. The lessee may use the property for any legal or reasonable purpose connected to the reason for which the property was leased unless the lease contains a specific restriction. For example, a lease of a residence may prohibit the operation of a business out of that residence. Moreover, the lessee is not entitled to use the property in any manner that will cause permanent damage to it. It is immaterial whether the damage was intentional or negligent. In general, a lessee has no right to make alterations to the property without consent; therefore, a business tenant who wishes to alter the property to suit his or her business must have specific consent of the lessor. In many states, the lessee must return the premises to the lessor at the end of the lease in the same condition in which it was received, except for normal wear and tear. If the lessee made any alterations to the property without the landlord's consent, the lessee must either put the property back in the original condition or pay the cost of putting it back into the original condition. If the lessee attaches something to the property in such a manner that it is construed to be a fixture, the fixture becomes part of the real estate and cannot be removed from residential property at the end of the lease; however, business or trade fixtures may be removed by a business tenant at the termination of the lease if it can be done without substantial damage to the real estate.

At common law, a lessee leased property as it existed at the time the lease was executed and had to make any subsequent repairs to return the property in the same condition at the termination of the lease. However, the lessee's duty to make repairs did not extend to major structural elements of the building unless it was an emergency repair necessary to protect the property from further damage. Minor repairs such as broken glass, dripping faucets, etc., are the responsibility of the lessee. If a lessee does not want to assume responsibility to make the repairs, he or she should insert an express covenant in the lease placing the responsibility for repairs on the lessor. In a shopping center or an apartment complex where the lessor maintains the common areas, he or she must maintain those areas in a reasonably safe condition and is responsible for making such repairs. The duty to make such repairs, though, extends only to those repairs that the lessor knows about or should have known about. Failure to inspect may make the lessor liable for any harm that results.

In the case of residential property, courts have been recognizing an implied warranty of habitability. This warranty requires the lessor to maintain residential property in such a manner as to be habitable or livable. This warranty runs through the entire term of the lease. The warranty of habitability does not apply to minor items such as painting, leaking faucets, defective venetian blinds or curtains, and other items that are not aesthetically pleasing but do not render the building uninhabitable. The defect must be of such a magnitude as to interfere with such things as sleeping, eating, safety, or health. The standard to which the lessor will be held varies with the age or condition of the building; an old building cannot be expected to have state of the art or modern conveniences.

If the lessor refuses to make the repairs that he or she is obligated to make, the lessee may sue for damages, make the repairs at his or her own expense and deduct the cost from the rent, withhold the rent until the repairs are made, or cancel the lease if the defects are of such a magnitude that the implied warranty of habitability is breached.

The lessor is not responsible for latent or hidden defects that he or she could not discover during a normal inspection. However, the lessor is responsible for repairs that are negligently made and result in injury.

If the lessee unjustifiably withholds rent, the lessor may seize and sell any of the lessee's property on the premises for nonpayment of rent. The landlord has a lien on all items physically on the premises. It is best not to use self-help but to file an action in a court of competent jurisdiction to execute the lien. In this case, the sheriff will be ordered to seize all of the lessee's property on the premises and sell them to satisfy the rent. If the lessee has made a security deposit, the security deposit may be forfeited to satisfy unpaid rent. If the landlord's lien and the security deposit are insufficient to satisfy the rent, the lessor may file suit to collect the remainder. Under common law, the lessor was allowed to leave the property vacant in case of abandonment or eviction during the remainder of the term of the lease and hold the lessee liable for all unpaid rent during the term. Today, states are requiring lessors to mitigate the damage. Mitigation requires a good faith effort on the part of the lessor to find another tenant to fill out the term of the lease.

Unless the lease expressly forbids it, a leasehold may be assigned or sublet. An assignment is a transfer of the entire estate held by the lessee to a third party. A sublease is a transfer of only a part of the estate held by the lessee. In the case of an assignment, there is essentially a substitution of the assignee (third party) for the original lessee; however, the original lessee is still obligated under the lease unless released by the lessor. If the assignee fails to pay the rent, the lessor may proceed against the assignee or the original lessee. In a sublease there is no legal relationship in existence between the lessor and the sublessee. In the absence of any legal relationship, there are no legally enforceable rights or obligations flowing from one to the other. The original lessor-lessee relationship continues in existence without alteration. The sublease creates a second lessor-lessee relationship between the original lessee as sublessor and the sublessee.

Nonpossessory Interests

Easement

An easement is a limited right to use property without taking possession. An easement may be an easement appurtenant or an easement in gross.

An easement appurtenant is one that relates to another piece of property. A right of way is a common example. An adjacent property owner without access to a public road may have an easement across a neighbor's land to gain access to the public road. The right of way should be recorded in the appropriate county records to insure recognition.

An easement in gross is not related to another piece of property. The right of a utility company to lay pipe or wire on property is an easement in gross.

Easements run with the land. The easement is not defeated or lost because the land over which the easement exists is conveyed to another. The new owner is required to accept or recognize all easements he or she knows exist or should have known exist. Recording in the county records is notice to all the world.

Profit à Prendre

A profit à prendre is a right to enter on property and remove something from it. A hunting or fishing right as well as the right to extract oil or minerals constitute a profit à prendre. Care must be taken to distinguish a profit à prendre from a fee simple interest in minerals or oil and gas in place in those states where minerals are capable of being owned while still in the ground.

License

A license is nothing more than the owner's permission to enter property. It is revocable at any time and merely prevents the licensee from being classed as a trespasser. Customers in a business are licensees. They have the owner's permission to enter the premises to transact business.

Lien

A lien is a property interest created to secure payment of a debt. The borrower creates a lien by executing a mortgage giving the lender the right to foreclose on the lien if the borrower defaults on the payments. The property will be seized and sold to pay off the debt; anything in excess of the debt, after expenses, is remitted to the borrower.

A lien may be placed on the land, a structure, or a fixture. Liens on personal property also known as security interests are discussed in detail in Chapter 6.

Joint and Concurrent Ownership

Tenancy in Common and Joint Tenancy

A tenancy in common and a joint tenancy are forms of co-ownership of property. Each of the tenants in common or joint tenants holds an undivided interest in the property. None owns a particular segment or piece. Moreover, each is entitled to all the rights appurtenant to the particular real estate interest in which they are tenants in common or joint tenants.

Should a dispute arise among the co-tenants, they may voluntarily partition the property by unanimous consent. Each co-tenant then becomes the sole owner of a particular designated segment of the original real estate interest. If they cannot unanimously agree how to divide the property, one or more may petition a court to partition the property in a fair and equitable manner.

The primary difference between a tenancy in common and joint tenancy is that, if a tenant in common dies, his or her interest devolves on the tenant's heirs, whereas in a joint tenancy the deceased joint tenant's interest goes to the surviving joint tenants by "right of survivorship."

Tenancy by the Entirety

A tenancy by the entirety is the same as a joint tenancy except that it can be created only by a conveyance to a husband and wife. The surviving spouse succeeds to the entire interest on the death of the other spouse.

Community Property

In a community property state, each spouse has an undivided one-half interest in property acquired during the marriage regardless of who earned the income used to purchase the property. Property brought into the marriage by a spouse remains the separate property of that spouse. Property acquired by gift or inheritance is also separate property. Separate property remains separate property even if exchanged, provided the newly acquired property can be traced to separate property or the proceeds from the sale of separate property. In some community property states, the gain on the sale of separate property is income to the community.

Condominium and Cooperative Ownership

In a condominium, the purchaser has sole title to his or her individual unit but is a tenant in common with the other condominium owners in the common areas such as a swimming pool, hallways, elevators, and parking facilities. The owner in most instances may mortgage or sell his or her unit without permission from the other owners. The common areas are maintained by a monthly fee paid by each unit owner. Taxes are assessed against each individual owner.

In a cooperative, the entire building is owned by the cooperative group collectively. Members buy stock in the cooperative which entitles them to an apartment under a renewable proprietary lease. When terminating, the stock is generally repurchased by the cooperative at the same price as issued. Such stock is not a security for securities law purposes.[1]

DOCUMENTS OF TITLE

Deeds

Title to real property is conveyed by a document called a deed. There are three principal types of deeds, and the choice depends on the rights available to be conveyed.

General Warranty Deed

A general warranty deed conveys the most complete set of rights of all deeds. The grantor warrants that

1. The grantor has good title to the land conveyed (Covenant of Seisin).
2. There are no encumbrances on the land except as stated in the deed (covenant against encumbrances).
3. No future rights will be created in favor of others and that there are no others having a better title or lien (covenant of quiet enjoyment).

Special Warranty Deed

A special warranty deed guarantees only that the title has not been diminished by any personal act of the grantor. There might be a lien or encumbrance on the property from a previous owner which is superior, or a previous owner may have conveyed an interest which is subsequently asserted by a third party.

Quitclaim Deed

A quitclaim deed only purports to transfer whatever present title or interest that the grantor might have. It is not sufficient performance under a contract of sale unless it is expressly provided for in the contract. A quitclaim deed is generally used only as a release of a questionable interest.

Requirements to Create a Valid Deed

Deed forms differ from state to state; however, there are six minimum basic requirements to create a valid deed.

The grantor and grantee must be named in the deed. In order to convey property, the grantor must not be incapacitated by reason of insanity or minority. It is prudent if not necessary to have the grantor's spouse to join in the conveyance even if the property is only in the grantor's name, particularly if the state is a community property state or the property was a "homestead." Otherwise, the grantor's spouse may have an interest in the property that survives the conveyance. Likewise, if the property is for residential use rather than business, the grantee's spouse should join in the conveyance to protect all rights.

Although consideration is not a requirement, since the property could be a gift, it is customary to insert a recital of consideration in a nominal amount. A sales contract must be supported by consideration to be enforceable. To make a gift, the deed must actually be delivered since a mere promise to make a gift is not enforceable.

The property must be legally described in the deed or incorporated by reference to another document. A street number may be sufficient for a sales contract, but it is not a sufficient description for a deed. Reference to a subdivision plat that has been properly filed in the land records or description by metes and bounds is sufficient. Metes and bounds descriptions are used primarily in rural areas and describe the boundaries of the property with reference to natural or artificial landmarks such as a stream, rock outcrop, or trees.

The document must contain actual words of conveyance such as manifests the grantor's intent to transfer ownership of the property. Words such as "grant," "sell," and "convey" are generally used in tandem.

The deed must be signed by the grantor and spouse, if necessary or desirable.

Many states require that the deed be acknowledged before a person such as a notary public that the deed is the act of the person who executed the document. While acknowledgement may not be a requirement to create a valid deed, it is necessary to record the deed.

Finally, the deed must be actually delivered to and accepted by the grantee. An executed and acknowledged deed in the possession of the grantor does not convey title to real property. Delivery may be accomplished by physically transferring the deed to the grantee or grantee's agent or by recording the deed in the appropriate land records.

Recording

After the grantee receives the valid deed, it should be recorded immediately to protect his or her rights with respect to third parties. A delivered valid but unrecorded deed is good as between the grantor and grantee, but there may be third parties with adverse interests. For example, the grantor may subsequently convey the same property to another person who is unaware of the first conveyance. The second grantee is a bona fide purchaser for value, and if the second grantee records his or her deed first, the first grantee's deed is void. To prevail, the first grantee would have to file first to put the second grantee on notice of the conveyance; therefore, the second grantee could not be a bona fide purchaser for value.

FINANCING INSTRUMENTS

A mortgage or trust deed arises out of debt financing of real property. The buyer/debtor executes a mortgage or trust deed which pledges the property as security for the loan. The mortgage or trust deed is a real estate interest (lien) which must be executed in writing and signed by the mortgagor (borrower). In some states, it must be acknowledged. It is then recorded in the appropriate records department with other real estate interests.

Mortgages

A mortgage is a conveyance of property to secure the performance of the debt obligation which conveyance is void if the obligation is performed.

A mortgage involves two parties, the mortgagor (borrower) and the mortgagee (lender).

If the loan is repaid according to schedule, the lien is released, and the borrower has the entire fee simple interest. In the case of default, the lender is required to give the borrower notice, and after the specified period of time required by law, the lender may proceed to foreclose. Foreclosure involves obtaining a court order to sell the property, generally at public auction, to satisfy the debt. The borrower still may redeem the property typically within a twelve-month period after the sale. If redemption is not made, the sale becomes final, and the purchaser at auction obtains all real estate interests held by the borrower. If the proceeds from the sale are not sufficient to cover the amount owed, the lender may get a deficiency judgment for the balance and proceed against the other assets of the borrower to satisfy the remaining balance.

Over the past 50 years, the fixed-rate, 30-year mortgage was virtually the only type of mortgage offered. As interest rates increased, many mortgagees were left holding paper that was bringing in interest at substantially below competitive market rates. In addition, inflation was increasing operating costs at alarming rates. Mortgagees began to find new ways to pass these increasing costs on to the borrower and obtain a higher interest rate of return. Variable rate, adjustable rate, and other new mortgage innovations are now commonplace.

A brief description of the traditional types of mortgages and newer innovations follows.

Junior Mortgages

Whenever a prior mortgage exists on a property and the owner needs additional financing, the owner may take out an additional mortgage or mortgages to obtain more money. These additional mortgages are known as junior mortgages. Because the primary mortgage has priority as to payment if default occurs, the cost of junior mortgages is higher than the primary.

Open End Mortgages

This type provides for additional funds to be available to the mortgagor over the term of the mortgage. It is generally used when the mortgagor does not need all of the funds at the beginning of the mortgage. The additional borrowing can then be amortized by a small addition to the monthly payments.

Problems may arise over determining the date of lien for the mortgagee. Questions arise concerning whether additional advances have the same priority as the original advance or whether priorities change as the advances are made. Most state laws stipulate that any future advances have the same priority of rights as the original, given that certain conditions are met. The main condition is that the total amount advanced cannot exceed the total amount dictated in the original mortgage. The intent is to prevent other liens, which may arise as more money is obtained, from taking priority.

An open end mortgage also allows for flexibility on the part of the mortgagee.

If the lender thinks that the funds already dispersed are not being used properly, it can withhold future dispersals until the terms of the mortgage are met.

Package Mortgages

This mortgage places a lien not only on the real property, but also on the personal property attached to the real property. Examples are carpeting, furnaces, and dishwashers. This allows the mortgagor to finance the fixtures over the life of the mortgage, as opposed to the shorter terms of most conventional household credit. However, this increases the overall cost of the personal property since it is financed over a longer period than usual.

Mortgagees benefit in that their offering becomes more attractive in the marketplace.

Construction Mortgages

Under a construction mortgage, the loan is dispersed to the builder in installments, which the builder is entitled to under the terms of the mortgage, provided that the builder is progressing within stipulated limits. For instance, the first quarter of the loan is dispersed after the foundation is laid, the second when the frame is built, etc., until the construction is completed.

Originally, the only collateral for the mortgage is the land. As the building is completed, all materials become part of the collateral. The rationale underlying construction loan mortgages is that the lender disperses funds only when its security has been increased and protected under the terms of the mortgage.

Blanket Mortgage

With a blanket mortgage, the borrower is able to put together several pieces of real estate and have all of them serve as security for a single loan. As the loan is gradually repaid, pieces of property are removed from the provisions of the mortgage. A blanket mortgage allows the borrower to obtain more money than if attempting to secure a mortgage on single pieces of property separately. The lender is given the added security of all the parcels.

Purchase Money Mortgages

Under a purchase money mortgage, the mortgage is given by the purchaser to the seller for all or a portion of the purchase price of the property. This is different from the traditional mortgage in that there is no third party lender involved. The seller has no rights other than being able to take back the property and cannot obtain a deficiency judgment.

A purchase money mortgage is often used when the purchaser does not have the equity funds available that a financial institution would require for a mortgage. When a purchase money mortgage is executed simultaneously with the deed conveying title, it takes precedence over liens, judgments, other mortgages, and all other debts of the mortgagor.

Leasehold Mortgages

Under the leasehold mortgage, a lease is mortgaged as security for a debt. Usually, the borrower has no ownership interest in real property to pledge as security for a loan but has an assignable lease. The borrower will offer a lease to the lender as security. The lender has security only during the term of the lease since the borrower's possessory interest terminates with the lease.

Participating Mortgages

In a participating mortgage, several investors pool their investment funds. The agreement states the ownership interest or shares that the parties own.

Lack of capital or experience could be the basis for generating a participation mortgage; this way individual investors benefit through collective participation. Recently, institutional lenders have acquired interests in mortgage participations as a way of expanding their loan portfolios. The Government National Mortgage Association (GNMA) guarantees securities backed by groups of federally underwritten mortgages to enter the public market for funds to finance real estate acquisition and development. This has led to an increase in the number of participating mortgages.

Balloon Mortgages

Under a balloon mortgage, periodic payments do not amortize the loan by its termination date. At the termination date, a lump sum payment is made.

This is usually done to accelerate the maturity and create a refinancing situation at a time considerably earlier than if the loan were amortized over a more traditional term. The purpose is hopefully to enter into a more favorable loan situation at the time of refinancing. Perhaps interest rates are high at the time of the original mortgage, and the borrower can possibly refinance later at a considerably lower interest rate. Of course, interest rates could be higher, and this strategy would not be beneficial.

Fixed Interest Rate Mortgages

The fixed interest rate mortgage was developed by the Federal Housing Administration (FHA) during the great depression of the 1930s.

In a fixed rate mortgage, the interest rate is established at the beginning of the loan and is fixed for its duration. This is advantageous to the borrower if interest rates rise after the beginning of the loan but can be disastrous for the lender. This led to the increased popularity of the variable loan.

Variable Interest Rate Mortgages

The interest rate in a variable rate mortgage is set for a short time, generally six months. After that time, it is adjusted upwards or downwards according to an index spelled out in the mortgage. The most common index is tied to treasury bill rates.

There are certain limits to how much a variable rate mortgage can be adjusted. Generally, 0.5 percent is the limit for any six-month period, and 2.5 percent is the limit for the entire contract.

Adjustable Rate Mortgages

The adjustable rate mortgage is very similar to the variable rate mortgage, with one major exception. In the adjustable rate mortgage, the interest rate has no limit as to how high or low it can move. It moves with the index no matter where the index goes.

The adjustable rate mortgage was developed because of the limits imposed on the variable interest rate mortgage. When interest rates approached 20 percent in the early 1980s, the variable rate mortgage was not adequate to keep lenders profitable.

Graduated Payment Mortgages

The graduated payment mortgage is one where the payments are lower in the first years of the mortgage and then increase over the term of the mortgage.

This is intended to benefit persons who expect their income to rise in future years. They can take out a large mortgage today even though they cannot afford a conventional mortgage payment in the hope that they will be able to afford it later.

Guaranteed Mortgages

A guaranteed mortgage is guaranteed as to payment by the federal government, usually the Veterans Administration (VA) or the FHA. Although private organizations can guarantee payment of a mortgage, it is not considered to be guaranteed. Only those mortgages that are guaranteed by the federal government are termed "guaranteed." All other mortgages are termed "conventional." Guaranteed mortgages are applicable to residential property and not to business property.

Renegotiated Mortgages

The renegotiated mortgage is a hybrid of the fixed and variable mortgage. Here, the interest rate is established at intervals dictated in the original mortgage, generally five years. The new rate is tied to the market rate. The borrower has the option to switch to a variable mortgage or pay off the mortgage in full, at these periods, as long as the option is spelled out in the original mortgage.

Accelerated Payment Mortgages

In most new mortgages, it is not uncommon to have the first few payments cover approximately 99.8 percent interest and 0.2 percent principal. This results in a substantial period of time passing before there is a substantial reduction in the principal.

The accelerated payment mortgage allows the borrower the option to pay additional money toward the principal (above what is called for in that payment) resulting in lower interest expense and early payment of the mortgage.

Deeds of Trust

Whereas a mortgage involves two parties, the deed of trust involves three parties. Many states still use the deed of trust as the principal real estate finance instrument.

The borrower, the lender, and the trustee are the parties in a deed of trust. The borrower acknowledges a debt by means of a note. The borrower receives a conveyance of the property, possession, and the loan proceeds. The lender extends credit to the trustee, receives the note and pledge of property as security for the debt, and conveys to the trustee rights to carry out the note's terms. The trustee holds legal title to the property for the benefit of the lender if the terms of the note are not met. The trustee can take possession of the property in case of default and may sell the property to recover any amounts still owed.

Under default of a deed of trust, the lender must notify the trustee in writing of the borrower's failure to meet the terms of the obligation. The lender then asks the trustee to sell the property. The trustee records the notice of default and publishes announcements of the default and intention to sell. For a period defined by each state's law, the borrower has the right to cure the default by paying all the money due on the note. If the default is not cured, the sale proceeds. The sale is performed at public auction. The highest bidder receives a trustee's deed to the property that was formerly held by the borrower, and title is conveyed to the purchaser.

The more important differences between the deed of trust and mortgage are that a lender cannot obtain a deficiency judgment and that the borrower cannot exercise any form of redemption after the period of time defined has passed.

Land Contracts

A land contract, or contract for deed, is used mostly to finance real estate where the buyer has little or no money for a down payment. The seller is not willing to transfer title by deed immediately and retains title until the debt is paid off, either substantially or in full, at which time the deed is given to the purchaser. A mortgage can also be used to replace the land contract after a specified amount of money is paid to the seller.

The major difference between the land contract and mortgage is who holds title to the purchased property. Under a mortgage, the borrower receives or retains title to the property against which the money has been lent, and the lender has a lien against the property.

Since the lender retains title under a land contract, it is not necessary to go through a court foreclosure proceeding in the event of a borrower's default, unless it is required by a state statute. The lender merely cancels the contract, keeping the payments already made.

Land contracts are commonly used for undeveloped property or for developed property where the property is not acceptable as security to the lender.

Vendor's Lien

When a trusting vendor transfers title to property in return for a part of the agreed-upon payment, the property is considered to be an implied security for the remaining payments toward the purchase price. This is known as a vendor's lien.

Promissory Note

A person who signs a promissory note incurs a personal liability to repay a debt. The person's assets can be seized and sold to pay the debt in event of default. The note does not pledge any specific assets, but it generally includes all the debtor's assets. The note is usually used along with a mortgage to secure a typical real estate loan.

Real Estate Syndication

Real estate syndication is a pooling of resources by investors to acquire or develop a particular parcel of real property.

The syndicate is usually formed by promoters who select the property to be acquired or developed and seek to finance it through syndication. The form that the syndication takes (partnership, limited partnership, or corporation) depends on several factors, primarily tax attributes.

A real estate syndicate is attractive because of historically high investment yields in real estate transactions. Many people believe that real estate is still the best investment. After annual investment yields, the investor looks forward to increased capital growth in the long term. On the other hand, the investment of a real estate syndicate is in a nonliquid asset that may be hard to sell. Further, the ordinary investor lacks management control and is along for the ride. More importantly, the federal government has made real estate syndication less attractive through changes in the tax law, securities regulation, and so on.

The syndication is terminated and dissolved after its objectives are accomplished.

Real estate syndication is not for the novice investor or anyone who may need to disinvest on short notice or cannot afford a loss. The typical investor is an individual in a high tax bracket who is interested in receiving immediate deductions from the real estate syndication to offset income from other sources.

GOVERNMENT REGULATION

Numerous state and federal laws govern real estate financing, many of which are discussed in Chapter 11. Most of the government regulations deal with lenders and disclosure. More importantly, government regulation concerns itself primarily with residential property and not business property.

Interstate Land Sales Full Disclosure Act

The purpose of the Interstate Land Sales Full Disclosure Act[2] is to provide full disclosure to consumers of all relevant or material facts prior to their decision to purchase a subdivision lot and to prohibit fraud in the sale of land in interstate commerce. In its purpose and operation, the act is similar to the Securities Act of 1933. In the act, Congress addressed three common abuses in land promotion schemes. The first abuse is the misrepresentation of the nature or general characteristics of the land offered for sale. Second, Congress discovered widespread fraud in the so-called site-unseen method of land sales promotion involving high pressure sales techniques. Third, Congress intended to prevent overuse of available resources such as water by preventing overcrowding or overdevelopment of particular areas.

Congress utilized the interstate commerce clause of the Constitution as its authority to regulate interstate land sales. Any sale to parties in different states or to parties in the same state if any instrumentality of interstate commerce such as the telephone, mail, or electronic media is used in the sales promotion is subject to the act. The act applies to all subdivisions divided into 50 or more lots which are sold or leased as part of a common promotional plan. The act applies not only to subdivisions containing 50 lots but also to subdivisions which may contain 50 lots in the future and to promotional plans which offer 50 or more lots in the aggregate whether contiguous or not. The term "lot" as used in the act does not require ownership so that a long-term lease on a particular lot would be covered. Similarly, a condominium unit is a lot, and any sale of condominium units in a complex with 50 or more units is subject to the act.

The act contains a rather lengthy list of exemptions provided the exemption is not used for the purpose of evading the rest of the act.[3] Exemptions may be had where the sale or lease of any improved land having a residence, commercial building, or condominium or the contract of sale requires the erection of such a building within a two-year period. A sale of property where there is an evidence of indebtedness secured by a mortgage or deed of trust is exempt from the act because it is otherwise regulated by the states and federal government. The sale or lease of cemetery lots is exempt as is the sale or lease of real estate by any government or governmental agency. Other exemptions exist, and the reader should check the act and the regulations promulgated under the act for current exemptions.

The act requires a registration statement to be filed with the Office of Interstate

Land Sales Registration in the Department of Housing and Urban Development.[4] Current regulations and requirements should be checked before any registration is attempted, and legal counsel should be sought if there is any question. As with the Securities Act of 1933, the Department of Housing and Urban Development does not pass on the desirability of buying any of the property advertised for sale but merely checks the information for accuracy and truth. If the registration is free of defects and inaccuracies, it becomes effective 30 days after filing.[5] Between the time that the registration statement is filed and it is approved, no sales to purchasers may be made; however, the developer may promote the property during that period.[6] The property report must be delivered to prospective purchasers as part of the disclosure requirement of the act.[7] Any property report which contains an untrue statement of a material fact or omits a material fact required under the act is fraudulent.[8]

A developer who violates the act may be required to make restitution to the purchaser.[9] Alternatively, the purchaser may retain the land purchased and sue for damages in the amount of the differences between the land as falsely advertised and its actual value.[10]

Truth-in-Lending Act

The Truth-in-Lending Act[11] requires full disclosure to a prospective borrower of any charges incident to a credit transaction. The heart of the truth-in-lending law is Regulation Z,[12] which is also discussed in Chapter 11. Regulation Z applies to most real estate financing transactions involving credit granted to a natural person for household, family, personal, or agricultural uses, and the creditor obtains a nonpossessory security interest in the property. Regulation Z does not apply to credit transactions involving dwellings containing more than four family housing units or property used for business purposes. Private transactions such as installment real estate contracts or purchase money mortgages are not covered by the act.

The lender in a real estate transaction is required to disclose information such as the total amount of the finance charge, the date on which the finance charges begin, the annual percentage rate, information regarding payments, any delinquency and penalty charges, the amount financed, the description of any security interest created for the benefit of the lender, any prepayment penalty, any prepaid finance charges, the total amount that will be paid, and the method used to refund any prepaid finance charge including interest. The disclosure must be made before the transaction is completed.

The disclosure requirements of the Truth-in-Lending Act and Regulation Z are limited regarding real estate transactions; however, Regulation Z is an important statute and care must be taken to comply with it. A more complete discussion of Regulation Z may be found in Chapter 11.

Real Estate Settlement Procedures Act

The Real Estate Settlement Procedures Act[13] applies to the purchase of one-to four-family residential dwellings, the financing of which is federally related. Federally related financing consists of loans insured by the Federal Housing Administration or Veterans Administration, loans administered through the Department of Housing and Urban Development, loans intended to be sold to the Federal National Mortgage Association, and loans through commercial lenders that are insured by the Federal Deposit Insurance Corporation or the Federal Home Loan Bank. The act is designed to provide more effective advanced disclosure to home buyers and sellers of settlement costs, to eliminate kickbacks or referral fees that tend to unnecessarily increase costs of settlement services, to reduce the amounts home buyers are required to place in escrow accounts to insure payment of real estate taxes and insurance, and to significantly reform and modernize recordkeeping on land title information.[14]

The act requires that each prospective borrower be given a copy of an information booklet at the time of loan application. The booklet contains details regarding the Real Estate Settlement Procedures Act and information required to be disclosed pursuant to the act.[15] The booklet is published by the Department of Housing and Urban Development and is made available to lenders.

The act requires that a good faith estimate of settlement charges that are likely to be assessed against the borrower with respect to a loan be disclosed in actual amounts or in ranges of amounts based on the actual experience of the lender in similar transactions.[16] Further, any special relationship which exists between the lender and an individual, such as a lawyer, who performs a service for a fee with respect to the loan must be disclosed.[17] Finally, a uniform settlement statement must be completed and provided to the borrower so that he or she has an opportunity to review the settlement statement at least one business day prior to the scheduled closing.[18] Detailed regulations and procedures are set out in Regulation X.[19]

Unlike the Interstate Land Sales Full Disclosure Act and Regulation Z, the Real Estate Settlement Procedures Act does not provide an equitable or law remedy for violation of the disclosure requirements or the limitations on the escrow account collection practices. The act does provide an action for violation of the abusive practices provision concerning kickbacks and unearned fees and allows the injured party to recover treble damages and attorney's fees.[20] There is also a criminal penalty for violation of the act.[21]

The act provides that its provisions shall not affect the validity or enforceability of any sale or contract for the sale of real property or any loan, loan agreement, mortgage, or lien made or arising in connection with a federally related mortgage loan.[22]

The Real Estate Settlement Procedures Act does not preclude the states from regulating in this area. There is concurrent jurisdiction of both federal and state laws, and, to the extent that the state law is stricter, it applies; however, to the extent that federal law provides greater protection, it applies.[23]

NOTES

1. United Housing Foundation v. Forman, 421 U.S. 837 (1975).
2. 15 U.S.C. §§ 1701–1717.
3. 15 U.S.C. § 1702.
4. 15 U.S.C. § 1704.
5. 15 U.S.C. § 1706 (a).
6. 15 U.S.C. § 1703.
7. 15 U.S.C. § 1703 (a) (1) (B).
8. 15 U.S.C. § 1703 (a) (2) (B).
9. 15 U.S.C. §§ 1703 (b)-(e).
10. 15 U.S.C. § 1709.
11. 15 U.S.C. §§ 1601–1677.
12. 12 C.F.R. § 226.
13. 15 U.S.C. §§ 2601–2617.
14. 15 U.S.C. § 2601.
15. 15 U.S.C. § 2604.
16. 15 U.S.C. §§ 2603 (a), 2604 (c).
17. 15 U.S.C. § 2607 (c).
18. 15 U.S.C. § 2603 (b).
19. 24 C.F.R. part 3500.
20. 15 U.S.C. § 2607 (d) (2).
21. 15 U.S.C. § 2607 (d) (1).
22. 15 U.S.C. § 2615.
23. 15 U.S.C. § 2616.

8

Negotiating and Performing Contracts

A business functions by negotiating and performing contracts. Indeed, "contract" has been described as one of the "basic institutions of our social fabric."[1] From the sale of a toothbrush to the takeover of a corporation, contracts facilitate every kind and variety of business transaction. The advertising, financing, sale, insuring, manufacture, processing, distribution, transportation, and storage of goods all depend upon contracts, as do the promotion, insuring, and rendering of services as well as the conveyancing, renting, subdividing, easement letting, and licensing of real estate. Wages are paid as a result of employment contracts, whereas construction work, government procurements, and franchises and other distributorship arrangements derive from consensual agreements.

This chapter discusses the general principles of law relevant to the negotiation and performance of contracts. Although these principles apply to all contracts, this chapter highlights employment, construction, and franchise agreements. Government contracts are examined in Chapter 9; contracts involving sales of goods are discussed in Chapter 10.

THE SIGNIFICANCE OF CONTRACTS: MAKING "PRIVATE" LAW

A contract is a mechanism which creates order where none previously existed by delegating responsibility for the happening of events in a predetermined rather than haphazard way. Contracts not only create definite expectations about future events, they also lessen anxieties by removing uncertainties.

The Principle of Private Autonomy

Contracting rests on the principle of private autonomy—the voluntary undertaking of responsibility for future events. Because contracting derives from the private autonomy principle, a contract has virtually unlimited uses and potential. Consequently, an agreement may be fashioned to respond to any business or commercial need provided the contract is not illegal and that it satisfies the legal requirements to be enforceable.

The Importance of Fine Print

Despite the significance contracts have in facilitating business transactions, they are frequently taken for granted. This is evidenced by the routine signing of agreements without bothering to read or understand the fine print. The print, regardless of its size, has a purpose and should be understood by those who put their (or their companies') names on the contract. A headline in the *Wall Street Journal* makes the point: "Write 100 Times on the Board: I Will Always Read the Fine Print." Indeed, contracting and contracts are and should always be considered serious matters.

A business must take its contracts seriously because they are a primary source of its legal obligations and rights and represent a source of potential liability. As a source of legal obligations, contracts are similar to statutes, regulations, and court decisions since contracts obligate parties to do or to refrain from doing specific tasks. As a source of legal rights, contracts are enforceable by courts allowing an aggrieved party to obtain compensation or other relief. Finally, a contract becomes a source of liability when repudiated, when carelessly negotiated or drafted, or when not performed in accordance with the agreement's terms.

The Importance of a Written Agreement

To enhance certainty while minimizing subsequent disputes, contracts should be evidenced by a writing and drafted in clear and precise language which both parties understand.[2] Contracts should speak to specific problems and concerns of the parties in addition to generalized legal matters. In this regard, contracts whenever possible should avoid "boilerplate." Boilerplate refers to printed, standardized legal clauses loaded with legal jargon which are copied or lifted from form books or purchased from business supply stores. Although generally allocating risks and responsibilities between the parties, boilerplate contracts in many instances do not create sensible or relevant allocations of rights and responsibilities within a specific business context. Normally, a business should use professionally drafted, tailor-made agreements whenever possible rather than rely on form agreements filled with jargonized boilerplate. Of course, transactional costs prohibit the hiring of a lawyer routinely to draft individualized contracts. Nonetheless, a lawyer should be hired to draft relevant and particularized forms to be used by the business to implement specific kinds of transactions.

THE NATURE OF CONTRACT AND CONTRACTING

Contract Defined

A contract is a bargain enforceable by a court. The bargain may result from an exchange of promises or from an exchange of a promise for a performance ("I promise to pay you $500 if you paint my store.") It should be understood that a contract is intangible; it is a concept; it cannot be seen or touched. To be sure, many contracts are written or, more properly stated, reduced to writing. But the writing is only evidence of the bargain; it is not the bargain or contract itself. Rather, the contract is the bargain in fact as evidenced by the parties' writings or by other relevant evidence. Relevant evidence may include the testimony of the parties or of other persons, written communications, and the parties' conduct consisting of prior course of dealing, course of performance, and usages of trade (discussed in Chapter 10). A contract is not only what the parties explicitly agree to, it also encompasses all the legal obligations and rights flowing from the contractual relationship as recognized under the common law or other legal rules.

The Law of the Contract versus Contract Law

An important distinction that should be kept in mind is the difference between "the law of the contract" and "contract law." The law of the contract consists of all the terms and conditions that the parties have agreed to in their bargain—the law that they have privately made and that applies primarily to them alone. These obligations spring *from* the agreement. They are to be distinguished from obligations which arise *because of* the agreement. The latter derive from contract law, the extensive body of legal doctrine consisting of statutory and common law rules which courts (and arbitrators) use to find, interpret, enforce, or otherwise adjust private bargains.

For example, the issue of whether an enforceable contract has been entered into between Jones and Smith turns on applying the principles of contract law—the rules of contract formation—to the facts peculiar to the Jones-Smith transaction. The question of whether under the contract (assuming it was formed) Jones is to pay Smith $500 or $10, however, turns on the law of the contract, more specifically, on the express price term upon which the parties agreed.

Although the law of the contract usually is clear, on occasion it is not, either because the parties failed to include a needed term (an omission) or because an included term is vague or ambiguous. In these instances, courts look to contract law to determine the law of the contract. In other words, the generalized rules of contract interpretation are used to determine legally what the parties intended as the law of their agreement.

Freedom of Contract and Social Well-Being

Under prevalent nineteenth and early twentieth century jurisprudential theory, so long as the parties having legal capacity to contract did not agree to commit or assist in the commission of an illegal act, they had the freedom to make whatever bargain (or law of the contract) they wished.

Today, modern contract doctrines increasingly are limiting the freedom of contract. Two doctrines in particular are used to place restrictions on contracting. These doctrines are known as the principle of unconscionability and the good faith obligation. (For a discussion of unconscionability and good faith, see Chapter 10). Also restricting freedom of contract today are various statutes, especially in the consumer protection area. (Several of these laws are examined in Chapter 11.) These doctrines and consumer-oriented statutes are predicated on notions of social well-being.

The theoretical battle over freedom of contract versus social well-being has practical consequences to both businesses and individuals. The controversy involves two opposing views concerning the role of courts in contract disputes. The older view considers contract as a mechanism for the private allocation of risks where a court should be concerned only with enforcing private agreements however made. A more recent view—as evidenced by scores of court opinions and enactment of various state and federal statutes—holds that a contract represents more than an allocation of private interests[3] but rather is an institution having broad social ramifications. Proponents of this view point out that most contracts do not result from arm's-length negotiations freely entered into by the parties but from a dominant economic party's imposing its will on a weaker one, typically by using standardized, printed, and, on occasion, legally one-sided forms. Thus, given the typical disparity in bargaining power, freedom of contract is a myth, they argue. It then follows that the role of the courts should include not only the enforcing but also the policing of agreements. Policing agreements may even necessitate adjusting a contract now and then by the courts "making law" for the parties by selectively enforcing only portions of an agreement or by reforming its terms.

The difficult task of reconciling certain contract cases which at times appear diametrical is explained in part by the divergent ways judges and lawyers conceive freedom of contract, private autonomy, the role of the courts, the contracting process, and social well-being. The way for a business to avoid the larger battle of contract theory is for it at all times to be reasonable and not to insist on one-sided agreements that maximize one party's legal rights, privileges, and prerogatives while minimizing the other party's. Being sensitive to the contracting party's legitimate commercial needs and reasonable expectations is not only ethically and practically good business, it is also good preventive law.

Sources of Contract Law

The Common Law

The most important source of contract principles is the common law. This body of legal principles is the result of tens of thousands of English and American court decisions which over the centuries have developed, defined, and redefined contract rules into a *theoretically consistent* doctrinal fabric. In fact, many contract decisions are inconsistent.

Although several reasons explicate this inconsistency, the foremost explanation is that the common law is a matter of individual state law. Common law principles are applied by state courts within their respective jurisdictions. Consequently, the most authoritative statements of contract principles of a given state are the pronouncements of that state's highest court, although decisions of that state's lower appellate courts also have authoritative value. On the other hand, decisions of other state courts have little if any precedential weight although they may be cited as "persuasive authority." Consequently, even though modern contract rules have their origins in the common law principles, as these were developed in England, many variations in the rules exist today among the 50 American states.

Restatement of the Law of Contracts

In an effort to attain a level of uniformity and consistency of contract principles among the states, a committee of the American Law Institute (ALI), a prestigious organization of eminent judges, lawyers, and academics, in the 1920s drafted the *Restatement of the Law of Contracts*—an enormous undertaking which attempted to systematize and articulate in a logical fashion all the principles of the common law applicable to contracts.[4] More recently the ALI has adopted a substantially revised *Restatement (Second) of the Law of Contracts.*[5]

It is important to understand three features about the restatements. First, they are not duly enacted laws. No state legislature has passed either the original restatement of contracts or its revision, although a few states have enacted portions of it.[6] Second, courts often treat the restatement, although not codified, as authoritative by quoting, citing, and adopting its rules. As a result, the restatements of contract have exerted a large influence on American courts in the judicial articulation of contract principles. Third, the name "restatement" is partially a misnomer since the provisions of the restatement, especially those of the *Restatement (Second)*, were drafted not entirely as an accurate reflection of contract law as it is or has developed, but rather as the ALI committee members, especially the official reporter, believed the law, to some extent at least, ought to develop.

The Uniform Commercial Code

Today, contracts involving the sale of goods are subject to the enacted and codified Uniform Commercial Code, notably Article Two (discussed in Chapter 10). Article Two[7] has altered in several significant respects many of the common law contract principles. Article Two only applies, however, to transactions involving goods.[8]

Other Relevant Statutes

Various statutes and regulations apply to a given contract depending on the type of the agreement. Government contracts are subject to specific statutes and regulations while contracts for the sale or shipment of produce must comply with other governmental regulations. In short, the law applicable to a given agreement often includes, in addition to the general principles of the common law of contracts, specific state or federal statutory and regulatory provisions. These laws at times alter the common law. New York and California, for example, have enacted general contract obligation statutes which have changed several common law rules.[9]

Types of Contracts: Specific Laws

Governmental Contracts

Contracts where one party is a governmental unit are referred to as public contracts. The common law of contracts and the Uniform Commercial Code apply to public contracts but so do other statutory laws and regulations. (These supplemental federal and state laws are discussed in Chapter 9.)

The Sale, Transportation, and Shipment of Goods

Contracts calling for the sale of goods are largely governed by UCC Article Two, titled Sales (see Chapter 10). When credit is extended pursuant to a sales agreement, several federal laws and regulations apply (see Chapter 11). Contracts calling for the shipment of goods are governed in part by Article Two, although the shipping documents themselves—bills of lading, dock warrants, ocean bills, and so on—are largely governed by federal statutes or by UCC Article Seven, Documents of Title.[10] Article Seven also applies to warehousing agreements (see Chapters 6 and 10).

Leases of Personal Property

Equipment leases and other lease contracts involving personal property are governed not only by common law contract and personal property rules but also by provisions of UCC Article Nine, Secured Transactions[11] (see Chapter 6) and by specific state or federal leasing statutes. In addition, courts have applied selective provisions of UCC Article Two to personal property leases.

Service Contracts

Service contracts run the gamut from the professional services of an architect, physician, lawyer, or accountant to those of a dry cleaner, building maintenance firm, security officer, or painting contractor. Although repair and maintenance contracts are largely governed by common law contract rules, specific Federal Trade Commission trade regulations rules may also apply. Examples include contracts involving funeral services, automotive sales, and door-to-door sales.

Professional service contracts, although subject to common law contract rules, in many cases are also subject to specific disclosure, billing, and dispute resolution requirements mandated under state licensing and professional regulation laws. Regulation of service contracts is illustrated by the extensive body of statutes and regulations that governs insurance agreements.

Construction Contracts

Common law principles apply to construction contracts including those between contractors and owners or developers and those between contractors and subcontractors. Nonetheless, several states have enacted statutes which apply specifically to construction contracts, especially to the bidding process. Moreover, certain common law principles as applied to construction agreements have been modified to meet the special needs of the construction industry.

Real Estate Contracts

Contracts involving the conveyancing of interests in real estate including easements, sales, licenses, rentals, and the like are subject to common law principles and, in many instances, to state and federal laws and regulations, especially if financing is involved. (See Chapter 7.)

Financing Contracts

Financing contracts involving personal property as collateral to secure payment obligations of purchasers or borrowers are very commmon. In addition to applicable federal laws (see Chapter 11), UCC Article Nine applies (see Chapter 6).

Payment Devices

All payment devices including checks, drafts, promissory notes, bank credit cards, point-of-sale debit cards, and letters of credit are contracts themselves or grow out of contracts. Various laws and regulations apply including UCC Articles Three, Commercial Paper, and Four, Bank Collections and Deposits.[12] (These payment devices and the applicable laws and regulations are discussed in Chapter 12.)

Franchises and Distributorships

Franchise agreements and other business ventures involving distributorships are the subject of a specific Federal Trade Commission disclosure rule, although other statutes and common law principles may also apply. Franchises and the FTC rule are discussed subsequently in this chapter.

Employment Contracts

Employment contracts collectively bargained between employers and their employees' exclusive representatives are subject to the federal labor laws and to the decisions of the National Labor Relations Board (see Chapter 15). Individual employment contracts, however, are subject for the most part to common law contracts rules and are discussed subsequently in this chapter.

Essential Terminology of Contract Law

Offer, Acceptance; Offeror, Offeree

An *offer* is a communication from an *offeror* which creates in the *offeree* the power of *acceptance*. If and when an acceptance is timely made and either manifested or communicated by the offeree, both offeror and offeree become legally bound to the contract. Offers are revocable prior to acceptance unless separate consideration has been promised by the offeree to the offeror to hold the offer open for a stated or otherwise reasonable period of time in which case the arrangement, under common law, becomes an option contract. An offer to sell goods, however, needs no separate consideration for it to be irrevocable when made as a *firm offer between merchants*. (A merchant includes one who deals in goods of the kind bought or sold.)

An offer is terminated by the death or other intervening legal incapacity of the offeree, by the offeree's rejection of the offer or by making a counteroffer, by the offer's lapse due to passage of a reasonable (or stated) time for its acceptance, or by the revocation of the offer by the offeror. A mailed revocation is effective, however, only upon the receipt by the offeree.

Consideration: Promisor, Promisee; Bilateral and Unilateral Contracts

For a contract to be enforceable by a court, it must include what the law refers to as *consideration*. Stated most simply, consideration is what the promisee either promises in exchange or does in exchange for the promisor's promise, provided in either case that it was bargained for.

Every contract involves at least one promise. The person making the promise, called the *promisor*, seeks either a return promise (a *bilateral* agreement) or a requested performance (a *unilateral* contract offer). The person to whom the promise is directed is the *promisee*. The promisee's consideration for a bilateral contract is his or her return promise provided the return promise was at least partially induced by the promisor's original promise. The promisee's consideration for a unilateral contract offer is his or her doing (or refraining from doing) what the promisor requested, and doing (or refraining from doing) it at least partially in response to the promise. In short, consideration is the heart of the important notion of bargain.

A *bargain* consists of either a reciprocally induced exchange of promises or an exchange of a promise for a performance.[13] Consequently, gift promises are not enforceable as contracts since nothing is promised or given in exchange. Similarly, a promise made in gratitude for services previously rendered by the promisee is not enforceable as a contract because the prior services were not bargained for. This is the situation where a company promises to pay an annuity to an employee in gratitude for the employee's long and faithful service. Furthermore, a promise to do something that the promisor is already legally obligated to do at the time of making the promise normally is not considered consideration for a return promise since the promisor has neither given nor offered to give up anything *new* in exchange. In this situation, a court may say that the promisor had a preexisting duty to perform the promise. In another variation, if an employee promises to drive a company truck to Seattle and back in return for the employer's promise to pay $200 for doing so, and then, when in Seattle, the employee demands an extra $100 before returning, the employer's promise to pay the additional $100 given under these circumstances is not enforceable since the employee was under a preexisting duty to drive the truck back anyway. The preexisting duty rule is used here to "police" the bargain, thereby allowing the court to avoid enforcing a coerced promise.

The notion of quid pro quo ("this for that") emphasizes the bargain aspect of the consideration requirement. One rationale for the requirement is that it separates economically significant and serious promises from those that are less so, thereby restricting courts to enforce only promises where mutual enhancement of values theoretically results.

Terms and Conditions; Express and Implied

A contract ordinarily consists of both terms and conditions. The *terms* establish the respective duties and rights of the parties to the agreement. The *conditions*, on the other hand, are specified events not certain to occur which the parties have agreed will affect their respective rights and obligations under the contract.

Take the case of a simple real estate offer. The prospective buyer (the offeror) promises to pay $10,000 for the prospective sellers' (the offeree's) property provided the buyer is able to obtain an 80-percent mortgage of twenty years or longer at no greater than a 10-percent annual rate of interest. Assume the seller "accepts" this offer by manifesting assent by signing his or her name to it, thereby causing the offer to become the sale contract. The terms of the agreement include the buyer's obligation to pay the $10,000 price and the seller's obligation to convey the described property to the buyer. The buyer's payment obligation, however, is conditional. The express condition is that the buyer procure the specified financing, an *event* not certain to occur. Although both buyer and seller have a binding contract between them, the buyer is not bound to perform (pay) until and unless the condition (obtaining the suitable financing) first occurs. Thus, the express duty to pay is a "conditional" one.

Duties and conditions may be implied as well as express. They may be *implied in fact* from the nature of the transaction as a whole and from all surrounding circumstances, or they may be *implied in law* by a court in an effort to "do justice" or as may be necessary for the agreement to be "workable."

Again, using the above hypothetical real estate sale, if the buyer makes no effort to obtain suitable financing (nothing in the written agreement, however, expressly indicates he or she must do so), a court would likely hold that the contract contains an implied in law term (or duty) that the buyer "must use reasonable efforts" to obtain financing. Similarly, even though the agreement is silent regarding how much time the buyer has to make such efforts, a court would likely find that the contract contains an implied or constructive condition that if the buyer fails to procure financing after making reasonable efforts for a reasonable time, the implied duty to make those efforts ceases to exist. Under this "constructive condition," the buyer is excused from making further efforts. A *constructive condition* is one which a court applies to a contract in construing the parties' rights and obligations under it. The stated rationale for a court's imposing a constructive condition on an agreement at times is to fulfill the parties' intentions and at other times to "do justice," an amorphous phrase which means to make the express contract terms workable and fair.

The Contracting Process

To understand many contract principles, it is helpful to conceptualize a contract in terms of a process of reaching and performing an agreement. Looked at in this manner, contracting involves six distinct phases: negotiating the terms, reaching an agreement, interpreting the agreement, performing the bargain, adjusting the bargain, and remedying possible disputes. This chapter examines each phase of the contracting process.

NEGOTIATING CONTRACTS

Legal Controls

With the exceptions of negotiating contracts with governmental agencies or with employee organizations, a business is free to negotiate how, when, where, for as long as, and with whom it pleases. Few legal regulations directly apply to the bargaining phase of a contract. The ones that do generally relate to contracts with consumers or with those who buy or borrow for a consumer object, defined as one primarily for personal, family, or household purposes. The federal Truth-in-Lending Act, for example, requires that certain disclosures be made in credit advertising or before point-of-sale purchases (see Chapter 11).

Although few laws directly regulate negotiations, several legal principles indirectly affect the process. An indirect control is one that permits one party to avoid a contract or affords other relief because of something that happened, or did not happen, in negotiations. Indirect controls which, under specific circumstances, may allow one party to obtain relief from performing a contract include contract and tort principles related to misrepresentations, omissions, concealments, mistakes, and duress.

Misrepresentations

One party during negotiations may either intentionally or innocently misrepresent some fact relevant to the contemplated transaction. A seller, for example, may state that a house being offered for sale is free of any termite infestation. If the facts are otherwise, a buyer who later discovers the infestation may be permitted to avoid the contract or obtain other relief, and, then again, he or she may not be afforded relief. As lawyers have the ingrained habit of saying, it depends.

It depends first on whether the misrepresented fact—the infestation—is deemed "material," that is, considered to be so relevant to a buyer that the buyer likely would not have purchased the house at all or at least not for the agreed-upon price had he or she known the truth. On the other hand, a misrepresentation deemed to be immaterial to a purchase decision is usually considered an insufficient basis for avoiding a contract. Still, if any misrepresentation is made with the fraudulent intention of deceiving the prospective buyer, the intentional tort of deceit (also known as fraudulent misrepresentation) normally will permit the aggrieved buyer to recover damages.

This raises a second relevant issue: whether a misrepresentation was knowingly (versus fraudulently) made. A misrepresentation innocently made due to a mistake (discussed below) raises different legal considerations than does a deliberate misrepresentation. Indeed, an analysis of misrepresentation cases reveals a continuum from clearly avoidable transactions at one end (a seller's deliberate, fraudulent, and knowing lie about information essential to the buyer) to clearly nonavoidable transactions on the other (a seller's innocent statement based on a reasonably based yet mistaken notion which in no way induced the buyer's decision). Most misrepresentation cases, however, fall between these points. Where to draw the line between allowing and not allowing relief for mistakes and misrepresentations presents courts with a difficult legal problem.

Legal remedies for material misrepresentation when actionable include the equitable remedy known as rescission and the tort remedy for damages for deceit (or fraudulent misrepresentation). For the tort remedy, which affords damages to compensate actual injuries sustained as a consequence of the misrepresentation, to be available, the challenged utterance must have been intentionally made with knowledge of its falsity. The rescission remedy based on a misrepresentation, on the other hand, requires neither an intention to deceive nor knowledge of the falsity of the utterance but only that the utterance induced the actual decision to enter into the contract or would so induce a reasonable person to do so. In other words, the misrepresentation must be deemed to have been material.

Concealments

Fraudulent misrepresentations in the bargaining process include both intentional utterances or statements designed to deceive and, on occasion, intentional conduct designed to prevent the other party from learning material facts. A seller of a building, for example, may plaster and paint over serious foundation cracks of the structure knowing that by doing so a prospective purchaser will be misled in believing that the building is safe and that the foundations are sound. Fraudulent concealment by conduct is a form of fraudulent misrepresentation and permits the aggrieved party to seek rescission or damages under the tort and equitable remedies noted above.

Omissions

As a general rule, no duty exists for either a prospective seller to disclose known defects or for a prospective buyer to divulge known assets of a property before concluding a sale. Although misrepresenting that a building is free of termites when it is in fact infested may be actionable, remaining silent about the infestation has been held in one state, at least, to be nonactionable.[14] Similarly, a prospective purchaser of a property which the buyer plans to develop normally is under no duty to inform the seller of the property about the planned development or, for that matter, of any adjacent prospective developments about which the prospective buyer has knowledge, but of which the seller knows nothing. This nondisclosure principle applies even though the planned development may render the seller's property potentially far more valuable than the seller presently understands.

Partial Disclosures

The no-duty-to-disclose principle is often circumvented by a "partial disclosure" rule recognized and applied by many courts. Under this rule, if one party discloses any information about a subject related to a prospective sale, that person must disclose all the information he or she has in reference to that subject. The rationale for the partial disclosure rule is that the giving of only selected information has the tendency to mislead and, thereby, to induce sales that would not have occurred had the full facts been known.

Courts sometimes talk about the failure to divulge all relevant data in terms of "half truths." For a seller to say that the local zoning ordinance permits a building to be used for commercial purposes, assuming it does, but not to say that the same ordinance requires sixteen off-street parking places before the commercial use can be implemented, asssuming it also does, is an example of a "half truth." The seller, in beginning to speak, must divulge to the prospective purchaser all the information he or she knows about the local zoning ordinance, even though it is available for public inspection.[15]

More troublesome for the courts has been the situation where one party in offering to sell a house or building knows of a defect—a serious roofing problem, for example—which a prospective buyer would not likely discover. The seller does not conceal the defect, rather, he or she just fails to mention it. Although not rendering the structure immediately uninhabitable, the defect could over time create a serious problem. Or consider the case of a cracked foundation known to, but not concealed by, the seller. Contract principles ordinarily afford the buyer of a commercial building little if any relief under these kinds of circumstances. Should the structure be a house, however, certain courts when applying real property law doctrines have held that a seller impliedly warrants that a house is habitable and has no serious structural defects. This is analogous to the implied warranty of merchantability which a merchant seller makes in offering goods for sale (see Chapter 10).

Mistakes

During negotiations, one party or both may operate under a mistaken notion. Just because one enters into a contract with a mistaken belief, however, normally is not grounds for avoiding contractual duties. Otherwise, contracts would rest on quicksand. Still, courts in attempting to "do justice" have developed a set of rules which under specific circumstances allow avoidance or reformation of a contract on the basis of mistake. In doing so, the courts have allocated mistakes into distinct categories in an effort to differentiate the types of mistakes that should afford relief from those that should not.

Mutual Mistakes

A mutual (or bilateral) mistake is one where both parties when entering into a contract hold the same mistaken notion about a fact or assumption related to the agreement. In a sale of goods, the fact or assumption might relate to the value or worth of the item sold, its very identity, the usefulness or functionality of the object, or any of its characteristics.

The mutual mistake may or may not relate to a basic assumption underlying the bargain, and it may or may not have been a material element in inducing one or both parties to enter into the exchange. Similarly, the mistake may or may not have been detectable with reasonable effort. All of these factors, however, are relevant when a court is asked to grant rescission of or to reform a contract on the basis of a mutual mistake.

Reformation is an equitable remedy by which a court in effect rewrites or reforms a contract to reflect accurately what the parties intended all along. It is an appropriate remedy when an agreement, which has been reduced to writing, contains either a term at variance with the parties' original understanding or omits a term which had been agreed upon by the parties.

In contrast to reformation, the equitable remedy of rescission involves a court-ordered cancellation of the bargain. In rescinding a contract, a court often attempts to put the parties in the economic position they were in at the time the contract was formed. Thus, in addition to rescinding the contract, which has the effect of extinguishing all legal obligations and rights under it, a court may also order restitution by directing that a down payment, for example, be returned. Restitution prevents what is called "unjust enrichment," where one party is deemed to be unjustly benefited at the expense of the other party.

Rescission is an equitable remedy traditionally within the discretionary powers of a court to grant or not grant as it deems appropriate. Thus, the surrounding facts become relevant in persuading a court either to invoke or to refrain from invoking the rescission remedy.

Nonetheless, mutual mistakes that concern only the value or worth of property sold are not normally considered bases for rescission, while mutual mistakes that go to the very identity or subject matter of the contract often are considered appropriate grounds for rescission and restitution. Litigation frequently occurs where a mistake may be characterized either as one of value or as one of identity. Cases in this area may go either way on similar facts. It is a truism that a lawyer is paid for arguing the particular legal characterization of facts which advances his or her client's interests.

Unilateral Mistakes

As the name suggests, a unilateral mistake occurs when only one party to a contract enters into it under a mistaken notion. Relief for unilateral mistakes typically is limited to cases where either the non-mistaken party to the contract contributed to or caused the mistake, or where he or she knew or had reason to know of the mistake.

The issue of unilateral mistake frequently arises in bidding situations where a contractor or subcontractor in preparing a bid for a project miscalculates or otherwise makes a clerical error which results in the bid's being under (or over) what it would have been but for the error. A contractor making an erroneous bid and being awarded the contract often will have to perform the contract (or pay damages for not doing so). This is not true, however, if the mistake was of such a magnitude that the other party did or should have suspected that an error had been made, for example, where the mistaken bid is so far below the next lowest bid as to alert the owner or developer that the contractor's bid is suspect on its face.[16]

Under government contract bidding and procurement statutes, the risks of clerical mistakes are typically allocated by clauses required to be included in the contract. In all cases, however, bidders should exercise caution in preparing and submitting bids both for governmental and nongovernmental projects. The cost for carelessness in bid preparations or submissions may be steep.

Duress

When one is forced to agree to a contract at gunpoint, the agreement is the result of duress and, as such, is not enforceable by the threatening party. Threats may take many shapes. They may be implied from words or conduct. Moreover, they may threaten either physical injury or, and more likely, the prospect of serious economic harm.

Economic Duress

Economic threats that induce contracts create a number of potential problems. Still, many economic threats are not actionable even when they induce contracts or contract modifications. Still, many are. The line is not easily drawn.[17] (See the discussion under the heading "Adjusting the Agreement" later in this chapter.)

The federal antitrust laws may also be relevant in this area. If a business, which has been purchasing goods from a firm, coerces the firm to agree to no longer sell goods to a competitor of the coercing party, the resulting contract will likely constitute an antitrust violation. Certainly, group boycotts of either a purchaser or a supplier—where through a contract, combination, or a conspiracy a group of buyers refuses to purchase goods from a particular seller or a group of sellers agrees not to sell goods to a particular buyer—are prohibited under the Sherman Antitrust Act as unlawful contracts in restraint of trade.[18]

The Relevance of Negotiations to the Contract

The most significant aspect of contract negotiations is the importance that they have both in creating and resolving later disputes. Negotiations create disputes when one party claims that a matter discussed and agreed to in negotiations was not included in the final writings evidencing the agreement. The party raising the issue usually wants the extrinsic matter to be controlling while the other party typically resists. The issue of whether items alleged to have been agreed to in negotiations should be even considered by a court when a written document purports to evidence the parties' full agreement involves the important contract rule known as the "parol evidence rule."[19]

Parol Evidence Rule

The parol evidence rule, in fact, is a set of substantive rules of law which regulate under what circumstances and for what purposes evidence of agreements reached in negotiations may be considered by a judge or jury to establish additional or different terms from those evidenced by the parties' written agreement. The parol evidence rules become applicable, however, only when an agreement has been reduced to writing.

If the written contract is deemed *integrated*, meaning that it evidences the parties' intention that it constitutes their complete agreement, a court ordinarily will not permit evidence of the negotiations to be admitted either to add to or contradict the terms set out in the written document. Before deciding to admit the evidence or not, however, a court first must determine whether the writings of the parties constitute "a final expression" of their agreement. If a court finds that it was so intended, the proffered evidence of other related agreements or terms will be excluded from the trier of fact.

Merger Clauses

It is legally desirable to draw a clean line between negotiations and the final agreement. One way to do this is to first reduce the final agreement to writing and then to include in that writing an express merger clause. A typical merger clause contains words such as: "This written contract represents the complete and total understanding of the parties to this agreement and is not to be supplemented by evidence of additional or contradictory terms." Another example: "All terms and conditions arising out of or related to this agreement are included and set out in this writing." Still another (and arguably the best): "The parties agree that this writing contains a full and complete recital of all the terms and conditions of their agreement as evidenced by their signatures which appear on the signature lines of this contract immediately following this clause."

A merger clause is intended to accomplish two objectives. First, it compels the parties to make sure that their entire agreement has, in fact, been reduced to writing. This promotes certainty as to the parties' respective obligations and rights under the agreement. Second, a merger clause makes operative in most situations the parol evidence rule, thereby precluding later attempts to alter or supplement the agreement based on one party's "convenient recollection."

The parol evidence rule does permit, however, evidence of negotiations to be admitted when the purpose is to interpret the meaning of written terms deemed to be ambiguous. (See Chapter 10 for a discussion of how extrinsic evidence of precontract facts such as a trade usage may be used to supplement and interpret the terms of a sales contract.)

Preservation of Negotiation Records

All correspondence, notes, and records of negotiations should be preserved to aid in resolving possible later ambiguities. In protracted or complicated negotiations, a negotiation diary should be kept. Certainly, any terms provisionally agreed upon in negotiations should be authenticated (commonly called "TA'd") by the agreeing parties signing their names or initials to identical copies of the provision or provisions.

AGREEING TO THE BARGAIN

The agreement phase of a contract is to be distinguished from the negotiation phase. Whereas the negotiation phase is generally free of direct legal controls, an extensive body of legal rules applies to a contract's agreement or formation phase. Overall, these rules require that the agreement process be evidenced by the parties' mutual manifestations of their willingness to be bound. What is crucial is not that the parties agree in their minds on a bargain, but that they *manifest* an agreement through their written and spoken words or conduct.

In this section, we briefly examine several of the more important formation rules concerning offer and acceptance. We begin, however, with a prerequisite for any agreement to be fully enforceable—the requirement that the parties to a contract have the legal capacity to contract.

The Legal Capacity to Contract

The rules regarding a person's legal capacity to enter into a binding legal contract require that the person be of legal age, not be suffering the disability of serious mental illness, and not be under the influence of intoxicants, either alcohol or drugs, or otherwise be incompetent to contract.

Minors

Every state has one or more statutes which set forth the minimum legal age for its citizens to enter into mutually binding contracts. The legal age in most states today is eighteen. If a person under the legal age, called a minor, enters into a contract, he or she has the power to avoid or disaffirm that contract at any time until and for a reasonable time period after attaining legal majority (in less jargonized words, after turning eighteen). To disaffirm a sales contract, the minor or his or her legal guardian must return the goods (regardless of their condition) to the seller. This is called the "restoration of the consideration" requirement.

Contracts entered into by minors do have legal significance, however. The other party must perform its obligations until and unless the minor disaffirms or otherwise ceases his or her performance (for example, stops making payments). The minor may, upon attaining majority, ratify or reaffirm the contract, rendering it fully enforceable and no longer voidable. Ratification may be by conduct (continuing to make payments after attaining legal age) or by simply not disaffirming the obligation within a reasonable time of attaining one's legal majority. A minor's remedy of disaffirmance is allowed even when the minor intentionally misrepresented his or her age. On the other hand, courts often permit a merchant whose contract with a minor has been disaffirmed to countersue for the tort of deceit to recover, or set off the merchant's actual damages caused by the minor's intentional misrepresentation of age.[20]

Mental Illness or Defect

Both in civil and criminal law contexts, the adjudication (or legal finding) of mental illness or defect involves many difficulties and uncertainties. Different tests are used in different jurisdictions and sometimes within the same jurisdiction. As a generalization, so-called weak-mindedness (or lower than normal mental cognitive abilities) does not itself render a person having this condition incompetent to contract. On the other hand, a history of mental illness or evidence of a psychotic episode at the time a contract was made is relevant in the determination. If a business person, in dealing with a customer or client, has reason to believe that the customer is or has been suffering from a serious mental illness or defect which might impair the person's ability either to make reasonable decisions or to understand the nature or ramifications of the contemplated transaction, the business person would be wise to move cautiously and to ascertain if any legal guardian for the individual may have been appointed.

Drugs and Alcohol

If a person becomes intoxicated through ingestion of alcohol or drugs and if the other person to a contract entered into under these conditions knew or should have known of the intoxication, the contract is voidable by the party who suffered the disability within a reasonable time either after the intoxication has ended or after the person comes to understand that he or she agreed to a contract while so intoxicated. In any event, the intoxication must be such as to make the person unaware of the nature or consequence of his or her actions.

Making a Contract Offer

The law differentiates an offer from preliminary negotiations. An offer manifests the willingness of the person making the offer, the offeror, to enter into a bargain and to confer upon the offeree the power to conclude that bargain. An offer may be either oral or written. It may consist of one or several communications. Regardless of its level of complexity, an offer must manifest the offeror's willingness to conclude a bargain. This means that the offer must be sufficiently definite and incorporate expressly or contextually the essential terms of the proposed deal.

In many transactions, an offer may incorporate contextually earlier communications. Thus, if B requests a price list from S stating in the request that it wishes to purchase 200 "oblets" depending on the price, and S then sends a price quote for 200 oblets followed by B's mailing in response a purchase order stating: "Please ship 200 at once; payment within 30 days," B's purchase order is an offer even though it fails to mention the product to be shipped. B's purchase order considered contextually in reference to B's earlier communication, which had stated 200 oblets, is sufficiently definite to constitute an offer.[21]

Definiteness

Although an offer should be as definite as possible to prevent later disputes, in many transactions it need not be "complete" for a valid contract to be formed. While financing and real estate contracts ordinarily require a high degree of specificity, sales of goods or services generally do not. In sales contracts, even the price terms may be left open or tied to an external price standard to reflect a fluctuating market price.[22]

Advertisements

Most advertisements are considered invitations to make offers rather than offers themselves. There are various reasons for this. For one, all essential terms normally are not set out in an advertisement. For another, there is no limitation on the number of people who might "accept." On the other hand, a newspaper advertisement, which declares that "the first ten people who come to Pauline's Department Store will receive a $100 gift certificate," will likely be deemed an offer because a stated number or a specific item is indicated along with the precise manner of acceptance, to wit, the coming to the store and being one of the first ten to do so.[23] The popular but erroneous notion that a store must sell at least one item of an object advertised at a mistaken price ($10, for example, rather than the correct $1,000) may result from the mistaken belief that advertisements are contract offers. Most are not.

Price Quotes

Price quotes normally are not intended to operate as offers. However, a price quotation in context of earlier communications may be an offer. Thus, if B writes S. "If you are willing at this time to sell me Blackacre under the following terms—cash, marketable title, closing within 90 days—please telegram your asking price," and S telegrams back "$50,000," S's price quote in this context would likely be an offer to sell Blackacre on the terms specified in B's inquiry. When submitting a price quote, it may be wise to state that the quote is not an offer but is being sent for information only.

Revoking an Offer

Since an offer creates a legal power of acceptance, an offer is good until it is revoked by the offeror, rejected by the offeree, or terminated by the death of the offeror or lapse of the offer. An offeror who wishes to revoke an offer should communicate the revocation directly to the offeree in unequivocal terms. An offeree's learning of the offeror's change of mind through an indirect communication from a third person usually will terminate the offeree's power of acceptance, particularly if the source is a reasonably reliable one.

The revocation of an offer is not effective, however, until and unless the offeree actually receives it. Thus, if A offers to sell Blackacre to B and then A changes his or her mind and mails B a revocation, but if B, before receiving the revocation accepts A's offer and puts the acceptance in the mail, A and B are bound, as a contract between them has been formed. The rationale is that an acceptance normally is effective on dispatch while a revocation is effective on receipt.

Irrevocability of Certain Offers

Offers or bids, which are submitted for public projects or procurements, ordinarily are irrevocable for stated periods of time under provisions of state and federal bidding laws. In nongovernmental contracts, if an offeree pays or promises to pay an offeror a sum of money or other consideration to keep an offer open for a stated time and the offeror agrees, an option contract is created prohibiting the offeror from revoking the offer during the option period.

On the other hand, firm offers made in compliance with the rules of UCC Article Two by merchants in the sales of goods do not need consideration to be irrevocable.[24] A few states, notably New York, enforce all written promises which state that they will be held open or are irrevocable, even though no separate consideration is promised or given.[25] A unilateral contract offer calling for a performance becomes irrevocable as an option contract once the performance has commenced.[26] Thus, if a firm wires a painting contractor: "We will pay you $3,400 if you paint our warehouse pursuant to our earlier discussions provided you finish the job within three weeks," and the painting contractor commences painting the building, the offer becomes irrevocable upon the commencement of the performance. Otherwise, the promisor could revoke the offer with one final paint stroke remaining to be performed and owe the painting contractor nothing.

Accepting an Offer

The important thing to remember about acceptance of contract offers is that the manner of acceptance is usually dictated by the offer itself. In other words, the offeror has the legal power to control the mode and conditions of acceptance by what is stated in the offer.[27] This means that an offeror may require either a performatory or a promissory acceptance. When the offer is unclear as to its mode of acceptance, the *Restatement (Second) of Contracts* position is that the offeree may accept either by a return promise or by rendering the performance.[28]

Responsiveness of the Acceptance

An acceptance must respond exactly to the terms set out in the offer. If any additional or contradictory terms are included in a purported acceptance, the common law considers it to be a rejection of the original offer while constituting a counteroffer. Under the common law, the acceptance must "mirror" exactly the offer. In contracts involving the sale of goods, however, the mirror image rule does not apply. Rather, a complex rule of Article Two governs acceptances which contain additional or different terms.[29] (This rule is discussed extensively in Chapter 10.)

Notification of Acceptance

Whenever a firm decides to accept an offer, it should communicate that acceptance back to the offeror. Although the law does not normally require a specific notification of acceptance, before an agreement becomes enforceable, the law does mandate that both parties manifest their assent to the bargain. Depending on the circumstances, an offeree's conduct, which is known or knowable to the offeror, may constitute a manifestation of the necessary assent. In the more typical case, however, an offeree should attempt to communicate directly its acceptance to the offeror. If done initially by phone or telegram, the offeree should send a followup letter which may serve as evidence of the notification to the offeror of the acceptance.

The "Mailbox Rule"

Unless an offer explicitly states when and how the acceptance becomes effective, an acceptance is effective upon its dispatch, for example, by placing a letter or notice of acceptance in the U.S. mails properly addressed to the offeror.[30] Upon dispatch, the contract is formed and the offeror's power to revoke his or her offer is terminated. This means that following dispatch of the acceptance, the offeror is bound to the bargain whether or not he or she actually receives the acceptance.

The way an offeror may protect itself from being bound without actual knowledge of the acceptance is to expressly, in the offer, make acceptance effective only on the offeror's actual receipt. Another way is for the offeror to contact the offeree to learn the status of the offer before offering the existing offer's subject matter to another person or firm.

The Statute of Frauds

To be enforceable, certain types of contacts must be evidenced by a written memorandum of the agreement and be signed by the party against whom enforcement is sought. All states, except Louisiana, have enacted or judicially adopted Section 4 of the 1677 English "Act for the Prevention of Frauds and Perjuries," more commonly called the Statute of Frauds. Types of contracts coming within the statute include those involving:

1. Promises of sureties and guarantors;

2. Agreements made upon consideration of marriage;

3. Any conveyance, rental, or sale of any interest in real estate; and

4. Contracts which cannot be performed within one year of their making.[31]

Several states have either expanded or clarified the above list. One example is a common statutory provision making it clear that real estate brokerage contracts come within the statute's scope. The UCC has several statute of frauds provisions including ones applicable to sales[32] and to secured transactions.[33]

Various doctrines have been developed to mitigate the potential harshness of the statute of frauds, which prevents a party from proving up and enforcing a covered transaction. One is known as the part performance doctrine where partial performance, for example, a change of possession of real estate following an oral sale of it, allows the oral promise to be enforced. Similarly, if it can be established that one reasonably and detrimentally relied on an oral promise otherwise unenforceable under the statute, the detrimental reliance may be a sufficient basis to allow the aggrieved party to enforce the contract or otherwise to recover damages based on the reliance.[34]

The Requirement of Consideration

The agreement to which the parties must manifest their assent must be in the form of a bargain to be enforceable. Under section 71 of the *Restatement (Second) of Contracts*, every promise to be enforceable must be given in exchange for consideration.[35] The exchange is the basis of the bargain. The *Restatement (Second)* provides that to constitute consideration, a performance or a return promise must be bargained for, which occurs when the performance or return promise is sought by the promisor in exchange for his promise and is given by the promisee in exchange for that promise.[36] Oliver Wendell Holmes, Jr., described the basic notion of consideration as one of reciprocal, conventional inducements, each for the other.[37]

Unjust Enrichment

Certain promises, which are not made in the form of an exchange and, therefore, are not given for consideration, may still be enforceable under two recognized noncontractual theories of liability. One is the theory of unjust enrichment under which a court may award restitution damages to one who has conferred a benefit upon a recipient where, under the circumstances, it would be "unjust" for the recipient to retain the value of the benefit.[38]

Detrimental Reliance: Promissory Estoppel

The second theory is known as promissory estoppel, also called the detrimental reliance principle. Under this principle, when a promisor has reasonably and justifiably changed his or her position detrimentally in reliance on a promise under circumstances where the promisor did expect, or reasonably should have expected, such reliance, the promisee may recover at least the cost of the reliance.[39] Not all states recognize the promissory estoppel theory. Nonetheless, these theories of liability are important and are gaining a wider acceptance by the courts. Still, these theories are not particularly significant to businesses which conduct their operations primarily through bargain-for-exchanges, in other words, pursuant to "normal" contracts.

INTERPRETING THE BARGAIN

The Problem with Language

A major source of contract litigation is the vague, generalized, and ambiguous language often found in written contracts. Disputes especially may result when the parties themselves try to draft their own agreements, but they arise also with lawyer-drafted documents. We noted earlier in this chapter why generalized boilerplate should be minimized or avoided. Not only does it rarely speak to the specific transactional context in a meaningful and practical fashion, the form language is rarely understood. The parties to boilerplate agreements typically sign without bothering to read the documents let alone learn what the printed language might mean. When disputes subsequently arise, a strong probability exists that the parties will interpret the boilerplate provisions in different ways, each arguing, naturally, for an interpretation which will justify his or her position in the underlying dispute. Such disagreements generate work (and fees) for lawyers.

Recitals and Definitions

It is helpful to consider a contract to be a plan. A good plan provides rules for its own execution. In a contract, rules of construction and interpretation are primarily found in the agreement's recitals and definitions. The recitals set out the reasons for and objectives of the contract, while the definitions particularize what specific words and terms mean within the agreement.

The Importance of Definitions

Although the parties to a contract should understand what the words used in the agreement mean, the problem is that the words do not have single meanings or meanings in themselves. Rather, the parties impute their own subjective meanings on the language used. Consequently, a word as a symbol may convey a clear meaning to one party to an agreement while conveying an equally clear but different meaning to the other party. The parties think they agree, but in fact they agree only on the symbol, not on what it means.

Consider the phrase "sufficient value." A loan contract might provide that the debtor must have collateral at all times on hand of sufficient value to collateralize the loan. What does "sufficient value" mean? Does it mean sufficient in the eyes of the lender? If so, various legal problems result. For one, the agreement may be deemed too indefinite to be enforceable, or it may be deemed illusory since it appears that the lender has the option of deciding what amount of collateral is sufficient. Even if neither illusory nor too indefinite, the agreement could be interpreted to permit a lender to be arbitrary should the lender suddenly demand a much greater amount of security than previously required. Sufficient value could also be interpreted to mean sufficient in relation to the outstanding loan balance. One cannot tell by merely looking at the writing. Thus, the phrase is both ambiguous and vague. It would have been better for the parties to have agreed on a specific collateral-to-loan-ratio such as: "Debtor agrees to maintain and have on hand collateral having a value equal to or greater than 150 percent of the amount of the loan's outstanding indebtedness as determined each month by certified reports furnished the lender."

The above language is an improvement, yet it still has several problems. Foremost is how "value" is to be determined. It may be by invoice price to the debtor, by suggested retail asking price, or by the rather amorphous, changing, and often difficult to prove "fair market" price. The parties should agree in their agreement on exactly what they mean by value by defining it: "Value under this agreement means the invoice price as determined by suppliers' original invoices to borrower." Another word used above in need of a definition is "collateral." "Outstanding indebtedness" should also be defined as should "certified report." And so goes the process of drafting a clear and definitive contract.

The Problem with "Common Words"

Common words—even more than legal jargon—often convey several possible meanings. Common words tend to be vague because of their generality. Consequently, certain common words used in a contract may need to be specifically defined, especially those which relate to the legal rights and duties of the parties. Such words include "price," "credit," "sale," "value," "valuation," "majority," "suitable," "good and proper," "guarantee," "substantial," "sufficient," "reasonable," or "commercially reasonable."

Under the UCC, the parties are obligated to perform certain obligations in a "commercially reasonable manner" or to act in "good faith" in performing a contract. Although these generalized obligations (also called "standards") may not be negated by the parties' agreement, they may be specifically defined. For example, a "commercially reasonable resale price" may be defined as any price obtained for the collateral after offering the collateral for resale at the XYZ Dealer's Auction, or at any other wholesale auction where dealers only are invited.

The Role of Counsel

Parties to contracts face two language challenges. On the one hand, there is the problem of jargonized boilerplate which, although conveying legal meanings which are generally understood by trained lawyers, is not generally understood or read by nonlawyers. On the other hand, simple, plain, and commonly used language also creates problems because so-called plain language does not always convey simple, precise, and unambiguous meanings. In fact, common words often convey vague, imprecise, and ambiguous impressions in the minds of people.

Drafting

Because of the imprecision of language and its potential for creating or contributing to later disagreements, a dispute-minimizing contracting process is needed. The best process is one in which the parties work side by side with their respective attorneys in drafting language which they mutually agree on and define as they proceed through the process of reducing their agreement to writing. Throughout, the attorneys routinely ask questions about what terms or words proposed to be written into the agreement mean to their clients. In many large transactions, the principals agree only on the concept and basic terms of the transaction, then the lawyers for each side meet to draft the detailed implementing language. In doing so, they typically expend many more hours on finalizing the language than on assisting the principals in reaching the core agreement. The time is well spent, however, since agreeing on the detailed language is crucial to prevent later misunderstandings. For example, a leading case involving language vagueness concerned a dispute between an American importer and a Swiss exporter over what types of "fowl" were to be included under the contract word "chickens."[40]

Incorporation by Reference

Counsel may recommend that the parties agree that certain technical terms or specifications which are used in the contract be defined by incorporating by reference specific documents, laws, regulations, or manuals which precisely define the terms or specifications. The kinds of extrinsic documents which may be incorporated by reference include trade association standards, an industry's tolerance manuals, or definitional regulations of a governmental agency such as the Department of Agriculture (which include a definition of "chicken").

Interpretation Problems in Litigation

When the parties do not resolve an interpretation dispute themselves, it often ends up in court. In contract interpretation matters, courts apply a set of interpretation rules but not necessarily in a consistent or predictable manner. Often, a court will turn to one or more of the traditional "axioms" of interpretation and construction.

The Plain Meaning Rule

Perhaps the best known interpretation axiom is the plain meaning rule, which certain courts prefer to apply because it allows a judge in looking at disputed language to offer his or her own subjective interpretation by declaring that the language has a "plain meaning" and then stating it. However, interpretation is not such an easy matter. As the highly respected late Chief Justice of the Supreme Court of California, Justice Roger Traynor, once wrote: "If words had absolute and constant referents, it might be possible to discover contractual intention in the words themselves. . . . Words, however, do not have absolute and constant referents.''[41] Despite this insightful view, the plain meaning axiom is still applied today, even though it may be an anachronism within the modern understanding of language and semantics.

Contra Proferentem

Another common maxim of contract interpretation is that a contract is to be interpreted *contra proferentem*—against its author. This maxim is applied by courts in situations involving ambiguities of either language or syntax so as to reject the author's meaning in favor of the other party's. The rationale is that the author was responsible for the ambiguity and should, therefore, be the one to bear the risk.

The Importance of Recitals

As noted earlier, contracts frequently contain recitals setting out the reasons for (and the objectives of) the contract. Recitals may be useful for construing or interpreting a contract. As a general rule, if the recitals are clear but the terms of the contract are ambiguous, the recitals govern the interpretation and construction of the terms. On the other hand, if the terms are clear, they will be given priority over the contract's recitals whether clear or not.

Usage and Custom

Usage or customs within a trade or industry may be used to resolve omissions, ambiguities, or vagueness in the stated terms. Indeed, an industry custom (called a usage of trade), a prior course of dealing between the parties, and prior negotiations and communications may all be admissible to supplement the agreement or to resolve language problems. Such evidence may normally be used to resolve ambiguities despite the presence of a merger clause (see earlier discussion) which, under the parol evidence rule, operates to exclude evidence of prior or contemporaneous agreements as well as claimed supplemental or additional terms.

Language may have a special or peculiar trade or territorial meaning not generally understood by the community at large. As any lumber dealer knows, a common "2 by 4" is more nearly a "1¾ by 3¾." Similarly, as probably every citizen of Great Britain knows (but most Americans do not), a "bonnet" is also worn by an automobile (the hood).

In sum, the importance of agreeing upon and understanding the language used in one's agreements can hardly be overstated. A business person should attempt to include definitions of both key legal phrases and important common words in all economically valuable contracts.

PERFORMING THE BARGAIN

Express and Constructive Duties of Performance

The fundamental significance of any contract is that the parties are legally obligated to perform the duties that the agreement sets out. Although, in some instances, no express duties arise until and unless a specified event or events first occur, implied or "constructive duties" are nearly always present. These judicially recognized obligations include the constructive duty to refrain from interfering or preventing the other party's performance, the constructive duty to cooperate with the other party in that performance, and the constructive duty not to impair the reasonable contractual expectations of the other party. Since a contract consists of all the legal obligations imposed on and rights granted to the respective parties by the agreement, a contract's obligations include constructive duties.

Conditions Affecting Performance Obligations

Most contractual duties are conditional; that is, they either become due on the happening of a specified event (a *condition precedent*), or they cease to exist following the occurrence of an event (a *condition subsequent*, otherwise known as an "event that terminates a duty"[42]). Since the occurrence of a required condition precedent is a necessary prerequisite for a party to be legally obligated to perform, the inclusion of specified conditions precedent within an agreement is an important way to qualify one's duties and, consequently, one's potential liability.

Dependent and Independent Promises

The performances called for in a bilateral contract (a promise for a promise) normally are dependent upon each other. Thus, a seller's promise to sell an art object for $100 given in exchange for a buyer's promise to pay $100 means that the seller's performance is dependent upon the buyer's tender of the $100, just as the buyer's tender is dependent upon seller's tender of the art object. In this situation and in others like it, the promises are said to be mutually dependent. A more modern doctrinal way of putting it is to say that the performance of the promise to pay is a construction condition of the performance of the promise to tender the goods, and vice versa.

Although mutually dependent promises typify many contracts, other bargains have independent covenants or promises, meaning that the performance or tendering of performance of one promise is neither an express nor constructive condition of the other party's obligation to perform. Whether one is obligated to perform when the other party has not performed is often a difficult legal question.

One way to minimize problems of knowing under what conditions specific duties under a contract must be performed is to expressly incorporate all of the express and constructive conditions for performance into the agreement. For example: "The borrower agrees to pay any and all premiums due or which may become due for casualty insurance on the collateral, regardless of whether the lender has defaulted or is in default in performing any of its obligations as specified in this agreement."

The Risks of Suspending Performance

The troublesome and important issues raised by one party's suspending or wishing to suspend its performance under a contract—because the other party has not performed, has performed badly, or has indicated that it will not perform—causes lawyers, let alone clients, trepidation. Indeed, a contracting party often walks a legal tightrope when it comes to suspending performance. Under certain circumstances, suspension of performance may be legally justifiable or even necessary to recover damages. On the other hand, a suspension may constitute a "material breach" of the contract giving the other party a right to sue for damages. The resolution of the legal issue depends both on the attending circumstances and on how a court would construe the contractual terms and conditions of performance. In a contract where the liability potential is significant, performance should be suspended only with the approval and advice of legal counsel. Several grounds for suspending performance are recognized under the law, but a lawyer's analysis and counsel are needed to ascertain if the grounds are present in a particular transaction. Moreover, a lawyer may protect the client's interests by drafting demands for assurance of performance or other documents which evidence an acceptable legal basis for the suspension of performance.

Excuses for Nonperformance

Both the common law and the UCC permit a party to avoid a contract if certain intervening events occur after the contract was formed but before its performance becomes due. Known under various doctrines such as "impossibility of performance," "commercial impracticability," and "failure of basic assumptions," the common basis for these excusing doctrines is that unexpected events have occurred which make the performance either impossible or, at least, commercially impracticable for at least one of the parties. The doctrines apply, however, only where the risk of the event has been neither expressly nor impliedly allocated in the parties' agreement. As a result of the event, one's performance must become commercially impracticable, meaning at an excessive cost of performance, or at a cost grossly disproportionate to the value of the prospective benefits.[43]

The easier cases involving excusing doctrines concern destruction of the subject matter of a contract prior to the time of its performance. Goods sold but not delivered might be destroyed, or a building reserved for a dance might burn down before the event.[44] The seller and lessor are excused from performing due to impossibility of performance.

The more difficult cases for excusing performance involve disruptive or sudden market changes not caused by either party but which have the effect of substantially increasing the cost of one party's performance or of lowering its value to the other. In cases where the value of the tendered performance has become commercially worthless (or nearly so) due to intervening unanticipated events, the courts speak of a "frustration of purpose."[45] The frustration of purpose, impossibility of performance, failure of basic assumptions, and commercial impracticability doctrines represent complex areas of contract analysis. Advice of counsel should be sought as to whether any of these excusing doctrines might be applicable to a given contracting situation where the parties' expectations have been altered by unexpected contingencies.

In summary, every party to a contract must perform all the duties specified in the agreement or be liable in damages for failing to do so unless the performance is excused or is suspendable under applicable legal doctrines. Before deciding not to perform or to suspend one's contractual obligations, competent advice should be obtained.

ADJUSTING THE BARGAIN

In many instances, events which occur between the execution of an agreement and its scheduled performance do not justify cancellation, suspension, or avoidance of the bargain. Nonetheless, external occurrences and market conditions affect the parties' duties and expectations. These events include the interruption of needed supplies or their availability only at increased and excessive cost. In such situations, completing performance may involve overcoming obstacles that neither party considered when negotiating the agreement. In addition, the market price of goods or materials may rise causing anticipated profits to vanish. These and other circumstances underscore that contracts should be drafted to provide for midcourse adjustments, particularly in regard to foreseeable marketplace changes which may significantly enhance or lower the value of one party's performance vis-à-vis the value to the other party.

Providing for Contingencies

Like any good plan, a contract should provide for contingencies which foreseeably might affect the parties' performances and expectations. One way to do this is to allocate the risks of specific contingencies to one party or the other. In a sale of a machine, for example, the parties may agree that the seller assumes the entire risk of loss for the theft, loss, or destruction of the unit until 12:01

A.M., July 21, 1988, at which moment the risk of loss will pass to the buyer. This risk-of-loss allocation not only answers the legal question of exactly when the risk passes, it also provides a convenient point in time for the seller to terminate any insurance on the machine it may have and for the buyer to commence its coverage.

Many risks may be allocated by the agreement including nonperformance due to strikes, failure of needed sources of supply, or legal inability to perform due to intervening governmental regulations or actions. In combination with a liquidated damage clause, which specifies an agreed-upon sum of money as damages, a risk-of-loss provision may effectively cause the parties to share the loss resulting from nonperformance of the contract due to destruction of property or the failure of a needed source of supply. The law permits the parties to agree to divide the risks and burdens of contingencies.[46] The parties may also incorporate a general "excuse for nonperformance" clause which excuses one party from performing the contract. Such a clause is called a *force mejeure* or *vis major* clause when it excuses performance because of acts of God or events that are beyond the control of either party.

Flexible Price Terms

A serious disruption that may occur following execution of an agreement is a significant change in the market price of the goods or services which either are the subject matter of the bargain or which are needed to perform the contract. The risk of fluctuating market prices is a serious one in a competitive economy as even a small price change may render a contract unprofitable. Consequently, parties often attempt either to delay setting the contract price until the last possible moment or to agree on a flexible price which will cause them to share the risk of market price changes that might occur during the life of the contract.

The UCC authorizes the use of both open price terms (where the parties say nothing about the price or leave it open for later agreement) and flexible price terms (where the contract prices are to be periodically fixed by some agreed market or other standard as set or recorded by a third person or agency).[47] A flexible price term is preferable to an open price term because it normally results in a definite price whereas the open price term could result in a dispute as to even if there is a contract if the parties fail to later agree on the price.[48] Should the open or flexible price term fail, the UCC provides that the price shall be a "reasonable price at the time for delivery," unless the parties intended a contract only if they agreed on the price.[49] That intention is often unclear, however.

Contract Modifications

Older cases typically held that certain agreements to modify a contract were unenforceable because of the preexisting duty rule (see the earlier discussion on consideration). More recent cases, however, have permitted contracting parties to agree to change their existing obligations by modifying their agreement. One method has been to use the legal fiction of "three separate contracts." Under this approach, a court considers the original contract to be cancelled by an implied or second contract of cancellation which allows the parties to agree on a third or modified contract where no preexisting duties exist.[50] A more honest approach is taken when courts simply disregard the requirement of consideration as it applies to contract modifications. This is the approach of the UCC in Article Two.[51]

On occasion, a party is coerced into agreeing to a modification by the other party's threat of suspending or interrupting its performance. This occurs, for example, when a supplier of goods who has entered into a fixed-price requirements contract with a buyer informs the buyer that no further goods will be furnished unless the buyer agrees to an upward adjustment in the price. This presents a difficult problem because the line between modifications agreed to for legitimate commercial reasons and modifications exacted under threats of economic harm is not always neatly drawn. In both sales and non-sales of goods, an obligation rests on each party to perform the contract in good faith.[52] This good faith obligation has been used by courts to differentiate enforceable modifications from those deemed unenforceable. Finding a good faith violation depends not only on the circumstances which compelled one party to seek the modification, it also depends on how that party went about getting the modification agreement.

If a business wishes to have a contract term adjusted in its favor because of a change in the market price of goods or materials needed either to perform a contract or to supply a customer, the business should proceed with caution in seeking a modification agreement. To suggest rather than to demand may be the difference between an enforceable and unenforceable modification. If a demand is coupled with an expressed or implied threat to stop supplying the customer under the contract, a resulting agreement will almost always be held to be unenforceable. In short, contract modifications should be bargained and never coerced by stopping or threatening to stop performance of an existing contract when the stoppage would cause the threatened party serious economic harm.

REMEDYING CONTRACT DISPUTES

When a dispute arises under a contract, the parties may work out the difficulty themselves, or they may litigate or arbitrate the matter. Certainly, the resolving of disputes without litigation or arbitration is preferable. Not only is a settlement or "workout" cheaper, it also minimizes the potential for hard feelings, which litigation engenders, while enhancing the likelihood of business relations between the disputants in the future. This section discusses several remedial options available following transactional breakdowns. Difficulties arise when one party commits either a breach (a failure to perform a specific obligation when it comes due) or a repudiation (a statement or conduct which clearly evidences that the party will not perform future obligations).

Negotiations and Assurances of Performance

On occasion, one party to a contract believes or has reason to believe that the other party may not perform its obligations when due, even though the contract has not yet been breached or repudiated. This occurs, for example, when a business learns that a supplier under a contract with the business is either having difficulty in supplying other firms or may be going through difficult financial times. Under these circumstances, it may be appropriate for the anxious party to request that the other party indicate that it will perform the agreed-upon contract.

Demand for an Adequate Assurance of Due Performance

In a sales contract, the anxious party has the right, whenever reasonable grounds for his or her insecurity exist regarding the other party's future performance, to demand in writing that the other party provide an "adequate assurance of due performance."[53] The worried party may suspend its performance while awaiting the reply, but *only if* under the circumstances it is considered "commercially reasonable" to do so. Once the written demand has been made, the other party must provide a timely reply. If it fails to do so or if the reply is deemed inadequate, the demanding party may treat the failure to give adequate assurance as one of repudiation, cease performance, and sue for damages under the UCC rule of anticipatory repudiation.[54]

The remedy of seeking an adequate assurance of due performance, however, is lined with sand traps. If a court later finds that the grounds for insecurity were not reasonable, that the demanding party's suspension of performance while awaiting the reply was commercially unreasonable, or that the reply was, legally speaking, an adequate assurance of performance (the demanding party's contrary interpretation notwithstanding), the anxious party who made the demand may be deemed the party who first materially breached the bargain. This means that the party who sought to invoke the remedy may itself end up being held liable in damages for breaching the contract.

The adequate assurance remedy must, therefore, be used cautiously. Its practical thrust should not be to accelerate remedies under the anticipatory repudiation principle but rather to foster and encourage communication and negotiation between the parties when there is reason to believe that one party may have difficulty in performing its obligations. The remedy is designed to precipitate adjustments, an extension agreement granting a debtor a longer period to pay back an indebtedness, for example. In short, seeking an adequate assurance of performance should be viewed as a step toward a possible negotiated adjustment to a bargain rather than as the first step in a rush to litigation.

Settlements; Accord and Satisfaction

The majority of disputes involving liability claims for alleged contract breaches are terminated without litigation through settlements. If the settlement involves an offer to do the promised performance followed by the doing of it, the arrangement is known as an *accord and satisfaction*. Contractual settlements are especially useful in compromising unliquidated damage claims (those where the amount of the liability is in controversy) but may also be used to settle liquidated contract claims (where the amount is clear but the liability is not).

Contract Damages: The Expectation Interest

The primary relief for breach or repudiation of a contract is damages. Contract damages rest upon the notion of compensation, that is, of making the aggrieved party economically whole. This means that an aggrieved party to the extent possible should be placed in the economic position that he or she would have been in had the contract been fully and properly performed. Contract damages, therefore, are rarely awarded either to penalize the breaching party or to act as a deterrent. This means that, even though one party may have breached a contract, the non-breaching party should not bring suit if, as a consequence, the non-breaching party is better off. This happens, for example, when a seller breaches a contract to sell goods at a time when the market price for the goods (assuming availability) is lower than the contract price. Under these conditions, the seller's breach actually saves the buyer money. Courts do not award windfall damages to contract claimants.

Damage Formulas

Various formulas have been used by courts in an effort to apply the compensatory, make-whole concept to concrete cases. These formulas all come down to the basic proposition that an aggrieved party's damages are measured by his or her loss of value (the expectation interest), plus any incidental and consequential damages caused by the breach, less any costs or expenses saved as a result of the breach. Broken down, the traditional notion regarding contract damages incorporates four distinct elements: expectation damages, consequential damages, incidental damages, and costs saved or avoided.

Expectation or Loss of Value Damages

Loss of value damages refers to the economic loss as measured by the aggrieved party's contract-induced expectations. In a sale, for example, a buyer's loss of value following a seller's breach is usually measured by either the difference between the market price of the goods and the actual contract price or the difference between the buyer's "cover" price and the contract price, meaning the additional amount the buyer had to pay to procure substitute goods from another seller.

Following a buyer's breach by non-delivery or repudiation, a seller's loss of value is measured either by the difference between the contract price and the market price or the difference between the contract price and what the seller obtained in proceeds as a result of a "commercially reasonable" resale of the goods. On occasion, however, a seller may be permitted to recover its lost profit when neither the resale contract price formula nor the market price contract formula works to make the seller whole. This occurs if the breached or repudiated sale represents a lost unit of sale. This is called the "lost volume rule." Simply to give the seller the resale contract price differential does not make the seller whole, for example, in the case of standardized goods held for resale where supply exceeds demand.[55]

Incidental Damages

Incidental damages are those costs resulting from a breach which reasonably are incurred by an aggrieved party to minimize an even greater loss. These include a seller's expense in redirecting shipments, in storing the goods, or in reselling or otherwise disposing of them. A buyer's incidental damages include the reasonable costs expended to buy substitute goods and the costs incurred to return nonconforming goods which have been rejected or when their acceptance has been revoked (see Chapter 10).

Consequential Damages

Consequential damages are those that are consequent to a breach and represent neither loss of value nor incidental damages. Consequential damages might include a buyer's expected lost profits on the resale of goods ordered but not delivered due to seller's breach or repudiation. We say "might" because not all lost profit damages are recoverable. Under the modern version of the rule of the famous case of *Hadley v. Baxendale*,[56] only those special damages, including anticipated profits from a resale which the breaching party knew or had reason to know at the time of contracting might result from its breach, are recoverable.[57]

Costs Avoided: Mitigation of Damages

Under any damage formula, the costs that the aggrieved party avoided or reasonably could have avoided must be deducted from the damages otherwise recoverable. Although known as the non-breaching party's "duty to mitigate damages," this mitigation rule does not obligate the aggrieved party to take any action. Rather, the failure to avoid or minimize one's damages means only that those damages that could have been avoided may not be recovered. Consider the situation where a contractor under contract is excavating footings for a new building. Assume the contractor learns that the owner, the other party to the contract, has repudiated the agreement. Under these circumstances, the contractor's continued performance after learning of the breach would be a failure to mitigate damages. The contractor could recover only the contract price less the cost of his or her entire performance beyond the point of learning of the repudiation since these post-repudiation costs could have been saved.

Reliance and Restitution Damages

Depending on the circumstances of a particular transaction, a court may award reliance damages, that is, damages based on one's actual costs or expenditures rather than loss of value or expectation damages. This occurs, for example, where no contract existed but where a promise was made which induced the promisee in reasonable reliance on it to change position to his or her detriment.

In contrast, restitutionary damages are awarded when a contract is ordered rescinded or cancelled. Restitution is also awarded under the theory of unjust enrichment or quasi-contract when a court finds that one who has received a benefit under circumstances, when it would be unjust for the recipient to retain the benefit, should be compelled to restore the value of the benefit to the party who conferred it. A doctor who comes to the aid of an unconscious victim, for example, may later recover restitution damages for the reasonable value of the medical benefits conferred.

Specific Performance

One might ask why, in every case of breach or repudiation, a court does not simply order the other party to perform his or her contractual obligations. The reasons why specific performance is not generally ordered are both legal and practical. From the legal standpoint, the traditional remedy for breach of contract is one of compensatory damages. Specific performance, on the other hand, developed in England as an equitable (meaning extraordinary) remedy available only when the legal remedy of damages was deemed insufficient as a matter of law.

The practical problem with specific performance in reference to breach or repudiation of contract is that it entails an affirmative order of a court mandating that the defendant do something. Not only may the ordered performance be difficult, the defendant may not be equipped or otherwise able or willing to perform. To be assured that the performance is being carried out properly, the ordering court, moreover, would have to supervise the defendant's performance over time. Courts do not have the resources to supervise contractual performances routinely.

Consequently, the remedy of specific performance is available under extraordinary circumstances or when monetary damages are insufficient to make the plaintiff whole. The latter situation occurs, for example, in the case of land sales where the law considers each parcel of land to be legally unique. Similarly, antiques, art objects, and other unique chattels such as a collector's automobile may also be the subject of specific performance decrees since monetary damages are inadequate to compensate an aggrieved buyer.

Under the "other proper circumstances" category, specific performance may also be available to order a supplier to furnish promised goods pursuant to its contract obligations where no alternative source of supply is reasonably available to the buyer (or is available only at a prohibitive cost) and when the buyer has an immediate and pressing need for the goods. This may occur, for example, when a coal supplier who supplies a utility under a requirements contract stops making deliveries and where other coal suppliers are either unavailable or available only at a prohibitive price.[58]

CONSTRUCTION CONTRACTS

The bidding process by general contractors on public projects normally is regulated by specific statutes and regulations (see Chapter 9). Here we discuss one of the more important contract doctrines as applied primarily to construction contract situations—the doctrine of substantial performance.

Substantial versus Full Performance

Under the doctrine of dependent promises, the performance of one promise often is a constructive condition for the return promise's performance. In a construction contract setting, this means that the complete performance of the contractor could be construed as a condition precedent for any duty of the owner or developer to pay. In fact, however, this is not the case, for the courts recognize that the constructive and express condition rules may create a genuine hardship on contractors who unintentionally omit a few details of performance or slightly "go off specs," or do not fully comply with the specifications as required by the blueprints or other contracting documents. In response to these hardships and the practical problems of demanding perfect performance in the construction area, courts developed what has come to be known as the "substantial performance doctrine." The doctrine does not allow, however, a contractor to perform only substantially. To the contrary, a contractor legally always must fully perform the contract. Rather, the doctrine allows a contractor who has substantially performed to enforce the owner's or developer's promise to pay the contract price, less damages for the incomplete or imperfect performance. What this means is that, although a contractor always is under a duty to perform fully all contract duties as specified in the contract, should the contractor's performance deviate from the full performance standards, he or she has a right to be paid although the owner's damages for the incomplete or nonconforming performance may be withheld from the payment, provided the contractor has substantially performed his or her duties. At what point a contractor has substantially performed is not always clear.

Cost of Completion versus Diminution in Value

One issue in substantial performance cases often concerns how the owner's or developer's damages, which are to be deducted from the amount otherwise owed the contractor, are to be measured. One formula known as the cost of completion rule measures the damages by the costs that have been or will have to be incurred to complete the project according to the contract's specifications. Another formula known as the diminution in value rule allows damages only in the amount of the difference between the value of the structure as built and the value that the structure would have had, had the contract been fully, rather than substantially, performed. The diminished value rule is applied in cases where the cost of completion would be excessive in comparison with the increased value that would result. Otherwise, the cost of completion formula is the more commonly used measure.[59]

Other legal problems, which tend to concentrate in the area of construction contracts, include the need for flexible pricing mechanisms such as cost plus clauses, liquidated damage clauses for delayed performances, mistakes in the bidding process (discussed earlier), and progress payment mechanisms often involving an agreed-upon release-of-funds procedure, for example, upon an architect's periodic certification of work completed. (The use of a standby letter of credit as a release-of-funds payment mechanism is described in Chapter 12.) Contractors, owners, and developers often become embroiled in contract disputes. Advice of counsel may be necessary at the first hint that things may not be going according to plan.

EMPLOYMENT CONTRACTS

Benefits of Individual Employment Contracts

Businesses need employees who are loyal and motivated to perform up to their capacities. Individual employment contracts with key sales, engineering, and management personnel may aid in achieving this business objective while at the same time protecting the firm should these valuable employees depart and go into competition with it.

Although business lawyers sometimes advise firms to avoid individual employment contracts since "employment at will" offers the business person the greatest range of options in dealing with employees, the reality is that the employment at will principle is being eroded as courts and legislatures are increasingly placing restrictions on an employer's managerial prerogatives to fire employees as it wishes. (For a discussion of employee terminations and the employment at will demise, see Chapter 15.) Moreover, employees with access to customer lists, trade secrets, and inventions need to be legally restrained from divulging or using that information. The individual employment contract may help accomplish this objective as well.

Restrictive Covenants

One of the more important aspects of an employment agreement is the section dealing with covenants not to compete (discussed more fully in Chapter 4).

Suffice it to note that restrictive covenants must be reasonable in all aspects under the attending circumstances or be held void and unenforceable under the public policy prohibiting unreasonable restraints on trade. The duration of the restrictive covenant, the defined scope of the area of noncompetition, and the geographic territory where it applies are all relevant factors in determining the reasonableness of a restrictive covenant not to compete.

Desirable Terms

An employment contract arguably should include but not be limited to the following subjects spelled out in sufficient detail to lessen the likelihood of later disputes:

1. The duration of the agreement;
2. Whether or not it is renewable;
3. If renewable, whether by unqualified option of the employer after an employer review-evaluation procedure, or by some other method;
4. The specific duties of employment (including "best efforts" language whereby the employee promises to use "best efforts" in working for the firm or company);
5. Whether the employee may work for compensation outside of the firm and, if so, the limits on outside work;
6. The employee's compensation including salary, fringe benefits, incentives, percentage of profits (profits must be specifically defined or a formula for calculation must be included), potential for and method of calculating bonuses, employee contributions to retirement or other deferred compensation plans, and method of earning commissions, including any formulas to be used;
7. To whom (or to what position) the employee is to report or otherwise be accountable;
8. The employee's title or designated position;
9. A listing of the employee's skills as agreed upon and a warrant by the employee that he or she possesses these skills;
10. A promise by the employee that he or she will devote substantially all of his or her working time to further the business's interests (including a definition of working time);
11. Restrictive covenants whereby the employee promises not to disclose trade secrets, inventions, customer lists, or other confidential business information of any kind, a violation of which subjects the employee to immediate dismissal;
12. Vacation, illness, and leave policies (these may be incorporated by reference from an employee handbook);
13. Restrictions dealing with the employee's non-competing directly or indirectly with the firm (or the non-joining of a competitor organization) following termination of the employment relationship (see Chapter 4);
14. Termination options setting out the various ways the agreement may be terminated (the employer may also want to include the phrase "and for any reason or no reason

whatsoever''), any notice requirements, and grounds for termination including the sale of the business;

15. The employer's right to change or add to the employee's duties and to reassign or transfer the employee at any time or upon reasonable notice;

16. Language which affords an employer flexibility in changing the agreement when necessary or desirable;

17. The effect of incapacity, illness, or death of either party on the employment contract;

18. The choice of law provision (what state law governs the contract);

19. A non-assignability clause;

20. A merger clause (discussed earlier in this chapter); and

21. A modification and rescission clause permitting the contract to be modified at any time, or to be rescinded and a new agreement substituted.

When drafting individual employment contracts, a business should enlist the assistance of legal counsel. Also, an employer should not offer individual employment contracts to employees while a unionization drive is unfolding. If unionization efforts are suspected, an employer should read Chapter 15 and hire a labor lawyer at once, whether the employer supports the unionization drive or not.

FRANCHISE AGREEMENTS

FTC Franchise and Business Venture Disclosure Rules

In late 1979, the Federal Trade Commission's trade regulation rule titled "Disclosure Requirements and Prohibitions Concerning Franchising and Business Opportunity Ventures" became effective.[60] The rule requires franchisors to furnish a presale disclosure document or booklet to prospective franchisees, setting out in the document information about the franchise, the franchisor's worth, the nature of the franchise business, and the terms of the franchise agreement.[61] The need for this information results from the franchisee's reliance on the franchisor's experience and expertise. The purpose of the FTC disclosure rule, in short, is to provide complete and accurate information about a franchise before it is entered into by a franchisee.

Franchises Defined

The FTC offers two alternative definitions of a covered franchise. The first definition contains three elements.

1. The franchisee sells goods or services which meet the franchisor's quality standards in situations where the franchisee operates under the franchisor's trademark, service mark, trade names, advertising, or other commercial symbol designating the franchisor or which are identified by the franchisor's mark.

2. The franchisor exercises significant control over, or promises to give the franchisee significant assistance in, the franchisee's method of operation.

3. The franchisee is required to make a payment of $500 or more to the franchisor or a person affiliated with the franchisor during the period from any time before to within six months after commencing operation of the franchise business.

Under this definition, the use of a mark requirement is met when a franchisor authorizes a firm to distribute goods or services which bear the franchisor's mark or authorizes another to operate under a business or trade name that includes, in whole or in part, the franchisor's mark. This definition makes it clear that the FTC rule applies not only to franchisors but also to firms who broker franchises.

The FTC's alternative definition of a franchise, also containing three elements, extends the rule's coverage to business opportunity ventures including distributorships, rack jobbers, and even vending machine route accounts:

1. The franchisee sells goods or services supplied by the franchisor or its affiliate, or by suppliers with which it is required by the franchisor to do business.

2. The franchisor secures retail outlets or accounts for the goods or services, or secures locations for vending devices or racks, or provides the services of a person to do either.

3. The franchisee is required to make a payment of $500 or more to the franchisor or to a person affiliated with the franchisor during the period from anytime before to within six months after commencing operation of the franchise business.

Exclusions include an individual trademark license granted to a single manufacturer to manufacture trademarked goods, leased department arrangements where an independent retailer sells goods or services from leased premises from another retailer who owns the premises, and fractional franchises where the franchise product line accounts for no more than 20 percent of the franchisee's gross sales.

Required Franchisor Disclosures

The FTC rule requires the covered franchisors at the "first (face-to-face) personal meeting" or at least ten business days prior to the execution of the franchise or payment of any consideration for a franchise, whichever is earlier, to submit a disclosure document setting forth information on the following topics:

1. Information about the franchisor
2. Business experience of the franchisor's directors and key executives
3. The franchisor's business experience
4. The franchisor's litigation history
5. The franchisor's bankruptcy history
6. Description of the franchise

7. Initial funds required to be paid by the franchisee

8. Recurring funds, if any, required to be paid by the franchisee

9. Persons affiliated with the franchisor

10. Any franchisee obligations to purchase or lease

11. Revenues received by the franchisor in consideration of purchases by a franchisee

12. Financing arrangements

13. Restrictions placed on a franchisee's conduct of its business

14. Personal participation required of the franchisee

15. Termination, cancellation, and renewal of the franchise

16. Statistical information about the number of franchises and their rate of termination

17. Site selection

18. Training programs, if any

19. Celebrity involvement with the franchise, if any

20. Financial information about the franchisor.

Along with this disclosure form or booklet and at the same time it is submitted, the franchisor must also furnish the prospective franchisee with the proposed franchise agreement and any related leases or other documents which are required to be signed. In addition, franchisors who discuss or make claims in reference to actual or potential sales or the income or profits of existing or prospective franchises must furnish a completed earnings claim form to the prospective franchisee setting out in the earnings or profits claim its bases and assumptions.

Violation of the disclosure rules could result in a cease and desist order, an injunction, and civil penalties up to $10,000 per violation. Franchisees under the rule have standing to bring suit for actual damages for alleged violations.

By late 1986, several states had also enacted their own respective franchise disclosure statutes. These states include California, Illinois, Indiana, Hawaii, Maryland, Michigan, Minnesota, New York, North Dakota, Rhode Island, South Dakota, Virginia, Washington, and Wisconsin.[62]

Termination of Franchises and Distributorships

One of the more litigated issues in the area of franchises and distributorships involves their termination. The issue arises especially under language which purports to allow a franchisor or manufacturer to terminate or cancel "for no reason" or "for any reason." Even when the language allows each party the same termination option and even though qualifying it upon reasonable prior notice, an agreement's terminable at will language is often the subject of litigation.

Although certain courts have held that the explicit "for any reason" language is qualified by the UCC's good faith obligation, other courts have suggested that terminable at will clauses may be unconscionable. Still other courts have interpreted "for any or no reason" language in the context of the entire franchise or distributorship agreement as meaning that the agreement may be terminated only for a commercial reason and not for one determined to be arbitrary or capricious. Finally, in some states, the courts have upheld even arbitrary terminations under "terminable at will" or for "any reason" language.[63]

Automobile dealerships and petroleum retail establishments, on the other hand, are afforded protection against arbitrary and sudden terminations under specific federal statutes, including the Dealers Day in Court Act[64] and legislation aimed at petroleum retailers.[65]

Arguably, distributors face greater dangers of abrupt terminations than do most franchisees since a franchise in most cases essentially involves a durational licensing agreement. A distributorship, however, often depends upon a constant supply of goods from a particular manufacturer. The dealer, moreover, often has invested large sums of money in developing a market for the manufacturer's goods. Consequently, distributors and jobbers should seek legal advice before signing agreements tendered by manufacturers with termination language that would appear to grant the manufacturer at any time the right to walk away for any reason from the joint business relationship.

ROLE OF COUNSEL

Throughout this chapter, the role of counsel in assisting a firm in negotiating, drafting, and legally performing a contract has been highlighted. By drafting contract documents, a lawyer is able to clarify language, expressly condition obligations, make sure that the contracting party is promising specific tasks rather than results, provide for both unforeseen contingencies (*force mejeure* clauses) and foreseeable contingencies (allocations of specific risks), and incorporate an efficient dispute resolution mechanism such as an arbitration of disputes clause. By using plain language, which is defined and understood by the parties, and by seeing to it that the agreement is fully and accurately reduced to writing with an incorporated merger clause, the business lawyer can be instrumental in his or her client's entering into a workable plan that minimizes misunderstandings as well as maximizes resolutions for contingencies.

NOTES

1. Friedrich Kessler, Grant Gilmore, and Anthony T. Kronman, *Contracts: Cases and Materials*, 3d ed. Little, Brown and Company (1986), p. 1.

2. Llewellyn, *What Price Contract? An Essay in Perspective*, 40 Yale L.J. 704, 704–8 (1931).

3. *See, e.g.*, Grant Gilmore, *The Death of Contract*. Ohio State University Press (1974); Patterson, *An Apology for Consideration*, 58 Colum. L. Rev. 929 (1958); Kennedy, *Form and Substance in Private Law Adjudication*, 89 Harv. L. Rev. 1685 (1976). *See also*, Henningsen v. Bloomfield Motors, Inc., 32 N.J. 358, 161 A.2d 69 (1960).

4. *See, Restatement of Contracts* §§ 1, *et seq.* (1932). *See also* Williston, *The*

Restatement of Contracts, 18 A.B.A. J. 775 (1932); Goodrich, *The Story of the American Law Institute*, 1951 Wash. U.L.Q. 283; and Wechsler, *Restatements and Legal Change: Problems of Policy in the Restatement Work of the American Law Institute*, 13 St. Louis U.L.J. 185 (1968).

5. *See*, *Restatement (Second) of Contracts* §§ 1, *et seq.* (1981).

6. *See*, *e.g.*, Ga. Code Ann. § 20–302.2 (supp. 1981).

7. *See*, U.C.C. §§ 2–101, *et seq.*

8. U.C.C. § 2–102.

9. *See*, *e.g.*, N.Y. General Obligations Law § 5–1105 (1941); and Cal. Civil Code § 1606 (1872).

10. *See*, U.C.C. §§ 7–101, *et seq.*

11. See, U.C.C. §§ 9–101, *et seq.*

12. *See*, U.C.C. §§ 3–101, *et seq.*, and 4–101, *et seq.*

13. *Restatement (Second) of Contracts* § 71.

14. Swinton v. Whitinsville Savings Bank, 311 Mass. 677, 42 N.E.2d 808 (1942); *contra*, Weintraub v. Krobatsch, 64 N.J. 445, 317 A.2d 68 (1974).

15. *See*, *e.g.*, Kannaves v. Annino, 356 Mass. 42, 247 N.E.2d 708 (1969).

16. *See*, *Restatement (Second) of Contracts* §§ 153 and 154. *See also*, Elsinore Union Elementary School Dist. v. Kastorff, 54 Cal.2d 380, 353 P.2d 713 (1960).

17. *See*, U.C.C. § 2–209, Official Comment 2.

18. 26 Stat. 209 (1980).

19. *Restatement (Second) of Contracts* § 213; U.C.C. § 2–202.

20. *See*, *e.g.*, Doenges-Long Motors, Inc. v. Gillen, 138 Colo. 31, 328 P.2d 1077 (1959); and Keser v. Chagnon, 159 Colo. 209, 410 P.2d 637 (1966).

21. *See*, *e.g.*, Fairmount Glass Works v. Crunden-Martin Woodenware Co., 106 Ky. 659, 51 S.W. 196 (1899).

22. *See*. U.C.C. § 2–305.

23. *See*, *e.g.*, Lefkowitz v. Great Minneapolis Surplus Store, 251 Minn. 188, 86 N.W.2d 689 (1957).

24. U.C.C. § 2–205.

25. New York General Obligations Law § 5–1109 (1941).

26. *Restatement (Second) of Contracts* § 45.

27. Arthur L. Corbin, *Offer and Acceptance, and Some of the Resulting Legal Relations*, 26 Yale L.J. 169, 199 (1917).

28. *Restatement (Second) of Contracts* §§ 30, 50, 60, and 62.

29. *See*, U.C.C. § 2–207.

30. Adams v. Lindsell, 1 B. & Ald. 681, 106 Eng. Rep. 250 (K.B. 1818); *Restatement (Second) of Contracts* § 63.

31. The Statute of Frauds, An Act for Prevention of Frauds and Perjuries, Stat. 29, Car. II, c.3 (1677): For a modern version, *see*, *e.g.*, N.J. Stat. Ann. § 25:1–5.

32. U.C.C. § 2–201.

33. U.C.C. § 9–203.

34. *See*, *e.g.*, Monarco v. LoGreco, 35 Cal.2d 621, 220 P.2d 737 (1950).

35. *See*, Fuller, *Consideration and Form*, 41 Colum. L. Rev. 799 (1941); and Lon L. Fuller, *Anatomy of the Law*. F.A. Praeger Co. (1968), pp. 36–37.

36. *Restatement (Second) of Contracts* § 71.

37. O. W. Holmes, *The Common Law*. Little, Brown and Company (1881), pp. 293–94.

38. *See, e.g.*, Paschall's Inc. v. Dozier, 219 Tenn. 45, 407 S.W.2d 150 (1966); and Cotnam v. Wisdom, 83 Ark. 601, 104 S.W. 164 (1907).

39. *Restatement (Second) of Contracts* § 90. *See also,* Swygert and Smucker, *Promissory Estoppel in Florida: A Growing Recognition of Promissory Obligation*, 16 Stetson L. Rev. 1 (1986).

40. Frigaliment Importing Co. v. B.N.S. International Sales Corp., 190 F. Supp. 116 (S.D.N.Y. 1960).

41. Pacific Gas & Electric Co. v. Thomas Drayage & Rigging Co., 69 Cal.2d 33, 34, 442 p.2d 641, 642 (1968).

42. *Restatement (Second) of Contracts* § 230.

43. *See*, Transatlantic Financing Corp. v. United States, 363 F.2d 312 (D.C. Cir. 1966).

44. Taylor v. Caldwell, 3 B. & S. 826, 122 Eng. Rep. 309 (K.B., 1863); and U.C.C. § 2–613.

45. Krell v. Henry, 2 K.B. 740 (Court of Appeal, 1903). *See also, Restatement (Second) of Contracts* § 265.

46. *See, e.g.*, U.C.C. § 2–303.

47. *See* U.C.C. §§ 2–305 (1) (a) and (b).

48. *See* U.C.C. §§ 2–305 (1) (C) and 2–305 (2).

49. U.C.C. § 2–305 (4).

50. *See, e.g.*, Schwartzreich v. Bauman-Basch, Inc., 231 N.Y. 196, 131 N.E. 887 (1921).

51. U.C.C. § 2–209.

52. *Restatement (Second) of Contracts* § 205; U.C.C. § 1–203.

53. U.C.C. § 2–609.

54. U.C.C. § 2–610.

55. U.C.C. § 2–708 (2).

56. 9 Ex. 341, 156 Eng. Rep. 145 (Court of Exchequer, 1854).

57. *Restatement (Second) of Contracts* § 351; U.C.C. § 2–715 (2) (a).

58. U.C.C. § 2–716 (1).

59. Jacob & Youngs v. Kent, 230 N.Y. 239, 129 N.E. 889 (N.Y. Ct. of Appeals, 1921).

60. 16 C.F.R. § 436. *See also,* 44 Fed. Reg. 49,966–49,992 (1979).

61. 16 C.F.R. § 436 (a).

62. Tifford, *The Federal Trade Commission Trade Regulation Rule on Franchises and Business Opportunity Ventures*, 36 Bus. Law. 1051, 1058–59 (1981).

63. *See, e.g.*, Corenswet, Inc. v. Amana Refrigeration, Inc., 594 F.2d 129 (5th Cir. 1979); *contra,* Shell Oil Co. v. Marinello, 63 N.J. 402, 307 A.2d 598 (1973), *cert. denied*, 415 U.S. 920 (1974).

64. 15 U.S.C. §§ 1221, *et seq.*

65. 15 U.S.C. §§ 2801, *et seq.* (the "Petroleum Marketing Practices Act").

9

Contracting with the Federal Government

When a business undertakes to supply goods or services to the United States, the commitment derives from a "public contract." As such, an extensive body of federal regulations applies. These regulations prescribe, among other things, the way a business must bid for a public contract, how the government may change the terms of the agreement, and what procedures must be followed if a dispute arises.

This is not to say that the common law rules of contract are inapplicable. For the most part they are, especially those that govern offer, acceptance, consideration, conditions, damages, and the interpretation of contract language. But the fact remains that supplemental rules apply to contracts between private contractors and the federal government. These rules have been enacted to assist the government in procuring needed supplies and services by establishing uniform and efficient contracting procedures.

The prescribed procedures are intended to respond to the needs of both the government and the contractor. This fairness objective is illustrated by the rule that, even though the United States is a sovereign power, suits may be brought against it by contractors seeking damages for breach of contract. A study of federal enabling statutes, implementing regulations, and court decisions underscores the intentions of Congress, the executive branch, and the courts to balance the interests of the government and the private contractor in public contract transactions. To this end, a contract between a contractor and the United States typically contains numerous standard provisions which, although appearing to be boilerplate, set out specific rights and prerogatives designed to protect the respective interests of both parties.

The federal law regulating aspects of public contracts has its genesis in two enabling statutes which confer the power and authority in the government's executive branch to bind the United States. The statutes are the Federal Property and Administrative Services Act of 1949 (as amended),[1] and the Armed Services Procurement Act of 1947 (as amended).[2] The primary implementing regulation for these enactments is the Federal Acquisition Regulation (FAR).[3]

Pursuant to these federal statutes, the United States of America contracts with businesses and individuals through its executive agencies. The person primarily responsible for exercising this power within an agency is called the "contracting officer." Unlike the manager of a private firm, who ordinarily would be considered to have apparent authority to bind the business beyond his or her actual authority, a contracting officer can bind the United States only to the extent of the actual authority conferred by statute or regulation. Moreover, the government—unlike a private firm—is not bound by the mistakes, misinterpretations, or misrepresentations of its contracting officers.[4] (See Chapter 16 for a discussion on the authority, power, and liabilities of principal and agent in a private context.)

THE PROCUREMENT PROCESS

"Procurement" is the process by which the federal government acquires goods and services. The process begins when an agency determines that it has a need for a specific property or service and culminates with completion of a procurement contract and closeout.

Various governmental departments and agencies enter into procurement contracts through formal advertising seeking competitive bids. Under enumerated circumstances where the bidding process is impracticable, procurements are made through negotiation.[5] Negotiated contracts, however, are the exceptions.

Competitive Bidding

The formal advertising method (also known as the competitive bidding process) for executive agency procurements is governed by federal statutes and regulations. This section discusses executive agency procurements under the Administrative Services Act.[6] A similar procurement procedure applies to agencies within the Department of Defense under the Armed Services Procurement Act.[7] Consequently, before bidding on either a Defense Department procurement or other agency contract, a company should carefully review the relevant statutory provisions and regulations.

The most important federal regulation is the Federal Acquisition Regulation.[8] The FAR was jointly promulgated by the General Services Administration, the Department of Defense, and the National Aeronautics and Space Administration. Prior to April 1, 1984, civilian and defense contracts were governed by separate and disparate sets of federal regulations. All procurement contracts entered into after April 1, 1984, however, must be executed in accordance with the standardized FAR.

An enterprise competing for procurement contracts should initially identify the governmental agency or department with which it wishes to do business. Many agencies have their own specific procurement regulations. These are located primarily in Title 48 of the Code of Federal Regulations.[9] The implementing regulations of the respective agencies together with the FAR make up the Federal Acquisition Regulations System.

The formal advertising process essentially consists of four steps. First, the procuring agency prepares an invitation for bids. Next, the agency solicits bids, usually by mailing the invitations to contractors on a predetermined list maintained by the agency. Third, contractors from the private sector submit their respective bids in response to the invitations. Finally, the agency or department awards the contract. Throughout this process, several practical measures should be taken by a business contractor desiring to bid on a procurement contract. These steps are mentioned in the following discussion.

Preparation of Invitations for Bids

"Full and open competition" is the objective of the government's formal advertising method for procurements. This means that all responsible sources are permitted to submit either sealed bids or, if appropriate, competitive proposals. In order to achieve this objective, an invitation for bids (IFB) must clearly and accurately describe the specific needs of the procuring agency. The invitation includes all documents used in connection with bidding. These documents typically include the specifications for the property to be acquired along with other attachments.

Invitations for bids prepared by executive agencies must list the factors that the agency expects to consider in evaluating the bids, the relative importance assigned to each factor, and the scheduled time(s) and place(s) for both submitting the bids and their opening. In addition, the invitations must indicate whether the bids will be evaluated with or without discussions with bidders. The FAR requires that most invitations for bids follow the *Uniform Contract Format* as closely as practicable.[10] This format includes background information regarding the time for receiving bids, the address of the procuring agency, and a description of the needed supplies or services. Also to be included are instructions to assist the contractor in preparing a bid, as well as various contract clauses expected to be incorporated in any final contract award.

Specifications, which normally form a part of the documentation of bid invitations, must clearly articulate the needs of the procuring agency. These specifications may take several forms depending on the agency's requirements.[11] Specifications may be stated in terms of performance standards, design requirements, or the end functions that the product must serve. The FAR delegates to contracting officers the responsibility of reviewing invitations for bids for ambiguities. Still, the prospective contractor responding to an invitation should check for ambiguities in the specifications and other terms. If the contractor discovers any ambiguities, it should carefully submit its bid explicitly identifying and interpreting the ambiguous matter. If a prospective bidder does not understand certain specifications, he or she should write or telephone the agency for an explanation, which the agency may (and then again, may not) furnish.

Solicitation of Bids

The policy of free and fair competition is reiterated in the FAR regulations relating to bid solicitations. The regulations require that invitations for bids be posted in public places, distributed to prospective contractors, and publicized by other appropriate means. Consequently, these requirements afford several avenues for a business to obtain information regarding prospective governmental contracts.

Contracting agencies of the federal government are required to maintain solicitation mailing lists. These lists are composed of names of contractors or sellers who either have applied to be on the lists or who are considered to be capable by the government (usually because of a prior course of dealing) of fulfilling the agency's procurement requirements. A business person who desires to have his or her firm compete for government contracts should file a "Solicitation Mailing List Application." The regulations require that each applicant be notified as to whether he or she is eligible to be placed on the solicitation list.[12] If the business is eligible, it will be listed according to the items it is deemed capable of furnishing both as to the specifications and the volume of goods or services required.

The solicitation listings are not permanent. A contractor's name may be removed from the list without notice if it fails to respond to an invitation. Therefore, once listed, a contractor should respond to each invitation either by requesting to be retained on the list for the future or by submitting a bid in response.

Even if a contractor is not listed on a particular solicitation mailing list, other methods are available for obtaining invitations.[13] The regulations require contracting officers to have copies of the invitations available in reasonable quantity to be picked up at the appropriate agency contracting office. Even if copies are no longer available, the invitations may be reviewed and duplicated by the contractor. In compliance with the enabling statutory framework,[14] the FAR also requires that notices of invitations for bids for most contracts in the amount of $10,000 or above be published in the *Commerce Business Daily*.[15] Businesses may subscribe to the *Commerce Business Daily* by contacting any Department of Commerce office.

Submission of Bids

Bidders responding to an invitation for bids must do so in timely fashion. In addition, the bids must be "responsive," meaning that they must comply in all material respects with the invitation so that all bidders may stand on an equal footing in the competitive assessment. Failure to respond in a timely and responsive manner normally will preclude a bidder from being eligible for the award.

The FAR requires that invitations for bids provide a reasonable time for respective bidders to prepare and submit their bids.[16] Several factors including anticipated mailing time, agency lead time, and the necessity of expediting a specific procurement determine the bidding period for a particular project. Bids received after the stated deadline in the invitation usually will not be considered. To prevent being held ineligible to receive a contract award, a bidder should timely submit its bid to counteract possible delays in the mail. In a situation involving a government procurement, the time of the bid's receipt rather than the time of mailing is the critical point for determining eligibility.

Where a late bid is received before the contract is awarded, it still may be considered under two circumstances.[17] The first is where the bid was sent by registered or certified mail at least five days before the deadline date. The second is where the government agency mishandles (for example, misplaces) the bid after its receipt. The government alone, of course, decides whether the bid is late due to mishandling. Thus, to be safe, a contractor should mail bids at least five days before the deadline by registered or certified mail.

Bids must be received in the agency office designated in the invitations for bids. Telegraphic bids, however, are sometimes authorized when insufficient time is given for submitting bids through the mail on the normally required bid forms. Telegraphic bids are also authorized when prices are subject to frequent fluctuations.

Submitting a timely bid is part of the responsiveness requirement. In addition, the bidder should meticulously follow all of the submission instructions set out in the invitation; this normally will ensure that the bidder is eligible for the award. Preparation of the bid dollar amount should be done with great care. Contractors generally are held to their clerical mistakes as well as to any errors in judgment reflected in their bids. Thus, the bidder should double and triple check all calculations and make sure that numbers from work sheets are precisely transcribed to the formal bid document.

Frequently, the invitation for bids requires that the bidder submit evidence of its financial strength, along with evidence and statements of nondiscriminatory employment practices. Also, a bidding bond, which guarantees the contractor's performance should the bid be accepted by the government, may be compulsory, particularly if construction services are involved.

Award of the Contract

On the date specified in the invitation, the bids will be publicly opened unless the bids concern a classified project. After opening, the procuring agency is directed to evaluate the bids solely on the factors specified in the invitations for bids.[18] Where sealed bids are deemed inappropriate by the awarding agency or department, the statutes permit executive agencies to request competitive proposals.[19] When the government evaluates competitive proposals, it bases part of its assessment on discussions it has with the bidders (the potential contractors) before rendering an award.

Under the competitive bidding process, the procurement contract must be awarded to the "responsible" source whose bid conforms to the solicitation and is most advantageous to the United States, considering only price and the other price-related factors specified in the solicitation.[20] The FAR lists the factors in addition to the price to be considered by the agency or department in evaluating the bids. These factors include taxes as well as foreseeable costs to the government resulting from differences in inspections, locations of supplies, and transportation facilities. Bidders' requests for changes or modification from those specified in the invitations are also considered.

Finally, the FAR requires the procuring agency to award the contract by furnishing an executed award document to the successful bidder. In addition, all the unsuccessful bidders are to be notified. The formal advertising process is completed with the award of the contract.

Negotiated Contracts

"Negotiation" is defined in the federal regulations as the process by which the government enters into procurements through proposals and discussions rather than by way of sealed bidding (IFB) procedures.[21] Negotiation consists of four steps: solicitation, receipt of proposals and quotations, evaluation and discussions, and contract award. Procurement by negotiation is not authorized unless the needed acquisition falls within one of the following circumstances:

1. The type of goods or services needed are available from only one responsible source;
2. There is such an urgent need for the particular acquisition that the delays inherent in the formal advertising method would seriously injure the government;
3. A particular source is needed to insure that the source will be available for supplying the property or services in a national emergency;
4. A particular source is needed to maintain essential engineering, research, or development capabilities;
5. The terms of a treaty require the use of negotiation procedures;
6. It is authorized by statute or the agency's need is for a brand-name commercial item for authorized resale;
7. Disclosure of an executive agency's needs would endanger national security; or
8. The head of an executive agency gives Congress written notification at least 30 days before the contract award that negotiation procedures are in the public interest.[22]

Once an executive agency determines that it is necessary to utilize the negotiation process, it proceeds through the four steps to complete the procedure.

Solicitations

An agency is authorized to issue solicitations in two principal situations. First, it may solicit proposals through "Requests for Proposals" (RFPs) when it intends to award a contract. Second, it may issue solicitations simply for informational and planning purposes. In the latter case, the government utilizes Requests for Quotations (RFQs) which seek prices, delivery, and other market information.[23] When the needed goods are perishable or when a delay in acquiring the supplies or services would be detrimental to the government, the solicitation does not have to be in writing and may be made orally.

Solicitations ordinarily must follow the Uniform Contract Format.[24] This format requires inclusion of the address of the agency, a description of the goods or services needed, the anticipated delivery and performance dates, various contract clauses to be incorporated, and instructions for making the proposal. The solicitation also sets out factors to be considered by the agency in awarding the contract. Of course, price or cost usually will be a priority concern. Contracting officers using the negotiation process must comply with the same solicitation distribution requirements as applicable to solicitations under the formal advertising procedure.

Receipt of Proposals and Quotations

A contractor responding to either an RFP or RFQ solicitation must submit its proposal or quotation in timely fashion. The responsiveness requirement which governs the formal advertising process also applies to the negotiation method of procurement. The proposal or quotation must be received on or before the time stated in the solicitation. If no time is stated, then 4:30 P.M. local time is the deadline for receipt.[25]

It is imperative that the contractor distinguish between a proposal and a quotation in preparing a response to a solicitation. A proposal is an offer which can be accepted by the executive agency to create a binding contract. A quotation, however, usually is not an offer. Its only purpose is to provide information to the government for planning purposes.[26]

Contractors should also be aware that it is the government's policy to encourage "unsolicited proposals," defined as an independently originated proposal prepared without government supervision. The FAR authorizes and encourages contractors to contact agencies for information on possible contracts prior to preparing unsolicited proposals.

Evaluation, Competitive Range, and Discussions

Following receipt of the bidders' proposals, the agency makes an evaluation and then enters into discussions with those offerors deemed eligible for the contract award. The evaluation includes an assessment of the proposal and of the offeror's ability to perform successfully the proposed contract. The contracting officer conducting the evaluation determines not only whether the price or cost is reasonable, but also whether it reflects the offeror's understanding of the work and evidences its capability of performing the contract work or service.[27] "Price" is defined in the FAR as cost plus whatever fee or profit is applicable to the type of contract to be awarded. The final price term is usually negotiated in detail during the discussions. Other evaluative factors include the offeror's

past performance record, specific expertise and experience, personnel qualifications, and management capabilities.

The purpose of the evaluation is to ascertain those proposals that are within
the "competitive range." This is important because offerors whose proposals
are within the competitive range are deemed to be eligible to enter into discussions
(or negotiations) with the executive agency. Offerors whose proposals are determined to be outside the range are notified by the agency that they are no
longer eligible to compete for the contract.

The eligible offerors are requested by the agency to bargain specific terms of
the proposed contract, including price, work schedule, and various technical
requirements. Bargaining is conducted through oral or written communications
during which the contracting officer may point out deficiencies in the offeror's
proposals and attempt to resolve uncertainties or mistakes. Throughout these
discussions, the contracting officer will permit the offeror to make revisions in
its proposal.[28]

Contract Award

After completion of the discussions, the contracting officer requests a best
and final offer from each offeror still within the competitive range. The officer
then selects the offer that is most advantageous to the government, evaluating
the offers in accordance with the factors listed in the solicitation. The offeror
whose final offer is selected is notified in writing by a "letter contract" of the
contract award.[29] Unsuccessful offerors may request information regarding the
basis of the award selection. This information normally includes an evaluation
of the unsuccessful offeror's proposal. This data may be particularly useful to
the contractor in making subsequent proposals (RFPs) for government contracts.

CONTRACT MODIFICATIONS

The FAR defines "contract modification" as any written change in the contract
terms.[30] Contract modifications may be made either unilaterally by the contracting
officer or bilaterally through the mutual agreement of the contracting officer and
the contractor. All contract changes must be within the general scope of the
agreement.

Bilateral Modifications

Bilateral modification contracts are agreements signed by both the contractor
and the agency's contracting officer. Besides being used to alter the original
contract terms, bilateral modifications are used to finalize letter contracts. A
letter contract is a binding commitment by the governmental agency which
authorizes a contractor immediately to begin manufacturing supplies or performing services.[31] Letter contracts are utilized when the execution of a full written
agreement affords insufficient time to meet the agency's procurement require-

ments. Subsequent to the letter contract, the parties enter into a bilateral modification agreement, which constitutes the final agreement between the parties, superceding the letter contract.

Unilateral Modifications

The private contractor should be aware that once a letter contract has been issued—but no final agreement has been reached on the contract price—the contractor is required to proceed with performance. If the parties still cannot agree on a price, the contracting officer may unilaterally determine the price. The price so "imposed" must be a "reasonable" one. Such a unilaterally set price is, however, subject to appeal by a dissatisfied contractor on the ground that it is not reasonable.

Unilateral contract modifications also result from administrative changes in the terms of the agreement imposed by the contracting officer. In these cases, only the officer's signature is required on a written modifications form. Administrative changes are those that do not affect the substantive rights of either the government or the contractor under the agreement. For example, the government may unilaterally change the location where the contractor is to be paid, commonly called the paying office. This change would be considered an administrative change.

Unilateral modifications are also used to alter existing contract terms pursuant to a "changes" clause. The FAR requires that solicitations and contracts include a changes clause.[32] The clause authorizes the contracting officer to alter or modify contract terms within the general scope of the agreement. When the contract is for supplies, authorized changes are restricted to the government's specifications, the method of delivery, and the place for delivery. When the contract is for services, the changes are restricted to the description of the services, the time of performance, and the place for performance.[33]

Contracting officers making unilateral modifications must issue a written "change order."[34] A change order directs the contractor to make a change without the contractor's consent. When a contractor receives a change order it must ordinarily perform the contract as modified. The contractor is entitled, however, to an equitable adjustment which modifies the contract price or time of performance, or both.[35]

Equitable Adjustments

The availability of equitable adjustments is not restricted to unilateral modifications resulting from the issuance of change orders. The FAR authorizes and even requires a contractor to notify the government in writing when the contractor determines that the government's conduct has constituted a change in the contract terms. The government will review and determine whether its conduct amounts to a change in terms. If the contracting officer confirms that the conduct constituted a change, the contractor is entitled to an equitable adjustment in the specific contract provisions affected.[36] In this situation, the contractor is required to continue performance during the time the equitable adjustment process runs its course.

In summary, the FAR regulations govern the way in which a contracting officer may modify contract terms both unilaterally and bilaterally. In addition, the regulations define the circumstances under which a contractor is entitled to an equitable adjustment. It should be noted, however, that the FAR neither authorizes nor empowers a contractor to alter the terms of its contract with a governmental agency, except through a bilateral modification agreement.

CONTRACT DISPUTE PROCEDURES

A significant difference between ordinary contracts and government contracts concerns dispute resolution procedures. While nongovernmental contract dispute resolutions often begin and end in court, governmental contract dispute resolutions begin under administrative law procedures. These procedures are established pursuant to provisions of the Contracts Disputes Act of 1978.[37] In furtherance of the governmental policy of avoiding litigation where possible, contractor claims initially are decided by the agency contracting officer. If the officer's decision is adverse to the contractor's claim, the contractor may appeal either to the agency board of contract appeals, or to the United States Claims Court located in Washington, D.C. Decisions by an agency board of contract appeals are appealable to the United States Court of Appeals for the Federal Circuit. The law also establishes procedures for expediting the appeal and resolution of small claims.

Submission of Claims

Any contractor who has a contract claim against the United States must submit the claim in writing to the contracting officer of the agency that awarded the contract.[38] A claim seeks the payment of a sum of money, an adjustment or an interpretation of a contract term or terms, or other relief arising under or relating to the contract.[39] A claim under $50,000 should include a request that the decision be rendered within 60 days of receipt of the claim. Without such a request, the contract officer is required to issue a decision within a reasonable time.[40]

Contract claims over $50,000 must be certified; this requires a statement by the contractor that its claim is made in good faith and that the information supporting the claim is accurate and complete to the best of his or her knowledge and belief. In addition, the contractor must state that the claim amount for which it believes the government is liable is accurate.[41]

The contracting officer as the person who initially decides claims relating to executive agency procurement contracts is required to furnish a written decision to the contractor.[42] Prior to rendering a decision, the contracting officer may in his or her discretion hold informal discussions between the parties. If the discussions do not result in a resolution of the dispute, then the contracting officer must render a decision.[43]

The FAR requires that the written decision describe the dispute, refer to the applicable contract terms, state and identify both stipulated and disputed facts, render a decision, and state the reasons for the decision. In addition, the contracting officer must furnish the contractor with information about the procedure for an appeal.[44]

Decisions regarding claims over $50,000 are also generally required to be issued within 60 days after the contracting officer receives the certified claim. However, the contracting officer does not have to issue the decision within 60 days if he or she notifies the contractor of the time within which the decision will be issued. In that situation, the decision must be issued within a reasonable time.[45] Where a contractor feels that there is an undue delay in issuing a decision, it may contact the agency board of contract appeals and request that the board order the officer to issue a decision within a specified period of time. If the contracting officer fails to comply with the board's directive, the failure will be considered a denial of the contractor's claim, authorizing the contractor to appeal to the board or to file suit.

Continuation of Performance

Despite deciding to appeal, a contractor may still be obligated to continue performance under the contract. If the procurement contract contains a "dispute" clause, the contractor generally must continue performance in accordance with the contracting officer's decision, pending a final resolution of the appeal.[46]

Two different varieties of dispute clauses are used by executive agencies.[47] One requires continued performance where the claim arises "under" or is "related to" the contract. A claim arising under the contract is one for which the relief sought by the claimant is available under a contract clause.[48] This clause requires continued performance where the claim arises solely under contract. On the other hand, if the contract dispute clause pertains to claims "related" to the contract, the contracting officer has discretionary power as to whether to finance the continued performance or not. Regardless, the contracting officer must see to it that the government's interests are protected.[49]

While the contractor often is required to continue performance pending its appeal, it is entitled to be paid any amounts determined payable under the contracting officer's decision. The contractor is not required to wait for the outcome of the appeal. Payment, moreover, does not affect the rights of either party.[50] When a judgment is rendered for the contractor, the contractor is entitled to interest on the judgment, starting from the date the contracting officer received the claim.[51]

Appeals

Upon receipt of the contracting officer's decision, a contractor may either appeal to the agency board of contract appeals or bring an action directly in the United States Claims Court. If the contractor decides to file suit, it must do so within one year of the date of receiving the contracting officer's decision.[52] If the contractor decides to appeal to the agency board of contract appeals, it must do so within 90 days.[53]

Board of Contract Appeals

Each executive agency either has its own board of contract appeals or can arrange for an appeal to be decided by the board of another executive agency. Each board is composed of at least three members. Members of a board of contract appeals have the same authority as administrative law judges. The Contract Disputes Act of 1978 requires that the agency board furnish the contractor with a written decision as quickly as possible.[54]

Expedited Appeals

Two alternative procedures are available for expediting the disposition of an appeal. These are known as the accelerated procedure and the small claims procedure. The accelerated procedure is available when the contract claim is for $50,000 or less. Under this procedure, the appeal is required to be resolved within 180 days from the date of the contractor's election to pursue the accelerated remedy.[55] Except for decisions made under the small claims procedure, decisions of the agency board of contract appeals are appealable to the Court of Appeals for the Federal Circuit. The contractor must do so, however, within 120 days of the agency board's decision.[56]

CHALLENGING CONTRACT AWARDS

An unsuccessful bidder for a government procurement contract, in addition to protesting to the agency that made the award, may also seek review of the decision in court or with the Government Accounting Office (GAO) under provisions of the Meritorious Claims Act,[57] as amended. If the GAO decides that the unsuccessful bidder's challenge is meritorious, it may render an advisory opinion, or the comptroller general may recommend to Congress that a private relief bill be enacted.[58] Note that the GAO is not involved in contract disputes but only in an unsuccessful bidder's protest challenging the award process.

The unsuccessful bidder may also have legal standing to challenge a contract award in the federal Claims Court, particularly since 1982 when the Claims Court was first granted the power to grant "declaratory judgments and such equitable and extraordinary relief as it deems proper."[59]

Deficit Reduction Act Procedures

The 1984 Deficit Reduction Act[60] mandates that the comptroller general, through the GAO, initially decide any "protest concerning an alleged violation of a procurement statute or regulation."[61] Once a protest is filed, the contracting agency must stay the procurement action until the protest is decided.[62] In signing the Deficit Reduction Act, however, President Reagan expressed reservations about the constitutionality of the new GAO powers. The problems with the new legislation have led one commentator to conclude that a disappointed bidder "has access to the courts only if an agency refuses to pay," a GAO favorable decision allowing recovery of bidding or proposal costs.[63]

The Competition in Contracting Act, otherwise known as Title Seven of Division B of the Deficit Reduction Act of 1984, also mandates the GAO promulgate implementing regulations. The GAO did so on December 20, 1984.[64] Known as the "Bid Protest Regulations," the rules are published in volume four of the Code of Federal Regulations.[65]

In summary, an unsuccessful or disgruntled bidder or proposer on a government procurement contract has standing to challenge the process (which culminated in an award to another contractor) in the agency, in a federal district court, in the Claims Court in Washington, D.C., with the Government Accounting Office, and, depending on the circumstance, with the General Services Administration. Bid challenges are allowed under law to encourage and to maintain both the integrity of the competitive bidding process and efficiency in government.

AFFIRMATIVE ACTION PLANS; WAGE AND HOUR LAWS

Affirmative Action

Pursuant to the rules of the Office of Federal Contract Compliance Programs, contractors must comply with strict nondiscriminatory requirements in reference to race, color, sex, religion, national origin, and age. Moreover, contractors procuring or negotiating contracts with a price greater than $50,000 must submit as part of their bid or proposal a written "Affirmative Action Plan" or AAP, which sets out specific compliance goals and time frames for their attainment. Also, most government contractors are required to have AAPs for handicapped workers, a plan which requires the contractor to make reasonable accommodations for them.

Area Wage Rates

Workers of contractors working on government contracts are entitled to certain protections under specific federal wage and hours laws, notably, the Walsh-Healey Act,[66] the Davis-Bacon Act,[67] and the Service Contract Act.[68] Pursuant to this legislation, workers generally must be paid either the specified minimum rate of pay in effect, or an area wage rate, whichever is higher. Also, for work performed beyond 8 hours per 24-hour period, overtime pay must be paid.

Before bidding on, or making a written proposal in response to any government procurement solicitation, a contractor should carefully calculate what its labor expenses will likely be in light of the area wage rate criteria. Both primary and secondary contractors are responsible for complying with applicable area wage rate pay schedules for all workers on a government project and also for complying with applicable affirmative action requirements. Primary contractors contract directly with the government; secondary contractors supply goods and services to the project through contracts with the primary contractor. In most instances, primary contractors are general contractors while secondary contractors are sub-contractors. No contractor dealing with the federal government may discriminate in hiring, retaining, or promoting workers on the basis of a worker's race or color, or other protected classifications.

STATE GOVERNMENT CONTRACTS

Contracts with state and local governments are often subject to specific yet diverse state statutes and regulations. Space limitations, however, prevent their treatment in this volume. Suffice it to note that the purpose of state public contracting statutes is also to enhance efficiency and integrity in the bidding process. One example of a state "public contracts" regulatory statute is the 1963 California Subleting and Subcontracting Fair Practices Act, which in part attempts to regulate bid shopping in state construction contracts.[69]

NOTES

1. 41 U.S.C. §§ 251, *et seq.*
2. 10 U.S.C. §§ 2301, *et seq.*
3. 48 C.F.R. § 14.205.
4. See, Smith, *Contracting with the Federal Government: Ten Key Areas*, Chi. Bar Record 240, 242 (Jan.–Feb. 1984).
5. 10 U.S.C. § 2304 (c); 41 U.S.C. § 253 (c).
6. 41 U.S.C. §§ 251–259.
7. 10 U.S.C. §§ 2301–2356.
8. 48 C.F.R. ch. 1.
9. 48 C.F.R. chs. 2–49.
10. 48 C.F.R. §§ 14.201–1 (a).
11. 41 U.S.C. § 253a (1984).
12. 48 C.F.R. § 14.205–1 (b).
13. 48 C.F.R. § 5.102.
14. 15 U.S.C. § 637 (7); 41 U.S.C. § 416.
15. 48 C.F.R. § 5.1.
16. 48 C.F.R. § 14.202–1.

17. 48 C.F.R. § 14.304.
18. 41 U.S.C. § 253b.
19. 41 U.S.C. § 253 (a) (2) (B).
20. 41 U.S.C. § 253b (c).
21. 48 C.F.R. § 15.101.
22. 41 U.S.C. § 253 (c).
23. 48 C.F.R. §§ 15.402 (a)-(f).
24. 48 C.F.R. § 15.406; 48 C.F.R. § 15.605.
25. 48 C.F.R. § 15.412.
26. 48 C.F.R. § 15.402 (e).
27. 48 C.F.R. § 15.608.
28. 48 C.F.R. § 15.610.
29. 48 C.F.R. §§ 15.1002, 15.1003.
30. 48 C.F.R. §§ 43.101, *et seq.*
31. 48 C.F.R. § 16.603.
32. 48 C.F.R. §§ 43.205, 43.103.
33. 48 C.F.R. § 52.243.
34. 48 C.F.R. §§ 43.101, 43.201.
35. 48 C.F.R. §§ 43.204, 43.104.
36. 48 C.F.R. § 52.243-7.
37. 41 U.S.C. §§ 601-603.
38. 41 U.S.C. § 605 (a).
39. 48 C.F.R. § 33.211 (b).
40. *Id.*
41. 48 C.F.R. § 33.207.
42. 41 U.S.C. § 605 (a).
43. 48 C.F.R. § 33.204.
44. 48 C.F.R. § 33.211 (a).
45. 41 U.S.C. § 605 (a).
46. *Id.*
47. 48 C.F.R. § 52.233-1.
48. 48 C.F.R. § 33.201.
49. 48 C.F.R. § 33.213 (b).
50. 48 C.F.R. § 33.211.
51. 41 U.S.C. § 211.
52. 41 U.S.C. § 606.
53. *Id.*
54. 41 U.S.C. § 607.
55. 41 U.S.C. § 607 (f).
56. 41 U.S.C. § 607 (g) (1) (A).
57. 31 U.S.C. § 3702.
58. G.A.O., *Principles of Private Appropriations Law*, 11-137 to 11-142 (1982).
59. 28 U.S.C. § 1491 (a); The Federal Courts Improvement Act of 1982, Pub. L. no. 97-164, 96 Stat. 25-58 (1982).
60. Pub. L. no. 98-369, 98 Stat. 1175 (1984), 31 U.S.C. §§ 3552, *et seq.* (The "Competition in Contracting Act.")
61. 31 U.S.C. § 3554.
62. 31 U.S.C. § 3553 (c).

63. Smith, *Government Contracts: Contesting the Federal Government's Award Decision*, 20 New Eng. L. Rev. 31, 52 (1984–85).

64. 49 Fed. Reg. 36,386–36,390 (1984).

65. 4 C.F.R. §§ 21.0–21.12.

66. 41 U.S.C. §§ 34–45.

67. 40 U.S.C. §§ 276a, *et seq.*

68. 41 U.S.C. §§ 351, *et seq.*

69. Cal. Gov. Code § 4104 (1963).

10

Buying and Selling Goods

This chapter focuses on legal problems that arise in buying and selling goods. These problems include disputes over the quality of the merchandise sold, who bears the risk of loss when goods are destroyed or damaged, and whether the buyer's or seller's printed forms control the terms of the agreement. From the design and manufacture of a good through its advertising, sale, and subsequent use by customers, potential liability may fall on each enterprise involved in the product's origin or movement through the stream of commerce. These include the designer, manufacturer, processor, distributor, jobber, and retailer. This chapter focuses on liabilities arising under the law of sales. Chapter 17 covers liabilities arising under tort theories.

An underlying theme of this chapter suggests that buyers and sellers have opportunities through properly drafted sales agreements to provide for most contingencies by allocating risks and agreeing on remedies, thereby minimizing future misunderstandings. Although such preventive law makes good sense, business realities frequently do not allow the negotiation and drafting of individualized contracts. Consequently, the use of standard, printed forms has become prevalent in many commercial settings. This chapter deals in part with the problems generated by the use of standard forms.

This chapter also discusses remedies of buyers and sellers following common transactional breakdowns. These include pre-performance repudiation as well as claims of improper shipment, tender, and the like. Although certain formation issues are discussed, more emphasis is placed on the creation and limitation of warranty obligations. The law of deceptive advertising and deceptive sales practices, areas principally regulated by the Federal Trade Commission, are also covered as are international sales.

Whenever a sales difficulty arises, the reader should remember that nonlegal considerations bear on the decision of whether or not to pursue an available legal remedy. Lawyers at times tend to forget that a business person, even in the midst of a hotly contested dispute, often expects to deal with his or her disputant in the future. The working out of difficulties through negotiation in most situations is preferable to litigation, especially when considering possible ramifications of a lawsuit on future business relations.

GOVERNING LAW: THE UNIFORM COMMERCIAL CODE

Although many federal, state, and local laws may apply to a given sales transaction, the most extensive legal principles are those contained in a lengthy and complex state statute enacted in 49 states and in the District of Columbia, known as the Uniform Commercial Code.[1] Several common law rules of contract law have been changed by the UCC as applicable to sales. Article Two of the UCC, titled "Sales," covers "transactions in goods." Given this broad scope language, courts on occasion have held that provisions of Article Two apply to leases (rentals), bailments, and consignments of goods in addition to sales.

Scope of Article Two

Article Two explicitly applies to sales of goods, including both current sales and those to occur pursuant to agreement in the future. Sales are defined as transactions where title to goods passes (or will pass) from the seller to the buyer for a price. Goods are defined as "all things" movable at the time the contract is formed.[2] Under this definition, all tangible objects and chattels including raw materials, work-in-process, building materials, standard as well as specially manufactured goods, farm products, inventory items, consumer goods, and equipment are covered. In addition, the unborn young of animals, growing crops, minerals (such as oil and gas) to be extracted by the seller, and timber to be cut—whether severed by the buyer or seller—explicitly are considered goods for purposes of Article Two.

A troublesome scope issue may arise upon a bulk sale of assets consisting of both tangible personal property (goods) and intangible assets (accounts, licenses, good will, and so on). This situation typically comes up in the asset sale of an ongoing business. While certain courts have considered combined asset sales severable, holding that the portion of the contract price represented by the sale of goods (equipment and inventory) falls under the applicable provisions of Article Two, others have held that Article Two does not apply. Regardless, in any sale of the assets of a business, the law seeks to protect the rights of the seller's creditors. Article Six of the UCC, titled "Bulk Sales," and Article Nine, titled "Secured Transactions," are relevant sources of these rights. Bulk sales are discussed in Chapter 4, and secured transactions are covered in Chapter 6.

A more frequent scope problem concerns whether Article Two's rules apply to a mixed sales/service transaction. Ordinarily, the UCC does not apply to renditions of services, for example, to a plumber hired to repair a broken pipe, a carpenter employed to fix a step, a lawyer retained to draft a will, or a physician engaged to set a broken bone. Each of these falls outside Article Two and generally would be subject to the principles of the common law of contracts discussed in Chapter 8. But what about a transaction where a plumber is hired to buy and install a new shower, or a carpenter to buy lumber and build a new deck, or a physician to aid a sick patient and to use whatever may be needed including blood transfusions in that process? In each of these examples, goods are part of the service, as is hair lotion when applied as part of a beauty treatment. In such mixed sales/service cases, the decisional trend has been to consider the goods, even when incidental to the service, to come under the rules of Article Two, particularly those dealing with implied warranties (discussed subsequently). Certain courts, however, have decided these cases on the basis of whether the goods or service predominate in the transaction. Only when the goods predominate, as determined by allocating the price between the goods and service, does the UCC apply, these courts hold. In all situations involving the serving of food or drink for value in a restaurant or elsewhere, the UCC explicitly provides these on-site food and beverage sales to constitute sales of goods for purposes of applying Article Two's implied warranty of merchantability,[3] meaning that the food must be wholesome and fit for human consumption.

UCC's Terminology

Familiarity with the code's essential terminology is necessary to understand the UCC rules. A "seller" is defined as a person (including any business enterprise) who sells or contracts to sell goods; a "buyer" is a person (or business entity) who buys or contracts to buy goods. A buyer or seller may or may not be a "merchant."

A "merchant" under Article Two is a person (or business entity) who deals in goods of the kind being sold or who, by his or her occupation, holds him- or herself out as having knowledge or skill peculiar to the trade or to the goods themselves.[4] The notion is one of a professional in business. Thus, every business that regularly deals in any manner with goods arguably comes within the UCC merchant definition. The designation is important because several code rules prescribe special obligations in the case of merchants. These special rules are applicable to manufacturers, processors, jobbers, distributors, repairers, storers, wholesalers, and retailers. Courts are divided, however, over whether those engaged in farming operations are to be considered merchants under the code.

In many sales transactions, a firm is hired to transport the goods, typically from the seller to the buyer. Transporters, referred to in the UCC as carriers, include railroads, airlines, and trucking companies. A carrier on occasion is denoted a "bailee" in the code. A carrier-bailee is a person who, following receipt of goods from a seller, issues a "bill of lading" (a form of "document of title") in reference to the goods and who thereby acknowledges both its possession of the goods and its contract to deliver them to the buyer or to some other designated person denoted the "consignee."

A document of title, of which a bill of lading is only one species, is any written document regularly used and recognized in business or financing as evidencing that the person holding the document is entitled to receive, hold, and dispose of the document as well as the goods that it covers. Bailees, including all common carriers and warehouse companies, are empowered to issue documents of title. Another widely used document of title is a "warehouse receipt," defined as a document issued by a person engaged in the business of storing goods for hire. In contrast, a "bill of lading," including an "ocean" bill of lading, evidences receipt of goods for shipment and is issued by a carrier engaged in transporting or forwarding goods. "Airbills" are bills of lading used for the air transportation of goods. The person who arranges a contract for transportation is called the shipper or "consignor." In most sales situations, the shipper will be the seller.

Documents of title, if they appear to be in proper form, ordinarily are taken at face value. Such documents are afforded prima facie evidence of authenticity and genuineness under the code. Although documents of title are commonly used in sales of goods, the law governing their issuance, use, and liability is found not only in Article Seven of the UCC but also in the Federal Bills of Lading Act[5] and in the Carmack Amendment to the Interstate Commerce Act.[6] To the extent that federal statutes do not govern, Article Seven of the UCC (state law) applies to determine the obligations and liabilities of issuers and holders of documents.[7]

In addition to the statutes noted above, Congress has enacted other laws regulating the transportation of goods. These include the Perishable Agricultural Commodities Act of 1938[8] and the Carriage of Goods by Sea Act of 1936.[9] Moreover, the Interstate Commerce Commission (ICC) has promulgated regulations applicable to carriers involved in the interstate transportation of goods. These ICC regulations are the basis of many obligations and, thus, are relevant to a carrier's potential liability.[10]

Core Concepts of Article Two

Agreement

Of the code's significant central or core concepts, one of the more important concerns the definitions of "agreement" and "contract." The words are not synonymous, although many lawyers and judges usually consider them to be equivalent.

The UCC defines "agreement" as the bargain of the parties in fact as found in their *language or by implication from other circumstances*.[11] The code's "other circumstances" consist of "course of dealing," "course of performance," and "usage of trade." What this means is that the obligations in a sales transaction may derive not only from the explicit, written agreement but also from the buyer's and seller's behavior prior to and following their written agreement. Certain obligations, moreover, may have their genesis in the patterns of behavior of the industry or trade as a whole, which the code refers to as a "usage of trade."

More specifically, a "course of dealing" is defined as a sequence of previous conduct between the parties to a sale which is to be regarded as establishing a basis for their respective expectations of the obligations to be performed under their present agreement. Thus, if a seller in previous transactions with a particular buyer paid the shipping costs and in the current contract with the same buyer (when the writings are silent as to who pays shipping) refuses to pay the shipping expense, the buyer may argue that the prior course of dealing between them adds the term, meaning that the seller is obligated to pay for the shipping. The prior course-of-dealing evidence is used to supply the silent or missing term. Course-of-dealing evidence may also be used to interpret or explain the written terms of the parties' agreement, especially if those terms are ambiguous. Course-of-dealing-generated obligations may become part of the parties' total legal undertaking either by explicit incorporation in the written agreement or by tacit recognition.

"Course of performance," on the other hand, refers to a pattern of conduct of one or both parties in performing the ongoing (existing) contract. For example, if in an installment contract calling for periodic deliveries by the seller, the first few deliveries are tendered late, and the buyer fails to object, the buyer subsequently may not be permitted to object to further late deliveries because of his or her acquiescence in the seller's earlier, dilatory course of performance. Thus, a specific obligation in a sales agreement may, on occasion, be modified by a subsequent course of performance.

"Usage of trade," in contrast, is a commercial practice having such regularity in a location, vocation, or trade as to justify an expectation that it will be part of the sales contract even when the written agreement is silent as to the specific trade usage. For example, the custom in the lumbering trade of having so-called 2 by 4's measure closer to 1¾ by 3¾ is a usage of trade. A usage of trade, like a course of dealing or course of performance, may either supplement or interpret the parties' written expression of their agreement.

Given the code's recognition that the terms of a sales agreement may be supplemented or affected by obligations which arise out of course of dealing, course of performance, and trade usages, a business should carefully review each of these areas to decide whether it should revise its contracting forms or procedures specifically to incorporate, negate, or limit such trade- or conduct-generated obligations. Certainly, if a lawyer is employed to draft or revise a sales agreement or form, he or she should be informed of all known courses of dealing and trade usages that might bear on the parties' total "agreement."

Contract

An important code word to be differentiated from "agreement" is "contract." Whereas agreement is the bargain of the parties as found in their writings and as supplemented and explained by possible trade usage, course of dealing, and course of performance terms, the sales "contract" is the total legal obligation of the parties, including those legal requirements supplied by applicable rules of law, principally, Article Two of the UCC.[12] These supplemental obligations result from the "gap filler" provisions of the code. For example, if the parties' agreement is silent as to the seller's time of performance, the code provides that it must occur within a reasonable time of the making of the agreement. If the agreement fails to specify the place of delivery, the code says it shall be at the seller's place of business. If the agreement is silent as to when the buyer is to pay for the goods, the code prescribes that payment shall be due at the time and place where the buyer is to receive the goods. Should the parties fail to agree on the price term but otherwise conclude a bargain and act accordingly, then the price will be a "reasonable price" at the time of tender. In addition to the ones just mentioned, the code has several other gap filler provisions. From a buyer's perspective, the most important gap fillers usually will be Article Two's implied warranty provisions (discussed subsequently).

Two other Article Two core concepts deserve explanation. One concerns what the code calls the good faith obligation and the other, the doctrine of unconscionability. Although these concepts are rather amorphous, it is fair to state that they tend to require the parties in any sales transaction to act in a commercially reasonable manner in both the negotiation and performance phases of the transaction.

Good Faith Obligation

Every business person who buys or sells goods should be aware of the code's good faith obligation. The UCC's general definition of good faith—"honesty in fact in the conduct or transaction concerned"—does not, however, explain the thrust of the obligation. For one thing, good faith violations extend beyond fraud, lying, and cheating. A separate UCC definition of good faith as applicable to merchants (all businesses buying or selling goods) is a bit more illuminating. It states that good faith means "honesty in fact and the observance of reasonable commercial standards of fair dealing in the trade."[13] This definition underscores a key point: Good faith is a normative standard by which courts appraise the reasonableness of a buyer's and seller's respective actions. A normative legal standard is a standard of conduct that the law considers normally is or should be followed. The law of torts, for example, consists largely of normative rules, framed typically in terms of the mythical reasonable person standard of due diligence. In the law of sales, however, the good faith obligation is a normative commercial standard of reasonableness which, although incapable of precise definition, can perhaps best be explained in economic terms. Thus, when two parties enter into a sales agreement they not only bind themselves, they also give up their freedom to enter into other bargains covering the same subject matter. Consider the following hypothetical situation.

On Monday, Buyer agrees to buy 1,000 widgets for $10 per widget from Seller, delivery to take place on Wednesday in exchange for the $10,000 total price. On Tuesday, Buyer learns he can buy identical widgets from a different supplier for $8 per widget. Should the Buyer attempt to avoid his $10 per widget contract with Seller, for example, by arguing that on Wednesday, Seller tendered only 998 widgets and, for that reason, Buyer does not have to perform, a court might conclude that Buyer under these facts acted in "bad faith," even though the UCC ordinarily allows a buyer to reject anything less than a "perfect tender." An economist, on the other hand, might point out that Buyer was attempting to "recapture a lost economic opportunity" by avoiding his contract with Seller so Buyer could obtain the desired goods at a cheaper price. Bad faith, in short, was trying to get out of a bargain because a prospective, more advantageous one became known to Buyer. The "perfect tender rule of Article Two" in this example would be held subject to the overriding good faith obligation.

Thus, it might be said that the good faith obligation makes relevant why a party under a sales agreement acted in a particular way to avoid or modify that agreement. Consider these examples: A buyer attempts to avoid a sales bargain because, subsequent to the agreement, he or she learns that it is possible to purchase the goods for a lower price from a different seller, a seller seeks avoidance because he or she learns that he or she could sell goods to another for a higher price than that agreed upon. Courts often find bad faith in these and other analogous situations.

Another area where the good faith standard applies is that of sales modifications. Article Two permits the parties to an existing sales contract to agree to change or modify the terms of their agreement, even when one of the parties receives nothing new in exchange for his or her promise to go along with the modification.[14] (This is at variance with the common law rule requiring new consideration.) If, however, the party seeking the change—for example, a seller who informs a buyer that it will not furnish the promised goods unless the buyer agrees to pay a higher price—coerces the modification, courts have held that the modification is unenforceable as it resulted from duress. Another reason given is that a coerced contract violates the good faith obligation of the UCC. Although most price adjustments in sales agreements are enforceable, the courts will grant relief when no legitimate commercial reason for the adjustment is present and if it resulted from economic coercion or duress. This occurs, for example, where one party extracts the adjustment under circumstances where the other party had a definite and immediate need for the goods and the seller, knowing of that need, took advantage of it.

In summary, to act in good faith means to act in a reasonably commercial manner keeping in mind the legitimate commercial needs of both parties to the agreement. What may be required as to specific conduct, of course, depends on the circumstances of the particular transaction. It should be noted, however, that the UCC's good faith obligation applies only to the post-agreement performance phase of a sales transaction; it does not apply to the negotiation phase. The concept of unconscionability has greater relevancy to the negotiation or pre-agreement phase of the transaction.

Unconscionability Standard

The UCC provides that if a court finds that a contract or any clause or term of a contract was "unconscionable" at the time the agreement was made, the court may refuse to enforce the contract, or it may give other appropriate relief.[15] The doctrine of unconscionability, like the obligation of good faith, is a normative standard which courts use from time to time to "police" bargains. As such, the doctrine is disfavored by certain scholars. The idea that courts should police bargains and decide which among them are "fair" and deserving of enforcement and which are not conflicts with the more traditional notion about the role of courts in private contracts. According to this view, courts should ascertain only whether a bargain has been formed, what the terms are, whether one party has breached an obligation, and, if so, what the appropriate relief, either by way of damages or through specific performance, reformation, or rescission, should be. The "fairness" of the exchange, according to the traditional view, is not a matter for judicial scrutiny. Yet, despite the controversial nature of the doctrine of unconscionability, it has been explicitly incorporated into the modern law of sales under section 2–302 of the UCC. Moreover, the doctrine in recent times increasingly has been applied by courts, particularly in sales involving consumer buyers and retail sellers.

The exact parameters of unconscionability—even more than in the case of the good faith obligation—defy easy demarcation. Still, it can be said generally that, while good faith applies to the performance phase of a contract, unconscionability often involves the bargaining or pre-agreement process leading up to the actual sale. Thus, when holding a contract or a clause to be unconscionable, a court typically evidences a concern not only with the fairness of the resulting bargain but also, and in many cases more importantly, with how that bargain came about. In assessing the contracting process, a court often will consider the educational backgrounds, positions, and levels of sophistication of the respective parties. On occasion, these socioeconomic factors become crucial to a court's finding of unconscionability.

A court might also look for evidence of "overreaching" where one party (usually the seller), having economic and knowledge superiority, uses that position of dominance to extract a legally one-sided agreement from the other. A legally one-sided agreement is one in which the dominant party puts into the agreement all the legal powers, rights, and prerogatives it (or its counsel) can think of, while limiting to the fullest possible extent its own responsibilities and, thereby, the rights of the weaker party. This one-sided "adhesion contract" usually involves printed forms containing small print coupled with a "take it or leave it" attitude by the merchant seller. These factors may preclude the possibility of any meaningful bargaining taking place by the economically weaker party who typically is a consumer buying goods or services on credit from a merchant seller or contractor.

This is not to say that all standardized, printed form agreements used by retailers and contractors routinely will be held to be unconscionable—far from it. But, depending on the circumstances, such form contracts may be attackable. For example, a consumer who buys a piano pursuant to a standard form and who at the time of sale did not understand that, if he or she missed a payment, the seller could repossess not only the piano but also the buyer's refrigerator (purchased six months earlier from the same seller) by reason of a cross-collateral clause in the piano sales agreement may be able to persuade a court that the cross-collateral clause was unconscionable. In some states, such cross-collateral consumer good clauses are prohibited by statute. In states not having statutes proscribing such clauses, a consumer's chances to avoid the contract will improve if it is found that he or she could not read the contract (poor education or lack of fluency in English); if he or she was told to "sign here, don't bother to read all the legal mumbo-jumbo"; if he or she is a member of a disadvantaged, low-income group; if he or she was subjected to high-pressure or deceptive sales tactics; if he or she was on welfare and the seller knew that fact when making the sale; or if the item sold is considered by the court to be a "frill," or non-necessity.

In short, unconscionability turns on all the circumstances present. Rarely does a court hold a contract clause to be per se unconscionable. Rather, a court will hold a contract or clause unconscionable only under the attending circumstances, especially if questionable or unethical seller conduct occurred at the point of sale. Significant exceptions to the non-per se principle are contract clauses which seek to limit consequential damages for personal injuries resulting from defective goods. The UCC provides that a damage limitation for personal injury is prima facie unconscionable but that limitation of damages where the loss is commercial is not.[16]

As to the more common situation, in which a clause is claimed to be unconscionable under the circumstances present, the gist of a consumer's argument will likely be that oppression or unfair surprise resulted. In the above hypothetical situation involving the cross-collateral clause, the unfair surprise to the consumer-buyer was his or her learning after the contract had been signed that the seller had given itself, through its form contract, the legal right to repossess not only the piano sold but also the buyer's refrigerator. It is this type of situation courts are referring to when they describe a seller's conduct as involving "overreaching." Given the potential for consumer claims of unconscionability, a retail business at a minimum should instruct its sales force to explain to prospective buyers of "big ticket items" the remedies available to the seller should the buyer default. This explanation should occur prior to the sales agreement's being signed by the buyer. Also, all the blanks should be filled in before the purchaser signs.

Two other aspects of unconscionability deserve noting. First, the code provides that a court may decide not to enforce an unconscionable contract. This language points out that the remedy is discretionary, not mandatory. Second (and related to the discretionary point), section 2–302 of the UCC provides that, before holding a contract or clause within a contract to be unconscionable, a court shall afford the merchant-seller an opportunity to present evidence regarding the contract's "commercial setting, purpose and effect to aid the court in making the determination."[17]

Although the unconscionability doctrine most frequently is invoked in consumer sales situations, on occasion it has been applied to commercial contracts between merchants. The issue, for example, has arisen in cases involving "at-will" franchise termination clauses which if literally enforced would allow a franchiser or manufacturer to terminate a franchisee or dealer at any time for any reason, even one deemed "arbitrary or capricious." Certain courts have found such at-will termination clauses to be either unconscionable or subject to the good faith requirement of the code. In effect, these holdings suggest that a franchise or dealership can be terminated only for a legitimate commercial reason and that the reason cannot be arbitrary or capricious. Several state or federal statutes also regulate the termination of certain categories of independent distributors, for example, automotive dealerships and petroleum retailers.

In summary, an unconscionable contract or clause is one that is deemed to be legally one sided and that has resulted from one party's having used its dominant position to the surprise or oppression of the weaker party. The doctrine predictably may gain a wider acceptability in the courts in the coming years as judges consider the fairness of bargains.

COMMON SALES TRANSACTIONS

Before delving deeper into the provisions of Article Two, we first review common varieties of sales transactions. These include closed-end sales, firm offers or options, requirements and output contracts, installment sales, sales on approval or return, auction sales, exclusive dealing contracts, and sales of specifically manufactured goods.

Closed-End Sale

A closed-end sale is one in which the buyer and seller pursuant to a sales agreement exchange money for goods. There is neither an ongoing sales relationship (as in requirements, output, and exclusive dealing arrangements) nor an overriding agreement covering a large number of future sales transactions. A closed-end sale may or may not be on open account, that is, where the seller relinquishes control over the goods prior to receipt of full payment, deferring his or her right for immediate payment upon delivery.

Typical Forms Sale

Although the closed-end sale can come about in several ways, a common method involves an exchange of forms between the buyer and seller as typified by the following pattern:

1. Buyer communicates with prospective seller seeking price quotations or price lists of seller's products.
2. Seller in response transmits price list or quotations to prospective buyer.
3. Buyer in turn transmits its printed purchase order to seller, specifying the items and amounts of each it desires to purchase.
4. Seller, following receipt of buyer's purchase order, sends back either a printed acknowledgement or a written confirmation indicating it has received the order and intends to fill it.
5. Seller then proceeds to identify and make ready the goods called for in the purchase order and arranges for their transportation to buyer's business by contracting with a carrier for shipment.
6. Seller tenders goods to carrier who transports them to buyer's city.
7. Buyer inspects and takes possession of the goods either by tendering proper documents (after having earlier paid against the documents) or by taking delivery on open (credit) account and later paying against the invoice transmitted from the seller.

In the sale just described, it should be noted that no single contract or writing constituted the parties' agreement. Rather, the sales agreement resulted from all the communications and conduct of the parties. The problem of ascertaining what the terms consist of in a "forms contract" is discussed subsequently in this chapter.

Auction Sales

In an auction sale the parties become bound when the auctioneer announces the fall of the hammer. The sale may be by item or lots. More importantly, an auction sale may be "with reserve," meaning that the auctioneer may withdraw the goods at any time until he or she announces completion of the sale. In an auction "without reserve," the auctioneer cannot withdraw the article after calling for bids unless no bids are received within a reasonable time of the item's being put up for sale. In either case, the UCC allows a bidder to retract his or her bid until the auctioneer's announcement of completion of the sale.[18] The code also allows sellers to make bids themselves or to have others bid for them, but unless this fact has been made known at the auction, a buyer whose bid was accepted may avoid the sale at his or her option.

Continuing Sales Arrangements

Article Two recognizes and validates several types of continuing sales arrangements[19] which extend over time and involve successive or periodic deliveries by the seller. These include requirements, output, and exclusive dealing contracts.

Requirements Contracts

A requirements contract is one in which the seller has obligated itself for a particular or indefinite time period to buy all of its actual requirements for a particular good from a specific seller who in return agrees to supply those requirements. The fact that the amount required for a given time period is or may be indefinite is not fatal so long as the buyer demands the seller meet only the buyer's actual requirements as occur in good faith. Manufacturers, utility companies, and processors, for example, enter into requirements contracts for needed supplies and raw materials.

Output Contracts

An output contract is one in which the quantity term is measured by the output of the seller. The seller agrees to sell its entire output of a product for a specified period of time to a particular buyer who agrees to purchase the goods. Again, the UCC's good faith obligation applies so that a seller must sell what it produces in good faith and, thus, cannot tender a quantity either far greater or lower or one unreasonably disproportionate to a stated estimate or, if none, to any normal or comparable prior output (for example, during the prior years of the agreement).

Exclusive Dealing Contracts

An exclusive dealing contract is one in which the buyer and seller agree to deal exclusively in the specific kind of goods (or brand) being sold, usually within a designated territory. Many varieties of exclusive sales contracts are commonly used. Under one form, a buyer may agree to purchase for resale the dishwashers of a particular manufacturer within a given marketing territory. In return, the seller, for example, a manufacturer, may agree to supply only that buyer within the specified territory with the particular brand involved. Under an exclusive sales agency, the UCC imposes an obligation upon a buyer to use its "best efforts" to expand the market and promote the resale of the seller's goods. Similarly, unless otherwise agreed, the UCC requires the seller in an exclusive dealing arrangement to use its "best efforts" to supply the goods required by its sales agent (the buyer) and not to supply any other dealer or agent within the designated exclusive territory during the duration of the agreement.

Although exclusive dealing is a recognized sales method under the code, if under a particular agreement the exclusive area is very large or in other respects the agreement has the effect of unreasonably restraining competition, a court may hold the arrangement to be violative of the federal antitrust laws, more specifically, either the Sherman or Clayton acts.[20] Apart from these laws, a court may hold the agreement to be unenforceable as against the public policy of promoting competition, reasoning that the exclusive dealing contract if enforced would result in an unreasonable restraint on competition.

Override Agreements

When a buyer and seller expect over a period of time to enter into a large number of sales transactions rather than exchanging purchase orders and acknowledgement forms for each sale, they may (and arguably should) negotiate an "override contract." An override agreement is intended to govern all future sales between the parties. It is referred to as an "override" because it replaces or alters specific boilerplate terms set out in the parties' forms. For example, it might be used when a Florida seller of fresh produce contemplates continuing sales over time to a Chicago produce jobber.

Sales on Approval or Return

Article Two provides that if delivered goods may be returned by the buyer, even when they conform to the agreement, the transaction is a "sale on approval" if the goods are delivered primarily for the buyer's own use or a "sale or return" if the goods are delivered primarily for resale by the buyer.[21] A sale on approval does not become final until the buyer accepts the goods either by so indicating or by failing to reject them within a reasonable time after having a reasonable opportunity to inspect.

Prior to acceptance, the risk of casualty loss to the goods remains on the seller. In a sale or return contract, the buyer has the option to seasonably return any goods not resold, but the buyer bears the risk of loss and expense of the return.[22] Generally, goods held on approval are not subject to the claims of buyer's creditors until acceptance, but goods bought on return are, unless the buyer posts signs in its store indicating it is holding goods on a consignment basis.

Sales of Specially Manufactured Goods

Sales include sales of existing goods and agreements to sell goods not yet in existence. In the latter case, a contract for goods not yet in existence is denoted a sale of "future goods." If the goods are to be manufactured by the seller pursuant to the buyer's specifications, then the goods are considered to be specially manufactured for the buyer. If the buyer repudiates a sales agreement before such goods are completed, the seller may, in the exercise of reasonable commercial judgment for the purpose of avoiding loss, either complete the manufacture of the goods or cease manufacture and resell for scrap or salvage value.[23]

Firm Offers

The UCC validates "firm offers." A firm offer is an offer to buy or sell which is irrevocable for the stated time or, if no time is stated, for a reasonable time (which in any event may not exceed three months). Although firm offers under common law are unenforceable unless supported by a separate consideration (in which case the offer becomes an option contract), the UCC has obviated the consideration requirement when the firm offer is made by a merchant in a potential sale of goods transaction.

Home Office Approval Sales

In certain sales situations, it is common for a seller of goods to use a "home office approval" form. In such a case, the seller has the buyer sign the seller's form after the seller has filled in the agreed-upon terms. According to the printed terms, the buyer is the one "making the offer." The seller then may reject or accept the buyer's offer by subsequent approval at the seller's home office. The purposes of home office approval forms are twofold. First, their use affords a seller time to investigate the creditworthiness of a prospective buyer prior to becoming bound. Second, and of greater significance, a seller may closely supervise its field personnel by retaining the power to reject disadvantageous deals tentatively struck by overzealous sales people.

When home office approval forms are used, it is common to include a term requiring the offeror (prospective buyer) to keep its offer open for a stated period. If such a term is included, UCC section 2–205 requires that the firm offer portion of the seller's supplied form be separately signed by the buyer to be enforceable.

Installment Contracts

The code defines an "installment contract" as one which requires or authorizes a seller's delivery of goods in separate lots and to be separately accepted, even when an override agreement provides that each delivery or lot is to be considered a separate contract.[24] Thus, the UCC rules applicable to installment contracts apply whenever the seller may perform its obligations by tendering separate deliveries.

The most frequent problem involving installment sales concerns a buyer's rights following tender or delivery of a nonconforming installment by the seller. If the nonconformity substantially impairs the value to the buyer of that installment, but not of the contract as a whole, then the buyer may reject that installment, provided the defect cannot be seasonably cured by the seller. If the seller gives an adequate assurance that it will correct the defect, the buyer must accept the nonconforming installment. On the other hand, if the nonconformity, with respect to one or more installments, is so great as to substantially impair the value of the whole contract, then there is a breach of the whole by the seller, and the buyer may suspend its own performance and pursue any remedies provided for under the code.

Retail Installment Sales Contracts

A retail installment sales contract is an agreement in which the seller has deferred its right to receive immediate payment for all or a portion of the price by allowing the buyer to pay off the balance in periodic installments. Although not specifically defined in the UCC, such contracts are widely used. In addition to defining "events of default," installment payment contracts often include a "default-acceleration" clause. An acceleration clause provides that, should the buyer default on any payment or other obligation, the entire indebtedness becomes immediately due and owing. Certain states have legislatively defined the circumstances under which default acceleration can occur in consumer transactions. Under these statutes, a grace period for payment is generally prescribed. Other problems involving these contracts are discussed in Chapter 11.

A retail installment sales contract ordinarily is one which the code describes as a security agreement by which a seller reserves a security interest in the goods sold (called the collateral) to secure the buyer's obligations as they become due. Unless the seller expressly reserves a security interest or includes words with similar import (for example, by reserving "title" to the goods sold), the sales contract is considered an unsecured sale.

Secured and Unsecured Sales

A seller, by simply selling goods on credit, does not thereby obtain a security interest or lien in the goods even if the buyer defaults in his or her payments. Consequently, an unsecured seller may not repossess the goods from the buyer through self-help methods. An unsecured seller in most cases will have to go to court to try to collect the debt. (Collection practices are discussed in Chapter 13.)

A "secured seller," on the other hand, is one who, through a security agreement, has reserved a security interest in the goods sold. A security interest under the UCC is defined as an interest in personal property or fixtures which secures the payment or performance of an obligation.[25] Regardless of what the particular form of the sales agreement might be, if the writings evidence the intention of the seller to reserve an interest in the goods sold to secure the buyer's obligation to pay the balance of the price, the UCC considers the sales transaction to include a security agreement. Many pre-UCC forms still in use today qualify as UCC security agreements. These include chattel mortgages, retail installment sales contracts, conditional sales agreements, trust receipts, and reservation-of-title contracts.[26] (Secured financing is discussed in Chapter 6.)

FORMATION OF THE SALES AGREEMENT

Sales agreements come about through three principal routes: by using forms, through negotiations, or orally. Of the three, the use of forms is the most common.

Battle of the Forms

Under the Common Law

As outlined earlier in this chapter, a typical forms sale results when the parties exchange a printed purchase order and a sales acknowledgement or other similar forms. Under the common law, if the offeree's acceptance does not mirror exactly the terms set out in the offeror's offer, the purported acceptance is deemed to constitute both a rejection of that offer and the proposal of a counteroffer.

When this common law contract formation principle was applied to "exchange of forms" sales transactions, uncertainty resulted. Because the printed forms used by the buyer and the seller were rarely identical, the parties often were not sure whose forms controlled. For one thing, it was not always clear which document was to be considered the controlling offer. For another, it was unclear when and how acceptance occurred. In applying the common law mirror image rule, courts often held that the last form sent prior to shipment or receipt of the goods prevailed. Why? Because the last form was deemed a rejection of the earlier form's counteroffer; the last form thus became the final counteroffer. Courts then held that the last form's terms were accepted either by the seller upon its shipment of the goods (when the buyer had sent the last form), or by the buyer upon its taking delivery of the goods (where the seller had sent the last form). In short, acceptance of the terms set out in the last transmitted form was deemed to have occurred by the receiving party's subsequent conduct.

Because the last form prior to shipment of the goods usually is the seller's printed acknowledgement or confirmation, the common law mirror image rule often made the seller's form the operative counteroffer, which the buyer was then deemed to have accepted by its subsequent taking delivery of the goods.

There is, however, one problem: Buyers and sellers normally do not read or pay the slightest attention to the boilerplate included on each other's forms, until, that is, something goes wrong. When applied, the common law mirror image rule tends to favor sellers, especially since sellers' forms often contain disclaimers of warranty, liability exculpatory clauses, and limitation of remedy clauses. Consequently, a seller's terms in most instances would prevail in the battle of the forms if the common law rules applied. The situation, however, has been reversed under the UCC.

UCC Section 2–207

Section 2–207 of the UCC was drafted specifically to address the battle of the forms problem. The section deals with two related problems: first, whether in an exchange of forms situation a contract has been formed and, second, if so, whether the buyer's or seller's terms govern.

The rules of the section are difficult and not happily drafted. It may be said that the UCC section favors the offeror rather than the offeree (who had been favored under the mirror image). Considering again the typical exchange of forms, under section 2–207, the buyer's purchase order would in most situations be considered the offer. The seller's subsequent acknowledgment or written confirmation form would then be considered an acceptance of the offer, even though the acceptance contained terms "different from or additional to" those contained in the original offer. Between merchants, the additional terms become part of the bargain unless: (1) the offer expressly limits acceptance to the terms of the offer (round two in the battle); (2) the additional terms materially alter the contract; or (3) the offeror timely objects.

What this means is that terms that normally would be considered material and important to the offeror—for example, price, quantity, and warranties—cannot be negated or altered by an offeree who mails a printed acknowledgement or written confirmation. Why? Because any such alteration would materially alter the offeror's expectations. This rule applies when the agreement is one between merchants. Consider a seller's attempt through its confirmation to disclaim warranties which otherwise would arise in the contract by way of the UCC's gap-filler implied warranty provisions.[27] Section 2–207 would in many cases render a seller's printed disclaimer ineffective on the basis that the disclaimer never became part of the parties' contract.

On the other hand, minor details of performance often will become part of the sales contract when a merchant offeree includes such additional terms in his or her confirmation. For example, a seller might add a specific delivery date, a term regarding insurance, or a method of shipment. These become part of the sales bargain because they are thought not to alter materially the offeror's obligations or expectations.

Understand that the rules of section 2–207 do not always favor buyers over sellers. Still, given that buyers tend more often than not to be the offerors in exchange of forms contracts, it might properly be said that buyers generally (but not always) have an important advantage under section 2–207.

Protecting the Seller in the Battle

If a seller wishes to fill a buyer's purchase order but also wants to avoid liability under the UCC's implied warranty gap fillers, simply having a conspicuous disclaimer properly worded on its form normally will not be sufficient, even if the seller's form is the last document sent prior to shipment.

Section 2–207 provides that the seller's confirmation serves as an acceptance of the buyer's offer unless the seller's "acceptance is expressly made conditional on assent to the additional [disclaimer] or different terms."[28] The best and perhaps only way for a seller-offeree to take advantage of this exception is to send its "unless form language," then to delay shipment and wait until it receives from the buyer the latter's assent in writing. This may require a phone call or two by the seller to the buyer, but, if the buyer is willing to buy under the seller's disclaimer term, the buyer should be made to evidence that agreement by assenting in writing before the seller ships the goods. Any other strategy is precarious from a seller's perspective, especially if it is trying to limit its liability under the UCC's implied warranty provisions. This is so because courts have been quick to invoke subsection (3) of section 2–207, which provides that, if the parties' writings do not evidence an agreement, then their sales contract consists of those terms on which the writings do agree, plus the supplemental, gap-filler provisions of the UCC. When this section is applied, one result is to negate a seller's efforts to disclaim warranty liability through its acknowledgement or confirmation forms. Although it was not the drafters' principal purpose, section 2–207 makes it more difficult for a seller of goods to escape potential warranty liability.

Oral Agreements

Following exchange of forms contracts, oral agreements constitute the second most common type of sales transaction whether made over the telephone or face to face. The UCC recognizes the validity of oral agreements although certain ones may be unenforceable under Article Two's "statute of frauds" provision.[29]

The UCC Statute of Frauds

In any possible statute of frauds application, three questions should be asked and answered. First, does the transaction come within the scope of the statute? Second, if it does, have the statute's requirements for enforceability been satisfied? Third, even if the requirements have not been satisfied, is the particular agreement nonetheless enforceable because events have occurred which take the transaction outside the rule prohibiting enforcement?

The UCC's Article Two statute of frauds provision states that any contract for the sale of goods "for the price of $500 or more is not enforceable . . . unless there is some writing sufficient to indicate that a contract has been made" and which is signed by the party against whom enforcement is sought.[30] Under this rule, only sales contracts for $500 or more need be evidenced by a writing. This is not to say that the entire agreement must be written. Rather, the rule requires only that there be a "sufficient writing indicating" that a contract has been made which evidences the intention of both parties to be bound. Consequently, the actual writing requirement is minimal. In transactions between merchants, not even a signature is required in all cases. Moreover, many essential terms may be omitted from the writing with one important exception. A sales contract coming under section 2–201 will be enforceable only to the extent of the quantity stated in the writing.

Events that may take a transaction outside the UCC's statute of frauds include a seller's acceptance of a buyer's payment or a buyer's acceptance of a seller's tendered goods. These rules represent a codification of the common law's part-performance exceptions, which made certain oral agreements, normally not enforceable, enforceable. Also, as between merchants, a form confirmation is deemed a sufficient writing if received and not timely objected to, even though it is not signed by the receiving party.[31] In the case of goods to be specially manufactured for a buyer, which are not suitable for sale to others, again no writing is required if the seller has made a substantial beginning of their manufacture at the time of the buyer's breach.[32]

Even though the UCC does not require all sales agreements to be in writing and requires only those having an original or modified price of $500 or more to be evidenced by a writing, good business practice and preventive law considerations dictate that agreements be written as completely and precisely as possible. Agreements skillfully reduced to writing often resolve or at least mitigate later disputes and misunderstandings. Only fully negotiated contracts ordinarily can accomplish this objective.

Negotiated Sales Agreement

Perhaps the most important advantage of a fully negotiated and competently drafted sales agreement is the minimization of subsequent disputes which might lead to costly litigation. The disadvantages are the time needed to negotiate and reduce to writing the details and contingency clauses of a specific sales agreement. A lawyer's time, of course, costs money. Consequently, the vast bulk of sales contracts are formed either through an exchange of forms, orally, or through "self-help drafting." Of the three, self-help drafting in time precipitates the greatest problems.

On the other hand, the competent negotiation and drafting of a tailor-made agreement with the assistance of legal counsel is advisable. This is especially true if either the buyer or seller in a prospective deal could stand to lose a substantial amount of money or future business or incur a damaged business reputation or serious disruption or peace of mind if things do not go as expected. And, things often do not go as expected.

In a properly negotiated and skillfully drafted written agreement, the parties themselves with aid of legal counsel agree ahead of time what should happen if things go wrong. This may include agreements for allocating the risk of loss if the goods become destroyed or damaged; for maintaining adequate insurance protection; for excusing a party's nonperformance due to strikes or other work stoppages; for resolving defects or nonconformities in the goods or documents; for price adjustments due to delays caused by weather, accidents, or other unforeseen problems; for excuses for nonperformance due to the failure of certain basic assumptions to the agreement (which are stated in the writing); for security interests; for commercial arbitration of disputes; for third-party inspections; for flexible price mechanisms; and for stipulated damages in the event of performance delays.

Understand also that, when parties decide with aid of counsel to negotiate and draft their individualized sales agreement, they are using freedom of contract to make their own law. Most of the UCC Article Two rules are changeable by agreement; for example, the risk of loss provisions. Through a negotiated, fully drafted agreement, the uncertainty that often results from the battle of the forms may be avoided, as may a statute of frauds defense. Moreover, identifiable trade usages may be either excluded or incorporated by reference (as may prior course of dealing practices) into the written agreement. Although the parties cannot disclaim the good faith standard under the code, they can define what good faith means under their agreement.

In short, future court costs, lawyer expenses, and, more importantly, damage liability can all be avoided or minimized when parties before finalizing economically important sales transactions utilize competent legal counsel to assist in negotiating and reducing to writing a fully integrated contract. Skillful drafting should lessen the chance that ambiguities in the agreement will lead to later misunderstandings. (Self-help drafting nearly always contains ambiguities.) Unfortunately, many business persons, lawyers, and, sadly, not an insignificant number of law teachers continue to view a business lawyer's role as primarily remedial in nature rather than preventive. Indeed, as strange as it may seem, in Florida in 1986, millions of dollars of fresh citrus and citrus concentrate were being bought and sold under long-term output and requirements contracts pursuant either to "oral understandings," or to mimeographed forms which contained not a single word about the impact of a possible freeze on the respective rights of the buyers and sellers to those agreements (despite several freezes during the 1980s). In North Dakota, it has been reported that a majority of large "futures" grain sales result from simple handshakes. Other examples could be cited. The point is, things do go wrong, even between honorable persons, and when they do, it is a real comfort for a business to have a comprehensive plan to fall back on. A fully negotiated and skillfully drafted sales agreement should incorporate such a plan.

RISK OF LOSS

As noted in the preceding sections, the parties themselves may agree on the precise time or event when the risk of loss or destruction of goods passes from seller to buyer. In the absence of a risk of loss clause in the sales agreement, the UCC's risk of loss rules govern.[33] Unlike the situation under prior law, the concept of "title" to the goods has no bearing under the UCC in resolving this issue. Rather, the code attempts to place the risk of loss, depending on the circumstances, on the party who was in the better position to have prevented the accident, on the party who was at fault, or on the party having effective insurance coverage.

More specifically, where the contract requires or authorizes the seller to ship the goods by carrier, the risk passes under the following rules:

1. If the parties have entered into a shipment contract which requires the seller to deliver the goods to the carrier and to arrange for their carriage, the risk passes to the buyer when the seller delivers the goods to the carrier.[34] "F.O.B." (meaning "free on

board'') place-of-shipment contracts come within this rule. Under an F.O.B. place-of-shipment arrangement, the buyer pays the carrier's charges in addition to the price.

2. If the parties have agreed on a "destination" contract (for example, an F.O.B. place of destination), requiring that the seller deliver the goods at a particular destination, the risk of loss passes when the goods are so tendered to enable the buyer to take delivery, regardless of whether delivery has been completed or not.

3. If the goods are not to be shipped by a carrier, then the risk passes in the case of a merchant-seller upon the buyer's receipt of the goods or if the seller is a nonmerchant, upon his or her tender of the goods to the buyer. Thus, if a merchant-seller using its own truck delivers furniture to a buyer's home or business but the buyer is not present to take possession and if the seller leaves the goods on the buyer's premises and an hour later they are destroyed or damaged in a heavy thunderstorm, the risk remains on the seller. The buyer does not have to pay the price since he or she had not actually taken receipt of the goods at the time of the storm.

4. When goods are held by a bailee at the time of sale, for example, by a warehouseman, risk of loss passes from the seller to the buyer either on the buyer's receipt of a negotiable or non-negotiable document of title covering the goods or upon the bailee's acknowledgement of the buyer's rights to the goods.

5. These rules change, however, when the seller has breached its duties under the sales agreement. Where either the manner of delivery or the goods so fail to conform to the contract requirements as to give the buyer a right of rejection, the risk of loss remains on the seller until either it cures the defect or accepts the nonconforming tender or goods.[35]

6. Finally, where there has been a breach by either the buyer or the seller, if the one in control of the goods is the aggrieved party, any loss not covered by that party's casualty insurance policy, if any, falls upon the party who breached the sales contract.[36]

SELLER'S GENERAL OBLIGATIONS

A seller is required to comply with all the obligations imposed by the sales contract. These include not only the terms that have been reduced to writing or orally agreed to but also those obligations resulting from course of dealing, usage of trade, and course of performance, as well as those arising under the law, notably the UCC. Fundamentally, both seller's tender of the goods and the goods themselves must fully conform to the contract, that is, must be in accordance with the obligations both under the agreement and under the law.[37]

Where, under the contract, the seller is required to send the goods to the buyer but does not require delivering them at a particular destination, the seller must first put the goods in the hands of a carrier, make a reasonable contract for their shipment, and then obtain and deliver any necessary documents (for example, a bill of lading) and promptly notify the buyer of the shipment.[38] The seller may reserve a security interest in the goods and maintain control over them if it procures a negotiable bill of lading to its own order. If it procures a negotiable bill covering the goods to the order of a financing agency or buyer, it also reserves a security interest in the goods.

Unless the sale involves payment against documents or a C.O.D. (cash on delivery) obligation, the buyer must be afforded the right to inspect the goods before payment or acceptance at a reasonable place and time. The parties may, however, fix the method of inspection (including a binding third-party procedure) in their agreement. Third-party inspections are commonly authorized in sales of agricultural commodities to determine the quality of goods at point of shipment, at destination, or at both.

The Perfect Tender Obligation

Should the seller fail to make a conforming tender of conforming goods, the buyer may reject the whole, accept the whole, or accept any commercial unit or lot and reject the rest.[39] This perfect tender rule of Article Two, upon first reading, appears to allow a buyer to reject an order if it is a day late or a pound short. But a buyer's right of rejection is not so absolute. First, the UCC's good faith obligation applies to the nonacceptance. Thus, if a buyer rejects a shipment on the basis of a minor nonconformity (which has little value to the buyer) because he or she wants out of the deal, a court may hold that the buyer's rejection and nonacceptance constitute a breach of good faith.

The perfect tender rule is also qualified by a seller's limited right to cure a nonconforming tender. Following a buyer's rejection of goods on the basis of a nonconformity, and provided the time for the seller's performance (as stipulated in the agreement or supplied by Article Two's gap filler) has not yet expired, the seller has the right to notify the buyer that he or she intends to cure the defect by substituting a conforming tender. Moreover, where a buyer rejects a nonconforming tender which, under the circumstances, the seller had reasonable grounds to believe would be acceptable, the seller may, if he or she seasonably notifies the buyer, have a further reasonable time to substitute a conforming tender.

One of the problems involving a seller's limited right to cure concerns the time period for seller's performance. If time is crucial to the buyer, the buyer should include a "time is of the essence" clause in the agreement along with the exact date on or before which the seller is to perform fully. The parties may also include a liquidated damage clause, which stipulates a specific dollar amount to be paid the buyer for each day the seller delays completing performance beyond the agreed-upon deadline. Such a sum, however, must be reasonably related to what the buyer's actual damages would likely be by reason of the delay. Of course, if the seller is too dilatory, the buyer may have to look elsewhere for the needed goods and then hold the seller liable for any added costs.

Documentary Sales

A contract requiring that a buyer tender payment against documents before taking receipt of the goods imposes special obligations on both the seller and the buyer. Before noting these obligations, a "documentary sale" is briefly described.

A documentary sales transaction is one of the more ingenious commercial devices made possible by the UCC. It allows a buyer and a seller located at a great distance from one another to each be assured that the other party is about to perform properly before performing him- or herself. For buyers, withholding payment is their principal leverage; for sellers, retaining control over the goods until payment is tendered is theirs. The documentary sale device permits a buyer to pay and a seller in effect to relinquish control at roughly the same moment, usually at a bank located in the buyer's home community.

There are many forms of documentary sales. One variation works like this. The parties provide for a documentary sale in their agreement, for example, by stipulating to ship the goods "C.I.F. (cost, insurance, and freight), payment against documents."[40] Under such an agreement, the seller typically procures from a carrier a negotiable document of title, called an order bill of lading, with delivery promised to the order of the procuring seller. The seller in addition draws a sight draft (governed by the rules of UCC, Article Three, "Commercial Paper") on the buyer. A draft is a form of negotiable instrument, a written, negotiable order, directing the buyer (the drawee) to pay the amount drawn (usually the contract price) to the order of the seller. (For a discussion of negotiable instruments, see Chapter 12.) The seller is both the drawer and payee of the draft. After execution, the seller takes these documents to a bank in his or her city and deposits them for collection. The bank forwards the items through banking channels (pursuant to the rules of UCC Article Four "Bank Deposits and Collections") to a presenting bank in the buyer's hometown.

Typically, but not always, the documents will arrive at the presenting bank before the goods. Even if the goods arrive in town first, the buyer will not be able to take delivery from the carrier because, in order to obtain possession of the goods, he or she will need to surrender the original, negotiable bill of lading covering them. The only way the buyer may obtain that negotiable bill or document, following notification of the presenting bank that the documents have arrived, is to go to that bank to pay (or honor) the amount of the attached sight draft (usually by tendering cash or a certified or cashier's check). The buyer's payment is due at the time and place at which the buyer is to receive the documents[41] regardless of where the goods are to be received.

Upon receiving payment against the sight draft, the presenting bank is obligated to endorse the negotiable bill of lading to the order of the buyer and to tender it to the buyer along with the other attached documents (for example, invoice and draft). The money paid is in time posted as a credit in the seller's hometown bank account. The buyer now has possession of the negotiable bill of lading, which describes the goods or packages that had been received by the carrier in the seller's city. By having the original negotiable bill, a buyer in the majority of situations has reason to feel confident that the goods are outside the control of the seller and are readily available (or soon will be) and that the buyer has the exclusive right to the goods by surrendering the negotiable bill to the carrier. The one significant disadvantage of a documentary sale from a buyer's perspective is that he or she gives up the right of inspection of the goods prior to payment. This problem may be avoided if a letter of credit or trade acceptance is used. Of course, a buyer in any event may still reject the goods if they fail to conform in any respect to the sales agreement. Other variations of documentary sales including the use of trade acceptances and letters of credit are described in Chapter 12.

SELLER'S WARRANTY OBLIGATIONS

Perhaps in no other area is Article Two more critical than in the area involving the creation and disclaimer of warranty obligations. Potential legal liability for warranty breaches abounds. Several legal issues are involved. First, has any warranty liability arisen in a particular sale? If so, how? Are the warranties express or implied? To whom do any of the warranties run? Is privity of contract required to sue for an alleged breach? May warranty liability be disclaimed? If so, how? Is a purported warranty disclaimer effective if the claimant seeks damages for personal injuries he or she sustained in having used the product? How does warranty theory differ from tort theories of recovery (negligence and strict liability)?

The following discussions seek to answer many of these questions. It must be noted, however, that variations exist among the states, particularly in reference to the judicial interpretation and construction of warranty obligations.

UCC Warranty Provisions

Article Two recognizes the existence of five distinct warranties which may arise singularly or in any combination. Two deal with the seller's property interest in the goods at the time of sale. The other three concern the goods, more specifically, their attributes of quality, fitness, and suitability.

Warranty of Title

A seller of goods, by the act of selling, warrants that he or she has good title to the goods and that the transfer is rightful. The only exceptions occur when the seller expressly disclaims ownership or the circumstances known to the buyer at the time of sale negate the seller's title.[42] Should a buyer subsequent to the sale be required to defend in court his or her right to the goods against the claims of a third party, the seller will have breached the warranty of good title and will be liable to the buyer for any damages the buyer may be ordered to pay if it is held the buyer's title was faulty.

Warranty against Patent or Trademarks Infringement

A merchant-seller (including a manufacturer, processor, jobber, distributor, or retailer) regularly dealing in goods of the kind sold warrants in the sale that the goods are free of the rightful claim of any third person.[43] Third-person claims include allegations of patent or trademark infringements. The seller is not liable to the buyer, however, for patent or trademark infringement if the seller manufactured goods pursuant to the buyer's furnished specifications.

Express Warranties

Of more practical significance to buyers than the property warranties are a seller's express warranties, since, in all cases, express warranties relate to the goods themselves.[44] The UCC describes three ways in which express warranties are created:

1. Any affirmation or promise by the seller to the buyer which becomes part of the basis of the bargain;
2. Any description of the goods which becomes part of the basis of the bargain; and
3. Any sample or model which is made part of the basis of the bargain.

On the other hand, any affirmation "merely of the value of the goods" or a statement purporting to be "merely the seller's opinion or commendation of the goods" does not create any express warranty under the code.[45] Courts refer to such innocent statements and opinions as to the value or general worth of goods as "puffing." Be warned, however, that the line between mere "puffing" and actionable affirmations of fact is not one neatly drawn, either by the courts in sales adjudications or by attorneys in attempting to advise a business client how far its sales staff may go before creating express warranty liability. Express warranties also may arise from advertisements. (Deceptive advertising is discussed subsequently in this chapter.)

Express Warranties and Merger Clauses

One method that a dealer may use to try to limit its liability for claims of express warranties is to include in its contracting forms or documents an express disclaimer of any express warranties together with what is called a "merger clause." A typical merger provision states that the entire agreement of the parties is set out and contained in the written contract (of which the merger clause is one part); that no other prior or contemporaneous agreements, promises, affirmations, descriptions, or understandings of any kind, express or implied, are included or relate to the written agreement; and that the written agreement supercedes all earlier discussions, understandings, and negotiations.

If a conspicuous merger clause is included within the written sales agreement, then Article Two's parol evidence rule will likely apply.[46] Under the parol evidence rule, if a court finds the written contract to have been intended as a "complete and exclusive statement of the terms of the agreement," then the court will not allow evidence to be admitted of either inconsistent or consistent additional terms (for example, evidence that might support a buyer's claim that a salesperson made a specific oral promise or affirmation in reference to the goods). In short, an important and often effective strategy for a firm to minimize its liability exposure that otherwise might be created by an overzealous salesperson is to include a conspicuous merger clause in either a fully drafted or standardized form sales agreement. In the latter case, the merger clause may be struck, however, under the battle of the forms rule, UCC section 2–207, discussed earlier.

Implied Warranties: Merchantability and Usage of Trade

Arguably, the most important and certainly the most litigated warranty under the UCC is the "implied warranty of merchantability."[47] Unless properly excluded or modified (as discussed below), a warranty that the goods shall be merchantable is implied in every contract for sale when the seller is a merchant (one who regularly deals in goods of that kind). Section 2–314 of the UCC provides that for goods to be merchantable, they must at least:

1. Pass without objection in the trade under the contract description;
2. Be of fair or average quality within the description in the case of fungible goods (for example, grain);
3. Be fit for the ordinary purposes for which such goods are used;
4. Run, within the agreement's permitted variations, of even kind, quality, and quantity;
5. Be adequately contained, packaged, and labeled; and
6. Conform to the promises or affirmations of fact made on the container or label, if any.

Of the above listed attributes, the one requiring that the goods must be fit for their ordinary purposes is most important; the drafters of the UCC have described it as the "fundamental concept."

To avoid potential liability under the implied warranty of merchantability, a seller must expressly disclaim the warranty in the sales agreement. The disclaiming language (which in the case of a writing must be conspicuous) must either mention by name "merchantability" or contain the expressions "as is" or "with all faults" or other similar language which calls the buyer's attention to the exclusion and makes plain that there are no implied warranties in the transaction.[48] (Limitation of warranty liability under the Magnuson-Moss Act is discussed in Chapter 17.)

Implied Warranty of Fitness for a Particular Use

Depending entirely on the circumstances present at a given sale, an implied warranty of fitness for a particular use may arise. Where the seller at time of contracting knows or has reason to know, first, of the particular purpose for which the goods are required and, second, that the buyer is relying on seller's skill or judgment to select or furnish suitable goods, the implied warranty of fitness for a particular purpose arises, unless excluded under section 2–316.[49] Unlike the implied warranty of merchantability, which goes to the product's fitness for ordinary uses, this warranty covers the situation when a buyer intends a specific use for a product which use the seller knows or has reason to know before the contract is concluded. The gist of the warranty is a buyer's reliance on a seller's skill or knowledge in furnishing a good suitable for the buyer's disclosed, specific use. To create this liability, the buyer must actually rely on seller's selection. Normally, the fitness for a particular use warranty arises only in the case of merchant sellers or under circumstances involving goods to be specially manufactured by a seller.

It may be more difficult to negate or avoid potential liability for breach of an implied warranty of fitness for a particular use than it is to negate the merchantability obligation under the exclusion and modification rules of section 2–316. Fitness for particular use warranties can be excluded only by a conspicuous writing which states in effect that all implied warranties are excluded, for example, by the statement: "There are no warranties, express or implied, which extend beyond the description on the face of this document."[50]

Extension of Warranties to Third Persons

Assuming express or implied warranties have arisen in a sales transaction, another important question concerns to whom they extend. Article Two includes a specific third-party beneficiary section,[51] which, unfortunately, is one of its least uniform provisions as several variations have been enacted by the states.

The most adopted variation provides that seller's warranties, express or implied, extend to any natural person who is in the immediate family or household of the buyer or is a guest in the buyer's home, provided it is reasonable to expect that the person would use, consume, or be affected by the goods and who, in fact, suffers personal injuries due to the seller's breach of warranty. A few states, Florida for example, extend the protection to servants and employees of the buyer. Note, however, that the warranty liability under this version of section 2–316, for the benefit of specified third persons not in privity of contract with the seller, covers only personal injuries and does not cover either property damage or commercial loss. Certain court decisions, however, despite the restrictive language of section 2–316 have allowed actions by third persons under warranty theories for property damage and commercial injuries under various circumstances.

A second version of UCC section 2–316 adopted by several states extends warranty protection for personal injuries to any natural person who may reasonably be expected to use, consume, or be affected by the goods. Finally, a third version recognizes an even broader potential liability for sellers by extending warranties to any person (including businesses) expected to use, consume, or be affected by the goods for any injuries consequent to the breach, including commercial loss and property damages in addition to personal injuries. Whichever version of section 2–316 a state has adopted, the seller, through the sales contract, may not exclude, negate, or limit this third-party warranty protection, *provided*, however, a warranty has been made or has arisen in the first place. As discussed earlier, the seller still may exclude all warranty liability if he or she follows the rules of section 2–316, as well as the Magnuson-Moss Act, as noted in Chapter 17. Consequently, sellers are able to avoid liability for third-party warranty claims provided the disclaimer becomes part of the sales contract. In certain cases, however, a total disclaimer has been held to be unconscionable.

The possible negation of product liability under the code does not extend, however, to a seller's or manufacturer's potential liability for personal injuries, particularly under tort theories of negligence and strict liability. These doctrines as applicable to defective or dangerous goods are discussed in Chapter 17. Suffice it to say that courts, in considering notions of public policy, do not permit a party through contract to disclaim obligations or limit liability for personal injuries resulting from a defectively manufactured product.[52]

Because of the growth in strict liability recoveries for injuries sustained from defective products, breach-of-warranty lawsuits tend to be limited to actions alleging economic loss. On the other hand, claims for personal injuries resulting from the use or consumption of goods more typically involve tort theories where the consensual negation and limitation of liability notions have less applicability. Even the UCC provides that a limitation of consequential damages for personal injuries in the case of the sale of consumer goods is prima facie unconscionable.[53] In short, the type of injury sustained by the product user or buyer is often a significant factor in determining which theory of liability may be invoked in a plaintiff's attempting to hold a manufacturer, processor, dealer, or other seller potentially liable.

BUYER'S OBLIGATIONS

Payment of the Price

A buyer's obligations arising out of a sale consist primarily of paying the price when it becomes due and accepting conforming goods when tendered in accordance with the agreement. The price may be payable fully upon tender, in installments, or at a later time in one sum. If the parties clearly intend to conclude a contract, even though they do not settle on the price, the UCC prescribes that the price will be a reasonable price at the time and place of delivery.[54] On the other hand, where the parties intend to be bound only if a price is agreed upon or fixed pursuant to their agreement and it is not so agreed upon or fixed, no contract results, and no price, reasonable or otherwise, will be imposed.

Unless otherwise agreed, payment is due at the time and place at which the buyer is to receive the goods.[55] Also unless otherwise agreed, a buyer's tender of payment is a condition of seller's duty to tender and complete any delivery.[56] Where the contract requires payment before inspection, the nonconformity of the goods does not excuse buyer's obligation to make payment unless the nonconformity appears without inspection, for example, by a description of nonconforming goods in the description on a bill of lading.[57]

Obligation to Accept Conforming Goods

If a seller tenders conforming goods, the buyer must accept them. When a buyer has a right to reject the goods because of a nonconformity, he or she must do so within a reasonable time after tender or delivery, and very importantly, must seasonably notify the seller of the rejection, pointing out the claimed defect or problem. Once the goods are accepted, the buyer must pay for them at the contract rate. A buyer may revoke his or her other acceptance of a lot or unit and thus "throw the goods" back on the seller only under specified circumstances, for example, when a buyer discovers a nonconformity that substantially impairs the value of the goods, a nonconformity the buyer had not earlier discovered either because of the difficulty of discovery or because of seller's assurances as to their conformity.[58]

Buyer's Obligation to Give Notice of Breach

One of the major sand traps for buyers under Article Two is the requirement that, following buyer's acceptance of the goods, the buyer must within a reasonable time after he discovers (or should have discovered) any breach notify the seller of the breach or "be barred from any remedy."[59] This applies to claims of improper tender, nonconformity, and breaches of express or implied warranties.

Courts in certain states have devised ways for a claimant to avoid the notice requirement, particularly in warranty suits involving personal injuries. Still, a buyer having a possible breach of warranty claim should notify the seller as soon as possible. A simple letter will do, preferably by certified, return-receipt-requested mail. The content of the notification only need let the seller know that the transaction is troublesome. There are no requirements to either threaten a lawsuit or to particularize the "legal" claim.

The purpose of the notice requirement is to inform the seller that a claimed breach has been made which, it is hoped, will lead to a settlement of the matter through adjustment, substitution of conforming goods, or negotiation. A buyer who fails to comply with the notice-of-breach rule of section 2–607 (3) (a) may be barred from later bringing a suit for a claimed breach, even when the breach substantially impairs the value of the goods to the buyer.

REMEDIES FOR BREACH

Article Two provides both for goods oriented remedies and for damages when a buyer or seller breaches or repudiates his or her obligations. A repudiation can be either an overt communication of an intention not to perform or an action which renders performance impossible or which demonstrates a clear determination not to continue performance.

Anticipatory Repudiation

A repudiation of an obligation before performance is due, the nonperformance of which will substantially impair the value of the entire contract to the nonrepudiating party, allows the aggrieved party to accelerate any remedies for breach and to suspend its own performance.[60] This is known as "anticipatory repudiation." The repudiating party, however, may retract its repudiation any time prior to the time its performance is due unless the aggrieved party, following the repudiation, has cancelled or materially changed its position.

Right to Adequate Assurance of Performance

When either the buyer or seller has reasonable grounds to feel insecure about the other party's being able or willing to perform its obligations under a sales agreement, the party whose expectations have been impaired may demand in writing "adequate assurance of due performance" and, until receiving such may, "if commercially reasonable," suspend its own performance.[61] Between merchants, the reasonableness of grounds for insecurity and the adequacy of any assurance offered shall be determined by "commercial standards."

The "right to adequate assurance of performance" remedy is designed to foster communications between the parties to help resolve doubts or difficulties as to performances still due. The party who invokes this remedy must do so with great caution, however. If a court later decides that no "reasonable grounds for insecurity" existed, the demand will be deemed to have been improper. If the party making the demand also suspended its own performance, then it will have breached the contract and be liable accordingly. If the party making the demand did not suspend its performance until after receiving an assurance which it then deemed to be inadequate and, at that point, suspended its performance, a court might again disagree and hold that the assurance furnished was adequate under the law. Thus, the "demanding party" by suspending its performance may end up itself being held to have breached the contract.

The point is that one may always request that the other party provide an assurance of performance, but it is dangerous to suspend or hold up one's own performance on the basis of the belief that the other party may not perform in the future. Section 2–609 of the code, which sets out this remedy, contains several amorphous phrases including "reasonable grounds," "commercially reasonable," "commercial standards," and "adequate assurance." Such abstract phrases in a statute invite disputes over their meaning when applied to a given situation. Thus, section 2–609 arguably may precipitate rather than prevent disputes.

Survey of Sellers' Remedies

Certain remedies available to a seller have already been mentioned in this chapter, including a seller's limited right to cure nonconformities under specified circumstances, the right to receive adequate assurance of due performance, the right to reserve a security interest in the goods, and the right to accelerate remedies in the event of buyer's repudiation.

The seller has also several "damage oriented" remedies plus a right of reclamation. The latter involves reclaiming goods sold (but not yet paid for) upon discovery that the buyer was insolvent at the time the sales agreement was formed.[62] In addition, if the seller learns of a buyer's breach before delivery, the seller can withhold delivery of the goods or stop or direct the delivery of a bailee and sue for damages.

Action for the Price

Under Article Two, the seller may sue for the contract price only as it becomes due for goods accepted or of conforming goods lost or destroyed within a commercially reasonable time after risk of their loss has passed to buyer.[63] The seller also may sue for the price of specially manufactured goods identified to the contract which the seller, after reasonable effort, is unable to resell at a reasonable price.

Damages for Nonacceptance or Repudiation

A seller may sue a buyer for damages for the buyer's nonacceptance of goods or repudiation of the agreement as measured by the difference between the market price at the time and place of tender and the unpaid contract price, plus incidental damages, less any savings caused by the breach. The purpose of this damage formula is to put the seller in the same economic position he or she would have been in had the buyer fully performed. Neither windfalls nor punitive damages are included under this formula. Incidental damages which are recoverable include reasonable charges, commissions, or expenses incurred to stop delivery and to take back and care for the goods following the buyer's breach.[64]

Article Two provides an alternative measure of damages if the above formula does not result in the seller's being made whole. This typically is the case in a "lost volume" situation where, as a result of a buyer's breach, the seller has lost a unit of sales volume for which either the resale or the market price formula fails to recover the lost "profit." The lost profits measure of section 2–708(2) typically will be applied in sales of standard priced goods. Under this measure, recovery is based on list price less cost to the dealer or list price less manufacturing cost to the manufacturers.[65]

Seller's Resale

A seller may resell conforming goods under section 2–706 that were not accepted by the buyer, provided the resale occurs in good faith and in a commercially reasonable manner. If a resale has occurred, the seller may recover as damages from the buyer the difference between the resale price and the contract price, plus incidental damages, less expenses saved as a result of the breach.[66] A seller's expenses saved following a buyer's breach or repudiation might include the costs of shipment (if the seller was to pay for shipping and the breach or repudiation occurred prior to shipment).

Seller's resale remedy is attractive for two reasons. First, the seller is able to recoup at least a portion of its loss relatively quickly. Second, the resale "fixes" the damages, thereby obviating the issue of what a "reasonable price" would have been at the time and place of delivery. Of course, if the seller resells the goods for a price equal to or higher than the contract price, no recovery is permitted unless the resale fails to make the seller whole, in which case the seller could seek damages under the lost profits measure.[67]

Survey of Buyer's Remedies

Various buyer's remedies have already been discussed including the buyer's right to demand the seller's adequate assurance of performance, the right to take possession of the goods on the seller's insolvency, the right of inspection prior to payment (other than in C.O.D. or documentary sales), and the rights to reject or, in a proper case, revoke acceptance of goods due to nonconformities. This section will focus on the buyer's damage oriented remedies.

Damages for Nondelivery

A buyer may recover from a seller damages for nondelivery of goods or for repudiation of the agreement, the difference between the market price at the time when the buyer learned of the breach and the contract price, plus incidental and consequential damages, less expenses saved.[68] Buyer's incidental damages include reasonable expenses incurred in the inspection, receipt, transportation, and care of goods rightfully rejected, plus reasonable expenses incurred in affecting cover (entering into a substitute purchase), plus any other expenses incidental to the delay or breach. Consequential damages which a buyer may recover include any commercial loss regarding its needs for the goods which the seller at the time of contracting had reason to know and any injuries to persons or property proximately resulting from any breach of warranty.[69]

Buyer's Cover Remedy

A buyer may "cover"—in the event of the seller's repudiation or nondelivery or for nonconforming goods rightfully rejected or where acceptance has been rightfully revoked—by purchasing substitute goods for those promised. If a buyer elects to cover, he or she may recover in damages from the defaulting seller, the difference between the cost of cover and the contract price, plus incidental and consequential damages (as defined above), less expenses saved.[70] Cover is not a mandatory remedy; a buyer may elect rather to sue for damages under the contract using the market price formula.

Damages for Accepted Goods

When a buyer has accepted goods, provided he or she has given the required section 2–607(3) notice of breach to the seller, the buyer may recover for any nonconformity the actual loss that resulted from the breach including, when appropriate, incidental and consequential damages. If seller's breach consists of a breach of warranty, the buyer may recover the difference at the time and place of acceptance of the value of the goods and the value they would have had if the goods had been as warranted.[71]

Buyer's Replevin of Goods

When the goods are unique or are "in other proper circumstances," a buyer may seek a decree of specific performance (a court order directing the seller to deliver the goods to the buyer). A buyer may also replevin (a court-assisted return of the goods) if, after reasonable effort, the buyer is unable to effect cover, or circumstances indicate such effort would be unavailing.[72] Courts have neither applied nor interpreted the specific performance and replevin remedies of the UCC in either a consistent or uniform manner. Suffice it to say that when a buyer seeks the goods after a seller's nondelivery, the remedy is less certain as it is considered to be within a court's "discretion." Normally, the goods either have to be unique or unavailable elsewhere for specific performance to be ordered.

DECEPTIVE ACTS AND PRACTICES

Congress, through enacting Section 5 of the Federal Trade Commission Act (and as amended by the Wheeler Lea Act), has delegated to the Federal Trade Commission the authority to identify and regulate deceptive acts and practices that affect commerce.[73] Toward this end, the FTC has established a Bureau of Consumer Protection,[74] whose powers extend to identifying and regulating:

1. Unfair acts or practices;
2. Deceptive acts or practices; and
3. False advertising.

This section focuses on the deceptive acts and practices including false advertising, since these matters may arise in the sale of goods.

False and Deceptive Advertising

It has been said that advertising comprises any method of attracting public attention to anything. Under Section 5 of the Federal Trade Commission Act, the FTC has the power to regulate false advertising. The jurisdiction of the FTC in this regard frequently overlaps that of the Food and Drug Administration (FDA)[75] and the Federal Communications Commission (FCC).[76] Pursuant to interagency agreements, however, the FTC remains the primary federal agency having responsibility for the regulation of deceptive and misleading advertising. The regulation of advertising is a complex matter. For one thing, a business has a constitutional right under the First Amendment to advertise, that is, to engage in commercial free speech. For another, a business has a recognized property right to be allowed to conduct its business, which includes advertising its products or services. Although product advertising cannot be banned (unless it is deemed inimical to public health or national security), it can be regulated by the FTC both to prevent and to correct false, misleading, and deceptive impressions which advertising may engender. Since false advertising is only one form of deceptive acts or practices the FTC seeks to minimize, a discussion of the law of deceptive acts and practices follows.

Evaluative Criteria

According to one FTC definition, which has been used for several years, an act or practice is deceptive if it: (1) has the tendency or capacity to mislead (2) a substantial number of consumers (3) in a material way. An advertisement which has the tendency or capacity to mislead, can arise out of an oral conversation or from any written literature or brochure. The tendency or capacity to mislead may be either explicit or implicit. Deception may result either from an affirmative statement or, on occasion, by omitting to convey certain information. Under these criteria, information set out in an advertisement need not be false to be considered deceptive.

Truthful information, moreover, may be represented in a misleading way, for example, information which is true only in unusual circumstances but which is presented to the public with no qualification. Further, consumers need not be actually misled for an action to be found deceptive. Nor is it relevant that a business intend to mislead. Rather, the key is the "tendency" or "capacity" of the advertisement to mislead even when the ad contains only an innocent misrepresentation.

The effectiveness of a disclaimer in correcting an innocent misrepresentation depends on the overall impression conveyed. A subsequent truthful disclosure, however, may not correct the deception. What is important to the FTC in finding a violation is that a deception resulted in a contract or created an initial interest in the product or service being advertised.

The second element of deception is that the advertisement has the capacity to mislead a substantial number of consumers. The FTC has never designated that a specific minimum number of consumers must be affected. Rather, the agency has focused on the nature of the claim and the probable consequences of the deception. Thus, if an advertisement is directed at a specific group, the issue becomes whether a substantial number within the targeted group would likely be misled by the advertisement.

Both the FTC and the courts have recognized that the most gullible consumer is afforded protection against misleading advertising under the FTC act. Similarly, the FTC does not require that the average consumer be on constant vigil in search of deception. Also, in considering the tendency to mislead a substantial number of consumers, the FTC takes into account the "normal inattentiveness" of the average consumer. Still, the FTC may not arbitrarily or capriciously find an advertising claim to be deceptive. A finding of deception must be based on the language used and circumstances present, together with reasonable inferences which may be drawn from them.

The traditional third element necessary for a finding of deception is materiality. To mislead in a material way means that the advertisement either did or had the tendency of inducing a purchaser to buy the advertised goods or service. Because various factors influence a consumer's decision to buy, thus making it impossible to always identify those factors that were important to a particular purchaser, no actual inducement is required. What is crucial is that the advertisement dealt with a topic either affirmatively or by omission which would, in light of an average consumer, likely serve as an inducement to purchase the product or service. Materiality, in short, relates to a hypothetical average, reasonable consumer's psychological reaction to the deceptive information. Although an intention to deceive is not required for materiality, if such an intention is established, the FTC will consider the deception to be material.

Newer Evaluation Standard

In the mid–1980s, the FTC began to apply a new standard for evaluating deceptive acts or practices.[77] Under this standard, an act or practice is deceptive if: (1) it is likely to mislead consumers (2) who are acting reasonably in the circumstances (3) to their detriment.[78] Respected commentators contend that, despite the differences in language, the two standards conceptually are substantially similar. Indeed, it appears that the newer standard is a reformation of the existing underlying legal principles. Still, changes in language formulations over time often result in changes in the legal principles.

Affect on State "Mini-FTC" Statutes

Compounding the uncertainty over what the definitional change of a deceptive act may mean for federal enforcement is the change's potential impact on state laws proscribing deceptive acts or practices. All states and the District of Columbia have enacted deceptive sales and practices laws, many of which are modeled after the Federal Trade Commission Act itself. These (sometimes called) "mini-FTC" state statutes are enforced by state officials who often look to federal enforcement and interpretative policies for guidance. Thus, a change in the federal law of deception over time will cause a change in state deceptive practice law as well.

The "likely to mislead" language of the newer standard arguably makes explicit what courts have for years been saying in applying the more traditional standard, that is, that a violation of section 5 of the Federal Trade Commission Act need not be based on an actual deception. The "consumer acting reasonably" requirement of the newer standard is a bit more troublesome but probably refers to the notion of the hypothetical, reasonable consumer of normal inattentiveness of the tradition standard. Finally, the "detriment" requirement arguably is another way of saying the "materiality" requirement. Thus, a misrepresentation would be to the detriment of a consumer if it "is likely to affect a consumer's choice of or conduct regarding a product."[79]

Deceptive Advertising: Untruths

An advertisement may be deemed deceptive or false under the above deceptive criteria either because it incorporates untruths or because it misleads by not conveying a truthful statement in proper context. On occasion, silence may be misleading and deceptive.[80] Certainly, a seller of a product that foreseeably might cause serious personal injury to a user by improper use who fails to alert a prospective buyer to that fact, may face liability for any resulting injuries. Similarly, proper instructions explaining how to safely use a product must be included with the product. Otherwise, the manufacturer or seller faces liability for injuries sustained by users who improperly assembled or used a product where the instructions were absent or incomplete.

In the realm of advertising, an untrue statement is not always deceptive. The notion of "fantasy" or "fanciful" advertising is well known and is widely used as a permissible method of promoting a good or service. Fantasy advertising, although untrue, is not likely to deceive or mislead a consumer. To say that "interesting people" drive car X, or that Y gasoline puts a "tiger in your tank" are examples of permitted, fanciful representations used in product promotions.

On the other hand, if a seller overstates a product's features by explicit representations of untruths or causes a consumer to have a mistaken notion about a product's attributes through implicit misrepresentations or makes statements consisting of half-truths, the seller's acts or statements are subject to findings of deception. An "implicit untruth" occurs when an advertisement conveys a meaning that distorts the truth. This may result when very technical or ambiguous language is used to confuse a consumer or to create the impression of product superiority. Moreover, statements that are true may be found to be nonetheless deceptive if a missing element of information is needed to overcome an inference which falls short of the truth.

Affirmative Disclosures

The FTC generally follows a comprehensive disclosure policy which mandates that an affirmation disclosure may be ordered if a particular advertisement has been found to be deceptive, provided the additional information is required to obviate and is reasonably capable of correcting the deception. Both the FTC and the courts have the power to order affirmative and corrective disclosures. Situations in which affirmative disclosures have been ordered include:

1. Advertisements containing half-truths;
2. Advertisements for products potentially dangerous to public health;
3. Advertisements for products easily capable of misuse, which misuse creates a potential risk of personal injury;
4. Products which are well-known to the public and which have suddenly been changed or altered in a significant way, where the change or alteration has not been made known through advertisements.

Although responsible for policing most advertising, the FTC especially scrutinizes advertisements for products making health claims or products that impact on public health, for example, alcohol and tobacco products.

Testimonials and Endorsements

Advertisers frequently use testimonials of users or endorsements of famous persons to promote products. In any testimonial or endorsement, an advertiser may not alter the words actually used to affect the substance of the statement so as to mislead the consumer. Use of any testimonial or endorsement containing incorrect statements is deceptive if the advertiser knew or should have known of the falsity. Although the advertiser need not disclose that the endorser was paid, if compensation was paid, it is a deceptive act for the advertiser to claim that the endorsement or testimonial was offered gratis (or was unsolicited, if in fact it was).

Miscellaneous Advertising Claims and Liability

Forty-four states have enacted a form of the 1911 "Printer's Ink Model Statute," which makes it a criminal misdemeanor to advertise a representation that is untrue, deceptive, or misleading. Despite these statutes, local prosecutors rarely enforce them.[81]

Use of an advertiser's own name, trademark, copyright, or patent may be deceptive even if it is true and properly registered, if the use creates a misleading impression to the detriment of consumers. Also, claims of uniqueness, performance capabilities, limited quantities, "special sales," or "special discounts" must have a reasonable basis in fact or otherwise will be considered deceptive.

Door-to-Door Sales

One area of seller abuse has involved door-to-door sales where unsolicited salespersons often, through high-pressure sales tactics, induce consumers to buy on credit everything from encyclopedias to grave plots. In response to these abuses, the FTC has promulgated a regulation entitled "Cooling Off Period for Door-to-Door Sales,"[82] which became effective June 7, 1974.

Under this rule, it constitutes an unfair and deceptive act or practice for any seller in any home solicitation sale to:

1. Fail to furnish the buyer with a fully completed receipt or copy of any contract pertaining to such sale at the time of its execution, which is in the same language, e.g., Spanish, as that principally used in the oral sales presentation and which shows the date of the transaction and contains the name and address of the seller, and in immediate proximity to the space reserved in the contract for the signature of the buyer or on the front page of the receipt if a contract is not used and in boldface type of a minimum size of 10 points, a statement in substantially the following form:

"YOU, THE BUYER, MAY CANCEL THIS TRANSACTION AT ANY TIME PRIOR TO MIDNIGHT OF THE THIRD BUSINESS DAY AFTER THE DATE OF THIS TRANSACTION. SEE THE ATTACHED NOTICE OF CANCELLATION FORM FOR AN EXPLANATION OF THIS RIGHT."

2. Fail to furnish each buyer, at the time he signs the door-to-door sales contract or otherwise agrees to buy consumer goods or services from the seller, a completed form in duplicate, captioned "NOTICE OF CANCELLATION", which shall be attached to the contract or receipt and easily detachable, and which shall contain in ten point bold face type the following information and statements in the same language, e.g., Spanish, as that used in the contract:

NOTICE OF CANCELLATION

_____

[Date]

YOU MAY CANCEL THIS TRANSACTION, WITHOUT ANY PENALTY OR OBLIGATION, WITHIN THREE BUSINESS DAYS FROM THE ABOVE DATE.

IF YOU CANCEL, ANY PROPERTY TRADED IN, ANY PAYMENTS MADE BY YOU UNDER THE CONTRACT OR SALE, AND ANY NEGOTIABLE INSTRUMENT EXECUTED BY YOU WILL BE RETURNED WITHIN 10 BUSINESS DAYS FOLLOWING RECEIPT BY THE SELLER OF YOUR CANCELLATION NOTICE, AND ANY SECURITY INTEREST ARISING OUT OF THE TRANSACTION WILL BE CANCELLED

IF YOU CANCEL, YOU MUST MAKE AVAILABLE TO THE SELLER AT YOUR RESIDENCE, IN SUBSTANTIALLY AS GOOD CONDITION AS WHEN RECEIVED, ANY GOODS DELIVERED TO YOU UNDER THIS CONTRACT OR SALE; OR YOU MAY IF YOU WISH COMPLY WITH THE INSTRUCTIONS OF THE SELLER REGARDING THE RETURN SHIPMENT OF THE GOODS AT THE SELLER'S EXPENSE AND RISK.

IF YOU DO MAKE THE GOODS AVAILABLE TO THE SELLER AND THE SELLER DOES NOT PICK THEM UP WITHIN 20 DAYS OF THE DATE OF YOUR NOTICE OF CANCELLATION, YOU MAY RETAIN OR DISPOSE OF THE GOODS WITHOUT ANY FURTHER OBLIGATION. IF YOU FAIL TO MAKE THE GOODS AVAILABLE TO THE SELLER, OR IF YOU AGREE TO RETURN THE GOODS TO THE SELLER AND FAIL TO DO SO, THEN YOU REMAIN LIABLE FOR PERFORMANCE OF ALL OBLIGATIONS UNDER THE CONTRACT.

TO CANCEL THIS TRANSACTION, MAIL OR DELIVER A SIGNED AND DATED COPY OF THIS CANCELLATION NOTICE OR ANY OTHER WRITTEN NOTICE, OR SEND A TELEGRAM, TO

——————————————, AT   ——————————————

[Name of Seller]   [Address of Seller's
                                                     place of business]

NOT LATER THAN MIDNIGHT OF ——————————

[Date]

I HEREBY CANCEL THIS TRANSACTION

——————————   ——————————————

[Date]   [Buyer's Signature]

3. Fail, before furnishing copies of the ''Notice of Cancellation'' to the buyer, to complete both copies by entering the name of the seller, the address of the seller's place of business, the date of the transaction, and the date, not earlier than the third business day following the date of the transaction, by which the buyer may give notice of cancellation.

4. Include in any door-to-door contract or receipt any confession of judgment or any waiver of any of the rights to which the buyer is entitled . . . including specifically his right to cancel the sale . . .

5. Fail to inform each buyer orally, at the time he signs the contract or purchases the goods or services, of his right to cancel.

6. Misrepresent in any manner the buyer's right to cancel.

7. Fail or refuse to honor any valid notice of cancellation by a buyer and within 10 business days after the receipt of such notice, to (i) refund all payments made under the contract or sale; (ii) return any goods or property traded in, in substantially as good condition as when received by the seller; (iii) cancel and return any negotiable instrument executed by the buyer . . . [83]

In addition to the above FTC regulation, approximately 40 states have enacted their own ''cooling off'' statutes as applicable to residential solicitations.

Other Deceptive Practices

Bait and Switch Selling

Pursuant to FTC guidelines on bait and switch advertising,[84] the practice of bait and switch (or bait advertising) is considered to be a deceptive act or practice. The typical bait and switch deceptive practice consists of:

1. An advertisement of an item at a very low price;

2. A refusal to show the advertised item, or disparagement of the product, or a failure to have the item available in reasonable quantity; and

3. A sales effort to convince the buyer to purchase a different, unadvertised, typically more expensive item.

The FTC looks for evidence of relatively few sales of the advertised item to establish a bait and switch violation. In an FTC enforcement action to abate a bait and switch practice, the agency normally issues a cease and desist order upon a finding of violation.

Referral Sales

A referral or pyramid sales practice involving consumer buyers is illegal under various state deceptive practice laws or is subject to regulation under others. Also, a referral sales practice often constitutes a violation of section 5 of the Federal Trade Commission Act.[85] Pursuant to a referral sales arrangement, a seller in selling goods to a buyer promises to compensate the buyer for each future customer referred by the customer to the seller.

Two problems exist with this sales device. First, the referral system is predicated on the illusion that an unlimited supply of potential customers exists. Second, the buyer's prospect of gaining "commissions" allows the seller to inflate the price of the goods to that buyer. Referral sales practices are particularly prone to pricing manipulation when used in selling goods to consumers. The practice is often difficult to control legally, however, because referral commissions are not per se illegal. Professionals and businesses frequently use them. Still, when used in selling merchandise or services to consumers, they ordinarily will be considered a deceptive referral sales practice.

FTC Adjudication Procedures

An FTC enforcement action typically begins either in response to a specific complaint received from a citizen or by a self-generated investigation. Investigations are conducted through the FTC's regional offices. The closing of an investigation with no further action is discretionary.

If an investigation suggests that further action is warranted, the bureau director will submit a proposed complaint to the commission. The commission normally will notify the parties concerned of its intention to issue a complaint. This opens the door to negotiations, which often leads to a settlement through a consent order. Should an agreement be reached, the consent order is made public and becomes final within 60 days.

If an agreement cannot be reached, the commission will issue a formal complaint. The case, upon assignment to an administrative judge, proceeds to trial. The decision of the administrative judge is subject to reversal or modification by the commission, whose decision in turn may be appealed to a United States Court of Appeals.

Defenses to Claims of Deceptive Practices

The most frequently used defense to a claim of deception is that of trade talk or "puffing." Puffing is exaggerated sales talk or opinion, the truth or falsity of which cannot be precisely determined. A certain level of puffing is always permissible (although the commission normally has less tolerance for puffing than do the courts). Decisional precedents in this area tend to be unreliable since the law in reference to puffing changes with the times. The general test is whether the consumer would recognize that the sales talk is puffing.

In evaluating a puffing defense, certain factors should be considered. First, the type of product or service involved will impact on the success of the defense. Health claims are rarely considered puffing. Second, the quality of the words used is important. Comparative words are considered to be specific and largely capable of objective measurement. Therefore, words such as "bigger," "safer," and "longer lasting" may not be within the realm of puffing. However, purely opinion-based words such as "big," "safe," "best," "prime," or "long lasting" are generally nonactionable.

Discontinuance of the deceptive practice may sometimes operate as a defense. This is only true, however, in situations where little possibility exists that the practice will be resumed in the future. Examples include a change in ownership, the discontinuance of the service or product, and the discontinuance of the practice upon the advice of counsel and stipulation that the practice will not be resumed.

A third defense may be available when the practice is engaged in on an industry-wide basis. It may be held that the deception must be corrected on an industry-wide level and that to proceed against an individual firm would be arbitrary and unfair because the individual would be at a competitive disadvantage if forced to refrain from the deceptive act. It must be cautioned, moreover, that prior approval of a particular practice by the FTC is not always a successful defense.

Liability for Violations

The usual enforcement device of the FTC is issuance of an administrative cease and desist order. When issued in final form, it must be obeyed as it has the full force and effect of law. Any person or business that violates a final order of the agency is subject to assessment of a penalty of up to $10,000 for each violation, with each day of noncompliance considered a separate violation. In assessing penalties for noncompliance, the defendant's good faith or lack thereof and the extent of public injuries are considered.

Criminal penalties may result for neglecting or refusing to attend, testify, or answer to any lawful inquiry of the commission. A fine between $1,000 and $5,000 or imprisonment of up to one year, or both is possible. Willful violation of the FTC labeling and identification requirements or the intentional placement or use of misleading advertisements likely to produce injuries to health are more likely to result in criminal penalties than are other varieties of violations.

INTERNATIONAL SALES

We live in an era when there is increasing emphasis on a global economy and interdependence of national economies. Yet, while free trade across international boundaries is a laudable goal, it is exactly that, a goal. Movement of goods across international boundaries is impeded and economies are distorted by restrictive trade devices such as import and export duties, quotas, licensing, and government subsidies.

Imports

Many goods are subject to import restrictions by the United States; for example, certain narcotics are prohibited and automobiles are limited by requiring conformance with the federal safety standards for automobiles. Imports may be limited by quotas which may be either global or bilateral. Global quotas apply to all goods of that class imported from any source whatsoever. Bilateral quotas are imposed by negotiation between two sovereigns and are generally reduced to a treaty. Some quotas are voluntary, such as the voluntary quotas on Japanese automobiles by Japanese firms with the agreement of the Japanese government.

Before the goods are available in the United States they must first pass through customs. Generally, the goods physically enter the country through customs. However, some goods physically enter certain locations called "foreign trade zones." The goods are exempt from tariffs while they remain in the foreign trade zone. There are more than 57 foreign trade zones located in the United States that are administered through the Foreign Trade Zones Board of the Commerce Department and the Customs Service. The foreign trade zones are primarily distribution centers or assembly points for certain manufactured goods such as foreign cars.

Passing through customs generally requires payment of the assessed tariff at the port of entry. The tariff schedule is complicated because its use requires identification of goods, their sources or origin, and a determination of their value.

The United States does not use the Brussels Tariff Nomenclature, which is in general use around the world. Rather, United States tariffs are set out in the Tariff Schedule of the United States, but the United States is taking steps to convert to a more common system, the Harmonized System, which was developed by the Customs Cooperation Council in Brussels.

United States customs assessments traditionally were based on the American

Selling Price (ASP), which is defined as the usual wholesale price at which similar U.S. manufactured goods freely sell in the United States plus shipping and preparation. Since 1979 valuations are supposed to be made based on "transaction value," which is the actual price paid for the goods when sold for export to the United States plus shipping, commissions, licensing or royalty fees paid, and any resale, disposal, or use proceeds accruing to the seller.

Tariffs are also based on country of origin. Difficulties arise in cases where a product is manufactured in one country from component parts manufactured in other countries and where a product is shipped from one country but was manufactured in a third. The Rule of Origin is contained in section 308 (4) (B) of the Trade Agreements Act of 1979, which provides that for a product to be from a particular country it must be wholly the growth, product, or manufacture of that country or the parts obtained from other countries must be substantially transformed into a new and different product having a different name and distinct use from the original articles transformed.

Exports

Exporters must meet all U.S. requirements before shipping goods. An export license must be obtained from the Commerce Department.

A validated license is required when the goods affect national security or foreign policy or are in short supply. The Export Administration Regulations, available from the Commerce Department, contain the licensing requirements and the complete list of commodities subject to licensing. Typical items subject to validated licensing are certain types of plastics, sophisticated electronic and communications equipment, and arms and munitions.

General licenses are published authorizations allowing export of goods not subject to validated licensing. No formal application is required, nor is written permission required, provided the correct general license symbol is on the export control document known as the "Shipper's Export Declaration."

The Commerce Department requires a "destination control statement" to protect against diversion of the goods from legally authorized destinations to restricted destinations. For instance, this requirement is to prevent items such as sophisticated electronics from being diverted to Eastern Soviet bloc countries from friendlier destinations such as a NATO ally. No destination control statement is required if the goods are shipped for consumption in Canada or under general license.

The use of letters of credit in international sales as a method of payment is discussed in Chapter 11.

Foreign Corrupt Practices Act

The Foreign Corrupt Practices Act of 1977 (FCPA) makes it illegal to offer to or make certain payments or make a gift to any foreign official, foreign political party, or foreign political candidate for the purpose of corruptly obtaining, retaining, or directing business to any person.[86] Administration of the act is the joint responsibility of the Securities and Exchange Commission and the Department of Justice. Companies required to report to the Securities and Exchange Commission under the Securities Exchange Act of 1934 are within the commission's jurisdiction; all others are subject to the Department of Justice. Companies must report and maintain adequate records and internal auditing procedures. The Department of Justice has an FCPA Review Procedure to advise businesses within its jurisdiction as to possible violations of the FCPA before the transaction occurs; however, the Securities and Exchange Commission refuses to make such pretransaction rulings.

Arab Boycott

The "Unified Law on the Boycott of Israel" was adopted by the Council of the Arab League in 1954 and was subsequently put into effect in the twenty member states of the Arab League. The response of the United States government to the boycott has been to try to ignore or downplay it. The Commerce Department has issued regulations,[87] which require a U.S. firm to report requests for boycott information and agreements in support of the boycott and whether or not the firm has or will comply. Compliance is not prohibited, but it is discouraged. Whether or not the Arab boycott violates the U.S. antitrust laws has not been determined. The primary boycott by command of Arab sovereigns may be exempt from U.S. antitrust law because of either sovereign immunity or act of state doctrine if the boycott is political in nature. However, antitrust problems do arise with respect to the secondary boycott, that is, the situation in which a firm doing business in or with an Arab country refuses to do business with a firm on the Arab blacklist. The United States brought suit against Bechtel Corporation for violation of the Sherman Act in a secondary boycott situation.[88] The issue was never tried. In the consent judgment, Bechtel agreed not to refuse to deal with (in the United States) blacklisted concerns or persons, to require subcontractors to boycott blacklisted concerns or persons, or to assist others in an agreement to boycott blacklisted U.S. firms. The state of the law then is uncertain. A firm may be in violation of U.S antitrust law if it participates in the secondary boycott. Such a warning is placed on Commerce Department forms provided to report boycott activities.

THE LAWYER'S ROLE IN SALES TRANSACTIONS

In any international sale or any other large or out-of-the-ordinary sales transaction, a lawyer knowledgeable about contracts and sales law should be consulted to advise what the law is and how it will likely be interpreted in reference to the proposed agreement. An attorney, moreover, can assist a business client in drafting override agreements when appropriate and can be very helpful in negotiating and drafting a fully integrated, written sales contract. In drafting an agreement, a lawyer should include language which reflects the parties' wishes on how foreseeable contingencies should be resolved. The attorney should also draft definitions and clarifications of terms which otherwise could give rise to disagreements.

Certainly, risk of loss, casualty to the goods, failure of basic assumptions, intervening contingencies, accidents, work stoppages, effects of weather, or unexpected price fluctuations can cause major disappointment and delay or nonperformance under a sales agreement. This may lead to costly litigation. To the extent a competent lawyer is involved in the "front end" of a sales transaction, the probability of serious transactional breakdowns may be significantly lessened through careful transactional planning.

NOTES

1. *The Uniform Commercial Code* (UCC) is the result of a joint undertaking by the American Law Institute (ALI) and the National Conference of Commissioners on Uniform State Laws (NCCUSL). Each state has enacted its own version. *See, e.g.*, Fla. Statutes §§ 671.101, *et seq.* Throughout this volume, the ALI–NCCUSL official 1978 version, as subsequently amended, is cited. Copies of the official draft of the UCC are available in libraries and at bookstores that sell law books.

2. U.C.C. § 2–105 (1).
3. U.C.C. § 2–314.
4. U.C.C. § 2–104 (1) (3).
5. 49 U.S.C. §§ 81–124.
6. 49 U.S.C. § 20 (11)
7. U.C.C. §§ 7–101–7–603.
8. 7 U.S.C. §§ 499a–499r.
9. 46 U.S.C. §§ 1300–1315. *See also*, 46 U.S.C. §§ 190–196.
10. 52 I.C.C. §§ 671, *et seq.*
11. U.C.C. § 1–201 (3). *See also*, U.C.C. §§ 1–205, 2–208.
12. U.C.C. § 1–201 (11).
13. U.C.C. § 2–103 (1) (b). *See also*, U.C.C. § 1–201 (19).
14. U.C.C. § 2–209 (1).
15. U.C.C. § 2–302.
16. U.C.C. § 2–719 (3).
17. U.C.C. § 2–302 (2).
18. U.C.C. § 2–328 (2) (3) (4).
19. U.C.C. § 2–306 (1) (2).
20. 15 U.S.C. §§ 1–7; 15 U.S.C. §§ 12–27.
21. U.C.C. § 2–326 (1) (a) (b).
22. U.C.C. § 3–327 (2).
23. U.C.C. §§ 2–610, 2–704 (2).
24. U.C.C. § 2–612 (1).
25. U.C.C. § 1–201 (37).
26. *See*, U.C.C. § 9–102 (2).
27. *See*, U.C.C. §§ 2–314 and 2–315.
28. U.C.C. § 2–207 (1).
29. U.C.C. § 2–207.

30. U.C.C. § 2–201 (1).

31. U.C.C. § 2–201 (2).

32. U.C.C. § 2–201 (3) (9).

33. *See* U.C.C. §§ 2–509, 2–510, and 2–319.

34. U.C.C. §§ 2–509 (1) (a) and 2–319 (1) (a).

35. U.C.C. § 2–510 (1).

36. U.C.C. § 2–510 (2) and (3).

37. U.C.C. § 2–503.

38. U.C.C. § 2–504.

39. U.C.C. § 2–601.

40. *See* U.C.C. § 2–320 (2) (a).

41. U.C.C. § 2–310 (c).

42. U.C.C. §§ 2–312 (1) (a), (b) and 2–312 (2).

43. U.C.C. § 2–312 (3).

44. U.C.C. § 2–313 (1).

45. U.C.C. § 2–313 (2).

46. U.C.C. § 2–202.

47. U.C.C. § 2–314.

48. U.C.C. § 2–316.

49. U.C.C. § 2–315.

50. *See*, U.C.C. § 2–316 (a).

51. U.C.C. § 2–318.

52. *See, e.g.*, Henningsen v. Bloomfield Motors, Inc., 32 N.J. 358, 161 A.2d 69 (1960).

53. U.C.C. § 2–719 (3).

54. U.C.C. § 2–305 (1) (b) and (c).

55. U.C.C. § 2–507 (1).

56. U.C.C. § 2–511 (1).

57. U.C.C. § 2–512.

58. U.C.C. § 2–606 (1).

59. U.C.C. § 2–607 (3) (a).

60. U.C.C. § 2–610.

61. U.C.C. § 2–609.

62. U.C.C. § 2–702.

63. U.C.C. § 2–705.

64. U.C.C. § 2–710. *See also*, U.C.C. § 2–708 (1).

65. *See*, U.C.C. § 2–708 (2).

66. U.C.C. § 2–706.

67. U.C.C. §§ 2–708 (2) and 2–703.

68. U.C.C. § 2–713.

69. U.C.C. § 2–715.

70. U.C.C. § 2–712.

71. U.C.C. § 2–714 (2).

72. U.C.C. § 2–716.

73. 15 U.S.C. §§ 41–58.

74. 16 C.F.R. § 0.17.

75. 21 U.S.C. §§ 301, *et seq.*

76. 47 U.S.C. §§ 151, *et seq.*

77. *See*, Bailey and Pertschuk, *The Law of Deception: The Past as Prologue*, 33 Am. U.L. Rev. 849 (1984).

78. Cliffdale Assocs., 3 *Trade Reg. Rep.* (CCH) ¶ 22,137, at 22,949 (F.T.C., March 28, 1984).

79. Letter from James Miller, Chairman, F.T.C., to John Dingle, Chairman, House Comm. on Energy and Commerce (Oct. 14, 1983), *reprinted in* 5 *Trade Reg. Rep.* (CCH) ¶ 50,455, at 56,077–78 (1983).

80. Posadas de Puerto Rico Associates v. Tourism Co. of Puerto Rico, _____U.S. _____(July 1, 1986).

81. *See*, David G. Epstein and Steve H. Nickles, *Consumer Law*. West Publishing Co. (1981), pp. 24, 25.

82. 16 C.F.R., ch. 1, subch. D, part 429.

83. 16 C.F.R. § 429.1.

84. 16 C.F.R. § 238.

85. 15 U.S.C. §§ 41–58.

86. 15 U.S.C. §§ 78m, 78dd, and 78ff.

87. 15 C.F.R. § 369.2 (b).

88. United States v. Bechtel Corp., Civ. No. C–76–99 (N.D. Cal. Jan. 16, 1976).

11

Extending Credit

Credit, it has been said, allows nearly everyone to participate in the marketplace. In America by the mid–1980s, nearly everyone was. According to one source, in 1985, over 200 million credit cards were in use, producing an annual charge volume of over $120 billion.[1] Changing attitudes about being in debt coupled with a proliferation of credit sources have resulted in a staggering growth of consumer accounts payable. By early 1984, the volume of consumer credit (excluding residential mortgages) reportedly was $400 billion, compared with $3.5 billion 50 years earlier.[2] This explosive growth has occurred despite enactment of several regulatory laws which control the manner, form, and, to a lesser degree, the terms of credit-extending transactions.

This chapter discusses the principal federal statutes and regulations applicable to credit extensions, notably the Fair Credit Reporting Act; the Truth-in-Lending Act and its implementing Regulations Z and M; the Equal Credit Opportunity Act and its implementing Regulation B; the Fair Credit Billing Act; and various Federal Trade Commission rules, including the Preservation of Consumers' Claims and Defenses, and Credit Practices rules. This chapter also considers state regulation of usury, balloon payments, late charges, default-accelerations, default-insecurity, rebates, and blanket and cross-collateral clauses in sales and loan agreements.

Congress, state legislatures, and the courts have closely scrutinized credit contracts. Arguably, this scrutiny reflects a paternalistic attitude that consumers need protection in dealing with creditors. This attitude recognizes that consumers often act in response to emotional needs and impulses to borrow or buy and, consequently, are prone to agree to anything creditors might demand. Although such reasoning supports regulations designed to protect consumer-debtors, it does not support the regulation of business borrowers who presumably are more sophisticated. Thus, many of the principal credit laws apply only to credit extensions for personal, family, or household purposes.

This chapter begins with a discussion of what a business may and may not do in investigating the creditworthiness of credit applicants. It then addresses credit disclosures, equal credit opportunities, usury, and the regulation of other substantive terms of credit.

CREDIT INVESTIGATIONS

The process which ends with the decision to extend credit usually begins with an investigation of the creditworthiness of the prospective borrower or buyer. The purpose of a credit investigation is to enable a creditor to acquire sufficient information so as to make an intelligent judgment on the risks of possible default, partial repayment, or delayed repayment by the credit applicant.

Credit management is an essential part of any business that sells (or leases) goods or services on credit or that lends money on a secured or unsecured basis to either a business or consumer borrower. Because a credit-extending decision usually turns on a credit manager's or committee's judgment and evaluation, reliable information about a credit applicant's financial situation is often critical.

Two related questions are involved in credit investigations. First, is the credit applicant *able to pay*? Second, does the applicant have a *willingness to pay* his or her bills on time? Information that concerns the applicant's current financial condition is relevant to the first inquiry; information on the applicant's past bill-paying practices is germane to the second.

Business Credit

Various sources of information concerning both a credit applicant's current financial condition and past payment practices exist. These include credit bureaus, banks, credit trade associations, commercial agencies, reports, attorneys, accountants, and, of course, information supplied by the applicant through an interview and as supplemented by other documents, including copies of tax returns, audited or unaudited financial statements, and letters of former or existing creditors. In the case of business credit, one source in particular is widely used—mercantile agencies.

Dun & Bradstreet Reports

Dun & Bradstreet, Inc., a general financial-services or mercantile agency, supplies credit reports on businesses of all sizes, regardless of location or business activities. The company reportedly maintains over 250 offices in the United States. Upon request, the company will issue a "Business Information Report" for a client on any American business that the client requests. A typical report contains information on a firm's payments record, finances, bank accounts, history, and operations, plus a summary of its recent financial condition. Credit reports from a commercial agency such as Dun & Bradstreet are also used to obtain updated information on existing accounts, especially those which are "slow pay" or "inactive," or which are being consolidated or refinanced.

In addition to specific credit reports, Dun & Bradstreet publishes a reference book which contains credit ratings of enterprises located in the United States and Canada. The book is issued periodically to paid subscribers. As Dun & Bradstreet learned in 1985, mistaken information in a published report may lead to liability for punitive as well as actual damages.[3] Despite an occasional error, the mercantile agencies provide valuable and reliable information, particularly in reference to a business's recent financial condition.

Credit bureaus, on the other hand, are not as helpful to credit managers in making creditworthiness judgments for business loans as they are for deciding on applications for consumer loans. Still, in many prospective business loans, information from credit bureaus often is useful when such information on individuals within a business organization is relevant to a credit granting decision; for example, when individual guarantees are required as added security or as a condition for granting a business loan or other credit extension.

Consumer Credit

Creditors who extend credit for a personal, family, or household purpose routinely use the services of credit bureaus and, less frequently, those of investigative reporting agencies. Credit bureaus maintain financial data files on millions of adults in the United States, especially those who have ever borrowed money or been extended credit in any form. It is reported that one company alone, TRW, Inc., maintains records on 90 million Americans.[4] The credit reporting industry obtains its data primarily from credit grantors themselves. Individual payment data practices are then coded and computerized because the process in recent years has become largely automated. It has also become regulated.

Fair Credit Reporting Act

Given the potential for both serious inaccuracies and the indiscriminate or other improper use of information about individuals, Congress in 1970 enacted the Fair Credit Reporting Act (FCRA), also known as Title Six of the federal Consumer Credit Protection Act.[5] Although purporting to be responsive to the individual's needs for privacy and fairness, the FCRA, in effect, validates the very existence of the credit reporting industry including the processes of collecting, evaluating, and disseminating consumer credit information. Given this authenticating ramification, it is little wonder that the credit reporting industry supported the FCRA's enactment.

Essential Terminology

The FCRA defines a "consumer reporting agency" as any person (or firm) which for money, or on a cooperative nonprofit basis, regularly engages in assembling or evaluating credit information about consumers for the purpose of furnishing consumer reports to third persons, where interstate means (for example, the mail or telephones) are used.[6] Thus, when a business gathers credit information only for its own use—not for transmittal to another person or firm—it is not a consumer reporting agency, and, therefore, is not subject to many of the FCRA's specific requirements. On the other hand, if a business gathers or evaluates consumer data from others which it then routinely reports to a consumer reporting agency, it may become a consumer reporting agency subject to the FCRA's requirements but only if the information transmitted meets the test for a "consumer report."

A consumer report is defined as any written, oral, or other communication of any information by a consumer reporting agency bearing on a consumer's creditworthiness, credit standing, credit capacity, character, general reputation, personal characteristics, or mode of living which is used or expected to be used in whole or in part for establishing a consumer's eligibility for:

1. Credit or insurance to be used primarily for personal, family, or household purposes;
2. Employment purposes;
3. Eligibility for a license or other benefit granted by government; or
4. A legitimate business need for the information in connection with a business transaction involving the consumer.[7]

The definition excludes any report containing information solely about transactions or experiences between the consumer and the business making the report.[8] Thus, when a business simply reports the history of its own credit experience with its own customers to a credit reporting agency, the reporting business does not become a credit reporting agency. Should a business, however, compile credit information about its customers received from others, transmittal of such data makes the business a consumer reporting agency under the FCRA.

A few other phrases in the regulation and act need to be understood. "Employment purposes" means a credit report used to evaluate a consumer for employment, promotion, reassignment, or retention.[9] An "investigative consumer report," on the other hand, includes information about a consumer's "character, general reputation, personal characteristics, or mode of living obtained through interviews with neighbors, friends, or associates of the consumer."[10]

Requirements for Business Users

Although the FCRA prescribes requirements applicable to both credit reporting agencies and to users of consumer reports, this discussion is limited to the requirements imposed on businesses that use credit reports. The requirements concern notification of adverse actions.

First, the FCRA requires a business to notify a consumer that his or her credit, employment, or insurance application has been denied or the cost has been raised, in whole or in part, because of information contained in a consumer report from a consumer reporting agency.[11] Second, whenever such an adverse decision is made, the business must also furnish the consumer with the name and address of the consumer reporting agency that issued the report.

When consumer credit is denied or the cost is increased, in whole or part, because of information a business has obtained from a source other than a consumer reporting agency, and that information deals with the applicant's character, creditworthiness, credit standing, credit capacity, mode of living, or general reputation, a business must within a reasonable time following receipt of the consumer's written request for reasons of the adverse action disclose the nature, but not the source, of the information to the consumer.[12] However, no business will be held liable for violating the above notification-of-adverse-action requirements if it establishes that at the time of an alleged violation the firm "maintained reasonable procedures to assure compliance."[13]

Liability

Criminal

Any business (or individual) that "knowingly and willfully" obtains information from a consumer reporting agency "under false pretenses" subjects itself to a fine of up to $5,000, imprisonment of up to one year in jail, or both.[14] In short, there must be a legitimate commercial need for the requested information.

Civil

A business user of either consumer or investigative reports that fails to give the required adverse notice requirements through negligence (carelessness) is liable for any actual damages sustained by a consumer plus costs for any successive enforcement action.[15] For willful or intentional noncompliance, a business is liable for punitive damages to be fixed by a court in addition to actual damages plus costs.[16]

Enforcement

A consumer may enforce the FCRA's compensatory and punitive provisions in any United States district court or state court of competent jurisdiction, within two years of the alleged violation;[17] the FCRA also authorizes administrative enforcement, primarily through the Federal Trade Commission.[18]

CREDIT DISCLOSURES

Prior to Congressional enactment of Title One of the federal Consumer Credit Protection Act of 1969,[19] consumers, in shopping for credit terms, frequently were not provided with meaningful information to enable them to evaluate comparatively what the true cost of offered credit would be. For one thing, lenders and credit sellers, in negotiating pending transactions, typically would not disclose all essential credit terms. For another, even when they were disclosed, the disclosures often would be confusing at best and seriously misleading at worst.

Consider an automobile purchaser who went to dealers A, B, and C in shopping for a particular model of a new car to buy on credit. Assume each dealer offered to sell on credit the car for the same base price, but dealer A said it would finance the sale at 9 percent, dealer B at 11 percent, and dealer C at 14 percent. Having no additional information, the prospective car buyer most likely would have accepted dealer A's offer. But if dealer A's 9-percent sales pitch turned out to be based on an add-on rate method of computation, while dealer B's was based on a discount method, and dealer C's reflected a simple interest rate based on the declining balances, the customer would have received the least expensive credit had he or she purchased the car from dealer C, even though C appeared to offer the most costly credit terms. If each rate were converted to a simple interest rate over the loan's four- or five-year duration, C's 14-percent rate would be the least costly.

Truth in lending (TIL) legislation was enacted not only to require full disclosure of all important credit terms in covered transactions but also to mandate that disclosures be made in a uniform manner. The required uniformity, significantly, applies to the finance rate. After TIL's enactment, dealers A, B, and C are required to disclose their respective interest rate charges in terms of a simple interest rate denoted the "annual percentage rate" or "APR." Congress believed that compelling full and uniform credit disclosures would enhance consumers' knowledge in the marketplace which, in turn, would promote the efficient and competitive offering of credit terms. Studies of marketplace behavior, however, conducted subsequent to TIL's enactment raise certain doubts as to whether the act has been successful in achieving its purposes.

The Applicable Law: Truth in Lending

Although several states have enacted their own consumer credit disclosure laws, the most important disclosure enactment is the federal Truth-in-Lending law, effective July 1, 1969, as amended by the Truth-in-Lending Simplification and Reform Act, effective October 1, 1982.[20] Although the TIL Simplification and Reform Act has made it a bit easier for a business to comply with the act's disclosure requirements, the 1982 amendments have made it a great deal easier for a business to avoid liability for slight or "technical" violations.

Regulations Z and M

Pursuant to the Congressional delegation in TIL, the Federal Reserve Board has promulgated two implementing regulations. Regulation Z,[21] a copy of which every business that extends consumer credit should have, sets out in detail the disclosure rules that creditors in consumer loans or credit sales must follow. Regulation M[22] does the same for consumer leases. The board in the past issued opinion letters and official interpretations but more recently has published an "Official Staff Commentary" on Regulations Z and M, which it revises periodically. Courts have held that the official positions of the board as set out in these interpretations and commentaries should be given deference "unless demonstrably irrational."[23]

TIL's Essential Terminology

TIL applies to most extensions of credit by creditors where the credit, goods, or services are for a consumer purpose. The act defines "credit" as the right granted by a creditor to a debtor to defer payment of debt or to incur debt and defer its payment.[24] "Consumer credit" is defined as credit extended to a *natural person* where the money, property, or services constituting the subject of the transaction are primarily for personal, family, or household purposes.[25]

A "creditor," who is obligated to comply with TIL and Regulation Z, is a person (or organization) who regularly extends consumer credit which is payable in more than four installments or for which the payment of a finance charge is or may be required. The creditor may be a firm which regularly extends consumer credit by way of loans, sales of property, or sales of service.[26] Credit card issuers are also included within the definition, although they are exempt from several of TIL's specific disclosure requirements.

"Credit sales" includes a lease if the lessee is obligated under the agreement to pay a sum of money substantially equivalent to or in excess of the aggregate value of the property involved and if the lessee will become or has the option of becoming the owner for nominal or no consideration upon compliance with the lease contract.[27]

Scope

Being primarily a disclosure statute, TIL does not regulate the substantive terms of a credit transaction. Rather, it mandates *timely* (before a consumer executes or signs the contracting documents) disclosure of credit terms. TIL applies to creditor extensions of consumer credit, including both credit sales and consumer loans, where the amount is less than $25,000 (except for "consumer real estate" or secured real estate transactions) so long as the debtor is a natural person and provided the transaction is primarily for personal, family, or household purposes.[28] The creditor, of course, must in the ordinary course of its business regularly extend or arrange for the extension of credit.[29] Arranging for the extension of credit occurs when a firm provides or offers to provide consumer credit that will be extended by another firm or person under a business relationship pursuant to which the arranger of credit either receives a fee or other compensation for such service or has knowledge of the credit terms and participates in the preparation of the contract documents.[30]

Four-Installment Rule

Provided the circumstances as described in the preceding paragraph are present in a consumer credit transaction, the creditor is subject to the TIL and Regulation Z disclosure requirements provided further that the contract either imposes a finance charge or requires the credit to be repaid *in more than four installments*.[31] The four-installment rule, originally promulgated by the board and subsequently upheld by the United States Supreme Court (and more recently amended into the act itself), is based on the recognition that a seller of goods who only or primarily sells on credit may bury the finance charge by raising the cash price to be equivalent to the credit or deferred price. Even though this is permissible, the "more than" four-installment rule (where the consumer is to pay for the goods in five or more installments) requires that a seller, before the sales agreement is signed, disclose all the required TIL data. Although the finance charge would be none and the APR zero, the most significant disclosure under these circumstances would be the total of all payments. This information effectively prevents a seller from advertising only the weekly or monthly charge without disclosing the total price of the goods or services.

Consumer Leases

Congress amended the Truth-in-Lending Act in 1976 by passing the Consumer Leasing Act.[32] The act defines a consumer lease as a lease or bailment of personal property by a natural person for a period in excess of four months for a total obligation of less than $25,000 where the leased property is primarily for personal, family, or household purposes and whether or not the lessee has an option to purchase or otherwise to become the owner of the property at the expiration of the lease.[33] To be subject to the disclosure requirements, the lessor must be "regularly engaged in leasing, offering to lease, or arranging to lease" property under a consumer lease.[34] Federal Reserve Board Regulations M and Z govern certain but not all consumer leases.

Rent-To-Own Agreements

Truth in Lending's disclosure requirements as of the mid–1980s do not apply to rent-to-own consumer contracts where a consumer agrees to rent, for example, a television set for however long he or she wishes for a stated weekly "rental" payment. (If the consumer rents for a stated number of consecutive weeks, however, he or she typically becomes the owner of the set.) It is not a covered transaction because first, the only payment that the consumer is obligated to pay under a typical rent-to-own contract is the first week's, so the agreement does not meet the four-month minimum period for a covered consumer lease. Second, the consumer is not *obligated* to pay a sum "substantially equivalent to or in excess of the aggregate value of the property," so it does not meet Regulation Z's requirements for a credit sale.[35]

A few states, nonetheless, have begun to enact consumer lease disclosure statutes which are written specifically to cover rent-to-purchase consumer contracts. One example is Michigan where its Rental Purchase Agreement Act became effective on March 30, 1985.[36] Also, in 1986 a similar bill had been proposed in New York. Congress in 1984, however, did *not* at that time enact the proposed Federal Consumer Lease and Lease-Purchase Act, which would have become Title Ten of the Consumer Credit Protection Act. This law had been strongly recommended for passage by the Federal Reserve Board.[37] A version of it seems likely to be enacted in the future, however, given the growth of the rent-to-own industry over the past several years.

Exemptions

As a result of the TIL Simplification and Reform Act of 1980, all agricultural credit extensions are now exempt. By far the most significant exemptions, however, remain those credit extensions used primarily for business or commercial purposes. Also credit to government or to governmental agencies and instrumentalities are exempt. Other exemptions include:

1. Transactions under public utility tariffs, including charges for delayed or late payments or discounts allowed for early payments;
2. Transactions in securities or commodities accounts by a broker-dealer registered with the Securities and Exchange Commission;
3. Loans made, unsigned, or guaranteed pursuant to a program authorized by Title Four of the Higher Education Act of 1965; and
4. Credit transactions where the amount financed exceeds $25,000, except when a security interest is or will be acquired in real or personal property used or expected to be used as the principal dwelling of the consumer.[38]

Disclosure Requirements

The complex TIL disclosure requirements applicable to a given transaction depend on the type of consumer credit being extended. Happily for businesses and lenders, the TIL Simplification and Reform Act mandated the Federal Reserve Board to publish model disclosure forms and clauses for common transactions to facilitate compliance. A creditor is deemed by law to be in compliance with the substantive (but not the numerical) disclosures requirements if it uses the appropriate model form published by the board.[39]

General Requirements

A creditor need not use the board's model forms but, if it does not, all the required disclosures must be made "clearly, conspicuously, [and] in meaningful sequence."[40] In addition to this general mandate, the most important disclosure requirements pertain to the finance charge and annual percentage rate.

Finance Charge

TIL articulates a "concept" of finance charge and describes how this concept should be used to determine the charge to be disclosed in a given credit transaction. Simply, the concept of finance charge is one of the total cost of either buying on credit or of borrowing or having credit extended. A finance charge is the sum of all charges payable directly or indirectly by the debtor and imposed directly or indirectly by the creditor as an incident to the extension of credit.[41] Included under this conceptual definition are

1. Interest, time price differential, plus amounts payable under a point, discount, or other system of additional charges;
2. Service or carrying charges;
3. Loan fees, finder fees, or similar charges;
4. Fees for credit or investigative reports; and
5. Premiums or other charges for any guarantee or insurance protecting the creditor against the obligor's default or other credit loss.

Section 106 of the TIL allows premiums for credit life, health, or accident insurance to be excluded from the finance charge *but only if*, first, the insurance coverage is not a factor in the creditor's credit-extending decision and this fact is clearly disclosed in writing to the credit applicant, and, second, the credit applicant gives a specific affirmative written indication that he or she desires the coverage after receiving written disclosure of its cost.[42]

Other charges which are excluded from the finance charge provided they are itemized and disclosed are license and registration fees, taxes, legal fees, and any other fees that must be paid to governmental officials.

Certain charges never have to be included in the disclosed finance charge. These include title examination, survey, document, and notary fees, as well as title insurance premiums, appraisal charges, credit reports, and required escrow payments for future taxes, utilities, or insurance costs.

Finally, the finance charge disclosure is one of two TIL-required disclosures that must be revealed *more conspicuously* than the other disclosures and terms set out on the form or contract used. The second TIL disclosure that must be portrayed more conspicuously is the annual percentage rate.

Annual Percentage Rate

The Truth-in-Lending Act requires that the finance charge be disclosed in terms of a rate of interest expressed as an annual percentage. In a closed-end installment contract, the annual percentage rate or APR must be computed by either the actuarial method or another accounting method authorized by the Federal Reserve Board. For practical purposes, most businesses use tables available from the board. To use the tables, one needs to compute the finance charge, the amount financed, and the number of payments and then follow the instructions that accompany the tables. Regulation Z contains "Annual Percentage Rate Tables" for monthly and weekly payment schedules.[43]

Other Disclosures

As noted above, the board has begun to publish forms that creditors and lenders may copy and use by filling in the correct numbers to comply with the TIL. The forms are still complex, despite the TIL Simplification and Reform Act. The correct form to use depends on the type of credit being extended. Forms have been published applicable to closed-end credit sales, closed-end loans, and open-end consumer credit plans.

Incidentally, nowhere does TIL or Regulation Z clearly define a closed-end transaction. By deductive elimination, it involves a single advance of credit or funds, for example, a lump-sum loan or a credit purchase of goods. In either case, the credit usually is repayable in installments. In contrast, open-end credit is typified by revolving credit, for example, a bank's line of credit or a consumer's revolving charge account with a credit granting merchant. In revolving credit arrangements, the billing method used affects the amount of the periodic finance charge.

A lender or credit seller of goods or services should obtain both Regulation Z and the model forms from one of the regionally located Federal Reserve Banks. To discuss in detail each of the disclosure requirements for each type of consumer credit sale, loan, or consumer lease would require a book in itself. Only the most important requirements are discussed here.

Right of Rescission

The Truth-in-Lending Act prescribes one significant substantive legal right— a consumer's right to timely rescind a consumer credit contract which *might* result in a security interest or lien in real property which is or expected to be used as the customer's principal residence.[44] This right to timely rescind does not extend to acquisition or construction mortgages or liens on principal residences, however. When applicable, the right of rescission may be exercised up to midnight of the third business day following the day on which the contract was formed or the day on which the required notice of the right to rescind and actual rescission forms were delivered to the debtor, whichever occurred later.[45] Note that the creditor *must supply* the rescission forms at the time the transaction is consummated. The required notice and rescission forms are published in Regulations Z and M.

Credit Advertising

Information given to potential credit customers through advertising is also subject to TIL-disclosure requirements. The extensive rules are collected in Chapter Three of Title One of the Consumer Credit Protection Act.[46] The most important provision is section 144, which states that the act applies to any advertisement designed "to aid, promote, or assist directly or indirectly any consumer credit sale, loan, or other extension of credit . . . "[47] Under this provision, any advertised rate of finance charge must be stated as an annual percentage rate. If *any* of the following "triggering data" is mentioned—a downpayment, the amount of any installment, the period of repayment, the number of installments, or the dollar amount of the finance charge—then the advertisement *must* also state:

1. The downpayment, if any;
2. The terms of repayment; and
3. The annual percentage rate.[48]

Under the TIL's advertising rules a dealer may use, but not advertise, add-on rates. If an advertisement contains any of the above triggering terms, the finance charge rate must be advertised and expressed as an annual percentage rate.

Fair Credit Billing Requirements

Congress, in 1974, enacted the Fair Credit Billing Act (FCBA) amendments to the Truth-in-Lending Act.[49] In revolving or open-end credit arrangements, accounting, clerical, and computer errors do occur which, if not resolved, can lead to disputes and loss of future business. To help alleviate these problems and to afford users of open-end credit a means "to talk with the computer," the FCBA established a procedure for questioning and resolving billing questions.

If a debtor or cardholder believes that a required billing statement contains an error, he or she may send a written notice to the creditor indicating the error, its amount, and the reasons supporting his or her belief that the challenged item is in error. If the creditor receives this written consumer notice within 60 days of transmitting the account statement, it must within 30 days of receiving the notice, respond in writing that it has received it. The creditor within 90 days or two complete billing cycles, whichever is shorter, must make the correction in the account or send to the customer its written explanation of why the original statement was correct. If a creditor fails to follow this procedure, it forfeits its right to collect the first $50 of the disputed charge.[50] If the creditor makes the "appropriate corrections," it must also credit any overpaid finance charge on accounts previously paid. A creditor who fails to comply with the FCRA's requirements is liable to the consumer for his or her actual damages, plus double the amount of the finance charge and costs plus attorney's fees.[51]

TIL Enforcement

Individual Civil Actions

The Truth-in-Lending Act allows a consumer to bring, within one year of a claimed violation, a direct action against the alleged violator of *any* TIL or Regulation Z requirement, no matter how trivial, in either a federal or state court of competent jurisdiction.[52] Despite this language, the TIL Simplification and Reform Act has restricted the liability of creditors to only those nondisclosures that, in effect, are deemed to have material importance to the consumer. These include the finance charge, annual percentage rate, notification of the right of rescission, and amount of all payments. Consumers who can establish a violation of one of the TIL-section-130 listed material disclosure requirements may recover actual damages plus double the amount of the finance charge up to $1,000 maximum but, in any event, at least $100[53] plus costs and attorney's fees. Multiple violations in a single disclosure statement or multiple violations of a single error in periodic statements in either case amount to a single violation and are limited to a single recovery.

Administrative Enforcement

Nine federal agencies have responsibility for the administrative enforcement of the TIL and Regulations Z and M:

1. Comptroller of the Currency (national banks)
2. Interstate Commerce Commission (carriers)
3. Civil Aeronautics Board (airlines)
4. Bureau of Federal Credit Unions (federal credit unions)
5. Federal Reserve Board (member, non-national banks)
6. Federal Deposit Insurance Corp. (insured banks, non-members of Federal Reserve system)
7. Federal Home Loan Bank Board (federally chartered savings banks)
8. Packers and Stockyard Administration (creditors under the Packers and Stockyards Act)
9. Federal Trade Commission (all creditors not coming within the eight previous categories).[54]

The FTC has the most expansive enforcement role of the nine agencies. The TIL enforcement agencies in 1979 published the Uniform Guidelines for Enforcement of Regulation Z in the Federal Register.[55] Although these guidelines have, in part, been superseded by the TIL Simiplification and Reform Act, they still serve as a resource for predicting the enforcement policies and measures that the agencies may follow in reacting to alleged violations of the TIL.

Creditor Defenses

If a creditor can show, by a preponderance of the evidence, that a violation was not intentional but rather resulted from a bona fide error, notwithstanding procedures designed to avoid such an error, he or she will not be held liable for damages in a civil action brought by an individual consumer. Such bona fide errors include mistakes caused by:

1. Computer malfunctions
2. Clerical staff mistakes
3. Miscalculations
4. Computer software
5. Printing mistakes.[56]

An error of legal judgment regarding what TIL requires is not an excusable error, however.

A creditor also may avoid liability if he or she can show that within 60 days of discovering an error, the creditor notified the consumer of the mistake and made the appropriate adjustments in the account.[57]

In summary, the TIL disclosure requirements are complex and pervasive. One commentator has estimated that over one million creditors in the United States are subject to the TIL requirements, and this figure excludes all federal and state banks.[58] Any business that sells goods or services or lends money to individuals on credit is likely to be subject to the TIL and Regulation Z or M requirements. Rather than calling in one's lawyer to draft appropriate and detailed disclosure forms, it may be prudent for a business to obtain a copy of the latest published edition of Regulation Z, along with the Federal Reserve Board model forms, and to carefully follow the instructions in using those forms to comply with the TIL's disclosure requirements.

EQUAL CREDIT OPPORTUNITIES

The Equal Credit Opportunity Act (ECOA)[59] was enacted by Congress in 1974 as an amendment to the federal Consumer Credit Protection Act.[60] ECOA makes it unlawful for a business to discriminate on the basis of sex or marital status in any aspect of a credit transaction.[61] In 1976, ECOA's scope was expanded to prohibit credit-oriented discrimination based on race, color, religion, national origin, age, or on the fact that the credit applicant was receiving income from a public assistance program.[62] Further, the 1976 amendments prohibit credit discrimination because a credit applicant in good faith exercised a right granted under the Consumer Credit Protection Act.[63]

Congress has delegated enforcement of ECOA to the Board of Governors of the Federal Reserve System.[64] Pursuant to this delegation, the board has promulgated Regulation B to implement the act.[65]

Covered Credit Transactions

Three issues must be considered in deciding whether ECOA applies to a transaction. First, does it qualify as a credit transaction? Second, is the credit applicant one who may initiate a claim under ECOA? Third, is the creditor subject to ECOA requirements? All three criteria must be met before the act applies.

Credit Defined

Both ECOA and Regulation B define credit as the right granted by a creditor to defer payment of a debt, incur debt and defer its payment, or purchase property or services and defer payment.[66] This definition is similar to that found in the Truth-in-Lending Act and Regulation Z discussed above. Although the TIL applies only to consumer credit, ECOA and Regulation B apply to nearly all business and consumer transactions. The exceptions are "special purpose credit programs" designed to help either the economically disadvantaged or a nonprofit organization,[67] transactions specifically exempted by the Federal Reserve Board,[68] and transactions in which information is requested by the federal government or by an agency with ECOA enforcement powers.[69]

Partial Exemptions

The Federal Reserve Board has partially exempted five types of credit transactions from all ECOA requirements: public utility, securities, incidental consumer credit, business, and governmental credit.

When a securities broker offers credit to a customer subject to the Securities and Exchange Act, certain provisions of Regulation B do not apply. Consequently, a broker may inquire as to whether the applicant has a spouse or former spouse, whether the applicant is married, and as to the applicant's gender. A broker may require an applicant to open an account in only one name or to have a co-signer. Finally, a broker is neither required to report credit information in both spouses' names nor to retain credit applications.[70]

"Incidental consumer credit" similarly is partially exempt from Regulation B's requirements. Incidental credit is primarily for personal, family, or household purposes; it is not made pursuant to the terms of a credit card account; it is not subject to any financial charge; and it is not payable in more than four installments.[71]

Although ECOA's prohibitions against discrimination on the basis of gender, race, national origin, religion, and sex are applicable to extensions of incidental consumer credit, Regulation B exempts the following requirements: section 202.5 (c), which limits inquiries about a spouse or former spouse; section 202.5 (d) (1), which forbids requests of creditors for marital status information; section 202.5 (d) (2), which limits creditor inquiries concerning alimony, child support, and separate maintenance payments; section 202.5 (d) (3), which forbids inquiries about the applicant's sex; section 202.7 (d), which restricts the creditor's requirement of a co-signer; section 202.9, which requires notification and reasons for an adverse credit action; section 202.10, which requires credit reporting information in both spouses' names upon request; and section 202.12 (b), which requires retention of credit applications. Certain commentators believe these exemptions considerably weaken the act's intended purpose of forcing creditors to disregard an applicant's sex.

Credit used for business purposes also is partially exempted from Regulation B, to wit: section 202.5 (d) (1), which forbids creditor requests for marital status information; section 202.9, which requires notification and reasons for an adverse credit action; section 202.10, which requires the reporting of credit information in the name of both spouses upon request; and section 202.12 (b), which requires retention of credit applications.

Credit Applicant

ECOA defines an "applicant" as a person who applies directly for an extension, renewal, or continuation of credit or applies indirectly by using an existing credit plan beyond the credit limit.[72] Regulation B further defines an applicant as any person who requests or receives credit.[73] A person becomes an applicant once the credit application is initiated even if the full application procedure has not been completed.

A credit applicant has a cause of action if he or she has been discriminated against on a prohibited basis provided the applicant requested credit, submitted an application for credit, opened an account, or requested an increased credit limit on an existing account.[74] A person who is a co-signer and shares primary liability for repayment in a consumer credit transaction is considered to be an applicant for purposes of the act.

Covered Creditors

ECOA lists three types of creditors who are subject to the act's requirements: first, any person (including a business) who regularly extends, renews, or continues credit; second, any person who regularly arranges for the extension, renewal, or continuation of credit; and third, any assignee of an original creditor who is involved in the decision to extend, renew, or continue credit.[75] Businesses that sell goods or services on open account or a deferred payment basis come within the definition. Regulation B further defines a covered creditor as a person who, in the ordinary course of business, regularly participates in deciding whether to extend credit or an assignee or transferee of an original creditor who participates in the credit decision and who had reasonable notice of the policy or practice of the original creditor that violated ECOA before participating in the credit transaction.[76]

Regulation B excludes from the creditor definition any person whose only participation in the transaction concerned honoring a credit card.[77] This means that a merchant honoring a customer's bank-issued credit card is exempt in that transaction from the ECOA requirements. Regulation B's definition of a covered creditor to include those persons who have knowledge of the original creditor's ECOA violation relates to the "close-connection" doctrine discussed elsewhere in this chapter.

Consumer Actions under ECOA

A credit applicant alleging an ECOA violation may bring an action in any state or federal court.[78] The litigant's remedies include actual and punitive damages, injunctive relief, and attorney's fees plus costs.[79] The act places no limits on the amount of actual damages recoverable. Consequently, civil actions are often attractive to rejected credit applicants.

A credit applicant may commence an ECOA-based action within two years from the date of the alleged violation. The infraction may occur at any stage of the transaction, from the applicant's initial application through the creditor's subsequent credit reporting and collection efforts.[80] Thus, the two-year limitation may not commence until long after the initial application has been completed.

Adverse Actions

ECOA defines an "adverse action" as "a denial or revocation of credit, a change in terms of an existing credit arrangement, or a refusal to grant credit in substantially the amount or on substantially the [same] terms [as those] requested."[81] Under Regulation B, adverse actions include:

1. Refusing to grant credit in the same amount or terms requested in an application (unless the applicant accepts or uses the credit as offered);
2. Terminating an account or changing an account's terms when similar accounts are not terminated or changed; and
3. Refusing to increase the credit limit when the creditor has procedures for such increase and the consumer has followed them.[82]

When an adverse action occurs, the applicant has the right to request and receive a written statement from the creditor of the reasons for the denial of credit or for the unfavorable terms offered.[83] Before an applicant may have this right, however, the creditor's application requirements must have been completed.

Regulation B describes five situations that do *not* constitute adverse actions:

1. Any agreed-upon change in the account terms;
2. Any action taken as a result of inactivity, default, or delinquency of an account;
3. Any refusal to approve a point-of-sale transaction;
4. Any refusal to extend credit because the creditor is not authorized by law to offer such credit; and

5. Any refusal to extend credit because the creditor does not offer the type of credit requested.[84]

Thus, a creditor would not violate the ECOA requirements if it accelerated payment on a defaulted or delinquent loan, refused to approve a credit card sale, refused to extend a loan for a consumer item it did not sell, or rejected an application for a long-term loan on a used car.

Protected Classes

The rule proscribing credit discrimination makes it illegal to treat an applicant less favorably than other applicants during any stage of a credit transaction because of the applicant's race, color, religion, national origin, sex, marital status, age, income based on a public assistance program, or exercise of rights granted under the Consumer Credit Protection Act.[85] In the categories of race, color, religion, national origin, sex, marital status, and age, ECOA also applies to an applicant's business partners and others with whom the applicant deals.[86]

Certain inquiries dealing with protected classes are permitted, including questions about marital status (to determine existing remedies for giving credit and having to institute collection procedures); the applicant's age or whether any income is in the form of public assistance (to determine amount and stability of income or credit history); and other information necessary for use in a statistically derived credit system, provided the system complies with requirements of Regulation B.[87]

Race and Color

A creditor cannot consider race and color in evaluating a credit applicant unless the credit program is specially aimed at benefitting the protected categories, for example, a loan program for minority-owned businesses. Information on race may be requested, however, to comply with federal monitoring, for example, in credit applications involving residential real estate sales.

The burden of proof rests on an applicant in any credit discrimination claim based on race. The credit applicant must prove that he or she is a member of a minority racial group and was treated less favorably than other applicants, that the creditor had knowledge of the applicant's race, and that the creditor treated the applicant in a different manner from other applicants of another race with the same qualifications.[88] A discriminatory action may be proved by disparate treatment. Proof of actual malice or an admission of discriminatory intent is not necessary to meet the burden of proof.

Religion

Regulation B prohibits both requests for information regarding the religious preference of a credit applicant (or of any person connected with the transaction) and the consideration of religion in evaluating the credit application.[89] The

Federal Reserve Board has allowed religious inquiries for marketing purposes, but the inquiries cannot be used to evaluate credit applications. Regulation B also allows a creditor to request information about an applicant's religious preference and to consider this information when extending credit under a special program for economically disadvantaged groups.[90]

National Origin

Discrimination based on national origin is discrimination predicated upon the country in which a person was born.[91] A creditor normally may neither request the national origin of any credit applicant nor use the information, if known, in a discriminatory manner.[92] However, it is permissible to inquire as to an applicant's permanent residence and immigration status and to evaluate such information when determining repayment remedies.[93] It is also permissible to request national origin disclosure on credit applications involving residential real estate purchases or when offering credit programs to benefit a specific national origin group.[94]

Sex

Regulation B prohibits a creditor from requesting or considering the applicant's sex during the application process or from using such information to discriminate against an applicant.[95] Creditors may request the applicant's sex to establish a prefix such as Ms., Mrs., or Mr., on an application. Moreover, a creditor should request the applicant's sex on a residential real estate credit application to comply with federal monitoring requirements. In these situations, the creditor should disclose to the applicant that providing the requested information regarding sex is optional.[96] A creditor may request and consider information regarding sex if it is providing a special credit program to benefit socially or economically disadvantaged groups, provided the program has not been established to avoid ECOA regulations.[97]

Examples of sex discrimination in credit transactions include a bank's giving preference to male co-signers on loans; a creditor's running credit checks on the spouses of married women who apply for individual accounts but not performing such reports on spouses of married male applicants, and a bank's denying loans to female account holders who are pregnant.

Marital Status

Marital status information may be requested in residential real estate credit applications and in special credit programs designed to benefit specific social needs. A creditor *must* allow a married applicant to apply for an individual account if the applicant so chooses.[98] When an applicant applies for an individual account, the creditor may not request marital status except in community property states.[99] The creditor may, however, ask about alimony and child support payments, income to be used to repay the account, any co-obligors on disclosed credit obligations, and who holds legal title to the assets disclosed by the applicant.[100] Such information cannot be used to discriminate against the applicant but only to evaluate the applicant's potential for repayment. In these situations the creditor may categorize applicants only as "unmarried," "married," or "separated."[101]

A creditor may inquire about an applicant's spouse whenever:

1. The spouse will use the account;

2. The spouse will be a co-signer on the account;

3. The applicant is using the spouse's income as a repayment source;

4. The transaction is in a community property state; or

5. The applicant is using alimony or child support payments as a repayment source.[102]

When an applicant has requested an individual account and meets the credit evaluation standards, the creditor may not require the applicant's spouse to co-sign the credit account[103] nor use information on marital status to consider only part or none of the applicant's income or that of his or her spouse.[104] Nor may a creditor refuse to aggregate the incomes of an unmarried couple applying for joint credit if the same couple would receive credit if married.[105]

A creditor may not automatically require reapplication on an open account when an account holder changes marital status.[106] The creditor may, however, request updates when the marital status changes. If the credit was originally granted based on a former spouse's income, the creditor may require reapplication.[107]

Age

ECOA makes it illegal to discriminate against a credit applicant on the basis of age provided the applicant has the legal capacity to enter into a contract.[108] Regulation B and the act focus on discrimination against elderly persons. Regulation B defines "elderly" as including all persons aged 62 or older.[109]

A creditor may use a credit evaluation system which considers age but may not assign a negative value on the basis of the age of the elderly applicant. However, a creditor may consider age "for purpose of determining an element of creditworthiness."[110] Elements of creditworthiness to which age might be pertinent include the applicant's occupation and time left before retirement for determining income and the duration of the applied-for credit in comparison with the applicant's life expectancy. On the other hand, a creditor may not require reapplication, change the terms, or terminate an existing account because the account holder has reached a certain age or retires. While a creditor may not disallow part-time employment or retirement benefits as income considerations, the creditor may consider the probable continuity of such income in evaluating the initial credit applicant.[111]

Public Assistance

It is unlawful to discriminate against a credit applicant on the ground that any or all of the applicant's income is from a public assistance program such as unemployment compensation, food stamps, or social security.[112] A creditor may inquire whether the applicant receives public assistance to determine the amount and probable continuance of income as pertinent to creditworthiness. Acceptable questions include how long the applicant has been receiving public assistance, the applicant's future plans concerning state residency, and the ages of the applicant's dependent children (to determine the duration of benefits).[113]

Exercise of Consumer Credit Protection Act Rights

A creditor may not discriminate against an applicant because that person has exercised in good faith a right granted under the Consumer Credit Protection Act.[114] This provision prevents retaliatory credit-related actions. The Consumer Credit Protection Act is an umbrella statute composed of a number of credit-oriented sections or titles,[115] several of which are discussed in this volume.

Subsequent Procedures

It is important for creditors to note that ECOA also applies to subsequent procedures pertaining to the granting of credit, including credit reporting and record retention. Reporting procedures are governed by Regulation B and the Fair Credit Reporting Act.[116] As to record retention requirements, Regulation B mandates creditors to retain records of credit transactions for 25 months following the date an applicant is notified of any action taken on the application or account.[117]

USURY LAWS

Usury laws regulate the costs a creditor may legally charge for extending credit. Usury generally is defined as the lending of money or the forbearance to collect a debt pursuant to an agreement which requires the debtor to pay back the indebtedness in full, plus an additional sum, usually denoted "interest," which exceeds the amount allowed by law. Certain, but not all, usury laws also require for a transaction to be usurious that the creditor intend to exact an unlawful rate of interest.

Until the twentieth century, personal debt was considered ill advised, even sinful. But in our increasingly commercialized society attitudes have changed to the point where today borrowing and buying on credit have become a way of life for nearly all segments of American society.

Early Usury Laws

Beginning with Massachusetts in 1641, most state legislatures eventually enacted lawful interest rate ceilings at between 6 percent and 8 percent.[118] By the mid–1980s, nearly all the states still had usury statutes in effect, although various legislative and judicial responses to the harshness of the traditionally low ceilings had by then occurred.

Loan-sharking

One might think that usury laws are needed to prevent loan-sharking—the lending of money or extending of credit at exorbitant rates. In fact, a good case has been made that the low rate ceilings, which were in effect around the turn of the century in America, foreclosed consumers from traditional lenders, thereby pushing many borrowers to seek other, less lawful sources of money. The typical lawful statutory ceiling rates were, in fact, quite low given the relative small amounts involved in consumer loans and their attending risks.[119] Thus, to meet the growing demand for consumer credit, loan-sharking began to flourish near the turn of the century.

To understand the truly oppressive nature of loan-sharking, consider the following (to be sure, extreme) example: Assume John needs to borrow $100 and no commercial bank is willing to extend him the loan because he is at the moment unemployed. John goes to a loan shark, Mary, who loans John $100 at the rate of "five for four," compounded weekly, repayment due in one year. Under the agreement, John is required to pay back the $100 loan plus interest in one lump sum, the total amount being due one year from the date of the transaction. The "five for four" rate simply means that John agrees to pay Mary five dollars for every four of the outstanding balance as determined at the end of each week, for fifty-two consecutive weeks. Under such an agreement, John would owe Mary the incredible but mathematically correct sum of $109,476,438. Not all loan-sharking was *that* profitable, however.

Small Loan Laws

Nonetheless, loan-sharking was clearly both profitable and oppressive. In response to the growing problem, the Russell Sage Foundation in 1915 drafted a Uniform Small Loan Law, which served as a model for the states to enact legislation designed to encourage and regulate small loans of $500 or less. This model law permitted a maximum annual rate of interest of up to 42 percent on balances within the first $300 of a loan. The model law was a success. Today, the lending rates of small loan companies and other lenders are regulated in part by similar small loan laws. These enactments represent statutory exceptions to a state's general usury rate statutes.

Small loan acts in effect today in numerous states cover loans up to $5,000. The interest rates are stratified depending on the amount of the initial loan. On the other hand, the Uniform Consumer Credit Code,[120] in effect in several states at the time of this writing (including Colorado, Idaho, Indiana, Iowa, Kansas, Maine, Oklahoma, Utah, and Wyoming), establishes various rate ceilings depending on the *type* of consumer loan, to wit: credit sale, revolving sale, consumer loan, revolving loan, and so on.

Time-Price Exception

Beginning with the 1861 U.S. Supreme Court decision of *Hogg v. Ruffner*,[121] the "time-price doctrine" has become a judicially recognized exception to the applicability of a state's general usury laws. Under this doctrine, a seller can sell an article for cash and ask one price or sell it on a deferred payment basis and ask a different or "time price." The difference between the cash price and the time price is called the time-price differential. Most courts considering the issue have held that a time-price differential is not interest as contemplated by the state legislature when enacting the state's usury statutes.[122]

Close-Connection Doctrine

The time-price doctrine applies only to bona fide credit sales made in good faith. Thus, a lender cannot avoid a state's usury limitations by arranging to extend credit through a retailer, even though the latter appears to be making a credit sale to a consumer, and then assigns the consumer's obligation to the lender. This is known as the "close-connection doctrine." It raises the issue of whether in a credit sale/subsequent assignment situation two separate arm's-length transactions have occurred or whether the transaction is to be considered an "arranged" or "conduit" loan. If the purchaser of the consumer obligation (the assignee) made the initial check on the prospective consumer-purchaser's creditworthiness, or if the assignee absorbs any credit loss by having taken the assignment "without recourse," a court may hold that the state's general usury limits apply and not the recognized time-price exception. Why? Because the court will likely find that there was no bona fide credit sale.[123] The assignee-creditor was too closely connected to the initial creditor-seller. Other factors courts consider in making this determination include the number of prior assignments between the merchant and assignee, whether the merchant is obligated to tender all its consumer paper to the assignee pursuant to a contractual right of first refusal, or whether the sales forms that the dealer-assignor uses in selling the goods or services have been provided by, or include the name of, the assignee-creditor.

State Sales Acts

The time-price exception to the general usury statutes has become less important in the past twenty years due to enactment of various state laws pertaining to sales of goods to consumers. Known under various titles such as retail in-

stallment sales acts, consumer finance acts, or consumer sales acts (as well as
the Uniform Consumer Credit Code noted above), these state statutes typically
incorporate specific rate ceilings applicable to both installment and open-end
credit sales. A state sales act's ceilings normally are higher than the legal rate
of interest ceilings prescribed by the state's general usury statutes.

Federal Preemptions

Certain types of credit extensions are subject to federal preemption in regard
to usury rates, meaning that the federal rules apply, not the state's. These include
real estate mortgage loans made since 1980 (see Chapter 7), most federally
insured loans and mortgages,[124] and all non-mortgage loans made by national
banks and other federally insured lenders. The latter institutions may charge for
loans a rate of interest 1 percent above the Federal Reserve Bank discount rate
on 90-day commercial paper.[125]

Computing Usury Rates

Not only does each state have its own usury laws—twelve separate rate ceiling
provisions are in effect in Florida, for example[126]—there is no uniformity among
the states in how the interest rate is to be calculated. Many state statutes are
drafted in terms of add-on rates (see the TIL discussion in this chapter), while
others are framed in a periodic rate, for example, 1.5 percent per month. But
even a periodic rate is unclear since at least four methods exist for the computing
of interest on revolving credit arrangements: ending balance, previous balance,
adjusted balance, and average daily balance. Also, certain state usury statutes
compute permissible interest on the basis of an allowable maximum discount,
usually calculated on an annual basis. To complicate the matter even more,
certain creditors calculate interest on the basis of a 360-day credit year, rather
than 365, a practice which appears to be permissible, even though it results in
a slightly higher rate than would otherwise be allowed. Many states require that
prepaid interest be spread over the expected duration of the credit transaction
and be included in computing the effective interest rate for purposes of usury.
Unfortunately, there is little uniformity as to what items are to be spread and
what may be disregarded for usury computations.

Variable Rate Loans

The Tennessee Supreme Court has held that "indexed principal" under a
variable rate loan is interest for purposes of the usury laws.[127] Variable rate loans
are designed to protect a lender from inflation and a borrower from possible
deflation. Indexing the interest rate is permissible so long as the rate does not
exceed the permissible ceiling. But indexing the principal, although also permissible, often will result in a required sum to be paid which will exceed the
usury limit during inflationary periods.

Included and Excluded Charges

For purposes of determining whether a given credit extension is usurious, the following charges normally will be excluded: late payment fees, recording fees, title examination fees, loan origination fees (except for points), and foreclosure or collection costs. The TIL definition of finance charge serves as a rough guide of what is to be included in determining the total amount of interest or finance charge in a particular transaction. Still, many usury statutes as well as court decisions do not necessarily follow the TIL when calculating interest under a state usury law. For example, no uniformity exists on the issue of whether unearned or unaccrued interest which may, under the terms of an agreement, become payable upon a debtor's default are to be included to determine if a default-acceleration payout is usurious or not. (See subsequent discussion in this chapter.)

Liability

Criminal

Several states render usurious credit extensions crimes if in excess of explicit statutory limits. For example, under a Florida criminal statute, a loan with an interest rate in excess of 45 percent is a felony, while one from 26 to 45 percent is a misdemeanor.[128] Liability under this statute includes forfeiture of the entire principal and interest. Loans that are extorted by threats or coercion whether usurious or not are prohibited and made crimes under a federal criminal statute.[129]

Civil

The civil liability of a person or business held to have made a usurious loan varies considerably from state to state. The most typical civil penalty is forfeiture of all interest. Other states limit the forfeiture only to that portion representing the excess or usurious interest. A few states require the defendant to pay the plaintiff multiples of the interest—for example, twice the amount of the interest, as a penalty. Still other states require a forfeiture of interest (all, a portion, or multiple) plus a forfeiture of a percentage of the principal.

Usury may come up as a defense to a debt collection action. If usury is found to exist, the plaintiff may be barred from foreclosing or from otherwise enforcing the remaining indebtedness. Other courts, however, will enforce a usurious loan but will order civil penalties to be deducted from any judgment for the plaintiff.

REGULATING THE TERMS OF CREDIT

While truth-in-lending and equal credit opportunity laws and regulations control the form and manner of many credit extensions, no comprehensive federal statute regulates the substantive terms that may be included in a credit sale or loan contract. The closest thing may be the Federal Trade Commission Trade

Regulation Rule on Credit Practices, which became effective on March 1, 1985.[130] Although it addresses several substantive terms, the FTC rule is far from being comprehensive.

As already noted, the cost of credit is regulated by a hodgepodge of state and federal usury rate laws which include state retail installment sales acts, judicial doctrines, small loan laws, sales finance acts, the Uniform Consumer Credit Code, and other interest rate ceiling legislation. Several other terms commonly included in credit contracts similarly fall within this hodgepodge regulatory environment. These include balloon payment clauses, blanket and cross-collateral security provisions, default-acceleration and default-insecurity clauses, waiver-of-defense provisions, co-signature requirements, rebating and late charge clauses, and confessions of judgments (or cognovit clauses). This section briefly addresses the regulation of each of these substantive terms.

Balloon Payments

Although balloon payments are often used in real estate financing, they are less common in consumer credit sales or loans. For one thing, balloon payments may be a deceptive selling practice. An official comment to section 2.405 of the Uniform Consumer Credit Code (UCCC) points out that balloon payments may be used to induce a buyer to enter into a burdensome contract by offering invitingly small installment payments until the end of the contract when the buyer is confronted with a balloon payment which the consumer often finds too large to pay. It is not surprising, therefore, that balloon payments in consumer credit sales either have been prohibited outright or their use has been restricted in several states.

The UCCC (in effect in ten states as of October 1, 1986) provides that, in a consumer sale, if any scheduled payment is more than twice as large as the average of the other earlier payments, the buyer has the right to refinance the balance without penalty at the time the balloon payment becomes due.[131] Other state statutes restrict the use of balloons or, like the UCCC, permit refinancing at no increased rate and with no penalty.

Blanket Security Clauses

A blanket security clause is one that covers all goods of a specified type or types and by which the goods become subject to a security interest of the lender or credit seller. Blanket security clauses are routinely used in business financing; for example, where a lender is granted a security interest in *all* the accounts or inventory of a firm.

When a blanket security clause is used in a consumer transaction, however, it is subject to attack, especially if, by its terms, it encompasses "household goods." The FTC's 1984 Credit Practices Rule declares it to be an unfair act or practice in violation of section 5 of the Federal Trade Commission Act for any lender or retail installment seller to include in any credit extension contract with a consumer a blanket security clause which creates a nonpossessory security interest in the consumer's household goods, except for a purchase money security interest.[132] A purchase money security interest as defined in Article Nine of the Uniform Commercial Code is an interest either taken by a lender who gives value to the debtor to enable the debtor to acquire the collateral or an interest retained by a seller to secure all or part of the purchase price of the goods.[133] Although a seller of household goods may retain a security interest pursuant to a security agreement in the goods sold, a lender may not secure a non-purchase money loan by taking out a security interest in the household goods of a borrower under the FTC rule.

Household goods are defined in the FTC rule as clothing, furniture, appliances, one radio and one television, linens, china, crockery, kitchenware, and personal effects of the consumer and of his or her dependents.[134] Excluded from the definition are art works, stereos, video-recorders, antiques over 100 years old, and jewelry (except wedding rings).[135]

In addition to the FTC Credit Practices Rule, several state statutes restrict the use of non-purchase money security interests in consumer goods in relation to lending and retail sales contracts. For example, the UCC (in effect in 49 states) provides that no security interest attaches under a blanket-after-acquired property clause to consumer goods when given as additional security except for consumer goods received by the debtor within the first ten days following the loan or sale.[136]

Cross-Collateral Clauses

A cross-collateral clause, like a blanket security clause, is used by a credit seller in an effort to extend the security interest beyond the immediate property being sold to the buyer. One form of cross-collateral clause extends the security interest back in time to include previously sold merchandise. For example, furniture dealer X sells a stereo to customer Y and, pursuant to the sales/security agreement, secures Y's future payments due for the stereo by retaining a security interest not only in the stereo but also in all the merchandise which X had previously sold to Y. Although there is no federal prohibition of such a backward-in-time, cross-collateral loan, certain courts have not enforced them if, under the circumstances, the add-on security clause is deemed to be unfair or unconscionable.[137]

Default-Acceleration Clauses

A default-acceleration clause is a provision of a lending or credit sales agreement which provides that, if any default event occurs, the entire remaining balance becomes immediately due and owing and which, as a result, accelerates the creditor's available remedies. No federal or state laws prohibit inclusion of a default-acceleration clause in a consumer loan or personal property sales contract. However, restrictions on the *use* of default acceleration provisions exist in several states. If the contract is worded so that a creditor may elect or choose to consider a single default occurrence (for example, a missed payment) as an acceleration event, several states' laws require that the consumer borrower or buyer be notified of the acceleration election before the creditor may invoke its remedies. In several states, moreover, the missing of a single payment does not become a default event under a consumer credit contract until a prescribed grace period for curing the default has expired. In such states, Wisconsin, for example, no acceleration of indebtedness or remedies occurs until the grace period's expiration.

Default-acceleration clauses, which include explicit waiver of notification language, are recognized as valid in some states but not in others. The UCC indirectly recognizes the validity of default-acceleration clauses in section 9–506's, "Official Comment"[138] which notes that a debtor, to redeem repossessed collateral, must tender the entire indebtedness if the security agreement contains a default-acceleration provision.

Default-Insecurity Clauses

A default-insecurity clause is a form of acceleration which, although as a general matter legally permissible, raises special problems. Under a default-insecurity provision in a loan, sales, or security agreement, the lender, seller, or secured party typically has an option to accelerate the debtor's payments or to require collateral or additional collateral whenever the creditor "deems himself insecure" in reference to the debtor's ability or willingness to make future payments or meet other obligations under the credit-extending contract.

The UCC validates default-insecurity clauses, which it denotes as options to accelerate in section 1–208. However, the UCC restricts the operation of these clauses to only those instances involving a creditor's insecurity when the creditor "in good faith believes that the prospect of payment or performance is impaired."[139] Thus, a clause, which purports to give a creditor the power to accelerate "at will" or "for any reason," will be construed under this UCC provision to mean that the creditor shall have the power to do so only when the creditor has a good faith belief that the prospect of the debtor's future performance is seriously in doubt.

Waiver-of-Defense Clauses

Creditors may transfer their rights to receive payments under existing credit-extending contracts to a third person for immediate cash or credit. Within the commercial community these transfers are variously referred to as discounting consumer paper, selling or factoring trade obligations, or assigning (for cash or security) retail installment or chattel paper. Assignable credit-extending contracts include most consumer leases, installment sales, loans, and security agreements.

Regardless of the form of the paper evidencing the obligation to pay, the lessor, installment purchaser, borrower, or debtor is legally considered the paper's obligor, in other words, the one having the duty to pay the balance due under the contract. The dealer, merchant, bank, lending company, or landlord is considered the obligee, the person (or legal entity) to whom the obligor owes the duty of payment and who, thereby, is the one under the contract having the initial right to receive the obligor's payments. The obligee may become an assignor when he or she transfers, sells, discounts or, more properly, assigns his or her right to receive payments from the obligor to a third person referred to as the assignee. The assignee (or transferee of the obligation) usually pays cash or advances credit to the obligee-assignor to obtain the obligee's rights to receive payments.

To make the contracts more marketable and, therefore, more easily assignable, they are often drafted to include waiver-of-defense clauses. A waiver-of-defense clause is a provision in a lease, sale, loan, or security agreement which states that the obligor (customer) agrees that he or she will not assert against any assignee of the contract any claim or defense which the obligor may have against the obligee-assignor. The clause makes the obligor's contract more marketable by assuring possible purchasers of the contract that the customer-obligor will continue to be legally obligated to pay the balance due regardless of what might go wrong between the customer and the merchant-obligee.

The principal legal effect of a waiver-of-defense clause (provided it is recognized as valid) is that it "cuts off" the obligor's or customer's defenses against making the payments when the contractual right to receive those payments has been transferred to a third person. A common example of this principle arises in the purchase of an automobile from a dealer who, after the sale of the new car, assigns or discounts the contract to a finance company.

Assume that the new car breaks down two weeks after the sale and that the dealer fails to honor its warranty obligations to the buyer. Although the UCC would allow the buyer to suspend making his or her payments to the seller, it does not allow the customer to stop paying the assignee. Since the sales contract had been assigned to the finance company for value and since the assignee took the paper without having actual knowledge of the buyer's breach of warranty defense in good faith and provided that the sales contract contained a waiver-of-defense clause, the buyer may not legally withhold payments but will have to tender all amounts as they become due under the sales contract to the finance company, the seller's breach of the sales contract notwithstanding. There is, however, a major exception to this defense cutoff principle: The rule does not apply if the buyer was purchasing the car for a consumer purpose. In that situation, the FTC steps in and changes the picture entirely.

FTC Preservation of Consumers' Claims and Defenses Rule

On May 14, 1976, the FTC trade regulation known as the Preservation of Consumers' Claims and Defenses rule became effective.[140] The rules as subsequently amended declare it to be a violation of section 5 of the Federal Trade

Commission Act for a covered seller or purchase money lender: (a) to take or receive a consumer credit contract which fails to contain the following notice in at least ten point, bold face type:

NOTICE

ANY HOLDER OF THIS CONSUMER CREDIT CONTRACT IS SUBJECT TO ALL CLAIMS AND DEFENSES WHICH THE DEBTOR COULD ASSERT AGAINST THE SELLER OF GOODS OR SERVICES OBTAINED PURSUANT HERETO OR WITH THE PROCEEDS HEREOF. RECOVERY HEREUNDER BY THE DEBTOR SHALL NOT EXCEED AMOUNTS PAID BY THE DEBTOR HEREUNDER.

or,(b) accept, as full or partial payment for such sale or lease, the proceeds of any purchase money loan (as purchase money loan is defined herein), unless any consumer credit contract made in connection with such purchase money loan contains the following provision in at least ten point, bold face, type:

NOTICE

ANY HOLDER OF THIS CONSUMER CREDIT CONTRACT IS SUBJECT TO ALL CLAIMS AND DEFENSES WHICH THE DEBTOR COULD ASSERT AGAINST THE SELLER OF GOODS OR SERVICES OBTAINED WITH THE PROCEEDS HEREOF. RECOVERY HEREUNDER BY THE DEBTOR SHALL NOT EXCEED AMOUNTS PAID BY THE DEBTOR HEREUNDER.[141]

The above FTC rule eliminates the effectiveness of waiver-of-defense clauses in most if not all consumer credit transactions.

The rule applies not only to sellers who extend consumer credit but also to lenders who make "purchase money loans" which, under the rule, include "interlocking loans," "body dragging," "vendor-related loans," and "specious cash sales." These latter categories refer to the close connection doctrine discussed earlier in this chapter in the section dealing with credit disclosures.[142] The purpose of including lenders who regularly participate in credit sales by arranging credit through, or by having customers referred from, a dealer was to prevent circumvention of the rule's intended reach. But for the purchase money rule, a seller could get just to the point of signing a credit contract with a prospective buyer and then either refer or physically take ("body drag") the customer to a lender who would then make a loan directly to the customer and be free of all defenses against payment. Because of the FTC rule, body dragging no longer may be used to insulate the lender from the underlying sales transaction.

Commercial Loans

Unlike the situation involving consumer loans or sales, credit extensions to businesses are not subject to the FTC preservation of claims and defenses rule. Thus, in extending a commercial loan to a business, a lender may include a waiver-of-defense clause in the contract. Moreover, even if the contract does not include an explicit waiver-of-defense clause, if a business in buying goods on credit executes both a negotiable instrument (typically, a promissory note—see Chapter 12) and a security agreement (one which creates a security interest in the goods sold in favor of the seller), the buyer is deemed under the UCC to have made implicitly a waiver-of-defense agreement.[143]

Co-Signature Requirements

The FTC Credit Practices Rule requires that, before a co-signer (or surety) becomes liable in reference to or under a consumer credit contract, the lender or credit seller must inform the co-signer "of the nature of his or her liability" as co-signer.[144]

The FTC rules prescribes a form which, if followed, avoids any liability for an FTC act section 5 violation. The form notice, a separate document from the consumer credit contract, reads as follows:

You are being asked to guarantee this debt. Think carefully before you do. If the borrower doesn't pay the debt, you will have to. Be sure you can afford to pay if you have to, and that you want to accept this responsibility.

You may have to pay up to the full amount of the debt if the borrower does not pay. You may also have to pay late fees or collection costs, which increase this amount.

The creditor can collect this debt from you without first trying to collect from the borrower. The creditor can use the same collection methods against you that can be used against the borrower, such as suing you, garnishing your wages, etc. If this debt is ever in default, that fact may become a part of *your* credit record.

This notice is not the contract that makes you liable for the debt.[145]

Late Charges and Rebates

Late Charges

The FTC Credit Practices Rule prohibits certain delinquency or late charges to be added on during the collection phase of a consumer credit indebtedness.[146] Nonetheless, courts have held most late charges to be legally permissible, noting that a late charge is in essence a penalty for delinquency and does not render the credit contract usurious even when the late charge is part of the credit-extending contract.[147] A late charge provision in a credit contract on occasion has been analyzed as a form of liquidated damages provision meaning that to be enforceable, it must be reasonably related to the creditor's actual damages caused by a late payment. An extension charge, on the other hand, has been held to be compensation for deferring payment, therefore, subject to a state's usury rate limits.

Rebate of Unearned Interest

In precomputed, closed-end credit transactions, the obligor's total credit obligations have been determined at the outset and included in the TIL-required total "Finance Charge." When an obligor prepays, however, under a typical state finance law, the creditor is entitled only to the interest earned up to the point of prepayment. The Uniform Consumer Credit Code, for example, affords any covered debtor the right to prepay at any time the unpaid balance of a consumer loan, refinancing, or consolidation but requires that any amounts representing an unearned portion of the finance charge must be rebated to the consumer.[148]

Many state finance laws requiring rebate or non-collection of unearned interest in the event of prepayment (or of default acceleration) use the "sum of the digits," also known as the "Rule of 78's," as the computational method. This method to some people appears to allow a creditor to concentrate near the front end of a consumer credit transaction a greater portion of the finance charge than in the later period. In fact, the Rule of 78's is an accounting method applicable to installment contracts where equal monthly payments are called for in the credit contract which accounting method approximates very closely the interest actually earned on a declining balance over time. The computation of rebates under the sum of the digits or Rule of 78's method is, however, a bit complex. Fortunately, financial publishing companies and most banks publish tables for computing rebates under the Rule of 78's.

Confessions of Judgment

Under a confession of judgment, also known as a cognovit clause or warrant of attorney provision, a debtor in a credit contract authorizes the creditor or the creditor's attorney to appear in court and enter judgment against the debtor without prior notice or any hearing. Such clauses have been judicially struck down in several states including California. There also have been serious constitutional questions raised about their use, although the United States Supreme Court has upheld their facial validity.[149]

More recently, the FTC Credit Practices Rule, effective March 1, 1985, declares that the inclusion of a confession of judgment, cognovit, warrant of attorney, or any other obligor waiver of rights to notice and hearing prior to judgment in a consumer credit contract affecting commerce is a violation of section 5 of the Federal Trade Commission Act.[150] Consequently, a lender or credit seller is advised not to include any waiver, confession, or warrant of attorney clause in any consumer credit contract. For that matter, a creditor would be well advised not to include either an explicit or implicit waiver of rights to notice or hearing language in any credit extending contract.

NOTES

1. Paul B. Rasor, *Consumer Finance Law*. Mathew Bender (1985), p. 6.
2. *Id.*

3. Dun & Bradstreet, Inc. v. Greenmoss Builders, Inc., 472 U.S. 749, 86 L.Ed.2d 593 (1985).

4. P. Rasor, *Consumer Finance Law* (1985), p. 17.

5. 15 U.S.C. §§ 1681–1681t.

6. 15 U.S.C. § 1681a.

7. 15 U.S.C. §§ 1681a, 1681b.

8. 15 U.S.C. § 1681a.

9. *Id.*

10. *Id.*

11. 15 U.S.C. § 1681m.

12. *Id.*

13. *Id.*

14. 15 U.S.C. § 1681q.

15. 15 U.S.C. § 1681o.

16. 15 U.S.C. § 1681n.

17. 15 U.S.C. § 1681.

18. 15 U.S.C. § 1681e.

19. 15 U.S.C. §§ 1601–1667e.

20. *Id.*

21. 12 C.F.R. part 226.

22. 12 C.F.R. part 213.

23. Ford Motor Co. v. Milhollin, 444 U.S. 555, 565 (1980).

24. 15 U.S.C. § 1602.

25. *Id.*

26. *Id.*

27. 12 C.F.R. § 226.2 (s).

28. 12 C.F.R. § 226.2 (m).

29. 12 C.F.R. § 226.2 (h).

30. 12 C.F.R. § 226.2 (k).

31. 15 U.S.C. §§ 1667–1667e.

32. 12 C.F.R. § 226.2 (mm); 15 U.S.C. § 1667 (1).

33. 15 U.S.C. § 1667 (z).

34. 12 C.F.R. § 213.2 (a).

35. Lemay v. Stroman's, Inc., 510 F.Supp. 921 (E.D. Ark. 1981).

36. Mich. Laws 1984, P.A. 424.

37. 5 *Cons. Credit Guide* (C.C.H.) ¶ 96,515 (1984).

38. 15 U.S.C. § 1603.

39. 15 U.S.C. § 1604.

40. 12 C.F.R. § 226.6 (a).

41. 15 U.S.C. § 1605.

42. *Id.*

43. 12 C.F.R. § 226.5.

44. 12 C.F.R. § 226.9 (a).

45. 15 U.S.C. § 1635.

46. 15 U.S.C. §§ 1661–1665a.

47. 15 U.S.C. § 1664.

48. *Id.*

49. 15 U.S.C. §§ 1666–1666j.

50. 15 U.S.C. § 1666e.

51. 15 U.S.C. § 1640.

52. *Id.*

53. *Id.*

54. 15 U.S.C. §§ 1607, 1608.

55. 44 Fed. Reg. 1222 (1979).

56. 15 U.S.C. § 1640; Mirabel v. General Motors Acceptance Corp., 537 F.2d 871 (7th Cir. 1976).

57. 15 U.S.C. § 1640.

58. David G. Epstein and Steve H. Nickles, *Consumer Law.* West Publishing Co. (1980), p. 158.

59. 15 U.S.C. §§ 1691 to 1691(s) (1974).

60. 15 U.S.C. §§ 1601 to 1681 (t) (1970).

61. 15 U.S.C. § 1691 (a).

62. 15 U.S.C. § 1691, as amended by ECOA amendments of 1976, Pub. L. No. 94–239, sections 7, 8, 90 Stat. 255.

63. *Id.*

64. 15 U.S.C. § 1691 (b) (1976).

65. 12 C.F.R. § 202.

66. 15 U.S.C. §§ 1691 (a) (d); 12 C.F.R. § 202.2 (i).

67. 15 U.S.C. § 1691 (c); 12 C.F.R. § 202.8.

68. 15 U.S.C. § 1691 (b) (a); 12 C.F.R. § 202.3.

69. 12 C.F.R. § 202.13.

70. 12 C.F.R. § 202.3

71. 12 C.F.R. § 202.3 (a) (3).

72. 15 U.S.C. § 1691a (b).

73. 12 C.F.R. § 202.2 (e). *See also,* Cragin v. First Federal Savings and Loan, 498 F. Supp. 379 (D. Nev. 1980).

74. 15 U.S.C. § 1691a (b); 12 C.F.R. § 202.2 (e).

75. 15 U.S.C. § 1691a (e).

76. 12 C.F.R. § 202.2 (1).

77. 12 C.F.R. § 202.2.

78. 15 U.S.C. § 1691e (f).

79. 12 C.F.R. §§ 1691e (a) to (f).

80. 12 C.F.R. § 202.2 (m).

81. 15 U.S.C. § 1691 (d) (6).

82. 12 C.F.R. §§ 202.2 (c) (1) (i), (ii), (iii).

83. 15 U.S.C. § 1691 (d); 12 C.F.R. § 202.9.

84. 12 C.F.R. § 202.2 (c).

85. 15 U.S.C. § 1691 (a); 12 C.F.R. § 202.4.

86. 12 C.F.R. § 202.2 (z).

87. 15 U.S.C. § 1691 (b) (1) (2); 12 C.F.R. § 202.2 (p) (2).

88. 12 C.F.R. § 202.8. *See also,* Steele v. Beneficial Finance Co., 5 *Cons. Cred. Guide* (C.C.H.) ¶ 97,481 (D. Kan. 1980).

89. 12 C.F.R. § 202.5 (d) (5).

90. *See,* Fed. Res. Bd., 5 *Cons. Cred. Guide* (C.C.H.) ¶ 42,102 (March, 1978); 12 C.F.R. § 202.8.

91. 15 U.S.C. § 1691 (a) (1); Fed. Res. Bd., 5 *Cons. Cred. Guide* (C.C.H.) ¶ 42,105 (June, 1978).

92. 12 C.F.R. §§ 202.4 and 202.2 (z).

93. 12 C.F.R. §§ 202.5 (d) (5) and 202.6 (b) (7).

94. 12 C.F.R. §§ 202.13 and 202.8.

95. 12 C.F.R. §§ 202.5 (d) (3) and 202.4.

96. 12 C.F.R. §§ 202.5 (d) (3) and 202.13.

97. 12 C.F.R. § 202.8.

98. 15 U.S.C. § 1691d (c); 12 C.F.R. § 202.7 (a).

99. 12 C.F.R. § 202.5 (d).

100. 12 C.F.R. § 202.5 (c) (2).

101. 12 C.F.R. § 202.5 (c) (d).

102. 12 C.F.R. § 202.5 (c) (2).

103. 12 C.F.R. § 202.7 (d) (1).

104. 12 C.F.R. § 202.6 (b) (5).

105. Markham v. Colonial Mortgage Service Co., 605 F.2d 566 (D.C. Cir. 1979).

106. 12 C.F.R. § 202.7 (c) (1).

107. Fed. Res. Bd., 5 *Cons. Cred. Guide* (C.C.H.) ¶ 42,080 (January, 1976).

108. 15 U.S.C. § 1691 (a) (1).

109. 12 C.F.R. § 202.2 (o).

110. 12 C.F.R. §§ 202.2 (v) and 202.6 (b) (2) (iii).

111. 12 C.F.R. §§ 202.7 (c) (1) and 202.6 (b) (5).

112. 15 U.S.C. § 1691 (a) (2); 12 C.F.R. § 202.2 (6).

113. 12 C.F.R. § 202.6 (b) (2) (iii).

114. 15 U.S.C. § 1691 (a) (3); 12 C.F.R. §§ 202.4 and 202.2 (z).

115. 15 U.S.C. §§ 1601 to 1693 (r).

116. 12 C.F.R. § 202.10; Fair Credit Reporting Act, 15 U.S.C. §§ 1681–1681T.

117. *See*, 12 C.F.R. § 202.12.

118. P. Rasor, *Consumer Finance Law* (1985), p. 313.

119. Haller and Alviti, *Loansharking in American Cities: Historical Analysis of a Marginal Enterprise*, 21 Am. J. Legal Hist. 125 (1977).

120. *See, e.g.*, I.C. §§ 24–4.5–1.101, *et seq.* (Burns).

121. 66 U.S.C. § 115 (1861).

122. *See, e.g.*, Schauman v. Solmica Midwest, Inc., 283 Minn. 437, 168 N.W.2d 667 (1969).

123. *See, e.g.*, Lee v. Household Finance Corp., 263 A.2d 635 (D.C. Ct. App. 1970).

124. 12 U.S.C. § 1709.

125. 12 U.S.C. § 85.

126. Oeltjen, *Usury: Utilitarian or Useless?*, 3 Fla. St. U.L. Rev. 169 (1975).

127. Aztec Properties, Inc. v. Union Planters Nat'l Bk., 530 S.W.2d 756 (Tenn. 1975), *cert. denied*, 425 U.S. 975 (1976).

128. *Fla. Stat.* § 678.971 (1986).

129. 18 U.S.C. § 892.

130. 16 C.F.R. Part 444.

131. U.C.C.C. § 2.405.

132. 16 C.F.R. § 444.2 (a) (4).

133. U.S.C. § 9–107 (a) (b).

134. 16 C.F.R. § 444.1 (i).

135. 16 C.F.R. § 444.1 (i) (j).

136. U.C.C. § 9–204 (2).

137. *See*, *e.g.*, Williams v. Walker-Thomas Furniture Co., 350 F.2d 445, 449 (D.C. Cir. 1965).

138. U.C.C. §§ 9–506 (Official Comment).

139. U.C.C. §§ 1–208.

140. 16 C.F.R. § 433.

141. 16 C.F.R. § 433.2.

142. 16 C.F.R. §§ 433.1 (c), (d), and (e).

143. U.C.C. § 9–206 (1).

144. 16 C.F.R. § 444.3.

145. 16 C.F.R. §§ 444.3 (b) and (c).

146. 16 C.F.R. § 444.4.

147. *See*, *e.g.*, Hayes v. First National Bank of Memphis, 256 Ark. 328, 507 S.W.2d 701 (1974).

148. U.C.C.C. § 2.510.

149. D. H. Overmeyer Co., Inc. v. Frick Co., 405 U.S. 174 (1972); Swarb v. Lennox, 405 U.S. 191 (1972).

150. 16 C.F.R. § 444.2 (a) (1).

12

Paying for Goods and Services

Paying for goods or services may be as simple as tendering cash or as complex as procuring an international confirmed letter of credit (where a foreign bank honors drafts drawn on it by a foreign seller to pay the price of goods sold to an American importer). Regardless of the complexity of the payment arrangement, goods and services may be sold for cash or on credit. Cash sales generally involve currency or a currency substitute such as a check, sight draft (an order directing a person or firm to pay the seller the price for the goods sold), or credit card. A buyer, moreover, may have previously arranged to have a third person make payment to the seller in its behalf. This occurs, for example, when a letter of credit is honored or when a bank credit card is accepted.

Regardless of whether a purchaser buys for cash or on credit and irrespective of the payment device used or agreed upon, various laws and regulations apply to the payment phase of a commercial transaction. This chapter discusses the laws applicable to payment devices used in business transactions. These devices include negotiable instruments (drafts, checks, and notes), documentary drafts, letters of credit, trade and banker acceptances, and electronic fund, automated teller machine, and wire transfers. Throughout the following discussions, the rights and obligations of the parties are highlighted, and the problems of forgeries and unauthorized use are considered.

SOURCES OF PAYMENT LAW

Unlike the situation involving business transactions subject to a single, comprehensive, and preemptive source of law, payment systems are governed by a diverse set of state and federal statutes and regulations. These laws include the Uniform Commercial Code, various federal regulations, and private agreements.

The specific laws and regulations applicable to a given transaction depend primarily on the mode of payment used or agreed upon by the parties. A brief survey of payment laws and regulations follows.

UCC Articles Three and Four

Negotiable Instruments

The most important sources of law applicable to negotiable checks, drafts, and notes (discussed subsequently in this chapter) are Articles Three ("Commercial Paper") and Four ("Bank Deposits and Collections") of the UCC.[1] These UCC provisions (enacted in all states and in the District of Columbia) prescribe the rights and obligations of parties to or transferees or assignees of negotiable instruments.

The rights and obligations of parties under instruments which do not meet the negotiability requirements are also subject to the rules of Article Three except for those dealing with the rights of holders in due course.[2] On the other hand, retail installment sales contracts, long-form notes, and security agreements are not subject to the rules of Article Three but come under the provisions of Article Two ("Sales") or Article Nine ("Secured Transactions") in addition to common law rules.

UCC Article Five: The Uniform Customs

Letters of Credit

Letters of credit (discussed subsequently in this chapter) are governed primarily by UCC's Article Five ("Letters of Credit")[3] or by the "Uniform Customs and Practice for Commercial Documentary Credits" (UCP) which are recognized as controlling in several states.[4] Although the UCP is the product of the International Chamber of Commerce, it has been enacted into or accorded the full force and effect of law in several jurisdictions.

The Electronic Fund Transfer Act and Regulation E

Electronic Fund Transfers and Automatic Teller Machines

In May 1980, the Electronic Fund Transfer Act became effective.[5] The act, along with the Federal Reserve Board's implementing Regulation E,[6] applies to electronic fund transfers with certain specific exemptions. Nonetheless, confusion remains over where the line should be drawn between electronic transfers subject to federal regulation and the more traditional (UCC Article Four) transfers and collections of payment obligations. In addition to negotiable instruments, Article Four applies to various payment items which do not meet Article Three's negotiability standard.[7]

Private Contractual Arrangements

Bank Credit Rules

Rules applicable to the rights and obligations of the parties to a bank credit card transaction (discussed below) for the most part derive from private contracts between or among those individuals and firms using the system. These agreements include contracts between a credit-card-issuing bank and its account cardholders as well as agreements between the system's member banks and the merchants who agree to accept the credit slips or drafts which result when cardholders use their cards. In addition to the private agreements among the parties, Article Four governs in part the collection of drafts or items generated by the use of bank credit cards.

Private agreements along with the rules agreed upon among the issuing member banks constitute the primary but not exclusive source of credit card law. In addition, many, if not most, bank credit card transactions are subject to selective disclosure requirements mandated by the federal Truth-in-Lending Act[8] and Regulation Z.[9] Credit card transactions are also regulated in part by Regulation E and are subject to specific usury (or interest rate ceiling) state laws.

Regulation J

Wire Transfers between or among Banks

The Federal Reserve Board has promulgated Regulation J, subpart B,[10] which in part deals with the federal banking system's wire transfers of funds among or between banks, particularly in reference to their liability for any errors or frauds that might occur. These rules are not particularly relevant to private businesses, however, and are not discussed in this volume.

U.S. Treasury Rules

Preauthorized Credits

The U.S. Treasury has promulgated rules applicable to preauthorized credits by which a bank posts a specific credit to a customer's existing deposit account. The credit, for example, may represent either the customer's salary or his or her government transfer or social security payment. Regulation E also encompasses rules applicable to preauthorized credits.[11]

New Payments Code

The New Payments Code (NPC) at this writing is *not* a source of law but deserves mentioning. The NPC represents an effort of major law reform not unlike the UCC 30 years ago. In 1978, a subcommittee, known as the 348

Committee of the Permanent Editorial Board of the Uniform Commercial Code, commenced work on what was hoped would become a comprehensive state statute covering both traditional as well as the more modern domestic and international payment devices including electronic and wire transfers.[12] By 1986, however, the NPC project had faltered and was given a back seat to the revision of existing UCC Articles Three and Four.

The objectives of the Articles Three and Four revision committee are both to expand the UCC's coverage and make it responsive to modern technology in the areas of electronic and wire transfers of funds. In coming years, several changes in the law relevant to payments and collections may be expected—changes that will allow banks to utilize better the electronic technology already developed.

"Float Period" Law

Check-Hold Laws

At the time of writing, pressure emanating primarily from consumer groups was gaining momentum in support of proposed federal legislation that would restrict the current check-hold rights of depository banks. The current situation largely is governed (except in California and New York which have enacted their own check-hold laws) by section 4–213 of the UCC, which allows banks to hold depository items for a reasonable time or float period. Many banks under this UCC section have restricted withdrawal of a customer's deposited funds drawn on an out-of-state bank for up to fourteen days or longer following deposit. The federal legislation, known in 1986 as H.R. #2443, would preempt section 4–213 if it becomes enacted and would mandate specific maximum check-hold time periods to be followed.

PAYMENT BY CHECKS

The most prevalent payment device used both in business and personal transactions is a draft drawn on a bank, more commonly known as a check. Reportedly, at least 35 billion checks are drawn on U.S. banks each year representing an aggregate payment value in excess of $20 trillion.[13]

Although a check is often used as a currency substitute, it is not the equivalent of cash. Not only may its payment be stopped by the drawer, but the drawer's signature may be forged or it may be drawn upon insufficient funds meaning that it will not be paid and will be returned to the depositor who will have to seek recourse from the drawer. Still, a check is often considered a close cash substitute. The reason for this is due to the special status a check has in the eyes of the law—a status denoted negotiability. Checks represent one form within a group of specialty contracts which are labeled negotiable instruments. Before exploring the rights and liabilities of the parties to a negotiable instrument, we first consider the kinds and requirements of negotiable contracts.

Negotiable Instruments

A negotiable instrument is a written engagement evidencing a promise or an order to pay a sum certain in money which writing fully complies with the UCC requirements for negotiability.[14] A negotiable instrument may be a two-party "promise to pay" writing, which the UCC labels a note, or a three-party "order to pay" instrument, which the UCC denotes a draft.

Promissory Notes

A promissory note is a writing in which a promisor, called the maker, promises to pay a sum of money to another person, denoted the payee. To be negotiable under Article Three, the promise to pay must:

1. Be a writing;
2. Be signed by the maker;
3. Contain an unconditional promise to pay a sum certain in money;
4. Contain no other promise, order, obligation, or power (with specific exceptions permitted under Article Three);
5. Be payable on demand or at a definite time; and
6. Contain the essential language of negotiation, for example, language that the obligation is *payable to the order of a named person* or *to bearer*.[15]

A simple I.O.U. may or may not be a negotiable note depending on the language used. Consider the following example. Mary Smith signs a writing which simply states: "I, Mary Smith, promise to pay Al Jones $100. [Signed] Mary Smith." This writing is *not* a negotiable instrument (although it may evidence a valid contract between Smith and Jones) because it contains no words of negotiability. Had Smith added the words "to the order of" so that her promise had read "I, Mary Smith, promise to pay to the order of Al Jones $100. [Signed] Mary Smith"—then the writing would have been a negotiable promissory note.

Drafts and Checks

A draft is an order directed to another to pay a sum of money to a third person. Unlike a note, which incorporates the maker's promise to pay directly a sum of money to a named person or firm, a draft involves three parties from the outset. In a draft, a *drawer*, the person who writes or draws the instruments, orders or directs a *drawee* to pay in the drawer's behalf, the indicated sum of money to a specified *payee* (who may be the drawer). The most prevalent form of draft, of course, is the bank check in which a depositor-drawer orders his or her drawee bank to pay a sum of money to a named payee or to cash.

To be negotiable, a draft including a check must comply with the following six requirements:

1. The draft or check must be in writing;

2. It must be signed by the drawer;

3. It must contain an *unconditional* order directing the specified payee to pay a sum certain in money;

4. It must not contain or evidence any other promise, order, obligation, or power (with certain exceptions noted below);

5. It must be payable on demand (a sight draft) or at a definite time (a time draft); and

6. It must be payable *to the order of a named payee* or *to bearer*.[16]

A draft is a modern form of negotiable instrument recognized in common and civil law systems since antiquity. Also known as bills of exchange, drafts drawn on banks represent the most prevalent payment device used in consumer and business transactions. Indeed, somewhere between 30 and 40 billion checks are drawn each year in the United States alone. While it is true that checks are not as final as cash—payment may be stopped, there may be insufficient funds, or the drawer's signature may be forged—they represent in the overwhelming majority of uses a safe and efficient means for paying (and getting paid) for goods and services.

Requisites of Negotiability

Unconditional Promise or Order

To qualify as an Article Three negotiable instrument, a check, draft, or note must meet all the requirements of section 3–104.[17] Although the promise or order must be unconditional, its consideration may be stated on the face of the instrument so long as the performance of the consideration is not a condition to the promise or order to pay. Thus, a drawer of a check may write on the check that it is "in reference to" or "per" a specified transaction, contract, agreement, or letter of credit and not affect thereby its negotiability. If the drawer, however, writes that the order to pay is made under the terms and conditions of a separate agreement and is conditional upon compliance with that agreement, the draft or check does not meet the section 3–105 requirement for the order to be unconditional on its face.[18] On the other hand, the order or promise to pay may be restricted to the entire assets of a partnership or unincorporated association.

Sum Certain

Although the sum payable must be a certain amount, the UCC permits the sum to be paid in stated installments with or without stated interest. Also, the amount payable may be subject to acceleration following default. The sum is considered certain even if a stated discount is allowed for early payment or a stated add-on charge for late payment.[19] The sum certain must be payable in money, which includes an order or promise to pay "in currency" or in "current funds.''[20] The promise or order to pay a sum in a stated foreign currency is permitted. The party liable under the instrument to pay the amount may pay it in U.S. dollars at the exchange rate in effect when the instrument becomes due or on the day of the demand for payment.[21]

A check, draft, or note is payable on demand (or "at sight") when it states that it is payable on presentment, at sight, or when no time for payment is stated.[22] An instrument is payable at a definite time even though, by its terms, it is payable on or before a stated date or at a fixed period after a stated date, or it is subject to acceleration but otherwise is payable at a definite time.[23] A time draft also may be payable upon passage of a fixed time after presentment (known as "after sight").[24]

An instrument is payable to order when it contains language such as "payable to the order of" or "to the assigns" of any person or when on its face it conspicuously contains the word "exchange" and names a payee.[25] The payee may be the maker, drawer, or even the drawee. Thus, a drawer may draw a check on a bank made payable to the same bank either to obtain cash or to pay for services, for example, a lockbox rental fee. If the instrument is made payable to a partnership or unincorporated association, it may be endorsed or transferred by any person authorized to do so.

An instrument made payable to bearer is one made expressly payable to "bearer," to a specified person or bearer, or to "cash." Bearer instruments should be avoided when possible as they may be transferred by delivery alone without any endorsements.

A further danger may arise if an instrument is not completed. For example, a check might contain the printed words: "Pay to the order of _____" where the blank has not been filled in. Such an instrument is called an "incomplete" order subject to the rule of UCC section 3–155[26] (see below). It is not, however, a bearer instrument. Incomplete instruments like bearer instruments are very risky since they afford opportunities for unauthorized completions which could result in serious financial loss to a business.

Signature Liability

The most important liability principle of Article Three is the principle that no person is liable on an instrument unless his or her signature appears thereon.[27] Signing one's trade name is considered a valid signature.[28] The principle of signature liability means that an undisclosed principal is *not* liable on an instrument signed by his or her agent when the principal's name does not appear on the instrument. Of course, the undisclosed principal may be liable on the underlying contract, but not on the instrument itself (see Chapter 16).

A signature on an instrument to be operative may be typed, printed, handwritten, or made in any other manner. It need not be subscribed but may appear anywhere on the body of the instrument. While one must have legally signed an instrument to be sued on it, one does not have to sign it to bring suit. Thus, a holder whose name appears on an instrument but who has neither signed nor endorsed it may sue to enforce the payment obligation.

Signature Capacities

Makers and Drawers

A party to an instrument who signs it may do so in various capacities. He or she may be the drawer of a draft or check or the maker of a note (discussed earlier). The signer may also be an acceptor, endorser, accommodation party, or guarantor.

Acceptors

An acceptor is a drawee's signed engagement to honor the draft or check as presented.[29] The acceptor's signature must appear on the instrument for it to become liable on it. The certification of a drawer's check by a drawee bank is an acceptance. Upon certifying a customer's checks, the drawee bank thereby becomes liable on the check as an acceptor.[30]

Endorsers

An endorser is one who signs the instrument either in blank or restrictively as part of its transfer or negotiation. Endorsers may include payers and banks through which a check passes in the collection process.

Accommodation Parties

An accommodation party is one who signs the instrument in any capacity for the purpose of lending his or her name to another party to it.[31] In other words, an accommodation party is always a surety to another party on the instrument. The scope of the accommodation party's liability generally is coterminous with that of the party for whom he or she is signing.

Guarantors

A guarantor, who writes following his or her signature on an instrument "payment guaranteed" or equivalent words, becomes a surety, meaning that the guarantor waives any required presentment, notice of dishonor, and protest (discussed below) and becomes primarily liable on the instrument.[32]

Primary Liability of Makers and Acceptors

It might be said that the party who is expected to pay the instrument when it is presented for payment is the party primarily liable to pay it. In the case of a promissory note that person, of course, is the maker. In the case of a draft or check, however, the party expected to pay is the drawee—the person ordered or directed to pay in behalf of the drawer. But since no person is liable on an instrument until he or she signs it, a drawee is not liable until and unless it "accepts" the instrument. Upon acceptance, the drawee (now called the acceptor) promises in writing that he or she will pay the instrument. Thus, only makers and acceptors are primarily liable on instruments along with their co-signers, who sign as accommodation parties or sureties. Normally, makers rather than acceptors have co-signers acting as accommodation parties.

Secondary Liability of Drawers and Endorsers

Under Article Three, drawers and endorsers are deemed "secondary parties."[33] As a general proposition, secondary parties are not liable on an instrument they have signed until and unless the party primarily liable on the instrument fails to pay it.

Drawer's Liability

A drawer becomes liable on a check or draft to a holder only after the drawee has "dishonored it," that is, only following the drawee's dishonor (non-payment upon presentment), notice of dishonor, and any required protest.[34] A drawer may disclaim this liability, however, by drawing a draft or check with the words "without recourse."[35] A potential payee of an instrument should insist that a drawer not disclaim his or her potential liability on the face of the instrument.

Endorser's Liability

Most transfers of negotiable instruments take place through the process of negotiation. Negotiation is the transfer of an instrument in such a manner that the transferee qualifies as a holder—one who takes possession of the instrument with any necessary endorsements.[36] If it is payable to order, it is negotiated by delivery plus a written endorsement of the transferor. The transferee of an order instrument for value to a transferee gives the transferee the right to have the *unqualified endorsement* of the transferor.[37] An unqualified endorser has secondary liability on an instrument he or she has signed. As in the case of a drawer, an unqualified endorser becomes liable only after the maker or acceptor has previously dishonored the instrument and the endorser has received notice of the dishonor and of any protest. Thus, an endorser becomes liable only following the primary party's failure to pay.

The order of endorser liability generally is that each endorser is liable to each subsequent endorser. In most cases involving checks, the secondary liability will ultimately fall on the original payee who would, consequently, be the first endorser in the chain.[38] An endorser may disclaim his or her potential liability on an instrument by adding the words "without recourse" above or below his or her signature.[39]

Rights of Transferees of Instruments

Holder in Due Course

The core concept of Article Three is the principle that certain transferees of negotiable instruments take them with greater legal rights than the transferor had to give. Known as a holder in due course (HDC), the transferee takes the instrument free of all claims and most defenses against paying it.[40]

Consider this typical situation: B in purchasing goods executes a note payable to the order of S, the seller, who then negotiates the note to H who gives value for it. If the goods turn out to be defective, B, the maker of the note, will still have to pay it upon presentment according to its terms. The defense of breach of the implied warranty of merchantability (see Chapter 10 for a discussion of implied warranties) which B could assert against S, the payee, is cut off as against a subsequent HDC. In this example, H is an HDC provided he or she gave value for the note and took it in good faith and without actual knowledge at the time of taking that any defense to paying it existed.[41] B, of course, can seek recourse against S, the seller, by suing for damages for breach of warranty. The HDC doctrine, however, only prevents B from withholding payments otherwise due under a negotiable instrument to a good faith holder of the instrument with whom B has not directly dealt, provided the holder paid value to his or her transferor in obtaining the instrument. In consumer credit sales or loans, however, the HDC doctrine has been sharply curtailed by the Federal Trade Commission's Preservation of Consumer Claims and Defenses trade regulation rule which is set out and discussed extensively in Chapter 11.

Non-HDC Holders

A transferee who does not qualify under section 3–302 as an HDC of instrument takes it subject to *all* valid claims and defenses of any party including the defenses of failure of consideration, non-delivery, breach of warranty, and so on.[42]

Defenses Assertable against HDCs

So-called real defenses of the kind that, under the law of contract, render the obligation void or voidable may be asserted against an HDC. These include infancy or other legal incapacity, duress, and such illegality as to render the promise of the promisor or order of the drawer a nullity. Also included within the category of real defenses is a fraud that has induced the maker or drawer to sign the instrument without knowledge of its essential terms.[43]

Unauthorized Use of Checks

Up to now, our focus has centered on the essential requirements of negotiable instruments, the liabilities of the parties to them, and the rights of holders or transferees. We now turn to common problems involving negotiable instruments.

The first is the unauthorized use of a check by a thief or an employee who forges the drawer's signature.

Unauthorized Signatures

An agent may innocently sign a check of his or her principal without having actual authority to do so. On the other hand, a company's checks may be stolen by a thief who forges the company's authorized agent's signature. In either case, the signatures are unauthorized under Article Three. The UCC's basic rule of liability provides that an unauthorized or forged signature does not bind the person or firm whose name appears.

If the company's bank pays one of the company's checks over a forged drawer's signature and if the company timely discovers this fact and notifies the bank, the bank will have to suffer the loss, not the company. The reason is that Article Four mandates that banks are not to pay items not properly payable. A check with a forged signature is one not properly payable. Still, the customer of the bank must exercise reasonable care and promptness to examine his or her statement or records to discover any unauthorized signature or alteration. Failure to discover and notify the bank may cause the loss due to the forgery to fall on the customer.[44] The lesson is clear that a business customer should routinely and promptly scrutinize all its checks in its monthly statements or, if the checks are truncated (left at the bank), check all statements against its own records and if any discrepancy appears should go to its bank and procure a microfiche or other printout of all checks to review the authenticity of the signatures and amounts drawn.

Material Alterations

A material alteration of an instrument if fraudulent will result in the discharge of liability of any party to the instrument unless assented to[45]; otherwise, the instrument is still enforceable against all parties to it according to its original terms. The discharge is inoperative, however, if any party by his or her negligence substantially contributed to the material alteration.[46]

Incomplete Instruments

An incomplete instrument, for example, when the amount is left blank, creates a special danger for parties who sign the incomplete form. If a person without authority fills in the amount (in other words, completes the instrument) which following the unauthorized completion is negotiated to a holder who qualifies as an HDC, the HDC may enforce the instrument *as completed*.[47] Again, the practical lesson is clear: Never sign an instrument until its essential terms have been written, typed, or printed on the face of the instrument rendering it complete on its face.

Fictitious Payee Problem

Employees from time to time are known to take advantage of their access to the employer's checkbook. Consider this example. The Iblet Co., a proprietorship and employer, authorizes its agent, John, to write checks on First Bank to pay the company's accounts payable. Assume that John signs Iblet's name to a check which he draws to the order of Mary Smith, a fictitious person. John then fraudulently endorses Mary Smith's name on the check and names himself as the endorsee. He then cashes the check (perhaps with many others) and becomes a former employee of Iblet Co. John, naturally, cannot be located. The problem is who should bear the loss—Iblet Co. or First Bank, which paid the check upon John's authorized drawer signature but over the unauthorized and fraudulent fictitious payee signature. In this instance, the UCC places the loss on the defrauded employer, not on the payor bank.[48] The policy, simply, is that the employer is in a better position to prevent the fictitious payee fraud than is the bank. The practical lesson again is clear: Choose one's employees having access to company checks with particular care.

Check Writing Machines

An employee's use of a check writing machine which imprints the facsimile signature of an authorized agent of the drawer by printing facsimile-signed checks creates another potential problem for an employer. Should the employee *without authority* use the machine to draw a number of facsimile-signed checks payable to itself or to a third person, although amounting to unauthorized forgeries, the employer may nonetheless have to suffer the loss, not the drawee bank. One court has held that the drawer was negligent in not better exercising control over accessability to and the use of the check-writing machine.[49] Other courts, however, have held that this situation amounts to a forged-drawer's signature claim against a depository payee bank and thus is barred under the Article Three's "finality of payment rule," meaning the loss falls on the drawee bank.[50]

Policies of Allocation of Loss for Forgeries and Alterations

According to two respected commentators, the UCC basically allocates the loss for alterations or forgeries when the perpetrator has vanished or is insolvent to the person who dealt with the culprit.[51] The person who dealt with the forger is considered to have been in the best position to have prevented the loss. That person is liable unless one of the innocent parties is held to have been negligent under the rules of section 3–406. These matters, however, are not always clear cut under the UCC. This uncertainty, in turn, has fostered litigation in reference to forgeries and alterations of negotiable instruments.

LETTERS OF CREDIT

Uses of Letters of Credit

A letter of credit is a special undertaking issued ordinarily by a commercial bank at the request of its customer for the benefit of a third person. A customer may seek to procure a bank letter of credit for any number of reasons, including:

1. To facilitate payment under an international or, less commonly, domestic sales transaction;

2. To guarantee standby credit which may at some later time be needed to pay the customer's creditors, especially those who supply goods or services;

3. To assist in the financing of real estate development projects;

4. To furnish protection to a governmental entity (or private owner or developer) in the contract bidding process (similar to the function of a bidding bond); and

5. To provide a guarantee or standby credit which may be drawn on by contractors in construction projects should the owner fail to meet its obligations to make progress payments upon periodic certifications of work completed in compliance with the contract's specifications.

In short, a letter of credit may serve a payment, financing, or surety function, or any combination of these three. By arranging for a bank's third-party credit, the procuring customer may significantly enhance its liquidity, especially for the short term.

Historically, the difficulties and risks involved in long-distance credit checks, foreign exchange controls, and foreign exchange fluctuations have made the letter of credit the primary financing mechanism for import-export transactions. Bank credits in recent years also have been increasingly used in various domestic transactions. We begin this section with a description of how bank letters of credit are used in a few specific transactions.

Sales of Goods: Documentary Drafts

A seller is often unwilling to take the risk of selling on open account to a remote buyer particularly if the buyer is located in another country. The seller may lack knowledge of the buyer's credit practices, creditworthiness, and general commercial reputation. In addition, reliable credit reports in the case of foreign buyers often are difficult to obtain. Moreover, sellers are aware of the impediments and costs of collecting overdue accounts or of instituting claims against insolvent or bankrupt buyers located in remote or foreign jurisdictions. Under these circumstances, the parties may likely agree upon a *documentary sale* with or without a letter of credit. There are many varieties of documentary sales. One form was briefly described in Chapter 10; another is described here.

Stated most simply, in a documentary sale not involving a bank letter of credit the buyer agrees to pay cash in exchange for documents, which give the buyer access to and control over the goods. The documentary sale often works like this: A seller ships goods to buyer's city and, upon deposit of the goods with the shipper procures an order, or a negotiable bill of lading. Under Article Seven of the UCC, the right to the goods covered by a negotiable document of title is locked up in the negotiable bill.[52] The bill directs the issuer to deliver the goods to the order of the seller who is the person entitled under the bill of lading to direct their disposition. The seller then draws a negotiable draft on the buyer in the amount of the sale price. Typically the draft is a sight draft, meaning the buyer must pay it at sight upon proper presentment. The draft, bill of lading, and other related papers such as certificate of origin, invoice, and delivery and shipping instructions together constitute the documentary draft recognized under both Articles Four and Five of the UCC.[53]

The collection of the documentary draft begins when the seller endorses over to its bank the sight draft and bill of lading. The documentary draft is then forwarded through customary banking channels to a "presenting bank" located in the buyer's hometown. There the presenting bank, after notifying the buyer, presents the documents to the buyer to be honored, in other words, to be paid or accepted. Accepted means that the buyer engages unconditionally to pay the draft at a later time.

Assuming the buyer honors the sight draft upon due presentment, the bill of lading is then endorsed over to the buyer who now, having the document of title, has legal access to and control over the goods. The payment meanwhile is credited back through banking channels and posted as a credit in the seller's account by its depository bank.

A documentary draft not involving a letter of credit, however, carries certain risks. Typically the documents arrive before the goods and, without an agreed-upon right of inspection prior to honoring the draft, the buyer must pay the price or accept the draft prior to inspecting the goods. Thus, the risk of prepaying for nonconforming goods is clearly on the buyer. Only in sales involving trade acceptances may a buyer accept the draft on presentment and then pay later, after inspecting the goods; even then, the buyer becomes obligated to pay the draft following its acceptance.

From a seller's perspective, the non-letter-of-credit documentary sale carries the risk that the buyer will be either unable (due to its insolvency) or unwilling (due to a change of mind) to pay the draft when presented. If this happens, the seller's goods will be located in a remote city or country where a substitute buyer might be impossible or difficult to obtain. This will likely cause great expense and inconvenience. What the seller really wants under these circumstances is the buyer's bank to substitute its credit for that of the buyer. It is not surprising, therefore, that the parties in international and even domestic sales frequently decide to use a bank letter of credit, sometimes referred to as a bank or commercial credit.

Commercial Credits: Letters of Credit

Pursuant to the underlying sales agreement, a buyer will go to its bank and seek to procure an irrevocable letter of credit naming the seller as beneficiary with authority to draw a draft on the issuing bank. The letter of credit commits the issuing bank to honor a draft drawn on it by the seller upon proper presentment of the draft and the specified required documents. The documents, of course, must evidence compliance with the conditions set out in the letter of credit (not with the terms of the underlying contract).

Under a letter of credit arrangement, a seller enjoys significantly lower risks than those present in a typical documentary sale. For one thing, the risk of a bank's inability to pay due to its insolvency versus the buyer's is considerably less. If the bank should fail, however, the loss will fall on the account party. A standby letter of credit was held by the U.S. Supreme Court in 1986 *not* to constitute a deposit account subject to the insurance protection of the Federal Deposit Insurance Corporation.[54] For another, the issuing bank is obligated to honor a presented draft under a letter of credit financed sale whenever the conditions specified in the letter are met. The bank cannot dishonor the seller's payment demand simply because the bank's customer (the buyer) has had second thoughts about the deal or has found less costly substitute goods. In short, an issuing bank *must* honor its issued credit so long as the tendered documents *strictly comply* with the terms of the credit.

Ordinarily, an issuing bank will not issue an irrevocable letter of credit in behalf of its customer (technically known as the "account party") if the bank has any serious misgivings about the customer's ability to repay the bank's commitment. In addition, under the UCC, the issuing bank in a sale of goods transaction has a perfected security interest in the goods upon receipt of a negotiable document of title covering them. This gives the bank added security. Should the customer default in repaying a commitment advanced or draft paid under a credit, the issuing bank may proceed against the goods (see Chapter 13) as well as invoke any setoff remedy which it may have allowing it to debit the deposit accounts of its customer. From the seller's perspective, he or she reaps the benefits of a solvent bank's primary obligation to honor the issued credit. Thus, letters of credit when used in conjunction with documents of title facilitate a high level of payment security in sales transactions.

Financing: Standby Credits

Since a letter of credit is one form of third-party credit—the situation in which one performs a service or sells a product to another person on the promise or guarantee of a third person to pay the price—it may also be used (and is with increasing frequency) to facilitate the financing of ongoing services such as construction projects, especially on a guarantee or standby basis. In a typical arrangement, the bank's payment obligation becomes due on presentment of documents including a draft, an authenticated certificate of work completed, and an executed affidavit of the account party's owing or overdue payment for the work.[55]

Thus, the letter of credit facilitates a certification-release of funds procedure. This procedure is one example of how a bank credit may be used to guarantee or finance an account party's payment obligations to third persons. In this manner, a letter of credit often combines both financing and guaranteed payment functions.

Legal Structure of a Letter of Credit Transaction

The legal structure of the letter of credit is tripartite. The structure results in a legally enforceable commitment by the issuing bank to pay, for example, the seller in an international trade transaction the price of goods sold in behalf of the buyer, the account party. The arrangement results from what appears to be three separate contracts between the buyer and the seller, the buyer and its issuing bank, and third, the issuing bank and the seller. In fact, the relationship between the issuing bank and the seller is not contractual since no privity exists between them (privity means consideration exists to support a contract; see Chapter 8). Certain courts have held that the named beneficiary in a letter of credit is not even a third-party beneficiary of the issuer-account party contract, meaning that the seller has no recourse against the bank if it fails to honor a credit. These decisions are correct, since the letter of credit is a "specialty" legal document recognized in the law as having independent status from the underlying credit-issuing contract. Consequently, the obligations of the issuing bank do not arise from any contract with the beneficiary.

Applying this structure to an international sale, the agreement between the buyer and seller constitutes the primary or underlying contract and contains the necessary terms and conditions with respect to the sale. The separate contract between the buyer and the issuing bank sets forth the terms under which the letter of credit will be opened and honored. The relationship between the issuing bank and the seller-beneficiary is one in which the bank's obligation to pay the letter of credit to the beneficiary stems in part from the contract between the buyer and the bank but more significantly from the UCC or other controlling law. To understand the rights and liabilities of the parties, a brief review of the essential legal terminology used in reference to letters of credits is presented.

Essential Terminology

Under the Uniform Commercial Code, a credit or letter of credit is defined as an engagement or a promise by a bank or other person made at the request of a customer (the account party) that the promisor or issuer will honor drafts or other demands for payment upon compliance with terms and conditions specified in the credit.[56] A letter of credit is one form of third-party credit, similar to the more common bank credit card situation. The *issuer* is the bank issuing the credit,[57] and the *beneficiary* of the credit is a person entitled under its terms to draw or demand payment.[58] The *customer* is a buyer or other person who causes a bank either to issue its own credit or to procure the issuance or confirmation of a credit by another bank in customer's behalf. A *confirming bank* engages or promises that it will honor a credit already issued by another bank or that the credit will be honored by the issuer or third bank.[59] Confirming banks frequently are used in international sales transactions. An *advising bank* is a bank that gives notice of the issuance of a credit by another bank.[60] A *docu-*

mentary draft or *demand for payment* is one in which payment is conditioned upon the presentation of necessary documents, for example, certificates of origin, invoices, ocean bills of lading, and so on.[61]

A *standby letter of credit*, on the other hand, is a credit that obligates the issuer to pay the beneficiary "on the account of any default by the account party—the customer in performance of an obligation."[62]

UCC Article Five: Uniform Customs, Choice of Law

Historically, the law governing letters of credit was developed through custom and by case law. Today the primary sources of letter of credit law are the codified Uniform Commercial Code and the Uniform Customs and Practice for Documentary Credits (1983 Revision), commonly known as the "Uniform Customs," as published by the International Chamber of Commerce in Brochure No. 400. In most states, Article Five of the UCC is the principal law governing letters of credit. Consequently, in these states the Uniform Customs are either relegated to an incorporation by reference in the state's UCC or used as evidence of custom when a dispute arises. Where Article Five of the UCC is silent with respect to a particular problem (which happens quite often), the prior custom as recognized in case law is applicable.[63] On the other hand, in Alabama, Missouri, and especially New York (where the majority of letters of credit have been issued), Article Five of the UCC does not apply. In these states the Uniform Customs are considered to be the governing law applicable to bank letters of credit.

The parties have discretion under UCC section 1–105 to choose the law that applies in cases of conflict. For example, even though an exporter is located in Florida, the contract between a buyer and a seller may call for New York law to govern the rights and obligations under their agreement. In that case, the Uniform Customs will apply even though the Uniform Commercial Code would be applicable in Florida.[64] The parties could have, however, decided by specific reference in their agreement to have Florida's UCC apply provided the transaction has minimal contacts with the state of Florida.

Revocable or Irrevocable Credits

A letter of credit may be revocable or irrevocable. The presumption under the Uniform Customs is that a letter of credit is revocable.[65] However, UCC section 2–325(3) declares that in a sales contract the term "letter of credit" means an irrevocable letter of credit. Whether or not a particular letter of credit is revocable or irrevocable may lead to a breach of contract. Consider, for example, an unlabeled letter of credit in New York where the Uniform Customs apply and which, therefore, is revocable. If the sales contract called for a letter of credit and the law of the state where the UCC is in force applies, then the existence of an unlabeled credit issued by a bank in New York would violate provisions of Article Five of the UCC.[66] Consequently, care must be taken to properly label a letter of credit.

Confirmed or Unconfirmed Credit

An *unconfirmed* letter of credit is one in which only the buyer's bank has direct liability to the seller. For example, a buyer opens a letter of credit with its local commercial bank for a seller's benefit. The buyer's bank will then mail or cable notification to seller's bank that a letter of credit for the benefit of the seller has been opened. The seller's bank is merely a conduit for information and has no liability on the letter of credit.

If the seller prefers to be additionally secured by the liability of its local bank, the issuing bank may instruct the seller's bank to hold itself out as being liable to seller. The seller's bank does this by becoming the *confirming* bank. Both issuing and confirming banks are liable on a confirmed letter of credit. This is typically the case of commercial credits involving international trade. The preferred situation from a domestic exporter's point of view is to require the foreign import buyer to have his or her foreign bank issue and arrange for an irrevocable letter of credit confirmed by a bank located in the United States.

Assignability

A letter of credit ordinarily may be assigned, provided the letter of credit so provides.[67] If the letter of credit is assignable, however, it may be assigned only once under Article 46(e) of Uniform Customs. UCC section 5–116, however, contains no such limitation. Therefore, the choice of applicable law once again becomes important.

Security

The seller-beneficiary of a letter may pledge the letter of credit for security for a loan or other credit extension. The seller's creditor may take physical possession of the letter of credit but cannot collect on the letter itself. A UCC Article Nine security interest may be perfected by the creditor's taking possession of the letter.[68] The pledge is valid even if presentment of the letter of credit is required for payment by an issuing or confirming bank. In that case, the seller will have to first redeem the pledge before obtaining payment. In short, the assignee must depend on the seller-assignor's performance of the conditions of the letter of credit for payment. While the assignment or transfer of the letter of credit itself may be restricted, there are no restrictions on the assignability of the proceeds.

Back-to-Back Credits

The *secondary* or *back-to-back* letter of credit is in wide use today. The seller-beneficiary of a letter of credit may have a confirming bank issue a secondary letter of credit which contains terms identical to the primary letter of credit except for the price term and invoice. Generally, a bank will open a secondary letter of credit only when the primary letter of credit is the bank's own credit, when the letters are literally identical except for price term and invoice, and when the bank is willing to accept some additional credit risk. The secondary letter of credit then is used by the seller-beneficiary to finance other transactions either foreign or domestic.

Minimization of Risks

Letters of credit both minimize a seller's risk of not receiving payment for goods shipped and give reasonable assurance to the distant buyer upon payment of the price that it will be permitted to obtain the goods from an international or domestic carrier. Under the UCC, the issuer of the credit must honor a draft drawn on it, which complies with the terms of the credit, even if the goods or documents fail to conform to the terms of the underlying sales agreement.[69] The issuing bank is not responsible for performance of the underlying contract between the customer (buyer) and the beneficiary (seller).[70] Although letters of credit minimize the risks of nondelivery and nonpayment, they are not particularly helpful for reducing the risks of a seller's late delivery or of breach of warranty.

Obtaining Payment under a Letter of Credit

A beneficiary of a letter of credit, whether a seller of goods or a supplier of services, must strictly comply with the conditions set out in the credit. This strict compliance rule is the heart of the credit because it promotes certainty in commercial transactions. An issuing bank's document examiners do not concern themselves with the underlying transaction. Rather, they carefully examine the documents that the beneficiary tenders along with its draft or demand for payment.

Independence Principle

The strict compliance rule is a corollary to the "independence principle," which holds that a letter of credit obligation is independent of the underlying contract between the account party and the beneficiary. Although courts in Illinois and Massachusetts have allowed the strict compliance rule to be weakened by ordering payments against relatively minor documentary defects, the majority of courts support the fundamental notion that the beneficiary must *fully*—not substantially—*comply* with the credit's documentary conditions. Compliance is determined by a facial scrutiny of the tendered documents. Since the issuing or confirming bank has a duty to pay only against conforming documents, an issued credit is subject only to its specified documentary conditions. It follows, therefore, that an issuing bank must agree to any change in the agreed-upon documentary conditions. Although an issuing bank may insist on strict compliance before honoring a beneficiary's draft or other demand for payment, if a bank pays over minor defects, it may still demand reimbursement from its account party.

Specification of Defect

When an issuing or confirming bank does not pay a beneficiary upon a documentary demand, the bank must specify the defect in the tendered documents. This means that a seller should submit the required documents as early as possible. Should they be objected to, the seller may still receive payment by curing the defect and resubmitting the package.

Fraud Defense

An account party, under both the common law and Article Five of the UCC, has the right to go to court and seek to enjoin an issuing or confirming bank from honoring a draft or other demand for payment upon allegations of fraud committed by the beneficiary. Known as the fraud defense, the defense itself is sometimes asserted with a fraudulent intent to avoid or delay the payment of an obligation that the account party owes.

A survey of litigation involving the fraud defense reveals that it is used more frequently in standby credits than in commercial credits because the customer of a standby credit often does not desire its bank to pay under the issued standby credit. For example, an owner (account party) may believe that a contractor fraudulently procured a certificate of work completed, tendered a forged certificate, or otherwise (and more commonly) did not perform to the satisfaction of the owner.

The fraud defense to honoring bank credits appears to be on the rise. Over time this may result in lowering the business community's faith in the reliability of letters of credit. The problem is made worse because the legal scope of the defense remains unclear. Does the claimed fraud which may be used to enjoin the issuing or confirming bank's payment include fraud in the underlying transactions or does it not?

Despite the level of uncertainty that the prospect of a claimed fraud defense injects, standby and commercial letters of credit overall still represent remarkably efficient and dependable payment devices. Indeed, their varied uses continue to grow despite their not inexpensive transactional costs.

Use of Counsel

A letter of credit required to facilitate a complex transaction requires considerable skill in its drafting. A competent attorney with experience in such matters should be used. Otherwise, later ambiguities and disputes may arise.

PAYMENT BY CREDIT CARDS

Payment by credit cards is commonplace today. Although bank credit cards had their origin in the 1960s, by 1980, the total revolving bank credit card volume had soared to over $27 billion.[71] In that same year, over 1.6 billion credit card transactions were executed in the United States.

The plastic credit card revolution continues to grow. Like checks, credit cards represent a convenient currency substitute. To a degree, they represent a check substitute as well. Certainly, they have enjoyed a wide acceptance, particularly by consumers, as a convenience for paying for goods and services. The convenience results from a distinctive feature of bank credit cards—they are honored by thousands of merchants or other sellers who do not as readily accept personal checks. The ease of using credit cards has not only contributed to their popularity and expanded use, but it also has encouraged their overuse by certain cardholders.

As one authority has described a credit card's essential functions, their use involves "both a convenient means of paying bills and the granting of a revolving line of credit to the cardholder, . . . "[72] The bank credit, in short, performs dual payment and credit functions comparable to those of standby letters of credit. In many ways, they are similar. For one thing, the bank letter of credit and the bank credit card both represent a dependable and solvent third-party credit device which sellers may safely rely on. For another, in each case, a maximum amount (or line) of credit is established. Finally, each device requires that certain conditions be met for the credit to be honored.

Merchant Credit Cards

Various kinds of credit cards are in common use today. One is the merchant or seller's card issued by sellers directly to their customers, principally by retailers and gasoline companies.

A merchant credit card is not a third-party credit device but rather is a means of implementing and policing a retailer's open account or credit selling of goods or services. Under a typical seller's credit card, the seller, following receipt of an application of a prospective cardholder, investigates the creditworthiness of the applicant and, if found to be satisfactory, issues a card. The card typically will be issued pursuant to a stipulated maximum amount of credit.

Bank Credit Cards

Although once issued on an unsolicited basis, bank credit cards today must be either requested or applied for by a prospective cardholder.[73] The issuance of the bank credit card along with the written cardholder agreement constitutes a contractual offer which a cardholder is deemed to accept by his or her initial use of the tendered card.

Although both state and national banks have the power to issue their own institutional credit cards, nearly all do so as an agent or member of one of the major bank credit card systems in existence today—Visa and MasterCard. Formerly known as BankAmericard and Master Charge, Visa and MasterCard represent multi-institutional associations. The central idea underlying each system is to market a single card with the widest possible geographic recognition and acceptability. The idea clearly has succeeded.

Implementing Agreements

Three separate agreements must be set up and in place before a merchant may honor a customer's bank credit card:

1. A cardholder-issuer agreement;

2. A merchant-bank agreement; and

3. An interchange or association agreement among member and agent banks.

Issuer-Cardholder Agreement

The issuer-cardholder agreement primarily consists of and is evidenced by the completed credit card application form along with terms which may be set out on the back of the card. The application form often includes all of the terms of the agreement. The fine print on a typical application provides for several issuer options for cancellation, withdrawal of credit, and acceleration of remedies, while requiring the cardholder to report the card's loss or theft and to make timely minimum monthly payments among other express terms and conditions.

Merchant-Bank Agreement

Pursuant to a typical merchant-bank arrangement, a merchant opens up a depository account with its bank. The bank, in turn, agrees to accept credit card sales slips within a specified number of days, usually five, of the sale transactions, and to post credits in the merchant's account for the total volume of sales slips submitted less an agreed-upon discount. The discount (often around 2 to 4 percent) may be deducted daily or monthly. Under this merchant-bank or discount agreement, the merchant must offer to sell its goods or services to any cardholder upon tender of his or her credit card provided the card has neither expired nor been placed on the system's published "hot" card list periodically provided to all merchant members within the system.

A merchant must also agree that it will not offer a legally defined "cash discount" in excess of 5 percent of the stated price of a good or service. This requirement grows out of a Truth-in-Lending Act provision which makes available cash discounts of greater than 5 percent a disclosable finance charge.[74]

Merchant's Liability

Normally, a bank accepting a merchant's submitted sales slips cannot obtain recourse from the seller should the cardholder fail for any reason to make his or her payments. There are exceptions, however, to this "without recourse" rule written into most merchant-bank agreements.

These exceptions, which place the loss on the merchant, include the following:

1. Illegible sales slips (for example, a cardholder's account number did not properly imprint on the form);

2. Expiration of the card at the time the merchant honored it;

3. Missing cardholder authorization number;

4. Cash advance slip or sales slip dishonored because the amount involved was not preauthorized as required;

5. Card honored while it was listed on the published hot list; and

6. Customer complaint that the amount was increased after the sales transaction.

In addition, the usual merchant-bank agreement allows the bank to "charge back" an item if, upon a customer's complaint, it turns out that the merchant failed to establish and maintain a fair policy for the exchange, return, or adjustment of merchandise sold.[75]

Merchants are required, under their agreement with their depository bank, to check the hot card list and the card's expiration dates, and to obtain preauthorizations for any sale, the price of which exceeds the agreement's "floor release" limit. Merchants, moreover, may not use two or more credit card slips to avoid the required "floor release—preauthorization" figure.

Fraud

As credit cards increasingly have been used for credit and payment functions, so have they become increasingly used to perpetrate fraud. Because no other identification normally is required upon the honoring of a bank credit card than the card itself, the risk of fraud is high, as reflected by the dollar amount resulting from fraudulent credit card use.

Cardholder's Liability

Under the federal Truth-in-Lending Act, a cardholder is liable for the unauthorized use of his or her accepted credit card whether lost or stolen to the amount of $50, and then only if the unauthorized use occurred prior to the cardholder's notification of the loss or theft to the card issuer.[76] The $50 limit on a cardholder's liability does *not* apply where a cardholder voluntarily and knowingly allows another person to use his or her card.[77]

Liability of Business Cardholders

The Truth-in-Lending Act in 1974 was amended to make it clear that bank credit cards issued to businesses are also subject to the $50 per card limit of liability.[78] The amendment allows, however, an issuer or a business, which furnishes cards to ten or more employees, to waive the federal limitation and stipulate its own liability amount provided the employees having company cards are not personally liable to the issuer for more than the $50 limit.[79]

Cardholder Defenses

In 1974, Congress enacted the Fair Credit Billing Act which in part covers the issue of the assertability of a cardholder's defenses against his or her credit card issuer.[80] The FCBA declares that issuers of bank as well as travel and entertainment credit cards (for example, American Express, Diner's Club, or Carte Blanche) are subject to all contract claims and defenses arising out of any transaction in which the card was used for payment; provided, first, that the cardholder has made a good faith effort to resolve the dispute; provided, second, that the amount of the transaction exceeded $50; and provided, third, that the sales transaction occurred within the issuer's state or within 100 miles of the cardholder's residence.

Debit Cards Distinguished

A debit card, unlike a credit card, upon use results in a point-of-sale transfer from the cardholder's deposit account to a merchant's deposit account. In reality, credit is not extended at all as a debit card represents an immediate payment device. From a consumer's perspective, debit cards allow no "window" in which either to stop payment or to subsequently assert a defense and withhold payment since the debit and crediting of the parties' accounts occur simultaneously. The use of debit cards likely will grow in the coming years as merchants would prefer to receive immediate payments rather than the more risky deferred payments for goods and services sold.

ELECTRONIC TRANSFERS

Electronic technology has effected major changes in the bank collection system. These include computerized off-premises data processing centers and the magnetic encoding of checks and drafts. Of all the various developments made possible by modern electronic technology, the most far reaching is the "computerized direct-funds-transfer system in which electronic impulses replace checks."[81] The electronic transfer technology portends to revolutionize the check collection system. This section discusses a few legal problems business should be aware of which are raised by electronic technology as applied to payment systems.

Magnetic Encoding

Nearly all banks today use magnetic ink character recognition (MICR), otherwise known as magnetic coding for checks. A bank "proof" machine operator at a drawer's depository bank may make an error of overencoding or underencoding an item to be posted for deposit. An important legal issue concerns what effect a drawer's failure to discover the error and notify his or her drawee bank may have. Certain courts have held that UCC section 4–406 does *not* apply to encoding errors, opening the door for other consumer law principles to apply.[82] Still, a strong UCC-based argument can be made that, if the drawer through negligence fails to timely discover and notify its drawee-depository bank of an underencoding error (where, for example, the bank credits the drawer's account an amount less than the correct amount, for example, by posting a $1,000 credit rather than a $10,000 credit), the drawer should be barred from any recovery.[83] Prudence dictates that a business should routinely and carefully scrutinize all statements and cancelled checks to see whether any encoding errors have been made in the posting process.

Electronic Fund Transfer Systems

Automated Clearing House

Electronic fund transfer (EFT) systems are proliferating. These include FED-WIRE, linking members of the Federal Reserve System; BANKWIRE, consisting of several New York and Chicago banks, a system owned by Western Union; and CHIPS, standing for Clearing House Interbank Payment Systems, composed of more than 80 banks located in New York.[84] In addition, automated clearing houses (ACHs) process electronic message items among member institutions. Reportedly, 33 regional ACHs are operating under the National Automated Clearing House Association.[85] The federal government uses ACHs for the direct deposit of transfer payments, principally, social security benefits. Checks are never issued. Direct deposits have considerably cut down on the number of forged, stolen, and misplaced social security checks to the benefit of social security recipients.

ACH systems include NYCE (New York Cash Exchange) and the Plus System, which in 1986 had 57 million cards giving access to 8,400 machines. Also, Cirrus reportedly involves a network of about 11,000 ACH machines in 46 states and Canada.

Corporations and other large business organizations also utilize automated clearing houses for the direct payment of payrolls into the employees' bank accounts. To use this payment system, each employee who desires the service must sign two authorizations: one allowing his or her bank (an ACH member) to receive the credit and the second authorizing the employer to initiate the wage credit through the ACH system. An employer initiates direct deposit credits by use of a specially encoded magnetic tape, which it tenders shortly before each scheduled payday to its depository bank. The tape is then sent to the regional ACH which processes it, resulting in credits eventually being posted in each covered employee's bank account.

Today, the ACH systems are expanding to include a multitude of business and consumer uses. This is not surprising because EFT is the most convenient of all payment systems. EFTs are especially useful when a consumer or business is obligated to make periodic or recurring payments. These include payments due under mortgages, utility bills, and life insurance premiums. An insurer, utility company, or lender, after receiving written debit authorizations, encodes a magnetic debit tape. Whereas an employer initiates a list of credits (on tape) representing wages to be posted to its employee bank accounts, a payee prepares a list of debits that will be deducted from its customers' bank accounts. If a customer's payments will be the same each month (as is the typical case of most fixed-rate mortgage obligations), then only one periodic debit authorization is needed. If, however, the payments will vary from month to month, as in the case of monthly utility bills, the payee each month must notify its customers of the amount before the debit tape is submitted to the ACH system through the payee's bank. The customer has the right to withdraw from the EFT system after notification of the amount due.

Point-of-Sale Systems: Automatic Teller Machines

Point-of-sale systems (POSSs) utilize debit cards described earlier in this chapter. Although more commonly used today in automatic teller machines (ATMs), debit cards (also known as access devices) may also be used in a POSS machine terminal (substantially similar to an ATM) located on the premises of a business. It may be only a matter of time before debit cards and point-of-sale terminals become the primary payment system used by consumers in purchasing goods and services. Each debit cardholder is assigned a personal identification number (PIN) to access either an ATM or an EFT point-of-sale system. Here is how it works.

To purchase shoes, a customer will take them to a clerk who will punch the price into a point-of-sale terminal. The customer will then insert his or her debit card into the terminal along with the appropriate PIN. The customer's bank account will be immediately debited for the price of the shoes while the merchant's bank account (probably a different institution) will be simultaneously credited the same amount.

In 1980, Congress enacted the Consumer Checking Account Equity Act,[86] which authorizes federally chartered savings and loan associations to offer point-of-sale terminals called "remote service units," which allow off-premise terminals for debit cards to be used to make payments on loans, mortgages, and so on. Point-of-sale systems are on the way.

Customer-Bank Communication Terminals

A 1985 U.S. Second Circuit Court of Appeals decision, which the U.S. Supreme Court refused to overturn in 1986, held that the use of a shared automated teller machine by a federal bank is not a branch bank if the point-of-sale terminal or automatic teller machine is neither rented nor owned by the bank.[87] Thus, customer-bank communication terminals, including automated teller machines, neither owned nor rented by national banks are not considered branch banks, which, if they were, would likely constitute illegal branch banking under the McFadden Act.[88]

Customers' Rights in Electronic Transfers

In 1978, Congress enacted as part of the Financial Institutions Regulatory and Interest Rate Control Act, Title XX, better known as the Electronic Fund Transfer Act.[89] The statute (which is located in Title IX of the Consumer Credit Protection Act), together with the Federal Reserve Board's implementing Regulation E,[90] establishes the basic rights, liabilities, and responsibilities of consumers who use electronic money transfer services and of the financial institutions that offer these services. Wire transfers of funds through the federal reserve communications system, however, are exempted.[91]

Access Devices

An access device is defined in Regulation E as any card, code, or other means of access to a consumer's account or combination of these that the consumer may use to initiate an electronic fund transfer.[92] A financial institution may issue an access device to a consumer only in response to a request or application or as a renewal or substitution of an existing device. An access device may also be distributed on an unsolicited basis provided that it is not validated and provided further that it is accompanied by a complete disclosure of the consumer's rights and liabilities along with a clear explanation that the device is not validated and how the consumer may dispose of it. The device may be activated only by the institution upon the request or application of the consumer after verification of the consumer's identity by reasonable means.[93]

Consumer's Liability

Under Regulation E, a consumer is strictly liable for an unauthorized electronic fund transfer or transfers for a maximum of $50 for those occurring before giving notice of the loss or theft of the access device to the issuing financial institution.[94] If, however, the consumer fails to give notice within two business days after learning of the loss or theft of the access device, the consumer's maximum liability could go up to a $500 limit under specified circumstances set out in Regulation E.[95]

Preauthorized Transfers

The Federal Reserve Board's Regulation J also sets out a number of rules applicable to preauthorized credits and debits to a consumer's bank (or other financial institution) account. All debits must be preauthorized in writing by the consumer with a copy provided to the consumer.[96] A consumer may stop payment on a preauthorized debit from his or her account by notifying the financial institution orally or in writing up to three business days before the scheduled date of the transfer.[97] A bank also must notify a consumer of periodic debits that vary in amount.[98]

The Federal Reserve Board in 1981 issued an official *Staff Commentary on Regulation E* in question and answer form. This document was subsequently updated, effective April 1, 1983. The FRB official staff commentary is available from one of the regional federal reserve banks.

Freedom of Choice

The Electronic Fund Transfer Act makes it clear that no business or person may require its customer or a consumer to repay a loan or other extension of credit by means of a preauthorized electronic fund debit transfer. An employer may require, however, that its employees receive their wages by direct, electronic fund credit transfer deposits, but an employer may not require as a condition of employment that its employee establish an account with a designated institution.[99]

Documentation

Finally, Regulation E requires that a receipt be made available for each electronic fund transfer initiated at an automated teller machine or point-of-sale terminal, except for those older terminals that cannot be modified to perform this function.[100] In addition, monthly statements must be furnished.[101]

CHANGING PAYMENT SYSTEMS IN COMING YEARS

America is in the midst of a revolution in payment systems. Having moved from barter to cash to checks to credit cards, payment systems are now rapidly moving toward a computerized, electronic impulse transfer system activated by a simple plastic debit card and a personal identification number. This revolution is evidenced by the explosive growth in automated teller machine transactions. Indeed, ATM debit card transactions are serving as a substitute for checks payable to cash, which have been traditionally cashed at banks and supermarkets.

The use of automated clearing houses both for preauthorized debits and for client deposit credits will grow in the coming years. Checks will be less frequently used while those that are will not be returned to the drawer at the end of the month but will be retained (truncated) by the banks where they were initially deposited. These changes will result in changes in many of the governing laws, especially the provisions of an increasingly outdated Article Four of the UCC.

Businesses will benefit from many of those technological developments in payment systems because of the efficiencies made possible by the electronic technology.

NOTES

1. *See*, U.C.C. §§ 3–101, *et seq.* and 4–101, *et seq.*
2. U.C.C. § 3–805.
3. *See*, U.C.C. §§ 5–101, *et seq.*
4. International Chamber of Commerce, *Uniform Customs and Practice*, Publication no. 400 (1980).
5. 15 U.S.C. §§ 1693, *et seq.*
6. 12 C.F.R. Part 205 (1981).
7. U.C.C. § 4–104 (1) (g).
8. 15 U.S.C. §§ 1601, *et seq.*
9. 12 C.F.R. Part 226 (1981).
10. 12 C.F.R. §§ 210.50, *et seq.*
11. *See, e.g.*, 12 C.F.R. § 205.10 (promulgated by the Federal Reserve Board).
12. *See, Survey: Consumer Financial Services*, R. Brandel and J. Soloway, Electronic Fund Transfers and the New Payments Code, 38 Bus. Law. 1355 (1983).
13. Barkley Clark, *The Law of Bank Deposits, Collections and Credit Cards.* Warren, Gorham & Lamont (1980), p. 10–3.
14. U.C.C. §§ 3–104 through 3–119.
15. U.C.C. § 3–104 (1).
16. *Id.*
17. U.C.C. §§ 3–104 (1) (a), (b), (c), and (d).
18. U.C.C. §§ 3–105 (1) and (2).
19. U.C.C. § 3–106 (1).
20. U.C.C. § 3–107 (1).
21. U.C.C. § 3–107 (2).
22. U.C.C. § 3–108.
23. U.C.C. § 3–109 (1).
24. *Id.*
25. U.C.C. § 3–110.
26. U.C.C. § 3–115.
27. U.C.C. § 3–401 (1).
28. U.C.C. § 3–401 (2).
29. U.C.C. § 3–401 (1).
30. U.C.C. § 3–411 (1).
31. U.C.C. § 3–415 (1).
32. U.C.C. § 3–416 (1).
33. U.C.C. § 3–102 (1) (d).
34. U.C.C. § 3–413 (2).
35. *Id.*
36. *See*, U.C.C. §§ 1–201 (20) and 3–202.
37. U.C.C. § 3–201 (3).
38. U.C.C. § 3–414 (2).

39. U.C.C. § 3–414 (1).

40. U.C.C. § 3–305.

41. U.C.C. § 3–302 (1). *See also*, U.C.C. §§ 3–303 and 3–304.

42. U.C.C. §§ 3–306 (a), (b), and (c).

43. U.C.C. § 3–305 (2).

44. U.C.C. § 4–406.

45. U.C.C. § 3–407 (2).

46. U.C.C. § 3–406.

47. U.C.C. § 3–407 (3).

48. U.C.C. § 3–405 (1) (b).

49. First Fed. Sav. & Loan Ass'n of Sioux Falls v. Union Bank & Trust Co., 291 N.W.2d 283 (S.D. 1980).

50. U.C.C. § 3–418.

51. Miller and Scott, *Commercial Paper, Bank Deposits and Collections, and Commercial Electronic Funds Transfers*, 38 Bus. Law. 1129, 1148 (1983).

52. *See*, U.C.C. §§ 7–502 and 9–304 (2).

53. U.C.C. § 4–104 (1) (f).

54. FDIC v. The Philadelphia Gear Corp., _____U.S. _____, 106 S. Ct 1931 (1986).

55. U.C.C. § 5–114.

56. U.C.C. § 5–103 (1) (a).

57. U.C.C. § 5–103 (c).

58. U.C.C. § 5–103 (d).

59. U.C.C. § 5–103 (1) (f).

60. U.C.C. § 5–103 (1) (e).

61. U.C.C. § 5–103 (1) (b).

62. Bradford Stone, *Uniform Commercial Code in a Nutshell*, 2d. ed. West Publishing Co. (1984), p. 509.

63. *See, e.g.*, Interco, Inc. v. Schwartz, 560 F.2d 480 (lst Cir. 1977).

64. U.C.C. § 5–103 (1) (a); International Chamber of Commerce, *Uniform Customs and Practice*, Article 1 (a) Publication no. 400 (1983).

65. *See, e.g.*, Beathard v. Chicago Football Club, Inc., 419 F. Supp. 1133 (N.D. Ill. 1976).

66. U.C.C. § 2–325 (3).

67. *See, e.g.*, U.C.C. § 5–116 (1).

68. U.C.C. § 9–305.

69. U.C.C. § 5–114.

70. U.C.C. §§ 5–109 (1) and (2).

71. Fed. Res. Bull. A42 (July 1980).

72. Clark, *The Law of Bank Deposits, Collections and Credit Cards* (1980), p. 9–3.

73. 15 U.S.C. § 1642.

74. 15 U.S.C. §§ 1666f (a) and (b).

75. Clark, *The Law of Bank Deposits, Collections and Credit Cards* (1980), p. 9–11.

76. 15 U.S.C. § 1643.

77. *Id.*

78. 15 U.S.C. § 1645.

79. *Id.*

80. 15 U.S.C. § 1666i.

81. Clark, *The Law of Bank Deposits, Collections and Credit Cards* (1980), p. 10–3.

82. *See, e.g.*, State ex rel. Gabalac v. Firestone Bank, 346 N.E.2d 326 (Ohio App. 1975); and Florida Federal Savings & Loan Ass'n. v. Martin, 400 So.2d 151 (Fla. App. 1981).

83. *See* U.C.C. §§ 4–406 (1), (2), and (4).

84. Frederick H. Miller & Barkley Clark, *Cases and Materials on Consumer Protection*. Michie-Bobbs Merrill Co. (1980), pp. 43–45.

85. *Id.*

86. Pub. L. 96–221, 96th Cong., 2d Sess.; 12 U.S.C. § 1464 (b) (1).

87. Independent Bankers Ass'n v. Marine Midland Bank, 757 F.2d 453 (2d Cir. 1985).

88. 12 U.S.C. § 36.

89. 15 U.S.C. §§ 1693–1693 (r).

90. 12 C.F.R. §§ 205.1, *et seq.*

91. 12 C.F.R. § 205.3 (b).

92. 12 C.F.R. § 205.2 (a) (1).

93. 12 C.F.R. §§ 205.5 (a) and (b).

94. 12 C.F.R. § 205.6 (b).

95. *Id.*

96. 12 C.F.R. § 205.10 (b).

97. 12 C.F.R. § 205.10 (c).

98. 12 C.F.R. § 205.10 (d).

99. 15 U.S.C. § 1693k.

100. 12 C.F.R. §§ 205.9 (a) and (f).

101. 12 C.F.R. § 205.9 (b).

13

Collecting Delinquent Accounts

When accounts receivable or other obligations to pay money are delinquent or otherwise in default, a business has several options in trying to collect the indebtedness. First, it may sell, assign, or discount the account to a debt collector or collection agency. Second, the firm may attempt through nonjudicial means to persuade or "dun" the obligor to pay the overdue obligation. Finally, the business may seek to collect the indebtedness by going to court or, if a secured creditor, by taking and disposing of its security (the collateral).

Regardless of the alternative pursued, the collection task becomes more complicated if the obligor becomes insolvent or goes into bankruptcy. In some instances, the collection efforts may be easier if the creditor has a lien or a security interest in specific property of the debtor, in other words, has collateral which the creditor may move against.

This chapter examines the laws and regulations that apply to a creditor's efforts to collect delinquent payment obligations. Included is a discussion of the federal Fair Debt Collection Practices Act[1] and state laws applicable to creditor remedies including attachment, execution, garnishment, and replevin. Certain self-help remedies are also discussed, especially those available under UCC Article Nine to secured creditors (see Chapter 6 for a discussion of how secured loans are created, documented, and made enforceable). This chapter also considers the impact of bankruptcy on collection efforts. Finally, the problems and possibility of writing off certain uncollectible receivables under the federal tax laws are discussed. We begin, however, with a brief description of the basic legal concepts of creditors' rights.

FUNDAMENTALS OF CREDITOR-DEBTOR LAW

Essential Terms

A *creditor* is a person, firm, organization, or other legal entity which is owed an obligation to pay money. The obligation to pay money is called the *debt*; the amount owed is called the *indebtedness*. The person who has the obligation to pay is called the *debtor* or, at other times, the *obligor*.

A creditor has a legal right to have an owed indebtedness *satisfied*, meaning to be paid in full. Reciprocally, a debtor has a legal duty to pay an owed indebtedness in full. A creditor's right to a satisfaction means that it may enforce and collect its claim through the courts. The right to go to court and to sue to collect the claimed amount owned is called the creditor's *chose in action*.

Categories of Creditors: Lien and Non-Lien Creditors

Although all creditors have a chose in action, they are not all on an equal footing or all treated alike under the law. A particular creditor's rights vis-à-vis those of other creditors depends on the priority or relative ranking of its claim which, in turn, largely depends on the category or type of claim involved.

Creditors are categorized or separated into different groups. Foremost is the separation of lien creditors from non-lien creditors. A *lien* is an interest in property which exists in favor of the *lienor* who does not, initially at least, have title to the property. In the case of a lien creditor, the lien arises to secure a legal obligation to pay a sum of money. A creditor's lien may attach in both real and personal property of the debtor, depending on the statute involved.

Liens arise in three different ways: through the consent or agreement of the parties, by operation of law, and through specific actions or events which occur during the judicial adjudication and enforcement of a debt.

Consensual Lienors: Mortgagees, Secured Parties

A debtor and a creditor may agree through contract to create a consensual lien in the debtor's real or personal property. In either case, the debtor conveys an interest in its property to secure an ongoing obligation or obligations to pay money (for example, a mortgage note calling for monthly payments over a number of years).

The real estate creditor (called a *mortgagee*) has a lien (designated a *mortgage interest*) in the debtor's (*mortgagor's*) legally described real estate. To maximize rights against third parties, the mortgagee usually *records* the mortgage instrument. This affords public notice of the mortgage relationship.

The personal property creditor (called a *secured party*) has a lien (an Article Nine *security interest*) in the personal property of the debtor as specified in a *security agreement*. The secured relationship may be publicly evidenced by the filing of a separate *financing statement*.

Liens by Operation of Law: Statutory and Common Law

A lien may arise automatically in a debtor's property simply because of the type of transaction involved. Liens which arise automatically are validated either under the common law lien or by specific state statutes and are referred to as either common law or statutory liens. The coverage and enforcement of these liens vary considerably from state to state. Common varieties include a *landlord's lien* for nonpayment of rent; an *artisan's lien* to secure payment for services supplied in connection with a chattel, for example, an automobile repair; a *warehouseman's lien* to secure the nonpayment of storage charges; and a *mechanic's lien* which attaches to real property for nonpayment of obligations for services and supplies related to the particular real estate or to its improvements.

Simply because a creditor has a lien which has attached automatically in the debtor's property does not mean that the lienor may proceed to dispose of the property to satisfy the indebtedness. A lienor's remedies today depend primarily on the provisions and judicial interpretations of a particular state's lien statutes. Many variations in a lienor's rights and remedies exist. For example, whether a lienor has the legal right to take the property ahead of another creditor depends on a state's priority laws and decisions. To have priority (outside of bankruptcy) means for one to have a better right than any other creditor or claimant to take the debtor's property and dispose of it to satisfy an indebtedness. Possible claimants include other creditors, purchasers of the property, and the United States and state governments (tax liens).

Judicial Liens

Judicial liens may result from a creditor's efforts to satisfy an indebtedness by going to court. Governed largely by state statutes, judicial liens arise from various events during the collection process including prejudgment remedies of attachment or garnishment (explained below); the rendition of a judgment for the creditor (or from the judgment's being docketed in the official records of the court); and, as a result of postjudgment collection remedies of execution, creditor's bill, and garnishment (also explained below). The filing of a legal complaint, however, does not elevate a general creditor's status to that of a lien creditor. Until a judgment, attachment, equitable, execution, or garnishment lien arises, the collecting creditor remains unsecured, meaning that it has no legal claim to or rights in any of the debtor's property.

General Scheme of Priorities

Although creditors are classified as either lien or non-lien creditors, lien creditors are further subdivided into subclasses. For example, creditors having security interests in specified personal property of debtors are classified as having either *perfected* or *unperfected* security interests (see Chapter 6 for definitions). Outside of the bankruptcy context, the law of creditor's rights places at the top of the priority ranking the claims of Article Nine secured parties having properly perfected security interests. Just below perfected secured parties are judicial lienors, referred to as "lien creditors" within Article Nine.[2] Below judicial lien creditors in many, but not all, instances are lienors whose liens arise by operation of law. This class is followed by Article Nine unperfected secured parties. At the bottom of the priority list are general (also called unsecured) creditors. This bottom group includes lenders who make "signature only" loans, wage claimants, and sellers of goods and services on credit who do not reserve security interests or reclaim the goods within ten days of their sale. To summarize, the general ranking or priority of creditors is as follows:

1. Perfected Article Nine security interests;

2. Judicial liens, including the interests of bankruptcy trustees and other representative creditors (creditors who represent the claims of other creditors);

3. Statutory or common law liens, for example, an artisan's lien asserted by an automobile mechanic for nonpayment of an amount due for repairs, or a mechanic's lien asserted by an artisan for nonpayment of services for working on a home;

4. Unperfected Article Nine security interests; and

5. The claims of general or unsecured creditors (who have only a chose in action to seek amounts owed through the courts).

This priority list, although generally accurate, is subject to numerous exceptions. Moreover, the list sets out general categories of creditors; it does not disclose the priority rights, if any, within each of the listed classes. Thus, although few priority rights exist among or between unsecured creditors (except in bankruptcy), perfected Article Nine secured parties are subject to definitive priority rules within their own classification as set out in UCC Article Nine.[3]

It should be remembered that the issue of priority becomes important when two or more creditors each assert an interest or lien in the debtor's property. Until such a conflict arises, however, a creditor is free to pursue both informal and formal judicial remedies to satisfy a delinquent indebtedness.

CREDITORS' INFORMAL COLLECTION EFFORTS

Reportedly, over 95 percent of consumer obligors pay their debts on time.[4] Of those who fail to do so, nearly half, according to one study, said that it was due to their loss of income or to their voluntary overextension.[5] On the other hand, the same study found that 20 percent of those who defaulted claimed either fraud or deception on the part of the creditor or payment misunderstandings between them as the bases for nonpayment.[6]

Such studies suggest that collection efforts should, when possible, be responsive to the reason or reasons why a particular debtor fails to pay. The uncharitable term sometimes applied to delinquent customers, "deadbeats," should be avoided because it tends to create the opinion that all debtors are alike and should be treated accordingly. This simply is not true. If a creditor wishes to maximize the collection of delinquent accounts, an understanding of customers' dissatisfactions and a sincere empathy in reference to legitimate hardships are desirable. With an understanding and constructively responsive attitude, many delinquencies may be worked out to both parties' satisfaction. This section deals with the process by which creditors themselves attempt to work out or otherwise collect delinquent accounts.

Dunning Letter

The first step a creditor normally takes when an account is overdue is to send a letter to its customer requesting payment. Although initial letters in reference to a delinquent account tend to be cordial, a level of hostility usually creeps into subsequent requests. Indeed, at some point, the "request" may be reworded as a "demand." When debtors fail to respond to polite or hostile dunning letters, many creditors follow up with telephone calls and personal visits, either at the debtor's residence or work place. Threats of lawsuits may also be made.

Few direct legal controls apply to a creditor's dunning efforts so long as the creditor uses its own name in the communications. However, if a creditor uses a name other than its own "which would indicate that a third person is collecting or attempting to collect the debt," the restrictions of the Fair Debt Collection Practices Act (FDCPA) govern.[7] The FDCPA applies primarily, however, to professional or full-time debt collectors, that is, to persons or companies that regularly collect debts owed to some other person or firm.[8]

Except for the possible but unlikely torts of negligent or intentional infliction of emotional distress, a dunning letter sent directly to the debtor may say whatever the creditor wishes it to say within limits. Although lawsuits ordinarily may be threatened, a statement that the debtor's life may be in jeopardy if payment is not forthcoming immediately, apart from constituting the possible crime of extortion, will likely be a violation of U.S. postal regulations as it arguably constitutes a misuse of the mails to carry out or threaten illegal or criminal actions.

Communications with a Debtor's Employer

Although no federal law prohibits a creditor vis-à-vis a debt collector from contacting a debtor's employer when the purpose is to inform the employer of the claimed overdue account, certain state laws restrict employer contacts. Moreover, if a creditor in contacting the employer mistakenly gives false information to an employer about one of its employees, the creditor could face liability for the tort of defamation—the publication (which includes mailing a letter) of false information. Truth, of course, is a defense to a defamation action. So too is privilege—a legally recognized right to say or publish information even if false. Normally, a communication is deemed privileged if it concerns a matter about which the recipient of the communication has a legitimate interest. Courts disagree, however, over the question of whether an employer has a sufficient interest in a creditor's communication regarding a claimed delinquent account of one of its employees.[9]

Wrongful Collection

One of the problems with a creditor's communicating with a delinquent debtor's employer is that the employer may subsequently order the employee to pay the account or face dismissal. This may raise various legal problems including a possible claim of denial of due process or even a defamation action, particularly if the employee had a legal defense to the creditor's claim. In short, telephoning, sending, or even threatening to send letters to a debtor's employer or third person about a debtor's delinquent account may be crossing the unclear line between legally permissive and impermissive collection efforts. Indeed, the courts in several states have recognized a relatively new tort sometimes called the "tort of wrongful collection." Any threat of physical harm falls into this category. Less clear are threats of lawsuits, complaints to employers, or statements such as: "You will never get credit again if you fail to pay within ten days!"

One of the authors of this book a few years ago when teaching a creditors' rights course to law students asked if they would furnish dunning letters for the instructor's files. One tendered form letter included a picture of what may be described only as a half-naked brute with the meanest face imaginable. Below the unpleasant picture were the words: "If you don't want this man pounding [yes, pounding] on your door, pay up at once!" Creditors should be aware that courts have awarded damages or issued injunctions against creditors who have tried to intimidate debtors or have used profanities, obscenities, and abusive language in letters, personal visitations, or telephone conversations.[10]

DEBT COLLECTORS' COLLECTION EFFORTS

Fair Debt Collection Practices Act

In 1982, by one source, more than 6,000 independent collection agencies operated in the United States.[11] Debt collection is a big and, on occasion, a somewhat nasty business. In 1977, Congress enacted the Fair Debt Collection Practices Act as Title VIII of the Consumer Credit Protection Act[12] in response to "abundant evidence of the use of abusive, deceptive, and unfair debt collection practices by many debt collectors."[13] Congress noted in section 802 of the act that abusive debt collection practices contribute to personal bankruptcies, marital instability, loss of jobs, and invasions of privacy.[14] The expressly stated purposes of the FDCPA include "to eliminate abusive debt collection practices" and "to insure that those debt collectors who refrain from using abusive debt collection practices are not comparatively disadvantaged."[15]

Coverage

The FDCPA applies only to the debt collector defined as a person (or firm) whose principal business is the collection of debts, or who "regularly collects or attempts to collect directly or indirectly, debts owed . . . to another."[16] Creditors who collect or attempt to collect their own delinquent accounts are excluded unless they use a name other than their own. Also excluded are officers and employees of creditors and fiduciaries under escrow arrangements.[17]

Contact with Third Persons

The FDCPA limits contacts with persons other than the debtor. If the whereabouts of the debtor (called a "consumer" in the act)[18] is unknown, a debt collector may contact other persons to acquire "location information" about the consumer.[19] Location information includes a consumer's place of abode, telephone number, or his or her place of employment.[20] The debt collector may not inform any person so contacted that the consumer owes or may owe a debt.[21]

With the exception of location information, a debt collector may not, without the consumer's prior consent or with the permission of a court, communicate with any person about the collection other than with the consumer, his or her attorney, and a consumer credit reporting agency. The act makes it clear that employers may not be contacted in reference to the debt itself.[22]

Communication with the Debtor

After verification of the debt with the consumer (which is required by the act), a debt collector, unless having the debtor's prior consent or with a court's express permission, may not communicate with the consumer except between 9 A.M. and 8 P.M. local time at his or her "normal location."[23] In any event, all communications with the consumer must cease if the debt collector learns that the consumer is represented by an attorney, if the consumer notifies the collector in writing that he or she refuses to pay the debt, or if the consumer informs the collector that he or she wishes the collector to cease further communications.[24]

Harassment or Abuse Prohibited

The act proscribes a debt collector from

1. Using or threatening violence or other criminal means;
2. Using obscene or profane language;
3. Publishing a list of debtors who allegedly refuse to pay debts (except to a consumer credit reporting agency);
4. Advertising for sale any debt to coerce its payment;
5. Harassing the debtor by causing his or her telephone to ring or harassing any person including the debtor through conversation over the telephone; and
6. Placing telephone calls without disclosing the caller's true identity.[25]

False or Misleading Representations Prohibited

A debt collector may not use any false, deceptive, or misleading representation or means in collecting a debt. Prohibited activities include the following:

1. Implying that the debt collector is in any way affiliated with the United States government or with any state by wearing a uniform, badge, or insignia;
2. Falsely representing the character, amount, or legal status of any debt;
3. Falsely representing or implying that the collector is an attorney or that a communication is from an attorney when it is not; and
4. Threatening to take any action that cannot legally be taken or that is not intended to be taken.[26]

The act lists several other examples of false or misleading representations. In addition, section 808 lists several unfair or unconscionable practices.[27] Any collection firm or person engaged in the business of collecting debts for others should carefully study these provisions.

Liability for Violations

A debt collector who violates any of the provisions of the FDCPA is liable for the debtor's actual damages regardless of the amount, plus "additional damages" which may not exceed $1,000, plus attorneys' fees and costs when deemed appropriate.[28] In addition to being subject to a direct action, which an aggrieved debtor may bring in court to redress a claimed violation of the act, a violator is subject to administrative proceedings initiated by the Federal Trade Commission. A violation of any of the FDCPA provisions is deemed an "unfair or deceptive act or practice" in violation of the Federal Trade Commission Act, rendering a violator liable for a fine up to $10,000 and to cease and desist orders, consent decrees, or other FTC administrative remedies.[29]

State Constraints on Debt Collections

Approximately 40 states have statutory provisions that regulate collection practices.[30] Although considerable variations exist among these state statutes, most allow private causes of action by debtors against debt collectors for alleged violations.[31] In several states, Florida for example, debt collectors who in the course of their duties repossess motor vehicles must be licensed.[32]

In California and Florida, state collection regulatory statutes apply to creditors as well as to third-party debt collectors.[33] New York's statute, on the other hand, specifically excludes creditors from its coverage.[34] Generally, a debt collector's compliance with provisions of the FDCPA will constitute compliance with a state's regulatory requirements.

REMEDIAL RIGHTS OF UNSECURED CREDITORS

In Chapter 6 we explained how creditors may condition extensions of credit by requiring that debtors convey Article Nine interests in personal property as security. Creditors, however, often do not so condition their credit extensions. In this section we focus on the important remedial rights of these unsecured or general creditors. In the following section we discuss the rights available to secured creditors.

Unsecured Creditor's Uncertain Path to a Satisfied Judgment

Assume that a creditor, when making a loan (although likely requiring that a promissory note be signed to evidence the credit and its repayment terms), does not require that a security agreement be executed. In short, the creditor is unsecured.

Dunning Efforts

Following the debtor's default, the unsecured creditor (assuming it does not assign the delinquent account to a debt collector or a collection agency) will likely attempt to dun the debtor through letters or telephone calls. If the debtor responds, it will either cure the delinquency or agree with the creditor to an extension (called a "workout"). The odds are, however, that the debtor will not respond, at least to the first letter. (These alternatives are diagrammed in Figure 3, which should be consulted throughout the following discussion.)

If the dunning efforts fail, the creditor either abandons its efforts or pursues the matter through the courts. Should the creditor decide to go to court, it should act to elevate its claim as quickly as possible from that of a general creditor to one of a judicial lien creditor. Having a lien affords a creditor an important legal advantage over unsecured creditors of the debtor.

In going to a court, a creditor first will need to file a legal complaint setting out the credit-extending contract and alleging that the plaintiff has complied with all the contract's terms and conditions but that the defendant has defaulted in its payment obligations. A collection suit is commenced as a civil action in a state court located in a state where the debtor either resides or has property. (See Chapter 2 for discussions of the state and federal court systems and of the procedure followed in civil lawsuits.)

Service of Process

The first of many obstacles that a creditor confronts along the judicial path toward the elusive goal of a satisfied judgment (where a creditor actually gets paid what is owed) is the possible failure of service of process. A failure of service means that the debtor (now defendant) has not been legally presented with a copy of the signed complaint and accompanying summons directing the debtor to answer in court the allegations contained in the complaint within a

Figure 3
An Unsecured Creditor's Path to a Satisfied Judgment

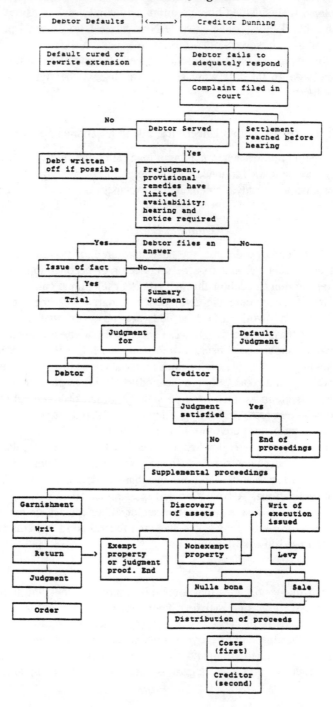

specified time. If service cannot be effected either because the debtor has "vanished into thin air" or for any other reason, then the creditor's only alternative is to wait and try again later or to write off the debt when permissible under the federal tax laws (see subsequent discussion in this chapter). If, however, the debtor has property that may be attached, the creditor may be able to reach the debtor through his or her property.

Let's assume that the debtor is served. The impact of becoming a defendant may cause the debtor to quickly pay the amount due or to reach an agreement with the creditor regarding how the delinquency is to be worked out. More likely, the served debtor will fail to answer the complaint or to otherwise appear in court either *pro se* (by him- or herself) or through an attorney within the required time under the relevant rules of civil procedure.

Default Judgments

When a debtor fails to answer within the required time, a default judgment will be entered for the creditor. A default judgment often, however, may be "opened up" should the debtor eventually appear and contest the creditor's claim. Although the majority of collection actions filed in court result in uncontested default judgments, a debtor, of course, may contest the lawsuit. (See Figure 3.)

Contested Actions

When a defendant answers a complaint either by filing a responsive pleading or by moving to dismiss the action with or without "affirmative defenses" (specified and recognized grounds why the complaint should be dismissed as a matter of law), he or she contests the action.

If a court decides that the creditor's complaint fails to state a cause of action, it will dismiss the complaint. More likely, a court may find that no genuine issue of fact exists (because the debtor's answer admits the nonpayment of a debt owed) and will enter a judgment for the plaintiff-creditor on the pleadings. The creditor may also be granted upon motion a summary judgment on the basis of the record of the case up until the time the motion is presented. The record may include affidavits (sworn *ex parte* statements), depositions (sworn statements where an opposing attorney usually asks the questions), interrogatories (sworn answers to written questions), and legal briefs (the lawyers' written arguments). In any of these situations except dismissals, a judgment or a judicial adjudication of liability or non-liability is entered. Any final judgment is subject to possible appeals.

When the defendant's answer to the complaint raises an issue or issues of fact, a trial usually is necessitated, which normally culminates in a judgment being entered either for the plaintiff (creditor) or defendant (debtor). If a trial is necessary, the creditor has the burden of convincing the trier of fact (the judge if a "bench trial," otherwise the jury) that his or her version of the facts is the true version. The burden of proof in civil cases is "by a preponderance of the evidence'' and normally falls on the plaintiff who in a collections' suit is either the creditor or a third-party debt collector.

Prejudgment, Provisional Remedies

Before judgment is rendered, a creditor may wish or need to invoke what are known as prejudgment or provisional remedies, particularly if the debtor is secreting or trying to dispose of his or her property by transferring it to others or by removing it outside the state. Prejudgment remedies are designed to protect a creditor's provisional interest in having the debtor's assets available should the creditor prevail on the merits. Also, the invoking of prejudgment remedies may cause a debtor to settle. The four most common provisional remedies are attachment, garnishment, replevin, and receivership.

Attachment

Attachment is a writ (or order) issued by a court official (today, usually a judge) directing the seizure of the debtor's property to secure the creditor's claim should judgment be entered for the creditor. The attachment remedy is entirely governed by state statutes, even when ordered by a federal court.[35] Attachment ordinarily is available only upon a creditor's showing of extraordinary circumstances as permitted by a controlling statute. The customary statutory grounds for attachment include the following:

1. Where the defendant is a nonresident, is out of state, or is concealing him- or herself;
2. Where the defendant is transferring or secreting property to defraud the plaintiff-creditor or other creditors generally; and
3. Where the nature of the claim (for example, one alleging fraud) entitles the creditor to special remedial considerations.

Because of four United States Supreme Court decisions,[36] prejudgment attachment and garnishment procedures are subject to the due process requirements of the federal constitution, meaning that the debtor is entitled to notice and an opportunity for a hearing before (or immediately after) the property is taken or seized. To obtain prejudgment attachment, in most states, a creditor must file a complaint and summons, plus an affidavit setting forth facts relevant to at least one of the statutory grounds, a bond, and the proposed writ of attachment. In a few states, clerks of the court still issue writs *ex parte*, but most states in response to certain U.S. Supreme Court decisions require the writ to be issued by a judge following notice and an opportunity for a hearing. The writ directs the sheriff or other court officials to attach and take control over nonexempt property of the debtor.

Exemption Laws

As discussed in Chapter 2, every state has exemption laws which exempt certain categories of a debtor's property from attachment or execution. Exemptions differ from state to state, ranging from "the family Bible" or the "family rifle," to "an automobile having a value of no more than $1,500."[37]

The most common exemption is the *homestead exemption*, which exempts the debtor's occupied or family home, at least up to a certain value. Even this exemption, however, varies considerably from state to state, and a creditor should consult its state's exemption laws to ascertain exactly what property is protected.

The exemption laws do not ordinarily apply to federal or state governmental creditors. Thus, the Internal Revenue Service, for example, generally is not hampered by state exemption laws when asserting a federal tax lien on a taxpayer's property. Other general creditors, however, may not so easily avoid the exemption laws. Purported "waivers" signed by consumer debtors in which they agree to give up or not assert their rights under state exemption laws are prohibited by the Federal Trade Commission under its 1985 Credit Practices Rule.[38]

Prejudgment Garnishment

Garnishment, called the "trustee process" in several New England states, is designed to allow a creditor to freeze the debtor's (called the *principal debtor* in garnishments) property when in the hands of a third person (called the *garnishee*). A potential garnishee is a person who owes a debt to the principal debtor or possesses property belonging to the principal debtor. Prejudgment garnishment involves notifying a garnishee that the garnishing creditor claims a right to have the debt or property in the garnishee's control applied to satisfy any judgment the creditor might obtain. Employers and banks of the principal debtor are the most likely garnishees in creditor prejudgment actions.

Other than the debtor's property being in the control of a third person, garnishment is similar to attachment. Both are statutory-based actions. Moreover, both remedies may be invoked to obtain jurisdiction over the property of a nonresident, and both are subject to the notice and opportunity of hearing due process requirements.

Prejudgment Replevin

Replevin is an action ordered or sanctioned by a court to recover possession of personal property in behalf of a creditor who either has title to or a right to the possession of property within the debtor's control. Normally, only secured creditors and sellers of goods have a right to seek prejudgment replevin and, then, only if notice and an opportunity for a hearing are furnished the debtor.

Receivership Pendente Lite

The fourth and final prejudgment remedy is receivership, in which a disinterested person is appointed by the court to care for or administer the defendant's property. Receivership is an equitable or discretionary remedy granted upon a showing that the defendant is unable to manage his or her affairs and that the value of the defendant's property as a consequence likely will be diminished.

A receiver appointed prior to judgment is called a receiver *pendente lite*. The receivership remedy under state law is used rather infrequently.

Meaning and Limitations of a Judgment

Today, the majority of judgments in collection cases are probably in the form of default judgments. The older practice of *confessions of judgment* (or cognovit judgments), which permitted a creditor to obtain a judgment upon a debtor's prior written authorization (or "confession"), has been prohibited in numerous states and is proscribed by the Federal Trade Commission's 1985 "Credit Practices Rules."[39]

Regardless of how a judgment comes about or what form it may take, every judgment in a collection's case represents an adjudication of the creditor's right to payment. The judgment once rendered does not, however, put money into the creditor's pocket although it does have legal significance for the creditor, especially since a judgment lien usually results.

Judgment Liens

Judgments result under the laws of many states in a *judgment lien* attaching nonexempt property of the judgment-debtor. This lien may result in the judgment creditor's moving ahead of the general creditors of the judgment debtor in priority, especially in the event of a bankruptcy proceeding. In certain states, a judgment lien arises automatically on rendition of the judgment while in others it attaches on the judgment's being docketed or recorded. A judgment lien has full effectiveness only in the state in which the judgment was rendered, however. Thus, when a creditor obtains a judgment against a defendant in one state but the defendant is in or moves to another state, to enforce the judgment, the judgment creditor may have to go to the debtor's state and sue on the judgment, that is, bring a new cause of action to enforce the judgment rendered in the "foreign jurisdiction."

In summary, the rendition of a judgment normally is only one step in the process of collecting a debt. Unless the judgment debtor voluntarily comes forth and tenders payment of the judgment amount, the judgment creditor may have to pursue postjudgment remedies and supplementary proceedings (See Figure 3).

Supplementary Proceedings

Even a judgment lien does not permit a creditor to seize the debtor's property subject to the lien him- or herself. Moreover, if a judgment debtor fails to pay a judgment which grew out of a contract debt (the situation involving accounts), he or she cannot be ordered to go to jail. Rather, the legal course of action that a judgment creditor may have to take in attempting to collect an unsatisfied judgment and to enforce its judgment lien is to pursue the postjudgment and supplemental remedies of discovery of assets, execution, creditor's bill, or garnishment.

Discovery of Assets

Under modern statutes, a judgment creditor may seek a writ of execution, which is an order directing a sheriff to seize and sell the debtor's personal and, in some states, real property to satisfy a judgment. Before seeking the writ, a creditor may first need to discover the assets of the debtor by obtaining an order or citation, which mandates the debtor to file with the court a sworn list of his or her real and personal property including any bank accounts, stocks, bonds, chattels, and interests in land. Failure to produce the sworn list (or committing perjury by knowingly filing a false or incomplete list) in some states could result in the judgment debtor's being ordered to jail for contempt of court. In contested actions, the debtor's assets may already have been "discovered" through pre-trial discovery devices—depositions and interrogatories, especially

Execution and Levy

A writ of execution normally is issued in response to a judgment creditor's request by the clerk of the court in which the judgment was rendered. No prior hearing or notice to the judgment debtor is ordinarily required. The writ orders the sheriff to levy on the property described in the writ and then to sell the property. The resulting "sheriff's sale" often involves a prior appraisal and general public notice of the pending disposition, typically by an advertisement in a local newspaper of general circulation which carries legal advertising. The proceeds of the sheriff's sale by statute must first go to pay all the costs of the sale before the remainder will be distributed to the levying judgment creditor.

Nulla Bonas

When the sheriff discovers either that the debtor has only exempt property (that is, property not subject to being levied upon under the state's exemption law) or that no tangible property exists (which happens frequently in collection cases), the sheriff must return the writ of attachment *nulla bona*. This means that the levy was unsuccessful. Subsequent (or alias) writs may then be issued.

In any event, the act of levying creates an *execution lien* on the levied property that is found. Over time, this execution lien may terminate under the doctrine of "dormancy." This occurs if the property is not sold within a reasonable time (at least within a few months) after the levy.

Creditor's Bill

A variation of execution recognized in several states is one in which a creditor files with a court a legal document typically denoted a *creditor's bill* compelling a judgment debtor to turn over his or her nonexempt intangible, beneficial, and equitable property assets. This may include contract rights, accounts receivable, and equitable and beneficial interests in real property. A creditor's bill (also known as a creditor's suit) is an equitable or extraordinary remedy which a court has discretion in granting and which, in any case, is available only if the creditor has no adequate remedy at law. In states where the distinction between legal and equitable remedies has been abolished by statute, the execution remedy may be used to levy on the beneficial and intangible property interests of a judgment debtor.

Garnishment

Postjudgment garnishment is similar to prejudgment garnishment (see earlier discussion). A judgment creditor files a motion and affidavit stating that the judgment is wholly or partially unsatisfied and that the garnishee (bank or employer) holds property of the principal debtor. A writ of garnishment is served on the garnishee, which creates a lien in the described property. The garnishee must answer the writ and summons within a stated time or face a default judgment. The garnishee in its answer states what, if any, property of the principal debtor it owes or possesses. If the garnishee admits it has nonexempt property of the judgment debtor and has no setoff right or other legal defense against paying it, a judgment for the admitted amount will be entered against the garnishee.

Restrictions on garnishment of an employee's wages have been imposed as a result of the Congressional enactment of Title III of the Consumer Credit Protection Act.[40] (These restrictions are discussed in Chapter 15.)

Risks of Collection

In pursuing available remedies through the courts, a creditor faces several serious risks which reduce the probability of obtaining a full satisfaction of the delinquent account. First, the debtor may have no property or income; in other words, he or she may be "collection proof." Second, as already noted, what property a debtor may have may be exempt from attachment, execution, a creditor's bill, or garnishment. Third, other creditors of the debtor may have a priority right in the debtor's property. Fourth, the property levied upon when sold may not produce sufficient proceeds to satisfy the indebtedness. Fifth, at any time prior to receiving the proceeds of the judicial sale, the collection efforts may be stopped or "stayed" if the debtor goes into bankruptcy. In short, the unsecured creditor's path to a satisfied judgment is uncertain, costly, and subject to numerous legal and practical pitfalls.

REMEDIAL RIGHTS OF SECURED CREDITORS

When a creditor conditions a credit extension on the debtor's giving of personal property security, the creditor is a UCC Article Nine secured party having a security interest. In Chapter 6 we discussed how a creditor lending against accounts may collect the indebtedness owed by the principal debtor by merely notifying the obligors of the accounts to make their future payments to the lender.[41] Here we consider a secured party's other remedies as authorized by UCC Article Nine.[42]

Options Available to a Secured Creditor

When a debtor defaults in making payments or in performing other obligations due under a security agreement, an Article Nine secured party ordinarily has three choices. First, the creditor may bring suit to seek satisfaction of the indebtedness (the chose-in-action remedy). Second, it may seek to gain possession of the collateral through a court-sanctioned replevin action. Or, third, the secured party may attempt to invoke the self-help remedies of taking possession and disposing of the collateral without court involvement.[43] These three options are discussed in this section. (Throughout the following discussion, it will be helpful to examine from time to time Figure 4, which diagrams the self-help remedies of a secured creditor available under Article Nine.)

Chose-in-Action Option

The most time-consuming, costly, and uncertain remedy for a secured creditor to pursue is the judicial chose-in-action route, the basic right any secured or unsecured creditor has to go to court to enforce one's legal claim. The problem is that the judicial collection route, when followed by a secured creditor, is subject to the same pitfalls and risks of failure as when pursued by an unsecured creditor save one—state exemption laws generally do not apply to consensual security interests in property otherwise exempt from attachment or execution. Despite this important difference, a secured creditor having a security interest in goods in most instances will prefer to invoke one of the two other remedial options available—judicial replevin or self-help repossession or sale of the collateral.

Judicial Sanctioned Replevin

When a security interest exists in and has attached to consumer goods, farm products, inventory, or equipment (as defined in Article Nine),[44] a secured party has the option to seek a judicially sanctioned replevin or court-ordered return of goods.[45] Replevin is a prejudgment remedy available to a plaintiff claiming either legal title to or the right to take possession of goods on the basis of an earlier conveyed security interest. Consequently, replevin is not available to unsecured creditors.

On the rationale of two United States Supreme Court decisions, *Fuentes v. Shevin*[46] and *North Georgia Finishing, Inc. v. Di-Chem, Inc.*,[47] replevin is subject to the constitutional due process requirements of prior notice and an opportunity for an adversary hearing before a debtor may permanently be dispossessed of its property. Replevin writs should be issued by judges, not by court clerks.

Figure 4
A Secured Party's Self-Help Remedies

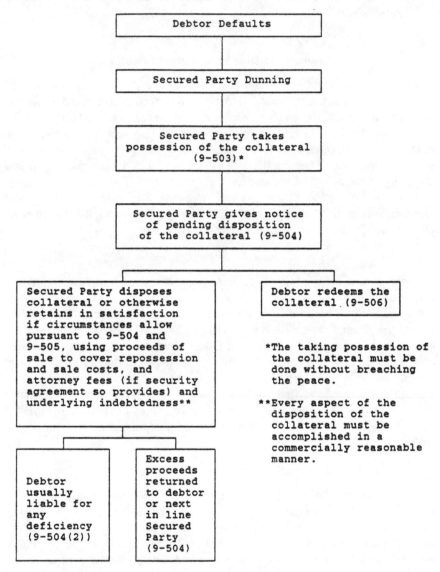

Debtor Defaults

Secured Party Dunning

Secured Party takes
possession of the collateral
(9-503)*

Secured Party gives notice
of pending disposition
of the collateral (9-504)

Secured Party disposes
collateral or otherwise
retains in satisfaction
if circumstances allow
pursuant to 9-504 and
9-505, using proceeds of
sale to cover repossession
and sale costs, and
attorney fees (if security
agreement so provides) and
underlying indebtedness**

Debtor redeems the
collateral (9-506)

*The taking possession of
the collateral must be
done without breaching
the peace.

**Every aspect of the
disposition of the
collateral must be
accomplished in a
commercially reasonable
manner.

Debtor
usually
liable for
any
deficiency
(9-504(2))

Excess
proceeds
returned
to debtor
or next
in line
Secured
Party
(9-504)

Moreover, prompt postseizure *adversary* proceedings must be held following any preseizure *ex parte* hearing (one in which the debtor is not in attendance).[48]

After a debtor's property has been seized and he or she has been given notice of the procedure and has been afforded an opportunity for an adversary hearing, the secured party, under certain state statutes, with a court's permission may take the seized property and dispose of it pursuant to the requirements of an applicable replevin statute or pursuant to sections 9–504 through 9–507 of Article Nine (discussed below). Under the statutes, however, a judgment must first be entered in favor of the creditor, after which the seized property may be disposed of only through a sheriff's sale.

Self-Help Remedies

Following a default and depending on the circumstances, the most expedient and least costly remedial course may be for the secured party to take the collateral and dispose of it without court involvement. These so-called self-help remedies of repossession and foreclosure are considered controversial, however, since they allow a creditor to determine unilaterally that a default event has occurred and to take and dispose of the debtor's property without a court's first determining whether the default had in fact taken place or, if it had, whether the defendant had a valid defense. One author of this volume has suggested that the concept of self-help runs against the jurisprudential notion that one is innocent (or has a legal right to continue to possess property) until proven guilty (or is found by a court to have committed a default).[49] Although the self-help repossession remedy was struck down in the 1960s by certain lower courts on the basis that it permitted the taking of property without due process of law, higher courts subsequently have upheld the constitutionality of self-help repossession, finding that state action is not involved. Constitutional due process restrictions apply to a taking of property whenever the machinery of the state is utilized. Self-help remedies involve neither the courts nor state officials and, thus, are considered private actions.

Although Article Nine's self-help remedies are assumed to be constitutional today, courts frequently find that the circumstances of a particular taking or sale cause a creditor's actions to constitute either an impermissible "breach of the peace" or a "commercially unreasonable" disposition. (These limitations are discussed below.) Consequently, self-help remedies tend to be monitored closely by courts. Of course, any monitoring which occurs, takes place after the fact because an aggrieved debtor must go to court to seek redress subsequent to his or her property's being taken.

Arguments supporting self-help remedies primarily go to remedial efficiency which arguably serves the interests of both parties. In addition, a persuasive rationale is advanced that it is not the actual taking and sale which are important, but rather it is the creditor's right to do so since the threat of repossession, the argument proceeds, causes obligors (especially consumers) to keep their payments current.[50] This argument is particularly persuasive in reference to big-ticket purchases like automobiles.

Right to Take Possession of the Collateral

Under section 9–503 of the UCC, following a debtor's default, a secured party may take possession of the collateral provided the taking is done without a breach of the peace. The only exception is if the parties' security agreement expressly prohibits the secured party from doing so. Although generally referred to as the "right to repossess," this phrase is misleading in two respects. First, the secured party does not have an absolute right to take possession of the collateral, but at most has only a qualified right—he or she may take possession only if it can be done without a breach of the peace. Second, the word "repossession" is misleading since a secured party who never had possession of the collateral in the first place, for example, a bank or finance company, has the option of "taking possession" following a debtor's default. In certain states, Wisconsin, for example, the right to take possession of collateral in consumer credit transactions is limited further by consumer-oriented statutes.

The qualified right to take possession of collateral does not depend on the right's being expressly set out in the parties' security agreement as the roots of the right predate Article Nine and are traceable far back in the common law. Thus, a secured loan or a sales agreement where title is reserved, for example, need not include an express reference to the secured party's rights to take possession and dispose of the collateral for the rights to be available.[51]

Breach of the Peace

Although section 9–503 limits the repossession remedy to circumstances where it can be done without breach of the peace,[52] the UCC does not define what this phrase means. Courts in interpreting the breach-of-the-peace limitation generally have held that if any resistence is offered or if any protest is voiced by the debtor, whether the resistence or protest threatens violence or not, a breach of the peace will result should the creditor or repossessor attempt to take possession of property in the debtor's control following such resistence or protest.

Repossessors of motor vehicles (who are required to be licensed in several states) may try to minimize the potential for debtor resistance by taking possession of vehicles in the middle of the night either with duplicate or master keys or by jump-starting the vehicles. This activity is generally permitted as is a repossessor's entering upon a debtor's private driveway, an activity considered to be privileged so long as the repossessor does not enter into the debtor's home or garage without authorization. Although certain courts have allowed entries into open garages or carports, breaking into a debtor's home or other building, obtaining permission to take goods from a minor child, or repossessing under the "color" or authority of law, for example, by having an off-duty police officer in uniform accompany the repossessor, have all been held to constitute violations of the breach of the peace standard. These situations illustrate the point that a breach of the peace need not involve actual violence nor even the threat of violence. Rather, the mere possibility of a disruption of the normal tranquility of a neighborhood may be sufficient for a breach. In sum, breach of the peace is a normative standard involving commercially reasonable conduct, fair dealing, and honesty in fact which courts demand when a creditor or repossessor takes possession of personal property held by a debtor.

Notification of Police

Although no notice must be furnished a debtor prior to a secured party's taking possession, police officials should be alerted before a repossession occurs. In certain states, prior notice of local police is required by statute. Even if it is not required, it should still be given. In one Florida case, a repossessed car (which had subsequently been resold) remained on the stolen car list because the police had not been informed of the repossession. Spotting the car on Collins Avenue in Miami Beach, police officers pulled the driver (the legitimate new owner) over and took him to a police station whereupon the distraught owner suffered a heart attack. Fortunately, he lived. Indeed, he soon was well enough to sue the repossessor for negligence in not notifying the police of the repossession. To repeat, whether legally mandated or not, it is wise to inform local police routinely of any repossessions of motor vehicles, television sets, furniture, appliances, and so on.

Foreclosure and Reasonable Notification

Under Article Nine, a secured party, after default, may sell, lease, or otherwise dispose of any or all of the collateral that is in its possession.[53] However, the self-help foreclosure remedy is qualified in several important respects.

First, the UCC requires that a "reasonable notification of the time and place of a public sale" or of the "time after which any private sale or other intended disposition is to be made" be sent to the debtor and to other secured parties who have submitted written claims or notices of their security interests to the secured party.[54] The claimed default event need not be identified nor the debtor's right to redeem explained in the notice. Even this minimal notification requirement is unnecessary if the collateral is perishable or may decline speedily in value, or if the debtor, after default, agreed in writing to waive his or her rights to notification or if the collateral is of a type subject to recognized market quotations (for example, equity or debt investments and commodities).

The reasonable notification requirement is not defined in Article Nine but is left for the courts to interpret. Indeed, the lack of a definition has precipitated many lawsuits. These cases have held that, although no notice of a disposition may have been received by the debtor, the UCC's notice provision requires only that it be sent, not that it be received. The more litigated issue, however, concerns allegations that a notice when received did not permit the debtor sufficient time to cure the default. Prior security laws required a waiting period following repossession of five to ten days before the collateral could be sold. The UCC is silent on the issue of reasonable time. The time period must relate, however, to the debtor's principal right in repossession situations—the right to redeem the collateral.

Debtor's Right to Redeem the Collateral

At any time before the secured party has disposed or has entered into a contract for the disposition of the collateral, under UCC Section 9–506, the debtor may redeem the collateral by "tendering fulfillment of all obligations secured," plus the secured party's retaking and holding expenses and reasonable attorney's fee (but only if attorney's fees are provided for in the security agreement).[55] Tendering fulfillment of all obligations secured means, according to UCC section 9–506 "Official Comment" (drafted by the authors of the UCC), the amount that is overdue, unless the security agreement contains a clause accelerating the entire balance in which case the entire balance must be tendered. (Default-acceleration clauses are discussed in Chapter 11.)

The debtor's right to redeem the collateral from the secured party relates to the reasonable notification which the secured party is usually obligated to give prior to disposing of the collateral. One reason for the notice is to permit the debtor a reasonable time to obtain the funds needed to redeem its property. The reasonable notice period, consequently, at a minimum should be such that the debtor will have sufficient time to take "appropriate steps to protect [his or her] interest."[56] This does not mean, however, that the debtor must be afforded time "to earn" the money.

Failure to Give Reasonable Notification

A secured party's failure to give reasonable notification of a pending public sale, where the general public is invited to participate, or a private sale, where the bidders are restricted (a dealer's-only auction, for example), has been judicially construed in several states to mean that the secured party may not bring a deficiency action against the debtor when the sale proceeds are insufficient to cover the indebtedness. Although the UCC is silent regarding the consequences of a failure to give reasonable notice, it explicitly authorizes a secured party's deficiency lawsuit by declaring that the "debtor is liable for any deficiency."[57] On the other hand, the secured party must account to the debtor for any surplus.[58]

Foreclosure Price

Under section 9–507, the fact that a higher price could have been obtained by a sale at a different time or in a different method than the one used does not mean that the sale was not made in a commercially reasonable manner.[59] Moreover, if a secured party sells the collateral "in any recognized market" or at a price "current" in such market, he or she is deemed to have sold in a commercially reasonable manner for a commercially reasonable price. Often a repossessing creditor will dispose of the property by selling it to or through a dealer and obtaining a dealer's wholesale price. UCC section 9–507 has been interpreted as permitting dealer or wholesaler dispositions.

On the other hand, if it appears that two dealers who repossess motor vehicles or other merchandise sell to each other their repossessed goods, such "cross-dumping" raises a strong suspicion that the dealers are not acting in good faith or in a commercially reasonable manner. Cross-sales schemes have been attacked in the courts and by the Federal Trade Commission.

Liability of Secured Party

When a secured party violates any of the provisions of Article Nine in the taking, maintaining, or disposing of the collateral or when the secured party breaches in any respect the commercially reasonable standard imposed by Article Nine, the debtor or any other person entitled to notification under section 9–504 may recover any actual damages resulting from the violation.[60] If the collateral in the hands of the debtor is consumer goods, under Article Nine, the debtor also has the right to recover the entire credit service charge (or interest) plus 10 percent of the principal amount of the debt plus 10 percent of the cash price.[61]

Effect of State Consumer Laws

Several states have enacted state consumer protection laws which have modified a secured creditor's remedial rights under Article Nine. The Wisconsin Consumer Protection Act, for example, restricts a secured creditor's right to move against collateral immediately following default. In certain states, a statutory minimum grace period is required before the creditor may act. Other statues define default as two or more consecutively missed payments.

IMPACT OF BANKRUPTCY ON COLLECTION EFFORTS

Bankruptcy is a federal court procedure designed largely to "relieve the honest debtor from the weight of oppressive indebtedness and permit him to start afresh . . . "[62] Its primary purpose is to afford an overextended debtor relief from creditors. Many of the fundamentals of bankruptcy law and procedure are discussed in Chapter 14. In this chapter, we focus on bankruptcy law from a creditor's perspective, especially on how bankruptcy affects a creditor's collection efforts.

Automatic Stay

The most immediate and significant impact of the filing of a bankruptcy petition (which begins the federal proceeding) is that all collection efforts of all creditors must cease, at least temporarily. Known as the automatic stay rule, the cessation covers the efforts of secured as well as unsecured creditors and extends to informal and self-help measures as well as to state and federal court actions. Even arbitration cases must be suspended.

Scope of the Automatic Stay

The filing of a bankruptcy petition either by the debtor or by one or several of his or her creditors under Chapter Seven (liquidation) or Chapters Eleven or Thirteen (rehabilitation) of the 1978 Bankruptcy Reform Act (BRA),[63] as amended by the Bankruptcy Amendments and Federal Judgeship Act of 1984,[64] automatically operates to stay (or prohibit) any creditor from taking further action to collect an indebtedness from or to enforce a security interest or other lien in the property of the debtor.[65] Notice to creditors is not required for the stay to be effective.

The breadth of the stay includes the filing of any new lawsuits, efforts to obtain or perfect a lien or security interest, or any attempts to enforce an existing judgment.[66] A creditor should not even ask a debtor to reaffirm a debt orally or in writing without permission of a bankruptcy judge. In short, the purpose of the automatic stay is to allow the debtor to have some breathing room, a period free of creditors' demands and actions.

Lifting the Automatic Stay

For Cause: Lack of Adequate Protection

A creditor may seek to have the automatic stay lifted under the BRA for cause. When applied to an Article Nine secured creditor, "cause" means essentially a "lack of adequate protection."[67] Since adequate protection is not clearly defined, a lawyer representing a secured creditor has an opportunity to argue a lack of adequate protection grounds for lifting the stay in nearly every case.[68] A court must either lift the stay upon a showing of inadequate protection or give the creditor something equivalent if harm appears likely.[69] The equivalency may be cash payments, additional security, or the lifting of the stay. If the stay is not lifted nor is additional security granted, and if the secured creditor later suffers damages as a result of the continuation of the stay (for example, the collateral is damaged, destroyed, sold, or declines in value), the creditor will be permitted additional compensation in the form of a *superpriority* unsecured claim for its damages. The superpriority status means that the damage claim must be paid ahead of all other secured claims including the expenses of the bankruptcy administration.[70]

Lack of Equity and Not Necessary for Rehabilitation Requirements

The second principal ground for a secured creditor to seek to have the automatic stay lifted is the claim that the debtor lacks equity in the collateral. The stay will be lifted, however, only if in addition to the debtor's lack of equity (the property is worth less than the claim), the debtor has no need to use the collateral in its rehabilitation. Although this second requirement has no application in a Chapter Seven liquidation proceeding, it is always a relevant factor in either a Chapter Eleven (business) or Thirteen (individual) rehabilitation action. Thus, a secured creditor will probably not be granted a lifting of the stay to replevin a debtor's automobile in a Chapter Thirteen proceeding so long as the debtor under the plan approved by the bankruptcy court may cure its prior defaults within a reasonable time and, thereafter, make payments to the creditor as they become due.[71] A creditor's patience in a Chapter Thirteen (individual rehabilitation) proceeding is a virtue indeed.

Procedure for Lifting the Automatic Stay

A creditor who seeks to have the automatic stay lifted must file a motion with the bankruptcy court. The BRA requires that a preliminary hearing be held before the bankruptcy judge within 30 days of the motion to lift the stay being filed.[72] If the hearing does not take place within that time, the stay is lifted as to the petitioning creditor. A court may, however, order the stay continued without holding a preliminary hearing pending a final hearing which must commence in any event within 60 days of the secured creditor's motion.

Stays against Guarantors

A guarantor of a debtor is not protected or affected by the automatic stay in a Chapter Seven liquidation proceeding. Thus, a creditor may demand payment of a surety, guarantor, or co-debtor when the principal debtor is in default and is in the midst of a Chapter Seven proceeding. If the bankruptcy petition, however, seeks rehabilitation under Chapter Thirteen, section 1301 of the BRA automatically stays all collection actions (including dunning letters) against guarantors and co-debtors if the debt is a consumer debt and the guarantor or co-debtor is not in the credit business.[73]

Debtor's Use of the Property

If a debtor is a business and is authorized to operate its business under Chapter Eleven of the BRA,[74] then it may sell, use, or lease its property in the ordinary course of business without notice or a prior hearing afforded any secured creditor.[75] An exception concerns "cash collateral," defined as "cash, negotiable instruments, documents of title, securities, deposit accounts or cash equivalents whenever acquired . . . "[76] A trustee or debtor in possession (a business operating under a Chapter Eleven reorganization) may use cash collateral only with the secured party's consent or with permission of the bankruptcy court after notice to the secured party and an opportunity for a hearing.[77] Businesses going through BRA Chapter Eleven proceedings continue to operate. (BRA Chapter Eleven reorganizations are discussed extensively in Chapter 14.)

Priorities in Bankruptcy

Unsecured Creditor's Priorities under Section 507

Under the BRA as amended in 1984, the expenses of administration of the bankrupt's estate in a liquidation or rehabilitation proceeding must be paid before any of the unsecured creditors,[78] except for the superpriorities available to secured creditors who suffered losses due to the automatic stay (see earlier discussion), or to postpetition creditors who fund the rehabilitation (discussed in Chapter 14). Next in priority are unpaid claims, which arose in the ordinary course before the trustee was appointed or the order for relief was entered, whichever occurred first (discussed in Chapter 14).[79] This group is followed by employee wage and fringe benefit claims earned within 90 days before the earlier of the petition filing or the closing of the debtor's business, up to a maximum of $2,000 per employee.[80] This group is followed by employee wage and fringe benefit claims within 180 days before the petition filing or closing of the business, whichever occurs first.[81] The next category, created by the 1984 amendments, is "consumer deposits," for example, deposits left with a merchant debtor, up to a maximum of $900 per customer.[82] The sixth and final priority in the BRA section 507 list regarding unsecured claims is the one for selected federal, state, and local taxes.[83]

In a Chapter Seven liquidation proceeding, all the section 507 priority claims are first paid in full. Next, the unsecured creditors who filed timely proofs of claims are paid, followed by claims for fines, then interest. Finally, the residue, if any, is paid to the debtor.[84]

Secured Creditors and Turn Over Rules

A "custodian" of any property of a debtor in a bankruptcy proceeding is obligated to turn over that property along with its profits or proceeds to the trustee or debtor in possession.[85] A custodian as defined by the BRA includes a secured party who is in or has taken possession of collateral under a secured loan or credit sale. In addition, third persons, such as an assignee for the benefit of creditors or a receiver to whom a debtor's property has been transferred, may be subject to this turn over requirement.

Secured Creditors and Proof of Claims

Since an Article Nine secured party may not proceed to enforce either its claim or security interest in the collateral due to the automatic stay and since it must turn over any collateral including proceeds and profits thereof which it holds to the trustee, the question of how a secured party protects its interest becomes crucial.

What the secured creditor must ordinarily do to protect its interest is to timely file a proof of claim in the bankruptcy proceeding. However, in a Chapter Eleven case, if the debtor listed the secured party's claim in the schedule of debts, which the BRA requires the debtor to file, and provided the listed claim is not in dispute and is not contingent, the secured party need not file a claim.[86] Once the claim has been filed by the secured party's lawyer or when the debtor lists the amount as undisputed, liquidated, and not subject to any conditions, it will be allowed. (It may still be a long time, however, before any proceeds or property reach the secured party.)

If the debt owed a secured creditor exceeds the value of that creditor's collateral, the creditor ordinarily will have two claims, one for the value of the collateral (the secured portion) and one for the balance of the indebtedness (the unsecured portion). Undersecured secured creditors may face another problem. The BRA allows a class of secured creditors who are undersecured in a rehabilitation plan to elect to have the claim of the class treated as secured to the full extent of the debt subject to what are called the "cramdown provisions" of the BRA. The cramdown provisions refer to the BRA sections that allow a reorganization or rehabilitation plan to be confirmed and implemented even when it impairs a class of secured claims[87] (see Chapter 14).

Trustee's Avoiding Powers

The trustee, as the representative of the bankruptcy estate, works primarily for the interests of the debtor's unsecured or general creditors. Consequently, trustees are natural enemies, if you will, of secured creditors, especially in Chapter Seven proceedings where secured creditors' claims when allowed permit segments of the debtor's estate to be removed from the bankruptcy estate to be liquidated.

Hypothetical Lien Creditor

The BRA contains several provisions that permit a trustee to set aside or avoid certain secured claims. Foremost, a trustee under section 544(a) of the BRA has all the rights of a hypothetical lien creditor under state law on the date of bankruptcy. This means that, if a security interest in collateral was unperfected for any reason on the day the bankruptcy petition was filed, the trustee has a right to retain the collateral in the bankruptcy estate and to eventually dispose of it for the benefit of general and unsecured creditors over the rights of the unperfected secured party.[88] A secured party's unperfected security interest may result from:

1. Failure to file a required financing statement;
2. Filing the financing statement in the wrong state or at the incorrect location within the right state;
3. Not including the necessary information or signature on the financing statement;
4. The lapse of the financing statement's effectiveness;
5. Filing the statement after the date of the petition; and
6. Filing as to collateral that is not subject to filing (for example, stocks and bonds).

In each of the above instances, the trustee prevails over the secured party. There is, however, one important exception available in most states—if the secured party perfects a purchase money security interest (discussed in Chapter 6) within ten days after the debtor receives the collateral, the secured party prevails even if bankruptcy intervenes.[89] This delayed perfection right is especially important for suppliers of goods.

Voidable Preferences

The transfer of the debtor's property to or for the benefit of a creditor for or on account of an antecedent debt, made while the debtor is insolvent and made within 90 days of the bankruptcy petition, which transfer enables the creditor to receive more than it would have received in a Chapter Seven liquidation proceeding through a *pro rata* distribution, is known as a *preferential transfer* or *voidable preference.*[90]

The trustee's power to avoid preferential transfers of property is one widely used in bankruptcy proceedings. Transfers subject to avoidance include *perfections* within 90 days of the petition of earlier created Article Nine security interests. The power to avoid security interests perfected within 90 days of the date of the bankruptcy but created prior to the 90-day period underscores the dangers of delayed perfection. The purpose of the provision, however, is not to penalize delayed perfections but to prevent a debtor from offering security "on the eve" of bankruptcy, thereby favoring one creditor over others. Obtaining a security interest at a later date is sometimes referred to as "after-thought" security. Understand, however, that a security interest created and perfected within the 90-day period prior to the petition, if given for reasonably equivalent new value (a new loan of money or other extension of credit), even if made while the debtor was insolvent, is neither a voidable preference nor a fraudulent conveyance. A preference requires that a transfer be for or on account of an antecedent debt. A fraudulent conveyance is one in which the debtor intends to hinder or delay its creditors or where the conveyance is not made for a reasonably equivalent value.

Preferences and Floating Liens

A secured party with a floating lien in a debtor's inventory (see Chapter 6) may not improve its position within the 90-day prepetition period. To the extent that improvement takes place, the improvement portion may be avoided as a preference by a trustee under section 547 of the BRA.[91]

Other Trustee Powers: Fraudulent Conveyances

Space permits only a brief mention of other trustees' avoiding powers. First, a trustee may avoid a transfer of any property of, or an obligation incurred by, the debtor within one year of filing the petition, provided the transfer was made with the intention to hinder, delay, or defraud a creditor or, if it was made when the debtor was insolvent, for less than a reasonably equivalent value.[92] This is the BRA's *fraudulent conveyance provision* and is similar to state fraudulent conveyance acts. A trustee has the power to avoid any transfer of property or obligation incurred by an insolvent partnership to a general partner that occurs within one year of the petition's being filed.[93] In addition, a trustee has what are called the *subrogation rights* of any actual creditor of the debtor. This means that a trustee has all the rights under state or federal law that any actual creditor may have had that would have allowed the actual creditor to avoid a security interest or mortgage in the debtor's personal or real property.[94]

Role of Counsel

A business needs the assistance of counsel in collecting delinquent accounts when going to court or when an important debtor of the business voluntarily or involuntarily enters a bankruptcy proceeding. Certainly, a business must cease all efforts to collect any indebtedness owed by a debtor upon the debtor's entering bankruptcy. Preferably, an experienced attorney knowledgeable about bankruptcy rules and procedures, including those pertaining to the filing of proofs of claims and the lifting of the automatic stay, should be hired. Bankruptcy laws and procedures constitute one of the more technical areas of commercial law. Understand, moreover, that bankruptcy is often a protracted matter. Creditors have little choice but to be patient with the court and with counsel.

BAD DEBTS AND THE TAX LAWS

A bad debt is a loan or debt due for services or for sale or rental of property that becomes worthless or uncollectible in a taxable year. Under the Internal Revenue Code, a bad debt may support a deduction used in the computation of adjusted gross income. To be deductible, the debt must have had value when acquired or created. No deduction is allowed for a worthless bad debt that arises from unpaid wages, rents, and so on unless the unpaid amount previously had been included in income. For a bad debt to be deductible, a genuine debtor-creditor relationship must exist. No deduction is allowed, for example, for a debt owed by a political party unless owed to a lending institution. Bad debts resulting from loans to relatives are strictly scrutinized by the IRS to determine whether the transaction was, in fact, a loan or a gift. To avoid these problems, the loan should be evidenced by a note and backed by collateral or other proof that the borrower is solvent. In addition, evidence should exist that repayment was contemplated and expected.

Characterization of Debt

A bad debt must be characterized as either a business or nonbusiness bad debt. This difference is important because a business bad debt is fully deductible against ordinary income whereas a nonbusiness bad debt currently is treated as a short-term capital loss subject to the capital loss limitation. A bad debt is a business bad debt if there is a proximate relationship between the creation of the debt and the taxpayer's trade or business. The United States Supreme Court has held that that relationship is proximate only if the taxpayer's motivation for making the loan is primary and dominant to his or her trade or business.[95] Significant motivation is not sufficient. Worthless securities are not treated as bad debts but are treated separately under the Internal Revenue Code. A non-business bad debt is a debt other than (1) a debt created or acquired in connection with a trade or business of the taxpayer or (2) a debt the loss from the worth-lessness of which is incurred in the taxpayer's trade or business. A loan by an officer or employee to a corporation which subsequently becomes uncollectible is a nonbusiness bad debt.

Forgiveness of Indebtedness

Voluntary cancellation or forgiveness of a debt does not support a deductible loss for bad debt. The debt must be actually worthless. If the debt is actually worthless, the deduction is allowed because the debt is worthless, not because it was forgiven or voluntarily cancelled.

Amount and Timing of the Deduction

To be deductible, the bad debt must become worthless in the taxable year in which the deduction is taken. If the bad business debt is only partially worthless, the taxpayer may deduct that part of the debt that is charged off within that taxable year. No loss is allowed for partial worthlessness of nonbusiness bad debts.

The amount of the bad debt deduction is equal to the adjusted basis that would be used in determining the loss from the sale or other disposition of property. No deduction is allowed if a basis cannot be established. In the context of an uncollectible account receivable for services rendered, the cost of adjusted basis of the services rendered by a professional such as an accountant or an attorney is zero; therefore, no bad debt deduction is allowed for an account receivable pertaining strictly to professional services rendered. A bad debt deduction is allowed, however, to the extent that part of the overhead expenses and salary expenses can be allocated to the rendering of the service.

Method of Deducting Bad Debts

A bad debt must be deducted by the specific charge-off method. The reserve method may not be used for taxable years beginning after December 31, 1986. The specific charge-off method allows for direct deduction of bad debts that have become worthless during the tax year.

Recovery of Bad Debts

A bad debt, which subsequently acquires value, must be accounted for in the year in which it ceases to be a bad debt. If the bad debt were deducted in a prior year under the specific charge-off method, the amount that is later recovered or collected must be included in gross income for the year in which it is received or recovered.

NOTES

1. 15 U.S.C. §§ 1692–1692o.
2. U.C.C. § 9–301 (3).
3. *See, e.g.*, U.C.C. §§ 9–312 (5) (a) and (b); 9–312 (3), and 9–312 (4).
4. Paul B. Rasor, *Consumer Finance Law.* Mathew Bender (1985), p. 489.
5. David Caplovitz, *Consumers in Trouble: A Study of Debtors in Default.* The Free Press (1974), p. 91.
6. *Id.*
7. 15 U.S.C. § 1692a (6).
8. *Id.*
9. David G. Esptein, *Debtor-Creditor Law in a Nutshell.* West Publishing Co. (1985), p. 9.
10. *See*, Sherman v. Field Clinic, 74 Ill. App.3d 21, 392 N.E.2d 154 (1979), *see also*, Note, *Debt Collection Practices: Remedies for Abuse*, 10 B.C. Ind. & Com. L. Rev. 698 (1969).
11. Geltzer and Woocher, *Debt Collection Regulation: Its Development and Direction for the 1980s.* 37 Bus. Law. 1401, 1402 (1982).
12. 15 U.S.C. §§ 1692, *et seq.*
13. 15 U.S.C. § 1692 (a).
14. *Id.*
15. 15 U.S.C. § 1692 (e).
16. 15 U.S.C. § 1692a (6) (emphasis added).
17. 15 U.S.C. § 1692a (6) (F).
18. 15 U.S.C. § 1692a (3).
19. 15 U.S.C. § 1692b.
20. 15 U.S.C. § 1692a (7).
21. 15 U.S.C. § 1692b (2).
22. 15 U.S.C. § 1692e (b).
23. 15 U.S.C. § 1692c (a) (1).
24. 15 U.S.C. §§ 1692c (a) (2) and (c).
25. 15 U.S.C. § 1692d.
26. 15 U.S.C. § 1692e.
27. *See*, 15 U.S.C. § 1692f.
28. 15 U.S.C. § 1692k.
29. 15 U.S.C. § 1692l.
30. Rasor, *Consumer Finance Law* (1985), p. 543.
31. *See, e.g.*, Md. Ann. Code art. 49, § 14–201 (Md. Consumer Debt Collection

Act), and N.H. Rev. Stat. Ann. 358-C (Unfair, Deceptive, or Unreasonable Collection Practices Act).

32. *See, e.g.*, Florida Statutes §§ 493.30 (6) and 493.304 (6).

33. Florida Statutes §§ 559.55–559.75; Calif. Fair Debt Collection Practices Act. c.907 § 1788.2 (c).

34. N.Y. Gen. Bus., c. 20 art. 29-H § 600.

35. Fed. Civ. Proc. Rule 64.

36. Sniadach v. Family Finance Corp., 395 U.S. 337 (1969); Fuentes v. Shevin, 407 U.S. 67 (1972); Mitchell v. W. T. Grant Co., 416 U.S. 600 (1974); and North Georgia Finishing, Inc. v. Di-Chem, Inc., 419 U.S. 601 (1975).

37. Epstein, *Debtor-Creditor Law* (1985), p. 16.

38. 16 C.F.R. § 444.2 (a) (2).

39. 16 C.F.R. § 444.2 (a) (1).

40. 15 U.S.C. §§ 1671–1677.

41. U.C.C. § 9–502.

42. U.C.C. §§ 9–501–9–507.

43. *See* U.C.C. §§ 9–501 (1), (2) and 9–207.

44. U.C.C. § 9–109.

45. U.C.C. § 9–501 (1).

46. 407 U.S. 67 (1972).

47. 419 U.S. 601 (1975).

48. *See* Epstein, *Debtor-Creditor Law* (1985), pp. 36–40.

49. Swygert, *Consumer Protection*, 23 De Paul L. Rev. 98, 104, n.24 (1973).

50. *Id.* at 106–07.

51. U.C.C. § 9–503.

52. *Id.*

53. U.C.C. § 9–504.

54. U.C.C. § 9–504 (3).

55. U.C.C. § 9–506.

56. U.C.C. § 9–504 (Official Comment no. 5).

57. U.C.C. § 9–504 (2).

58. *Id.*

59. U.C.C. § 9–507 (2).

60. U.C.C. § 9–507 (1).

61. *Id.*

62. Local Loan Co. v. Hunt, 292 U.S. 234, 244 (1934).

63. Pub. L. No. 95–598, 92 Stat. 2549 (the "Bankruptcy Reform Act of 1978"), 11 U.S.C. §§ 101, *et seq.*

64. Pub. L. No. 98–353, 98 Stat. 333 (the "Bankruptcy Amendments and Federal Judgeship Act of 1984").

65. 11 U.S.C. § 362.

66. *See in re* Elder, 12 B.R. 491 (Bankr. M.D. Ga. 1981).

67. 11 U.S.C. § 361.

68. *See generally*, Melanie Rouner Cohen and Faye B. Feinstein, *The Bankruptcy Reform Act of 1978 as Amended by the Bankruptcy Amendments and Federal Judgeship Act of 1984*, in *Bankruptcy Practice* (I.I.C.L.E.) 1–1, 1–23 (1985). *See also, in re* Alyucan Interstate Corp., 12 B.R. 803 (Bankr. Utah 1981) and *in re* American Mariner Industries, Inc., 734 F.2d 426 (9th Cir. 1984).

69. 11 U.S.C. § 361.
70. 11 U.S.C. § 507 (b).
71. 11 U.S.C. § 1322 (b) (5).
72. 11 U.S.C. § 362 (e).
73. 11 U.S.C. § 1301. *See also*, 11 U.S.C. § 105.
74. *See*, 11 U.S.C. §§ 721, 1108, and 1304.
75. 11 U.S.C. § 363 (c) (1).
76. 11 U.S.C. § 363 (a).
77. 11 U.S.C. § 363 (c) (2).
78. 11 U.S.C. §§ 507 (a) (1) and 503 (b).
79. 11 U.S.C. § 507 (a).
80. 11 U.S.C. § 507 (a) (3).
81. 11 U.S.C. § 507 (a) (4).
82. 11 U.S.C. § 507 (a) (5).
83. 11 U.S.C. § 507 (a) (6).
84. 11 U.S.C. § 726.
85. 11 U.S.C. § 543. *See also*, 11 U.S.C. § 542.
86. 11 U.S.C. §§ 501 (a) and 111 (a).
87. 11 U.S.C. § 1129 (b).
88. *See*, 11 U.S.C. § 544 (a) and U.C.C. §§ 9–301 (1) (b) and (3).
89. *See*, U.C.C. § 9–301 (2).
90. 11 U.S.C. § 547.
91. 11 U.S.C. § 547 (c) (5).
92. 11 U.S.C. §§ 548 (a) (1) and (2).
93. 11 U.S.C. § 548 (b).
94. 11 U.S.C. § 544 (b).
95. U.S. v. Generes, 405 U.S. 93, 103 (1972).

14

Obtaining Relief from Creditors

When a business is not able to pay its bills (even though the firm may be solvent), relief from creditors may become necessary. This chapter considers the various alternatives that a firm may take in seeking relief from creditors. We start with a discussion of private agreements called "workouts" between business-debtors and lending institutions. Next we consider various state-sanctioned remedies designed to relieve debtors, including extensions, compositions, and assignments for the benefit of creditors. The majority of this chapter, however, deals with remedies available under the federal bankruptcy laws. The alternatives include the drastic but at times necessary liquidation of a firm's assets as well as the more common (and usually more sensible) restructuring of its debts through a reorganization plan.

WORKOUT PLANS

Indications of a firm's financial trouble include shrinking profits, anxious auditors, and threats of cutting off credit. Before a financial crisis develops to the point of a complete loss of credit, however, a firm should explore with an existing or potential lender a possible workout arrangement. An existing lender is a more likely candidate for a workout because of the stake it has in the success or failure of the plan. The object of a workout is for a bank or other lending institution to fund the rehabilitation of a business to enable the firm to generate sufficient revenues to pay off its creditors with interest over a relatively short time period.

At the first sign of a business customer's financial difficulty, an existing lender typically will make an internal audit of the customer's credit to determine if the account is slow or delinquent. The lender may also analyze the loan's legal documentation including any promissory notes, security agreements, guarantees, and so on. The lender may want to review every aspect of the customer's business and may invite a business consultant to analyze the firm's strengths and weaknesses with a particular focus on its operating costs. As a part of the analysis, the lender or consultant will seek to ascertain current labor, material, and overhead expenses for each unit or division of the ailing firm. A study of the firm's cash flow is especially crucial.

As a result of the financial and legal analyses, the potential workout lender reaches the decision of whether its customer is worth saving. If the decision is yes, the lender will offer a workout plan. The plan may require that a firm with a cash flow problem trim down to survival size through closing unprofitable divisions or offices, reducing staff, cutting overhead, discarding unprofitable product lines, or leasing cheaper facilities.

In larger workout arrangements, it is typical for the business and lender to each draft its own workout plan and to meet together to negotiate a joint workout agreement. Consultants proficient in crisis management may be especially valuable to a firm in preparing a financial workout proposal. Any plan that is adopted should deal with the management of loan losses due to delinquencies and the adequacy of reserves for future losses. To be enforceable under the doctrine of *Foakes v. Beer*,[1] a debtor's obligations to repay loans earlier made by the lender and subject to the debtor's pre-existing duty to repay should be either extended or otherwise modified to minimize possible objections of a lack of consideration.

A workout plan approved by the lender and its business customer should be reduced to writing and be signed by both parties. The principles of the common law of contracts govern workout agreements (see Chapter 8). Nonetheless, included language such as value, valuation, collateral-to-loan ratio, interest, subordination, reserves, and the like should be precisely defined in the written workout agreement.

EXTENSIONS AND COMPOSITIONS

An *extension* is a state-law-sanctioned remedy designed to afford a debtor relief from two or more creditors. An extension *agreement* is a legal contract between a debtor and two or more creditors, which extends the time period for the debtor to pay off balances owed the creditors. Normally, extension agreements are enforceable and are not considered preferences in bankruptcy (see subsequent discussion).

Composition Agreements

A *composition of creditors* is an agreement between a debtor and two or more creditors, which authorizes the debtor to pay a partial payment to each of the creditors in full satisfaction of their claims. An agreement may combine both composition and extension aspects meaning that a debtor will be obligated to pay less than originally owed over a longer period of time. A composition and extension agreement privately entered into and recognized as a valid contract under state law is similar to a federal bankruptcy Chapter Eleven or Thirteen debt adjustment plan except that the common law composition and extension may be less costly to creditors. From a debtor's perspective, however, a common law debt adjustment plan may not necessarily contain the same discharge safeguards that a Chapter Eleven confirmed reorganization plan typically affords under the bankruptcy laws.

Composition Terms

Composition agreements may contain clauses whereby the creditors agree to waive their rights to receive future interest on their respective claims. In addition, the creditors usually agree to take a stated percentage of the total amounts owed in full satisfaction. A composition agreement should indicate the partial portion of the original principal indebtedness which the debtor has agreed to repay and whether repayment is to be in one lump sum or in installments. Moreover, the agreement should state that the debtor's performance of its obligations under the composition will be in full satisfaction of its original obligations to each of the participating creditors. Creditors typically demand that a "reinstatement" clause be included providing that if the debtor defaults or breaches any of its obligations under the composition, the original indebtedness becomes due and owing.

Since a composition typically involves installment obligations to pay a stated percentage of the original indebtedness, a resulting agreement is often referred to in an installment, percentage form. Thus, a 24-installment, 60-percent agreement means that the obligor must pay 60 percent of the original indebtedness in 24 equal installments. Certain composition agreements, however, contain a large final or balloon payment. Debtors are advised to avoid, if possible, balloon payments in compositions.

Effect on Other Creditors

State law does not require that all the debtor's creditors participate in a proposed composition. Indeed, two or more creditors and the debtor may agree on a composition over the express opposition of one or more other creditors. To go forward with the arrangement under these conditions is risky, however. First, any collection action brought by a nonagreeing creditor may prevent completion of the composition agreement by depleting the debtor's funds below a level necessary to meet its composition obligations. Second, a composition may force nonagreeing creditors to file an involuntary bankruptcy petition claiming that the composition constitutes a preference. The filing of the bankruptcy petition results in an automatic stay, meaning that the composition becomes immediately unenforceable.[2] Consequently, all creditors having significant claims against a debtor should be encouraged to participate in any proposed composition.

Common Law Preferences

When one creditor is given favored treatment over other creditors by way of a secret consideration, the other creditors under the common law may avoid the agreement as a preference. For example, if two creditors of a debtor enter into an agreement whereby the debtor agrees (usually under duress) to pay the two creditors' claims off entirely before paying the claims of its other creditors, the arrangement may be a preference and as such would be voidable by the other creditors. The agreement, moreover, is nonenforceable by the agreeing creditors and is subject to the debtor's remedy of restitution for the return of any payments already made.

Advantages of Composition over Bankruptcy

A composition agreement, when legally effective, works to discharge totally the debtor and its sureties or guarantors from their original obligations in contrast to bankruptcy which, in Chapters Seven and Eleven, only works to discharge the debtor, not its sureties.[3] Debts discharged in bankruptcy may be revived by reaffirmation after discharge,[4] while the only way to revive a debt discharged in a composition is through the debtor's giving new consideration. Compositions, moreover, do not bar bankruptcy as an available debtor remedy following the composition, whereas a discharge under BRA Chapter Seven bars any subsequent bankruptcy discharge relief for six years.[5] The chief disadvantage of a composition, however, is that, since it is voluntary in nature, not all the creditors of a debtor have to take part. As noted earlier, the nonparticipation of all a debtor's creditors could cause the composition agreement to fail in achieving its purpose.

ASSIGNMENTS FOR THE BENEFIT OF CREDITORS

An assignment for the benefit of creditors occurs when a debtor voluntarily transfers assets to another person in trust to liquidate the assets and distribute the proceeds to the debtor's creditors. As the state law counterpart to a federal BRA Chapter Seven liquidation proceeding, an assignment conveys legal title in the assets transferred to the trustee. This prevents the creditors of the debtor-transferor from attaching or executing on the property transferred (see Chapter 13). The title, however, is subject to the claims, encumbrances, and liens of the transferor's creditors.

Priority Rights of the Assignee

Under UCC Article Nine, an assignee of property for the benefit of creditors is considered under state law a "lien creditor"[6] and, as such, has priority rights over both general creditors and unperfected security interests.[7] Consequently, except for property subject to an earlier perfected Article Nine security interest (see Chapter 6 for a discussion of security interests), an assignee trustee ordinarily has a priority interest in all the debtor's transferred property as against most other creditors. Upon disposal of the assets, the trustee makes a pro rata (proportional) distribution of proceeds to the transferor's unsecured creditors.

Fiduciary Duties of Trustee

Assignments for the benefit of creditors in most states are considered trust relationships and are subject to the laws applicable to trusts. The law of trusts places special duties on a trustee who is deemed to be a *fiduciary*, one who stands in a special position of trust (usually of a pecuniary nature) in reference to another. A fiduciary trustee is accountable to the debtor's creditors and may be removed or held personally liable for breach of its fiduciary duties of honesty, candor, commercial reasonableness, reasonable professional judgment, and good faith.

Assignments and Fraudulent Conveyances

Assignments for the benefit of creditors may be attacked as fraudulent conveyances when the transfer is to hinder or delay collection by the debtor's creditors. Courts will uphold an assignment provided no ownership rights or uses have been reserved by the debtor-transferor. Thus, the debtor must give up all property rights in and contract rights to the transferred property. In some states, an assignment of anything less than the debtor's entire, nonexempt property is deemed a fraudulent conveyance. Other states require that the debtor be insolvent (current obligations exceed current market value of all assets) at the time of the assignment, holding that a solvent debtor's transfer may be interpreted only as one to delay or hinder collection efforts.

State statutes also usually require that the assignment be recorded, a schedule of the debtor's property be filed, notice of the assignment be given the debtor's creditors, and the trustee be bonded. Finally, a trustee under an assignment for the benefit of creditors may not grant a preference to any creditor.

Advantages in Comparison with Bankruptcy

Assignments for the benefit of creditors are normally less costly and more expeditious than federal bankruptcy liquidations. They are less costly because assignments generally produce better liquidation prices than do Chapter Seven liquidations, and the administrative costs of assignments tend to be lower.[8] On the other hand, if a debtor has given creditors preferential treatment, has allowed liens to attach to its property (which might constitute voidable preferences in bankruptcy), or has made fraudulent conveyances of any of its assets, an assignment for the benefit of creditors may not adequately protect the debtor's creditors.[9] Under any of these circumstances, the creditors would probably be better off to force the debtor involuntarily into a federal bankruptcy proceeding. In the majority of bankruptcies, however, the debtor initiates the proceeding.

DEBTOR'S RELIEF THROUGH BANKRUPTCY

Bankruptcy is the culmination of an individual's or a business' financial deterioration over time. In the case of a business, the downturn is seldom sudden. Rather, the effects of unwise expansion, tort liability, poor management, overextending credit, ruinous competition, and imprudent contracts eventually take their toll. When debt extensions are no longer given or when credit lines are cut off and the possibility of a workout is past, bankruptcy may be the debtor's only reasonable alternative.

Bankruptcy, particularly Chapter Eleven reorganizations or "rehabilitations,"[10] offers business debtors, which are no longer able to pay debts as they mature, an opportunity to freeze the collection of those obligations while working out a plan of reorganization with their lenders, suppliers, employees, and equity holders. This section explores the various alternatives available to debtors under the bankruptcy laws. We begin with a discussion of the basic provisions and structure of the 1978 Bankruptcy Reform Act, commonly referred to as the "Bankruptcy Code."

The Bankruptcy Reform Act of 1978 and the 1984 Bankruptcy Amendments

The statutory successor to the Bankruptcy Act of 1898,[11] the Bankruptcy Reform Act of 1978[12] is the first major bankruptcy law enactment since the Chandler Act of 1928.[13] The BRA incorporates major reforms in both liquidation and reorganization proceedings. Clearly, the BRA's changes reflect, as one commentator has put it, a "swing of the pendulum from the spirit of creditor protection to the spirit of debtor protection in the legal age of the consumer."[14] The BRA may have swung too far in the debtor's direction, however, as Congress tightened the eligibility requirements in the 1984 bankruptcy amendments signed into law on July 10, 1984, by President Reagan.[15]

Under Title I of the 1984 amendments, federal bankruptcy courts are established as units within the federal district courts (see a discussion of the court system in Chapter 2). Also as a result of the 1984 amendments, the federal district courts have original and exclusive jurisdiction of all bankruptcy cases arising under Title II of the United States Code, including both liquidation and debt adjustment or rehabilitation matters.[16]

Bankruptcy Judges and Core Proceedings

Bankruptcy judges are authorized to hear and enter judgments in "core proceedings." Core proceedings are defined by examples to include the following:

1. Allowing or disallowing claims
2. Determining claims of exempt status in reference to the debtor's property
3. Conducting hearings to determine whether orders should be issued directing that property be turned over to the debtor's estate
4. Deciding issues of trustee and equitable subordinations
5. Hearing counterclaims
6. Deciding motions to lift, modify, or annul the automatic stay
7. Ruling on objections to discharge
8. Determining the validity of secured claims and other liens
9. Determining priorities among claimants (see Chapter 13)
10. Determining the dischargeability of debts
11. Confirming submitted reorganization or rehabilitation plans
12. Adjudicating voidable preferences and fraudulent conveyances (see Chapter 13)
13. Approving or disapproving the use, disposal, or lease of property within the debtor's estate
14. Overseeing liquidation proceedings.[17]

Under the 1984 amendments, bankruptcy judges are judicial officers of the district court under Article III of the federal Constitution[18] and are appointed for fourteen-year terms.[19]

Structure of the Bankruptcy Reform Act

Title II of the United States Code is divided into eight odd-numbered chapters. Chapter One includes a list of definitions[20] along with a list of who is eligible to be a debtor under the various reorganization and liquidation chapters.[21] Chapter Three's provisions cover the mechanics of filing petitions,[22] the appointment of trustees,[23] and the rules for the meetings of creditors (discussed below).[24] Chapter Five sets out the rights and duties of the creditors, the debtor, and the trustee.[25] Chapter Seven deals with liquidation, which was formerly called "straight" or "ordinary" bankruptcy.[26] Chapter Nine deals with insolvencies of state and local governmental units.[27] Chapter Eleven, which deals with reorganizations, is often the most suitable remedy for a business in serious financial difficulty.[28] Chapter Thirteen also involves reorganizations but is available only to individuals and sole proprietors having regular income. Like Chapter Eleven, Chapter Thirteen involves debt adjustment or rehabilitation plans.[29] Finally, Chapter Fifteen governs the duties of a new federal official, the United States Trustee, who handles many of the administrative matters in a bankruptcy proceeding. The U.S. trustee program has been tried out on an experimental basis in eighteen judicial districts within the United States.[30]

Interim and Permanent Trustees

In most bankruptcy proceedings, an active trustee is appointed as a representative of the debtor's estate.[31] The debtor's estate, also called the bankruptcy estate, is considered a separate and distinct legal entity. In liquidation proceedings, a trustee is obligated, among other duties, to collect the debtor's property (the "property of the estate"); challenge all transfers of property from the estate and claims made against the estate considered to be improper; and liquidate (oversee the sale or disposition of) the estate property.

The trustee may be appointed or elected on either an interim or permanent basis. An initial or "interim" trustee generally is a private citizen chosen from a panel established and maintained by the Administrative Office of the United States Courts.[32] In a Chapter Seven proceeding, the interim trustee is often replaced by a trustee elected at the first meeting of the creditors provided that the creditors holding at least 20 percent of the value of all unsecured claims vote in the election.[33]

Although trustees serve in Chapter Thirteen reorganization proceedings, they are not elected. Only the bankruptcy judge may appoint the trustee from a group of "standing" Chapter Thirteen trustees from within the district. A Chapter Thirteen trustee oversees the individual debtor's performance under the approved ("confirmed") rehabilitation plan.[34] Trustees are rare in Chapter Eleven reorganizations and are normally appointed only upon either a showing of good cause or on the basis that the appointment is in the interests of creditors. Since a Chapter Eleven proceeding typically involves a business that continues to operate following the petition's filing, a trustee is not needed if the debtor continues to operate its business. Such a debtor is referred to in the BRA as a debtor in possession.

LIQUIDATION VERSUS REORGANIZATION

Liquidations: Chapter Seven

Chapter Seven (liquidation) affords relief especially to an individual debtor as it allows the individual to have a fresh economic beginning, free from most of its previous debts. For a business, however, liquidation has little advantage except as a means of going out of business in an orderly way.[35] Non-individuals, including all business entities other than sole proprietorships, receive neither exemptions nor discharges in federal liquidation proceedings.[36] Thus, the only reason for a business to file a voluntary Chapter Seven petition is to provide for an orderly sale and distribution of its proceeds to its creditors. A business may, however, liquidate under a Chapter Eleven plan if the plan is approved and confirmed by the bankruptcy court (discussed subsequently).

Business Reorganizations: Chapter Eleven

Although not strictly limited to business debtors, Chapter Eleven is "clearly intended to facilitate business reorganizations."[37] In most business reorganization proceedings, the debtor remains in possession and control of the business and its assets during the course of the reorganization. Trustees, as noted earlier, are rarely appointed. By freezing the creditor's efforts to collect debts, a debtor along with its creditors, may work out a plan of reorganization including the necessary funding that affords the debtor "a chance to reestablish himself again."[38]

The remainder of this chapter deals with both the mechanics and substantive law of a Chapter Eleven reorganization proceeding, although BRA Chapter Thirteen debt adjustment plans are also briefly discussed. (The problems that creditors face because of a debtor's bankruptcy are discussed in Chapter 13 of this volume.)

BUSINESS REORGANIZATIONS: CHAPTER ELEVEN

Commencement of a Chapter Eleven Proceeding

A reorganization proceeding is commenced by the debtor or its creditors filing a petition with the federal bankruptcy court.[39] A petition that commences a bankruptcy action is not a complaint (the pleading which is used to commence most civil actions) but rather is a request for relief under the bankruptcy laws. Petitions may be voluntary or involuntary. A voluntary petition is one filed by the debtor; an involuntary petition is filed against a debtor by its creditors. The filing of either a voluntary or involuntary petition stays other creditor actions and creates a bankruptcy estate.[40] Any partnership, corporation, not-for-profit association, sole proprietorship, or individual may file for relief under Chapter Eleven.[41] Sole proprietorships, however, having regular income are also eligible to file for reorganization under BRA Chapter Thirteen.[42]

Voluntary Petitions

A voluntary petition must conform with Official Form One.[43] In the case of a debtor corporation, an additional Exhibit A must be completed and attached to the petition for the benefit of the Securities and Exchange Commission. Form One along with Exhibit A (if required) must be filed in the district where the debtor was domiciled, resided, or had either its principal office or its principal assets for more of the 180 days before the filing of the petition than in any other district.[44] Filing must be at the office of the clerk of the bankruptcy court (if one), otherwise in the office of the clerk of the district court. In a Chapter Eleven case, the petition plus five copies must be filed,[45] along with a statement of current income and expenditures,[46] plus lists of creditors and shareholders,[47] and appropriate schedules of assets and liabilities.[48] Also a $200 filing fee for a Chapter Eleven must be submitted with the petition.

Assistance of legal counsel is recommended when initiating a Chapter Eleven proceeding. The forms, schedules, lists, and statements must be expertly assembled and properly submitted along with the petition.

A voluntary petition automatically acts as the *order for relief* (formerly known as an "adjudication in bankruptcy"). The most immediate aspect of the order is the automatic stay, which insures that the debtor will be free from creditor collection efforts and debt collection harassment throughout the bankruptcy proceeding.

Involuntary Petitions

Creditors usually are better off if they proceed outside of bankruptcy. Thus, involuntary bankruptcy is threatened more than it is used. Still, if a debtor is making fraudulent conveyances, has incompetent or dishonest management, or is paying certain creditors but not all, involuntary bankruptcy may occur. Involuntary petitions, when they do occur, are usually filed against corporate or partnership debtors.

In the case of a partnership, an involuntary petition must be filed when some, but not all, of the general partners want the partnership in a bankruptcy proceeding.[49] On the other hand, objections of limited partners do not prevent general partners from filing a voluntary petition if all the general partners agree to the filing.

An involuntary petition filed by creditors must allege one of two possible grounds for obtaining relief: either a general failure by the debtor to meet its current obligations or the appointment of a custodian to take possession of the debtor's property within 120 days of the petition.[50] A failure to pay debts as they become due means that the debtor is insolvent in the equity sense, not necessarily in a balance sheet assessment. Thus, the key is the debtor's liquidity. The fact that the debtor's assets may be greater than its liabilities makes no difference so long as the debtor is not generally meeting its current obligations. "Generally" refers to a pattern of defaults, not to isolated instances of delinquent payments.

If a debtor at the time of an involuntary petition has twelve or more creditors, three or more must join in the petition. If the creditors number eleven or fewer, then only one creditor need file.[51] Employee creditors, insiders, and creditors with preferences are not counted in this tabulation. In either event, the claims of the petitioning creditor or creditors must total at least $5,000 in noncontingent, undisputed, and unsecured claims against the debtor.[52]

An involuntary petition must conform to Official Form 11 (partners must use Form 12) and be filed along with five additional copies. Upon filing, a summons is issued for service on the debtor. Service may be effected by mail or by personal delivery anywhere within the United States.

Debtor's Response to Involuntary Petition

A debtor has twenty days after receipt of service to respond unless he or she is residing out of the state of issuance, in which case a longer response time is permitted.[53] A debtor may respond to the merits of the involuntary petition, for example, by denying the petition's claim that it is not generally making payments on maturing obligations. A contested involuntary petition is to be resolved as quickly as possible. Although a debtor does not have a right to a jury trial, it may request a jury trial. While the decision on the request is within the discretion of the bankruptcy judge, an actual jury trial would likely be conducted by a federal district judge. Whether a petition is contested or not, a bankruptcy judge may dismiss a voluntary or involuntary petition if the judge believes that the dismissal would serve the interests of the debtor and its creditors.[54]

Automatic Stay

The filing of a voluntary or involuntary petition automatically results in a stay of all creditor actions.[55] (The scope of the automatic stay as well as the grounds for its being lifted are discussed in Chapter 13.)

Notification of Creditors

Creditors of a business debtor ordinarily will learn of a Chapter Eleven filing because the BRA requires that each creditor listed on the debtor's filed list of creditors[56] be sent appropriate notice of the order for relief.[57] Significantly, a creditor ordinarily does not need to file an individual proof of claim in a Chapter Eleven proceeding if the claim is listed on the debtor's filed schedule and is uncontested, liquidated, and noncontingent.[58] It is safe to do so, however.

Committee of Creditors

Under the BRA, a committee of unsecured creditors normally is appointed as soon as practicable by either the bankruptcy court or, when appropriate, by a United States Trustee.[59] In certain instances, a prepetition committee may have already been formed which the court may allow to continue in operation if the committee is deemed to have been fairly chosen and to be "representative of the outstanding creditors."[60] Otherwise, the court appoints the seven most owed unsecured creditors who are willing to serve as the committee members.[61]

The creditors' committee investigates the debtor's financial condition and business operation, consults with the debtor in possession about the management of the firm, participates in the formulation of the reorganization plan, and performs other services that may further the interests of creditors represented by the committee.[62] The committee may also request that the bankruptcy court appoint a trustee to run the business rather than the debtor in possession. The creditors' committee is authorized to hire attorneys, accountants, or other agents.[63] Responsibility for other creditors rests with the committee as it acts in a fiduciary capacity in behalf of all the unsecured creditors of the debtor.[64]

Meeting of Creditors

A meeting of creditors is required in all Chapter Eleven proceedings at which the debtor may be examined under oath about its assets, liabilities, current financial conditions, and related matters.[65] The bankruptcy judge is not permitted to preside over or attend any of the meetings in which the debtor is examined by its creditors.[66] The officers of the debtor's business organization, including its board of directors, attorneys, accountants, and consultants, if any, are expected to meet with the creditors or with the creditors' committee to discuss the business operations of the debtor.

Running the Business

During a Chapter Eleven proceeding, a debtor in possession has all the rights of a trustee including the powers to avoid preferences. Unless the bankruptcy court orders otherwise, the debtor in possession may operate its business as it sees fit.[67]

Credit extended to a postpetition debtor business in a Chapter Eleven case is given a special priority status as it qualifies as an administrative expense priority to be paid before any prepetition creditors are paid.[68] If a debtor in possession is unable to obtain credit needed to run its business during a reorganization, a bankruptcy court has the power to authorize the debtor to grant prospective postpetition creditors a superpriority, one which is at least equal to or superior to all existing lienors (although prepetition *secured* parties must be afforded "adequate protection" if a superpriority is created).[69]

Purpose of Reorganization

The primary purpose of Chapter Eleven is to permit a business to be rehabilitated. By restructuring its finances, a firm may be able to continue its operations, provide its employees with jobs, pay its creditors, and produce a return for its owners. Moreover, a business's assets, when used for the purposes for which they were designed, are more valuable than when sold in liquidation. Often a business may be returned to a healthy state, provided the firm is allowed to reduce or extend its debts to both trade creditors and long-term lenders. As such, it usually is more efficient to reorganize than to liquidate.

The purpose of the reorganization is to formulate and have confirmed a debt adjustment plan of rehabilitation. The plan determines the amounts creditors will be paid and in what form (cash, property, or securities, for example); what interest, if any, the equity holders will continue to have in the company; and what form the business will take following the reorganization. Reorganization plans are quite versatile. They may even incorporate a partial or total liquidation of a firm's assets.[70] The liquidation may be designed to trim down the firm, to raise cash, or to enable the firm to go out of business over time in an orderly fashion.

Throughout the reorganization, the debtor is relieved from paying its prepetition debts on the premise that the additional cash flow freed up will be used to meet current operating expenses. The most significant aspects of a Chapter Eleven reorganization are the preparation of a plan of rehabilitation, the disclosure of the plan to creditors and stockholders, and the court's hearing and confirmation of the plan—matters which are next discussed.

Step One: Preparation of the Rehabilitation Plan

Although any party of interest (including any creditor) may file a proposal in a Chapter Eleven proceeding, the debtor is given the exclusive right to propose a plan of rehabilitation for the first 120 days of the proceeding if no trustee is appointed.[71] If the debtor does not file a plan or if its filed plan is not confirmed within 180 days, any party of interest may then file its own proposed plan. These time limits may be extended or reduced by order of the bankruptcy court.[72]

Contents

A Chapter Eleven rehabilitation plan must contain several provisions as specified in BRA section 1123(a). First, the plan must designate and classify all claims or interests asserted against the debtor's property.[73] Classification of claims is necessary since, before a plan is confirmed (made legally binding), certain classes of claims or interests must ordinarily accept it.[74] Acceptance of a class occurs when the proposed plan is accepted by a majority of the number of creditors in the class voting on the plan, provided those creditors hold at least two-thirds in dollar amount of the total claims in the class which voted.[75]

All small claims regardless of their nature may be segregated into a single class "if reasonable and necessary for administrative convenience."[76] It may be advantageous for a debtor in possession to segregate and pay all grouped small claims in full since a class of claims that receives full payment on the effective date of the plan is not "impaired" and, as such, is deemed to have accepted the plan thereby negating the BRA's requirement of a solicitation of acceptance of the class (discussed below). Importantly, all claims within a designated class must be "substantially similar."[77] Thus, secured claims may not be put in the same class as unsecured claims. On the other hand, claims or interests which are substantially similar do not have to be placed in the same class. Thus, unsecured creditors' claims could be placed in several classes depending, for example, on their amount. Although certain BRA defined "priority" claims may not be placed in classes (prepetition tax claims, for example[78]), other priority claims must be placed in separate classes according to the BRA's priority classification.[79] An attorney should always be hired by a debtor in possession or by an appointed trustee to prepare the claims and interests classifications since the BRA's complex rules dealing with impaired and nonimpaired classes (and other matters) require the assistance of a specialist.

Funding of the Plan

Debtors typically need to borrow additional funds to make payments to creditors in executing a rehabilitation plan. To obtain the necessary funding of the plan, business assets may have to be sold (authorized by the BRA)[80] or creditors paid by distributing the debtor's equity (stocks) or debt securities (bonds). A distribution of securities in a Chapter Eleven case normally is not subject to registration requirements under state or federal securities laws.[81]

To save money, a debtor under certain circumstances may be permitted to reject or modify a collective bargaining agreement. Although an early 1984 U.S. Supreme Court decision held that a collective bargaining agreement could be rejected under Chapter Eleven when "the agreement burdens the estate,"[82] this holding has been restricted by the subsequent 1984 bankruptcy amendments that limit a debtor's right of rejection of a collective bargaining agreement to those where the affected employees approve the proposed rejection or modification.[83]

Step Two: Disclosure of the Plan

Following preparation of a plan of rehabilitation, the plan proponent must prepare and submit a disclosure statement which offers to those whose claims or interests are impaired by the plan "sufficient information" about the debtor, the debtor's history, the prospects for the business, the plan proponent, and the plan itself to enable the parties of interest to cast an intelligent vote for or against the plan.[84] The premise of the disclosure requirement is that, if adequate disclosure is provided to all creditors and equity holders whose rights are to be impaired, then they should be able to make an informed judgment. Consequently, a bankruptcy court does not review a Chapter Eleven plan prior to its submission to creditors, but rather examines the information furnished to the parties of interest to determine whether their judgment will be an informed judgment.[85]

The disclosure statement must be submitted before the solicitation of acceptances. All creditors and shareholders are to be provided with a copy or summary of the plan along with a "written disclosure statement approved, after notice and a hearing, by the court as containing adequate information."[86] What constitutes adequate information depends on various factors including the relative sophistication of the creditors and shareholders, the complexity of the plan, the condition of the debtor's business, and the reliability of its financial records.[87]

Step Three: Solicitation of Acceptances

The third major step in a Chapter Eleven proceeding is the submission of the plan for approval to the impaired creditors and shareholders. The plan must be submitted to all impaired classes for a vote. Two classes of creditors, however, need not be solicited. First, if a class is to be fully paid, the class is not impaired, and it is deemed by the BRA to have accepted the plan.[88] Second, if a class is to receive nothing under a plan, the class is deemed to have rejected the plan.[89] All other creditors or shareholders having claims or interests, which will in any way be adjusted, must be solicited as impaired claims.

Impairment

Under the the provisions of the BRA,[90] a class of claims or interests is impaired unless:

1. The legal, equitable, and contractual rights of the holder are left (for better or worse) unaltered; or

2. The only alteration of rights is a reversal of a default-acceleration provision by curing the default and reinstating the installment obligation; or

3. Cash payment to a creditor on the plan's effective date equals the legally allowed amount of the claim; or

4. Cash payment to a shareholder on the plan's effective date is equal to the greater of the share's redemption price or any fixed liquidation preference.[91]

The proponent of a reorganization plan may propose to impair any class of claims, both secured and unsecured, as well as the interests of equity security holders.[92] A plan may also contain provisions rejecting executory (still to be performed) contracts previously entered into by the debtor.[93] Moreover, the debtor in possession or the trustee may assume or reject prepetition executory contracts any time before a plan's confirmation.[94]

Step Four: Approval or Rejection of the Plan

A class of creditors accepts a plan if the plan is approved by creditors that hold at least two-thirds of the dollar amount and more than one-half the allowed claims of the class that actually voted.[95] Similarly, if the plan is approved by two-thirds in amount of equity securities held by a class of shareholders voting on the plan, that class of shareholders accepts the plan.[96] If the plan is accepted by a class of impaired creditors or shareholders, the bankruptcy court may then hold a hearing to consider confirming the plan.

Step Five: Confirmation of the Plan

Confirmation is the legal event in a bankruptcy reorganization that legally binds the debtor, its creditors, and its equity security holders to the terms and conditions of the plan.[97] All parties having interests in the proceeding must be given notice of the confirmation hearing.[98] If more than one plan has been submitted, the bankruptcy court must consider the preferences of the debtor's creditors and equity security holders in determining which plan to confirm.[99]

Requirements for Confirmation

If a plan has been accepted by every class of claims and every class of interests, ordinarily it must be confirmed by the bankruptcy court provided all the following listed requirements of BRA section 1129(a) are met:

1. The plan must comply with Chapter Eleven's requirements.

2. The proponent of the plan must have complied with the Chapter Eleven provisions.

3. The plan must be proposed in good faith.

4. All payments made or promised in connection with the plan must be disclosed to the court.

5. The proponent must disclose certain persons who will be involved in the reorganization.

6. Public regulatory agencies having jurisdiction over any rates the debtor may charge must have approved the plan's rates, or the scheduled rates must be conditioned upon such approval forthcoming.

7. Each holder of a claim or interest has either accepted the plan or will receive on the plan's effective date property having a value that is not less than the amount the holder would have received if the debtor were liquidated in Chapter Seven proceeding.

8. Each class has accepted the plan, is not impaired under it, or has not been discriminated against unfairly and has been treated equitably.

9. Certain priority creditors have been treated in accordance with the BRA's requirements (these include employees, administrative expense claimants, and governmental tax claimants).

10. At least one class of claims has accepted the plan.

11. Confirmation is not likely to be followed in the near term for a need of further financial reorganization of the debtor or of any successor-in-interest.

Plans Accepted by Less than Every Class: "Cram Downs"

If not all classes accept the plan, the plan may be confirmed only if the plan "does not discriminate unfairly" and is found to be in the "best interests of the creditors."[100] Known as the "cram down" method of confirmation, the BRA provision allows a plan to be confirmed over the objections of an impaired class or classes (including those of secured creditors). Although the requirements for a cram down are highly technical,[101] the BRA's basic standard of fairness provides that a secured party realizes under the plan the "indubitable equivalent" of its claim.[102] A cash payment of the present value of collateral may not be the indubitable equivalent because the secured creditor may be denied the potential appreciation value of the collateral.[103] Also, a plan that does not offer dissenters full compensation may be crammed down if classes beneath that of the dissenters' class are denied any participation in the debtor's assets. In short, the standards used in making a cram down determination involve complex financial analysis.[104] Experienced bankruptcy counsel should be consulted in drafting and seeing through a proposed cram-down reorganization.

Debtor's Discharge

One of the legal effects of a plan's confirmation is the discharge of the debtor's prepetition obligations unless the plan is one of liquidation, which terminates the debtor's business.[105] Although corporations and partnerships are not eligible to have their debts discharged in a Chapter Seven liquidation, they are eligible for such relief when a nonliquidating reorganization plan is confirmed in a Chapter Eleven proceeding.

CHAPTER THIRTEEN REHABILITATIONS

Chapter Thirteen of the BRA offers individual debtors (but not corporations or partnerships) an alternative to a Chapter Seven liquidation. Sole proprietorships and self-employed debtors are eligible, however, for Chapter Thirteen treatment.[106]

Because of the 1984 "consumer amendments" to the BRA, a Chapter Thirteen proceeding is required to be considered by a consumer debtor in any bankruptcy action.[107] Chapter Thirteen is limited to small debtors who owe less than $100,000 in fixed unsecured debt or less than $350,000 in fixed secured debt. Also, the debtor must have sufficient regular income from any source to support a Chapter Thirteen rehabilitation.[108]

A Chapter Thirteen proceeding is strictly voluntary. The filing of the petition causes the automatic stay to go into effect, which in this BRA chapter, extends to stay efforts to collect from the debtor's guarantors and cosignors.[109] Although a trustee is always appointed in a Chapter Thirteen proceeding, the debtor remains in possession of its property and, if a business, will usually continue to operate it.[110]

Only the debtor may propose a plan of rehabilitation under Chapter Thirteen. Although priority administrative expenses and unsecured claims of employees must be paid in full, the claims of other unsecured creditors may be paid only partially.[111] The plan may be funded in part from the debtor's future earnings and in part from sale of its assets.

Like a Chapter Eleven plan, a Chapter Thirteen reorganization must be confirmed by the bankruptcy court.[112] The court may force the plan on an unwilling, secured creditor (other than the mortgagee of the debtor's principal residence) if the payments the debtor is scheduled to make under the plan to that creditor have a present value at least equal to the amount of the creditors' secured claim.[113]

If the debtor completes all the payments required under the confirmed plan, the debtor will receive a discharge of its prepetition debts[114] which were specifically provided for in the plan. If a debtor defaults under the plan, the bankruptcy court may dismiss the proceedings, modify the plan, or even convert it to a Chapter Seven liquidation.[115] The BRA limits the payment period under a plan to three years although the court may extend that period to five years.[116]

ROLE OF COUNSEL

In representing a sole proprietorship or self-employed debtor seeking relief from its creditors, an attorney often will compare with the client the advantages and disadvantages of Chapters Eleven and Thirteen. From the point of view of a sole proprietor or self-employed individual, Chapter Thirteen offers certain advantages. Permission to continue to operate one's own business seems nearly certain under Chapter Thirteen but is less certain under Chapter Eleven. Moreover, there is neither a creditor's committee nor the requirement of creditor acceptance of a plan in Chapter Thirteen as there are in Chapter Eleven. Chapter Eleven, however, has its advantages including no requirements to pay all claims in full or to commit all of the debtor's disposable income for the next three years to the plan as are required by Chapter Thirteen.

Depending on the availability of bankruptcy or other debtor relief options (such as a composition of creditors or an assignment to a trustee for their benefit), the debtor's attorney will weigh the advantages and disadvantages of each remedy before making a recommendation to the business client. A business needing relief from creditors should not hesitate to call in experienced commercial counsel for assistance.

NOTES

1. 9 App. Cas. 605 (1884).

2. *See,* Arnold B. Cohen, *Bankruptcy, Secured Transactions, and Other Debtor-Creditor Matters.* Michie, Bobbs-Merrill (1981) p. 231–32.

3. 11 U.S.C. § 524 (e).

4. 11 U.S.C. § 524 (c).

5. 11 U.S.C. § 727 (a) (8).

6. U.C.C. § 9–301 (3).

7. U.C.C. § 9–301 (1) (b).

8. David G. Epstein, *Debtor-Creditor Law in a Nutshell.* West Publishing Co.(1985), p. 133.

9. *Id.* at 132.

10. *See,* 11 U.S.C. §§ 1101, *et seq.*

11. Ch. 541, 30 Stat. 544 (1897–98) (codified in 11 U.S.C. (1976), [repealed (1979)]).

12. Pub. L. No. 95–598, 92 Stat. 2549 [codified in part in 11 U.S.C. (1979)].

13. Ch. 575, 52 Stat. 840 (1938).

14. Ginsberg, *The Bankruptcy Reform Act of 1978—A Primer,* 28 De Paul L. Rev. 923, 923 (1979). *See also* Stefan A. Riesenfeld, *Cases and Materials on Creditors' Remedies and Debtors' Protection.* 3rd ed. West Publishing Co. (1979): "[B]oth the legislative and decisional law have shown an increasing preoccupation with the protection and relief of debtors." *Id.* at xii.

15. Pub. L. No. 98–353, enacted July 10, 1984.

16. 28 U.S.C. § 1334.

17. 28 U.S.C. §§ 157 (b) (1), (2), and (3).

18. 28 U.S.C. § 151.

19. 28 U.S.C. § 152 (a) (1).

20. 11 U.S.C. § 101.

21. 11 U.S.C. § 109.

22. 11 U.S.C. §§ 301–306.

23. 11 U.S.C. §§ 321–331.

24. 11 U.S.C. §§ 342–344.

25. 11 U.S.C. §§ 501, *et seq.*

26. 11 U.S.C. §§ 701, *et seq.*

27. 11 U.S.C. §§ 901, *et seq.*

28. 11 U.S.C. §§ 1101, *et seq.*

29. 11 U.S.C. §§ 1301, *et seq.*

30. 11 U.S.C. §§ 15101, *et seq.*

31. 11 U.S.C. § 323.

32. 11 U.S.C. § 701.

33. 11 U.S.C. § 702 (c).

34. 11 U.S.C. § 1302.

35. Robert E. Ginsberg, *Bankruptcy.* Prentice-Hall, Inc. (1985), p. 1016; *see also,* Benjamin Weintraub, *What Every Executive Should Know About Chapter 11.* National Association of Credit Management (1985), pp. 11–15.

36. Robert E. Ginsberg, *Bankruptcy.* Prentice-Hall, Inc. (1985), p. 1016.

37. Benjamin Weintraub, *What Every Executive Should Know About Chapter 11.* National Association of Credit Management (1985), p. 1.

38. Vogel v. Mohawk Electrical Sales Co., 126 F.2d 759, 761 (2d Cir. 1942).

39. 11 U.S.C. §§ 301–303.

40. 11 U.S.C. § 541 (a).

41. *See,* 11 U.S.C. §§ 101 (33), 101 (8), and 109 (d).

42. *See,* 11 U.S.C. §§ 109 (e) and 101 (27).

43. Bankruptcy Rule 1002 (a).

44. 28 U.S.C. § 1408 (1).

45. Bankruptcy Rule 1002 (b).

46. 11 U.S.C. § 521 (1).

47. Bankruptcy Rule 1007.

48. Official Forms 6–8; Bankruptcy Rule 1007 (a) (b); *see also,* 11 U.S.C. § 1106 (a) (2).

49. 11 U.S.C. § 303 (b) (3) (A).

50. 11 U.S.C. § 303 (h).

51. 11 U.S.C. § 303 (h).

52. 11 U.S.C. §§ 303 (b) (1)–(2).

53. Bankruptcy Rule 1011 (b).

54. *See in re* Every, 17 B.R. 685 (Bankr. W.D. Wis. 1982). *See also,* 11 U.S.C. § 305.

55. 11 U.S.C. § 362.

56. *See,* 11 U.S.C. § 521.

57. 11 U.S.C. § 342. *See also,* Bankruptcy Rule 2002.

58. 11 U.S.C. § 1111 (a).

59. 11 U.S.C. § 1102.

60. 11 U.S.C. § 1102 (b) (1).

61. 11 U.S.C. § 1102 (b).

62. 11 U.S.C. § 1103.

63. 11 U.S.C. § 1103 (a).

64. *In re* Johns-Manville Corp., 26 B.R. 919 (Bankr. S.D.N.Y. 1983).

65. 11 U.S.C. §§ 341 and 343.

66. Bankruptcy Rule 2004.

67. 11 U.S.C. § 1108.

68. 11 U.S.C. § 364.

69. 11 U.S.C. § 364 (d).

70. 11 U.S.C. § 1123.

71. 11 U.S.C. § 1121.
72. 11 U.S.C. § 1121 (d).
73. 11 U.S.C. § 1122.
74. 11 U.S.C. § 1129.
75. 11 U.S.C. § 1126.
76. 11 U.S.C. § 1122 (b).
77. 11 U.S.C. § 1122 (a).
78. 11 U.S.C. § 507 (a) (6).
79. 11 U.S.C. § 1123 (a) (1).
80. 11 U.S.C. § 1123 (b) (4).
81. 11 U.S.C. §§ 1145 (a) and (b). *See also*, 11 U.S.C. § 1125 (d), and *in re* The Stanley Hotel, Inc., 5 C.B.C.2d 64 (Bankr. D. Colo. 1981).
82. N.L.R.B. v. Bildisco & Bildisco, 104 S.Ct. 1188, 1196 (1984).
83. 11 U.S.C. § 1113.
84. 11 U.S.C. § 1125. *See also*, Ginsberg, *Bankruptcy* (1985), pp. 1017–18.
85. 11 U.S.C. § 1125.
86. 11 U.S.C. § 1125 (b).
87. Epstein, *Debtor-Creditor Law* (1985), p. 334.
88. 11 U.S.C. § 1126 (f).
89. 11 U.S.C. § 1126 (g).
90. 11 U.S.C. § 1124.
91. For a detailed discussion of impaired versus nonimpaired claims in Chapter Eleven, *see* Cohen, *Bankrutpcy, Secured Transactions, and Other Debtor-Creditor Matters*. Michie, Bobbs-Merrill (1981), pp. 284–86.
92. 11 U.S.C. § 1123 (b) (1).
93. 11 U.S.C. § 1123 (b) (2).
94. 11 U.S.C. § 365 (d) (2).
95. 11 U.S.C. § 1126 (c).
96. 11 U.S.C. § 1126 (d).
97. 11 U.S.C. § 1141 (a).
98. 11 U.S.C. § 1128.
99. 11 U.S.C. § 1129 (c).
100. 11 U.S.C. § 1129 (b).
101. 11 U.S.C. § 1129 (b) (2) (A).
102. 11 U.S.C. § 1129 (b) (2) (A) (iii).
103. Lake, *Representing Secured Creditors under the Bankruptcy Code*, 37 Bus. Law. 1153, 1180 (1982).
104. Melanie Rouner Cohen and Faye B. Feinstein, *The Bankruptcy Reform Act of 1978 as Amended by the Bankruptcy Amendments and Federal Judgeship Act of 1984*, in *Bankruptcy Practice* (I.I.C.L.E.) 1–1, 1–57 (1985). *See also*, Klee, *All You Ever Wanted to Know about Cram Down under the New Bankruptcy Code*, 53 Am. Bankr. L.J. 133 (1979).
105. 11 U.S.C. § 1141.
106. 11 U.S.C. § 109 (e).
107. 11 U.S.C. § 342 (b).
108. 11 U.S.C. § 101 (24).
109. 11 U.S.C. § 1301.
110. 11 U.S.C. § 1304.

111. 11 U.S.C. § 1332.
112. 11 U.S.C. § 1325.
113. 11 U.S.C. § 1325 (a) (5) (b).
114. 11 U.S.C. § 1328 (a).
115. *See*, 11 U.S.C. §§ 1307 (c), 1328 (b), and 1329.
116. 11 U.S.C. § 1322 (b) (2).

15

Employment Laws and Regulations

Various federal laws and regulations apply to a business' employment practices, from the hiring of employees through their possible discharge. Although millions of workers are members of labor unions and thus are afforded protections under the federal labor laws, the majority of American employees have not joined labor organizations. Nonetheless, several important federal laws and regulations affect the employment relations between employers and employees whether the employees are unionized or not. Chief among these are the federal wage and hour laws (notably, the Fair Labor Standards Act),[1] Title VII of the Civil Rights Act of 1964,[2] the Welfare and Pension Plans Disclosure Act of 1958,[3] as supplemented by the Employee Retirement Income Security Act (ERISA) of 1974,[4] the Consumer Credit Protection Act of 1968,[5] and the Occupational Safety and Health Act of 1970.[6] The last listed act established the Occupational Safety and Health Administration (OSHA), which is discussed in Chapter 18. The pension plan legislation is discussed in Chapter 21.

This chapter first discusses the federal labor laws dealing with unionized workers, focusing on unionization and duty to bargain issues. It then covers in more detail the federal wage and hour regulations, followed by a survey of the employment discrimination laws. Included is a discussion of the federal restrictions on garnishment of an employee's wages. It should be understood that the federal laws and regulations pertaining to wages and hours, employment discrimination, and garnishment apply to businesses that have even the remotest connection with interstate commerce—in effect, all commercial enterprises—with exceptions noted in the following text.

FEDERAL LABOR LAWS

The complexity of the federal labor statutes together with the numerous decisions of the National Labor Relations Board precludes any comprehensive discussion in this volume. Certainly, an employer facing a union organizing effort, certification election, jurisdictional dispute, collective bargaining impasse, or charge of an unfair labor practice should consult with an attorney knowledgeable and experienced in labor law matters. In this section we simply note the principal labor laws and their respective regulatory thrusts.

The most important of the federal statutes affecting labor relations is the 1935 National Labor Relations Act,[7] also known as the Wagner Act. The United States Supreme Court held the act to be constitutional in 1937.[8] This statute permits employees to organize and form employee organizations or unions for purposes of collective bargaining of wages, hours, and other working conditions of employment. The act also prohibits various "unfair labor practices" *by an employer*, including:

1. Any interfering, restraining, or coercing of employees in the exercise of their rights to organize or elect a bargaining representative, to bargain collectively, or to engage in other protected activities under the act for their mutual benefit;

2. Any encouragement or discouragement of membership in any labor organization directly or indirectly by discriminating in regard to hiring decisions or regarding tenure or conditions of employment;

3. Any efforts to interfere with or dominate the administration of any labor organization, for example, by contributing financial or other support to it;

4. Any discipline, change of employment conditions, or discharge of an employee because of his or her involvement in protected activities under the act or under a decision of the National Labor Relations Board, including an employee's organizing activities or filing of an unfair labor practice charge; and

5. Any refusal to bargain or to bargain in good faith with the certified representative of the employees.

As established by the Wagner Act, the National Labor Relations Board (NLRB) oversees the unionization, collective bargaining, and unfair labor practice processes. The NLRB as an administrative agency of the federal government has rulemaking powers in addition to its adjudicatory functions. Consequently, there has evolved over the past several decades an extensive body of labor law decisions interpreting what an employer may and may not do in reference to protected employee activities. For example, scores of NLRB decisions have dealt with claims of employer interference with the employee's free choice to organize and bargain collectively and to engage in other protected, peaceful, and concerted activities. Given an employer's potential legal liability, coupled with the prospective disruptive impact on one's business for violating an established labor law principle, the employer is well advised to hire a labor law expert at the earliest possible stage of a brewing labor dispute.

Following the Wagner Act, Congress enacted, in 1947, the Labor Management Relations Act, more commonly known as the Taft-Hartley Act,[9] which sought to curb certain union abuses in affecting work stoppages that threatened public health and safety. The Taft-Hartley Act also amended the Wagner Act, especially those provisions dealing with representation elections. More importantly, the Taft-Hartley Act, for the first time, prohibited *unions* from engaging in certain specified unfair labor practices. By its explicit terms, unions could no longer:

1. Restrain or coerce an employer in selection of either grievance or collective bargaining representatives;
2. Restrain employees in the exercise of their rights under the Wagner Act;
3. Cause an employer to discriminate against an employee or group of employees on account of membership or nonmembership in the union, with the exception of recognizing legally enforceable union-shop agreements;
4. Promote strikes or work stoppages to force an employer or other person to cease doing business with any other person (the secondary boycott provision);
5. Promote work stoppages to force an employer or a self-employed person to join a union or to force his or her employees to join a union;
6. Refuse to bargain in good faith with an employer through the union's designated bargaining representatives or agent or to recognize another union as the employee's exclusive representative (in bargaining), as determined by a majority vote in a certification election of the employees;
7. Induce or encourage employees to stop work or take other disruptive job actions to force an employer to recognize and bargain with a union where another labor organization had previously been certified as the exclusive bargaining agent;
8. Encourage or cause employees to stop work to force an employer to assign work to members of the union rather than to members of another union (jurisdictional disputes); and
9. Force or attempt to force an employer to pay employees for services not to be performed (the antifeatherbedding provision).

Under the Taft-Hartley Act, the NLRB was expanded from three to five members. Through the act's provisions, Congress declared that unfair labor practices were not to be based on any employer expression of opinion or argument that contained *no* threat of reprisal. In short, employers within limits, were allowed to attempt to disuade their employees from joining or engaging in union activities. Known as the "employer free speech" section, this declaration has produced a great deal of litigation regarding the permissive limits of an employer's free speech.

In 1959, the Labor-Management Reporting and Disclosure Act,[10] more commonly known as the Landrum-Griffin Act, was enacted by Congress. Its provisions primarily focused on the internal management of labor unions in response to the public's concern with widespread corruption existing in several labor organizations. A union member's "bill of rights" was included, and all unions had to promulgate both a constitution and corresponding bylaws. Annual reports on the union's policies had to be disclosed to the membership and filed with the secretary of labor.

The 1959 Landrum-Griffin Act also contained several amendments to the earlier Taft-Hartley Act. These provisions closed several loopholes in the secondary boycott area, including the elimination of "hot cargo" agreements. A hot cargo clause in a collectively bargained contract required the employer to cease doing business with any nonunion company. Such a prohibition amounted to a form of secondary boycott.

The Wagner, Taft-Hartley, and Landrum Griffin acts are primarily administered by the National Labor Relations Board through 31 regional offices. The staff of each regional office includes a director, a regional attorney, trial lawyers, and field examiners. Nearly all disputes presented to the NLRB initially go through (and most culminate at) the regional office level. Administrative appeals, however, often are taken to higher levels including the full National Labor Relations Board, which has the authority to render a final agency decision. These board decisions, in turn, are subject to judicial review by one of the United States courts of appeals.

In addition to the three "basic" labor law statutes, Congress in 1926 (and by later amendments in 1934, 1951, and 1966) enacted the Railway Labor Act,[11] regulating the bargaining and other concerted activities of the nation's railway and airline employees. One other significant federal law in effect governing union and employer activities is the 1932 Norris-LaGuardia Act,[12] which places limitations on the granting of injunctions by federal judges as a means to quell labor disputes. The act also proscribes so-called "yellow dog" contracts under which an employee agrees either not to join or not to leave a union as a condition of employment.

UNIONIZATION DRIVES

Because of the federal labor laws, employees have the right to organize into a bargaining unit and to bargain collectively with their employer. A business facing a unionization drive is restrained by law as to the responses it may make. First, the employer may not circumvent unionization efforts or NLRB election procedures by negotiating individual employment contracts which either explicitly or implicitly require employees to waive their organizational rights.[13] Nor may an employer discharge employees for promoting or joining a labor organization.[14]

Employer's Tightrope

Once an employer learns about a unionization drive (perhaps by noticing solicitation cards circulating among its workers), a labor law specialist should be brought in immediately. In any unionization effort, the employer walks a tightrope in terms of what it may or may not do. Nowhere is the employer's position more precarious than it is when it talks to employees in an effort to disuade them from their unionization efforts. Generalizations about the law in this area are dangerous. To say that an employer has free speech to disuade employees, or that the employer may place reasonable restrictions on solicitations and distributions of literature inside its plant or office, although generally true, does not begin to tell the whole story. Such generalizations are dangerous, in part because they tend to give an employer a mistaken notion about how far it may go in resisting a unionization drive, and in part because they oversimplify the matter. What an employer may or may not do depends on all the circumstances present at its particular plant, office, or firm in light of countless NLRB and court decisions. The board, moreover, has developed a complex set of rules (confusing even to a skilled labor specialist), which attempts to differentiate permissible from impermissible employer conduct in response to unionization efforts.

Before the labor lawyer arrives, *one thing an employer should always avoid doing is looking at the authorization cards* supposedly signed by those employees who seek to engage in collective bargaining. If an employer is tendered the cards by its employee representatives, a lawyer will advise that the employer should at once seal the cards in an envelope and have a third person hold them until the firm's labor lawyer takes over. By not looking at the cards, an employer avoids a possible charge of discrimination brought by those employees who signed. Also, by not knowing how many employees actually signed the cards, an employer may maintain a good faith doubt about whether 50 percent or more of its employees supported the unionization effort. With this good faith doubt, an employer may force a representation election. In the mid–1980s, a majority of representation elections were being won by employers who were resisting unionization efforts.

In any unionization drive, an employer should never talk with *any* employees about confidential union matters, for example, where meetings will take place, the names of outside organizers, or even the names of the company's prounion leaders. Furthermore, an employer, in an effort to resist a unionization drive, should never discharge, lay off, or discriminate in any way against any employees who are, or might be, involved in unionization efforts. This prohibition includes any explicit or implicit threats of discharge, punishment, or discrimination of any employee or group of employees, present or future. In short, an employer should never threaten, promise, coerce, discriminate, or ask employees questions about their union efforts, sympathies, or involvements. Moreover, threats to close or move the business are illegal, even if they are meant sincerely.[15] (Actual plant or company closures versus removals raise different problems.)

During organization drives, employers are allowed to pass on to their employees information regarding existing employment benefits; opinions regarding the general disadvantages of unions (dues, strikes, and so on); their own views (pro, con, or neutral) on unions and union procedures; and corrections of untrue or misleading statements made by the prounion organizers.

As to solicitations and distributions of literature, normally an employer may require that these activities be conducted during nonworking time and outside normal working areas. There are, however, recognized exceptions to this rule. Outside (nonemployee) organizers under two sets of circumstances are permitted to come on company property to solicit employees: first, when the union is unable to solicit through other means and, second, where the employer allows other groups to solicit or distribute but does not permit the particular union organizers to do so.

Finally, an employer should understand that it is an unfair labor practice for it in any manner to promote, assist, or dominate a union. In reference to union-ization drives, this means that an employer may not promote one possible union over another or try to institute a so-called company union.

Election and Certification

Regional directors of the National Labor Relations Board are responsible for conducting representation elections within their respective geographic areas. The procedure begins with the filing of a petition for a representation election. The petition can be filed by a union, an employer, or by a group of employees. If a union files the petition, it must be supported by at least 30 percent of the employees in the bargaining unit designated in the petition. (This does *not* mean 30 percent of all the firm's nonsupervisory personnel.) The required support typically is evidenced by authorization cards signed by the employees. (The NLRB authenticates the signatures.) An employer may petition for an election in two circumstances: first, following a union's claim that the latter represents more than 50 percent of the employees and, second, if the union requests to bargain collectively.

Once the petition is filed and provided the NLRB asserts jurisdiction, the board typically encourages the parties to agree to a "consent" election. If the parties do not agree that the proposed bargaining unit is appropriate, a "representation" hearing will be required at one of the NLRB's regional offices to determine which employees will be within the bargaining unit and to resolve other issues regarding the pending certification election. The appropriateness of a proposed bargaining unit is a complex legal and practical issue requiring the assistance, skill, and knowledge of a labor law specialist. Suffice it to say that any proposed unit of a portion of a firm's nonsupervisory employees affords an employer a basis for a prima facie challenge, in other words, an opportunity to litigate the issue.

Once the election is held, if a majority of those eligible vote for the union, the board will "certify" that the bargaining unit is the exclusive representative of the employees for bargaining purposes. Of course, an employer may volun-tarily recognize a union without a board-conducted election. Whether based on an election, or on the voluntary recognition of the employer, once the bargaining unit is legally established the employer must engage in collective bargaining with it.

DUTY TO BARGAIN

Under the National Labor Relations Act and Taft Hartley amendments, both the employer and the certified or recognized employee organization are obligated to bargain in good faith.[16] Bargaining in good faith, however, does not require one side's agreeing to the other party's proposals or to making concessions. Thus, the meaning of good faith bargaining has been (and likely will remain) unclear. Still, the obligation minimally requires that the parties meet at reasonable times and discuss certain mandatory topics—wages, hours, and other terms and conditions of employment. The scope of mandatory bargaining is not, however, as wide as it first appears. The United States Supreme Court has held that the good faith bargaining mandate does not mean that the parties must bargain every matter that might impact or have an effect on the employees' terms of employment.[17]

On the other hand, an employer should not make a unilateral modification in an existing bargaining agreement if it pertains either to a mandatory subject of bargaining or to a subject covered in an existing labor agreement. Such a unilateral modification has been held to constitute a Section 8(a)(5) refusal to bargain violation.[18] Employer violations of the duty to bargain in good faith have also been found in the following circumstances:

1. Refusals to meet with the union and discuss its proposals at reasonable times;

2. A pattern of postponing scheduled bargaining sessions;

3. Withdrawing proposals tentatively agreed to in the bargaining process;

4. Negotiating directly with individual employees within the bargaining unit;

5. Engaging in what is called "mere surface" bargaining; and

6. Refusing to furnish the union with financial information within the exclusive control of the employer which data is reasonably necessary for "intelligent bargaining" by the exclusive representative.

When an employer violates its duty to bargain in good faith, the NLRB may issue a cease and desist order mandating that the employer return to the table. A so-called make whole remedy, once recognized and used by at least one court,[19] has been totally discredited by the board. Under this former procedure, an employer would have to compensate employees for the probable damages resulting from the employer's refusal to bargain in good faith.

Apart from the legal considerations involved in collective bargaining, the need for harmonious labor relations often plays a determinative role in the process. A competent labor law specialist not only understands the law but also is sensitive to the political and personality dynamics that play strategic roles in labor relations.

FEDERAL LAW OF WAGES AND HOURS

Congress has regulated what it considers to be substandard labor conditions on the theory that these conditions burden the free flow of interstate goods. It has done so primarily through enactment of four federal statutes pertaining to wages and hours: the Fair Labor Standards Act (FLSA),[20] the Walsh-Healey Act,[21] the Davis Bacon Act,[22] and the Service Contract Act.[23] Only the Fair Labor Standards Act, however, affects all interstate industry. The other laws affect only contracts made with or financed by the federal government. Thus, the most important of these acts—because of its wide applicability to businesses—is the Fair Labor Standards Acts. The FLSA provisions primarily regulate four basic areas: hourly wage rates, overtime compensation, child labor, and equal pay for equal work. The following discussion deals with the FLSA, commonly referred to as "The Wage and Hour Law."

Administration

Principal responsibility for administration and enforcement of the FLSA rests in the Department of Labor, Division of Hours and Wages. Overseeing the department is the secretary of labor, who has the authority to delegate the duties mandated by the act. The secretary has delegated many of his statutory duties to an appointed administrator of the Division of Hours and Wages. Thus, it is the administrator and his assistants who perform most FLSA administrative and enforcement functions. Administration of the equal pay provisions of the FLSA, however, has been transferred to the Equal Employment Opportunity Commission (EEOC).

Although he is the chief enforcement official of the FLSA, the administrator of the Division of Hours and Wages has minimal authority to promulgate regulations except in limited instances. He does from time to time, however, issue bulletins stating how the division interprets the FLSA for enforcement purposes. Even though these bulletins do not have the full force and effect of law, they do represent informed opinions of the Department of Labor. Thus, employers should look to these pronouncements for guidance regarding the department's positions on specific issues. The administrator also periodically issues rulings on individual cases appealed to his office.

In reference to the employment of minors, the Child Labor Branch of the Bureau of Labor Standards conducts research, determines standards, and assembles statistics on child labor matters. The administrator becomes involved in child labor situations only it is when necessary to obtain compliance with the child labor provisions of the act.

Coverage

Geographically, FLSA coverage extends to all states, the District of Columbia, Puerto Rico, the Virgin Islands, the outer Contintental Shelf lands, American

Samoa, Guam, Wake Island, Eniwetok Atoll, Kwajalein Atoll, Johnston Island, and the Canal Zone. The FLSA applies to all employees who participate in interstate commerce, whether the commerce involves trade, transportation, transmission, or communications activities. FLSA coverage also extends to American trade and commerce with other nations, whether import or export in nature.

The FLSA wage and hour rules are designed to protect only employees. They do not apply to independent contractors. An employee is defined as a person over whom an employer has the right to control the means by which the employee accomplishes his or her task. Whether the right of control is exercised or not is not determinative of the status. On the other hand, if a worker has been hired to do a specific task, and the worker so hired has sole control over how he or she accomplishes it, that worker likely would be classified as an independent contractor, particularly if a specified time limit to accomplish the task is involved. In addition, certain persons who functionally are noncompensated trainees are not covered. More specifically, workers hired as trainees are not deemed covered employees if no benefit is derived by the employer and no wages are paid to the trainee. Understand, however, that simply calling a novice worker a trainee will not affect that worker's FLSA protection. Moreover, a covered, nonexempt employee may not waive his or her statutory right to protection under the FLSA. Any purported waiver by a covered employee is null and void, notwithstanding that it is in writing or given for a valuable consideration. Effective April 15, 1986, the FLSA provisions also became applicable to most state and local governmental employees.

Although the FLSA applies to most private workers, not all employees of all businesses are covered. Two tests exist to determine whether an employee comes within the protection of the FLSA. Under the "individual employee" test, when an employee's duties directly involve interstate commerce, for example, by being required to drive a truck across state lines or by selling goods out of state, he or she is subject to the FLSA protections.

A second, broader test extends coverage to those employees who perform all of their job-related tasks within a single state but who are employed by businesses engaged in interstate commerce. This measurement, known as the "enterprise" test, in effect extends coverage to all employees of the enterprise, even those having purely local or intrastate duties. A business will satisfy the enterprise test if any of its activities, which are performed by one or more persons for a related business purpose, involves interstate commerce. Therefore, any intrastate activity with any reasonable connection to an interstate business activity can confer enterprise status. The effect of the enterprise test is to make the FLSA provisions applicable to virtually all industries and businesses but with certain significant exceptions noted below.

The FLSA was amended in 1977 with respect to enterprise coverage.[24] The amendment adds an additional gross sales requirement for the act to be applicable to certain enterprises. Businesses are divided into five categories. The standards applying to each category are as follows:

1. Dollar-test enterprises (businesses not falling within subcategories two through five): To be subject to FLSA's provisions these firms must meet the commerce requirement and have yearly gross sales of at least $250,000.

2. Enterprises that are entirely retail or service establishments: These businesses must meet the commerce requirement and have yearly gross sales of at least $362,500.

3. Laundry and dry cleaning enterprises: These firms must meet only the commerce requirement, regardless of receipts.

4. Construction business enterprises: These companies must meet only the commerce requirement.

5. Hospital, nursing home, and school enterprises: These enterprises, too, must meet only the commerce requirement.

Under the enterprise test, the FLSA applies to an employee regardless of how limited the firm's interstate activity might be so long as the activity occurs on a regular basis. Sending one shipment per month out of state would suffice. Thus, in actuality, it is difficult for any American employer involved in trade to avoid the applicable regulations of the FLSA. On the other hand, a purely intrastate service-oriented business may not be subject to the federal law. Still, many states have enacted legislation similar to the FLSA to apply to intrastate business activities not otherwise subject to the federal legislation. In situations where a state's statute prescribes a stricter standard than that mandated by the federal statute, compliance with the FLSA provisions does not excuse noncompliance with stricter state law standards. Only where the state standards would be less protective of the worker's interests does the federal statute preempt the inconsistent state law provisions.

Wages and Hours

With the important exception of child labor, the FLSA does not limit the numbers of hours an employee can be directed to work. Rather, the act prescribes a minimum wage to be paid for regular hours, and requires that a covered employee be compensated at the rate of time and half the regular rate for any overtime worked. Since January 1, 1981, the minimum wage has congressionally been set at $3.35 per hour.[25] This figure, of course, may and likely will be raised by Congress in the near future. (A reader may ascertain the minimum wage in effect at the time of reading by calling the nearest Department of Labor, Division of Hours and Wages office.) Wages may be paid either in cash or by bank draft (check). Compensation paid in the form of lodging, board, or other facilities may be deducted in computing the actual cash payments to be made so that the cash payments actually may fall below the minimum rate. Examples of other facilities include fuel, clothing, and household effects. The amount of such deduction should equal the reasonable cost to the employer in furnishing the facilities. Although reasonable cost is defined as actual cost, in no event may the deduction exceed the fair market value of the services or facilities provided.

To determine whether the minimum wage is being paid, a weekly wage rate must be determined. A workweek is defined as seven consecutive 24-hour periods. Thus, if a covered employee works only 27 hours in a seven consecutive day period, he or she must be compensated at a minimum in the amount of $90.45, or $3.35 times 27 hours. If an employee is paid on some schedule other than on a weekly basis, the pay rate must still meet the minimum wage requirement when expressed in weekly terms. Even when an employee is paid solely on a commission basis, his or her weekly earnings must equate to at least $3.35 per hour of time actually worked.

Employees who routinely receive gratuities for their services are sometimes treated differently regarding minimum wage compensation. An employee is considered a tipped employee if he or she customarily and regularly (greater than occasionally, but less than constantly) receives at least $30.00 per month in gratuities. An employer is allowed to credit 40 percent of the employee's actual tip income received against the minimum wage standard.

Federal and state income taxes as well as employee Social Security contributions, of course, are to be deducted from the wages actually paid the employee, even when the deductions drop the employee's take-home pay below the minimum hourly rate. What is crucial is what is earned, not what is received as take-home pay. Any deductions authorized by the employee, such as pension or health plan contributions, may also be deducted from the employee's check. However, if a deduction, which cuts into the minimum wage standard, is for the benefit of a third party—for example, a voluntary wage deduction for the benefit of a creditor or a union dues checkoff—the employee must assent to the deduction, and the employer must derive no benefit to allow it to be deducted from the wages actually paid when the amount paid, due to the deduction, falls below the minimum wage amount. With union employees, the assent of the union is deemed the assent of the employee.

Overtime Compensation

Overtime compensation must be paid for all hours worked in excess of 40 hours per week. The hourly rate of pay required for overtime is one and one half times the employee's regular hourly rate of pay. The regular rate of pay may be more than the statutory minimum, currently $3.35 per hour, but never less. In calculating overtime, a workweek may be staggered to avoid overtime pay.

The FLSA defines hours worked as:

1. All the time an employee is required to be on duty or to be on the employer's premises or at a prescribed work place; and

2. All the time during which an employee is suffered or permitted to work, whether or not he or she is required to do so.

Therefore, to calculate the total number of hours an employee has worked, the employer must include all the employee's time spent on his or her principal duties as well as the time expended on tasks incidental to the principal duties. Incidental tasks would include time spent waiting for, preparing for, or concluding principal duties. On the other hand, time spent on call away from the business need not be included in work time if the only restriction upon the employee is that he or she keep the employer notified of his or her whereabouts. Required on call time at the plant or business, however, is a different matter and must be included. Similarly, employee training sessions, seminars, and analogous functions must also be included in computing an employee's total work time.

The law does not require that an employee be given a rest period or times for meals. Thus, meal periods are not considered as working time if an employee is relieved of all duties during the break. Neither does the FLSA require that an employee be paid for time not worked. Thus, vacations, holidays, and absences need not be compensated. In addition, the "Portal-to-Portal Act" allows employers not to pay workers to and from their home and their place of employment.

The regular rate of pay, used in the overtime pay calculations, includes all compensation (in cash and as deductions for lodging or other facilities) consequent to the employment relation. Reimbursement for expenses incurred on the employer's behalf, premium payments, discretionary bonuses, gifts, and vacation, holiday, or absence pay may be excluded in calculating the regular rate of pay.

A bonus is considered discretionary if the employer retains control over whether a bonus will be paid, when the bonus will be paid, and how much the bonus will be. A bonus designed to encourage increased efforts by tying it either to the hours worked or to the employee's productive output is not discretionary and must be included in computing the regular rate. To avoid the distinction between discretionary and nondiscretionary bonuses, a bonus may be paid as a percentage of an employee's total earnings. With percentage bonuses, the bonus is a percentage of the sum of straight time wages plus overtime wages. Therefore, overtime is already included in the bonus, and the distinction between discretionary or nondiscretionary becomes less important.

In furtherance of the policy of promoting employer contributions to benefit plans, the act provides that such payments may be excluded from the regular rate. To qualify for exclusion, the benefit plan must be classified as a welfare plan (a plan that provides old age, retirement, accident, life or health insurance, or similar benefits), a profit sharing plan, trusts, or a thrift or savings plan. Regardless of the type of plan, it must meet other requirements specified by statute or regulations.[26] Advice of counsel in this area is highly recommended before structuring and implementing any plan of employee benefits. Many other laws may apply including ERISA and other provisions of the Internal Revenue Code.

If an employee is paid a fixed salary although he or she is working fluctuating hours, the fixed amount will constitute straight time pay for all hours worked. The regular rate would then vary each week dependent upon the hours actually worked, and overtime would be paid at one and one half times that regular rate, as determined weekly.

There are exceptions to the general rule that overtime must be compensated at one and one half times the regular rate. To simplify the computations when an employee works under two or more differing rates, the FLSA permits two shortcuts, which are really exceptions to the general rule. First, pieceworkers may be paid at one and one half the piece rate in effect during the overtime hours. Second, hourly employees working at two or more rates during one week may be paid at one and one half the hourly rate in effect during the overtime hours.

An important exception also arises when the employee and employer agree before overtime work is performed on a specific rate of overtime pay. Also, employees of wholesale petroleum distributors (jobbers) who satisfy certain qualifications may be paid overtime at the standard minimum wage rate.

Child Labor

The FLSA affords protection to minors from oppressive child labor, particularly when the labor involves children under the age of sixteen.[27] Child labor is deemed legally oppressive when a child below the minimum statutory age for the specified type of job is employed. The minimum age standards depend upon the type of work involved. The standards distinguish between agricultural and nonagricultural work. Eighteen years of age is the minimum age allowed for hazardous nonagricultural occupations. The secretary of labor has defined seventeen hazardous occupations including the operation of heavy industrial or manufacturing machinery, manufacture of explosives, exposure to radioactive substances, and operation of motor vehicles.[28] Sixteen years of age is the minimum age for employment in hazardous agricultural occupations.

A sixteen-year-old boy or girl may be employed during school hours, even when school is in session, in nonhazardous undertakings. Employment of fourteen- and fifteen-year-olds, however, is strictly limited so that their employment cannot interfere with their health and well-being. Children fourteen or fifteen generally may not be employed during school hours and may not work more than 3 hours per school day or 8 hours per nonschool day, 18 hours per school week, or 40 hours per nonschool week. Moreover, all work of this age group must be performed between 7 A.M. and 7 P.M., except during the summer when the children may work until 9 P.M. Fourteen- and fifteen-year-olds in retail food and gas service establishments may be employed in light labor such as cashiering, selling, tagging, delivery work by foot or bicycle, kitchen work, gas dispensing, and stocking. Such children may not, however, be employed in maintenance or repair of any equipment or premises or in nonclerical warehouse occupations.

Generally no child younger than fourteen may be employed. Exceptions include those involved in newspaper deliveries and the like. Employers engaged in farming operations, however, may apply for a waiver of age restrictions and hire children as young as ten-and eleven-years-old as hand harvest laborers.

Employers should seek to protect themselves from possible violation of the child labor provisions by obtaining age certificates for each minor employed. These certificates, often called work permits, must be acquired from the Department of Labor, Wage and Hour Division regional offices.[29] Reportedly, age certificates are accepted as legal proof of age in 45 states.

Equal Pay for Equal Work

The FLSA prohibits discrimination in the payment of wages on the basis of sex.[30] There are no recognized exemptions to the equal pay provisions as there are to the other provisions. Though the FLSA provides no protection from racial, age, religious, or other types of discrimination, Title VII of the 1964 Civil Rights Act requires that jobs be made available on a nondiscriminatory basis.[31] These matters are discussed subsequently in this chapter.

The equal pay standard relates to the job itself and not to the person holding it. Further, it is applied on a distinct physical location basis rather than throughout an entire enterprise. For example, each branch store of a retailer would be considered a separate location. Thus, there could be different pay scales for the same job among the different stores.

The requirement of equal pay extends to overtime as well as to straight time pay rates. Exclusions allowed in computing overtime pay must be considered when evaluating compliance with the equal pay provisions. To measure compliance, an employer must describe each job within a particular establishment. The standard may be divided into four equal pay tests: (1) equal skill, (2) equal effort, (3) equal responsibility, and (4) similar working conditions.

Equal skill involves a determination of the skills required to perform the assigned job successfully. Factors such as experience, training, education, and ability are considered. The skills that a particular employee may have but that are not required in the particular job are not relevant in this determination.

Equal effort is a measurement of the degree of physical or mental exertion required in performance of the job. Equal effort is the most difficult to evaluate as two jobs may require equal effort even though one requires physical exertion and the other mental. Reliance upon practical judgment appears to be the best guide.

Equal responsibility involves a measure of the degree of accountability required and the importance of the obligations involved in the performance of the job. Similarity of working conditions involves an assessment of the situations under which a particular task or job is performed. It is worth considering that equal does not necessarily mean identical. Slight or inconsequential differences in any of the four areas will not justify a difference in wage rates. Equal pay issues represent a problem area for businesses today. Given the lack of more definitive guidelines, an employer is left to common sense to determine when a difference is substantial. When a violation of the equal pay standard is deemed to have occurred, an employer may not correct the error by reducing all other hourly wage rates. Rather, he or she can bring his or her business into compliance only by increasing the wage rates of all jobs falling within the equal pay category to the highest rate then being paid to an employee within that category.

The FLSA exempts payments made on the basis of a seniority, merit, or any other system based on quantity or quality of production, provided the system is applied fairly to both men and women. It must be proven that the criteria upon which the system is based are known by each affected employee. Formal written documents are preferred as they provide the best evidence of employee awareness of the merit pay or productivity plan.

An exception is also allowed for trainees who may perform various types of work in furtherance of their training. The training program, however, must be bona fide. Programs that appear to be available to only one sex will be carefully scrutinized by the Department of Labor, as single-gender programs are suspect on their face.

Exemptions

The FLSA provides for several exemptions of all or part of its provisions, but mostly from the overtime rules.[32] Most exemptions are narrowly defined and do not affect large numbers of workers. The trend has been to eliminate slowly many exemptions previously recognized. Thus, this section will focus on the most significant remaining exemptions. These are the "white collar exemptions"; the special rules for learners, apprentices, students, and handicapped workers; and agricultural exemptions. Because any exemption under the FLSA is strictly construed, only those employees who exactly come within the stated exemption requirements will be exempt. The burden of proving the exempt status of the employee is always upon the employer. An exempt employee must be exempt for an entire workweek in order for the employer to claim the exemption status.

Employees with white collar jobs are exempt from both minimum wage and overtime requirements of the FLSA. White collar jobs are defined as executives, administrative employees, professional employees, and outside salespersons. Each defined category has specified tests that must be met to claim the exemption.

Six tests must be satisfied to exempt an executive employee:

1. The employee's primary duty (greater than 50 percent of employee's time) must be management of all or part of the business.

2. The employee must regularly direct the work of two or more employees.

3. The employee must have the authority to hire and fire or to recommend the promotion and demotion of other employees.

4. The employee must regularly exercise discretionary authority.

5. The employee must receive at least $155 per week, exclusive of board, lodging, or other facilities.

6. The employee must devote no more than 20 percent of his or her time to nonexempt work (40 percent for retail or service businesses).

If the employee is paid at least $250 per week, only the first and second requirements need be met.

To qualify for exemption, administrative employees must satisfy a five-part test:

1. The employee's primary duty must be the performance of nonmanual work directly related to management or to general business operations.

2. The employee must regularly exercise discretion and judgment.

3. The employee must regularly and directly assist an executive employee or must perform, under only general supervision, work requiring special skill, or must execute special assignments under only general supervision.

4. The employee must earn at least $155 per week.

5. The employee must devote no more than 20 percent of his or her time to nonexempt work (40 percent in retail or service businesses).

If the administrative employee is paid at least $250 per week, he or she need only satisfy the first two requirements.

Professional employees must satisfy a five-part test to be exempt:

1. The employee's primary duties must require advanced knowledge in a scientific field or specialized study.

2. The work must require the constant exercise of discretion and judgment.

3. The work must be predominantly intellectual and so varied that the output cannot be standardized.

4. No more than 20 percent of the employee's time can be spent on nonexempt work.

5. The employee must earn at least $170 per week.

When the professional employee earns at least $250 per week he or she need satisfy only the first requirement.

The exempt outside sales person must satisfy a three-part test:

1. The employee must be employed to and must, in fact, customarily and regularly work outside the employer's business premises.

2. The employee must be engaged in selling goods or in obtaining orders or contracts for services or the use of facilities.

3. The employee must devote no more than 20 percent of his or her time on nonexempt work.

Apprentices, learners, students, and handicapped workers may under certain conditions also be exempt from the minimum wage provisions of the FLSA. To pay at a rate below the minimum wage, the employer must obtain a certificate from the wage and hour administrator. Generally, wages may not be less than one half the standard minimum wage. Under certain conditions, however, equitable wage rates below 50 percent of the standard may be paid.

An apprentice is defined as a worker at least sixteen years of age employed to learn a skilled trade. The trade must require at least 4,000 hours to learn. There must be an apprenticeship agreement between the employer and the employee, and the agreement must be approved by a local, state, or federal apprenticeship council.

Handicapped workers are defined as those whose earning capacity is impaired. The impairment may have come about by age, physical or mental deficiency, or injury.

Learners may be employed at subminimum wages. To do so, the employer must prove that opportunities for employment within the firm would otherwise be reduced.

Retail and service establishments may employ full-time students at subminimum wages. The wage rate must be no less than 85 percent of the standard minimum wage. The student must be at least fourteen years old and attend a bona fide educational institution full time. The students may be employed for no more than twenty hours per week, and the work hours must be outside normal school hours. However, the student may work 40 hours per week (no more than 8 hours per day) during school vacation periods. The student's employment must be of the type not ordinarily given to full-time employees to prevent displacement of adult workers in favor of cheaper student labor. If an employee plans to employ more than six students, he or she must first obtain a special certificate; otherwise, the employer need only inform the Department of Labor of his or her intent to hire students at subminimum wages. This notification is designed to allow the administrator to determine whether student employment will reduce full-time employment.

In the past, agricultural employees were totally exempt from the protection of the FLSA. Agriculture is defined as "farming and all its branches." Thus, the exemption covered a great number of workers. In recent times, Congress has severely narrowed the exemptions available to agricultural employers. Today, agricultural workers are generally exempt only from the overtime pay provisions of the FLSA, and only five exemption categories are recognized under the minimum wage provisions:

1. Employees whose employer did not use more than 500 man-days of agricultural labor in any quarter of the preceding year. (A man-day is defined as any day an employee performed at least one hour of agricultural labor. This provision is a function of Congress's desire to encompass the large farms within the FLSA.)

2. Employees who are members of the employer's immediate family. (These employees are also exempt from the equal pay provisions of the FLSA.)

3. Hand harvesters who are paid at piece rates, commute to work, and were employed in agriculture for less than thirteen weeks during the preceding year.

4. Pieceworkers who are under seventeen years old and are employed on the same farm as their parents.

5. Cowboys and shepherds. (These employees are also exempt from the equal pay provisions.)

Record Keeping and Enforcement

To assist the enforcement of the FLSA, the law requires that employers keep records reflecting wages, hours, and other conditions concerning their employees, including even those persons who are or who might be exempt.[33] There are no requirements as to the form of the records to be maintained. Any reasonable method will be accepted as long as the information is both accurate and complete. The essential information that must be recorded and preserved includes the following:

1. Identifying information: Employee's name, address, birthdate (if under nineteen, age certificates should be on file for all minor employees), sex, and occupation.

2. Hours: When employee's workweek begins, hours worked per day, and hours worked per week.

3. Wages: Basis or formula on which the employee's wages are paid, overtime pay rate (one and one half the regular rate or other stipulated rate), amount and nature of payments excluded from the overtime rate, daily or weekly straight time pay, overtime pay per week, any additions or deductions from wages per pay period, and dates of payments.

An employer, moreover, must keep actual payroll records, age certificates, employee-employer agreements, plan notices (collective bargaining agreements, benefit plans, trust plans, etc.), as well as volume of sales data for at least three years after the events. Employment earnings records, which substantiate other records, must be kept for at least two years. An employer, however, may petition the administrator for authority to change or modify the requirements for record keeping.

Personnel from the regional offices of the Division of Hours and Wages have the right to enter an employer's premises and conduct investigations and inspections to determine compliance with the FLSA, including compliance with the requirements for making and preserving records. Investigations may be and usually are prompted by employee complaints. Investigations also result from reinspections of previous violators, spot checks in high violation business areas, or as part of a random audit of industry members. Employers are advised to cooperate with these investigations fully as the secretary of labor has the power to subpoena witnesses and records without establishing that the employer's business and employees are subject to the FLSA. Upon notice of an impending investigation or inspection, an employee is advised to seek consultation with legal counsel. An employer should never destroy any required records. Willful violations of FLSA may lead to severe penalties.

The following steps are typically involved in an FLSA investigation:

1. A compliance officer will identify him- or herself with official credentials.

2. The officer will arrange to meet with the employer or its representative. He or she will explain what records the officer will need to review and may ask the employer to designate a staff member to aid in explaining any records.

3. The officer may investigate and transcribe any records he or she chooses. The officer may conduct interviews with any of the business's employees in private. Often this is done to confirm the information in the records and to check on possible equal pay, discrimination, or child labor violations.

4. Usually the officer will, in an exit interview, again meet with the employer and will tentatively advise whether any possible violations were found. If violations were determined to exist, the employer normally will be advised on ways to correct them.

Employer's Rights

An employer accused of being in violation of the FLSA may request a conference with Department of Labor personnel and, of course, may be represented by counsel throughout any investigative and enforcement proceedings. Although a compliance officer may request an employer to comply with FLSA, only a court of competent jurisdiction can *order* compliance. The employer who believes that the investigator was in error in finding a violation may pursue the matter with higher officials within the Labor Department. A field office supervisor has the authority to overrule or modify an investigator's findings. The field officer, moreover, has authority to compromise disputed claims if reasonable to do so. If an employer remains unsatisfied with the field officer's actions, the employer may take the complaint higher to the regional director's office. The employer may even appeal to the administrator's office in Washington, D.C., for an administrative ruling. The appeal to Washington may be accomplished in person or through written correspondence. Of course, the Department of Labor may go to court to enforce compliance at any time once it believes an FLSA violation has occurred. Thus, the employer may have to defend his or her position in court.

Liability for Violations

The FLSA provisions are enforced through civil actions commenced against employers for back wages by (or in behalf of) employees themselves, injunctive suits commenced by the secretary of labor to restrain repeated violations, and criminal proceedings prosecuted by the attorney general to punish alleged willful violators.[34] Enforcement actions may be brought in any state or federal court of competent jurisdiction. The statute of limitations for all actions is two years from the date of a claimed violation. If the alleged infraction is deemed to have been willful, the statute of limitations extends to five years from the alleged occurrence.

If an employee brings a civil action for back wages, he or she may recover not only the overdue wages but also an equal amount as liquidated damages plus a sum for reasonable attorney fees and costs of the action. Liquidated damages in this sense are not considered a penalty but rather are deemed to be compensation for delay in the payment of the wages due the employee. If the civil suit for back wages in behalf of an employee or former employee is brought by the secretary of labor, the attorney fees and costs are not recoverable, but the employee may no longer commence suit individually. An employer may avoid paying back pay if it can prove reliance on a written ruling of the wage and hour administrator. Employers may also avoid liability for the double payment as liquidated damages by showing reasonable grounds for believing that the firm's payment practice was in compliance with FLSA even though in fact it was not.

Courts are divided over the issue of whether arbitration clauses in an employment contract or specific arbitration awards will bar an employee's right to seek recovery in a wage suit filed in court. A 1974 federal appellate court decision ruled that such wage suits would be barred by an arbitration award in light of the federal labor law policy of favoring arbitration.[35] The issue remains unsettled, however.

As to injunctive actions, only the secretary of labor may sue for an injunction. Such an action does not cut off an employee's individual right to sue. The secretary need not prove a violation was willful or repeatedly and knowingly done to obtain an injunction. Once an injunction has been issued, it may run indefinitely, leaving an employer open to contempt of court proceedings for subsequent violations. Thus, criminal contempt sanctions including fines and imprisonment could occur for violations of an injunctive order. When the Department of Justice pursues a willful criminal violation, the criminal penalties may not exceed $10,000 for first offenders. A second offense, however, may result in a prison term not to exceed six months. Such convictions are rare, but they do occur. It is the policy of the Wage and Hour Division to refer only aggravated violations to the Department of Justice for prosecution.

The FLSA also provides other measures to promote compliance.[36] Civil and criminal penalties exist for an employer's violation of a ban on transporting in interstate commerce goods produced in violation of the FLSA, for an employer's taking reprisals against employees who complained or commenced FLSA proceedings, and for employers who fail to keep or who falsify records. Also, an employer is required to display, in a conspicuous place, a poster apprising workers of minimum wage and overtime pay rights and how to collect back wages. Posters are available at the Department of Labor's local wage and hour office.

In summary, the provisions of the FLSA apply to most enterprises. It is better for the business person to comply with the FLSA requirements regarding minimum wage, overtime pay, equal pay for equal work, and child labor than to face the potential civil and criminal liability for noncompliance.

WAGE GARNISHMENTS

To curb the unrestricted garnishment of an employee's compensation, a practice that Congress believed encouraged the predatory extension of credit, Title III of the Consumer Credit Protection Act of 1968[37] was enacted. It seeks to control in a uniform manner among all the states the garnishment of an employee's wages. Title III both limits the amount (or proportion) of an employee's wages subject to garnishment and prohibits an employer from discharging an employee because of a wage garnishment because of a single indebtedness. This title is enforced by the Department of Labor through the Wage and Hour Division.

Garnishment is defined in Section 302 of Title III as any legal or equitable proceeding through which the earnings of any individual are required to be withheld for the payment of any debt.[38] Garnishments include executions, attachments, and court orders. For a discussion of civil court procedure, see Chapter 2. Earnings are defined as compensation paid or payable for personal services, whether denominated as wages, salary, commission, bonus, or otherwise, and includes periodic payments pursuant to a pension plan or retirement program.

The Consumer Credit Protection Act allows garnishment of no more than 25 percent of disposable earnings for a workweek or the disposable earnings for a workweek in excess of 30 times the minimum wage (30 × $3.35/hour in 1986 = $100.50), whichever is less.[39] Disposable earnings are defined as that part of the earnings of any individual remaining after the employer has deducted any amounts required by law to be withheld. Thus, the disposable earnings in many but not all cases will be what the employee considers take-home pay.

A greater (up to 50 percent) garnishment of disposable earnings per workweek is allowed pursuant to court orders for child support and alimony where the employee has a second family to support. For court orders for child, dependant, or former spousal support, a maximum garnishment of up to 60 percent of disposable earnings per workweek is allowed where the employee does not have to provide for a second family. Also, the 25-percent restriction does not apply to any attachment orders issued by a federal bankruptcy court or to any garnishment of an indebtedness owed on account of state or federal taxes.

States with garnishment laws substantially similar to the federal Consumer Credit Protection Act's provisions are exempt from its coverage. In determining whether a state law is substantially similar, the scope of the state statute and the state's methods of computation and procedural burdens are considered. In 1986, only Kentucky and Virginia had become exempt from the federal presumption because of having enacted substantially similar state laws. State garnishment laws in most cases have been held not to be substantially similar to the federal statute's limitations. Certain state statutes would, in effect, allow a 100-percent garnishment. A Kansas statute, for example, allows garnishment of all property and indebtedness owed a debtor in possession of a garnishee (including an employer). In states having such laws, the federal limitations control. As of this writing, the garnishment statutes of Illinois, Kansas, Louisiana, Minnesota, New Hampshire, North Carolina, North Dakota, Ohio, South Carolina, and Utah have been held neither to be substantially similar to the federal statute nor to be more protective of employee's interests, thus the federal Consumer Credit Protection Act's limitations clearly apply in these states.

Where state garnishment statutes are not substantially similar but contain more stringent provisions, the stricter state laws govern. In other words, the employee is entitled to the greatest protection possible, be it federally or state based. The most common differences between a state's garnishment provision and that of the federal law concerns the maximum amount that may be withheld and the method of computing that maximum amount.

As previously indicated, the federal Consumer Credit Protection Act prohibits the discharge of an employee for the garnishment of any single indebtedness, regardless of the number of levies. The protection is renewed with each new employer. Still, the act seeks to protect the employer from the unreasonable inconvenience of reacting to multiple garnishments. Nonetheless, the wage and hour administrator has stated that an employee's discharge by an employer because of the garnishment of two distinct debts separated with a considerable time interval would be unlawful.

Discharge of an employee in violation of the Consumer Credit Protection Act may result in a criminal penalty of $1,000, one year in prison, or both. The act further provides that no court or state may make, enforce, or execute any process in violation of the federal restrictions.

Whether a creditor of an employee has the legal right to garnish an employee's wages and, if he does, what procedures it must follow are matters controlled principally by state law. The applicable regulations vary considerably from state to state.

Wage assignments which typically result from contractual agreements between the employee and creditor are not covered or proscribed by the federal act. An explicit federal credit practices rule, which places limitations on consensual agreements relating to wage assignments, however, became effective in 1985.[40]

The Department of Labor has ruled that a wage assignment is subject, more-over, to the Title III restrictions, provided it is enforced through a court order that directs the employer to withhold wages or that imposes liability on an employer for its failure to withhold the wages.

In 1969, the United States Supreme Court, in *Sniadach v. Family Finance Co.*, held that a prejudgment garnishment of an employee's wages by court order is subject to the due process mandates of the federal Constitution, thereby requiring prior notice to the debtor and a judicial hearing before any such court order could be issued, state statutory provisions to the contrary notwithstanding.[41] The Supreme Court commented that wages are a specialized type of property and deserve greater protection from overbearing creditors. Although creditors, as a result of *Sniadach*, cannot in most cases judicially enforce ex parte (without the debtor's presence in court) their claims through a court-ordered garnishment prior to judgment, they can do so through available court processes affording due process after receiving a favorable judgment. Moreover, a creditor at the time the debt arose may have extracted from the debtor a consensual wage assignment authorizing the debtor's employer to withhold part of the employee's wages for the creditor's benefit in the event the debtor defaults in repayment of the debt. Such a wage assignment generally is permissible under the law.

As to enforcement of the Title III protections, courts are divided on whether an individual has a right of action for an alleged employer violation, for example, for having been discharged because his wages had been garnished on account of a single debt. One United States court of appeals (the Ninth Circuit in the West Coast region), has held that the discharged employee can sue. Other courts, however, have held that only the Department of Labor has the standing to enforce the Title III provisions. Either way, an employer faces penalties for noncompliance with Title III's mandates.

WRONGFUL DISMISSALS

An employment of indefinite duration, terminable by either the employee or the employer at any time, is denoted an employment-at-will. Although this status traditionally has been the characteristic, legal relationship between an employer and its employees, the principle is being eroded by courts and legislatures. In the nineteenth century, if an employer chose to discharge an at-will employee, generally no cause for the discharge was required under any theory or rule of law. This is less true today. The initial erosion of the employment-at-will legal status began with various civil service protections afforded federal employees in 1912.[42] Subsequently, employees represented by trade unions began to demand and receive employment security, particularly under provisions of collective bargaining agreements as validated and protected by the federal labor laws. Next, members of specified classes of employees subjected to unlawful discriminatory practices received protection under federal antidiscrimination laws, especially from their removal or discharge without cause.[43] Finally, in the late 1950s, further protection against wrongful dismissal began to be recognized in certain state courts, which held that an implied contract obligation existed requiring an employer to act in good faith in dealing with his employees.[44]

Erosion of the at-will concept continued to expand in the 1970s and 1980s under a relatively recent tort theory known as wrongful dismissal. Presently, judicially recognized restrictions are recognized and imposed in several states on employers' freedom to discharge their employees. Thus, a former employee may have the right under state law to file suit for what he or she claims to have been a wrongful or unjust discharge. Causes of action based in tort or contract for wrongful dismissal were recognized in the mid–1980s in Alaska, California, Colorado, Connecticut, Florida, Hawaii, Idaho, Illinois, Indiana, Kansas, Kentucky, Maryland, Massachusetts, Michigan, Minnesota, Montana, Nebraska, New Hampshire, New Jersey, New York, Oklahoma, Oregon, Pennsylvania, South Dakota, Virginia, Washington, West Virginia, and Wisconsin.[45]

The states following the employment-at-will rule were Alabama, Arkansas, Delaware, the District of Columbia, Georgia, Iowa, Louisiana, Maine, Mississippi, Nebraska, New Mexico, North Carolina, North Dakota, Ohio, Rhode Island, South Carolina, Tennessee, Texas, Utah, and Vermont.

Regardless of whether state law recognizes the employment-at-will notion or not, all employees are protected by federal statute from dismissal for defined characteristics or specific conduct under Title VII of the Civil Rights Act of 1964 or the Age Discrimination in Employment Act of 1967, together with the enforcement guidelines issued by the Equal Employment Opportunity Commission.[46] Many states have statutes affording substantially similar protections to employees from certain discriminatory actions including discharges.

In the states that recognize the tort of wrongful dismissal, an action arises if an employer dismisses an employee following the employer's prior verbal statements or promises of employment tenure. Such tenure or job security may also be implied from the employer's conduct. For example, implied tenure arose in one case where an employer gave an employee raises and promotions for thirteen years based on his job performance. The employer then fired the employee so the latter would not gain a vested interest in the company pension plan, which provided for vesting of benefits upon fifteen years' service. The court found an implied promise by the employer to continue the employee in his job without a legitimate, job-related reason for termination. The court stated that an implied obligation of good faith and fair dealing exists in employments-at-will relationships as well as in negotiated employment contracts.[47]

Other courts also have held that, if an employer acts in violation of a good faith relationship with an employee or in violation of some specific public policy, an action for wrongful dismissal arises. In *Monge v. Beebe Rubber Company*, the plaintiff employee was promised a promotion by a foreman if she would be "nice" to him.[48] When the employee refused the foreman's advances, she was demoted to a janitorial position and was subjected to verbal harassment by the foreman. When she was out of work in the hospital, the company terminated her employment for failing to call in sick. The court upheld the employee's wrongful termination suit, stating that the employer was not free to discharge the employee if the termination was based on malice or retaliation.

When an employer fires an employee for the employee's refusal to commit an unlawful act in the course of employment, the termination is violative of public policy. For example, in *Parliss v. First National Bank in Fairmont*, an employee was terminated in violation of public policy when his employer discharged him for attempting to comply fully with federal and state consumer credit laws.[49]

A particularly strong case of wrongful termination can be made if a discharged employee establishes that his or her former employee breached a promise contained in a policy statement or employee handbook. In one case, an employer made a company policy statement in an employee handbook supporting community involvement and encouraging employee community participation. When an employee informed a supervisor of a jury summons requiring one month of duty, the employee was told the one-month period was too long and to get out of serving. The employee was successful in reducing the time period to two weeks, but she told the court she wanted to serve on a jury. When the employer learned of her remark, she was fired. The court held that the employer had breached its promised support of employee civic involvement and also had breached public policy by its discharge.[50]

The growth and momentum of wrongful dismissal suits supports the conclusion that an employee who is dismissed and goes to court to challenge the dismissal will be given an opportunity to rebut the employment-at-will argument. Tort and contract theories available to the former employee in reference to a claim of wrongful dismissal are well established and increasingly utilized by courts. Still, judges in these cases attempt to balance both employee and employer interests.

To minimize potential liability for wrongful discharge, employers are advised to place in their employee personnel files all instances of unsatisfactory performance as soon as possible after they occur. This should be done even in the case of model employees since difficulties could arise in the future. In such a situation, a record of job infractions and unsatisfactory work may be necessary to defend a wrongful dismissal action. Employers, of course, should never fabricate claimed job inadequacies. For one thing, a possible libel or slander action might result. More importantly, it is unethical.

Also, an employer should be cautious in making promises having possible job security implications. If a dismissal procedure has been established, it should be followed exactly. The alternative is to face a possible breach of contract or a wrongful dismissal action. Any established grievance procedure also should be exactly adhered to. Short cuts may lead to a court- or arbitrator-ordered reinstatement of a dismissed employee.

To further minimize liability for wrongful dismissal, an employer should establish clear termination procedures and make them known to all employees. An employer should also review employee handbooks or company policies and delete any statements that could be interpreted as promises of job tenure. In addition, employers should consider establishing and publishing progressive disciplinary procedures for employees who violate employment rules. Above all, an employer should always attempt to be fair and reasonable in dealing with its employees. Such a concerned approach to employee relations establishes good faith. To this end, employers also should consistently follow the Equal Employment Opportunity Commission's employment guidelines, set out in volume 29, Code of Federal Regulations.[51]

In summary, both courts and legislatures are expanding employees' rights in reference to their employment security as the at-will rule is being replaced in many states by an implied promise of good faith and fair dealing.

EMPLOYMENT DISCRIMINATION

Title VII and EEOC Procedure

The most important statutory framework dealing with employment discrimination is Title VII of the Civil Rights Act of 1964.[52] Although not all businesses come under Title VII or the other federal employment statutes, many state legislatures have enacted substantially similar antidiscrimination employment laws to cover employees not protected by the federal law.[53]

Title VII prohibits employment discrimination based on race, color, sex, religion, or national origin. Under Title VII, it is unlawful to refuse to hire, to fire, or to discriminate against an individual as to wages or conditions of employment based on that person's race, color, sex, or national origin. It is also unlawful to segregate or classify employees or job applicants in a way that limits their career opportunities based on any of the protected classifications.

To come under Title VII, an employer must be engaged in a business affecting commerce who has fifteen or more employees for each working day in twenty or more weeks in the current or immediately preceding year. The weeks need not be consecutive. The employer can be an individual, partnership, profit or not-for-profit corporation, trust, or union. Exempted employers are the United States government, political subdivisions of the United States government, American Indian tribes, governmental agencies within the District of Columbia, and certain tax-exempt private clubs. Foreign employers doing business in the United States are included under Title VII to the extent that their business activities take place within the United States. State and local governments and private educational institutions are also included under the Title VII antidiscrimination mandates.

When formulating hiring criteria, the employer must determine whether any of the qualifications might eliminate certain of the protected classes of applicants and thereby trigger a potential Title VII discrimination problem. An intention to discriminate is not required for a Title VII violation.

This does not mean that hiring criteria must never impact a protected class. An employment qualification that adversely impacts a protected class must be necessary for the job's performance if that qualification is to be held to be nondiscriminatory. This is called the Bona Fide Occupational Qualification Requirement (BFOQ)[54] and is a valid employer defense to a discrimination claim. The BFOQ must be reasonably necessary to the normal operation of the business. Moreover, the burden is on the employer to establish its necessity. The test seeks to ascertain whether the job requires that the employee be of one sex, national origin, age group, or religion and, if so, whether such a requirement is necessary to the employer's business.

For example, requiring a high school diploma to be a janitor is a qualification that is not reasonably related to job performance and necessary to the employer's operation of business.[55] However, a church employer may require that its minister be of a certain faith,[56] and an employer may exclude an individual from employment for failure to meet applicable security requirements.[57] Females may be excluded from prison guard positions in a violent maximum security male prison.[58] Nonpregnancy has been found to be a valid BFOQ for flight attendants.[59]

Race Discrimination

Most employment discrimination cases are filed under claims of race or color discrimination. When an employer is sued on charges of racial discrimination in an employment decision, the issue is whether the discharge, nonpromotion, or employment rejection would have occurred had the employee been of a different race or color. This is referred to as disparate impact or disparate treatment.[60] The minority applicant, employee, or former employee will attempt to prove that he or she was qualified to perform the job but was denied the opportunity on account of his or her race or color. The employer may attempt to prove that it did not hire, promote, or retain the employee for a legitimate, nondiscriminatory reason. The permissible reasons, for example, may be excessive absenteeism or a lack of qualifications. The employee must then prove that the employer's stated reasons were merely a pretext for the discriminatory hiring, firing, or promotion. Courts often consider that the best evidence of discrimination or lack thereof is the employer's past action in comparable situations. Job statistics are frequently used in this regard in an attempt to establish a discriminatory pattern.

The Title VII prohibition against race discrimination includes supporting affirmative action programs to increase black employment opportunities.[61] It also includes giving preferential treatment to American Indians by employers on or near reservations. Employment discrimination against these racial groups is prohibited under Title VII.[62] Race or color cannot be a bona fide occupational qualification.

National Origin Discrimination

Title VII also prohibits discrimination based on national origin, but not based on alienage or citizenship. National origin refers to the country of birth of a person.[63] While discrimination against aliens is not a violation of Title VII, an employer cannot discriminate on the basis of origins of citizenship. National origin discrimination is not a citizenship requirement. It is a denial of employment because of a person's place of birth or because the person has physical characteristics associated with national origin. Similarly, a language qualification cannot be used to disqualify a person from employment unless the job performance requires fluency in a certain language.

Courts approach national origin discrimination in the same way they analyze race cases. The burden of proof and preferred statistical evidence used are similar to those used in the racial and national origin cases.

Sex Discrimination

Title VII prohibits sex discrimination. The courts have interpreted sex to mean gender and not sexual preferences or practices.[64] Sex also includes pregnancy and childbirth, and Title VII requires that these conditions be treated in the same manner as other disabilities affecting ability to work. Any medical plans provided by an employer must treat pregnancy and childbirth under those plans in the same fashion as other medical conditions and disabilities.[65] An employer is not required to provide a health plan for employees but if one is provided, pregnancy must be treated as other similar temporary disabilities.

Height and weight requirements must be related to the performance of the job. If such a restriction is not necessary to perform the normal tasks of the position, then it is discriminatory. Many height and weight requirements have been dropped by employers because they were determined to be sexually discriminatory.[66]

Although discrimination against homosexuals is not included in the protections of Title VII, certain state statutes and city or county ordinances prohibit discrimination against persons because of their sexual preference.[67] If no state statute or other local law exists prohibiting such discrimination, an employer may use the sexual preference factor in its hiring decisions.

Subsequent to a 1978 amendment, Title VII forbids disqualifying a woman for employment for pregnancy, unless danger would result to the woman or fetus from the employment.[68] The prohibitions against sex discrimination have fostered extensive litigation in recent years regarding hiring, promotion, and discharge. The sex discrimination issues are similar to the issues found in the race and color cases. The most controversial of the recent sex discrimination cases involve charges of sexual harassment in the workplace.

Sexual Harassment

When a supervisor of one sex demands or requests sexual favors from an employee of the opposite sex, a Title VII violation has occurred if the request is viewed as a term or condition of employment and the person making the request is acting with actual or constructive authority over the employer, according to the U.S. Supreme Court.[69] By constructive authority is meant authority inferred or assumed to have been given by the employer because of the grant of authority inherent in a supervisory position. For example, when a foreman tells an employee to do something, it is an instruction given with the constructive authority of the employer. In other words, it is as if the employer were giving the order to the employee. Thus, when a supervisor demands sexual favors or harasses an employee, the employer becomes liable for the supervisor's conduct. If the employer is unaware of the sexual harassment, certain courts have held that the conduct cannot be imputed to the employer. If the employer becomes aware of the misconduct and does not take immediate corrective steps, the employer is liable. Even when the employer is unaware of the sexual harassment, if the harassing employee has supervisory power and makes employment decisions, the employer may be liable.

Two federal agencies are actively involved in sexual harassment cases—the Office of Federal Contract Compliance Programs (OFCCP) and the Equal Employment Opportunity Commission. OFCCP, which is within the Department of Labor, derives its authority from Executive Order 11246 issued by President Johnson in 1965 (amended by E.O. 11375 in 1967 to include sex as a prohibited discriminatory basis).[70] The OFCCP regulates government contractors.[71] The regulations provide that it is a violation of the executive order for a supervisor to take any personnel action because of an employee's participation or refusal of participation in sexual acts with a supervisor or co-worker and for an employer not to take corrective action to deal with such situations that it knows about or should have known about.

Under Title VII, employers can be held liable for sexual harassment acts that occur within the scope of employment. The relevant EEOC regulations went into effect on April 1, 1980.[72] The agency's guidelines define sexual harassment as "unwelcome sexual advances, requests for sexual favors, and other verbal or physical conduct of a sexual nature."[73] If this conduct adversely affects the individual's employment status, it becomes actionable. Under the EEOC's regulatory approach, liability is not limited to acts that directly affect a term or condition of employment. Included are acts that create "an intimidating, hostile, or offensive working environment." According to the EEOC guidelines, the employer has "an affirmative duty to maintain a workplace free of sexual harassment and intimidation." Under the corresponding EEOC regulations, if it is shown that an employee was forced to resign to avoid "an intimidating, hostile or offensive working environment," a Title VII action may be instituted.

The EEOC guidelines also point to liability on the employer for discriminatory acts of supervisors, regardless of the employer's knowledge of the acts or any antiharassment policy in place at the time.[74] The guidelines also suggest that employers will be liable for nonsupervisory employee conduct. If the employer shows that when it became aware of the sexual harassment by a nonsupervisory employee it took immediate corrective steps, it may avoid liability. Also, under the EEOC regulations, an employer may be held liable for acts of sexual harassment by nonemployees if the acts occur on the employer's business property and if the employer should have known of the conduct or did know of it and failed to take immediate corrective action.

To avoid liability based on sexual harassment claims, the EEOC recommends that companies institute prevention programs. It is suggested that these programs incorporate an antiharassment policy statement which includes specific disciplinary consequences for violations, an internal system of reporting harassments, and prompt actions to correct any alleged misconduct through investigation and disciplinary actions.

Religious Discrimination

Employment discrimination based on religion is prohibited by Title VII. It is unlawful on the basis of religion to refuse to hire a person because of clothing or appearance required by their religion.[75] Also, it is unlawful discrimination to discharge a person from employment because of a refusal to work on his or her day of worship. If an employer cannot reasonably accommodate an employee's or applicant's religious practice without undue business hardship, this fact can be a defense to a discrimination claim.

Only religious institutions (including religious affiliated schools, colleges, and universities) may use a person's religion in a hiring decision. Employers generally should not discuss religious beliefs with job applicants. Even an atheist is protected from job discrimination because of his or her lack of religious belief.

The issues and analysis used by the courts in this area are similar to those used in the race and sex cases. The religious discrimination cases usually fall under the disparate treatment category. Thus, the evidence will often consist of statistics of comparative treatment of employees of different religions.

Age

The Age Discrimination Act prohibits the discharge or discriminatory treatment of an employee age 40 to 70 because of the employee's age.[76] EEOC procedures of enforcement are similar to those under Title VII. They require, first, a complaint or claim by the employee against the employer, followed by resolution efforts through conference and negotiation, and, as a final resort, a lawsuit in federal court filed by either the EEOC or the employee.

The issues and analysis are similar to the other protected classes, and the remedies include reinstatement, back pay, attorney's fees, and an additional amount equal to the back pay if the employer's action was a willful violation taken by the employer with a discriminatory result in mind.

In age discrimination cases, the employee must show he or she is within the protected age range of 40 to 70 and must give evidence to establish his or her qualifications for the job. The employer must establish that the personnel action was based on a factor other than age. The employee then must show that the employer's stated reason was a pretext for age discrimination.

Handicap Discrimination

Recent state and federal regulations have prohibited employment discrimination against handicapped persons.[77] Litigation regarding personnel actions against handicapped employees is increasing. Though the handicapped employee has not been protected under Title VII, the Vocational Rehabilitative Act of 1973 is an affirmative action program for government contractors to hire qualified handicapped individuals.[78] This statute also prohibits discrimination against a qualified handicapped person under any federally assisted program.

The main issue raised in handicap discrimination cases is whether the handicap is protected under the law. The Rehabilitative Act defines a handicapped person as someone who "has a physical or mental impairment which substantially limits one or more major life activities." This broad definition encompasses impairments such as alcoholism, epilepsy, arthritis, a heart condition, and even a chronic back condition.

The covered employer should avoid terminating an employee or refusing to hire or promote an employee solely because the employee is handicapped. The qualifications of the employee to do the work are what the employer must rely on in making personnel decisions regarding handicapped employees. If the employer can reasonably accommodate the employee's handicap, provided it does not affect the employee's ability to perform the job, then the handicap may not be a factor in the employer's personnel decision. An employer may not limit the handicapped person's job opportunity in an area unaffected by the handicap. Generally, the statutes provide that if the handicapped person is qualified to perform the job, he or she should not be excluded because of the handicap.

Discriminatory Employment Qualifications

Requiring an educational degree for employment can have an adverse impact on a protected group. Before requiring a degree as an employment qualification, the employer should apply the Bona Fide Occupational Qualification test.[79] If not filling a professional position, an employer should state that a degree is preferred but not required.

When interviewing and screening job applications, an employer must maintain an equal employment opportunity. Although an employer may consider the applicant's experience, it may not use an experience criterion to eliminate protected classes. If the experience is essential to performance of the position applied for, the employer may use this factor in its employee selection.

An employer may not advertise any sex, race, color, religion, or national origin preference or limitation in a job notice. If a BFOQ exception exists, only then may such a preference be stated by the employer. Neither race nor color can be used as a BFOQ exception in any job notice.

While an employer may conduct background investigations of applicants, it may not eliminate an applicant from consideration simply because of negative information. Rather, the adverse information should be evaluated as to its potential effect on the applicant's job performance. For example, a criminal conviction might sufficiently impact an applicant's qualifications to disqualify that individual if the position is one involving a high degree of trust and responsibility, but it would not be sufficient to automatically eliminate the applicant from consideration for a job less fiduciary in nature.

The disqualification of an applicant based on a poor credit report is discriminatory unless it is directly job related. However, an employer may use an employee's false statements on his or her application as a basis for disqualification.

The employment application should not request religious, race, color, national origin, or political affiliations. Even if known, this information may not be used in the consideration of applicants for a position. Nor should photographs be requested on the applications.

Additionally, any preemployment tests that discriminate against protected classes and are not directly job related are proscribed. Thus, language barriers in tests given to persons whose language has nothing to do with job fitness are discriminatory.

Polygraph tests are widely used in employment screening; however, their credibility is seriously questioned. Before incorporating a polygraph test into an employment screening procedure, local regulations regarding the use of the test should be checked. In any event, employers are advised not to ask personal questions in a polygraph test unless directly job related. Also, written permission should be obtained from the applicant prior to taking the test.

Finally, Title VII protects employees from retaliation by employers for filing a charge, testifying, or participating in any manner in a Title VII investigation or proceeding conducted by the EEOC.

Equal Employment Opportunity Commission Procedure

Section 705 of the Civil Rights Act of 1964 established the EEOC.[80] Its initial purpose was to administer and enforce Title VII. Since 1979, however, the EEOC also has enforcement responsibility for the Age Discrimination in Employment Act[81] and the Equal Pay Act.[82]

Before an employee may file a court action based on an employment discrimination complaint under Title VII, the employee must first file a claim with the EEOC or with a state or local equal opportunity employment agency. Discrimination claims must be filed within 180 days of the alleged incident. The EEOC will then notify the employee of the complaint and the alleged unlawful employment practice. This action must take place within ten days after the claim is filed with the EEOC.

If there is a state agency that administers a state law prohibiting the alleged act, then the complaint must first be filed with that agency. The state agency has 60 days to settle the matter before a claim can be filed with the EEOC. If the complaint is first filed with the EEOC, the EEOC will forward the complaint to the existing state or local agency and wait 60 days before taking action on the complaint.

If no resolution has been reached in 60 days, the EEOC then asserts jurisdiction. Once the EEOC asserts its jurisdiction, the initial step is an informal conference between the employee and the employer. The EEOC objective at this stage is settlement without liability. If, however, no resolution is reached at the conference and if, as a result, the EEOC decides that there may be some substance to the complaint, then the EEOC will begin an investigation to determine if there is reasonable cause to believe that a Title VII violation has occurred. Upon completion of its investigation, if the EEOC decides no reasonable cause exists, it will notify the complaining employee and will take no further action.

The complaining employee may still file a suit in federal court within 90 days of receiving notice from the EEOC of no further action. This notice is called the "right-to-sue" letter because it gives the employee permission to pursue the matter in court.[83] The EEOC must make a determination as to reasonable cause within 120 days from the filing of the employee's complaint.

If the EEOC determines that reasonable cause exists that an unlawful employment practice has occurred, it must first try to settle the matter through conference and negotiation. If during its investigation the EEOC determines that other parties should be added to the complaint, it may add them in its discretion.

If the matter is not resolved by conference and negotiation, then the EEOC may file a lawsuit against the employer and any other parties added during the investigation. If the EEOC decides not to file a suit, the complaining employee is notified and receives a right-to-sue letter. The employee may then file a suit within 90 days of notification. If the EEOC has had a complaint for 180 days, the complaining party may request a right-to-sue letter and file suit even if the EEOC investigation is not complete.

If the employee is successful in his or her suit against the employer, the court may order the employer to stop the unlawful employment practice and to take appropriate corrective action, including an order to reinstate or promote the employee with or without back pay. Courts have broad powers to correct discriminatory employment practices.

The EEOC has published detailed guidelines regarding lawful and unlawful conduct under Title VII.[84] Courts have held that these EEOC guidelines are not binding on employers but constitute the EEOC's opinion on lawful and unlawful conduct under Title VII. The United States Supreme Court has stated, however, that the EEOC guidelines are to be given great deference.[85] Thus, if an employer follows the guidelines, he can reasonably argue good faith and nondiscriminatory employment practices. If in doubt as to an employment practice, an employer may request an opinion letter from the EEOC. The request should be written, signed by the person making the request, and addressed to the EEOC Chairperson, 2401 E Street, N.W., Washington, D.C., 20506. The request should contain a statement of all relevant facts and a statement of the employer's reasons why the EEOC opinion should be given.

Record Keeping Requirements

An employer subject to Title VII must make and retain all records and reports that are relevant to the determination of whether or not an unlawful employment practice has been committed as prescribed by the EEOC Regulations.[86] The EEOC consults with other state and federal agencies in coordinating requirements of record keeping.[87] Thus, record-keeping requirements under equal opportunity laws tend to overlap. For a full discussion of the EEOC record-keeping requirements, see Chapter 19.

NOTES

1. 29 U.S.C. §§ 201, *et seq.*
2. 42 U.S.C. §§ 2000e, *et seq.*
3. 29 U.S.C. §§ 301, *et seq.*
4. 29 U.S.C. §§ 1001, *et seq.*
5. 15 U.S.C. §§ 1601, *et seq.*
6. 29 U.S.C. §§ 651, *et seq.*
7. 29 U.S.C. §§ 151, *et seq.*
8. National Labor Relations Board v. Jones & Laughlin Steel Corp., 301 U.S. 1 (1937).
9. 29 U.S.C. §§ 141–197.
10. 29 U.S.C. §§ 401, *et seq.*
11. 45 U.S.C. §§ 151, *et seq.*
12. 29 U.S.C. §§ 101–115.
13. J.I. Case Co. v. NLRB, 321 U.S. 332 (1944).
14. 29 U.S.C. § 158 (a) (3).
15. 29 U.S.C. § 158 (a) (1); Gissel Packing Co. v. NLRB, 395 U.S. 575 (1969).
16. 29 U.S.C. §§ 8 (a) (5) and 8 (b) (3).
17. NLRB v. Wooster Div. of Borg-Warner Corp., 356 U.S. 342 (1958).
18. 29 U.S.C. § 158 (a) (5); American Ship Building Co. v. NLRB, 380 U.S. 300 (1965). *See also,* NLRB v. Katz, 369 U.S. 736 (1962).
19. Electrical Workers (IUE) v. NLRB (Tiidee Products), 426 F.2d 1243 (D.C. Cir. 1969), *cert. denied,* 400 U.S. 959 (1970), *md'd,* 194 NLRB 1234 (1972), *md'd,* 502 F.2d 349 (D.C. Cir. 1974), *cert. denied,* 421 U.S. 991 (1975). *Contra,* Culinary Alliance & Bartenders Union Local 703 v. NLRB, 488 F.2d 664 (9th Cir. 1973), *cert. denied,* 417 U.S. 946 (1974).
20. 29 U.S.C. §§ 201–219.
21. 41 U.S.C. §§ 35–45.
22. 40 U.S.C. §§ 276a, *et seq.*
23. 41 U.S.C. §§ 351, *et seq.*
24. 29 U.S.C. § 203 (s).
25. 29 U.S.C. § 206 (a) (1).
26. 29 C.F.R. ch. V, parts 549 and 547.
27. 29 U.S.C. § 212.
28. 29 C.F.R. ch. V, part 570, subpart E.
29. 29 C.F.R. ch. V, part 570, subparts A and B.
30. Pub. L. No. 88–38, 77 Stat. 56. *See also,* 42 U.S.C. § 2000e.
31. 42 U.S.C. § 2000e, Title VII Civil Rights Act of 1964.
32. 29 U.S.C. § 213.
33. 29 C.F.R. ch. V, part 516.
34. 29 U.S.C. § 216.
35. Satterwhite v. United Parcel Service, Inc., 496 F.2d 488 (10th Cir. 1974).
36. 29 U.S.C. § 216.

37. Pub. L. No. 90–321, as amended, 15 U.S.C. §§ 1671, *et. seq.*

38. 15 U.S.C. § 1672.

39. 15 U.S.C. § 1673.

40. 16 C.F.R. § 444.2 (a) (3).

41. 395 U.S. 337 (1969).

42. The Lloyd-LaFollette Act of 1912.

43. Unemployment Relief Act (1933), 48 Stat. 22, 23; Executive Order 8587, 5 Fed. Reg. 4445 (1940); Ramspeck Act, 54 Stat. 1211 (1940).

44. Peterman v. Teamsters, 174 Cal. App. 2d 184, 344 P.2d 25 (1959).

45. Henry H. Perritt, *Employee Dismissal Law and Practice*. Wiley Law Publications (1984), p. 18.

46. 42 U.S.C. §§ 2000e, *et seq.*; Age Discrimination in Employment Act, 81 Stat. 602 (1967), 29 U.S.C. § 621. *See also*, Uniform Guidelines of the Equal Employment Opportunity Commission, 29 C.F.R. subpart 1607.

47. Savodnik v. Korvettes, Inc., 488 F.Supp. 822 (E.D.N.Y. 1980).

48. 316 A.2d 549 (N.H. 1974).

49. 246 S.E.2d 270 (1978).

50. Nees v. Hocks, 536 P.2d 512 (1975).

51. 29 C.F.R. subpart 1607.

52. 42 U.S.C. §§ 2000e, *et seq.*

53. *See, e.g.*, New York Human Rights Law (1945). A comprehensive discussion of state fair employment laws can be found in *Fair Employment Practices (F.E.P.) Manual 8A, Labor Relations Reporter*.

54. Title VII of the Civil Rights Act of 1964 Section 703 (e) (1). *See also*, Griggs v. Duke Power Co., 401 U.S. 424 (1971).

55. Donnell v. General Motors Corp., 576 F.2d 1292 (8th Cir. 1975).

56. 42 U.S.C. § 200e–2 (e) (2).

57. 42 U.S.C. § 200e–2 (g).

58. Dothard v. Rawlinson, 433 U.S. 321 (1977).

59. Condit v. United Air Lines, Inc., 558 F.2d 1176 (4th Cir. 1977).

60. 29 C.F.R. § 1607.16 (1978). *See also*, Griggs v. Duke Power Co., 401 U.S. 424 (1971); McDonald v. Santa Fe Trail Transportation Co., 427 U.S. 273 (1976); and McDonnell Douglas Corp. v. Green, 411 U.S. 792 (1973).

61. *See*, EEOC Affirmative Action Guidelines, 29 C.F.R. § 1608.1 (1978). *See also*, United Steelworkers of America v. Weber, 443 U.S. 193 (1979).

62. Title VII of the Civil Rights Act of 1964, Section 703 (a) (1).

63. National origin is not defined in Title VII or in the EEOC Guidelines; however, in the EEOC Guidelines on Discrimination Because of National Origin, 29 C.F.R. subpart 1606 (b), national origin is referred to as a circumstance in which English is not the "mother tongue" of a person discriminated against.

64. *See, e.g.*, Sommers v. Budget Marketing, Inc., 667 F.2d 748 (8th Cir. 1982); and Smith v. Liberty Mutual Ins. Co., 569 F.2d 325 (5th Cir. 1978).

65. 42 U.S.C. § 2000k, 29 C.F.R. subpart 1604.10 (b).

66. *See, e.g.*, Blake v. Los Angeles, 595 F.2d 1367 (9th Cir. 1979), where the minimum height requirement for employees was found to be discriminatory. Compare Dothard v. Rawlinson, 433 U.S. 321 (1977).

67. *See generally*, Siniscalco, *Homosexual Discrimination in Employment*, 16 Santa Clara L. Rev. 495 (1976).

68. Pregnancy Discrimination Act of 1978, 92 Stat. 2076 (1978).

69. EEOC Sexual Harassment Guidelines, 29 C.F.R. subpart 1604.11.

70. 3 C.F.R. subpart 169 (1965), as amended, 32 C.F.R. subpart 14303 (1967).

71. *See*, OFCCP's Testing and Selecting Employees by Government Contractors, 41 C.F.R. subpart 60.3 (1971).

72. 45 Fed. Reg. 25,024.

73. 29 C.F.R. subpart 1604.11 (a).

74. 29 C.F.R. subpart 1604.11 (c).

75. EEOC Decision No. 71–1529; EEOC Decision No. 71–2620; EEOC v. Rollins, Inc., 8 F.E.D. 492 (N.D. Ga. 1974).

76. 29 U.S.C. §§ 12 (a), 631 (a).

77. *See, e.g.*, Vocational Rehabilitation Act of 1973, 29 U.S.C. § 701; Department of Labor's Affirmative Action Regulations on Handicapped Workers, 401 *F.E.P. Manual 3021. See also, F.E.P. Manual 8A, Labor Relations Reporter (BNA)*, for list and discussion of state fair employment practices laws.

78. Section 503 of the Vocational Rehabilitation Act of 1973, 29 U.S.C. § 793.

79. *See*, Griggs v. Duke Power Co., 401 U.S. 424 (1971).

80. 42 U.S.C. § 2000e–4 (a).

81. 81 Stat. 602 (1967), 29 U.S.C. § 621.

82. 29 U.S.C. § 206 (d).

83. 29 C.F.R. subpart 1601.25.

84. Equal Employment Opportunity Commission's Uniform Guidelines, 29 C.F.R. subpart 1607 (1978).

85. *See, e.g.*, Griggs v. Duke Power Co., 401 U.S. 424 (1971); Albemarle Paper Co. v. Moody, 422 U.S. 405 (1975).

86. 42 U.S.C. § 2000e–8 (c).

87. 42 U.S.C. § 2000e–8 (d).

16

Employer's Responsibility for Employees' Acts

The relationship between an employer and its employees is one of agency or master-servant. The compilation of rules governing this legal relationship is called the law of agency. An agency relationship is a consensual agreement between two parties, one of which is called the principal and the other the agent. Under the agreement, the agent agrees to represent or act in behalf of the principal. During the relationship, the agent remains subject to the control of the principal. In a master-servant or employment situation, the power of the master or employer extends to control over the means or way in which the servant physically performs his or her duties.

An agency relationship is a fiduciary relationship which is one of trust. It exists where there is a special confidence placed in the agent who in equity and good conscience is bound to act in good faith and with due regard for the interest of the principal. The agent agrees to act primarily for the benefit of the principal and has a duty at all times to obey the principal. The agent may not act adversely to the principal's interest nor in the agent's own behalf or benefit.

An agency relationship is consensual but not necessarily contractual; therefore, the principal does not necessarily have to have the capacity to enter into a contract. Nevertheless, the principal must have the capacity to do the act delegated to the agent to perform. Hence, if the principal lacks capacity to give a legally effective consent, because of insanity or other reason, he or she may not appoint an agent to act for him or her. A corporate principal can act only through an agent; therefore, corporations necessarily must have the capacity to appoint an agent. Corporate officers are agents of the corporation.

On the other hand, almost any person has the capacity to act as an agent in behalf of another, as long as he or she has the physical or mental capability to do the act that has been delegated. However, an agent who lacks capacity may not be subject to the fiduciary duties and liabilities that normally arise from the agency relationship. Corporations may act as agents within the scope of their powers.

A person may be a general or a special agent. A general agent is normally empowered to act in behalf of his or her principal over a period of time during which he or she conducts a number of transactions as agent. A special agent, however, is restricted to more specific acts for a limited duration.

It is not uncommon for an agent to have authority to appoint an agent who may be either an agent of the principal or merely a subagent. In an employment relationship, an agent, who has the power to employ others to perform in behalf of the principal, employs others as agents of the principal. Such persons do not become agents of the agent but owe a fiduciary duty to the principal. Nonetheless, it is possible for an agent to be authorized to appoint his or her own agents to perform the work delegated by the principal. A corporation acting as an agent in behalf of a principal is in this position. Since the corporation can act only through its agents, its agents are not agents of the principal but are subagents of the principal and are directly responsible to the corporate agent. In this case, the subagent is responsible to the appointing agent who, in turn, is responsible to the principal for the conduct of the subagent. The subagent, in effect, is a dual agent of both the principal and the appointing agent and owes a fiduciary duty to both. While either the appointing agent or the principal may terminate the agency relationship with the subagent, only the appointing agent is responsible for compensating the subagent.

A careful distinction must be made between an agency relationship and certain other relationships such as partnership, trusteeship, and corporate directorship. Partners by definition are co-owners of a business carried on for profit. In the general partnership, each partner is a general agent for the partnership which, in turn, makes the partner both agent and principal since the partners are principals as well as agents. A trustee is a fiduciary but not necessarily an agent. A trustee may be an agent, but in a normal trust situation trustees are not subject to beneficiaries' control although they act in behalf of the beneficiaries. Corporate directors are elected by the shareholders of a corporation and are responsible for the management of the corporation. However, once corporate directors are elected, they are not under the control of the shareholders, and fiduciary duties are owed to the corporation not to the shareholders. Moreover, corporate directors are not principals. The corporation is the principal. Corporate employees are agents of the corporation and not the board of directors.

AUTHORITY

An agent's authority may be express, implied, or apparent. The agent's authority is the power to act and must be manifested in some way for the power to exist.

Express Authority

Express authority is derived from some manifestation of authority which flows from the principal to the agent. A unilateral act of the principal is sufficient to create express authority if it reasonably leads the agent to believe that the principal wants or desires the agent to act in his or her behalf. The most straightforward forms of express authority are oral or written forms which manifest the principal's intent to grant authority to the agent. It is not necessary that the agent respond or consent to the principal's unilateral delegation of authority. It is what the principal does that is important. However, certain transactions require a writing to be valid. A statute which requires that the principal personally acknowledge a particular kind of document requires the agent's authorization also to be acknowledged. Certain state statutes of frauds require that an agent's authority be in writing. But, unless required by statute, a written authorization is not required for the execution of a writing.

In interpreting the principal's intention as to the scope of the agent's authority, the agent is authorized to do that which he or she could reasonably believe to be authorized from the manifestation of the principal's intent. The agent is limited by what he or she knows or should know of the principal's desires under all of the attendant circumstances. Moreover, the agent's fiduciary duty requires that he or she not act contrary to the manifested intention of the principal.

If the agent's authority is written, the parol evidence rule applies. In substance, the parol evidence rule assumes that the final written document manifests the complete agreement of the parties; therefore, any other evidence extraneous to that document is not admissible in evidence in interpreting the document. Evidence is admissible, however, to show fraud, mutual mistake, or condition precedent. Of course, evidence is admissible to show any agreement subsequent to the written document which changes or modifies the agent's authority. The parol evidence rule was not designed to preclude evidence of subsequent agreements but only evidence of negotiations or agreements that precede or are contemporaneous with the written document.

Implied Authority

Implied authority is actual authority derived from the principal's words or actions. Implied authority is the power to do those things that are usual and incidental to the actual authority and that are reasonably necessary to accomplish the goal assigned by the principal. In a trade or business context, an agent has implied authority to act in accordance with customs or usages of the trade or business in question provided that the principal is aware of the customs and usages of the trade of business and that they do not expand the scope of the authority of the agent. In case of ambiguity as to the specific instructions of the principal, the principal is liable for any mistakes made by the agent in reasonably interpreting his or her authority. Nonetheless, the agent should not act until he or she has clarified his or her authority with the principal, unless an emergency situation arises requiring immediate action to protect the principal's interests, and the agent is unable to communicate with his or her principal. In an emergency situation, the agent should act in a manner consistent with what the agent could reasonably believe the principal would wish him or her to do.

Apparent Authority

Unlike express or implied authority, where the manifestation of the principal's intent flows from the principal to the agent, in an apparent authority situation, the manifestation of the principal's intent to appoint an agent flows from the principal to a third party and is interpreted from the viewpoint of the third party rather from that of the agent. If the principal leads a third party to believe that an agent has the power to act in behalf of the principal, the agent has apparent authority to bind the principal. Similarly, a principal who places an agent in a position that ordinarily carries with it certain authority is bound when a third party relies upon that manifestation, unless the third party knows the agent not to have such authority. Indeed, the agent need not know of the principal's manifestation of apparent authority to a third party.

Specific Authorizations

In a business context, where an agent is placed in complete control of the principal's property or business, the agent may have express, implied, and apparent authority. The agent may have received express instructions regarding the business or property and may do whatever is reasonable and appropriate to carry out those express instructions giving rise to implied authority. By placing the agent in charge of the principal's property or business, the principal is placing an agent in a position where third parties could reasonably believe that the agent has the authority to act in behalf of the principal. In carrying out his or her duties, the agent in the normal course of business operations may do whatever is usual and necessary to operate the business including entering into contracts; purchasing equipment and supplies; employing, supervising, or discharging employees; offering for sale or selling the principal's product; and receiving and disbursing funds of the business. Generally, an agent has no authority to borrow money or issue negotiable paper. Authority to borrow money on behalf of the principal must be express. Implied authority to borrow money is almost never found by the courts. A similar rule exists for endorsing negotiable instruments. While the authority need not always be express and written, it is not readily implied. When it is implied, it is generally in a situation regarding an endorsement for deposit in the principal's account rather than where the instrument is to be drawn on that account.

A principal may authorize an agent to buy or sell land or goods. Depending upon the attendant circumstances, an authorization to buy may authorize the agent only to find a seller with whom the principal can complete the purchase, or under other circumstances may authorize an agent to execute a contract of purchase. The same is true of an authorization to sell. The agent may be restricted merely to finding a customer. However, the agent may, in fact, be authorized to complete the contract for sale and convey the property. Although an agent may merely have authority to find a purchaser or buyer, the agent generally has the authority to make representations concerning the land or personal property to be sold, to state the principal's terms, and to solicit offers or orders from third parties. Two common examples of this type of authority are the realtor and the outside salesman who is merely an order taker. An agent whose authority extends to completing a contract of purchase has the authority to negotiate the terms of the contract under the usual and customary terms and to execute the contract in writing when required. If the agent's authorization is required by law to be in writing, the third party may hold only the principal liable to the extent of the agent's actual authority. An agent who is authorized to complete a contract for sale is restricted to the terms and conditions fixed by the principal but may make any usual or customary warranties and representations concerning the property. A sales clerk in a department store is an agent authorized to complete a contract for sale.

KNOWLEDGE AND NOTICE

The issue often arises as to when a principal has been given notice or has knowledge of a particular fact, particularly when that knowledge or notice affects the legal relationship between the principal and third parties. In general, a principal has notice of a fact when the agent knows the fact, has reason to know of the fact, has a duty to know the fact, or has been given actual notification.

An agent has reason to know a fact if he or she possesses information from which an ordinary person would infer that the fact existed or that there is a substantial likelihood that the fact exists. Under circumstances in which an agent has a duty to know certain facts, the agent will be held to know those facts if a person of ordinary intelligence would discover the fact in the performance of his or her duty.

The same rules apply to servants, subservants, and subagents provided that they have a duty to report receipt of notice to the principal or the agent who appointed them.

Notifications between principal and agent may be made in any acceptable manner. The most direct form of notification is for one of the parties to tell the other all pertinent information in his or her possession. If notification is made in a writing, the delivery may be made to the other party or to his authorized agent. If the writing is to be delivered to the party's place of business or residence, notification will be effective only when read by that party or after passage of a reasonable amount of time for the party to have read the contents of the message. The mailbox rule is not in effect. Merely posting the letter is not sufficient.

Moreover, if the notice is sent in any manner other than first class mail or its equivalent, the receiver will not be deemed to have knowledge of the contents unless he or she has actually read it.

In notifications given by third parties to an agent who has actual, implied, or apparent authority to receive the notification, the principal has effectively been given notice. Notice given to the agent of an undisclosed principal is effective notice to such principal even if the agent is not authorized to receive such notification. However, notice given to an agent who is no longer authorized to act in behalf of the principal is ineffective.

Only agents who have actual, implied, or apparent authority may give effective notice to third parties. However, the defect may be cured by ratification by the purported principal, and the notice given or received is effective.

It is often important in agency relationships to determine the knowledge of either the principal or the agent and how much of that knowledge should be imputed from one to the other.

In business and professional relationships, persons are normally expected to know what any person of ordinary intelligence and experience engaged in that profession or business would know. A principal is deemed to know the ordinary and customary business usages in the locality in which he conducts the business. Moreover, a principal is expected to know the contents of all communications sent to the place of business. An agent who is a professional or business agent is expected to know the customary and usual business usages associated with that business or profession. If an agent proposes to act in a situation where special knowledge is required, the agent is expected to have the special knowledge required.

Any knowledge acquired by an agent while acting in behalf of the principal is imputed to the principal and will be treated as if the principal had direct knowledge. However, the rights and liabilities of the principal are affected only if the agent has had a reasonable opportunity to communicate the knowledge to the principal. If the agent, through no fault of his or her own, has been unable to communicate the knowledge to the principal, the principal is not liable. A principal may remain liable where an agent has received information but has actually forgotten the information and has not conveyed it to the principal.

Information which an agent should have acquired but did not may not be imputed to the principal unless the principal was under an obligation or duty to others to discover the information. A common example is a master-servant situation wherein the servant fails to discover a defect in the premises or machinery which injures a third party to whom the principal owed a duty of care.

If the principal is required to have personal knowledge or actual knowledge, the failure of the agent to convey such knowledge to the principal will not bind the principal. If the agent receives information that is confidential and privileged, that knowledge is not imputed to the principal.

If the agent intends to commit or commits an unauthorized act or acts in a manner adverse to the interest of his or her principal, the principal is not bound by the agent's knowledge. Similarly, if the agent and third party conspire to conceal information from the principal, the principal is not bound by the agent's knowledge. However, in any situation where the principal receives the benefit of the bargain, the principal is bound by the agent's knowledge, unless he or she received the benefit as a bona fide purchaser for value.

Generally, knowledge is not imputed from a principal to the agent, unless the principal had reason to believe that the knowledge was relevant and that another person might be harmed as a result of his or her failure to inform the agent. But this rule will not apply if the principal did not have an opportunity to convey the information to the agent in sufficient time to prevent the act that caused the harm.

UNDISCLOSED PRINCIPAL

If an agent acting within the scope of his or her authority and in behalf of an undisclosed principal enters into a contract or conveyance, such contract or conveyance may be enforced by or against the undisclosed principal. This rule does not apply to negotiable instruments that the undisclosed principal has not signed and those contracts that specifically exclude an undisclosed principal.

An undisclosed principal is a principal whose existence is not known to the third party. A partially disclosed principal is a principal whose existence is known to the third party but not his or her exact identity. Partially disclosed principals are treated the same as fully disclosed principals since the third party knows of the existence of a principal.

The use of an undisclosed principal is neither illegal nor immoral and may be expedient, particularly in business transactions where knowledge that a particular person or corporation is about to engage in a particular transaction would have the effect of dramatically increasing prices. This is not detrimental to a third party because a third party can protect itself by stating specifically that it will not deal with an agent acting in behalf of an undisclosed principal. If the agent of the undisclosed principal, as a part of the contract, represents that the agent is dealing in his or her own behalf and represents no undisclosed principal, the third party is entitled to rescind the contract when it proves to be false.

The undisclosed principal becomes a party to the contract without consent of the third party, and the undisclosed principal becomes liable if the agent was authorized to act and did indeed act in behalf of the undisclosed principal. However, if the agent did not intend to act in behalf of the undisclosed principal but in behalf of him- or herself or another undisclosed principal, the first undisclosed principal is not liable. An agent who purports to act in behalf of an undisclosed principal and then tries to appropriate the benefits of the contract to his or her own purposes violates his or her fiduciary duty to the principal, and any property acquired will be held under a constructive trust for the benefit of the principal.

In the event of breach of contract or dispute arising out of the contract, both the agent and the undisclosed principal may be held liable by the third party. The agent's liability arises directly out of the agent's promise in the contract whereas the principal's liability arises out of the agency relationship itself. Since either the agent or the undisclosed principal may be held liable under the contract, the third party must make an election as to which of the parties it wishes to hold liable. However, if the third party does not know of the existence of the undisclosed principal, it may proceed against the agent as if the agent were the principal. If the third party to the contract knows of the existence of the undisclosed principal and obtains a judgment against either one, the third party is subsequently barred from bringing suit against the other. The third party is entitled only to one judgment on the contract. But, if the third party obtains a judgment against the agent without knowing of the existence of the undisclosed principal, the third party may subsequently bring a suit against the principal after discovering his or her identity before execution of the judgment against the agent. If the third party knows of the existence of the undisclosed principal, the third party should join both undisclosed principal and agent in the same suit. An election only need be made when one of the parties to the suit moves for an election. The election may be made at any time before the entry of judgment. If the third party elects to recover from the agent, the principal is discharged from liability to the third party, but the agent has a right of indemnity against the principal. Collection of a judgment against the agent will bar any subsequent lawsuit against the undisclosed principal even if the third party was unaware of the existence of the undisclosed principal at the time.

An undisclosed principal is barred from bringing an action against the third party to the contract if the third party has obtained a judgment against the agent and the undisclosed principal actively participated in the action. However, if the undisclosed principal's identity is known, but he or she did not participate in the action, the undisclosed principal is not bound by a judgment for or against the third party. If the identity of the undisclosed principal is not known, a judgment against the agent destroys any claim that the undisclosed principal has against the third party. Should the undisclosed principal bring an action against the third party, the third party may assert all defenses that he or she may have against the agent. This result is equitable because the third party should not be subjected to any greater liability than that which would have been imposed had the agent proceeded against the third party.

Ratification by a principal is not allowed regarding contracts that the agent had no authority to enter into in behalf of the principal and did not purport to act in behalf of the principal. The principal is, however, liable for unjust enrichment as a result of the agent's actions.

Any contract that excludes a particular person as principal or any undisclosed principal is not binding on the third party. This does not mean, however, that an agent may not deny that he or she is acting on behalf of another. Such a representation is not binding. The contract may be enforced against the third party if neither the agent nor the undisclosed principal knows or has reason to know that the third party would not deal with a particular undisclosed principal or any undisclosed principal. However, if the agent knows that the third party would not deal with his or her particular principal, the agent has an affirmative duty to disclose the identity of his or her principal. Failure to do so results in fraud, and the contract may be rescinded by the third party. Similarly, if the agent purports to be acting in behalf of an undisclosed principal but is really acting for him- or herself, the purported agent remains liable on the contract, but the third party has a right to rescind the contract if he or she would be unwilling to deal with the purported agent as principal.

If a principal puts an agent in complete charge of his or her business under conditions where it appears to third parties that the agent is the owner of the business, the principal becomes bound by any transactions entered into by the agent, whether authorized or not, if the transactions are usual, necessary, or customary for that particular business. In such situations, however, the principal's liability is limited to the assets of the business or the benefit actually received. Likewise, a principal who conveys title to his or her property to an agent under conditions that make it appear that the agent is the owner of the property, the property may be conveyed to a bona fide purchaser for value even though the agent's actions were unauthorized. This rule does not apply to situations in which the principal entrusts the agent with possession but not indicia of ownership or title.

An undisclosed principal may not substitute his or her personal services for the performance of the agent. The agent must perform under the contract. In instances in which personal services of the promisor-agent are not required, the principal may substitute his or her own performance under the contract. Likewise, once the identity of the undisclosed principal is known, the third party may be required to render performance, other than personal services, to the principal instead of the agent. If the contract calls for the third party to render performance to the agent, the principal cannot require that the performance be rendered to the principal instead of the agent. A typical example of this prohibition is an attempt by an agent to negotiate a loan on behalf of an undisclosed principal where it appears to the third party that the agent is negotiating the loan for him- or herself. In this case, the third party, who is relying solely on the credit of the agent, is not required to extend the loan to the principal.

The rules regarding satisfaction or performance of the contract follow the law of agency. Payment or performance by the third party to the agent is deemed to be payment to the principal. However, payment from the principal to the agent is not in satisfaction of the principal's obligation to pay the third party. Discharge of the principal's obligation occurs only when the third party actually receives payment. Should the principal pay the agent and instruct the agent to convey payment to the third party but the agent absconds or through negligence fails to pay, the principal is still liable to the third party; however the principal does have a cause of action against the agent.

In case of any dispute that may result in a lawsuit, the statute of limitations begins to run when the cause of action accrues and not when the existence of the undisclosed principal is discovered.

RATIFICATION

Ratification is an after-the-fact affirmation, by word or deed, of a prior unauthorized act or deed purportedly done in behalf of the ratifier. Ratification relates back to the time of the original act or deed. It is treated as if the act or deed had been originally authorized by the ratifier. The ratifier need not have been the principal of the purported agent at the time the act or deed was performed, although clearly a principal may ratify unauthorized acts of the agent performed outside the scope of the agent's authority. Further, the third party need not know that the agent's act was unauthorized. Ratification may be direct or indirect. The ratifier may expressly or directly indicate an intention to treat the act or deed as if authorized or indirectly by conduct that is inconsistent with treating the act as if it were unauthorized. Ratification does not require new consent to the transaction by the third party. Moreover, no new consideration is required by the ratifier nor must any communication that ratification has been accomplished be made to the third party.

There are five requirements for ratification to be effective. First, the act or deed to be ratified must constitute a valid act or deed if it had been authorized at the time that it was executed. Second, the purported principal must be an existing, legally competent person at the time the act was done. This precludes ratification of a promoter's contract or deed by a corporation that was not in existence at the time the promoter executed the contract or performed the deed. Third, the purported agent must have acted in behalf of the individual or person who attempts to ratify it. Fourth, ratification requires the same formalities that would be required for an authorization to execute the contract or perform the act. Fifth, a purported principal may ratify only an act or deed of which he has knowledge of the material facts.

The clearest form of ratification is a direct, express manifestation of the purported principal's consent to the act or agreement. Ratification may be inferred from the purported principal's silence if he or she has knowledge of the unauthorized act. Ratification by silence will be inferred under circumstances such that a reasonable person would be expected to repudiate the act if he or she did not consent. Ratification must be of the whole transaction and not piecemeal. The ratifier must either accept the complete or whole transaction or disaffirm; he or she may not benefit from only part of the transaction and reject other parts more undesirable or burdensome.

Ratification may be accomplished by bringing or defending a lawsuit concerning the transaction. This is true even though the purported principal disclaims any liability for the act. However, any attempt to gain the benefit of the contract by suit while repudiating obligations or liabilities of the contract will fail. The contract has to be accepted in total. A suit on part of a contract will constitute a suit on the whole of the contract.

A purported principal who receives or retains benefits from a purported agent's action will be held to have ratified the act if he or she fails to return the benefits within a reasonable time, unless it is not possible to return the benefits, for example, if they have been consumed or have become an inseparable part of the principal's property. The principal must know that he or she has received the benefits. Ratification takes place only after the purported principal has learned the true state of affairs and refuses to return the benefits.

Ratification is ineffective in certain instances. Until ratification has been accomplished, the transaction is in the form of an offer which the purported principal may reject by not ratifying and which the third party may withdraw until ratified. If the third party, in fact, does withdraw the offer before ratification, ratification is ineffective. Withdrawal will be effective even though the third party does not know that the act was unauthorized. Once ratification is effective, neither the principal nor the third party may withdraw in the absence of fraud or illegality. Death or loss of capacity of the third party will render ratification ineffective if the transaction imposes an affirmative duty upon the third party. If the transaction does not require any affirmative action by the third party, his or her death or loss of capacity will have no effect on ratification. A principal may not ratify where there has been a basic change in material circumstances surrounding the transaction. Where it would be manifestly unfair to the third party to hold him or her liable to the original transaction, ratification is not effective; however, a change of circumstances occurring after ratification does not affect ratification.

Once an act is ratified, it is treated as if it were an authorized act from the beginning. Therefore, liabilities of the parties to the transaction are determined at the time that the unauthorized act was originally performed and not at the time of the subsequent ratification. Moreover, the principal after ratification cannot subject the agent to liability for exceeding his or her authority since the effect of ratification is to transform the unauthorized act into an authorized act.

Since ratification treats the act as if it were originally authorized, the principal succeeds to all of the rights and liabilities arising out of the agent's conduct. If the third party refuses to perform, the principal may bring an action for breach of contract or specific performance.

LIABILITIES

Tort

A tort is defined as a private or civil wrong or injury independent of contract. There are three necessary elements of every tort action: (1) the existence of a legal duty owed from one party to another, (2) breach of that duty, and (3) damage as a proximate result of the breach. Torts include such legal actions as negligence, defamation, slander, interference with a business relation, battery, assault, and trespass.

Liability of Principal

Any person is liable for a tort committed by another which he or she intended, directed, or otherwise caused. Hence, where a principal directs an agent to commit a physical tort or to act negligently, the principal is personally liable for any and all consequences resulting from the directed act. Such liability arises out of the law of tort and not out of the agency relationship. A principal is liable for the conduct of an agent where the conduct was authorized by the principal even though the principal may have been unaware of the tortious result, unless there is an unanticipated change in circumstance which materially alters the intended or expected result.

A principal is directly liable for negligence in directing the manner in which the job is to be performed, hiring someone with dangerous propensities which results in harm, utilizing dangerous premises or instrumentalities, or failing to correct or control the dangerous conduct of others on the premises.

If a person has a duty of due care to protect another, he or she may not relieve him- or herself of that obligation by delegating the duty to another. For example, a landlord cannot satisfy an obligation of due care to tenants by delegating the authority to either an agent or an independent contractor. So that, if the premises degenerate into a dangerous situation for persons in the area or business visitors, the landlord is liable for any harm that occurs. Similarly, certain inherently dangerous activities such as blasting or demolition of a building give rise to strict liability—liability without fault—and the principal or delegator is liable for any harm resulting from the inherently dangerous activity.

A principal will be liable for the torts of an agent if he or she authorized the act, if the agent had apparent authority, or if the agent mistakenly believed that he or she was authorized. Generally, the conduct of the agent must occur while acting in behalf of the principal, and the agent must be subject to the principal's right to control. If either one of these conditions is missing, the principal would not be liable; hence, a principal may be liable for the unauthorized conduct of an agent if the agent was acting in behalf of the principal and was subject to the principal's right of control. The same result would follow if the principal subsequently ratified an unauthorized act of the agent that was purported to be in behalf of the principal. However, a different set of rules applies in a master-servant situation, which is discussed in the next section.

A principal may be liable to a third party even though the agent would not be liable if acting in his or her own behalf. If the agent had a nondelegatable privilege to act or has an immunity from liability arising out of a relationship between the agent and the third party, the agent would escape liability, but the fact that neither the immunity nor the privilege is transferable results in the principal's being held liable.

In the normal situation, both principal and agent would be jointly and severally liable for the tortious conduct of the agent that occurred while the agent was acting in behalf of the principal and was subject to the principal's right of control. Consequently, they both may be joined in a single suit, and a judgment may be obtained against each. However, the judgments may not be inconsistent; for example, a judgment rendered against the principal but in favor of the agent must be set aside unless there is some ground for the principal's liability such as a nondelegatable duty or immunity. Where a judgment is rendered against each, the amount of the compensatory damages must be the same; however, punitive damages may be awarded against the principal in an amount different from that awarded against the agent.

Respondeat Superior

The master-servant relationship is distinguished from a principal-agent relationship by the right of the master to control the means by which the servant physically performs his or her duties. This increase in control gives rise to the doctrine of *respondeat superior*. In exchange for the privilege of controlling the means by which the servant physically performs his or her duties, the master becomes liable for the tortious conduct of the servant while acting within the scope of his or her employment even though the master may be without fault. The doctrine of *respondeat superior* has also been justified under the "deep pocket" theory. Under this theory, the risk of loss sustained by the victim of the tortious conduct is transferred to the party best able to pay for the damage. In a master-servant relationship, the probability is that the servant is judgment proof or unable to pay for the victim's damage; liability then is transferred or imputed to the master whom society assumes does have the capability of paying the damages.

It is important to distinguish between a servant and an independent contractor. An independent contractor by definition is one who is hired to perform a particular task or service, but the employer does not have the right to control the means by which the task is accomplished. In such cases, the employer is not held liable for the tortious conduct of the independent contractor even though the conduct was ostensively performed in behalf of the employer. However, in cases involving inherently dangerous activity, the employer may be held liable for the tortious conduct of the independent contractor. This is so because the employer has a nondelegatable duty of care with respect to inherently dangerous activity.

In determining whether a person is a servant or an independent contractor, the critical element is the right of control whether it is actually exercised or not. Other factors which may be considered in making the determination include whether the employer provides the tools and workplace, the length of time of the employment (customarily an independent contractor is hired on a short-term basis), whether the employee or the independent contractor can be discharged at will, the intent of the parties, and whether the person employed has a particular skill or occupation that is generally considered to be that of an independent contractor since unskilled laborers are most often servants while highly skilled persons and professional persons are almost always independent contractors.

The tortious conduct of a subservant may be imputed to the master if the servant who hired the subservant was authorized to do so or had inherent power to do so. This is true even if the subservant does not know of the existence of the undisclosed master.

The doctrine of apparent authority is also applicable in a master-servant relationship. If a person makes representations to third parties or leads third parties to believe that another person is his or her servant that person may be an apparent servant whose tortious conduct may then be imputed to the master if the third party actually relied on the misrepresentation and was harmed as a result of that reliance.

Allocation of liability among masters arises in situations where a servant is acting for two masters at the same time. Most often, this arises in a loaned servant context. In general, the loaned servant remains in the general employment of the first master; however, if the borrower of the servant has primary right of control when the act is performed, the liability for the tortious conduct of the loaned servant is imputed to the borrower and not to the original master.

The key to imputing liability to the master for tortious conduct of the servant is scope of employment. The servant must be acting within the scope of his or her employment for liability to be imputed to the master. Unfortunately, the term scope of employment is nebulous; however, the activity of the servant must be motivated by an intent to serve the master, and the manner, place, and time during which the activity is performed must not vary substantially from the normal or authorized elements. A servant who is negligent while performing an authorized act is clearly within the scope of his or her employment. The difficulty arises in cases where the servant is performing an unauthorized act or, in fact, has been forbidden by the master to perform a specific act. Generally, if the crime or tort committed by the servant is minor and is reasonably related to the authorized conduct of the servant, the master will be liable. Substantial deviation from the servant's authorized conduct, however, will generally relieve a master of liability for the servant's tortious conduct.

A master may be liable for omissions of the servant as well as commissions of tortious conduct within the scope of the servant's employment. A servant is required to act in accord with the standards of due care and renders the master liable if the servant fails to uphold the standard of due care with resulting harm to a third party.

A troublesome concept in the master-servant relationship is that of frolic. If the servant has left the scope of his or her employment and is off on a frolic of his or her own, the master is not liable because the master no longer has the right of control of the servant. Normally, the master is liable only for the tortious conduct of the servant performed in the authorized workplace during ordinary working hours excluding lunchtime and commuting time from home to work. Obviously, the risk of imputed liability is greatest when servants are authorized to leave the place of employment and conduct the master's business elsewhere. The prime example is the servant who is authorized to operate the master's motor vehicle. A servant who deviates from a specified route or plan for his or her own purposes is no longer within his or her scope of employment. The question of liability arises at the point where the servant reenters his or her employment. Reentry is generally held to be the time at which the employee or servant intends to return to his or her employment and is reasonably close to the authorized route or plan; however, the servant need not return to the place from which he or she deviated from the scope of employment. A servant who merely borrows the master's vehicle for his or her own purposes is not acting within the scope of employment but is acting for his or her own purposes.

If a servant or employee allows a third party to operate a vehicle that the servant or employee is authorized to operate to serve the master, the master is liable for the negligence of the third party if the servant is authorized to transfer control of the vehicle or if such assistance is customarily sought as in an emergency situation and the third party operates the vehicle in behalf of the master. Where the third party operates the motor vehicle for his or her own purposes, the master is not liable for the negligence of the third party even if the servant were authorized to transfer control.

A master is not liable to passengers riding in the vehicle unless the servant is authorized or is apparently authorized to invite riders. If the servant is authorized or has apparent authority, the rider is treated as a guest or as a business visitor if the rider were invited for business purposes.

Liability of Third Party to Principal

A third party may not tortiously interfere with the principal's interest by inducing the agent to breach his or her fiduciary duties to the principal. If a third party does induce an agent to breach his or her fiduciary duties, the third party is jointly liable with the agent for any secret profits made as well as damages for tortious interference with the contractual relation between the agent and the principal. Likewise, it is tortious interference with the interests of the principal for a third party to employ another person's agent in a transaction adverse to the agent's first principal. Dual agency generally is a breach of duty by the agent unless the principal has knowledge of the agent's dual employment and agrees to it.

A third party may be liable for tortious interference with the principal's interests even in situations where an agent has no authority or in fact is not an agent unless the principal is responsible for apparent authority.

A principal may bring an action in deceit against a third party who is responsible for fraudulently inducing an agent to enter into a contract or unknowingly breach his or her fiduciary duty to a principal. Likewise, fraud perpetuated on the principal, which results in authorizing an agent to enter into a contract with a third party, is actionable.

Liability of Agent to Third Party

In general, neither the liability of the principal for the tortious conduct of an agent nor the doctrine of *respondeat superior* will relieve the agent-servant tortfeasor from liability to the third party. In certain cases, the agent may not have possessed the required state of mind him- or herself and is not liable for the tort. It is no defense by the agent that he or she was ordered by the principal or master to commit the tort even if the order took the form of physical or economic coercion by the principal. An agent or servant may interject any defenses that the principal may have that are delegatable; however, since most defenses or immunities are personal they are nondelegatable.

An agent or servant is not liable for negligence when a tool or instrumentality provided by the principal or master is defective and causes injury to a third party, unless the agent or servant knows or has reason to know of the defect. In this case, knowledge of the principal is not imputed to the agent. Where an agent is in complete control of the principal's land or chattels, he or she is liable for any harm caused to third parties arising out of the condition of the land or the chattels.

Where principal-agent or master-servant are joint tortfeasors they may be joined in a single action, and a separate judgment may be obtained against each. However, the judgments must be consistent in an action based solely on the agent's conduct. If not, one or the other of the judgments must be erroneous and must be corrected.

Contracts

Liability of Principal to Third Party

A disclosed or partially disclosed principal is liable to third parties on contracts executed by his or her agent if the agent was acting within the scope of his or her authority and if the contract is executed in the proper form and indicates that the principal is a party to the contract. Even if the contract purports to be the contract of the agent, a disclosed or a partially disclosed principal may still be considered a party to the contract unless the terms of the contract specifically exclude the principal. The disclosed or partially disclosed principal is subject to any legal or equitable action available to third parties to enforce the contract. In essence, the contract is treated as if the principal had executed the contract and was a party thereto. Normally, the authorized agent of a disclosed principal is not a party to the contract but may be if the contract purports to be the contract of the agent even though the principal still may be considered a party to the contract.

A principal is not liable on a negotiable instrument unless he or she is named in the instrument. However, if the principal is using a fictitious name or is doing business in the name of the agent and the agent executes the negotiable instrument in the business name of the principal, the principal will be liable on the instrument if given by the agent in the ordinary course of business.

If a state statute of frauds requires an instrument to be in writing, the principal is liable on the instrument where the memorandum has been signed by an authorized agent, whether or not the principal is identified in the document.

A principal may be liable for the unauthorized acts of a person acting in his or her behalf if that person has either apparent or implied authority. If the principal cloaks a person with apparent authority and that person makes a contract in the proper form indicating that the principal is the party to be bound, the principal will be liable.

A principal will be liable on a contract executed by an agent who has violated secret instructions from the principal provided the third party has no notice of the secret limitations on the agent's authority.

A principal is liable in contract for acts, performed on his or her account by a general agent, that are incidental to or are usually part of the transaction that the agent is authorized to perform, even though the particular act has been forbidden by the principal. The principal escapes liability if the third party had actual knowledge that the agent was unauthorized or had no reason to believe that the agent was authorized. This situation generally occurs where a general agent has been entrusted with the principal's business. The principal is then liable to third parties with whom the agent deals in the usual conduct of the business, even if the agent is acting contrary to the principal's direction.

In the case of a special agent who is authorized only to conduct a transaction or a series of transactions that is limited in scope, the principal is not bound by any contracts executed by the special agent that are not authorized or apparently authorized. A consequence of the principal's being treated as a party to the contract is that the liability of the principal is unaffected by any rights or liabilities existing between third party and agent. Nonetheless, the principal may interject any and all defenses arising out of the transaction except those considered personal to the agent. If both the agent and the principal are parties to the contract, a judgment recovered against the agent does not discharge the principal in the absence of showing that both were joint obligors. In any case brought against both the principal and the agent, judgments must be consistent. The principal's liability is extinguished if the claim has been satisfied by an agent authorized to settle or who is a party to the contract.

Liability of Third Parties to Principal

In those situations in which a principal is held to be a party to the contract, the third party is liable to the principal on such contracts as if the principal had personally executed the contract. The third party, like the principal, has benefit of all defenses arising out of the transaction in addition to any defenses that he or she may have against the principal personally. In cases of an undisclosed principal where the third party intended to deal with only the agent, the principal takes the contract subject to the defenses that the third party has against the agent until such time that the principal is discovered by the third party. A third party is not liable to a principal if the principal is undisclosed on a sealed contract or a negotiable instrument on which the principal's name does not appear. Naturally, if the terms of the contract specifically exclude the principal as a party, the principal may not proceed against the third party. However, a third party may not escape liability where the principal's identity is unknown unless the contract specifically excludes the principal as a party. Misrepresentation of the existence of the principal or of the identity of the principal by the agent is not a defense unless the principal or agent is aware or should be aware of the fact that the third party does not want to deal with that particular principal.

If the third party has contracted for the personal performance of the agent, the undisclosed principal cannot force the third party to accept his or her performance. The third party may still seek specific performance by the agent. However, an undisclosed principal may require a third party to render a personal performance to him or her rather than to the agent unless the contract specifically excludes the principal as a party to the contract. A third party is protected by rendering performance to the agent if done before learning of the existence of the principal or if the principal does not direct that performance be rendered to him or her.

DUTIES

While the principal-agent relationship is not necessarily contractual in nature, most duties arise out of the agreement between the parties, although some duties are implied by law. If the relationship is in fact contractual, normal contract rules apply in interpreting the duties.

Agent's Duty of Obedience

An agent has a duty of care and skill. The agent is under a duty to act with reasonable care, and he or she may be held liable for negligence in failing to do so. The standard to which the agent will be held in exercising his or her duty is that skill and knowledge standard to the place where the act or transaction is to be performed. If an agent has a particular skill, he or she must exercise that skill.

An agent has a duty of good conduct. The agent is under a duty to act in such a manner as not to bring dishonor to the principal or his or her business and to maintain friendly relations between principal and agent.

An agent is under a duty to report any information he or she receives within the scope of his or her agency to the principal, unless the agent acquired the information confidentially. In connection with this duty, the agent is required to report any adverse interest that the agent may have regarding the principal.

An agent has a duty to account for any profits that might arise out of the agency or for any money or property received from the principal for his or her benefit.

An agent has a duty of obedience. He or she is required to perform in accordance with his or her authorization and any reasonable customs regarding the business or locality. An agent is under a duty to obey the reasonable commands of the principal even if the principal had promised not to issue such commands. However, an agent is not required to perform any act which is illegal, unethical, or unreasonable.

An agent has a duty to terminate acting in behalf of his or her principal after receiving notice that his or her authority is terminated by the principal or if notice of termination is given to the principal by the agent.

Agent's Duty of Loyalty

The duty of loyalty arises out of the fiduciary duty owed by the agent to the principal and is the same as the fiduciary duty owed by a trustee to his or her beneficiary. An agent must act exclusively for the benefit of his or her principal in all matters within the scope of the agency. This is a duty of undivided loyalty. An agent may not speak disloyally, act disloyally, or use any information or property acquired by virtue of the agency relationship to the detriment of the principal or his or her business.

An agent has a duty to account for profits in money or property he or she receives from a third party within the scope of his or her employment. An agent is liable for any profit he or she has personally made as a result of using or selling confidential information or property of the principal including bribes received from third parties.

It is also a breach of the fiduciary duty for the agent not to reveal any adverse interest he or she has regarding the principal, and the agent may not act adversely to the interests of the principal unless the principal has acquiesced. In this regard, the agent is required to act fairly with the principal. Similarly, the agent may not act in behalf of any adverse party without disclosing such fact to the principal and obtaining the principal's consent.

An agent has a duty not to compete with his or her principal in matters within the scope of his or her authority. If the agent is an exclusive agent, the obligation not to compete is absolute; however, a nonexclusive agent has no such duty. The duty not to compete terminates with the agency relationship unless a restrictive covenant is contained in the agreement. Regardless, the agent may not use any confidential information acquired during the agency relationship within the scope of his or her authority nor attempt to solicit the principal's customers.

An agent may not reveal or use any confidential information acquired within the scope of his or her authority to the detriment of the principal whether the agent uses the information directly or conveys it to a third party.

An agent is under a duty not to mingle his or her own property with that of the principal's nor make it appear to third parties that the agent actually owns the principal's property.

If an agent breaches one or more of his or her duties owed to a principal, the principal may be entitled to restitution, an accounting, an injunction, or a discharge of the agent. The appropriate remedy to be sought depends on the factual situation and the damage sustained by the principal as a result of the breach.

Duties of Principal to Agent

If the relationship between the principal and agent is one of contract, the principal has an obligation to perform fully that contract and may be liable for breach thereof. If the breach is material, the agent has the right to terminate the contract.

If a principal ratifies an unauthorized act by an agent, that agent subsequently will have the same rights against the principal as any other agent unless the ratification was obtained by misrepresentation.

A principal is not under an obligation to provide an opportunity to the agent to work unless the agreement specifically states or may be reasonably inferred from the agreement. If such an opportunity to work exists, the principal is also under an obligation not to unreasonably interfere with the work of the agent.

A master ordinarily has a duty to keep an account of money due his or her servant; however, a principal is not under the same duty to account for amounts he or she owes an agent. Whether or not a principal has a duty to keep accounts depends on the customs of the trade or business and the ability of the agent to determine any amounts due him or her.

A principal also has a duty of good conduct to avoid discrediting or harming the agent's personal or business reputation or otherwise demeaning the agent. If after being employed the agent learns that the principal is engaged in an illegal or unsavory activity or has an unsavory reputation, the agent may terminate the relationship; however, if the agent does not terminate the relationship after learning of the nature of the principal's business or reputation, the agent may not unilaterally terminate the relationship for those reasons later.

In any consensual or contractual relationship, either party has the power to terminate the relationship at any time. If either party terminating the relationship repudiates or terminates the contract, he or she may be liable for breach of contract.

Generally, one person serves another in expectation of being compensated for doing so; however, some agents are in fact gratuitous agents. Again, the contract or the agreement between the parties determines what compensation shall be paid, if any. Nonetheless, if an agent believes he or she is to be compensated, but the principal reasonably believes that the agent is acting gratuitously, the agent is not entitled to be compensated. If the contract calls for compensation, but no amount is specified, the agent is entitled to the amount customarily paid for the services rendered or the reasonable value of such services under the circumstances. Once the agency relationship is terminated, the agent is not entitled to compensation, unless the principal is aware that the agent is continuing to act in his or her behalf and makes no objection.

A principal has a duty to indemnify the agent for any loss or damage sustained while acting in behalf of the principal. The right to indemnification should be spelled out in the contract or agreement to avoid later disputes. However, a right to indemnification may be inferred under certain circumstances by the courts to avoid inequities. An agent is generally entitled to indemnification when he or she has made a payment authorized by the principal which was necessary for the agent's performance, losses due to the principal's breach of duty, or benefit conferred upon the principal. Indemnification is not the proper claim to be made for reimbursement when the agent pays another party. The agent's right to reimbursement arises when the payment is made, and it is limited to the actual amount paid. The agent bears the burden of loss on any unauthorized payments, unless the payment was incidental to some authorized act or the principal benefited by the agent's action.

TERMINATION

The agency relationship may be terminated by an act of one of the parties or by operation of law on the occurrence of certain events.

The agency relationship, being a consensual one by agreement or contract, may be terminated by the express terms of the contract or on some happening or event specified in the contract. The contract itself may contain a specified term of weeks, months, or years during which period the agency relationship is valid. In the absence of an express agreement, the authority of the agent may terminate at the end of a reasonable time based on the totality of the circumstances. For example, an agent's authority to sell property belonging to the principal will terminate on the conclusion of the sale. Instead of specifying a particular time period, principal and agent may agree that the agency relationship will terminate on the happening of a particular event. In this case, the agent's authority terminates when he or she has notice of or should have known of the occurrence of the event.

The consensual agreement between principal and agent may be terminated by mutual consent of the parties provided that a third party does not rely on the existence of the agency relationship as security for the benefit of that third party.

One or the other of the parties to the agreement may terminate. The principal may revoke the agent's authority unilaterally even if the original authorization was irrevocable. Likewise, an agent may terminate his authority by refusing to act or by notifying the principal that he refuses to act thereby renouncing the relationship. However, if the principal revokes the agent's authority or if the agent renounces his or her authority, the other party may have a cause of action for breach of contract.

Termination by operation of law usually arises when unforeseen events occur which make it impossible for the agent to perform or would make it unlikely that the principal would desire the agent to perform. For example, changes in the general business climate which would make the agent's action undesirable, acquisition by the agent of an adverse interest in the subject matter of the authorization, breach of the duty of loyalty to the principal by the agent, bankruptcy or insolvency of either of the parties, loss or destruction of the subject matter of the authority, extinguishment of the principal's interest in the subject matter, loss of license or some other qualification of the agent, or a change in the law that makes the act illegal, impossible to achieve, or nonbeneficial.

Death or loss of capacity of either the principal or the agent will terminate the agency relationship. Death of the principal is an automatic termination whether the agent has knowledge of the death or not. Clearly, the death of the agent terminates his authority and that of any subagent appointed by him or her. Permanent loss of capacity of the principal is treated the same as the principal's death; however, brief periods of insanity do not terminate an agent's authority whether the principal could reappoint an agent at that time or not. Nor does insanity of the agent necessarily terminate the authority of the agent unless capacity is required for the particular act or transaction in question.

Apparent authority, which is based on a representation by the principal to a third party that an agent is authorized to act on behalf of the principal, will terminate upon the death or incapacity of the principal or agent or where the transaction becomes impossible to perform. Likewise, the agency relationship will terminate once the third party knows or has reason to know that the agent is no longer authorized. It is the intent of the principal that controls since apparent authority cannot exist in the absence of a representation by the principal, whatever may be expressed or implied in the principal's representation controls. To avoid inequities, the apparent authority of a general agent continues until the third party has been notified of the termination of the agent's authority. Third-party creditors of the principal are required to be individually notified of the termination of the agent's authority either orally or by mail. Notification by mail must actually be delivered at the home or place of business where the third party ordinarily receives communications. This is a change in the ordinary mailbox rule, which only requires posting. Here, actual receipt is necessary. Where the third party is not a creditor, public notice by publication in a newspaper of general circulation or some other appropriate method is sufficient.

17

Liability for Carelessness in Conducting a Business

TORTS

In the development of the English common law, criminal law and contract law preceded the development of the law of torts. The criminal law developed as a priority of the nation-state's need to regulate conduct considered to be undesirable or immoral in an organized society. Criminal law consists of wrongs against the state which the state then undertakes to prosecute and punish those found guilty either by fines or by imprisonment. Contract law developed to regulate transactions between individuals in freely negotiated bargains. Contract law deals with the rights and duties of the parties to a contract and specified remedies in the event that one or the other of the parties breaches the contract. It became obvious in the development of the common law that there were many persons who suffered harm or injury from conduct other than criminal conduct but which was equally unjustifiable from a social standpoint and was not covered by contract law. Tort law, which developed on a case-by-case basis, represents a broad range of activities which the courts have deemed to be unjustifiable or unacceptable social conduct.

In the early tort cases, courts utilized the concept of strict liability. Under the doctrine of strict liability, the person committing the conduct is liable without regard to whether or not they are at fault or blameworthy in the incident. It became obvious that such a strict liability approach could impose draconian liability on the members of the society. Around 1800, the strict liability doctrine gave way to the fault approach, but it has been resurrected in product liability cases. As the concept of fault developed, courts equated fault with moral turpitude. A tort consisted of conduct that violated the generally held moral standards of the community. These early torts, such as defamation, misrepresentation, and conversion of property of others without consent, still exist in today's law.

The law of torts encompasses such a broad area that it is difficult to provide a definition. In general, a tort may be defined as a private civil wrong committed against a person or his or her property which is not a breach of contract or criminal act. The primary aim of tort law is compensation of persons injured by the tortious acts of others. Unlike contract law, which requires privity of contract, which is the relationship existing between the parties to the contract, any person injured by the tortious act of another may file a civil suit to recover damages for the injury. The plaintiff in a civil tort suit may recover actual or compensatory damages including damages for direct or immediate harm such as bodily injury, medical expenses, lost pay and benefits, damage to property and for such intangibles as loss of privacy, pain and suffering, and emotional distress. In addition to actual or compensatory damages, the plaintiff may recover punitive damages if the action of the wrongdoer is particularly reprehensible. Punitive damages are designed to deter particularly reprehensible conduct by the wrongdoer and others engaged in similar conduct.

The entire development of tort law represents a constant shifting and balancing of competing social interests. The protection of one societal class may mean a corresponding limitation on the liberty or freedom of another class of the society. The balancing process continues as the courts continue to deal with the growing tensions of an increasingly interdependent urban industrialized society.

Negligence

The tort of negligence has become the most common of the different tort actions. Negligence focuses on the conduct of the hypothetical reasonable person in society. Tortious conduct is conduct that falls below the reasonable person standard and results in harm or injury to another person. The elements of a negligence case are a duty owed by one person to another, breach of that duty, and damages that result as the proximate cause of the breach of the duty.

Duty

Every person in today's society is under an obligation to conduct his or her affairs in such a manner as not to cause harm to others. The standard of conduct required is that of the reasonable person of ordinary prudence in similar circumstances. This standard is objective in that it compares conduct with that of a hypothetical person who is always thoughtful and cautious and never unreasonably endangers another. The qualification, in similar circumstances, allows for flexibility in the standard. Similarly, courts take into consideration the personal characteristics of the individual against whom the complaint has been filed. Thus, children are not held to the same standard as adults but are held to the standard of the reasonable child in similar circumstances. However, mental defects or deficiencies are not taken into consideration and do not relieve the wrongdoer from the duty to conform to the reasonable person standard.

Some duties exist as a matter of law. A contractual relationship may give rise to a duty that might not otherwise exist; for example, medical malpractice cases are based on the contractual relationship between the doctor and the patient who has contracted with the doctor to perform certain professional duties and who relies on the competent performance of those duties. Other special relationships have developed in case law and include duties owed to customers by common carriers and innkeepers who are held liable for damage or loss of property of their customers. Further, the relationship among the parties may affect the level of duty that is owed from one person to another. For example, a merchant or business owes a higher level of duty to business invitees—persons who are on private property for purposes connected with the business—than to trespassers who are there without any legal right or privilege to be there. If the plaintiff is unable to establish that the defendant owed him or her a duty, no tort has been committed.

Certain statutes may create a legal duty the violation of which may result in a tort. Negligence per se results if someone violates a statute and, in the violation of that statute, harms a person of the class that the statute was intended to protect. The violation of the statute, however, must be the cause of the injury.

Breach

Once the duty has been established, the plaintiff must prove that the defendant breached that duty. The duty is breached by substandard conduct on behalf of the wrongdoer. Substandard conduct consists of conduct that presents an unreasonable, foreseeable risk of harm to another. There is no breach of duty if a person is acting reasonably and inflicts harm on another that was unforeseeable. The conduct must be unreasonable and the harm must be foreseeable to be tortious. In determining whether or not the conduct was reasonable, the courts balance the social utility of the conduct against the risk of harm. As the risk of harm increases so does the level of the duty required to prevent any harm from resulting from the conduct.

In a negligence per se case, the violation of the statute is sufficient to establish the breach of duty.

Oftentimes, it is not possible for the injured party to establish who breached the duty. These cases often involve situations in which the wrongdoer is in complete control of the attendant circumstances such as in an operating room or during aircraft maintenance. In the typical medical malpractice case involving an operation, the injured party was unconscious and unaware of the attendant circumstances. All the injured party knows is that when he or she regained consciousness some unexpected bodily injury occurred in a situation under the control of the defendant. In order to facilitate the plaintiff's cases under such circumstances, the doctrine of *res ipsa loquitur* was developed by the courts. Freely translated it means "the thing speaks for itself." To avail one's self of the doctrine of *res ipsa loquitur*, the plaintiff must prove that the defendant was in exclusive control of the instrumentality of harm and that the harm would not have ordinarily occurred in the absence of negligence. If the plaintiff can prove those two items, the breach of duty is presumed. In those states in which *res ipsa loquitur* creates a presumption of negligence, the burden of proof is on the defendant to rebut the presumption, and, if the defendant fails to do so, a directed verdict will be entered for the plaintiff. The general rule in most states is that *res ipsa loquitur* gives rise to an inference that the defendant was negligent, and the burden of proof is shifted to the defendant. The trier of fact, judge or jury, then decides the issue using the preponderance of the evidence rule. This rule simply requires the trier of fact to decide which of the parties best proved his or her case.

Damages

Next, the plaintiff must prove that he or she sustained an injury that the law protects against. Bodily harm, loss of wages, injury to property, lost pay or benefits, and medical expenses are recoverable to the extent incurred. The difficulty arises in cases in which purely emotional harm has been inflicted. Traditionally, most courts would allow a plaintiff to recover only from emotional injuries resulting from negligent conduct if there had been an actual contact with or an impact on the plaintiff's person. The impact or contact rule is gradually being abandoned, but a large number of courts require proof that some physical injury resulted from the emotional distress before allowing recovery. The growing trend is to allow recovery for emotional distress where it was a foreseeable consequence of the defendant's behavior.

Emotional distress inflicted on a third party is even more troublesome. Suppose a third party witnesses an injury negligently inflicted upon another person. Recovery for emotional distress of the third party in many jurisdictions depends upon the relationship between the third party and the direct victim of the negligence, for example, one spouse witnessing the other spouse's horrible injury or parents seeing their child injured or maimed. Moreover, the third party must show that the emotional distress was a result of witnessing the accident or the injury. As with emotional distress inflicted upon victims, a third party in some jurisdictions may recover only if some physical injury resulted from the infliction of the emotional distress.

Proximate Cause

The legal connection between the breach of duty and the injury or harm inflicted is proximate cause. The breach of duty must be the cause in fact of the injury. Proximate cause is a slippery concept on which the courts have not reached any agreement. Some courts impose a "but for" test. The issue is framed in terms of whether or not the injury would have occurred but for the breach of duty. In cases of intentional torts, courts have long held that the wrongdoer is liable for all of the direct consequences of the act however unforeseeable; however, courts have been reluctant to place such draconian liability on a person for negligence. To limit liability in negligence cases, some courts have adopted a standard of proximate cause that a person is liable only for the natural and probable consequences of the act, which is to say that the consequences were foreseeable.

Often a person's negligence will set into motion a chain of events that leads to injury of another person. The initial negligence in these cases may not be the direct cause of the injury, but rather an intervening or superseding force or cause may be present. For example, a person negligently leaves a car engine running, and the car is subsequently stolen by a joyrider who runs down an innocent third party. The initial wrongdoer will be liable if the intervening or superseding cause was foreseeable but not otherwise. If a person is negligent, he or she is also legally responsible as the cause of aggravating any preexisting physical characteristic of the victim. For example, if the victim of a negligent act had a preexisting heart condition, and as a result of the negligence, suffered a heart attack, the wrongdoer is liable for the damage even though that negligent act would not have produced a heart attack in an otherwise normal person. The wrongdoer is also jointly liable for any harm sustained by the victim as a result of negligent medical care of the injuries inflicted. Similarly, a person who is injured trying to avoid the negligent consequences of an act has a cause of action against the negligent party even though he or she was not injured as a direct consequence of the act. Liability also extends to any person who is injured trying to rescue the victim of the negligent act as long as the rescuer is not reckless in making the attempt.

Defenses

Contributory negligence and assumption of the risk are the two primary defenses available in a tort action. These defenses are based on the theory that a person should not recover for his or her own contribution to the negligence.

The doctrine of contributory negligence produces harsh results. A plaintiff who fails to exercise reasonable care for his or her own safety may not recover for an injury resulting from the negligence of another. If the plaintiff's own contributory negligence was a substantial factor in producing the harm, the plaintiff is absolutely barred from recovery.

A plaintiff who is guilty of contributory negligence may be able to overcome that handicap by the doctrine of last clear chance. Under the doctrine of last clear chance, the court will inquire as to who was last negligent. If the plaintiff was contributorily negligent but the defendant had a last clear chance to avoid the harm, then contributory negligence is not a bar to recovery.

To mitigate the harshness of the contributory negligence rule, many state legislatures have adopted comparative negligence statutes. In essence, the statutes require the finder of fact to determine the relative fault of the parties. The application of the comparative fault system varies from state to state. In some states, the relative fault of the parties is determined, and the party who is more at fault sustains the loss. If the defendant was more at fault than the plaintiff, the plaintiff recovers all compensatory and punitive damages awarded. On the other hand, if the plaintiff was more at fault than the defendant, the plaintiff is barred from recovery. Other states allocate damages based on the relative fault. For example, if plaintiff sustains damages of $100,000 and the relative findings of fault are defendant 60 percent and plaintiff 40 percent, then the plaintiff will recover 60 percent of the amount of damages, or $60,000.

A person who voluntarily exposes him- or herself to a known danger knowingly assumes the risk of harm. Assumption of the risk is an absolute bar to recovery by the injured party. For a person to assume the risk, however, he or she must fully understand the nature and the extent of the risk involved. In those states that have adopted comparative negligence systems, the doctrine of assumption of the risk has been abolished and is incorporated into the comparative negligence system.

Strict Liability

Strict liability or liability without fault was used as the basis of tort liability into the eighteenth century. After 1800 the doctrine of negligence replaced strict liability. Today, the doctrine of strict liability has been resurrected particularly in products liability cases, which are discussed below. The other area in which strict liability is still utilized today is ultrahazardous activities. An ultrahazardous activity is one that involves a risk of harm that cannot be mitigated by the exercise of reasonable care. Such activities include blasting, crop dusting, and stunt flying. The underlying rationale of strict liability is that certain activities that are ultrahazardous may have social utility, but society will hold the person who engages in the ultrahazardous activity strictly liable for any harm that results from that activity. In a strict liability case, plaintiffs do not have to prove duty or breach of duty but only proximate cause and damages.

Intentional Torts

Intentional torts are torts in which the wrongdoer's behavior indicates either a conscious desire to cause harm to a legally protected interest or knowledge that such harm is substantially certain to be the result of his or her actions.

Assault and Battery

Each member of society has a fundamental right to be free from intentional, harmful, or offensive physical attacks on one's person. The corresponding duty is to refrain from making such physical contacts. Physical injury is not required; offensive contacts that offend a reasonable sense of personal dignity are actionable.

A battery is the actual physical touching of the person or anything connected to the body such as a cane or a dog on a leash. Anyone who is touched may bring an action whether they were the intended victim or not. Under the doctrine of transferred intent, the person who is actually touched or harmed has a valid claim against the wrongdoer for battery.

Consent is a defense to a claim of battery. Consent must be freely and intelligently given to be effective. Willfully engaging in a contact sport implies consent to physical contact within the rules of the game. Another defense to a claim of battery is privilege. Privilege is present under certain socially accepted conditions when the use of force is justified such as self-defense; however, the extent of the force used must be no more than reasonably necessary under the circumstances. A storeowner may use reasonable force to remove an intruder from the premises.

Assault consists of a threat to commit a battery which causes reasonable apprehension in the mind of the victim that the battery is imminent, but the actual battery need not be committed. Threats of future battery do not constitute assault. The fear must be of an imminent battery. Likewise, a mere verbal threat under circumstances that indicate that there is no intent to carry out the threat is not an assault.

False Imprisonment

Individuals have a fundamental right to move about or travel. Anyone who unjustifiably interferes with that right commits the tort of false imprisonment. False imprisonment consists of confining a person to a space where there is no reasonable means of escape or of denying entrance to a space where the person otherwise has a legal right to go. Confinement or denial of entry must be complete. Merely blocking one entrance when others are open is not false imprisonment. Confinement may be by physical barriers, assertion of legal authority to detain, detention of property, or threat of harm to another. The detainee must know that his or her freedom to move about or travel is restrained.

False imprisonment has been a common complaint arising out of suspected shoplifting cases. If the suspected shoplifter was detained either by store officials or police and the person was innocent, the merchant was held liable for false imprisonment. Today, most states have enacted antishoplifting statutes which give merchants a conditional privilege to detain a person reasonably suspected of shoplifting provided that the merchant acts in a reasonable manner and detains the suspect only for a reasonable amount of time. If the merchant acts unreasonably, a cause of action for false imprisonment arises.

Defamation

All of us have an interest in our reputation and a corresponding right not to have that reputation defamed. Defamation is the unprivileged publication of false and defamatory statements. Defamation is really two torts: libel and slander. Libel and slander differ in form of publication. Libel consists of written, printed, or other physical forms such as photographs or statues. Slander is an oral defamation. Of the two, libel is more onerous because of its more permanent nature and potentially broader audience. Libel is actionable without proof of special damages, i.e., monetary damages. However, certain kinds of slanderous statements are also actionable without proof of special damages as slander per se. Slander per se consists of statements that the person has committed a crime involving moral turpitude or carrying a prison sentence, that the person has a loathsome disease such as leprosy or venereal disease, that the person is professionally incompetent or guilty of professional misconduct, or that the person has engaged in serious sexual misconduct.

The defamatory statement must be published to be actionable; however, widespread publication is not necessary. Transmittal of the defamatory statement either orally or in writing to one person other than the person defamed is sufficient for publication. A person is not defamed in direct confrontation in a private conversation with or private letter to the person who is the subject of the statement.

Corporations and other business entities have limited rights to reputation. Defamatory statements must harm the entity in the conduct of its business or deter others from dealing with the business. Statements made about corporate employees, officers, or directors must reflect upon the manner in which the corporation does business to be actionable.

Truth is an absolute defense to a claim of defamation regardless of the motive or intent of the perpetrator. Certain statements are privileged if made within the context of socially desirable activities such as in courtrooms, legislative proceedings, and communications between spouses.

Appropriation of Name or Likeness

The tort of appropriation of name or likeness for a commercial purpose is part of the recently developing right of privacy. In essence, an individual has a right to be left alone. Use of a person's name or likeness without his or her consent in an advertisement or endorsement of a product, which implies a nonexistent relationship between the product or business and the person whose name or likeness is used, is an intentional tort. This area of the law is developing and fluctuates widely from state to state. An attorney in the particular locality should be consulted before using a name or likeness in advertising.

Interference with Business Conduct

A person engaged in business has a right not to be maliciously interfered with by another. This tort does not require a showing of ill will or intent to injure as an element of maliciousness; all that is required is that the intentional action was unjustified or unlawful and that it was carried on for an improper purpose or by the use of improper means. If there is ill will or an intent to injure the business, it is clearly tortious even if the means used are lawful or proper. Conversely, even if the purpose is proper, it may be wrongful interference to accomplish the proper purpose by improper or wrongful means such as bribes, fraudulent conduct, or threat of a groundless lawsuit.

Interference with Contractual Relationships

Parties to a contract have a right to be free from wrongful interference with an existing contract. Wrongful interference may consist of trying to induce one of the parties to breach the contract or interfering in the lawful performance of the contract. This tort requires an existing contract, knowledge of such contract by the wrongdoer, and unjustified, intentional conduct which results in harm. Justifiable conduct is proper conduct undertaken by proper means. Interference using improper means such as blackmail or bribes is wrongful as is improper conduct such as intent to injure or embarrass even if undertaken by proper means.

A director who advises its own corporation to breach a contract with another party does not commit the tort of interference with a contractual relationship. Such advice is privileged insofar as the advice is rendered for the benefit of the corporation and not the director's own personal advantage.

Appropriation of Trade Secrets

It is a tort to acquire or use wrongfully another's trade secret. A trade secret is a manufacturing process, formula, customer list or other information, or any other device known only to the business that created or compiled it. The device or information must be secret, and proper precautions must be taken by the owner to safeguard it. General information freely circulated in a business is not secret. Care must be taken to restrict access by employees and warn against disclosure. The device or information must be wrongfully acquired either illegally or by breach of a confidential relationship or substandard commercial morality.

Trademark Infringement

At common law, trademark infringement was a tort. Today trademark infringement is the subject of federal statutory law which is a technical specialty of a number of lawyers who should be consulted regarding any trademark problem.

A trademark is defined as any distinctive word or words, symbol, device, or design used to identify goods of a particular manufacturer. Certain terms or potential trademarks are not recognized as registerable. Generic, descriptive, and geographical terms and surnames, unless they have a secondary meaning, are not registerable.

Generic terms such as aspirin are names of a particular class or genus of which the item is merely one member. Aspirin represents the classic case of a trademark's losing its protection and becoming a generic term. This accounts for the millions of dollars spent to protect "Coke" and "Xerox."

Descriptive terms describing attributes such as color, odor, function, size, or ingredients are not registerable. Similarly, use of geographical terms such as direction, states, or countries is not protectable.

Surnames and other terms generally not registerable may become so if they acquire a secondary meaning. Examples are Bavarian beer, Waltham watches, Chevrolet automobiles, and Safeway stores.

Most infringement cases involve similar trademarks. One party is deliberately using a trademark similar to an established one to take advantage of the goodwill and advertising of the original.

Questions involving trademarks and trademark infringement should be referred to a competent trademark attorney.

Common Law Fraud

Common law fraud is a misrepresentation of a material fact knowingly made with the intent to deceive which is reasonably relied upon by the victim to his or her detriment. To recover under common law fraud, the plaintiff must be able to show each of the elements.

First, there must be a misrepresentation or misstatement which includes any word or conduct that causes an innocent person to reach an erroneous conclusion of fact. The misrepresentation or misstatement must be of a material fact. A material fact is a statement of fact on which the reasonable person would rely in making his or her decision regarding the transaction. The statement must be one of fact, not prediction or opinion. Predictions are mere speculation about what may or may not happen in the future. Since no one can reasonably predict what will happen in the future, such statements do not constitute fraud. Likewise, statements of opinion are subjective and merely represent personal feelings or judgments on the matter about which reasonable persons may disagree. Thus, representations regarding beauty, color, speed, and soundness are generally opinion. However, if the person making the statement is considerably more knowledgeable than the party to whom the statement is made, it is conceivable that statements regarding safety or soundness may be fraudulent if they prove to be false. The same is true with respect to an article's value. Generally, courts hold the view that an article's value is a matter of opinion rather than fact. Therefore, a statement that this particular piece of merchandise is easily worth $200,000 is a matter of opinion and not fact. Puffing by salespeople does not rise to the level of common law fraud because their statements generally are subjective and a matter of opinion rather than fact. As paradoxical as the two theories may seem, statements made by nonlawyers concerning the law are not fraudulent because a statement made by a nonlawyer should not be relied upon and because everyone is presumed to know the law. Two notable exceptions to the rule are statements made by real estate brokers and bank cashiers as to legal matters within the scope of their employment.

In general, misrepresentation or misstatement of a material fact requires an affirmative statement. However, there are certain instances when silence may be considered misrepresentation. Ordinarily, a person has a right to remain silent unless there is a legal duty to speak. While courts are not consistent in their decisions as to what situations impose a duty to speak, there are certain instances that are generally agreed upon. A latent or hidden defect in the sale of property that simple or casual inspection by a prospective purchaser would not ordinarily disclose, situations in which one of the parties occupies a special duty of trust and confidence in relationship to the other party such as a corporate officer vis à vis his or her corporation, situations requiring the utmost good faith such as the sale of life insurance contracts, and situations in which statements made during preliminary negotiations may be true but subsequently become false are situations in which the failure to speak or disclose the changed circumstances gives rise to common law fraud.

The misrepresentation or misstatement of the material fact must be knowingly made with the intent to deceive. This is the scienter requirement. The defendant must prove that the person making the misrepresentation or misstatement knew, or should have known, that it was false or not true at the time it was made. The scienter requirement is also satisfied if a person makes a statement with a reckless disregard of the truth whether or not he or she knew the statement to be false. The person making the statement must intend to deceive either by knowingly making the misrepresentation or misstatement of the material fact or by exhibiting a reckless disregard for the truth.

If the person reasonably believed the statement to be true, he or she is guilty of innocent misrepresentation, not fraud. In this event, the victim can rescind the contract but does not have a cause of action for damages. It often happens that both parties to the contract are mistaken as to a material fact at the time the contract was entered into, in which event either party may rescind the agreement. If only one of the parties was mistaken, the contract may not be rescinded unless the person who was mistaken can show that the other party knew or should have known of the mistake at the time the contract was made. Mistakes regarding things other than fact such as prediction or value are not grounds for rescission of a contract.

The person to whom the misstatement or misrepresentation is made must reasonably rely on the misrepresentation. If the party to whom the misrepresentation or misstatement was made knows the truth, he or she could not reasonably rely on the misrepresentation or misstatement. Likewise, a misrepresentation or misstatement that is unreasonable or is of something that is within the common knowledge is not sufficient to support a charge of fraud.

Finally, there must be detrimental reliance as a result of the misrepresentation by the party to whom the statement was made. Ordinarily, that party must show that he or she suffered monetary damages as a result of the misrepresentation. The measure of damages is the difference between the actual value of the property that the buyer received and the value of the property if it had been as misrepresented. An alternative remedy to money damages is rescission of the contract in which event the innocent party is not required to show monetary damages.

PRODUCT LIABILITY

The nineteenth century saw the industrial revolution take firm root in the United States. As a matter of social and economic policy, industrialization was promoted. To allow the greatest possible growth of industry, protectionism and economic freedom were the order of the day. Economic freedom found its counterpoint in the law in the doctrine of freedom of contract.

Freedom of contract presumed face to face negotiations between persons having relatively equal bargaining power. In the sale of goods, freedom of contract meant that manufacturers should get the benefit of the bargain struck; therefore, they should not be liable for any defect or harm which they did not knowingly and willingly assume through a direct, express promise. As a result of the doctrine of freedom of contract, manufacturers were favored before the law over consumers. Infant industries were protected from foreign competition and from burdensome costs at home. Imposition of liability for defects in manufactured goods would increase costs dramatically and might result in business failures. Freedom of contract coupled with the policy of protectionism resulted in the doctrine of *caveat emptor*: "Let the buyer beware."

In twentieth-century America, the industrial revolution reached maturity. Protectionism no longer seemed necessary. Moreover, the presumptions under which freedom of contract operated were no longer true. The consumer no longer negotiated with the manufacturer face to face. Bargaining power had long since shifted in favor of large corporations. Goods became more complex, and the average person lacks the expertise to determine whether or not the goods are well made or defective. The risk of harm from defective goods is far greater today than it was in the nineteenth century.

Traditional laissez-faire economics has given way to increased government intervention and regulation further reducing freedom of contract. In many areas, the government dictates certain terms of the contract.

Consumer advocates such as Ralph Nader awakened the public conscience to the inequities of the marketplace. The consumer protection movement of the middle twentieth century resulted in socialization of the risk. The manufacturer is directly liable, often without fault, for harm caused by defective goods. However, these costs become part of the cost of goods sold and, in turn, are passed on to the consumer in the form of higher prices. The consumer representing society at large underwrites the losses sustained by consumers who are injured or harmed by defective products. The pendulum of risk of loss has shifted from *caveat emptor* to *caveat venditor*: "Let the seller beware."

Many observers feel that the pendulum has swung too far in favor of consumers to the detriment of business. Costs associated with product liability such as judgments, attorney's fees, and insurance are hard to pass on in a relatively stagnant economy. Moreover, the cost of liability insurance is prohibitive for many smaller businesses which often elect to be self-insured and risk bankruptcy in case of a large adverse judgment.

Several efforts have been made in Congress and state legislatures to limit the burgeoning judgments awarded by juries in product liability cases. It seems only a matter of time before the pendulum swings back again hopefully toward equilibrium.

Warranty

Historically, the consumer's redress for a defective product was based on contract law. To recover damages, the consumer had to prove a breach of promise by the seller. Since parties were liable only for promises freely made, consumers were by and large unsuccessful.

To recover under contract law, the plaintiff had to have privity of contract. Only the parties to the contract, which may include a third-party beneficiary, have standing to file suit based on the contract. Many ultimate consumers such as other members of the household, friends, or relatives did not enjoy privity of contract. If the injured plaintiff wins the contract case, damages are limited to actual or loss of bargain damages and limited, reasonably foreseeable consequential damages. Personal injury, property damage, lost profits, or punitive damages are not recoverable in contract actions, only in tort cases.

Warranty theory today is primarily contained in the Uniform Commercial Code and the Magnuson-Moss Warranty Act.[1] The Uniform Commercial Code substantially is in effect in each of the states except Louisiana, which has adopted only parts. The three primary warranties described in Article 2 of the UCC are the express warranty,[2] the implied warranty of merchantability,[3] and the implied warranty of fitness for a particular purpose.[4] Only the express warranty is found in traditional contract law; the other two warranties, as their names connote, are implied by operation of law. For a full discussion of Article 2, see Chapter 10.

The Magnuson-Moss Warranty Act was enacted by Congress in 1975. The act applies to sales of consumer products, which are defined as any tangible personal property used for personal, family, or household purposes. Notice that goods purchased for resale or used in a business are not consumer products; however, it is not the goods' actual use that determines whether or not they are consumer products. If it is not uncommon for the particular item to be used for personal, family, or household purposes, it is a consumer product. Magnuson-Moss applies only to the sale of consumer goods costing more than $10 per item to an ultimate consumer and applies only to written warranties. Thus a seller may avoid Magnuson-Moss by failing or refusing to give a written warranty.

If a written warranty is given to a consumer for a consumer product costing more than $15,[5] Magnuson-Moss and the Federal Trade Commission regulations implementing Magnuson-Moss require that the warranty must contain the following kinds of information in a simple, clear, and conspicuous presentation: (1) the identity of persons covered by the warranty if limited to particular persons such as original purchaser; (2) a description of warranted products, parts, characteristics, components, or properties; (3) the remedies provided by the warrantor in case of defect; (4) the duration of warranty including the beginning date if it is different from the date of purchase; (5) the detailed procedure the purchaser is to follow to obtain satisfaction under the warranty.

If the warranty is limited, the warranty must disclose the limitations and any attempt to limit consequential damages or other remedies. All warranties must contain the following statement: "This warranty gives you specific legal rights, and you may also have other rights which vary from state to state." You should check the law of your state to determine whether or not warranties may be limited.

Enforcement of Magnuson-Moss is by means of various civil actions provided private parties and actions taken by the Federal Trade Commission under section 5 of the Federal Trade Commission Act.[6]

Section 5 of the Federal Trade Commission Act prohibits unfair or deceptive practices in or affecting interstate commerce.

Section 5 is enforceable only by the Federal Trade Commission and not by private parties; however, anyone such as a consumer, business, government agency, Congress, or the Federal Trade Commission may file an informal complaint to start the enforcement process. Inquiries may be made to and complaints filed with any regional office of the Federal Trade Commission.

The informal complaint may be in any form. A letter is sufficient, but it should be accompanied by any supporting data such as a copy of the warranty, bill of sale, etc. The identity of the complainant is kept confidential except as required by law. Unfortunately, the Federal Trade Commission's resources are limited, and it must be selective in pursuing complaints. If a complaint is investigated, the FTC will try to negotiate a settlement, dismiss the complaint, or file a formal complaint. It would be prudent to secure legal counsel as soon as possible after receiving notice of a complaint filed against you.

A formal complaint is the beginning of the formalized adjudicatory process within the FTC. The FTC may also seek an injunction in a federal district court to halt the practice until the matter is resolved through the formal complaint process.

A copy of the formal complaint is sent to the respondent (person against whom the complaint is made) along with a copy of the proposed order. The proposed order sets out the alleged violation and what the FTC wants the respondent to do to rectify matters. A hearing before an administrative law judge will be scheduled. Prior to the hearing, the respondent may negotiate a cease-and-desist order. If agreement is reached, the respondent is not required to admit guilt but does promise to stop the challenged practice. The proposed cease-and-desist order must be published for 60 days for public comment before it becomes final.

If no agreement can be reached, the matter is tried before an administrative law judge. The judge's decision becomes the FTC's decision in 30 days if no appeal is taken to the FTC commissioners. Notice that the first appeal is within the FTC itself. The commissioners may sustain, modify, or reverse the administrative law judge's decision. If a cease-and-desist order is issued by the commissioners, the respondent has 60 days to appeal to a United States court of appeals.

The FTC only has the power to issue cease-and-desist orders. If a cease-and-desist order is violated, the FTC seeks enforcement in a United States district court. The court may order civil penalties up to $10,000 per violation of the cease-and-desist order. Each day that a violation continues may be a separate offense.

Magnuson-Moss is the sleeper among product liability laws. It is not widely used by lawyers in product liability cases although it has the potential to become a powerful weapon in the consumer protection arsenal.

Negligence Theory

Negligence theory has played an important role in the development of product liability law. As was discussed above, negligence is a separate tort, and for a plaintiff to recover he or she must be able to prove the necessary elements of the tort of negligence. The necessary elements of the tort of negligence are a duty owed to another, a breach of that duty, and damages sustained by the person to whom the duty was owed as the proximate cause of the breach.

The most difficult problem proving negligence in a product liability case is to establish a duty owed and breach of that duty. A manufacturer of goods commonly owes a duty to properly design the goods, properly manufacture or handle the goods, adequately inspect the goods, and adequately warn the consumer of all foreseeable hazards that may be associated with the use of the goods.

A product must be designed so that it is safe for any reasonably foreseeable use. In most states, not only is there the duty to use reasonable care in designing a product but there is also a duty to design it so that injuries will be minimized in the event that an accident should occur. However, a defendant may be relieved from liability by virtue of several court-recognized defenses. If a product has social utility and there is no feasible way of making the product safer, all that is required of the manufacturer is that the consumer be adequately warned. If the manufacturer complies with state or federal product safety standards or with existing industry standards or contemporary state-of-the-art manufacturing, the defendant may be relieved of liability. Some states have created a state-of-the-art defense by statute. Under such statutes, the manufacturer is held to the prevailing product standard in effect at the time that the product was manufactured and not by some subsequent standard or state of the art. Some states will still relieve a defendant of liability in cases in which the design risk is so obvious that the purchaser/plaintiff should have recognized the design defect or risk. However, if the problem is not readily evident to the unsophisticated purchaser, the manufacturer will not be relieved of liability. An increasing number of states, but still a minority, are developing a risk/benefit analysis in design defect cases. In such cases, the courts weigh the social utility of the product against the risk of injury or harm that the product poses. Liability for negligent design is imposed only when an unreasonable danger or risk is created by the manufacturer.

A manufacturer has a duty to manufacture, handle, and inspect goods properly. Negligence cases involving improper manufacturing or handling are extremely difficult to prove because the elements of the case are within the control of the manufacturer and are not readily available to the consumer/plaintiff. Moreover, in such a case, the manufacturer may introduce into evidence quality control methods in place and in use in the manufacturing facility. The doctrine of *res ipsa loquitur* may be applied if the accident is one that would not have ordinarily occurred had someone not breached the duty and the defendant was in exclusive control of the instrumentality that caused the harm. If the doctrine of *res ipsa loquitur* is applicable, the plaintiff need not prove breach of duty. In some states it is presumed, and the defendant must rebut the presumption to prevail. In other states, breach of duty is merely inferred, and the burden of proof shifts to the defendant. Liability for improper manufacturing, handling, or inspection may be imposed upon a wholesaler or a retailer. If the wholesaler or retailer is merely a conduit for the goods, he or she is not liable in negligence for failure to inspect unless he or she knew or had reason to know of the defect. This is particularly true if the product is packaged in a sealed container and is not to be opened before sale. If the wholesaler or retailer is involved in the preparation of the product or its installation, the wholesaler or retailer is liable for failure to discover any reasonably apparent defects. In the event that a wholesaler or retailer is held liable for negligence he or she has recourse against the manufacturer for indemnification or contribution.

Sellers are under an obligation to warn purchasers if they know or have reason to know that the product is likely to be used in a reasonably foreseeable dangerous situation and the seller has no reason to believe that the user realizes the danger. A seller who fails to give adequate warning may be liable for negligence. In determining liability, courts look not only to the reasonable foreseeability of harm but also to the seriousness of the foreseeable harm and the feasibility of a warning in preventing the harm. Clearly, there is no duty to warn if the danger connected with the product is obvious. Note that a warning is not a substitute for proper design. A seller who manufactures and markets a product that is extremely unsafe may be liable for defective design whether or not an adequate warning is issued with the product.

Negligence per se may be an alternative to a negligence action. In a negligence per se case, the duty and the breach of duty involve the violation of a statute, but not all statutes will suffice in a negligence per se case. The plaintiff must be within the class of persons intended to be protected by the statute and must suffer the kind of harm that the statute was intended to protect against.

Strict Liability

In the development of product liability law, negligence actions have not always proved satisfactory. In many cases, plaintiffs have been unable to prove specific elements of negligence on the part of the manufacturer, particularly a breach of duty. A more formidable weapon for product liability is the strict liability theory, which is a resurrection of an earlier strict liability theory beginning in the early 1960s. Today it is probably the most common ground for imposing liability on manufacturers. A plaintiff may recover for injuries sustained by a defective product by simply showing that the product was defective, that the defect was the proximate cause of the injury, and that the defect caused the product to be unreasonably dangerous. Under strict liability, the plaintiff does not have to establish a duty or breach of the duty. A showing that the product was defective and unreasonably dangerous and was the proximate cause of the injury are all that are required under strict liability. The strict liability theory, in effect, is an extension of the implied warranty of merchantability to the ultimate customer in cases involving all kinds of goods. Strict liability then represents a mingling of tort and contract law with the result of imposing liability on manufacturers unprecedented in the history of product liability law. Consequently, almost one half of the states have enacted statutes placing limits on a consumer's right to sue and the amount of the damages that can be awarded in a product liability case.

The rule of strict liability in most states is formulated in section 402A of the Second Restatement of Torts. The Second Restatement of Torts was drafted by the American Law Institute in 1965. While section 402A of the restatement does not have the force of law, it has been recognized by most states as the current state of the law. Under section 402A, anyone who sells a product in a defective condition unreasonably dangerous is subject to liability for the harm caused provided that the seller is engaged in the business of selling that product and the product is expected to and does reach the consumer or ultimate user without substantial change in the condition in which it is sold. Note that strict liability under section 402A is imposed only on persons engaged in the business of selling the product in question. This is similar to the merchant requirement in UCC's section 2–314. Occasional sales by nonmerchants in the particular product in question are not covered by section 402A. Second, the product must reach the consumer without substantial change in the condition in which it was sold. Thus, there is no strict liability on a manufacturer of parts that are to be incorporated in another manufactured product or where the merchandise is substantially altered before being purchased by the ultimate consumer.

Section 402A liability is imposed even if the seller has exercised all possible care in the preparation and sale of the product and even if the user or consumer did not buy the product from or enter into any contractual relationship with the seller.

The major problem with section 402A is the definition of "defective condition unreasonably dangerous to the user or consumer or his property." To establish such condition requires proving first that the product was defective and second that it is unreasonably dangerous to the user or consumer or his property. In general, a product is defective if it does not meet the expectations of the average or reasonable consumer. Again, this standard is similar to the merchantability standard in UCC section 2–314. To prove unreasonably dangerous involves proving that the product had some significant and unexpected capacity to cause personal injury or property damage; that is, the article must be dangerous beyond the reasonable contemplation of the reasonable consumer. A product with a positive social utility which is unavoidably unsafe is not unreasonably dangerous under section 402A. A further pro-consumer step by some courts has been to dispense with the unreasonably dangerous element of the case and require only proof that the product was defective.

Section 402B of the Restatement Second of Torts imposes liability on sellers of chattels who make misrepresentations of material facts in advertising, labels, or otherwise to the public concerning the character or quality of the chattel sold. Chattels are generally defined as articles of personal property that do not amount to a freehold or fee in land. The misrepresentation must be of a material fact which is a fact that the ordinary consumer or user would consider important in purchasing the chattel. Moreover, the consumer must have suffered physical harm as the result of justifiable reliance on the misrepresentation. It is not a defense by the seller that the misrepresentation was not fraudulently or negligently made or that the consumer had not purchased the chattel from or entered any contractual relationship with the seller. Section 402B of the restatement is similar to an action under an express warranty made to the general public and represents another blurring of tort and contract theories.

Consumer Product Safety Commission

In 1972, Congress enacted the Consumer Product Safety Act, which established the Consumer Product Safety Commission. The commission is made up of five members appointed by the president. The commissioners select a fifteen-member Product Safety Advisory Council. The advisory council has representatives from industry, government, and consumer groups. The commission with the aid of the advisory council conducts studies, research, and investigations of consumer products for safety purposes. It promulgates safety standards for consumer products based on its research and studies. The commission may order manufacturers to conduct their own safety tests to insure the safety of consumer products.

In the case of an unsafe consumer product, the commission may order the manufacturer to:

1. Repair the defective product
2. Replace it with a safe product
3. Refund the purchaser's money.

There are severe penalties for violation of the act. Criminal penalties for willful violation include a fine of up to $50,000, imprisonment, or both on conviction.

NOTES

1. 25 U.S.C. §§ 2301–2312.
2. U.C.C. § 2–213.

3. U.C.C. § 2–314.

4. U.C.C. § 2–315.

5. The statute itself contains a figure of $5; however, the regulations promulgated provide for a $15 amount. Ten dollars is the amount that triggers the full and limited warranty provisions.

6. 15 U.S.C. §§ 41–58.

18

Keeping the Workplace Safe

The two primary subjects of this chapter are the duty to keep the workplace safe and liability for failure to do so. Liability for breach of the common law duty to keep a reasonably safe workplace was imposed by way of an employee's suit against the employer for negligence. Such suits were unsatisfactory remedies from the employee's perspective since most failed because of the powerful defenses of the fellow-servant rule, assumption of the risk, and contributory negligence. The common law development was influenced by the need to protect the infant industry of the industrial revolution in the nineteenth century. The common law was biased in favor of the employer. Early in the twentieth century, states began to provide compensation for job-related injuries through worker's compensation systems. But worker's compensation systems did not deter employers or make the workplace safer, and compensation rates are too low to make the injured worker whole. Finally in 1970, Congress passed the Occupational Safety and Health Act[1] to make the workplace safer. The controversy over the cost of OSHA versus its benefits continues.

In this chapter, safety in the workplace will be discussed first, followed by the consequences and liability for failure to keep it safe.

OCCUPATIONAL SAFETY AND HEALTH ACT

Until relatively recently, no uniform or comprehensive provisions existed for the protection of workers from safety and health hazards in the workplace. In terms of lost production and wages, medical expenses, and liability compensation, the burden on the nation's commerce is staggering. The Congressional hearings on the Occupational Safety and Health Act of 1970 revealed that 14,500 persons were killed annually as a result of industrial accidents and that conservatively 2.2 million people were disabled on the job, resulting in a loss of 250 million man-days of work. Economically, $1.5 billion was wasted on lost wages, and the annual loss to the gross national product was calculated at over $8 billion. The Occupational Safety and Health Act was passed by Congress ". . . to assure so far as possible every working man and woman in the nation safe and healthful working conditions and to preserve our human resources."

OSHA's Purpose

Under the act, the Occupational Safety and Health Administration (OSHA) was created within the Department of Labor to

1. Encourage employers and employees to reduce workplace hazards and to implement new or improved existing safety and health programs.
2. Provide for research in occupational safety and health and develop innovative ways of dealing with occupational safety and health problems.
3. Maintain a reporting and record-keeping system to monitor job-related injuries and illnesses.
4. Establish training programs to increase the number of occupational safety and health personnel.
5. Develop mandatory job safety and health standards and enforce them effectively.
6. Provide for the development, analysis, evaluation, and approval of state occupational safety and health programs.

Coverage

General

Coverage of the act extends to all employers and their employees in the 50 states, the District of Columbia, Puerto Rico, and all territories under the jurisdiction of the United States.

As defined by the act, an employer is any "person engaged in a business affecting commerce who has employees, but does not include the United States or any state or political subdivision of a state." The language "affecting commerce" justifies the act under the Commerce Clause of the Constitution and virtually extends the act to all employers except those specifically exempted.

The following are not covered under the act:

1. Self-employed persons
2. Farms at which only immediate members of the farm employer's family are employed
3. Workplaces already protected by other federal agencies under other federal statutes.

When OSHA develops safety and health standards of its own, standards issued under the following laws administered by the Department of Labor are superseded: the Walsh-Healey Act,[2] the Service Contract Act,[3] the Construction Safety Act,[4] the Arts and Humanities Act,[5] and the Longshoremen's and Harbor Worker's Compensation Act.[6]

Federal Employees

Federal agencies are covered by the act. Each agency is required to establish and maintain an effective and comprehensive job safety and health program. The program must be consistent with OSHA standards for private employers. The secretary of labor must provide federal agencies with guidance to assist them in maintaining an effective program for their employees.

State and Local Governments

OSHA provisions do not apply to state and local governments in their role as employers. The act does provide that any state desiring to gain OSHA approval for its private sector occupational safety and health program must provide a program that covers its state and local government workers and that is at least as effective as its program for private employees.

Standards

General Duty

The general duty clause of the act states that each employer "shall furnish . . . a place of employment which is free from recognized hazards that are causing or are likely to cause death or serious physical harm to his employees."[7]

In carrying out its duties, OSHA is responsible for promulgating legally enforceable standards. It is the employer's responsibility to become familiar with standards applicable to its establishment and to insure that employees have and use personal protective gear and safety equipment. Even where OSHA has not promulgated specific standards, employers are responsible for following the intent of the act's general duty clause.

Standards Development

OSHA may begin standards-setting procedures on its own initiative or on petitions from other parties, including the secretary of health and human services (HHS), the National Institute for Occupational Safety and Health (NIOSH), state and local governments, any nationally recognized standards-producing organization, an employer or labor representative, or any other interested person.

If OSHA determines that a specific standard is needed, any of several advisory committees may be called upon to develop specific recommendations. There are two standing committees, and ad hoc committees may be appointed to examine special areas of concern to OSHA. All advisory committees must have members representing management, labor, and state agencies, as well as one or more designees of the secretary of HHS. The two standing committees are the National

Advisory Committee on Occupational Safety and Health (NACOSH) and the Advisory Committee on Construction Safety and Health.

Once OSHA has developed plans to propose, amend, or delete a standard, it publishes its intention in the Federal Register. The notice must include the terms of the new rule and provide a specific time for the public to respond.

Interested parties who submit written arguments and pertinent evidence may request a public hearing when none has been announced in the notice. If a hearing is required, OSHA must schedule one and give adequate notice by publishing its date in the Federal Register.

After the close of the comment period or public hearing, OSHA must publish in the Federal Register the full text of any standard amended or adopted, along with the effective date and the reasons for implementation.

Under certain conditions, OSHA is authorized to set emergency temporary standards which take effect immediately. To do so, OSHA must determine that workers are in grave danger due to exposure to toxic substances or new hazards and that immediate action is needed to protect them. A final standard must be adopted according to established procedures within six months.

Any person who may be adversely affected by a final or emergency standard may file a petition for judicial review of the standard with the U.S. court of appeals. Enforcement of a standard is not delayed unless the court of appeals specifically suspends enforcement.

Employers may ask OSHA for a variance from a standard or regulation if they cannot fully comply by the effective date due to shortages of materials, equipment, or professional or technical personnel or can prove their facilities or methods of operations are "at least as effective as" those required by OSHA.

In order to continue to operate under existing conditions until a variance decision is made, the employer must apply to OSHA for an interim order. Application for an interim order may be made at the same time or after application for a variance.

Standards for Toxic Materials and Harmful Physical Agents

Section 6(b)(5) of OSHA requires that the secretary of labor set standards dealing with toxic materials or harmful physical agents that most adequately insure, *to the extent feasible*, on the basis of best available evidence, that no employee will suffer material impairment of health or functional capacity even if such employee is regularly exposed to the hazard.[8]

Before any regulation may be promulgated, OSHA must first establish that it is reasonably necessary or appropriate to provide safe or healthful employment.[9] If such a finding is made, OSHA may proceed to define standards.

The feasibility requirement has been the subject of a considerable amount of controversy. Feasible means capable of being done, but it must be examined in terms of both economic and technological feasibility.

Many have argued for a cost/benefit analysis, but the U.S. Supreme Court has dismissed this argument on the grounds that Congress has already done the cost/benefit analysis in Section 6(b)(5) by placing the benefit of employees' health above all other considerations.[10] The Court's position is that, since the cost/benefit analysis decidedly comes down in favor of the employee if the standard is capable of being done technologically, cost is irrelevant short of making financial viability impossible.

OSHA cannot require protection devices or equipment that are not technologically feasible. The technology must be available to make the workplace safer.

Record Keeping

Before OSHA, no centralized and systematic method existed for monitoring occupational safety and health problems. Statistics on job injuries and illnesses were collected by some states and private organizations; national figures were based on unreliable projections. With OSHA standards came the first basis for consistent, nationwide statistics.

Employers of eleven or more employees must maintain records of occupational injuries and illnesses as they occur. The purpose of keeping records is to permit the Bureau of Labor Statistics (BLS) survey material to be compiled, to help define high hazard industries, and to inform employees of the status of their employer's record. An occupational injury is defined as any injury such as a cut, fracture, sprain, or amputation that results from a work-related accident or from exposure involving a single incident in the work environment. An occupational illness is any abnormal condition or disorder, other than one resulting from an occupational injury, caused by exposure to environmental factors associated with employment.

For greater detail on OSHA record-keeping requirements see Chapter 19.

Information to Employees

Employers are responsible for keeping employees informed about OSHA and about the various safety and health matters with which they are involved. OSHA requires that each employer post the following materials in a prominent location at the workplace:

1. Job safety and health protection posters informing employers of their rights and responsibilities under the act. (Besides displaying the poster in the workplace, the employers must make available upon request copies of the act and copies of relevant OSHA rules and regulations.)
2. Summaries of petitions for variances from standards or record-keeping procedures.
3. Copies of OSHA citations for violations of standards.

Occasionally, OSHA standards or NIOSH research activities will require an employer to measure and record employee exposure to potentially harmful substances. Employees have the right (in person or through an authorized representative) to be present during the measuring and to examine records of the results.

Each employee or former employee has the right to see his or her examination records and must be told by the employer if exposure has exceeded the levels set by standards. The employee must also be told what corrective measures are being taken.

Recently there has been greater concern with the employee's right to know about physical or health hazards in the workplace. OSHA's Hazard Communication Standard[11] requires chemical manufacturers and importers to determine the physical and health hazards associated with any chemicals they manufacture or sell. This hazard information is passed along by container labels and material safety data sheets (MSDS) to the user. Additionally, certain employers are required to provide employees with special training in the use of the hazardous materials in the workplace. Some states, such as Michigan, are enacting even stricter right-to-know acts.

Inspection of the Workplace

Authority to Inspect

To enforce its standards, OSHA is authorized under the act to conduct inspections of the workplace. Every establishment covered by the act is subject to inspection by OSHA compliance officers. Under the act, "upon presenting appropriate credentials to the owner, operator or agent in charge," an OSHA compliance officer is authorized to

1. Enter without delay and at reasonable times any factory, plant, establishment, construction site or other areas, workplace, or environment where work is performed by an employee of an employer, and

2. Inspect and investigate during regular working hours, and at other reasonable times, and within reasonable limits and in a reasonable manner, any such place of employment and all pertinent conditions, structures, machines, apparatus, devices, equipment and materials therein, and to question privately any such employer, owner, operator, agent, or employee.[12]

With very few exceptions, inspections are conducted without advance notice. There are, however, special circumstances under which OSHA may indeed give notice to the employer, but even then, such a notice will be less than 24 hours. Employers receiving advance notice of an inspection must inform their employees' representative or arrange for OSHA to do so.

An employer may refuse to admit an OSHA inspector to a nonpublic area of the business without a warrant. OSHA inspections are subject to the Fourth Amendment prescription against unreasonable searches. To obtain a warrant, OSHA must have probable cause and specifically describe the place to be searched and matter to be seized, if any. The U.S. Supreme Court has stated though that OSHA does not have to meet the same high rigid standards as in a criminal case.[13] Presumably probable cause exists when an employee, even if unidentified, provides information initiating a search.

Two recent cases decided by the United States Supreme Court indicate that no warrant is needed to fly over a plant or business and take aerial photographs of violations that are used to issue citations.

Inspection Process

Prior to inspection, the compliance officer becomes familiar with as many relevant facts as possible about the workplace, taking into account such things as the history of the establishment, the nature of the business, and the particular standards likely to apply. Preparing for the inspection also involves selecting appropriate equipment for detecting and measuring fumes, gases, toxic substances, noise, and so on.

An inspection begins when the OSHA compliance officer arrives at the establishment. He or she displays official credentials and asks to meet an appropriate employer representative.

The compliance officer then explains the purpose of the visit, the scope of the inspection, and the standards that apply. The employer will be given copies of applicable safety and health standards as well as a copy of any employee complaint that may be involved. If the employee has so requested, his or her name will not be revealed.

The route and duration of the inspection are determined by the compliance officer. The compliance officer observes conditions, consults with employees, perhaps takes photos, takes instrument readings, and examines records.

Employees are consulted during the inspection. The compliance officer may stop and question workers, in private if necessary, about safety and health conditions and practices in their workplaces. It is unsettled as to whether the employer or OSHA must pay the employee's compensation for the time spent with the OSHA inspector. Each employee is protected, under the act, from discrimination or discharge for exercising his or her rights under the act.

Some apparent violations detected by the compliance officer may be corrected immediately. When they are corrected on the spot, the compliance officer records such corrections to help in judging the employer's good faith in compliance. An inspection tour may cover part or all of the establishment, even if the inspection resulted from a specific complaint, fatality, or catastrophe.

After the inspection tour is completed, a closing conference is held between the compliance officer and the employer or the employer's representative. The compliance officer relates his or her findings and indicates all apparent violations for which a citation may be issued or recommended. The employer is advised of its right of appeal. The compliance officer may not indicate any proposed penalties. Only the OSHA area director has authority to determine penalties and only after having received a full report.

Citations and Penalties

After the compliance officer reports his or her findings to the OSHA office, the area director determines what citations and penalties, if any, will be issued within six months of the inspection. Citations inform the employer and employees of the regulations and standards alleged to have been violated and of the time set for their abatement. The employer must post a copy of each citation at the place of violation until the violation is abated. A notice instead of a citation may be sent if the violation is minimal.

A compliance officer may issue citations at the worksite after he or she has discussed each violation with the area director and has received permission to issue citations. Such permission is granted to provide the employees with immediate knowledge of the violations. If deemed necessary, OSHA may seek an immediate injunction if there is imminent danger that death or serious injury could result and enforcement procedures are inadequate to protect the employees.

There are four levels of violations which may be cited by OSHA.

A citation may be issued where the violation presents "imminent danger." Imminent danger results from a situation in which there is reasonable certainty that a danger exists that can possibly cause death or serious physical harm immediately or before the danger can be eliminated through normal enforcement procedures. A violation that constitutes imminent danger results in a mandatory penalty ranging from $300 to $1,000 for each violation.

A "serious violation" is one in which there is a substantial probability that death or serious physical harm may result and that the employer knew or should have known of the hazard. A serious violation results in a mandatory penalty of from $300 to $1,000 per violation.

A violation "other than serious" is one that has a direct relationship to job safety and health, but it is improbable that death or serious harm would result. A discretionary penalty of up to $1,000 may be imposed for each other than serious violation.

A "willful violation" is a violation that the employer commits intentionally and knowingly. The employer either knows that the violation exists or is aware that the hazardous condition existed and made no reasonable effort to eliminate it. The penalty for a willful violation is a fine of up to $10,000 per violation.

Although criminal penalties are provided in the act there have been few prosecutions.

Appeals

Appeals by Employees

If an inspection was initiated as a result of an employee complaint, the employee or an authorized representative may request an informal review of any decision not to issue a citation.

Employees may not contest citations or amendments to citations or penalties or lack of penalties. They may contest the time allowed for abatement of a hazardous condition and an employer's petition for extension of the abatement period as unreasonable.

Employees may request an informal conference with OSHA to discuss any issues raised by an inspection, citation, notice of proposed penalty, or employer's notice of intention to contest.

Appeals by Employers

Employers are notified of an assessed penalty by certified mail and have fifteen working days to give notice to contest the citation or proposed penalty. If no notice of intent to contest is served, the penalty becomes final.

When an employer is issued a citation, it may request an informal meeting with OSHA's area director to discuss the case. The area director has the authority to agree to settlements that mitigate citations and penalties to avoid prolonged legal disputes.

After receiving a citation, an employer is required to correct the hazard by the prescribed date. Failure to correct is a violation subject to a penalty. If circumstances beyond an employer's control prevent the completion of the required corrections on time, an employer, who has made a good faith effort to comply, may file for a Petition of Modification of Abatement. The petition should specify all steps taken to achieve compliance, the additional time needed to comply, the reasons the time is needed, and all temporary steps being taken to protect employees against the hazard until it can be corrected.

If a citation or penalty is contested by either an employer or employee, a hearing must be held under the Administrative Procedures Act before the Occupational Health and Safety Commission. The commission's decision becomes final unless an appeal is taken to a U.S. court of appeals.

Criticisms of OSHA

Many employers severely criticize OSHA for promulgating vague regulations that are too subjective. Issuance of a citation depends more on the inspector's mood than on safety considerations. For example, whether or not a hallway or passageway is clean and orderly is debatable.

Another criticism of OSHA is that it has too many trivial or nit-picking regulations. In 1977, Congress ordered OSHA to withdraw its "nuisance standards," which were unrelated to safety and health objectives. Reduction of government regulation is a campaign promise heard every election year.

Third, there are considerable costs involved in complying with OSHA regulations. Naturally, businesses complain that these costs increase the cost of doing business and that, in some cases, OSHA regulations have forced businesses to close.

Some complain that OSHA spends too much of its limited resources on inspecting the "little guy" instead of high-risk industries.

There is an adversary relationship between business and OSHA rather than a spirit of cooperation, which is unfortunate because the common goal of both should be increased safety in the workplace.

LIABILITY OF EMPLOYER FOR INJURED EMPLOYEE

Common Law

An employer is liable for any negligence that results in an injury to an employee who is acting in the scope of his or her employment. An employee owes certain duties to its employees, breach of which may result in imposing liability for injury on the employer. However, the employer's liability is mitigated by the existence of the defenses of fellow-servant, assumption of the risk, and contributory negligence.

Duty to Employ Reasonably Competent Employees

An employer owes its employees a duty to select reasonably competent employees as fellow-servants. If the employer fails to perform this duty, the fellow-servant rule does not apply. Moreover, if the employer becomes aware or knows that an employee has become so incompetent as to be dangerous to other employees, the employer has an obligation to discharge the incompetent employee. The employer also has a duty to employ a sufficient or reasonable number of employees to perform the job safely.

Fellow-Servant Rule

The fellow-servant rule is particularly damaging to an injured employee's case. An employer is not liable for injury to an employee who is harmed by another employee's negligence acting within the scope of his or her employment and engaged in the same enterprise. In such case, the employee's only recourse is against the employee who negligently injured him or her. The rule does not apply, however, if the employee is assaulted or defamed by a superior acting within his or her authority in supervising the employee's conduct or protecting the employer's property. The fellow-servant rule applies not only to physical injury sustained by the employee but also to any injury to the employee's property that is used in his or her employment. The rule does not apply to any of the employee's property not used in his or her employment nor to any member of the employee's family who is injured by a fellow employee.

It is essential that both employees be employed by the same employer and be engaged in the same general type of enterprise. For example, if an employer carries on several lines of work, which are unconnected and distinct from one another, an employee of one line of work is not a fellow-servant of an employee in one of the other lines of work. The mere fact that the employees are in different departments or perform different kinds of services, though, is irrelevant. Moreover, employees do not have to be of equal rank to be fellow-servants, even supervisors are fellow-servants of the employees they supervise unless they are performing nondelegatable duties of the employer.

The rule does not apply to partners nor to independent contractors. The fellow-servant rule is not applicable where it is the employer himself who is responsible for the employee's mistake or where the employer is aware of the mistake. The rule does not apply to a person who is compelled or coerced into serving another, who is illegally employed, or who does not have the capacity to appreciate adequately the risk of harm from fellow employees.

The rule is not limited to compensated personnel. The rule applies equally to a volunteer who gratuitously offers his or her service to assist the employee in performing the employer's business.

Duty to Provide Safe Working Area

An employer has a nondelegatable duty to provide and maintain a reasonably safe working place. Moreover, the employer is under a duty to warn its employees of any unsafe conditions that do exist or that it should be aware exists and that the employees are not capable of discovering on their own. An employer who provides a reasonably safe working place is not liable for injury to an employee because the employer is not negligent. The employer is liable for harm caused only by its negligent conduct and which is reasonably foreseeable. This means that an employer is not required to provide the safest possible working place but only one that is reasonably safe.

Assumption of the Risk

Another debilitating defense is the assumption of the risk doctrine. The general rule is that employees by accepting employment assume the risk of harm for any existing dangers that are inherent in the business and that they are aware of or should be aware of. An employer, although it has a duty to provide a reasonably safe place of employment, is not liable for injuries resulting from temporary danger caused by the negligence of employees. Both the fellow-servant rule and the assumption of the risk doctrine would protect the employer under this circumstance. In general, the employer has a duty to protect its employees while working on the premises against such things as fires, floods, and other foreseeable harms against which the employees are unable to protect themselves. But this duty does not include other natural conditions such as heat and cold where the employees know of the conditions of employment and are employed outdoors. They accept those risks as conditions of employment.

An employer who provides its employees with tools has an obligation to exercise reasonable care in their selection and inspection. However, an employer is not liable for any harm caused by a hidden defect in the tool which could not be reasonably discovered. If the employer discovers a defective tool or dangerous condition on the premises, the employer is under an obligation to have it repaired or order its disuse. If an employee, who has a reasonable opportunity to inspect the tool or premises and such inspection would have revealed the defect, uses the tool or enters the premises, the employer is not liable for any injury sustained by the employee as a result. Similarly, an employer is not liable if an employee is injured by an unreasonable use of a tool.

Contributory Negligence

An employee who unreasonably uses a tool, fails to inspect, or unreasonably places him- or herself in a dangerous situation is contributorily negligent. In some states, contributory negligence is an absolute bar to recovery by the employee, but, in other states utilizing comparative negligence, the relative negligence of the employer and the contributory negligence of the employee are determined according to the relative weights of each. Under one version of comparative negligence, if the employee is more than 50-percent negligent, no recovery is allowed. Other comparative negligence systems merely reduce the amount of the award for damages by the percentage that the employee is found to be contributorily negligent.

Duty to Supervise

The employer has a duty to regulate and supervise employees and to establish rules and regulations necessary for the reasonable safety of the employees. With regard to new employees, the employer has a duty to provide them with work suitable to their level of accomplishment, instruct them in the performance of the work, and warn them of any concealed dangers. If an employee is put into a position of imminent danger or is rendered helpless during the course of employment, the employer has an obligation to come to the aid of the employee, whether or not the dangerous situation was caused by the negligence of the employer. The employer must act reasonably to rescue the employee and to provide first aid to any injured employee until competent medical help arrives.

Common Law and Worker's Compensation

Under the common law, it is extremely difficult for employees to recover damages caused as a result of the employer's negligence because of the existence of such powerful defenses as the fellow-servant rule, assumption of the risk, and contributory negligence. The result is that the common law rules have been abolished in most states in favor of worker's compensation laws. Worker's compensation laws generally make the employer liable without fault; therefore, the defenses of fellow-servant rule, assumption of the risk, and contributory negligence have been abolished. Some states still retain the option for the injured employee to bring an action against the employer for negligence, in which event the defenses of fellow-servant rule, assumption of the risk, and contributory negligence are still available to the employer. Those states that allow the injured employee an option of either worker's compensation or bringing a cause of action in negligence against the employer do so because of the monetary limitation on damages under the worker's compensation act. The tradeoff in worker's compensation laws has been between certainty of recovery and the amount of the monetary award for damages.

Worker's Compensation

The models for worker's compensation statutes in the United States were the German system adopted in 1884 and the British legislation of 1897, which was also modeled after the German system.

Federal Legislation

Interstate railroad employees are covered by the Federal Employer's Liability Act.[14] Liability is predicated on employer fault, but neither the fellow-servant rule nor assumption of the risk is allowed as a defense by the employer. Contributory negligence is not allowed as a defense but is taken into consideration in assessing damages. Coverage was extended to seamen in 1920 under the Jones Act.[15] Seamen are also covered by the Death on the High Seas Act.[16]

The Federal Employees Compensation Act[17] covers all civilian employees of the United States government.

The Longshoremen's and Harbor Worker's Compensation Act[18] covers non-seamen maritime workers and an assortment of other workers such as PX employees and offshore drilling workers. In addition, it is the worker's compensation statute of the District of Columbia.

Worker's Compensation Plan

All states have a worker's compensation plan of one kind or another which compensates injured employees for medical or hospitalization expenses and lost income resulting from job-related injuries. This section discusses worker's compensation systems in general. For more specific information concerning the worker's compensation system in your state, you should contact the state administrator or your attorney.

Worker's compensation is essentially an insurance program. Worker's compensation insurance coverage is generally regulated by the state insurance department. Insurance rates are set in each state by rating bureaus for each industry covered. Worker's compensation insurance rates are different from other liability and casualty rates because they are completely noncompetitive; however, a few states are beginning to permit ratings based on the employer's loss experience. Most states require an employer to fulfill its obligation under the state worker's compensation system through the purchase of commercial insurance or, under certain conditions, to act as a self-insurer. A few states have instituted state funds which act as insurers for covered employers. Some of these states make the state fund the exclusive means of providing coverage under the state worker's compensation system while others provide the employer with a choice between the state fund or a private commercial insurer. Louisiana is the exception; covered employers are not required to have insurance under the Louisiana statute.

Failure of an employer to provide coverage as required under a worker's compensation act is generally a misdemeanor punishable by a fine, imprisonment of generally not more than one year, or both. In addition to a criminal penalty for failure to provide adequate coverage, an employer may be subject to suit by an injured employee for negligence. In this event, the defenses of fellow-servant, assumption of the risk, and contributory negligence are not available to the employer.

The worker's compensation system in every state except Alabama and Louisiana is administered through a state agency. In Alabama and Louisiana, the worker's compensation system is judicially administered.

Most claims under worker's compensation statutes involve relatively small amounts for medical payments and are uncontested. These cases are handled without formal proceedings. A worker who is injured reports the injury to his or her employer, and the employer in turn reports it to its insurance carrier or the state fund whichever is applicable.

In contested cases where no agreement is reached among employer, employee, and insurance carrier or state fund, the state administrative agency has exclusive jurisdiction to hear the case. The state agency charged with enforcement of the worker's compensation act has authority to hear and determine claims, make awards, conduct investigations, assess penalties, and perform all necessary non-administrative tasks. Referees may be appointed to assist with the hearing case-load. The hearings are generally governed under the state administrative procedures act, and judicial review is allowed only after exhausting the administrative procedure.

An employee injured on the job or in a job-related activity is required to notify the employer within the specified number of days. If the claim cannot be satisfactorily settled among the employer, employee, and insurance carrier, the claim may be presented to the state agency.

If the claim is contested by either party, a hearing will be held where evidence will be collected from both sides. The administrative law judge or referee may issue subpoenas, examine witnesses, and take testimony.

The burden of proof is on the injured employee or his or her representatives. The employer has the burden of proof for defenses which may be appropriate to the claim.

The administrative law judge or referee will make a decision which is final with respect to the state agency unless new evidence is uncovered and the case is reopened at a later date.

Judicial appeals, as is generally the case in an appellate review, are limited to issues of law and not findings of fact.

The worker's compensation system is the exclusive remedy if the employer, employee, and injury are all covered by the worker's compensation system. The exclusivity of the compensation remedy is imposed on the employer and employee in exchange for the more limited liability without fault imposed on the employer and the certainty of recovery without regard to fault or defenses on behalf of the employee. The exclusivity rule provides immunity for the employer from tort liability to the injured employee. Some states extend the immunity from tort liability to supervisors, fellow-servants, and the employer's insurance carrier. The grant of immunity, however, does not extend to any third party who may be responsible for the injury. Exclusivity also extends on the injured employee's side to his or her spouse or other dependent for damages arising out of the injury to the employee. However, suit is not barred for breach of an independent duty owed by the employer to the spouse or dependent. A growing trend is to bar suit by a spouse for loss of consortium. Consortium is the conjugal fellowship of spouses which consists of their rights to companionship and services of each other.

Worker's compensation benefits are payable to employees who suffer accidents arising out of or in the course of employment. Some states have replaced the word accident with injury, but almost all states still retain the language "arising out of and in the course of."

An accident is defined to be an event that is unexpected or not according to the usual course of things. The word "accident" still occurs in most worker's compensation statutes. A great deal of litigation is centered around the definition of an accident. The primary issue revolves around the suddenness of the event. Occupational injuries, such as loss of hearing due to protracted exposure to loud noise, were traditionally not accidents because they occurred over a long period of time and could not be attributed to any specific traumatic occurrence. The trend is toward covering injuries that gradually occur such as loss of hearing, but a minority of states still continues to use the unexpected or sudden traumatic event concept.

Occupational disease has now become a compensable injury in almost all states. Some states have amended their worker's compensation statute to include occupational diseases; other states have enacted separate legislation. Occupational disease statutes vary from those that list and schedule various diseases to those that rely on a more general definition of occupational disease. The former schedule type of statute is more restrictive in that it requires that the injured employee be able to bring the disease within the definition on the schedule. An occupational disease is defined to be a disease or illness that is contracted or caused by the nature of employment or occupation, the process or employment in which an employee is exposed or a characteristic peculiar to a particular trade. Generally, worker's compensation is paid only when the employee is disabled or dies as a result of the occupational disease. Disability means that the employee is unable to earn full wages at the work at which the employee was last employed.

Worker's compensation coverage is limited to employees. "In the course of employment" is similar to the concept of scope of employment in the master-servant area. A worker or employee whose employment is casual and is not in the course of the employer's regular trade or business is not covered. Moreover, some states exempt from coverage activities that are not in pursuit of pecuniary gain. The nonbusiness exception is extended to exclude work done on private dwellings. The nonbusiness exception also excludes from coverage domestic servants. Only a few states provide worker's compensation coverage for agricultural workers. Nearly half the states exempt employers with fewer than four or five employees based on administrative convenience.

To be within the course of employment, the employee generally must be injured on the job during normal working hours. On the job or job-related is liberally construed by courts. For example, an employee injured in an athletic event at a company picnic is covered by worker's compensation since it is job related. As with scope of employment, injuries which occur on the way to or home from the workplace generally are not covered by worker's compensation, but there are exceptions.

The employee's negligence is not a bar to compensation if the injury is otherwise compensable. However, about half of the states prohibit compensation for an injury resulting from the employee's willful misconduct or violation of a safety rule or failure to use safety equipment provided. In almost every state, compensation is prohibited if the employee was intoxicated and such intoxication was a contributing factor to the injury. Most worker's compensation systems do not compensate employees for self-inflicted wounds. However, some states allow recovery for suicide whether it occurs at the workplace or not if an industrial accident was the precipitating cause.

The phrase "arising out of" has its parallel in a negligence action in proximate cause. Some courts have adopted a "but for" standard. Under this test the purpose of the statute is satisfied if it appears that but for the employment, the employee would not have experienced the injury.

If a worker is injured as a result of an accident arising out of employment and in the course of the employment, the employee or his or her estate may be entitled to the following benefits:

1. Medical and hospital expenses
2. Lost wages
3. Compensation for lost body members
4. Rehabilitation following the injury
5. Prosthetics
6. Death benefits.

By far the greatest majority of worker's compensation claims are for medical or hospital expenses, but these constitute less than one third of worker's compensation benefits paid. Generally, the injured employee may go to any professionally qualified person he or she chooses for treatment. The professionally qualified person may be paid either through the worker's compensation system or directly by the employer. Most worker's compensation claims are satisfied and terminate at this point.

Lost wages or claims for income replacement generally involve claims for *temporary total disability*. Income replacement benefits for temporary total disability are calculated by multiplying a percentage, usually 66-2/3, times the average weekly wage prior to the injury times the number of weeks of temporary total disability. Another type of income replacement benefit is *permanent partial disability*. Permanent partial disability cases are generally contested because they depend upon the opinion testimony of physicians as to the extent of the impairment. Payments for permanent partial disability may be either according to a schedule of the injuries providing for a lump-sum payment or for a percentage of the employee's total disability payment. Most income replacement cases are either temporary total disability or permanent partial disability, and *permanent total disability* cases are uncommon. Permanent total disability payments are made according to schedules in a lump sum.

Most states have schedule payments for lost body members such as loss of an eye or loss of a limb. Compensation for rehabilitation and prosthetics is also included.

All states pay a death benefit in a lump-sum payment independent of the employee's earnings record and include an allowance for funeral and burial expenses.

Developing Trend: Criminal Liabililty of Corporate Officers

Traditionally, courts have employed the business judgment rule and have refrained from interfering in business decisions. The business judgment rule presumes that the directors of a corporation act on an informed basis, in good faith, and in the honest belief that the action taken is in the best interests of the corporation. The rationale for the rule is that the directors know better than the courts what is best for the corporation. In the absence of fraud or self-dealing, the business judgment rule applics.

Recent cases indicate that the courts may be reconsidering their deference to the corporate decision-making process. The more notable of these cases involve workers' safety on the job and their right to know about hazards in the workplace.

The president and four other corporate officials of Film Recovery Systems, a suburban Chicago company, were indicted and three were convicted of homicide for the death of a worker. Most of Film Recovery Systems' workers were people of Polish and Mexican descent who were working illegally and could not read or speak English. The workers were exposed to cyanide on a regular and continual basis. The corporation knew of a number of cases of cyanide poisoning among the workers but did nothing to warn them of the hazards. In 1983, a worker collapsed and died of cyanide poisoning. This case represents a turning point in prosecutors' attitudes toward corporate defendants because this is the first case in which the charge was as serious as homicide. Moreover, the charges arose out of conduct considered to be in the ordinary course of business.

The Cook County prosecutor has also filed criminal actions for reckless conduct and aggravated battery for failure to take adequate safety precautions to protect workers baking enamel on insulated wire against Chicago Magnet Wire Company of Elk Grove Village.

Film director John Landis and others have been charged with manslaughter for criminal negligence in filming the tragic helicopter scene in the movie "Twilight Zone." Actor Vic Morrow and two children were killed during the staging of the scene by a crashing helicopter. Prosecutors charge that the defendants did not adequately protect the actors from the dangers involved.

It is still too early to be able to define the parameters of prosecutorial zeal in prosecuting this kind of case, but other considerations such as budgetary limitations and public pressure to prosecute street crime will probably limit the number of these cases to the more reprehensible ones.

Liability Insurance and Indemnification

This growing trend will have an effect on liability insurance and indemnification of corporate officers by the corporation. Every business corporation statute in the United States has an indemnification provision for reimbursement of expenses incurred by directors, officers, and other corporate personnel. There are two general forms of statutes: some speak to the power of a corporation to indemnify, and others are drafted in terms of a right of indemnification.

Most indemnification statutes are traceable to the original Model Business Corporation Act,[19] the 1967 Model Act Delaware version,[20] the 1980 Model Act revision,[21] the 1963 New York statute,[22] and the 1977 California statute.[23]

The statutes distinguish between actions by or in the right of the corporation to procure judgment in its favor and other proceedings. Most statutes are not limited to derivative actions. A shareholder derivative suit is an equitable action designed to allow shareholders to enforce corporate rights against the corporation's own management or third parties when management refuses to enforce those rights of its own volition. The shareholder sues the corporation on behalf of the corporation. All judgments are in favor of the corporation, not the individual shareholder. Legislatures have been more liberal with indemnification for liability arising out of third-party actions than for derivative suits.

To be eligible for indemnification, the person must meet the prescribed standard of conduct which generally requires good faith and reasonable belief that the conduct was in or at least was not opposed to the best interests of the corporation. In an action by or in the right of the corporation, negligence or misconduct in the performance of the duty owed to the corporation is a bar to indemnification. In a criminal proceeding, the person must have reasonable belief that the conduct was lawful. Self-dealing is also a bar to indemnification.

Unless court ordered, indemnification must be authorized; therefore, a finding must be made that the person to be indemnified met the required standard of conduct. That determination is typically made by the board of directors by majority vote of a quorum present, who were not parties to the conduct or action or legal counsel, in a written opinion submitted to the board of directors. Sometimes the decision is made by the shareholders if they were not parties to the conduct or action, or infrequently the determination is made by a court. Success on the merits or otherwise in defense affords the person seeking indemnification the right to indemnification.

If the state corporation act is unclear or general in content, the corporation should provide detailed indemnification procedures and guidelines in its bylaws.

Most modern corporate statutes expressly provide that a corporation may purchase and maintain liability insurance on behalf of corporate personnel even if the corporation would not have the power to indemnify such persons against such liability.

Insurance coverage has two aspects whether in a single policy or several. First, the policy provides for reimbursement of amounts paid by the corporation for indemnification of corporate personnel. Second, the policy provides for payment of liabilities of directors and officers who are not indemnifiable by the corporation. The latter aspect generally covers judgments and settlements in derivative actions for negligence but not claims arising out of self-dealing, bad faith, and knowing violations of federal securities law and other willful misconduct. The policies generally have high deductibles, and some have co-insurance provisions.

NOTES

1. 29 U.S.C. §§ 651–678.
2. 29 U.S.C. § 557; 41 U.S.C. §§ 35–45.
3. 41 U.S.C. §§ 351–357.
4. 40 U.S.C. § 333.
5. 20 U.S.C. §§ 951–960.
6. 33 U.S.C. §§ 901–950.
7. 29 U.S.C. § 654.
8. 29 U.S.C. § 655 (b) (5).
9. 29 U.S.C. § 652 (8).
10. American Textile Mfrs. Institute, Inc. v. Donovan, 452 U.S. 490 (1981).
11. 29 C.F.R. § 1910.1200.
12. 29 C.F.R. § 1903.3.
13. Marshall v. Barlow's, Inc., 436 U.S. 307 (1978).
14. 45 U.S.C. §§ 51–60.
15. 46 U.S.C. §§ 688.
16. 46 U.S.C. §§ 761–768.
17. 5 U.S.C. §§ 8101–8193.
18. 33 U.S.C. §§ 901–950.
19. 1959 ABA-ALI Model Business Corp. Act, § 4 (0).
20. 1967 ABA-ALI Model Business Corp. Act, § 4A.
21. ABA-ALI Model Business Corp. Act, § 5.
22. N.Y. Bus. Corp. Law §§ 721–26 (McKinney).
23. Cal. Corp. Code § 317 (West).

19

Record Keeping

SMALL BUSINESS RECORDS

Adequate records are necessary to prepare tax returns; to provide financial data to banks or other financial institutions, suppliers, or creditors; and to determine the financial status of the business at any given point.

A good record-keeping system must be simple to use, easy to understand, reliable, accurate, consistent, and designed to provide information on a timely basis.

Revenue and Expense Records

A simple revenue and expense record-keeping system requires four basic records for

1. Sales
2. Cash receipts
3. Cash dispersements
4. Accounts receivable.

Sales may be divided into categories such as wholesale, retail, and services. Cash receipts represent cash sales and collections of accounts receivable. Cash dispersements should be a record of all cash outflows. Accounts receivable represent monies due on account. In order to balance a cash receipts book easily, all receipts for the day should be deposited in the bank in a night depository. The exact amount received should be deposited. Do not pay out small amounts from receipts, instead use a petty cash account. All dispersements other than small amounts made out of petty cash should be made by check. The checkbook serves as a record of all expenditures, and the check stubs should be completely filled out to complete the record.

A petty cash account should be set up and used to make payment of small amounts not covered by invoices. Payments made from petty cash for such items as postage, freight, and bus or taxi fares should be listed on a printed form or blank sheet of paper located with the petty cash account. The petty cash on hand plus the listed expenditures should equal the amount of the petty cash account at all times.

Accounting System

An initial decision must be made as to the type of accounting system to be utilized by the business. The business may choose either a cash or accrual accounting basis and an appropriate accounting period. Most small businesses use a calendar year as the accounting period; however, corporate and noncorporate taxpayers may choose a fiscal year ending on the last day of any month. The election is made by filing an initial tax return. The elected accounting period must be used until permission to change is obtained from the IRS. Under a cash basis accounting system, entries for revenues and expenses are made when cash is received or dispersed. Under an accrual basis accounting system, revenues and expenses are recorded when each item is earned or incurred without regard as to when actual payments are made or received. Income is recognized when all events that fix the right to receive it have occurred, and the amount is reasonably estimatable. An expense is deductible in the tax year in which all events have occurred that determine that the liability exists, and the amount is reasonably estimatable. A cash basis accounting system is simpler to operate and should suffice for a small business; however, under certain circumstances, an accrual basis accounting system must be used. For example, a business that utilizes an inventory system must use an accrual basis accounting system unless otherwise authorized by the IRS.

A business needs some type of simple record book, which can be obtained easily at most office supply stores.

Preparation of financial statements should be done by an outside accountant. The principal financial statements are the balance sheet, the income (profit and loss) statement, and the retained earnings statement. These financial statements are prepared from the basic records of the business. Each contains information useful to both management and outside creditors and investors.

Equipment Records

A careful list of permanent equipment used in the business should be kept. Equipment that has a useful life of a year or longer and is of appreciable value should be listed. The information listed should include the date purchased, the name of the supplier, a description of the item, a record of the means by which it was paid, and the amount paid. If the business owns a large number of individual items of equipment, separate lists breaking the equipment down into particular categories would be helpful. These lists provide the basic information for calculating depreciation and provide the supporting data for fixed-asset accounts. Fixed assets are items normally in use for one year or longer, such as buildings, automobiles, equipment, tools, furniture, and fixtures.

Benefits of a Good Record-Keeping System

A good record-keeping system should provide the owner-manager of the business with essential periodic information. On a daily basis, the owner-manager should know the amount of cash on hand, the bank balance, the daily summary of sales and cash receipts, and a daily summary of all monies paid out by cash or check. On a weekly basis, the owner-manager should know the amount of the accounts receivable account, the amount of the accounts payable account, payroll obligations, and taxes due. Good records will allow the owner-manager to calculate and prepare a profit and loss statement for each month showing the income for the business for the month, the expenses incurred in obtaining the income, and the profit or loss resulting. This information may be used to take action to eliminate losses by adjusting markup, reducing overhead expenses, and reducing pilferage; to correct any deficiencies in tax reporting; to correct errors in buying procedures; and to enable the business to take advantage of cash discounts. The bank statement should be reconciled on a monthly basis as well as the petty cash account.

The balance sheet, which may also be prepared monthly, will provide information concerning accounts receivable which should be aged each month to determine their collectibility. To keep accounts receivable current, they should be aged each month. Accounts should be listed according to the length of time that they are outstanding. Accounts should be put into categories of current, unpaid for 30 days, and unpaid for 60 days or more. The owner-manager should work on all bad and slow accounts by contacting the customer and by obtaining a promise of payment on a definite date. Uncollectible accounts may be written off directly or charged against an allowance for uncollectible accounts. Knowing the amount of uncollectible accounts helps to establish the allowance for uncollectible accounts. Screening of customers' creditworthiness will insure that unwarranted credit is not extended.

Inventory control should be worked on a monthly basis to remove dead stock and order new stock.

TAX RECORDS AND REPORTING

Records

The Internal Revenue Service does not prescribe specific accounting records, documents, or systems. Although no particular form of records is required, the records must be accurate and must reflect taxable income and allowable deductions. Records must be kept available for inspection by agents of the IRS. It is necessary then to maintain permanent books of account or records which may be used to identify income, expenses, and deductions. Where inventories are involved in determining income or when travel or entertainment deductions are taken, special supporting details are required. Since the burden of proof lies with the taxpayer in almost all tax matters, the records must reflect all income and all expenses to support the tax return in case of audit. Lack of supporting documentation may result in an increase in income, disallowance of a deduction, and an additional tax payment and penalty. Maintenance of an adequate records system will generally prevent allegations of willful negligence and fraud by the IRS.

The simple record-keeping system described above consisting of a checkbook, a cash receipts journal, a cash dispersements journal, and a petty cash fund is generally sufficient for a small business such as a sole proprietorship. As the business becomes more complex, a more sophisticated record system will be required. A fixed-asset record will be needed to record all equipment, buildings, vehicles, and other depreciable assets. If the business is a partnership or corporation, the records required to be kept increase in complexity. A publicly held corporation is required to keep extensive financial records not only for tax purposes but also for the shareholders and various government agencies such as the Securities and Exchange Commission.

Employers who withhold taxes from wages have to keep additional and more extensive records. Employer records must show the names of persons employed during the year, their identification numbers, addresses, wages and reported tips subject to withholding, periods of employment, and amounts and dates of payments and deductions. Withholding allowance certificates and changes in status filed by employees should also be kept.

Retention

Records used to prepare taxes should be retained for varying periods depending upon their nature. In general, the statute of limitations under the Internal Revenue Code is three years following the date that the return is due or filed, whichever is later. Therefore, records should be kept for a minimum of four years after the due date or the tax is paid, whichever is later. However, the statute of limitations is six years if the taxpayer omitted over 25 percent of gross income or filed a false or fraudulent return. Certain records should be considered permanent. Cash books, depreciation schedules, general ledger, journals, financial statements, and audit reports should be kept permanently. Other records such as accounts payable, accounts receivable, cancelled checks, inventory schedules, payroll records, and sales vouchers and invoice details should be retained for six or seven years. Copies of income tax returns should be permanently retained. Records for a claim for refund, credit, or abatement should be retained for four years after filing.

Federal Income and Social Security Tax Reporting

The owner-manager of a small business has a dual role in managing taxes. The owner-manager is both a debtor and an agent. As a debtor, the owner-manager is liable for various taxes that must be paid as part of the business obligations. As an agent, the owner-manager of a business collects various taxes and remits the funds to the appropriate governmental agency. The result is that the owner-manager is responsible for paying taxes not only owed by the business but also those collected from others such as sales taxes, federal income and social security withholding taxes, and property taxes.

The mechanics of withholding may be handled by an agent, but the legal responsibility rests with the employer. Fiduciaries, agents, and others who have control of or pay wages of employees may perform the employer's duties when authorized by the IRS. Lenders, sureties, or other persons who pay wages directly to employees of another are liable to the government for withholding plus interest. Any creditor who lends money knowing that the loan will be used to meet payrolls is subject to a limited liability.

Taxpayer Identification Numbers

All taxpayers must have a taxpayer identification number (TIN) which must be shown on returns, statements, and other documents filed with the IRS. The identifying number for individuals and decedent's estates is the taxpayer's social security number. Taxpayers must obtain an employer identification number (EI) if they are engaged in a trade or business or withhold taxes from employees' wages. Corporations and partnerships must use an employer identification number. An employer identification number may be obtained from the IRS by filing Form SS–4 within seven days after wages are first paid. A $5 penalty may be imposed for each failure to use the proper taxpayer identification number.

Employer's Federal Income and Social Security Taxes

In paying income taxes and social security taxes owed by the business, the owner-manager is a debtor. The amount of federal income taxes owed by the owner-manager depends on the earnings of the business and the type of business organization. Sole proprietors and partners are required by law to make estimated quarterly tax payments on their federal income tax and self-employment tax liability. A Declaration of Estimated Tax (Form 1040 ES) must be filed on or before April 15 of each calendar year. The declaration is an estimate of the income and self-employment taxes expected to be owed based on expected income and exemptions. Payments on the estimate of one quarter each are due April 15, June 15, September 15, and January 15. Any necessary adjustments to the estimated tax should be made at each quarter.

Corporations also are required to make payments on account quarterly. A corporation whose estimated tax is expected to be $40 or more is required to make estimated tax payments by the fourth, sixth, ninth, and twelfth months of the corporation's fiscal year.

Employee Withholding

In essence, employees make federal income tax payments each payday through the employer. The employer, in turn, passes those payments on to the government.

Withholding is required only when the payment is for services as an employee, but the recipient need not be an employee at the time of payment. An employer-employee relationship exists if the payor has the right, whether he or she exercises it or not, to control and direct the worker, both for an end or a means to something. There is no withholding on the earnings or drawings of a partner, independent contractor, or self-employed person.

All employees regardless of class are subject to withholding. Superintendents, managers, corporate officers, and blue collar employees are subject to withholding, but director's fees are not ordinarily subject to withholding. Minors are treated the same as other employees, but there are special rules for newspaper carriers and employees who file a withholding allowance certificate (W–4).

Individuals properly substituting for regular employees are considered employees. However, if a person is engaged without the company's knowledge or consent, that person is not an employee. Employees who perform services in illegal as well as legal activities are subject to withholding.

Wages whether in cash or in kind are subject to withholding. Noncash wages are measured by their fair market value at the time of transfer.

Items not subject to withholding include: facilities or privileges of small value furnished to employees generally to promote health, goodwill, or efficiency, such as entertainment, medical service, and courtesy discounts on purchases; merchandise of nominal value, such as turkeys and hams, distributed at holidays to promote goodwill; scholarship and fellowship grants; union strike benefits; compensation paid to former employees in the Armed Forces or National Guard; meal reimbursements; supper money; payment for employee's tuition job-related courses.

The amount to be withheld is figured on gross wages, before any deductions, by using either the percentage method or the wage-bracket withholding tables. Tables and instructions may be obtained from the IRS. The percentage method may be used for some employees and the wage-bracket for others. The method first adopted may be changed without the Internal Revenue Service's approval. However, the percentage method must be used for quarterly, semiannual, or annual payroll periods, unless an authorized alternative method is used. The amount of withholding under the percentage or wage-bracket method depends on the schedule used (referring to the payroll period and the employee's marital status), the number of withholding allowances claimed by the employee on the withholding allowance certificate, and on the amount of the employee's earnings.

In addition to the percentage and wage-bracket methods, several alternatives are available. Employers can use their own method of figuring withholding without IRS approval if it gives the same results as the percentage or wage-bracket methods.

In addition, rules have been prescribed for employers to withhold, on the basis of annual wages, cumulative wages, wages for part-time employment, or any other method of computing withholding that comes within the maximum permissible deviation amounts set forth in the regulations. Employers may also withhold quarterly on the basis of the employee's average estimated wages.

Withholding on payments made without regard to a specified payroll period, or for a period not provided for in the tables, is figured by using the table for a "daily or miscellaneous payroll period," or, if the percentage method is used, by applying the allowance for such period. If wages are paid for a period that is not a payroll period (wages paid on completing a project), the withholding allowance allowed is that for a miscellaneous payroll period containing a number of days (including Sundays and holidays) equal to the number of days in the period the wages cover. If paid without regard to any particular period (commissions paid on completing sale), the withholding allowance is measured by the number of days elapsed (including Sundays and holidays) since the date of the last wage payment to that employee during the calendar year, the date work began during the calendar year, or January 1 of the calendar year, whichever is the latest. If the payments cover less than a week, the employer may determine the withholding by use of the weekly payroll period table if he first obtains a written, sworn statement from the employee that he or she works for no other employer during the week and will notify the employer within ten days after starting any other job. If other work is secured, the weekly payroll period table cannot be used, but the daily or miscellaneous table will take effect as of the beginning of the first payroll period ending, or the first payment of wages made without regard to a payroll period, on or after 30 days from the date on which such employee notifies the employer that he or she has secured additional work.

Withholding can be computed on the basis of annualized wages by: (1) multiplying wages for the payroll period by the number of such periods in the calendar year, (2) determining the tax required to be withheld from the first step on an annual basis, and (3) dividing the result by the number of payroll periods.

The local office of the IRS can provide you with tables and instructions for their use.

Each new employee is required to complete and sign a Form W-4, Employee's Withholding Allowance Certificate. On it, the employee lists the exemptions and additional withholding allowances that the employee claims. The completed certificate is the employer's authority to withhold income tax in accordance with the withholding tables issued by the IRS. If an employee claims fourteen or more allowances or exemptions from withholding and is paid more than $200 per week, the employer must submit a copy of the W-4 to the IRS. The copy should be attached to the quarterly return but may be filed sooner. If found defective, the employer must withhold on the basis of the maximum allowances specified in an IRS notice and disregard any inconsistent W-4 on file. If an employee should fail to furnish a certificate, the employer is required to withhold taxes as if the employee were a single person with no withholding exemptions. Before December 1, of each calendar year, the employer should request that all employees file new exemptions for the following year if there have been any changes in their exemption status since they filed the last certificate.

At the end of the year, the employer is required to furnish each employee with copies of Form W-2, Wage and Tax Statement, for each tax jurisdiction and the employee. Employers are required to furnish the Form W-2 to employees no later than January 31. The employer is required to furnish a copy of the Form W-2 to the Internal Revenue Service on or before February 28. Penalties may result from failing to provide a W-2.

If employees are covered by certain deferred compensation plans, Form W-2P, for withholding on annuities, pensions, or other deferred income payments, must also be furnished to employees by January 31, regardless of whether income or social security taxes are otherwise withheld, if wages equal or exceed one withholding exemption.

Form W-2 must show the wages paid (including tips reported) and the taxes deducted during the preceding year for income and social security taxes and any advance payments of earned income credit. It must include the name, address, and identification number of the employer and employee.

Employers may furnish a Form W-2 anytime after an employee's employment ends but not later than January 31 of the following calendar year. However, an employee may request that the employer furnish the form within 30 days after such request or last payment of wages, whichever is later, if both do not expect further employment. The IRS may extend for a reasonable time the due date for furnishing the employee's W-2. It cannot be more than six months except for taxpayers abroad. The application to extend must be filed when the W-2 would be given to the employee. It must be signed by the employer or its agent and state the reasons for the request.

Employees must attach the tax return copy of each W-2 statement they receive to their income tax return for the year. If the employee gets an additional W-2 after filing his or her return, he or she must file an amended return with the W-2 attached. An employer may replace lost or destroyed copies, marked "Reissued Statement." Employers must make a reasonable effort to deliver the W-2 or Form W-2c to each employee; however, mailing it to the last known address is sufficient effort. If the W-2 cannot be delivered, it should be kept as part of the employer's records for at least four years.

Social security taxes are deducted at the rate set by law, which is usually a percentage of an employee's base wages. The percentage and base are set by Congress and have been increasing dramatically over recent years. The employer pays a matching amount which is also remitted to the government. An employer is not required to match social security tax deductions on tips even though they must be reported for income tax and social security purposes if the cash tips exceed $20 or more per month. Employees are required to report the amount of tips to the employer on or before the tenth day of the following month.

Remitting Federal Taxes

An employer is required to report income and social security taxes withheld from employees' pay and to deposit those funds with the appropriate government agency. A Form 941 is used to report withholding and social security remittances to the government. The return for each calendar quarter is due on the last day of the following month, namely, April 30, July 31, October 31, and January 31. In some cases, remittance of taxes is required before the due date of the return. To make deposits, preinscribed Federal Tax Deposit Coupon Form 8109-B is used. The form and the check in the amount of the taxes due are sent to the federal reserve bank that serves the district in which the business is located or to a commercial bank that is authorized to accept tax deposits. Generally, a local bank or federal reserve bank can provide you with the names of such commercial banks authorized to accept deposits. Do not send the form and deposit to an IRS center because a penalty will be assessed if you do so.

The amount of tax determines the frequency of deposits. Large employers must make eight deposits of federal income and social security taxes each month; medium-size employers make monthly deposits; and small employers make quarterly deposits. An employer who has $3,000 or more in undeposited taxes after the end of an eighth-monthly period must make the deposit within three banking days. An eighth-monthly period ends on the third, seventh, eleventh, fifteenth, nineteenth, twenty-second, twenty-fifth, and last day of the month. An employer, for whom an eighth-monthly deposit is not required, is required to make a monthly deposit by the fifteenth day of any month where the accumulated liability is $500 or more. If no eighth-monthly or monthly payment is due, the payment must accompany the quarterly return.

The date of receipt by the authorized bank determines the timeliness of the deposit. A deposit mailed two or more days before the due date is timely even if it was actually received by the bank after the due date. However, a deposit of $20,000 or more must actually be received by the due date.

Withholding Adjustments

Errors made by employers in withholding or paying the tax for any quarter may be adjusted without interest in a later quarter of the same year.

If an error is found before the quarterly return is filed and too little was withheld, the correct amount should be shown on the return and the undercollection should be deducted from the employee's next wage payment. If too much was withheld, a receipt should be obtained from the employee showing the date and amount of repayment to him or her. If repayment to the employee is not made before the Form 941 is filed, the amount collected must be included in the return, and the adjustment is made in the return for a following quarter.

If an error is found after the quarterly return is filed and the employer collected too much, it may repay the employee in a later quarter of the same year. Care should be taken to get a receipt for the employer's files. An employer may apply the overcollection against the tax to be withheld for a later quarter of the year. The adjustment is made by a deduction on a return for a later quarter of the year.

The employer may report an underpayment in a return for a later quarter of that year or may file a supplemental return for the period when the wages were paid. If the employer reports it by the due date of the return for the period when the error was found, there is no penalty; if it is reported afterward, interest is due.

Employers may reimburse themselves for an undercollection of tax from employees by deductions from the employees' pay on or before the last day of the calendar year. The employer and employee can settle the item between themselves within the year if the deduction is not made.

If an employer pays the IRS more than the correct amount withheld from its employees, it can obtain a refund or credit. Credit for overpayment of tax not withheld from employees may be taken as a deduction on Form 941; an explanatory statement must be attached to the return.

Taxes withheld from employees are credited against their total tax liability. If the amount withheld exceeds the tax, the excess will be refunded upon application. Fiscal year taxpayers must claim credit for the entire tax withheld during the calendar year that ends in the fiscal year for which the return is filed.

Penalties

Employers may be liable for payment of the tax that they must withhold, unless the employee later pays the tax. However, the employer is liable for interest or other penalties for failure to withhold, to file the return, and to pay the amount withheld to the IRS. They can be penalized an amount equal to the total amount of the tax not collected or paid over, if the failure is willful. A stay against collection of this penalty is permitted if a bond is posted, if payment is made to start a refund suit, if a refund claim is filed, and if court proceedings are brought within 30 days after denial of the refund claim. Interest runs from the preinscribed date for payment on the form to the next April 15 or the date the employee pays the tax, whichever is earlier.

Employers are not liable for withholding on cash tips not reported to them by their employees on written statements.

There may be penalties for failure to file a return. Unless due to reasonable cause and not to willful neglect, the penalty is 5 percent of the net amount due for delay up to one month, with an added 5 percent for each additional month or fraction of a month (25 percent maximum penalty). The penalty runs from the return due date (including extensions) until the payment date. If this penalty is assessed for an employer's failure to file Form 941, it runs from the return's due date to the date the form is filed. It is considered filed by the employer when it is prepared and executed by the IRS. This stops the delinquency period.

An additional penalty of $50 must be paid for each copy of Form W–2 that the taxpayer, without reasonable cause, fails to file on time. The maximum penalty is $50,000 for any one year. For intentional failures, the penalty is not less than 10 percent of the aggregate reportable amount, and the $50,000 limit does not apply.

For failure to pay taxes unless an adjustment is made, interest is charged at the current rate from the date the tax becomes due until paid. An additional penalty is imposed for failure to pay the amount shown as tax on any return to which the penalty for failure to file applies and for failure to pay a deficiency after notice; the penalty is one-half of 1 percent of the unpaid tax (less credits) for each month or fractional month of delinquency with a maximum of 25 percent, unless failure is due to reasonable cause and not willful neglect. If the amount demanded is paid within ten days after the notice and demand, interest will not be imposed for the period after the date of notice and demand. If the deficiency results from fraud, the penalty is 50 percent plus interest on the deficiency attributable to fraud. The 50-percent penalty does not apply if the penalty for failure to withhold applies.

Criminal penalties are provided for willful failure to withhold, account for, and pay over the required taxes to be withheld; or for a willful attempt to evade or defeat the tax. Criminal penalties can also result from willful failure to make a required return. However, these penalties do not apply if there is no addition to tax because of underpayment exceptions.

For a fraudulent withholding statement or a failure to furnish a withholding statement, the employer will be subject to a civil penalty of $50 and a fine of not more than $1000, imprisonment for not more than one year, or both. These penalties are instead of any other that might otherwise be imposed.

On underpaid or overstated deposits, failure to deposit the full tax in a government depository results in a penalty of 5 percent. Also, an additional penalty of 25 percent is imposed on an overstated deposit claim. The penalty does not apply if the claim is due to reasonable cause and not due to willful neglect.

Federal Excise Taxes

Federal excise taxes are imposed on the sale or use of certain items, on certain transactions, and on certain occupations. For example, there is an occupational tax on retail dealers in adulterated butter, retail dealers in beer, retail liquor dealers, and wholesale beer and liquor dealers. Diesel fuel and certain special motor fuels carry a retailer's excise tax. Information concerning excise tax liability may be obtained from the nearest Internal Revenue Service office. If a business is liable for any excise tax, it must file a quarterly return on Form 720. If more than $100 per month is owed in excise taxes, monthly deposits of that tax must be made in the federal reserve bank or other authorized depository in the same manner as federal income tax. Semimonthly, rather than monthly, deposits of excise taxes are required if the business was liable for more than

$2,000 of all excise taxes reportable on Form 720 for any month during the previous quarter.

If the business owns and operates trucks, it will have to pay the federal highway use tax. If as an owner-manager you are engaged in an occupation involving gaming devices, liquor, narcotics, gambling, or firearms, you must pay an occupational excise tax. For more information concerning the federal highway use tax and occupational excise taxes, contact the local office of the Internal Revenue Service.

Unemployment Taxes

A business is liable for federal unemployment taxes if wages of $1,500 or more were paid in any calendar quarter or if one or more persons were employed at least some portion of one day in each of twenty or more calendar weeks. The twenty weeks do not have to be consecutive.

If the liability for undeposited federal unemployment tax exceeds $100 for any calendar quarter and any preceding quarter, the tax must be deposited with an authorized commercial bank or federal reserve bank within one month following the close of the quarter. Each deposit must be accompanied by a preinscribed Federal Unemployment Tax Deposit Form (Form 508). A supply of Form 508's is furnished to employers who have applied for a federal employer identification number automatically, but, in any case, they may be obtained from any Internal Revenue Service office.

An annual return must be filed on Form 940 on or before January 31, following the close of the calendar year for which the tax is due. Any tax still due is payable with the return. It is necessary to file Form 940 on a calendar year basis even if you operate on a fiscal year basis. Form 940 may be filed on or before February 10, following the close of the year if all required deposits were made timely and full payment of the tax due is deposited on or before January 31. Payment of state taxes after the due date limits the credit otherwise available.

The basic unemployment tax rate is set by law, but the actual rate paid should be less because the federal government allows a credit for unemployment taxes paid to states. A small number of states have a slight surcharge because of the above average unemployment experience within the state itself.

State Taxes

Although state taxes vary from state to state, the four major types of state taxes are unemployment taxes, income taxes, property taxes, and sales taxes.

Each state has unemployment taxes. Usually, unemployment taxes are based on the taxable wage base of a quarter. The rate of a tax charge is usually determined by the employer's unemployment experience and the unemployment experience of the state. Because the rules and requirements vary from state to state, state authority should be consulted to determine the basis of your unemployment tax obligation. In some states, employees, through payroll deductions, are also assessed an unemployment tax. See the prior discussion on federal unemployment taxes.

Most states impose an income tax. In those states with income taxes the employer is generally required to deduct or withhold tax due from employees' wages. The form and content of state tax returns and withholding statements can be determined by consulting your local state tax authority. If the requirements for records are different from federal income tax requirements, adjust your record-keeping scheme accordingly. Failure to remit state withheld taxes will result in a charge of embezzlement.

Most states also have sales taxes. In the collection of a sales tax, the employer is acting as an agent. The employer collects the tax on the sales and remits the money to the appropriate state agency. The system that the taxing jurisdiction has set up must be used. You should check your system of collecting, reporting, and paying sales taxes with local and state authorities to make sure it complies with their requirements.

Many counties, towns, and cities impose various kinds of taxes including real estate taxes, personal property taxes, taxes on gross receipts of businesses, and unincorporated business taxes. A license to do business is also a tax even though it is not commonly thought of as such. Some localities, particularly large cities, also impose an income tax.

Admonitions

Make sure that all tax reports are timely filed when they are due and pay the tax on time. Failure to file or pay taxes when due may result in penalties ranging from fines to jail terms and interest on the tax money that is involved. In certain cases, the officers of a corporation may be held personally liable for taxes due from the corporation if the corporation does not pay the taxes. In addition, criminal charges may be imposed, particularly when monies—such as income tax withholdings—that are held in escrow for others are not available on the due dates. Make sure that the cash is on hand and available when a particular tax is due. This may be accomplished by depositing funds in a separate bank account on a systematic basis or by arranging for loans at appropriate times.

Good record keeping is essential in determining proper tax liabilities. For that reason, business records should be reviewed by an accountant for acceptability for audit by the various taxing authorities. It is good management and common sense to coordinate your overall accounting with tax due dates so that tax liabilities may be ascertained without substantial additional work. Moreover, an accountant can relieve you of time-consuming paperwork. An accountant can also research tax problems with a view to saving money for the business.

EQUAL EMPLOYMENT OPPORTUNITY COMMISSION

Record-Keeping Requirements

An employer subject to Title VII must make and retain all records and reports that are relevant to the determination of whether or not an unlawful employment practice has been committed as prescribed by the EEOC regulations.[1] The EEOC consults with other state and federal agencies in coordinating requirements of record keeping. Thus, record-keeping requirements under equal opportunity laws tend to overlap.

The EEOC requires an employer who makes personnel or employment records to keep them for at least six months from the date the record was made or the personnel action generating the record occurred. If a complaint is filed by an employee, the employer must keep all relevant personnel records as long as necessary to make available to the EEOC.

As required under the Equal Pay Act, the EEOC requires maintenance of employee earning records for at least two years and payroll records for at least three years. The Age Discrimination in Employment Act requires that all employee information as to address, date of birth, occupation, and rate of pay be kept for three years and that all application forms and test results be kept for one year.

Each year, employers subject to Title VII, who have 100 or more employees, are required to file an Employer Information Report with the EEOC. Title VII employers, who employ 100 or fewer employees and other employers not required to file an Employer Information Report, must maintain and have available records for each year showing the number of persons hired, promoted, and terminated for each job, by sex, race, and national origin. They must also have records showing the number of applicants for hire and promotion by sex, race, and national origin. These records must include a description of the selection procedures utilized.

An employer subject to Title VII must post in a conspicuous place any notices prepared or approved by the EEOC concerning the provisions of Title VII pertaining to the filing of an employee complaint.

EEOC Reporting

The EEOC has seven required forms to be filed. The EEO–1 must be filed by all employers covered by Title VII that have 100 or more employees and by government contractors covered by Executive Order 11246 that have 50 or more employees and government contracts of $50,000 or more. The EEO–2 must be filed annually by joint labor management committees that have five or more trainees in their programs and at least one employer having 25 or more employees and one union sponsor having 25 or more members covered by Title VII. The EEO–2–E must be filed annually by every business with 25 or more employees if the employer has a total employment of 100 or more employees, conducts an apprenticeship program, and has five or more active apprentices in the program. The EEO–3 must be filed annually by local unions that have had 100 or more members at any time since the end of the previous calendar year. An international union is excluded unless it operates a local chapter. The EEO–4 must be filed annually by state and local government jurisdictions with 100 or more employees. The EEO–5 must be filed biennially by every public school system, including every separately administered school with 100 or more employees. Selected schools with fifteen or more employees are required to file biennially as determined by the reporting committee. The EEO–6 also must be filed every two years by every institution of higher learning with fifteen or more employees.

For a discussion of employment laws and regulations, see Chapter 15.

FAIR LABOR STANDARDS ACT

Record-Keeping and Enforcement

To assist the enforcement of the FLSA, the law requires that employers keep records reflecting wages, hours, and other conditions concerning their employees, including even those persons who are or who might be exempt.[2] There are no requirements as to the form of the records to be maintained. Any reasonable method will be accepted so long as the information is both accurate and complete. The essential information that must be recorded and preserved includes the following:

1. Identifying information: Employee's name, address, birthdate (if under nineteen, age certificates should be on file for all minor employees), sex, and occupation.
2. Hours: When employee's workweek begins, hours worked per day, and hours worked per week.
3. Wages: Basis or formula on which the employee's wages are paid, overtime pay rate (one and one half the regular rate or other stipulated rate), amount and nature of payments excluded from the overtime rate, daily or weekly straight time pay, overtime pay per week, any additions or deductions from wages per pay period, and dates of payments.

An employer, moreover, must keep actual payroll records, age certificates, employee-employer agreements, plan notices (collective bargaining agreements, benefit plans, trust plans, etc.), as well as volume of sales data for at least three years after the events. Employment earnings records which substantiate other records must be kept for at least two years. An employer, however, may petition the administrator for authority to change or modify the requirements for record keeping.

Personnel from the regional offices of the Division of Hours and Wages have the right to enter an employer's premises and conduct investigations and inspections to determine compliance with the FLSA, including compliance with the requirements for making and preserving records. Investigations may be and usually are prompted by employee complaints. Investigations also result from reinspections of previous violators, spot checks in high violation business areas, or as part of a random audit of industry members. Employers are advised to cooperate with these investigations fully as the secretary of labor has the power to subpoena witnesses and records without establishing that the employer's business and employees are subject to the FLSA. Upon notice of an impending investigation or inspection, an employee is advised to seek consultation with legal counsel. An employer should never destroy any required records. Willful violations of the FLSA may lead to severe penalties.

The following steps are typically involved in an FLSA investigation:

1. A compliance officer will identify him- or herself with official credentials.

2. The officer will arrange to meet with the employer or its representative. He or she will explain what records the officer will need to review and may ask the employer to designate a staff member to aid in explaining any records.

3. The officer may investigate and transcribe any records he or she chooses. The officer may conduct interviews with any of the business' employees in private. Often, this is done to confirm the information in the records and to check on possible equal pay, discrimination, or child labor violations.

4. Usually the officer will, in an exit interview, again meet with the employer and tentatively advise whether any possible violations were found. If violations were determined to exist, the employer normally will be advised on ways to correct them.

For a discussion of employment laws and regulations, see Chapter 15.

OCCUPATIONAL SAFETY AND HEALTH ACT

Sections 8(c)(1) and (2), 8(g)(2), and 24(a) and (e) of the Occupational Safety and Health Act of 1970 provide for record keeping and reporting by employers covered under the act as necessary or appropriate for enforcement of the act, for developing information regarding the causes and prevention of occupational accidents and illnesses, and for maintaining a program of collection, compilation, and analysis of occupational safety and health statistics.

Who Must Keep Records

OSHA applies to any person engaged in a business affecting commerce who has employees, but it does not apply to the United States or any state or political subdivision of a state. Certain exceptions are made.

Any employer who employs no more than ten persons at any time during the calendar year need not comply with the record-keeping and reporting requirements for that year, except for:

1. Reports of fatalities and multiple hospitalization incidents.

2. A log of occupational injuries and illnesses from which to prepare reports for the statistical part of the OSHA program after being notified by the Bureau of Labor Statistics that the employer has been selected to participate in a statistical survey of occupational injuries and illnesses.

3. Reports required by the state.

Mining employers report to the Department of the Interior. Their required report was developed with the cooperation of the Bureau of Labor Statistics and contains essentially the same information required by OSHA.

Employers of domestics in the employer's private residence for housekeeping or child care purposes are exempt.

Farm employers who employ only members of their immediate families are exempt. The exemption is not lost if neighbors work for a farm employer at specified times of the year as a neighborly gesture.

Employers in religious activities need not keep records regarding employees participating in the conduct of religious services or rites. Records must be kept of injuries or illnesses occurring to employees performing secular duties. Records are required for private hospitals, schools, orphanages, and commercial entities owned and operated by religious organizations.

Records Maintenance

Log and Summary of Occupational Injuries and Illnesses

Each employer shall maintain in each establishment a log and summary of all recordable occupational injuries and illnesses for that establishment on OSHA Form 200 or an equivalent which is as readable and comprehensible as the Form 200 to a person not familiar with it. Recordable cases are defined on the reverse side of the form. Each recordable injury and illness shall be entered on the log and summary form as early as practicable but no later than six working days after receiving information that an injury or illness has occurred. The log and summary shall be completed in the detail provided in the form and the instructions on the reverse side.

An employer may maintain the log of occupational injuries and illnesses at a place other than the establishment or by data processing equipment, or both, if

1. There is sufficient information available at the place where the log is maintained to complete the log within six working days after receiving information that a recordable case has occurred.

2. There is a copy of the log available at each of the employer's establishments which shows all injury and illness cases of the previous 45 days.

Supplementary Record

Supplementary records of injuries and illnesses recorded in the log must be kept at each establishment and must be completed within six working days after the employer has been notified of an injury or illness. This record must be available for inspection by OSHA and Department of Health, Education, and Welfare (HEW) officials.

The Supplementary Record (OSHA Form 101) requires the following: (1) employee's name and address, occupation, and vital statistics; (2) where and how the accident occurred; (3) extent of the injury or illness; (4) fatality (if any); and (5) name and address of physician or hospital. Other reports are acceptable if they contain the information required by OSHA Form 101. Worker's compensation or insurance forms may be used if they contain all of the required information.

Annual Summary

Each employer must conspicuously post an annual summary of occupational injuries and illnesses for each establishment. This shall consist of a copy of the year's totals from OSHA Form 200's and the following information from those forms: calendar year covered, company name, establishment name, establishment address, certification signature, title, and date. OSHA Form 200 is also used for the summary. If no injuries or illnesses occur in the year, zeros must be entered on the totals line, and the form must be posted. The summary must be completed by February 1 of the following year.

Each employer, or the employee who supervises the preparation of OSHA Form 200 and Form 101, shall certify that the annual summary is true and complete. The certification is made by signing at the bottom of the last page of the summary or by attaching a separate signed statement.

The summary must remain in place until March 1. For employees who do not primarily work or report at a single establishment or who do not report to any fixed establishment on a regular basis, employers may satisfy the posting requirement by presenting or mailing a copy of the summary during February to each employee who receives pay that month. For multiestablishment employers, if operations have closed down in some establishments during the year, it is not necessary to post summaries for those establishments.

Failure to post a copy of the annual summary may result in the issuance of citations and imposition of penalties as described in sections 9 and 17 of OSHA.

Retention of and Access to Records

The log and summary, along with the annual summary, must be retained in each establishment for five years after the end of the year they represent.

Each employer must furnish, upon request, the required records for inspection and copying by any representative of the secretary of labor for the purpose of carrying out the provisions of the act, by representatives of the secretary of Health, Education, and Welfare during any investigation conducted under the act, and by any representative of a state-accorded jurisdiction for occupational safety and health inspections.

The log and summary must be made available to any employee, former employee, or their representatives for inspection or copying in a reasonable manner and at a reasonable time.

Employers of employees who are engaged in physically dispersed operations such as construction, repair, or service activities and who do not report to any fixed establishment on a regular basis but are subject to common supervision may satisfy the record-keeping requirements by:

1. Maintaining the required records for each operation that is subject to common supervision in an established central place.
2. Having the address and telephone number of the central place available at each work site.
3. Having personnel available at the central place during normal business hours to provide information from the records maintained there by telephone and by mail.

Reporting of Fatality or Multiple Hospitalization Incidents

Within 48 hours following the occurrence of an employment accident that is fatal to one or more employees or which results in hospitalization of five or more employees, the employer must report the accident orally or in writing to the nearest OSHA area director. The report must relate the circumstances of the accident, the number of fatalities, and the extent of any injuries. The area director may require additional reports, in writing or otherwise, as he or she deems necessary concerning the accident.

Enforcement and Penalties

Failure to maintain the records or file the reports required by OSHA or to fill in the details required by the OSHA forms and instructions may result in the issuance of citations and an assessment of penalties as provided for in sections 9, 10, and 17 of the act.

An employer who violates a record-keeping requirement may receive a citation issued under authority of section 9 of OSHA. The citation will specify a reasonable amount of time in which to correct the violation. If the violation is not cured within the specified time period, the employer may be subject to the penalties of section 17. The employer has fifteen working days after receiving notice of an assessed penalty to contest it. Failure to contest makes the assessment final and no longer subject to review by any court or agency. If notice to contest is given, a hearing will be held to determine the correctness of the citation.

An employer who fails to correct the violation for which the citation was issued within the specified time period (exclusive of the time required for review) may be assessed a civil penalty of not more than $1,000 per day that the violation continues.

An employer who violates any of the posting requirements may be assessed a civil penalty of not more than $1,000 for each violation.

Knowingly falsifying an application, record, report, plan, or other document filed or required to be maintained under OSHA is punishable under section 17(g) by a fine of up to $10,000, by imprisonment for up to six months, or both.

Record Keeping under Approved State Plans

Records maintained by an employer and reports submitted pursuant to and in accordance with the requirements of an approved state plan under section 18 of OSHA shall be regarded as compliance with the record keeping and reporting guidelines of OSHA.

Petitions for Record-Keeping Exceptions

Any employer who wishes to maintain records in a manner different from that required may submit a petition to the regional commissioner of the Bureau of Labor Statistics in the employer's region.

Affected employees or their representatives have the opportunity to submit written data, views, or arguments concerning the petition to the regional commissioner involved within ten working days following the receipt of notice from their employer.

The petition must include:

1. The name and address of the applicant.
2. The address of the place or places of employment involved.
3. The reasons for seeking relief.
4. A statement of the different record-keeping procedures proposed by the applicant.
5. A statement that the applicant has informed his or her affected employees of the petition and of their right to comment by giving a copy of the petition to them or their representative and by posting a statement giving a summary of the petition.
6. A list of all of the employer's establishments and of the states in which they are located. If some of the establishments are not affected by the petition, the employer must identify all the establishments that are affected by the petition and the states in which they are located.

If a regional commissioner receives a petition from an employer having one or more establishments beyond the boundaries of the region, the regional commissioner must refer the petition to the assistant commissioner for action.

After review of the petition and any comments submitted, a necessary, appropriate investigation concerning the petition may be instituted. If the regional or assistant commissioner finds that the proposed alternative procedure will not hamper or interfere with the purposes of the act and that it will provide equivalent information, the commissioner may grant the petition. It may be subject to such conditions as the commissioner determines appropriate and is subject to revocation for cause.

Whenever any relief is granted to an applicant under the act, notice of relief and the reasons therefor shall be published in the Federal Register.

Statistical Reporting of Occupational Injuries and Illnesses

Section 24 of OSHA directs the secretary of labor, in consultation with the secretary of health, education, and welfare, to develop and maintain a program of collection, compilation, and analysis of occupational safety and health statistics. The commissioner of the Bureau of Labor Statistics has been delegated this authority by the secretary of labor. The program consists of periodic surveys of occupational injuries and illnesses. In addition to the information recorded on the annual summary (OSHA Form 102), information concerning the establishment's principal product or service, employment size and hours worked, support activities, monthly data of recordable cases, and medical provisions in case of accident must be reported.

Upon receipt of an Occupational Injuries and Illnesses Survey Form (OSHA Form 103), the employer must promptly complete the form in accordance with the instructions and return it within the specified time period.

Nothing in any state plan approved by the act shall affect the duties of employers to submit a statistical report.

The sample design encompasses probability procedures, detailed stratification by industry and size, and a systematic selection within strata. Stratification and sampling will be carried out by states and other jurisdictions in order to provide the most efficient sample for state estimates.

NOTES

1. 42 U.S.C. § 2000e–8; 29 C.F.R. part 1602.
2. 29 C.F.R. ch. V, part 516.

20

Taxation of a Business

In keeping with the transactional approach adopted in this book, the tax treatment of particular business transactions is given contemporaneously with the transaction. For example, acquisitive reorganizations and their tax treatment are covered in Chapters 3 and 4. Certain planning tools and their tax treatment are discussed in Chapter 21.

This chapter discusses the primary concepts and building blocks of federal income taxation—income, adjustments to gross income, deductions, taxable income, and credits.

INCOME

Definition

It is important to remember that the United States tax system is a self-assessing system for which the government relies on the honesty of its citizens in reporting their income. To that extent, the tax system in use should be perceived by the citizenry to be fair and workable. It is, therefore, necessary that the taxpayer have some rudimentary understanding of the tax system in order to accurately self-assess his or her tax liability.

The Internal Revenue Code (I.R.C.) defines gross income as all income from whatever source derived.[1] The legislative history indicates that Congress intended to include within the definition of gross income the full extent of its tax power under the Sixteenth Amendment.

Income may be derived from any source, not just from capital or labor. The phraseology "from whatever source derived" means that income derived from illegal sources as well as legal is included in gross income. The United States

Supreme Court in *Commissioner v. Glenshaw Company*[2] set forth criteria for determining income. Income is an accession to wealth which is fully realized and within the complete dominion of the taxpayer. An accession to wealth is clearly any increase in the economic position of the taxpayer. Realization is a term of art of accountants and lawyers, which establishes a rule for when an item should be included in income. An item should be included in income when all of the necessary events have taken place that establish the taxpayer's right to receive the income and the amount of the income is reasonably determinable. The requirement that the accession to wealth be within the dominion of the taxpayer means that the taxpayer has the right to receive or control the disposition of the item. Mere power to dispose is sufficient receipt. Actual receipt is not necessary for the item to be within the complete dominion of the taxpayer.

An accession to wealth need not be in the form of money. A taxpayer may have income without receipt of cash or property. For example, receiving an interest-free loan from a taxpayer's corporation will result in recognition of income to the taxpayer for the imputed interest.[3] A shareholder or corporate officer who occupies a building or apartment owned by the taxpayer's corporation realizes income to the extent of the fair market value of the rent and maintenance above normal operating expense.[4]

Exclusions

In order to understand the concept of gross income, it is necessary to understand what is not gross income. A return of capital is not gross income because there is no accession to wealth. The taxpayer is merely recovering the investment which does not result in any increase in the taxpayer's wealth. Loan proceeds received by a taxpayer who has an obligation to repay are not included in gross income. The taxpayer does not have a net increase in wealth because the loan proceeds are offset by the obligation to repay. However, if the taxpayer does not intend to repay the loan, then the receipt of the loan proceeds constitutes gross income because there is no offsetting obligation. Other items are not included in gross income by specific statutory exclusion in the Internal Revenue Code. There is a last category of exclusions from gross income that have arisen as a result of administrative practice in the IRS such as the long-standing exclusion of certain tax-free fringe benefits.

Gifts

Gross income does not include the value of property acquired by gift, bequest, devise, or inheritance.[5] It is important to note that the concept of a gift in the Internal Revenue Code is not the same as the common law definition of a gift. The concept of a gift is important to business because most of the cases dealing with the exclusion of a gift from income arose in a business context. A gift in the statutory sense proceeds from a detached and disinterested generosity arising out of affection, respect, admiration, charity, or like impulses.[6] The critical consideration is what the transferor intended. In a business context, the presumption is that any transfer of property between persons having a business relationship is income and not a gift because it is not detached or disinterested generosity. The burden of proof is on the taxpayer to establish that the transferor's intent was to make a gift rather than to compensate the recipient.

As with the concept of gift, what constitutes property acquired by inheritance is also a federal question, not a matter of state law. To demonstrate the importance of this concept, assume that an attorney performs services for a client without charging the client. The client agrees to leave the attorney certain stock in the client's will as compensation for services rendered. On the client's death, the attorney receives the stock pursuant to the client's will. Under state law, this is a testamentary disposition. However, for federal income tax purposes, the fair market value of the stock is gross income as compensation for services rendered. Merely using a testamentary instrument to convey it is not sufficient; there must be a similar intent as in the gift situation to constitute a bequest or a devise.

Employee's Death Benefits

A surviving spouse or other beneficiary may exclude from gross income up to $5000 paid by the employer of the deceased spouse or beneficiary to the estate or beneficiary by reason of the death of the employee.[7] To be excluded, the $5000 must be a death benefit paid by reason of the death of the employee and not intended as further compensation of the deceased employee, for services to the deceased's spouse or beneficiary, or by reason of any other relationship between the spouse or beneficiary and the employer. Any benefit paid by the employer in excess of $5000 may be excluded from gross income by the surviving spouse or beneficiary if the surviving spouse or beneficiary can prove that the amount in excess of $5,000 constituted a gift under I.R.C. section 102.

Meals and Lodgings

The Internal Revenue Code allows an exclusion from gross income for the value of meals provided to employees, spouses, and dependents that are made by or on behalf of the employer if provided for the convenience of the employer and furnished on the business premises.[8] A similar provision allows for the exclusion from gross income of the value of lodging, provided it is for the convenience of the employer, the employee is required to accept the lodging as a condition of employment, and the lodging is on the business premises.[9]

Employees who receive meals provided by the employer at a cut rate price that are not otherwise excludable from gross income must recognize income to the extent of the difference between the fair market price of the meal and the cut rate price.[10] The benefit is excluded from income if provided on the business premises, if the revenue equals or exceeds direct operating costs, and if the meals are provided to all employees regardless of amount of compensation.

Fringe Benefits

Certain employee fringe benefits have not been included in gross income by reason of long-standing administrative practice by the Internal Revenue Service, some of which is more than 60 years old. The treatment of employee fringe benefits is currently in a state of flux since the Congressional moratorium on Internal Revenue Service regulations concerning fringe benefits expired at the end of 1983. The IRS suspended issuance of regulations on fringe benefits pending further Congressional action. Section 132 excludes from gross income certain fringe benefits that do not impose substantial additional costs on the employer, that are *de minimis* in value, that are working condition fringe benefits otherwise deductible by the employee as an ordinary and necessary business expense or as depreciation, and that qualify as qualified employee discounts not to exceed the gross profit margin or 20 percent of the price of services offered to customers. Congress is addressing fringe benefits on a piecemeal basis.

Gains from Dealings in Property

The Internal Revenue Code specifically includes within the definition of gross income gains derived from dealings in property. A gain derived from dealings in property is the excess of the amount realized (cash plus the fair market value of any property received) over the adjusted basis of the property.[11] In computing the amount realized there may be some valuation problems, but generally the amount realized is equal to the cash plus the fair market value of any property received in the exchange. The computation of basis is more complicated. Basis is not equivalent to value. The general rule is that the basis is equal to the historical cost of the item, that is, the amount paid.[12] However, if property is exchanged for property, the basis is determined by the fair market value of the property given up by the taxpayer in the exchange or the fair market value of the property received by the taxpayer in the exchange, whichever is the more easily determinable and objective.[13]

Discharge of Indebtedness

A corporation may recognize a gain on a discharge of indebtedness by repurchasing previously issued bonds at less than face value. The difference between the face value and the purchase price is a gain, which must be included in gross income.[14] This rule is known as the Kirby doctrine and has many exceptions. For example, no income is recognized if the taxpayer can establish that the holder of the bond intended to make a gift of the difference between the face amount of the bond and the repurchase price. Likewise, no income is recognized if the taxpayer can establish that the adjustment was a renegotiation of the sale between the debtor and the creditor because of a decline in value.

DEDUCTIONS

Under the Sixteenth Amendment, Congress has the absolute power to tax gross income; however, it does not exercise the full power as a matter of legislative grace. Congress allows certain deductions for both business and nonbusiness activities. Deductions, however, must be grounded in a particular section of the Internal Revenue Code, and each deduction section is narrowly construed by the courts.

Business Deductions

Ordinary and Necessary Expenditures

The Internal Revenue Code provides for a deduction for ordinary and necessary expenditures directly connected with or pertaining to the taxpayer's trade or business.[15] An expenditure is necessary if it is appropriate and helpful and is ordinary if it is common and accepted.

The expenditure must be an expense and not a capital outlay. A capital outlay is one that is designed to provide future benefits. An expense is an expenditure that is not anticipated to result in a significant increase in future service potential. A capital expenditure extends the useful life of an asset, increases the quantity of services provided by the asset, or increases the quality of services provided by the asset. A capital outlay is included in the cost of the asset and is generally recovered by depreciation of the asset. An expense, if it is ordinary and necessary, will support a deduction in the tax year in which the expense is incurred. In many cases, the controversy turns on the characterization of the expenditure as a repair or replacement. A repair is an expense whereas a replacement is a capital outlay. A repair is an expenditure made to restore an asset to a sound state or to mend it. A replacement, on the other hand, is a substitute of one asset for another. An expenditure that keeps an asset or property in an ordinarily efficient operating condition does not add value to the property and does not appreciably prolong the asset's life is a repair expense. In general, no deduction is allowed for a permanent improvement or betterment or restoration or adaption to new use.

One of the major ordinary and necessary business expenses incurred by any business is for reasonable compensation and salaries. A deduction is allowed for reasonable salaries or other compensation paid for personal services actually rendered.[16] Reasonable compensation is the amount that would ordinarily be paid for the same type of services by similar enterprises under the same circumstances. Each set of circumstances is different and depends on the facts of the case. Factors that the IRS considers in determining reasonableness are the character and amount of the responsibility of the employee, the ease or difficulty of the work, the amount of time required, working conditions, future prospects, standard of living in the locality, individual ability, education of the employee, and market availability of persons of similar ability. Only reasonable compensation is deductible, and any amount in excess of what is determined to be reasonable is disallowed as a deduction. The disallowance of the employer's deduction does not change the fact that the employee has income for the full amount of the payment. In long-term contingency contracts which are entered into by arm's-length agreements the reasonableness of the salary is determined in the year in which the contingency contract is entered into and not in any subsequent year.[17]

The ordinary and necessary expense must be directly connected to the carrying on of the taxpayer's business. There is no deduction allowed for personal, living, and family expenses.[18] Carrying on of a trade or business means that the taxpayer must be in the trade or business when the expense is made or incurred or at least be in the initial investigation stage of starting up the business.

Travel expenses incurred away from home are deductible if three conditions are met.[19] First, the travel expense must be reasonable and necessary. Second, the expense must be incurred while away from home. Third, the expense must be incurred in pursuit of business. The purpose of this deduction is to defray expenses incurred in addition to the regular, nondeductible living and family expenses of the business traveler.

The requirement that the taxpayer be away from home means away from the taxpayer's normal place of business not residence. Normal commuting expenses from home to office or factory are not deductible. Where the taxpayer chooses to live in relationship to his or her place of employment has no bearing on travel status away from home.

If the requirements are met, transportation, meals, and lodging are deductible. Meals and lodging are deductible, however, only if the traveler is staying overnight. To justify staying overnight, the business traveler must be far enough away from the business home that he or she could not reasonably return that day. Business meals and entertainment deductions are limited to 80 percent of cost for taxable years beginning after December 31, 1986.

Other ordinary and necessary business expenses are necessary rental and similar payments made in connection with the trade or business.[20] To be able to deduct rental or similar payments, the taxpayer may not take title or acquire equity in the property which is the subject of the lease. Lease agreements with options to purchase at the termination of the lease are scrutinized to make sure that the lease actually represents a rental with a reasonable option to purchase at termination rather than a disguised purchase agreement. Sale-leaseback agreements, particularly among family members, are the subject of careful scrutiny by the courts. If the leaseback has the effect of transferring ownership rights back to the grantor who takes the deduction, the sale-leaseback transaction will be treated as a sham and disallowed.

Educational expenses may be deducted as ordinary and necessary business expenses (1) if the expenditure for education meets the express requirements of the individual's employer or applicable law or regulations imposed as a condition to retention by the individual of established employment relationship, status, or rate of compensation or (2) if the expense for education maintains or improves skills required by the individual in his or her employment, trade, or business.[21] Transportation, meals, and lodging are also fully deductible when incurred in connection with a deductible educational expense.

Entertainment expenses may be deducted if they are directly related to or associated with the taxpayer's trade or business either by conducting business during the entertainment or by conducting business immediately before or after the entertainment. Deductions for business lunches and dinners are restricted to expenses of the client and not the taxpayer or taxpayer's family. Deductions for business meals and entertainment are limited to 80 percent of cost for taxable years beginning after December 31, 1986. To substantiate expenses, taxpayers must have a receipt for all items that exceed $25.

Uniform expenses are allowed as deductions if the uniform is specifically required as a condition of employment and the uniform is not of a type adaptable to general or combined usage to the extent that they take the place of ordinary street clothing.[22]

Restrictions on Business Deductions

Certain expenses otherwise allowable as a deduction are limited by Congress. Losses incurred by a corporation are fully deductible, but losses incurred by individuals are limited to losses incurred in a trade or business that are not otherwise compensated by insurance or other means and which are both realized and recognized losses.[23] A loss incurred by an individual on the sale of a personal residence is not deductible whereas a loss incurred by an individual on the sale of business premises is deductible.

Congress also requires that the activity be engaged in for profit before the deduction is allowed for the loss even if incurred in a trade or business.[24] This restriction applies to individuals and subchapter S corporations. There is a rebuttable presumption in favor of the taxpayer that an activity is engaged in profit if it shows an excess of income over deductions for at least three years out of the previous five years. If the activity is engaged in for profit, there is no limit on the deductions. However, if the activity does not show a profit in at least three years out of the previous five, the deductions are allowed only to the extent of the excess of gross income over deductions otherwise allowable without regard to the conduct of a trade or business such as taxes and interest.

Congress has further limited the amount of deduction for losses to amounts "at risk."[25] This restriction applies to all activities engaged in by a taxpayer in carrying on a trade or business or for the production of income except for equipment leasing by closely held corporations. The restriction applies to individuals, subchapter S corporations, and closely held corporations, which are defined as having more than 50 percent of the value of the stock owned by five or fewer individuals. The amount at risk is the amount of money plus the adjusted basis of any property contributed by the taxpayer in addition to any amounts borrowed, provided that the taxpayer is personally liable or that the taxpayer pledged property other than the property used in the activity as security for the loan.

Illegality or Impropriety

In determining income, illegally or unlawfully obtained income must be included in gross income. The converse is not true for deductions. No deduction is allowed for any activity that is against public policy that has been declared by any governmental agency. No bribes or kickbacks are deductible.[26] Fines and similar penalties are not deductible.[27] For example, trucking firms may no longer deduct traffic fines as a cost of doing business. However, attorney's fees are deductible for both civil and criminal actions if the activity is related to a trade or business whether the trade or business is illegal or legal.

Deductions for Profit-Making Nonbusiness Activities

As originally enacted, the provision allowing ordinary and necessary business deductions did not extend to other profit-making activities that were nonbusiness in nature, such as investment activities. Subsequent amendments to the Internal Revenue Code allow deductions for expenses made for (1) the production or colleclection of income, (2) the management, conservation, or maintenance of property held for the production of income, (3) or in connection with the determination, collection, or refund of any tax.[28] To be deductible, the expense must be ordinary and necessary as defined in ordinary and necessary deductions in connection with carrying on a trade or business. Examples are ordinary and necessary expenses incurred in holding rental income and incurred in investment activities.

Other Deductions

Certain deductions are not limited to business or profit-seeking activities. Of primary importance are deductions for interest, taxes, casualty and theft losses, and bad debts.

Interest

A deduction is allowed for interest paid or accrued within the taxable year on indebtedness other than consumer debts.[29] Interest is defined to be the amount one has contracted to pay for the use of borrowed money and is compensation paid for the use or forbearance of money. Examples of interest are as follows:

1. Ordinary interest on loans and mortgages of principal residences
2. A negotiated bonus or premium paid by a borrower to a lender in order to obtain a loan
3. A loan charge paid by a seller of a residence to assist the purchaser in obtaining a mortgage loan

4. A loan origination fee paid by borrower to lender

5. A discount on bonds

6. Amounts and installment payments where a carrying charge is separately stated, but the interest charge is not ascertained

7. Points on a mortgage to the extent not included in the loan amount.

Certain items are not considered to be interest:

1. Points on loans where amounts are withheld from mortgage proceeds

2. Interest paid where the recipient does not include the interest in gross income

3. Loans to purchase single premium life insurance or an endowment or annuity contract

4. Interest on indebtedness used to purchase tax exempt obligations

5. Service charges on loans

6. Personal interest other than interest on debt incurred or carried in connection with a trade or business or investment activity, qualified residences' interest, interest connected to income or loss from passive activities, or interest payable on certain estate tax deficiencies.

Taxes

A deduction is allowed in a taxable year in which taxes are paid or accrued for the following:

1. State, local, and foreign real property taxes

2. State and local personal property taxes

3. State, local, and foreign income, war profits, and excess profits tax.[30]

No deduction is allowed for the following:

1. Federal income taxes

2. Social security withholding taxes from employees

3. Withholding taxes withheld by the employer

4. Federal war profits and federal excess profits taxes

5. Estate, inheritance, succession, and gift taxes

6. Taxes on public foundations and real estate investment trusts

7. State and local general sales taxes.[31]

Casualty and Theft Losses

A deduction is allowed for losses sustained during a taxable year which are not compensated for by insurance or otherwise.[32] There are severe limitations on the deduction of casualty and theft losses that are not incurred in a trade or business or a transaction entered into for profit.[33] Casualty and theft losses incurred in carrying on a trade or business or incurred in a transaction entered into for profit are deductible in full.[34] A taxpayer must be able to prove theft to claim the deduction. Mere loss of an item is not deductible. To be a casualty loss, the loss must be sustained by a sudden and unexpected or catastrophic event. The amount of the loss sustained is the adjusted basis of the property that would be used for determining loss from the sale or other exchange of property; however, that loss is limited to the difference between the value of the property immediately before and after the casualty or theft and not replacement cost.[35]

Bad Debts

For discussion of the bad debt deduction see Chapter 13.

ADJUSTED GROSS INCOME

Adjusted gross income is gross income less certain deductions allowed directly against gross income. These are the so-called above the line deductions. The concept of adjusted gross income allows taxpayers who otherwise could not itemize deductions to get the benefit of certain specified deductions. Of particular importance to the businessperson are the deductions for employer expenses incurred in carrying on a trade or business, expenses arising out of transactions entered into for profit, IRA and Keogh plan payments, and certain employee expenses.[36]

The concept of adjusted gross income does not create new deductions. It merely allows certain deductions, primarily those expenses that are directly incurred in carrying on a trade or business, to be deductible without itemizing, but it does not allow double deduction of the items. An item that is allowed as an adjustment to gross income is not deductible in another part of the taxpayer's return. Further, the concept of adjusted gross income is applicable only to individual taxpayers. It has no significance as far as corporate taxpayers, partnerships, or estates and trusts are concerned. In essence, the concept of adjusted gross income puts individual taxpayers with business expenses on a parity with other business entities.

CREDITS

A credit is an allowance made directly against taxes owed whereas a deduction is an offset against adjusted gross income to determine taxable income. For a business, the most important tax credit was the investment tax credit which was used to stimulate capital investment by businesses. The Tax Reform Act of 1986 repealed the investment tax credit. Another important credit for multinational operations is the foreign tax credit.[37] Foreign taxes paid are credited, directly or indirectly, against U.S. tax liability. The effect is a shift of tax revenue from the U.S. Treasury to foreign treasuries.

COMPUTATION

Once gross income is determined, the adjustments to gross income are subtracted to arrive at adjusted gross income. Allowable deductions are then subtracted from the adjusted gross income to find taxable income. The taxable income is the amount of income that is subject to tax liability. Tax liability is computed by applying the applicable tax rates to taxable income. After determining the amount of tax due, any allowable credits are then subtracted from the computed tax liability to determine the amount of payment to be made or overpayment made.

CAPITAL GAINS AND LOSSES

Historically there is no mention in the Sixteenth Amendment of a capital gain or loss. It merely legitimatizes taxation of income from whatever source it is derived. Courts early on decided that profit gained from the sale or conversion of capital assets was income. In response, Congress has given capital gains favorable tax treatment since 1921.

There are essentially three reasons for giving capital gains favorable tax treatment. First, an exchange of one investment for another is a continuation of an investment in a different form, but no proceeds or gain are withdrawn. Second, the gain on a sale or exchange may be largely a change in overall price structure because of inflation. Third, the gain accumulates over a period of years, and it would not be fair to tax the entire gain in a single year at high rates.

If capital gains are given favorable tax treatment an accommodation must be made for capital losses. If capital losses were treated as ordinary losses, the taxpayer would receive a tax benefit on both sides of the transaction. The solution was to restrict capital losses so that there is nearly a balance between capital gains and losses.

There are three factors to be considered when determining whether or not an item is a capital gain or loss—capital asset, sale or exchange, and holding period.

Capital Asset

A capital asset is defined in section 1221 as property held by the taxpayer except:

1. Stock in trade (inventories) or property primarily held for sale to customers.
2. Property used in a trade or business on which depreciation is allowed.
3. Copyrights, literary, musical, and artistic compositions, letters, memoranda, and similar property.
4. Accounts or notes receivable acquired in the ordinary course of a trade or business.
5. Certain free or discounted government publications.

Classification largely depends on the purpose for which property is acquired. For example, stock or securities are generally capital assets in the hands of the owner, but they are inventory items to a stockbroker and are not capital assets.

In an unincorporated business, such as a sole proprietorship or partnership, the business is not a single asset owned by the proprietor or partners. The property held by the business must be classified separately. Some property will be capital assets; other property such as inventories will not be capital assets. The ownership interest in a corporation—the common stock—is a capital asset in the hands of the owner.

Sale or Exchange

A sale is a bilateral agreement to transfer property for money or its equivalent. An exchange is a swap of property often with boot (cash) being paid or received to compensate for differences in fair market value.

Some transactions are treated as a sale or exchange even though they are, in fact, not sales or exchanges. Examples are a transfer of property by a trustee or executor to discharge a cash legacy, an involuntary conversion, severance of timber, liquidating dividends, worthless debts or securities, and foreclosures of mortgaged property. Conversely, some sales or exchanges are not considered as such. Examples are settlements of accounts receivable that were retained after the sale of a business and transactions involving judgments at a gain.

Holding Period

Congress is continually changing the holding period required to classify a capital gain or loss as a long- or short-term capital gain or loss.

Assets held one year or less are short term except assets acquired after June 22, 1984, but before January 1, 1988, where the holding period is six months or less.[38] Those assets held for more than one year are long term except assets acquired after June 22, 1984, but before January 1, 1988, where the holding period is more than six months.[39] The rule for commodity futures is six months regardless of acquisition date.[40]

To determine the holding period, calendar months are counted, not days. The counting convention used by the IRS is to count the last day of the period but not the first day. There are special rules for certain assets.

For stocks and bonds purchased over the counter or on an exchange, the significant date is the trade date, not the settlement date. If stock is sold in a block where it is impossible to identify which individual shares are sold, a first-in-first-out (FIFO) rule is used. The oldest securities are deemed to have been sold first. A short sale against the box (sale of borrowed securities) is always a short-term gain.

The holding period date for real estate sold on an unconditional contract for sale is the date title passes or possession is obtained with all the burdens and privileges of ownership attached, whichever occurs earlier.

Section 1223 provides tacking rules which, in general, add the prior owner's holding period to the new owner's holding period if the new owner acquires a carryover basis from the prior owner.

Tax Treatment

Because of the new lower individual rates in the Tax Reform Act of 1986, capital gain preferential tax treatment is not accorded to individuals any more. The loss limitation of $3,000 is still in effect for individuals.

Corporations include capital gains in their income and are taxed as ordinary income but subject to a maximum tax rate of 34 percent.[41] A corporation may deduct its capital losses only from capital gains.[42] Capital losses may be carried back three years and carried forward for five years but only to offset capital gains and subject to special limitations.

DEPRECIATION

Depreciation for accounting purposes is a method of matching revenues and costs when the item has a service potential of more than one year or an accounting cycle, whichever is greater. The straight line method is generally used.

Under the straight line method, three pieces of information are necessary—the cost, salvage value, and useful life. The cost is the historical cost of the property plus any other costs incurred to get the property in place for use. Salvage value is an estimate of what the property will be worth when its service potential is gone. Useful life is an estimate of length of service potential. The difference between cost and salvage value is the depreciation base. The depreciation base is divided by the useful life in years to determine the annual depreciation expense.

Depreciation is not a source of funds; it is merely a matching of costs against revenue. The only cash flow involved is derived from its tax benefit as a deductible item. A firm generally uses one method such as straight line for financial accounting purposes and an accelerated system for tax purposes.

The Economic Recovery Tax Act of 1981 replaced the depreciation system for property put into service after December 31, 1980, with the accelerated cost recovery system (ACRS).[43] The ACRS permits the recovery of capital costs for most tangible depreciable property over generally shorter periods than section 167 had and is hopefully less complex.

Under ACRS, the cost (without consideration for any salvage value) of eligible personal property is recovered over a fifteen-year, ten-year, seven-year, five-year, or three-year period depending on the type of property involved. Most eligible property is five-year property. The annual deduction is determined by multiplying the cost times the percentage rate provided in section 168 tables.

Residential real property put in service after December 31, 1986, is 27½-

year real property. Nonresidential real property placed in service after December 31, 1986 is 31½-year property. Raw or undeveloped land is not depreciable. The taxpayer depreciates the unadjusted basis. No distinction is made between new or used real property.

A taxpayer may elect to use the straight line method over the specified recovery period or an optional period provided. Useful life has no meaning in tax depreciation today.

Section 179 provides for first year bonus depreciation. If section 179 is used the section 179 deduction reduces the basis available for depreciation under section 168. Section 179 applies to property that is acquired by purchase for use in the active conduct of the taxpayer's trade or business. Section 179 does not apply to real property.

NOTES

1. I.R.C. § 61.
2. 348 U.S. 426, *rehearing den.*, 349 U.S. 925 (1955),
3. Hardee v. U.S., 708 F.2d 661 (Fed. Cir. 1983).
4. Dean v. Commissioner, 187 F.2d 1019 (3d Cir. 1951).
5. I.R.C. § 102.
6. Commissioner v. Duberstein, 363 U.S. 278 (1960).
7. I.R.C. § 101 (b).
8. I.R.C. § 119.
9. *Id.*
10. I.R.C. § 132.
11. I.R.C. § 1001
12. I.R.C. §§ 1012 and 1016.
13. Philadelphia Park Amusement Co. v. U.S., 126 F. Supp 184 (Ct. Cl. 1954).
14. U.S. v. Kirby Lumber Co., 284 U.S. 1 (1931).
15. I.R.C. § 162.
16. I.R.C. § 162 (a) (1).
17. Harolds Club v. Commissioner, 340 F.2d 861 (9th Cir. 1965).
18. I.R.C. § 262.
19. I.R.C. § 162 (a) (2).
20. I.R.C. § 162 (a) (3).
21. Treas. Reg. § 1.162–5 (a).
22. Mem. 6463, 1950–1 C.B. 29.
23. I.R.C. § 165.
24. I.R.C. § 183.
25. I.R.C. § 465.
26. I.R.C. § 162 (c).
27. *Id.*
28. I.R.C. § 212.
29. I.R.C. § 163.
30. I.R.C. § 164.
31. I.R.C. § 275.

32. I.R.C. § 165 (a).
33. I.R.C. § 165 (c) (3).
34. I.R.C. §§ 165 (c) (1) and (2).
35. I.R.C. §§ 165 (b) and 1011.
36. I.R.C. § 62.
37. I.R.C. §§ 901–904.
38. I.R.C. § 1222.
39. *Id.*
40. *Id.*
41. I.R.C. § 11.
42. I.R.C. § 1211 (a).
43. I.R.C. § 168.

21

Business Planning

No business can or should operate very long without a plan. A plan consists of goal setting and mapping a path to your goals by accomplishing a series of objectives designed to reach the overall goals. To a large extent, this entire book is about business planning and making informed choices—decisions such as organizational form, financing, buying or selling a business concern, and business planning. Tax planning is merely evaluating the business decision in terms of the impact of taxes on the alternative choices and choosing the alternative that represents the best overall choice, taking all factors including taxation into consideration. Business planning is nothing more than integrating the various chapters of this book and making conscious choices based on the information contained in relation to your goals and objectives.

INCOME SPLITTING

Because the U.S. tax system is a progressive tax system, there is an incentive to split or reallocate income particularly among family members and entities such as partnerships, corporations, and trusts which are in lower tax brackets. Some income splitting is sanctioned by Congress. The two biggest examples are the joint return, in which spouses equally divide the income regardless of who earns it, and the alimony provisions, which allow an ex-spouse a deduction for alimony included in income by the other.

Income from Services

These are the easy cases because a person who receives income from services rendered to an employer is subject to withholding. The identity of the wage earner and the amount of wages are reported directly to the IRS. There is generally no opportunity for reallocation. Income is attributed to the person who earns it without regard to disposition of the income even if plans to dispose of it are made in advance of earning it. Thus, directions to an employer to make the actual cash payment to a third person does not shift the attribution of the income from the person who earned it. The right to control the disposition is equivalent to receipt. To avoid attribution, there must be an absolute and definite refusal of any right to receive income before it is earned.

Certain exceptions exist for faculty and resident physicians who render services on behalf of the employer and are paid a full-time salary. Some laws require that compensation be paid to the professional rendering the service rather than the employer, for example, a law professor working in the law school legal aid clinic. The professional must, in turn, endorse the payment over to the employer. The professional does not recognize income from the payment under these circumstances.

Income from Property

Disposition of income from property such as stock, bonds, other interest payments, and leases is more easily manipulated. The taxpayer recognizes income with the exercise of the power to dispose, which is equivalent to ownership. One cannot legally dispose of something that one does not earn. The income is attributed to the person who earns or otherwise creates the right to receive the income and who enjoys the benefits when paid. The right to dispose is an economic benefit.

To avoid attribution of income from property, the income-producing property, not merely the income, must be disposed of by transferring ownership before the income is earned. Any income earned before disposition is attributable to the prior owner.

Partnerships

Remember that a partnership is not a taxable entity but merely a conduit through which income is passed to the owners, the partners. A partnership may be used as an income-splitting device by making family members partners. There is no benefit in making a spouse a partner since the joint return accomplishes the same thing.

In general, the IRS gives effect to partnership agreements that follow the Uniform Partnership Act provisions. However, close scrutiny is given to family partnerships because of the income-splitting potential.

A partnership is an organization created for the production of income to which each partner contributes one or both of the ingredients of income—capital or services.[1] An intent to provide future capital or services is not sufficient. The partners must have joined together in good faith to conduct a business, having agreed that the services or capital to be contributed presently by each is of such value to the partnership that the contributor is entitled to participate in the profits.

The capital contribution may be derived by gift.[2] For example, a parent may give a child a capital interest in a partnership. Recognition of the partnership for tax purposes is independent of its validity under state law. If the family member is a partner, then the earnings are divided as provided in the partnership agreement and attributable to each partner for tax purposes. The distributable portion must not be disproportionate to the other partnership shares.

A partnership interest may not be acquired by gift in a service partnership. For example, a physician may not make a child who is not a physician a partner in a partnership for the practice of medicine. The partnership must be one in which capital is the material income-producing factor.[3] Capital is a material income-producing factor if a substantial part of the partnership's gross income is derived from capital such as inventories, plant, and equipment.

Creating a family partnership not only results in a decreased income tax burden but also permits an accelerated buildup of the child's estate. Gift tax liability is lessened by giving the child the interest when the value of the partnership is lower in the beginning stages.

Corporation

The use of a corporation as an income-splitting device is diminishing since personal and corporate tax rates are decreasing. As corporate tax rates decrease and become closer to personal tax rates, the incentive disappears particularly in light of the fact that income is taxed to the corporation and then to individual shareholders when distributed.

The IRS particularly scrutinizes personal service corporations where substantially all the corporation's income is attributable to services performed by the owner-employee. These corporations have been attacked by the IRS using three different approaches—assignment of income, sham corporation, and section 482.[4]

The assignment of income doctrine attributes income to the person who earns it or who owns the property that produces it. In the case of personal service corporations, the rationale is that, since the owner-employee actually earns the income, he or she should recognize it rather than the corporation.

An entity that conforms to state law requirements for incorporation may not be a corporation for tax purposes. The corporate form is disregarded if the IRS considers it to be a sham. The sham corporation test requires that the business purpose be the equivalent of business activity or be followed by carrying on a business. Unless the corporation is a purely passive dummy or is used for tax avoidance purposes, it will be recognized as a corporation for tax purposes. Tax avoidance is not a business purpose.

Section 482 is a powerful weapon in the hands of the commissioner and has been abused. Section 482 overrides every other section of the Internal Revenue Code. Under section 482, the commissioner may apportion or allocate gross income if:

1. Two or more organizations, trades, or businesses are owned or controlled, directly or indirectly by the same interest, and

2. Apportionment or allocation is necessary to prevent tax evasion or more clearly reflect income.

The commissioner's determination will be upheld even if the method by which the apportionment or reallocation is made is defective. The result may be attacked only if it is arbitrary or capricious.

In general, a corporate employee is not engaged in a separate trade or business from the corporation so that the first criterion of section 482 is not met. The owner-employee must be engaged in a separate business activity apart from the corporation for section 482 to be applied.[5] The danger area occurs when the owner-employee incorporates but continues to operate as if the corporation did not exist except as a conduit for the income. For the corporation to be recognized, the corporation must have the right to direct and control the owner-employee, and the service user must recognize that right through contract or other means.

The other area of potential for income splitting is the purchase-gift-lease. An owner-employee may purchase equipment individually and make a gift of the equipment to a child or trust who then leases the equipment to the corporation. The child or trust has income hopefully taxed at a lower rate or not at all, and the corporation takes a deduction for an ordinary and necessary business expense. When these arrangements are attacked, the courts sometimes find a lack of necessity for the rental payments without any business purpose for the arrangement.[6] If a real, rather than a sham, ownership interest is created in the leased property and a fair rental value is paid, the deduction should be allowed. Courts outside the Fifth Circuit adopt this approach. The benefits of transferring income-producing property to children under 14 years of age are diminished by the Tax Reform Act of 1986. Under the act, the child's unearned income (generally income from passive investments) in excess of $1,000 is taxed at the parent's marginal tax rate instead of the child's.

CORPORATE FORMATION

Debt/Equity Ratio

In forming a corporation, an initial decision must be made regarding the relative amounts of debt and equity in the capital structure. Corporation statutes generally require a *de minimis* amount of equity to incorporate. A common figure is $1,000.

There are obvious advantages to using debt rather than equity. Debt holders have priority over equity holders in liquidation and bankruptcy. From the corporation's viewpoint, interest paid on debt is deductible;[7] dividends paid on equity securities are not. Moreover, interest paid does not reduce earnings and profits while dividends do. From the holder's perspective, repayment of the debt obligation does not result in any income recognition whereas a stock redemption might be treated as a dividend to the extent of earnings and profits.[8] However, if the recipient of the dividends is a corporation, it is entitled to an 80-percent intercorporate deduction.[9]

Because of the tax advantages of having debt in the corporate structure, shareholders have an incentive to classify as large a percentage as possible of their contribution as debt rather than equity. There has been a tendency by courts to treat shareholder debt as equity regardless of how carefully the contribution has been structured as debt.

A threshold problem is often presented as to whether the particular instrument in question is a debt or equity instrument. This type of instrument is referred to as hybrid stock because it has attributes of both debt and equity. The following factors are considered in characterizing the instrument as debt or equity:

1. The name on the instrument (bond, common stock, preferred stock).

2. The existence of a maturity date, which is a characteristic of a debt instrument.

3. The source of the payments such as earned surplus in the case of an equity instrument.

4. The right to enforce the payment of principal and interest, which is an attribute of debt.

5. The right to participate in management, which is a prerogative of equity holders except in case of default.

6. Priority vis-à-vis creditors.

7. The intent of the parties.

The debt/equity ratio, which is the ratio of shareholder-held debt to equity holdings, is an important factor in determining how the instrument will be treated for tax purposes.

After *Talbot Mills v. Commissioner*,[10] tax experts thought that a 4:1 ratio was a safe harbor, but subsequent lower court decisions were inconsistent. The IRS has been struggling for years with debt/equity regulations but has failed to adopt one yet. Nonetheless, today it is but one factor in the characterization of the instrument, and some courts ignore it altogether.

The most suspect situation is the one in which the debt is held pro rata with the equity. Courts generally are inclined to treat debt as equity in these situations since the debt/equity structure is obviously fabricated to take advantage of the tax laws.[11] However, disproportionate holdings are not necessarily safe.[12]

While there is no safe harbor, a good test to use is whether the shareholder intended to treat the debt in the same manner as an outside creditor would.[13] An outside creditor would require security and a higher return to compensate for the risk involved. If an outside creditor would not advance money on the same terms as the shareholder, the inference is that the instrument is equity. This test works against shareholders who try to save a failing enterprise by advancing money to it. Nevertheless, any deviation from normal business patterns combined with a tax avoidance motive will cause the debt to be treated as equity for tax purposes.

Section 351

Often a business will start as a sole proprietorship or partnership and evolve into a corporation. Section 351 governs transfers of property from one or more persons to a corporation in exchange for its stock or securities. Without section 351, a person who transferred property to a corporation in exchange for its stock or securities may have to recognize a gain or loss on the exchange.[14] Section 351 provides for nonrecognition of the gain or loss under certain circumstances. It may be advantageous to avoid the nonrecognition provisions of section 351 in order to recognize a loss, in which event, the transferor should take care not to qualify for section 351 treatment.

The three requirements for nonrecognition are as follows:

1. One or more persons must transfer property to a corporation, either a newly incorporated or preexisting one.
2. The transfer must be solely in exchange for the corporation's stock or securities.
3. Immediately after the transfer, the transferor or transferors must be in control of the corporation.

If these requirements are met, the transferor recognizes neither gain nor loss on the transfer, the corporation recognizes neither gain nor loss on the exchange,[15] the transferee corporation takes the property with the transferor's basis,[16] and the transferor's basis in the acquired stock is equal to the basis in the property transferred.[17]

Property

For purposes of section 351, property includes money. A purchase of stock as part of a plan to transfer property qualifies, and the stock purchased counts toward the control requirement.

Services are not property. If stock is received solely as compensation for services rendered, it does not count as a transfer under section 351 unless stock or securities are also exchanged for property, in which case, all stock or securities acquired as compensation for services and exchanged for property count toward the control requirement.

Exchange for Stock or Securities

An exchange is required by the statute and incorporates the sale or exchange requirement for a capital asset in section 1222. Retention of a substantial economic interest in the property by the transferor will defeat the exchange requirement. This problem frequently arises with transfers of intangibles such as patents.

The transferor must transfer all rights in the patent. Merely granting the corporation a license is insufficient.[18]

The term "stock or securities" has taken on a specialized meaning since the Supreme Court decision in *Pinellas Ice & Cold Storage Co. v. Commissioner*.[19] Short-term notes are not considered to be securities because of their pending satisfaction. For notes to be considered securities, they should have a term of ten years or more. Moreover, debt securities do not give the holder an interest in the affairs of the corporation.

The Court also imposed a continuity of interest test in *Pinellas Ice*, which is now part of Treasury Regulations section 1.368–1(b). Because the transferors must be in control of the corporation immediately after the transfer, the continuity of interest test should be satisfied at least with respect to a transferor who receives stock or securities.

Solely in Exchange

If a transferor receives cash or other property (such as short-term notes) in addition to stock or securities of the transferee corporation, gain must be recognized by the transferor to the extent of the cash plus the fair market value of the other property (boot); however, no loss is recognized.[20] Gain or loss, if any, is calculated separately on each asset, and the boot is allocated to each asset based on relative fair market values.

If a corporation assumes a liability or accepts property subject to a liability in a section 351 exchange, the corporation's assumption of liability does not constitute boot with two exceptions.[21] If the sum of liabilities assumed plus the liabilities to which property is subject exceeds the aggregate basis of the property transferred by one transferor, the excess constitutes a gain.[22] Any liability transferred for a tax avoidance or nonbusiness purpose constitutes boot.[23]

Control

Control means that, immediately after the transfer, the transferors must own 80 percent or more of the total combined voting power of all classes of stock entitled to vote plus at least 80 percent of all other classes of stock. Revenue Ruling 59–259 requires an 80-percent ownership of each class not merely 80 percent in the aggregate.

Control may be held by the group of transferors. The transfers do not all have to be at the same time if a plan exists to transfer property in exchange for stock or securities. When determining stock or securities held for control purposes, all stock owned is counted however acquired.

1244 Stock

Section 1244 provides relief for shareholders of small corporations who suffer a loss if their stock becomes worthless. The ordinary treatment of such a loss is as a capital loss rather than an ordinary loss. Since capital losses are not fully deductible, these shareholders are in a worse position than a sole proprietor or a partner whose business fails and who has ordinary losses. Under section 1244 the loss is treated as a ordinary loss.

Section 1244 applies only to individual taxpayers, not to trusts or estates. Moreover, section 1244 protects only the original issue shareholder, not vendees or donees.

The corporation has to be a domestic corporation that is classed as a small business corporation. A small business corporation, for purposes of section 1244, has to have an aggregate amount of money and other property received by the corporation for stock, as a contribution to capital, and as paid in surplus of less than $1 million. This test has to be met when the corporation is formed and when the stock becomes worthless. Moreover, for the five taxable years (or the life of the corporation if less than five years) immediately preceding the year in which the stock became worthless, the corporation must have derived more than 50 percent of its aggregate gross receipts from sources other than royalties, rents, dividends, interest, annuities, and sales or exchanges of stock or securities.

The stock has to be voting or nonvoting common stock. No stock convertible to common stock and no common stock convertible to other stock is allowed to be treated as common stock. The stock has to be issued for money or property not in exchange for services or other stock or securities.

The aggregate amount of loss treated as an ordinary loss for any taxable year is $50,000 per individual or $100,000 for spouses filing a joint return.

NONACQUISITIVE REORGANIZATIONS

Corporate reorganizations, defined in section 368(a)(1), range from statutory mergers to corporate divisions. One common element is the exchange of stock and securities of one corporation for the stock and securities or property of another. Since these exchanges result in realized gain or loss,[24] the gain or loss is recognized unless accorded nonrecognition by the reorganization provisions. As a matter of policy, a reorganization is considered to be a continuation of business in another form so that recognition is postponed to a later date.

The acquisitive reorganizations are briefly discussed in Chapter 3. This section deals with the nonacquisitive reorganizations.

D Reorganizations

D reorganizations are primarily amalgamations and corporate divisions. A primary user of the D reorganization is the IRS, which uses it to attack liquidation-reincorporation schemes.

To qualify for a D reorganization, a corporation must transfer assets to another corporation controlled by the transferor corporation, its shareholders, or both. The transfer must be pursuant to a plan, and the transferee's stock or securities must be distributed to the transferor's shareholders in a tax-free exchange under section 354, 355, or 356.

Under section 354, all or substantially all the assets of the transferor corporation must be exchanged for stock or securities of the transferee corporation. This is the same requirement as for a C reorganization.[25]

Section 355 governs corporate divisions. The three types of corporate divisions discussed here are the spin off, the split off, and the split up.

To visualize a spin off, suppose two shareholders A and B own the common stock of P corporation. P corporation owns 100 percent of the common stock of S corporation. To accomplish a spin off, P corporation distributes its S stock to A and B. After the distribution, S is no longer a wholly owned subsidiary of P corporation but is a separate corporation held by A and B who also still hold P corporation. Without the protection of section 355, this transaction would be treated as a dividend to the extent of earnings and profits.

In a split off, the starting point is the same as in a spin off. A and B own the stock of P corporation, which owns the stock of S corporation. Now, instead of distributing its S stock to A and B, it distributes its S stock to A in exchange for A's P stock, which is transferred to B. After the transaction, A owns the S stock, and B owns the P stock. They are no longer shareholders in common. Without the protection of section 355, this would be treated as a stock redemption under section 302 or as a partial liquidation under section 346.

Finally, in a split up, again, the starting position is the same as in a spin off or split off. This time P distributes its S stock to A and B in exchange for its own (P) stock, and then P terminates. After the transaction, A and B own S corporation, and P corporation is dissolved. Without the protection of section 355, this would be treated as a complete liquidation.

The statutory conditions for nonrecognition under section 355 are as follows:

1. The distribution must consist solely of stock or securities of a controlled corporation.
2. The distribution is not a device for distribution of earnings and profits.
3. The businesses must be actively conducted for five years prior to the reorganization and continue after the reorganization.
4. All stock or securities of the controlled corporation, or at least a controlling interest, must be distributed.

Control in reorganizations means the same as in section 351. Control means ownership of at least 80 percent of each class of voting and nonvoting stock.

In addition to statutory requirements for section 355, the courts have added continuity of business and personal interests and a valid business purpose. The principal purpose of the reorganization must not be tax avoidance, but any purpose germane to the business will be sufficient. Problems arise in trying to distinguish between a corporate business purpose and a shareholder purpose in a small, closely held corporation. Continuity of the business requires that either the transferee corporation continue the historic business of the transferor or the transferee use a significant part of the transferor's historic assets in a business. If the transferor has more than one line of business, the transferee need only pursue one significant line. Continuity of personal interest is assured by the control requirement.

As with section 351 exchanges, gain is recognized in a D reorganization if the aggregate liabilities assumed or to which property transferred is subject exceeds the aggregate bases of the transferred property to the extent of the difference.

Boot

If property other than stocks or securities is received by a shareholder in a reorganization, the other property is boot, and gain is recognized but not in excess of the fair market value of the boot.[26] If the exchange has the effect of a distribution of a dividend, the gain recognized is treated as a dividend to the extent of the shareholder's ratable share of the accumulated earnings and profits.[27]

E Reorganizations

An E reorganization is a recapitalization of a corporation. Shareholders of the corporation exchange their stocks and securities for different stocks and securities of the same corporation. There are no tax consequences to the corporation since all changes are internal and no tax consequences to the shareholders unless boot is involved. Boot is the excess of the principal amount of stocks and securities received over the principal amount of the stocks and securities given up.[28] Notice that principal amount (face value) is used, not the fair market value.

E reorganizations must also satisfy the business purpose and shareholder continuity tests. Valid business purposes are a change in voting control, a reduction of interest expense, an increase in the debt structure, estate planning, and elimination of arrearages. Since the same shareholders exist before and after the reorganization, the continuity of shareholder interest requirement is met.

Types of Exchanges

If common stock is exchanged for common stock or if preferred stock is exchanged for preferred stock, there are no tax consequences. A problem with section 306 stock (see corporate distributions below) arises if common stock is exchanged for preferred. Since no gain or loss is recognized, the preferred is section 306 stock if the receipt is substantially the same as a dividend. Any preferred stock received by a continuing common shareholder whose proportionate interest is not substantially changed is treated as section 306 stock.[29]

If a preferred shareholder with dividend arrearages exchanges preferred for other stock and, as a result, increases his or her proportionate interest in the assets and earnings and profits, section 305(b) applies, and the transaction becomes taxable.

A recapitalization where stock is exchanged for stocks and bonds on a pro rata basis is not an E reorganization. The bonds are not securities but are boot and constitute a dividend.[30] This rule is designed to prevent dividend distributions under the guise of a reorganization. However, a disproportionate distribution of stocks and bonds is an E reorganization.[31]

An exchange of bonds for bonds is an E reorganization, but boot is received if the principal amount of bonds received is greater than the principal amount of bonds surrendered. The fair market value of the difference is boot.[32]

It is quite common in E reorganizations to exchange bonds for stock. There is no recognition of gain or loss.[33] The benefit from this type of exchange is that it removes fixed liability costs (bond interest) and replaces them with equity interests on which no fixed obligation exists. This is a good move for a corporation facing possible involuntary bankruptcy in the future if the bonds are left outstanding.

F Reorganizations

An F reorganization is a mere change in identity, form, or place of incorporation of one corporation. The typical F reorganization is a change in state of incorporation to take advantage of a particular state's corporation laws. A recapitalization or corporate division might also be an F reorganization. If a reorganization could be classed as an F reorganization and another type of reorganization, it will be treated as an F reorganization for tax attributes.[34]

To satisfy the continuity of business requirement the pre-reorganization business of the transferor corporation must be continued by the transferee corporation, and virtually all the transferor's assets, other than liquid assets, must be distributed to the transferee corporation.

The continuity of shareholder interest requirement is satisfied if shareholders of the transferee corporation are substantially the same persons who were shareholders of the transferor corporation, and there are no significant changes in proprietary interests. Revenue Ruling 66–284 allows an inconsequential change in shareholder interests (1 percent). However, the Fifth and Second Circuit Courts of Appeal have allowed a significant portion of the transferor corporation stock to the redeemed.[35]

CORPORATE DISTRIBUTIONS

For purposes of this section, corporate distributions are nonstock dividends, stock dividends, stock redemptions, and partial liquidations.

Two different sets of rules apply to corporate distributions. The first set of rules consists of the state corporation law. State corporation law determines shareholders' rights to certain distributions, management's obligations with regard to distributions, availability of funds for distribution, and other aspects that are largely financial in nature. The second set of rules consists of the federal income tax law. These rules are not the same although they overlap. For instance, under state corporation law, the board of directors of a corporation may declare a dividend which complies with the state requirements; however, the distribution of the property may not be a dividend for tax purposes. This section discusses corporate distributions in terms of both sets of rules. Because each state's corporation law is different in some respects, state corporation law will be discussed in terms of the Model Business Corporation Act (MBCA)[36] and any significant deviations from the MBCA by major states. Federal tax law discussion is based on the Tax Reform Act of 1986.

Nonstock Dividends

This section discusses corporate distributions called "dividends" payable in cash or property other than the stock of the declaring corporation. Stock dividends are discussed below. A dividend is a distribution of cash or other property, except the corporation's own stock, to the shareholders by virtue of their stock ownership. In essence, a dividend is a financial return on the stockholders' investment in the corporation.

Discretion of Board of Directors to Declare a Dividend

The board of directors has the discretion to pay dividends or not. This discretion falls within the business judgment rule. Under the business judgment rule, the board of directors is presumed to know what is best for the corporation. A court will not interfere with the board's judgment unless there is an abuse of discretion such as fraud, bad faith, or a clear case of unreasonableness. The burden of proof is on the complaining shareholder and is almost insurmountable.

A mandatory dividend provision may be inserted in the articles of incorporation, one which obligates the directors to declare a dividend in any year in which legal funds are available. "Guaranteed" dividends may be construed by the courts as mandatory dividends, but the language must be clear and express since judges are reluctant to substitute their judgment for that of the board of directors.

Restrictions on Dividends

The directors' discretion to declare a dividend is not unfettered. State statutes impose limitations.

Almost every state either expressly in the corporation statute or by case law imposes a solvency requirement. The declaration and distribution of a dividend must not cause a corporation to become insolvent. Insolvent means that the corporation is not able to pay its debts as they become due in the normal course of business.[37] An alternative test of insolvency is the balance sheet test. If the corporation's total assets would be less than its total liabilities plus any amount necessary to pay preferences on priority stock in case of dissolution, then the corporation would be insolvent for purposes of declaring a dividend.[38] The insolvency requirement is for the protection of both creditors and shareholders.

Some states have an earned surplus test. Earned surplus includes all of the undistributed net profits each year during the life of the corporation. If the corporation is otherwise solvent, dividends may be declared on the unreserved and unrestricted earned surplus. Every state allows payment of dividends out of earned surplus; some states restrict dividends to earned surplus.

In addition to earned surplus, some states allow a dividend on net profits or earnings. The terms "net profits" and "net earnings" do not mean the same thing in every state. Some states define net profits or earnings as earned surplus. In this event, it is equivalent to an earned surplus test. Other states allow dividends to be declared out of current year profits even if the earned surplus account shows a deficit or even in the face of capital impairment. This rule allowing dividends to be declared out of current profits even if stated capital is impaired is called the "nimble dividend" rule.

Some state statutes include nonimpairment of capital with the insolvency test. Restricting dividend distributions to surplus (capital or earned) is, in effect, a nonimpairment rule. Net assets must exceed stated capital (paid in capital in exchange for stock at par value or, if no par, at stated value). The excess of net assets over stated capital is either capital surplus or earned surplus. Capital surplus is the amount of capital paid in exchange for stock in excess of the par value or, if no par, stated value. Under a nonimpairment test, dividends may be declared on earned surplus, to its extent, then on capital surplus, to its extent.

Other restrictions on the declaration and distribution of dividends may be contained in the articles of incorporation or imposed by creditors. Some creditors insist that a corporation agree not to pay dividends until its obligation to the creditor is satisfied. Preferred stock contracts provide that no dividend may be declared on the common stock until current dividends have been paid on the preferred and, if cumulative preferred, until all arrearages are made up.

The board of directors may be liable both civilly and criminally for unlawful distributions to shareholders. A shareholder who knowingly receives an unlawful distribution may also be liable.

A director who votes for or assents to an unlawful distribution is jointly and severally liable with other directors who voted for or assented to the unlawful distribution. Minimally, the directors are liable for the amount of the unlawful distribution and may be subject to criminal sanctions. Such directors are entitled to contribution from shareholders who knowingly received the unlawful distribution. Good faith reliance on the corporate books as prepared by a lawyer or accountant is a defense to a charge of an unlawful distribution.

Mechanics

Assuming that legal funds are available for dividends and that there are no preferences or other limitations, the board of directors may declare a dividend in either cash or property payable at a future date to shareholders of record on a certain date. Provisions for setting the record and payment dates may be contained in the articles of incorporation. The record date is generally ten days after the declaration date with the payment date following the record date by 30 days. The importance of the record date is to determine the actual identity of the shareholders entitled to the dividend. Since stock is freely transferable, the process must be frozen in time to determine entitlement.

Once declared, the dividend may not be revoked without the consent of the shareholders. All shareholders of record immediately become creditors of the corporation. The debt is enforceable in a court of law.

Unclaimed dividends are forfeited to the state of the shareholder's address of record on the corporate books if that state has escheat laws, otherwise to the state of incorporation. The corporation may not reclaim the declared dividend.

Tax Dividends

For tax purposes, a dividend is any distribution of property (other than the stock of the distributing corporation) by a corporation to its shareholders out of the accumulated earnings and profits or current earnings and profits.[39]

Earnings and profits for tax purposes are not equivalent to retained earnings or earned surplus used in financial accounting. Ironically, earnings and profits are not defined in the Internal Revenue Code even though the term first appeared in the code in 1916. The starting point in determining earnings and profits is taxable income. Taxable income is then adjusted by (1) adding back certain items excluded from taxable income, (2) restoring certain allowable deductions that are artificial in the sense that they do not relate to actual expenditures, and (3) allowing deductions from earnings and profits not otherwise allowed against taxable income but which deplete funds available for distribution. Accurate computation of earnings and profits requires a professional tax lawyer or accountant or both. Current earnings and profits are computed at the end of the taxable year without regard to distributions made out of earnings and profits during the year. Accumulated earnings and profits consist of undistributed earnings and profits from 1913 to the current year.

Distributions are considered to be made out of current earnings and profits first, to the extent thereof, then out of accumulated earnings and profits. Distributions reduce the earnings and profits to the extent thereof. This means that earnings and profits cannot be reduced below zero as a result of a distribution, but a negative balance can otherwise be obtained.

It is not necessary to have earnings and profits to make a corporate distribution; however, the distribution is a dividend for tax purposes only to the extent that the corporation has earnings and profits. The distribution may be a corporate dividend under state law whether the corporation has earnings and profits or not.

The general rule is that a corporation does not recognize a gain or loss on the distribution to its shareholders.[40] There are several statutory and judicially created exceptions to the rule. Professional advice should be sought in this area.

The tax treatment of a distribution by distributees depends on whether they are noncorporate or corporate shareholders.

To determine the distributee's tax liability, the amount distributed must be calculated. If the distributee is a noncorporate shareholder, the amount distributed is equal to the cash plus the fair market value of other property distributed.[41] The amount distributed to a domestic corporate shareholder is the amount of cash plus the lesser of either (1) the fair market value of other property received or (2) the basis in the hands of the distributing corporation of other property plus any gain recognized by the distributing corporation as a result of the distribution.[42]

To the extent that the amount distributed is covered by earnings and profits, the distribution is treated as ordinary income.[43] If the amount distributed exceeds the amount of earnings and profits, the distribution represents a return of capital and reduces the basis of the stock in the hands of the distributee.[44] The basis in the stock cannot be reduced below zero. Hence, there is no immediate tax consequence on this portion of the distribution. Any tax consequence is delayed until the stock is sold or is otherwise disposed of. Any amount distributed in excess of earnings and profits and basis of the shareholder's stock is treated as a sale or exchange of property.[45]

Constructive or Disguised Dividends

Unlike interest paid on corporate bonds, a corporate dividend is not deductible as an interest expense. It would be to the tax advantage of a corporation to recharacterize a dividend to be able to take advantage of a deduction. Often a corporation will try to transform a dividend into a salary expense, which is deductible as an ordinary and necessary business expense, or into a loss on the sale of property.

In the case of salaries paid to shareholders, if the salary is reasonable and purely for services rendered, no part of the payment is a dividend regardless of the amount of the corporation's earnings and profits. An earlier court decision had set out an automatic dividend rule which required that part of a shareholder employee's salary be designated as a dividend to the extent that earnings and profits existed if the corporation had not otherwise declared and paid a dividend. The automatic dividend rule has been repudiated.[46]

To the extent that a shareholder's salary is unreasonable, it may constitute a dividend if the corporation has earnings and profits. The following factors are considered in determining reasonableness:

1. Amounts paid by similar enterprises for services of a like character;
2. Type and extent of the services rendered;
3. Scarcity of qualified persons for the position;
4. Prior earnings capacity of the shareholder-employee;
5. Peculiar characteristics of the taxpayer's business;
6. General economic conditions of the period.

To avoid having part of a salary being treated as a dividend, it must be reasonable.

Bonus payments to shareholder-employees are sometimes used to disguise dividends. Factors to be considered when analyzing a bonus are as follows:

1. Whether the bonus payments made to shareholder-employees are in proportion to their stock ownership;
2. When there is a complete absence of a dividend;
3. Whether the payments are made in a lump sum or in connection with services rendered;
4. Whether the system of payments is completely unstructured or is on a prescribed basis;
5. Whether payments are made only to shareholder employees;
6. Whether the corporation consistently has negligible taxable income.

Another method of disguising a dividend is to sell corporate property to the shareholders at bargain prices. Whenever a corporation sells corporate property to shareholders or their assignees at less than fair market value, it constitutes a corporate distribution since it diminishes the net worth of the corporation. The difference between the fair market value of the corporate asset and the sales price is a distribution, which is a dividend to the extent that the corporation has earnings and profits.

Not only are dividends disguised, but sometimes other forms of compensation are disguised as dividends. Salaries paid to employees whether shareholders or not may be called dividends by the corporation to avoid paying social security and unemployment taxes and collecting withholding from wages.

Constructive or disguised dividends are treated as dividends for tax purposes. The name applied to the distribution by the taxpayers is irrelevant and not determinative.

Stock Splits and Dividends

General

Stock splits and stock dividends are distributions to shareholders of additional shares of the distributing corporation.

In a stock split, the issuing corporation issues an additional number of shares depending on the split ratio. A two for one split, for example, means that each shareholder will receive one additional share for each share held so that after the split there are twice as many shares outstanding as before. As a result of the split, the par or stated value of each share is reduced pro rata; that is, the same par or stated value of the original stock must be proportionately spread over all stock issued. A stock dividend is a distribution of stock to shareholders where the par or stated value of the stock issued as a dividend is the same as the original stock.

A stock split differs from a stock dividend in that there is no transfer from earned surplus to stated capital as a result of the stock split. If a stock dividend is declared, a corresponding increase in stated capital must be made by transferring the par or stated value of the stock to stated capital from earned surplus and a corresponding transfer to capital surplus from earned surplus to the extent that fair market value exceeds the par or stated value.

It is important to understand that a stock dividend is not a real dividend in the sense that the total equity of the corporation is subject to more claims thereby diluting the equity. Only the nature of the equity is changed by transferring earned surplus to stated capital. The net effect of a stock dividend is to retain earnings in the corporation thereby reducing surplus available for cash or property dividends. Stock splits and stock dividends, if large, generally result in a reduced market price for the stock.

There is no insolvency test for declaring a stock dividend because a stock dividend alone cannot affect solvency either in an equity or in a bankruptcy sense.

Stock splits require action not only by the board of directors but probably also by the shareholders because a stock split involves a change in par or stated value. The articles of incorporation may have to be amended to charge par or stated value and to authorize additional shares, if necessary.

In the case of both stock splits and stock dividends in which the stock is traded on a national exchange, the issuing corporation must comply with any applicable exchange rules.

Section 305 Distributions

Straightforward pro rata distributions of stock or rights to acquire stock to a corporation's common shareholders are ordinarily tax free, especially if only common stock is outstanding.[47] However, there are five exceptions to the rule. If the distribution falls within one of the five exceptions, it is treated as a corporate distribution and constitutes a dividend to the extent of earnings and profits available.

The entire distribution of stock is treated as a corporate distribution of property if:

1. The distribution is, at the election of any one or more shareholders, payable in either stock or property whether so elected or not.
2. The distribution is disproportionate in that one group of shareholders receives property and another group has an increase in their share of the assets or earnings and profits.
3. Common stock is distributed to one group of common stockholders and preferred is distributed to another group of common stockholders.
4. There is any distribution on preferred stock except to take account of a stock dividend or stock split concerning a convertible preferred.
5. There is a distribution of convertible preferred unless it is approved by the Treasury Department.

The tax basis, in the hands of the shareholder of the old stock, must be allocated between the old stock and the stock rights or new stock received as a split or dividend. The allocation is made by proportioning the basis based on fair market value. The new basis in the old stock is equal to the old basis times the ratio of the fair market value of old stock held to the total fair market value of old and new stock held by the shareholder. Similarly, the basis allocated to the new stock is equal to the original basis times the ratio of the fair market value of the new stock to the total fair market value of the old and new stock held by the shareholder.

Section 306 Stock

Section 306 of the 1954 Internal Revenue Code was enacted to close the preferred stock bailout. The preferred stock bailout worked wonderfully well until section 306 was enacted. A corporation with earnings and profits would distribute preferred stock to its shareholders in a tax-free distribution. The shareholders subsequently would sell the preferred stock to a third party or the issuing corporation and report the gain as a long-term capital gain. The corporation would redeem the preferred stock sold to a third party generally at a premium. The stockholders received preferential tax treatment, and the third-party purchaser made money on the premium. The net result was the same as a cash dividend.

So-called 306 stock is defined as stock other than common stock distributed to a shareholder in a tax-free distribution either as a stock distribution or in a corporate reorganization or division of stock including common stock for which the shareholder exchanged 306 stock tax free. A corporation must have earnings and profit for any stock to be classified as 306 stock because without earnings and profits there could have been no dividend.

When a shareholder disposes of 306 stock, the tax consequence depends on whether the disposition is a redemption or other sale and whether it is exempt under section 306 or not.

If the issuing corporation redeems the 306 stock, the amount received is treated as a property distribution and is a dividend to the extent of earnings and profit at the time of the redemption. If the stock is disposed of in any other way, it is treated as a dividend to the extent of earnings and profits available at the time that the stock was issued.

Five transactions are exempt from section 306 dividend treatment:

1. A termination of a shareholder's interest in the corporation;

2. A complete liquidation;

3. A transaction not in avoidance of tax;

4. A disposition not involving recognition of gain or loss such as a gift;

5. Conversion of 306 stock to the common stock of the issuing corporation.

Stock Redemptions

A stock redemption is a repurchase by a corporation of its own outstanding stock. A stock redemption occurs only at the discretion of the corporation. A shareholder does not have the right to require the corporation to buy back its stock.

The effect of a stock redemption is similar to a dividend distribution in that there is a corporate distribution to the shareholders with regard to their stock. The difference is that, in a stock redemption, the shareholders surrender some or all of their stock in exchange for the distribution.

When a corporation buys its own stock, it may cancel or retire the stock or hold it as treasury stock. Treasury stock is stock held by the issuing corporation that is authorized and issued but not outstanding. Generally, treasury shares may not be voted by the corporation and do not participate in distributions. The Model Business Corporation Act has abandoned the classification of treasury stock, but it still exists in many states.

Funding of Redemptions

A corporation may redeem stock with funds legally available from surplus. Depending on the state, the funds may include surplus, earned surplus, unreserved and unrestricted surplus, and, sometimes, capital surplus. The insolvency test used for corporate dividends applies to stock redemptions also.

Tax Treatment

Stock is treated as redeemed by a corporation if the corporation acquires its stock from a shareholder in exchange for property, whether or not the acquired stock is cancelled, retired, or held as treasury stock.[48] A redemption is virtually equivalent to a sale or exchange by the shareholder to the corporation. The gain or loss on the "sale" is the difference between the amount of cash plus the fair market value of the property received and the taxpayer's adjusted basis in the stock. Remember that the adjusted basis in the stock is affected by corporate distributions in excess of earnings and profits.

To qualify for tax treatment as a sale, the sale or exchange must be one of the following:

1. Not essentially equivalent to a dividend
2. Substantially disproportionate
3. A termination of the shareholder's interest in the corporation.[49]

Otherwise, the distribution is treated as a dividend to the extent of earnings and profits.

To be able to make a determination of whether or not the redemption qualifies for treatment as a sale, we must examine the requirements in light of the stock attribution rules.[50] Under certain circumstances, stock actually owned by one person will be attributed or treated as if owned by another person. Under the family attribution rule an individual is deemed to own stock owned, directly or indirectly, by or for the spouse, children, grandchildren, and parents. Stock owned by a trust or partnership is deemed to be owned by the beneficiaries or partners proportionately. Stock owned by a corporation is attributed to any shareholder having at least a 50-percent interest in the corporation in proportion to that interest. The converse is also true. Stock held by a trust or estate beneficiary, partner, or 50-percent or more shareholder is attributable to the entity. The holder of a stock option is deemed to own the stock relative to the option. These rules are strictly applied.

A purchase of stock by the issuing corporation will be treated as a sale if it is not essentially equivalent to a dividend. The issue is whether or not the circumstances resulting from the redemption are significantly different from the circumstances resulting from a dividend distribution. In order to satisfy this test, there must be a meaningful reduction of the shareholder's proportionate interest in the corporation by a reduction in voting rights and control, the right to participate in current earnings and accumulated surplus, and the right to share in assets on liquidation.

Any redemption of a sole shareholder's stock is essentially equivalent to a dividend because the shareholder's position remains the same before and after the redemption. The sole shareholder remains the sole shareholder without any reduction in proportionate interest. Redemption of preferred stock (nonvoting and nonconvertible) is a meaningful reduction in the shareholder's proportionate interest, provided the shareholder owns no stock of any other class, either directly or indirectly.

The substantially disproportionate redemption test is an objective test which is treated as a safe harbor. If the shareholder meets the percentage tests, the redemption is treated as a sale. This provision applies only to shareholders who own less than 50 percent of the total combined voting power of all classes of stock entitled to vote immediately following the redemption. This provision does not apply to redemptions of only nonvoting stock.

Substantially disproportionate means that, immediately after the redemption, the shareholder owns less than 80 percent of the percentage of outstanding voting stock of the corporation owned by the shareholder immediately prior to redemption. The 80-percent rule also applies to the shareholder's interest in the common stock. If there is more than one class of common stock, the 80-percent rule applies to the fair market value of the common stock and not the number of shares.

A complete termination of a shareholder's interest is treated as a sale. The primary obstacle here is the attribution rules which may trip the shareholder.

If the redemption is not treated as a purchase of stock, the entire amount distributed is treated as a corporate distribution, which constitutes a dividend to the extent of the earnings and profits, then a return of capital, which reduces the basis in the shareholder's stock. Any excess is treated as a sale.

Partial Liquidations

Since 1982, partial liquidations to corporate shareholders have not received preferential tax treatment. A partial liquidation to a noncorporate shareholder is treated as part or full payment in exchange for the shareholder's stock. If the stock is a capital asset in the hands of the noncorporate shareholder, the gain or loss on the distribution is a capital gain or loss.

There are three categories of partial liquidations:

1. Not essentially equivalent to a dividend at the corporate level and pursuant to a plan under which the distribution takes place in the taxable year in which the plan is adopted or within the succeeding taxable year.
2. Termination of one of two or more active businesses conducted by the distributing corporation.
3. A series of partial liquidations, which results in a complete liquidation.[51]

Not Essentially Equivalent to a Dividend

The determination is made at the corporate level for partial liquidations not at the shareholder level as when classifying stock dividends. The typical partial liquidation in this category is a contraction of the corporation's business as a result of casualty loss followed by a distribution of the insurance proceeds to the shareholders. Voluntary contraction also qualifies. The following factors should be considered:

1. Business purposes
2. Motives of the corporation
3. Size of the corporate surplus
4. Past dividend policy
5. Special circumstances relating to the distributing corporation.

The distribution must be made pursuant to a plan. The plan may be informal, but do not take chances. A formal plan recorded in the corporate minutes is recommended.

The distribution in partial liquidation includes net proceeds, assets, and a portion of the working capital attributed to the terminated activity. The distribution must be made in the taxable year in which the plan was adopted or in the next succeeding taxable year.

Termination of One of Two or More Active Businesses

To qualify as a partial liquidation, the distribution must be attributable to the distributing corporation's cessation of conduct of a qualified trade or business or the assets of that trade or business. A qualified trade or business is one that was actively conducted during the preceding five-year period (or life of the corporation if less than five years) and that was not acquired within five years in a transaction in which gain or loss was recognized. Immediately after the distribution, the distributing corporation must be actively engaged in the conduct of a qualified trade or business.

The shareholder's stock need not actually be redeemed. A constructive redemption will be based on the fair market value of the distribution, and the stock basis will be reduced accordingly.

DEFERRED COMPENSATION

Almost everyone has, as the ultimate goal, future financial security. The subject of deferred compensation has been left to the end since it is a goal rather than a transaction. Many of us find that, because of the current tax structure and inflation, we are unable to provide adequately for the future by saving or investing with after-tax dollars. Four forms of deferred compensation will be discussed in this section—pension plans, profit-sharing plans, stock option plans, and deferred compensation agreements.

Pension Plans

A pension plan is designed to provide for the payment of definitely determinable benefits for the covered employees over a period of years or life after retirement. The key element of a pension plan, as opposed to a profit sharing plan, is that the retirement benefits are definitely determinable. Definitely determinable means that the ultimate benefits to the retiree are defined benefits set out in the plan.

Qualified Plan

A qualified pension plan is one that qualifies under the provisions of the Internal Revenue Code.[52]

The pension plan must be for the exclusive benefit of former or present employees and their beneficiaries. This does not mean that all employees must be eligible to participate, but rather that the plan not be a subterfuge for the distribution of profits to the shareholders or other disqualified person such as a trust fiduciary, the employer, officers and directors of a corporation, a person who provides services to the employer, or a 10-percent or more shareholder. Disqualified persons may not engage in the following prohibited transactions with the pension trust:

1. Sell, exchange, or lease property
2. Lend money or extend credit
3. Furnish goods or services
4. Transfer assets to or for the benefit of a disqualified person from the plan.

The pension plan fiduciary may not:

1. Treat or use the plan's income or assets for its own account

2. Accept consideration from a third party dealing with the income or assets of the plan.

The pension plan must be set up in such a way that it is impossible to divert any of the funds for purposes other than the exclusive benefit of past or present employees and their beneficiaries. The trust agreement itself must clearly state that diversion cannot occur, whether by operation, termination, amendment, or revocation of the trust. The only exception permitted is for a plan that is terminated in which the trust assets exceed obligations due to an erroneous actuarial computation. In this case, the excess may revert to the employer after all obligations and liabilities have been satisfied.

A qualified plan must meet the minimum coverage requirements of both the mathematical test and the nondiscrimination test.

To satisfy the mathematical test, at least 70 percent of nonhighly compensated employees must be eligible to participate, or the percentage of covered nonhighly compensated employees must be at least 70 percent of the percentage of highly compensated employees who are covered. Certain employees are excluded from the computations. Employees who have not attained the minimum age requirement or who have not completed the minimum service requirement, if over the minimum age, may be excluded. In addition, part-time employees who work less than 1,000 hours per year may be excluded. If the mathematical test is not met, the IRS may consider the coverage requirement met if a classification for eligibility is set up that is not discriminatory in favor of employees who are officers, shareholders, or highly compensated employees under the classification test of prior I.R.C. section 410 (b) (1) (B), and if the average benefit percentage for nonhighly compensated employees is at least 70 percent of the average benefit percentage for highly compensated employees.

A qualified plan may not discriminate in coverage in favor of officers, shareholders, or highly compensated employees.[53] Highly compensated is determined solely with reference to co-workers and not compared to outsiders. A plan may be restricted to salaried employees and exclude hourly wage employees provided that the salaried employees are not predominantly officers, shareholders, or highly compensated employees. A plan restricted to salaried employees will be strictly scrutinized by the IRS.

Contributions to or benefits provided under the plan may not discriminate in favor of officers, shareholders, or highly compensated employees.[54] This requirement, although closely related to the nondiscrimination test for coverage, is independent of the coverage test and must be independently satisfied. The emphasis is on the operation of the plan rather than on eligibility.

Tax Benefits

The employer's contribution to a qualified plan is deductible, subject to the maximum limitations set out in the Internal Revenue Code and treasury regulations.[55] The deduction is allowed for the taxable year if it is actually paid in the taxable year or no later than the due date (including extension) for filing the employer's tax return if the liability accrued as of the end of the taxable year. Any plan that is discretionary from year to year requires that an appropriate resolution or commitment to contribute to the plan be made before the end of the taxable year. A contribution made by the employer's promissory note payable to the trust will be disallowed unless the note is paid on or before the due date for filing the employer's tax return.

The employee does not recognize any income on the employer's contribution to the plan whether the employee's share is irrevocably vested or not.[56] There is one important exception to this rule regarding the purchase of life insurance on a participating employee, which is payable to the employee's beneficiaries either directly or through the trust. In this case, the employee recognizes income in the amount of the portion of the total premium that represents the net one-year term cost of the pure insurance protection.

Income received by the trust fund from employer and employee contributions is tax free.[57] This allows the funds in the trust to be compounded tax free over the period of investment, which represents a substantial tax savings.

Benefits distributed are taxed to the employee or beneficiaries at the time of receipt to the extent that such benefits exceed the employee's own contributions to the plan.[58] The amounts paid out in installment payments are classed as ordinary income. The tax benefit is that presumably the benefits will be received by the employee or beneficiaries at a time when they are in a lower tax bracket.

Establishing a Plan

It is absolutely essential that an employer contact an experienced pension plan lawyer to draft the trust agreement. Establishing a plan is a lengthy and time-consuming process that requires a knowledgeable person to negotiate successfully. Experienced lawyers have a "pattern plan." A pattern plan is a form plan which has been preapproved by the IRS. Use of a pattern plan will cut down on the amount of time spent dealing with the IRS. It is unwise to institute a plan before receiving approval from the IRS.

When a plan is submitted for approval, the employer must notify all employees of the application for approval.[59] The employees have 45 days in which to make comments on the application to the IRS. If the employer is a corporation, it is best to have the plan approved by both the board of directors and the shareholders at legally constituted meetings.

The plan must be communicated to the eligible employees by brochure or pamphlet as well as in a meeting during which the plan is explained. The communications to employees requirement continues after the approval of the plan.

Profit-Sharing Plans

A profit-sharing plan is a plan in which the eligible employees participate in the profits of the business. The contribution by the employer may be a fixed percentage of the annual profits or may be discretionary with the employer as to the amount of the annual contribution without regard to annual profits. A profit-sharing plan is primarily an incentive program intended to spur the employees on to higher productivity to increase profits which employer and emloyees share.

Qualification, establishment, and tax treatment are essentially the same for profit-sharing plans as for pension plans.

Employee Stock Option Plans

Stock option plans are generally better suited to widely held public corporations than to closely held corporations. For a closely held corporation, an employee stock option plan represents a dilution of the shareholders' equity.

Stock options must be made available on a nondiscriminatory basis to all eligible employees.[60] Part-time employees, employees with less than two years of service, and supervisory and highly compensated employees may be excluded from coverage. To qualify, not more than one third of the employer contributions for the taxable year may be allocated to officers, 10-percent or more shareholders, and highly compensated employees.

A corporation was entitled to a tax credit of up to one-half of 1 percent of the aggregate compensation paid or accrued to eligible participating employees before December 31, 1986.

The employer must transfer the employer's securities to the plan not later than 30 days after the due date for the employer's tax return for the taxable year involved. A cash contribution may be made to the plan if the cash is used to purchase the employer's securities within 30 days.

Deferred Compensation Agreements

Deferred compensation agreements are better suited to closely held corporations than are employee stock option plans, but they are also well suited to publicly held corporations.

Under a deferred compensation agreement, an employee agrees to accept less compensation than he or she could command in exchange for a promise to pay the employee or his or her beneficiaries an agreed-upon sum in the future. This results in lower taxable income in early years and postponement of the income until later years when presumably the employee will be in a lower tax bracket.

The employee will be taxed on the deferred compensation only when received if:

1. The employer's contractual promise to make future payments is unsecured and nonnegotiable.
2. The promise is made before services are rendered by the employee.
3. The employee does not have the unrestricted right to draw down the amount of the deferred compensation earned.
4. The employer has not funded its commitment by placing funds outside of its control.

From the employer's perspective, current cash outflows are reduced. The employer takes the salary deduction when it is actually paid. There is no preferential tax treatment accorded.

Deferred compensation agreements can be restricted to a few employees. They do not have to be made available to all employees. No prior approval is needed from the IRS, but nonrecurring disclosure to the Department of Labor is required within 120 days of the execution of the agreement.

NOTES

1. Commissioner v. Culbertson, 337 U.S. 733 (1949).
2. I.R.C. § 704(e).
3. *Id.*
4. *See, e.g.*, Foglesong v. Commissioner, 691 F.2d 848 (7th Cir. 1982).
5. *Id.*
6. Mathews v. Commissioner, 520 F.2d 323 (5th Cir. 1975).
7. I.R.C. § 163.
8. I.R.C. § 302 (b).
9. I.R.C. § 243.
10. 1432 Broadway Corp. v. Commissioner, 4 T.C. 1158 (1945), *aff'd per curiam*, 160 F.2d 885 (2d Cir. 1947).
11. The Colony, Inc. v. Commissioner, 26 T.C. 30 (1956).
12. 326 U.S. 521 (1946).
13. Gilbert v. Commissioner, 248 F.2d 399 (2d Cir. 1957).
14. I.R.C. § 1001.
15. I.R.C. § 1032.
16. I.R.C. § 362.
17. I.R.C. § 358.
18. Rev. Rul. 69–156.
19. 287 U.S. 462 (1933).
20. I.R.C. § 351 (b).
21. I.R.C. § 357 (a).
22. I.R.C. § 357 (c).
23. *Id.*
24. I.R.C. § 1001.
25. Rev. Proc. 77–37.

26. I.R.C. § 356 (a) (1).

27. I.R.C. § 356 (a) (2).

28. I.R.C. § 354 (a) and 356 (d).

29. Rev. Ruls. 56–116, 59–84, and 59–197.

30. I.R.C. § 356.

31. Daisey Seide, 18 T.C. 502 (1952).

32. Rev. Rul. 59–98.

33. *Id.*

34. Rev. Rul. 57–276.

35. Reef Corp. v. Commissioner, 368 F.2d 125 (5th Cir. 1966), *cert. denied*, 386 U.S. 1018 (1967) and Aetna Cas. & Surety Co. v. U.S., 568 F.2d 811 (2d Cir. 1976).

36. The Model Business Corporation Act is a model law jointly drafted by members of the American Law Institute and American Bar Association. It has served as the model for many state corporation acts.

37. ALI-ABA Model Business Corp. Act § 6.40 (c) (1)

38. ALI-ABA Model Business Corp. Act § 6.40 (c) (2).

39. I.R.C. § 316.

40. I.R.C. § 311.

41. I.R.C. § 301 (b) (1) (A).

42. I.R.C. § 301 (b) (1) (B).

43. I.R.C. § 301 (c) (1).

44. I.R.C. § 301 (c) (2).

45. I.R.C. § 301 (c) (3).

46. Rev. Rul. 79–8.

47. I.R.C. § 305.

48. I.R.C. § 317.

49. I.R.C. § 302.

50. I.R.C. § 318.

51. I.R.C. § 346.

52. I.R.C. Subchapter D.

53. I.R.C. § 401 (a) (5).

54. I.R.C. § 401 (a) (4).

55. I.R.C. § 404 (a).

56. I.R.C. § 402 (a).

57. I.R.C. § 501 (a).

58. I.R.C. § 402 (a).

59. Treas. Reg. §§ 1.401–1 (a) (2) and 1.404 (a) (2) (a) (1). *See also*, I.R.S. Publication 778 (2172), part 2 (i) and Rev. Rul. 72–509.

60. I.R.C. § 423.

Bibliography

American Law Institute, *Restatement of the Law of Contracts*. (1932).

American Law Institute, *Restatement (Second) of the Law of Contracts*. (1981).

American Law Institute, *Restatement (Second) of the Law of Torts*. (1965).

American Law Institute, *The Uniform Commercial Code*. National Conference of Commissioners on Uniform State Laws (1978).

Bailey and Pertschuk, *The Law of Deception: The Past as Prologue*, 33 Am. U.L. Rev. 849 (1984).

Berendt, Gerald E., *Collective Bargaining*. The Michie Company (1984).

Brandel and Geary, *Electronic Fund Transfers*, 36 Bus. Law. 1219 (1981).

Burby, William E., *Real Property*. 3d ed. West Publishing Co. (1965).

Burton, *Breach of Contract and the Common Law Duty to Perform in Good Faith*, 94 Harv. L. Rev. 369 (1980).

Campbell, *Regression Analysis in Title VII Cases: Minimum Standards, Comparable Worth, and Other Issues Where Law and Statistics Meet*. 36 Stan. L. Rev. 1299 (1984).

Caplovitz, David, *Consumers in Trouble: A Study of Debtors in DeFault*. The Free Press (Macmillan, Inc.) (1974).

Clark, Barkley, *The Law of Bank Deposits, Collections and Credit Cards*. Warren, Gorham & Lamont (1980).

————, *The Law of Product Warranties*. Warren, Gorham & Lamont (1984).

Cohen, Arnold B., *Bankruptcy, Secured Transactions, and Other Debtor-Creditor Matters* (with 1985 supplement). Michie, Bobbs-Merrill (1981).

Cohen, Melanie Rouner, and Faye B. Feinstein, *The Bankruptcy Reform Act of 1978 as Amended by the Bankruptcy Amendments and Federal Judgeship Act of 1984*, in *Bankruptcy Practice*. Illinois Institute for Continuing Legal Education (1985).

Cohen, *"Value" Judgments: Accounts Receivable Financing and Voidable Preferences under the New Bankruptcy Code*, 66 Minn. L. Rev. 639 (1982).

Comment, *Modern Bank Card Systems*, 18 U. Kan. L. Rev. 871 (1970).

Consumer Credit Guide, vol. 5. Commerce Clearing House (1984).

Corbin, Arthur L., *Corbin's Text on Contracts*. West Publishing Co. (1952).

————, *Offer and Acceptance, and Some of the Resulting Legal Relations*, 26 Yale L.J. 169 (1917).

Cribbet, John E., *Property*. 2d ed. Foundation Press (1975).

Davidson, *The Definition of "Employee" under Title VII: Distinguishing between Employees and Independent Contractors*, 53 Cin. L. Rev. 203 (1984).

Davis, Kenneth Culp, *Basic Text on Administrative Law*, 3rd ed. West Publishing Co. (1972).

Denis, *Subjective Decision Making: Does It Have a Place in the Employment Process?*, 11 Empl. Rel. L.J. 269 (1985).

Dickerson, Reed, *The Fundamentals of Legal Drafting*. Little, Brown and Company (1965).

Edelman, Charles D., and Ilene C. Siegler, *Federal Age Discrimination in Employment Law*. The Michie Company (1978).

Epstein, David G., *Debtor-Creditor Law in a Nutshell*. West Publishing Co. (1985).

Epstein, David G., and Steve H. Nickles, *Consumer Law*. West Publishing Co. (1981).

Farnsworth, E. Allan, *Contracts*. Little, Brown & Company (1982).

Farnsworth, E. Allan, and William F. Young, *Cases and Materials on Contracts*. The Foundation Press (1980).

Farrar, *Letters of Credit*, 38 Bus. Law. 1169 (1983).

Federal Employment Practices Manual, 8A, Labor Relations Reporter. Bureau of National Affairs (1984).

Frankel, Lionel H., Julian B. McDonnell, and Raymond T. Nimmer, *Commercial Transactions: Payment Systems*. The Michie Company (1982).

Fuller, *Consideration and Form*. 41 Colum. L. Rev. 799 (1941).

Fuller, Lon L., *Anatomy of the Law*. F. A. Praeger Co. (1968).

Geltzer and Woocher, *Debt Collection Regulation: Its Development and Direction for the 1980s*. 37 Bus. Law. 1401 (1982).

Gerber, Michael A., *Business Reorganizations*. Matthew Bender (1986).

Gilmore, Grant, *The Death of Contract*. Ohio State University Press (1974).

Ginsberg, Robert E., *Bankruptcy*. Prentice-Hall, Inc. (1985).

Ginsberg, Robert E., and Michael I. Swygert, *Bulk Transfers in Illinois*, in *Bankruptcy Practice*. Illinois Institute for Continuing Legal Education (1986).

Ginsberg, *The Bankruptcy Reform Act of 1978—A Primer*, 28 De Paul L. Rev. 923 (1979).

Goodrich, *The Story of the American Law Institute*, 1951 Wash. U.L.Q. 283.

Haller and Alviti, *Loansharking in American Cities: Historical Analysis of a Marginal Enterprise*, 21 Am. J. Legal Hist. 125 (1977).

Hawkland, *Documentary Transactions: New Solutions to Old Problems*, 18 U.C.C. L.J. 291 (1986).

————, *Proposed Revisions to U.C.C. Article 6*, 38 Bus. Law. 1729 (1983).

Henn, Henry G. and John R. Alexander, *Corporations*, 3d ed. West Publishing Co. (1983).

Holmes, Oliver Wendell, *The Common Law*. Little, Brown and Company (1881).

International Chamber of Commerce, *Uniform Customs and Practice*. Publication no. 400 (1980).

Jones, James E., Jr., William P. Murphy, and Robert Belton, *Cases and Materials on Discrimination in Employment*, 5th ed. West Publishing Co. (1986).

Kahn, Douglas A., *Corporate Taxation*, 3rd ed. (with 1983 supplement). West Publishing Co. (1981).

Keeton, Robert E., *Insurance*. West Publishing Co. (1971).

Kennedy, *Creative Bankruptcy? Use and Abuse of the Bankruptcy Law—Reflection on Some Recent Cases*, 71 Iowa L. Rev. 199 (1985).

Kennedy, *Form and Substance in Private Law Adjudication*, 89 Harv. L. Rev. 1685 (1976).

_____, *The Uniform Fraudulent Transfer Act*, 18 U.C.C. L.J. 195 (1986).

Kessler, Friedrich; Grant Gilmore, and Anthony T. Kronman, *Contracts: Cases and Materials*, 3rd ed. Little, Brown and Company (1986).

Keye, W. Noel, *Government Contracts in a Nutshell*. West Publishing Co. (1979).

Klee, *All You Ever Wanted to Know About Cram Down under the New Bankruptcy Code*, 53 Am. Bankr. L.J. 133 (1979).

Klein, William A., *Business Organization and Finance: Legal and Economic Principles*. Foundation Press (1980).

Kohl, *Equal Employment Opportunity in America: An Historical Past and Emerging Trends*, 36 Lab. L.J. 835 (1985).

Lake, *Representing Secured Creditors under the Bankruptcy Code*, 37 Bus. Law. 1153 (1982).

Larson, Arthur, *Workers' Compensation Law*. Matthew Bender (1984).

Lashbrooke, *Tax Liability: A Case for Compelling a Dividend*, 10 Stetson L. Rev. 272 (1981), reprinted in 2 National Law Review Reporter 625 (1981).

Lattin, Norman D., *Corporations*, 2d ed. Foundation Press (1971).

Leonard, *Employment Discrimination against Persons with AIDS*, 19 Clearinghouse Rev. 1292 (1986).

Llewellyn, *What Price Contract? An Essay in Perspective*, 40 Yale L.J. 704 (1931).

Lo Pucki, Lynn M., *Strategies for Creditors in Bankruptcy Proceedings*. Little, Brown and Company (1985).

Loss, Louis, *Fundamentals of Securities Regulation* (with 1985 supplement). Little, Brown and Company (1983).

Macaulay, *Non-Contractual Relations in Business*, 28 Am. Soc. Rev. 55 (1963).

_____, *The Use and Non-use of Contracts in the Manufacturing Industry*, 9 Prac. Law. 13 (1963).

Manning, Bayless, *Legal Capital*. Foundation Press (1977).

Miller, Frederick H., and Barkley Clark, *Cases and Materials on Consumer Protection*. Michie-Bobbs Merrill Co. (1980).

Miller and Scott, *Commercial Paper, Bank Deposits and Collections, and Commercial Electronic Funds Transfers*, 38 Bus. Law. 1129 (1983).

Mooney, *Personal Property Leasing: A Challenge*, 36 Bus. Law. 1605 (1981).

Morris, William Otis, *Revocation of Professional Licenses by Governmental Agencies*. The Michie Company (1984).

Murphy, Edward J., and Richard E. Speidel, *Studies in Contract Law*, 2d ed. The Foundation Press, Inc. (1977).

Nassberg, *Loan Documentation: Basic but Crucial*, 36 Bus. Law. 843 (1981).

Nolan, Dennis R., *Labor Arbitration Law and Practice in a Nutshell*. West Publishing Co. (1979).

Note, *Debt Collection Practices: Remedies for Abuse.* 10 B.C. Ind. & Com. L. Rev. 698 (1969).

Note, *Employment Discrimination against the Handicapped and Section 504 of the Rehabilitation Act*, 97 Harv. L. Rev. (1984).

Note, *New Payments Code; Consumer Financial Services Law*, 38 Bus. Law. 1360 (1983).

Oeltjen, *Usury: Utilitarian or Useless?*, 3 Fla. St. U.L. Rev. 169 (1975).

Osborne, George E., Grant S. Nelson, and Dale A. Whitman, *Real Estate Finance Law.* West Publishing Co. (1979).

Patterson, *An Apology for Consideration.* 58 Colum. L. Rev. 929 (1958).

Perritt, Henry H., *Employee Dismissal Law and Practice.* Wiley Law Publications (1984).

Peters, Ellen A., *A Negotiable Instruments Primer*, 2d ed. The Michie Company (1974).

Posin, Daniel Q., Jr., *Federal Income Taxation of Individuals.* West Publishing Co. (1983).

Posner, Richard A., *Economic Analysis of the Law*, 3d ed. Little, Brown and Company (1986).

Prosser, William L., Page Keeton, Dan B. Dobbs, Robert E. Keeton, and David G. Owen, *Prosser and Keeton on Torts*, 5th ed. West Publishing Co. (1984).

Rasor, Paul B., *Consumer Finance Law.* Matthew Bender (1985).

Riesenfeld, Stefan A., *Cases and Materials on Creditors' Remedies and Debtors' Protection.* 3d ed. West Publishing Co. (1979).

Schaber, Gordon A., and Claude D. Rohwer, *Contracts in a Nutshell*, 2d ed. West Publishing Co. (1984).

Schultz, *The Firm Offer Puzzle: A Study of Business Practice in the Construction Industry*, 19 U. Chi. L. Rev. 237 (1952).

Sell, W. Edward, *Agency.* Foundation Press (1975).

Shaffer, Thomas L., *American Legal Ethics: Text, Readings and Discussion Topics.* Matthew Bender (1985).

Siegel, *Employment Equality under the Pregnancy Discrimination Act of 1978*, 94 Yale L.J. 929 (1985).

Simon, Peter N, *The Anatomy of a Lawsuit*, The Michie Company (1984).

Siniscalco, *Homosexual Discrimination in Employment*, 16 Santa Clara L. Rev. 495 (1976).

Smith, *Contracting with the Federal Government: Ten Key Areas.* Chi. Bar Record 240 (Jan–Feb 1984).

————, *Government Contracts: Contesting the Federal Government's Award Decision*, 20 New Eng. L. Rev. 31 (1984–85).

Stanley-Elliott, *Sexual Harassment in the Workplace: Title VII's Imperfect Relief*, 6 J. Corp. L. 625 (1981).

Stone, Bradford, *Uniform Commercial Code in a Nutshell.* 2d. ed. West Publishing Co. (1984).

Sweet, Justin, *Legal Aspects of Architecture, Engineering and the Construction Process*, 3d ed. West Publishing Co. (1985).

Swygert, *Consumer Protection*, 23 De Paul L. Rev. 98 (1973).

————, *Revised Article Nine: Recognition of Legal Issues through Identification and Phase Analyses*, 22 De Paul L. Rev. 317 (1972).

Swygert and Smucker, *Promissory Estoppel in Florida: A Growing Recognition of Promissory Obligation*, 16 Stetson L. Rev. 1 (1986).

Tifford, *The Federal Trade Commission's Trade Regulation Rule on Franchises and Business Opportunity Ventures*. 36 Bus. Law. 1051 (1981).

Weber, Charles M., and Richard E. Speidel, *Commercial Paper in a Nutshell*, 3d ed. West Publishing Co. (1982).

Wechsler, *Restatements and Legal Change: Problems of Policy in the Restatement Work of the American Law Institute*, 13 St. Louis U.L.J. 185 (1968).

Weintraub, Benjamin, *What Every Executive Should Know About Chapter 11*. National Association of Credit Management (1985).

Whaley, Douglas J., *Problems and Materials on Negotiable Instruments*. Little, Brown and Company (1981).

White, *Contract Law in Modern Commercial Transactions, An Artifact of Twentieth Century Business Life?* 22 Washburn L.J. 1 (1982).

White, *The Use of EEOC Investigative Files in Title VII Actions*, 61 B.U.L. Rev. 1245 (1981).

Williston, *The Restatement of Contracts*. 18 A.B.A. J. 775 (1932).

Index

About the Authors

E. C. LASHBROOKE, JR., is Professor and Chairperson of the Department of General Business and Business Law at Michigan State University. He is the author of *Tax Exempt Organizations* (Quorum Books, 1985). His articles have appeared in such publications as the *Duke Law Journal*, *National Law Review Reporter*, and *Oil and Gas Tax Quarterly*.

MICHAEL I. SWYGERT is Professor of Law at Stetson University College of Law. He is the coeditor of *Maximizing the Law School Experience*. His articles have appeared in such publications as the *Hastings Law Journal*, the *Journal of Legal Education*, and the *Houston Law Review*.